L.A. Noir

JOHN BUNTIN

L.A. Noir

The Struggle
for the Soul
of America's
Most Seductive City

Harmony Books / New York

Copyright © 2009 by John Buntin

All rights reserved.
Published in the United States by Harmony Books, an imprint of the
Crown Publishing Group, a division of Random House, Inc., New York.
www.crownpublishing.com

Harmony Books is a registered trademark and the Harmony Books
colophon is a trademark of Random House, Inc.

Library of Congress Cataloging-in-Publication Data is available upon
request.

ISBN 978-0-307-35207-1

Printed in the United States of America

DESIGN BY ELINA NUDELMAN

10 9 8 7 6 5 4 3 2 1

First Edition

To Melinda
—and the boys

"This is the city—Los Angeles, California. I work here. I'm a cop."
—Sgt. Joe Friday, *Dragnet*

"A cop-syndicate rules this city with an iron hand."
—Mickey Cohen, gangster

"The only time to worry is when they tell the truth about you."
—William H. Parker, chief, Los Angeles Police Department

Contents

Prologue

OTHER CITIES have histories. Los Angeles has legends. Advertised to the world as the Eden at the end of the western frontier, the settlement the Spaniards named El Pueblo de Nuestra Señora la Reina de los Ángeles turned out to be something very different—not the beatific Our Lady the Queen of the Angels advertised by its name but rather a dark, dangerous blonde.

> *She got up slowly and swayed towards me in a tight black dress that didn't reflect any light. She had long thighs and she walked with a certain something I hadn't often seen in bookstores. She was an ash blonde. . . .*
> *Her smile was tentative, but could be persuaded to be nice.*
>
> —*Raymond Chandler,* The Big Sleep

For more than sixty years, writers and directors from Raymond Chandler and Billy Wilder to Roman Polanski and James Ellroy have explored L.A.'s origins, its underbelly, and (yes) its blondes in fiction and films like *The Big Sleep, Double Indemnity, Chinatown,* and *L.A. Confidential.* In the process, they created the distinctive worldview known as noir, where honor is in short supply and where Los Angeles invariably proves to be a femme fatale. Yet this preoccupation with a mythic past has obscured something important—the true history of noir Los Angeles.

For more than forty years, from Prohibition through the Watts riots, politicians, gangsters, businessmen, and policemen engaged in an often-violent contest for control of the city. Their struggle shaped the history of

Los Angeles, the future of policing, and the course of American politics. In time, two primary antagonists emerged. The first was William H. Parker, Los Angeles's greatest and most controversial chief of police. His nemesis was Los Angeles's most colorful criminal, featherweight boxer-turned-gangster Mickey Cohen.

IN 1920 Los Angeles surpassed San Francisco as California's largest city. It was a moment of triumph for *Los Angeles Times* publisher Harry Chandler, who had arrived four decades earlier when the city of angels was a dusty, water-starved pueblo of ten thousand souls. Chandler and his associates worked tirelessly to build a metropolis, relentlessly promoting the fledgling city and ruthlessly securing the water needed to support it (a campaign made famous by the film *Chinatown*). Yet 1920 was also the year that witnessed the emergence of a major threat to their authority. The threat came from Prohibition. For years, Harry Chandler and the so-called business barons had supplied local politicians with the advertising, the publicity, and the money they needed to reach the city's new residents. In exchange, they gained power over the city government. But with the imposition of Prohibition, a new force appeared with the money and the desire to purchase L.A.'s politicians: the criminal underworld. To suppress it, the business community turned to the Los Angeles Police Department. The underworld also looked to the LAPD—for protection.

In 1922, Bill Parker and Mickey Cohen entered this drama as bit players in the struggle for control of Los Angeles. In 1937, Parker emerged as a protégé of Los Angeles's top policeman while Mickey became the enforcer for L.A.'s top gangster. In 1950, they became direct rivals, each dedicated to the other's destruction. Two characters more different from each other would be hard to imagine. Parker arrived in Los Angeles in 1922 from Deadwood, South Dakota, a proud, ambitious seventeen-year-old, one of the tens of thousands of migrants who were moving west to Southern California in what the journalist Carey McWilliams described as "the largest internal migration in the history of the American people." He hoped to follow in the footsteps of his grandfather, a pioneering prosecutor on the western frontier, and make a career for himself in the law. But instead of opportunity, Parker found in Los Angeles temptation. Instead of becoming a prominent attorney, he became a cop, a patrolman in the Los Angeles Police Department. Coldly cerebral (*Star Trek* creator Gene Roddenberry, a onetime LAPD officer and Parker speechwriter, reputedly based the character Mr. Spock on his former boss), intolerant of fools, and famously incorruptible (in a department that was famously corrupt), Parker persevered. Gradually he rose. Between 1934 and 1937, he masterminded a campaign to free the police department from the control of gangsters and politicians, only to see his efforts undone by a blast of dynamite and a sensational scandal. Then, in 1950, another scandal (this one involving 114 Hollywood "pleasure girls") made Parker chief of the Los Angeles Police Department, a position he would hold for sixteen controversial years.

In contrast, Mickey Cohen wasn't troubled by self-examination until much later in life (when he would grapple with the question of going "straight"). Born Meyer Harris Cohen in 1913 in the Brownsville section of Brooklyn, Mickey arrived in Los Angeles with his mother and sister at the age of three. By the age of six, he was hustling newspapers on the streets of Boyle Heights. At the age of nine, he began his career in armed robbery with an attempt to "heist" a movie theater in downtown L.A. using a baseball bat. His talent with his fists took the diminutive brawler to New York City to train as a featherweight boxer. His skill with a .38 took him into the rackets, first in Cleveland, then in Al Capone's Chicago. In 1937, Mickey returned to Los Angeles to serve as gangster Benjamin "Bugsy" Siegel's right-hand man. It was a job that put him on a collision course with Bill Parker.

For three decades, from the Great Depression to the Watts riots, Parker and Cohen—the policeman and the gangster—would engage in a struggle for power, first as lieutenants to older, more powerful men, then directly with each other, and finally with their own instincts and desires. In 1956, Chief Parker's war against Mickey Cohen and organized crime in L.A. attracted the attention of a young Senate investigator with political ambitions named Robert Kennedy. It also antagonized FBI director J. Edgar Hoover and created an extralegal, wiretap-driven style of policing that eerily prefigures the tactics being used in today's war on terror. In the 1960s, it would incite the Watts riots and help propel Ronald Reagan into the governor's mansion in Sacramento. Their contest would involve some of the most powerful—and colorful—figures of the twentieth century: press magnates Harry Chandler and his nemesis, William Randolph Hearst; studio head Harry Cohn of Columbia; entertainers Jack Webb, Frank Sinatra, Lana Turner, and Sammy Davis Jr.; and civil rights leaders Malcolm X and Martin Luther King Jr. The outcome of their struggle would change the history of Los Angeles, set race relations in America on a dangerous new path, and chart a problematic course for American policing.

Parker and Cohen's struggle for control of the city also changed them. Ultimately, like any good noir tale, the story of the rivalry between the young hoodlum with a second-grade education who became the king of the L.A. underworld and the obstinate young patrolman from Deadwood who created the modern LAPD brings us back to the question that Los Angeles always seems to pose: Is Our Lady the Queen of the Angels the dark angel, or do we simply bring our own darkness to her?

part one/

The Fallen City

The Mickey Mouse Mafia

*"[A] dead-rotten law enforcement setup rules
in this county and city with an iron hand."*
—LAPD Sgt. Charlie Stoker, 1950

MICKEY COHEN was not a man used to being shaken down. Threatened with handguns, blasted with shotguns, strafed on occasion by a machine gun, yes. Firebombed and dynamited, sure. But threatened, extorted—hit up for $20,000—no. Anyone who read the tabloids in post–World War II Los Angeles knew that extortion was Mickey's racket, along with book-making, gambling, loan-sharking, slot machines, narcotics, union agitation, and a substantial portion of the city's other illicit pastimes. In the years following Benjamin "Bugsy" Siegel's ill-fated move to Las Vegas, Mickey Cohen had become the top mobster on the West Coast. And the tart-tongued, sharp-dressed, pint-sized gangster, whom the more circumspect newspapers described tactfully as "a prominent figure in the sporting life world," hadn't gotten there by being easily intimidated—certainly not by midlevel police functionaries. Yet in October 1948 that is precisely what the head of the Los Angeles Police Department vice squad set out to do.

Cohen was no stranger to the heat. During his first days in Los Angeles as Bugsy Siegel's enforcer, he had been instructed to squeeze Eddy Neales, the proprietor of the Clover Club. Located on the Sunset Strip, an unincorporated county area just outside of Los Angeles city limits, the Clover Club was Southern California's poshest gaming joint. It reputedly paid the L.A. County Sheriff's Department a small fortune for protection. The squad that provided it, led by Det. George "Iron Man" Contreras, had a formidable reputation. People who crossed it died. According to Cohen, one member of the unit had been the triggerman on eleven killings. So when Neales sicced Contreras's men on Cohen, he undoubtedly expected that the sheriff's men would scare Mickey stiff.

Contreras tried. Cohen was picked up and brought in to receive a warning: If he didn't lay off Neales, the next warning would come in the form of a bullet to the head.

Mickey wasn't impressed. A few nights later, he sought out Contreras's top gunman.

"I looked him up and said to him, 'Let me tell you something: to me you're no cop. Being no cop I gotta right to kill you—so come prepared. The next time I see you coming to me I'm going to hit you between the eyes.'"

It was an effective warning. "He felt I was sincere," Mickey later reported. The cops backed down. Until now.

THE FACT OF THE MATTER was, Mickey Cohen was in an uncharacteristically vulnerable position that fall. Two months earlier, on Wednesday, August 18, as Cohen was putting the final touches on his newest venture, a swank men's clothing shop on Sunset Boulevard named Michael's Haberdashery, three gunmen had charged into the store and opened fire, wounding two Cohen henchmen and killing his top gunman, Hooky Rothman. Mickey himself was in the back bathroom washing his hands, something the obsessive-compulsive gangster did fifty or sixty times a day. Trapped, he hid in a stall, atop a toilet, awaiting his death. But instead of checking to see that they'd gotten their man—item number one on the professional hitman's checklist—the gunmen fled. A few minutes later the incredulous driver of the gunmen's crash car saw Mickey scurry to safety out the front door.

Cohen had survived, but great damage had been done. As Siegel shifted his attention to Las Vegas, Mickey had taken over his old boss's Los Angeles operations—as well as Siegel's organized crime connections back East. The attempted hit on Cohen not only showed that Mickey was vulnerable, it suggested that Bugsy's powerful friends had no particular commitment to his protégé's survival. In short, Mickey looked weak, and in the underworld, weakness attracts predators. So when the head of the LAPD administrative vice squad called just weeks after the attempted rub-out to inform Cohen that they "had him down for a ten to twenty thousand dollar contribution" for the upcoming reelection campaign of incumbent mayor Fletcher Bowron, Mickey knew what was happening. This was not an opportunity for good, old-fashioned graft: Bowron had devoted his career to eradicating the underworld. Rather, this was a sign that the vice squad now viewed him as prey rather than predator.

"Power's a funny thing," Cohen would later muse. "Somebody calls your hole card, and [if you can't show you aren't bluffing] it's like a dike—one little hole can blow the whole thing."

Paying would only confirm his weakness. Cohen refused.

Administrative vice's response was not long in coming. Just after midnight on the evening of January 15, 1949, five officers watched two Cadillacs depart from Michael's Haberdashery. They set off in pursuit. At the corner of Santa Monica and Ogden Drive, two miles west of Los Angeles city limits, the police pulled over the Cadillac containing Cohen, his driver, and Harold "Happy" Meltzer, a sometime Cohen gunman who also had a jewelry shop in the same building as Cohen's haberdashery. A firearm was conveniently found on Meltzer, who was arrested. (It later disappeared, making it impossible to determine whether or not the gun had been planted.) Several days later, Mickey received a phone call offering to settle matters for $5,000. The vice squad was sending Cohen one last message: Hand over the cash or the gloves come off.

Mickey was furious. For years he had helped cops who got injured on the job and dispensed Thanksgiving turkeys to families in need at division captains' request. He'd given municipal judges valuable horse tips. He'd wined and dined the administrative vice squad's commanding officers, Lt. Rudy Wellpot and Sgt. Elmer Jackson, at the Brown Derby and Dave's Blue Room, presented their girlfriends with expensive gifts, and treated them as VIPs at his nightclub-hangout on Beverly Boulevard, Slapsie Maxie's. The police had responded by breaking into his new house in Brentwood, stealing his address books, and swaggering around town with almost unbearable arrogance, routinely telling waiters who arrived with the check at the end of evening to "send it to Mickey Cohen." It was time to teach the LAPD a lesson it would never forget about who was running this town. The vice squad had called his hole card; now Mickey would show them he was holding the equivalent of a pair of bullets (two aces)—in the form of a recording that tied the vice squad to a thirty-six-year-old redheaded ex-prostitute named Brenda Allen.

BRENDA ALLEN was Hollywood's most prosperous madam, in part because she was so cautious. Rather than take on the risks that came with running a "bawdy house," Allen relied on a telephone exchange service to communicate with her clients, clients who were vetted with the utmost care. While Allen would occasionally insert chaste ads in actors' directories or distribute her phone number to select cabbies, bartenders, and bellhops, she prided herself on serving the crème de la crème of Los Angeles. It was rumored that she even ran a Dun & Bradstreet check on prospective customers to ensure their suitability. Those who were accepted were rewarded with Allen's full and carefully considered attention. All of her girls were analyzed as to their more intimate characteristics, which were then carefully noted on file cards for cross-tabulation with her clients' preferences. The selection Allen offered was considerable. By 1948, she had 114 "pleasure girls" in her harem. She also had a most unusual partner and lover: Sergeant Jackson of the LAPD administrative vice squad, the same policeman who was trying to shake down Mickey Cohen.

Needless to say, Sergeant Jackson's connection to Brenda Allen was not common knowledge. Even someone as well informed as Mickey Cohen might never have learned of it—but for the fact that another member of the police department had recently blackmailed Mickey with a transcription of certain sensitive conversations that Mickey had conducted at home. The shakedown tipped Mickey off to the fact that the LAPD had gotten a bug into his house. So he asked his friend Barney Ruditsky for help. Ruditsky, a former NYPD officer, was now Hollywood's foremost private eye. He specialized in documenting the infidelities of the stars (then as now, a business that relied heavily on illegal electronic surveillance). Cohen asked Ruditsky if he could recommend someone to sweep his house in Brentwood for eavesdropping devices. Ruditsky could: an electronics whiz named Jimmy Vaus. Vaus found the bug, and Mickey hired him on the spot. Soon thereafter, Vaus let Mickey in on a little secret: He was also a wiretapper for a sergeant on the Hollywood vice squad. Vaus told Cohen he had recordings linking Sergeant Jackson to Brenda Allen. That information was Cohen's ace in the hole. He decided to play it at henchman "Happy" Meltzer's trial.

The trial began on May 5, 1949. In his opening statement, attorney Sam Rummel laid out Meltzer's defense. "We will prove through testimony that the two men first sought $20,000, then $10,000, then $5,000 from Cohen in return for their promise to quit harassing him," Rummel declared. As a defense, this was ho-hum stuff: Gangsters were always insisting they'd been framed. But when Cohen appeared with "sound expert" Jimmy Vaus and a mysterious sound-recording machine, the press took notice, especially after Cohen confidentially informed them that he had recordings that would "blow this case right out of court."

The timing of Cohen's accusation was potentially explosive. Incumbent mayor Fletcher Bowron was up for reelection on June 1. The mayor had based his entire reelection campaign on his record of keeping Los Angeles's underworld "closed" and the city government clean. Now Mickey was claiming that he had evidence that would show that senior police officials were on the take. Fortunately for Mayor Bowron, most of the city's newspapers strongly supported his reelection. So did the county grand jury impaneled every year to investigate municipal wrongdoing. A mistrial was hastily declared. Cohen's allegations received only light coverage. Mayor

Bowron was handily reelected. Only then did the *Los Angeles Daily News* break the story: BIG EXPOSÉ TELLS VICE, POLICE LINK: INSIDE STORY TELLS BRENDA'S CLOSE RELATIONS WITH THE POLICE, BY SGT. CHARLES STOKER!

It turned out that Vaus's contact on the Hollywood vice squad, Sgt. Charles Stoker, had gone before the criminal complaints committee of the county grand jury the day before Cohen and Vaus showed up in court with the wire recordings. There Stoker had told the committee about overhearing Brenda Allen's conversations with Sergeant Jackson. It then emerged that Sgt. Guy Rudolph, confidential investigator for the chief of police, had gotten wind of Jackson's connection to Allen fourteen months earlier and had asked police department technician Ray Pinker to set up another wiretap. But that investigation had mysteriously stalled, and the recordings had then disappeared.

Spurred by these revelations and by Cohen's charges, the county grand jury opened an investigation. In mid-June it began subpoenaing police officers. Chief Clarence B. Horrall insisted that he had never been informed of the allegations swirling around the vice squad; high-ranking officers stepped forward to insist that he had been. Brenda Allen volunteered that Sergeants Stoker and Jackson had both been on the take. The head of the LAPD gangster squad abruptly retired. Every day brought a new revelation. The *Daily News* revealed that the LAPD had broken into Mickey's house in Brentwood and installed wiretaps. Columnist Florabel Muir accused Mayor Bowron of personally authorizing the operation and implied that the transcriptions were being used for purposes of blackmail. Shamefaced, Mayor Bowron and Chief Horrall were forced to concede that they had OK'd a break-in. What was worse was that no charges against Cohen had come of it. On June 28, Chief Horrall announced his retirement. One month later, the grand jury indicted Lieutenant Wellpot, Sergeant Jackson, Asst. Chief Joseph Reed, and Chief of Police C. B. Horrall for perjury. Cohen had won his bet—if he could survive to collect.

JUST A FEW WEEKS LATER, Mickey was driving home to his house in Brentwood for dinner with his wife, LaVonne, and the actor George Raft. Mickey had outfitted his $150,000 home at 513 Moreno Avenue with the most advanced security gear of the time, including an "electronic eye" that could detect intruders and trigger floodlights. The goal was to illuminate anyone who approached the house. But of course the security system also illuminated *him* when he got home in the evening. This was a serious problem when there was a hitman hiding in the empty lot next door, as there was that night.

As Mickey started to swing into his driveway and the lights came on, the gunman opened fire, pumping slugs into Mickey's car. Mickey dropped to the floorboard. Without looking over the dashboard, he wrenched his blue Caddy back onto the road and floored it. He made it about two blocks before beaching the car on a curb. Fortunately, the gunman was gone. So Mickey went home. Despite bleeding from cuts inflicted by the shattered glass, Mickey waved off the questions about what had happened and insisted on proceeding with dinner—New York strip and apple pie, Raft's favorite. The actor would later say that Mickey had looked "a little mussed up."

Cohen didn't report the matter to the police. (Why advertise his vulnerability further?) The attack might never have come to light but for a tip from Cohen's auto-body shop to the police . . . and Mickey's decision to commission a $25,000 armored Cadillac and test it at the police academy firing range. When the press broke the story, Cohen replied nonchalantly, "Well, where else? You can't test it [by opening fire] . . . on the street for Christ's sake!" Posed before his massive new armored car, the sad-eyed, five-foot-three-inch gangster (five-foot-five in lifts) looked like nothing so much as Mickey Mouse. Gangsters in other cities marveled about Mickey's good luck—and sniggered about L.A.'s "Mickey Mouse Mafia."

Still, someone clearly was trying to kill him, albeit rather ineptly. It might have seemed like a good time to lie low. But that was a feat Cohen seemed constitutionally incapable of. Thanks to the tabloids, Mickey was a celebrity, one of the biggest in town, and he acted the part, courting the press, squiring "budding starlets" around town (although in private his tastes inclined more to exotic dancers), and frequenting hot nightclubs like Ciro's, the Trocadero, and the Mocambo.

The evening of Tuesday, July 19, 1949, was a typical one for Mickey. After dining with Artie Samish, chief lobbyist for the state's liquor interests and one of the most powerful men in Sacramento, Mickey and his party of henchmen, starlets, and reporters repaired to one of his favorite hangouts, Sherry's, a nightclub on the Sunset Strip that was owned by his friend Barney Ruditsky. Standing watch outside was a curious addition to Mickey's crew: Special Agent Harry Cooper, from the state attorney general's office. After the attempted hit at Michael's Haberdashery, the L.A. County Sheriff's Department had insisted—somewhat counterintuitively—on disarming Cohen's men and checking them frequently for weapons, to make sure they stayed unarmed. As a result, Mickey was essentially unprotected. Samish had arranged to provide a little extra protection in the form of Special Agent Cooper.

By 3:30 a.m., Mickey was ready to call it a night. Ruditsky went outside and did a quick sweep of the parking lot. Everything looked clear. Two of

Cohen's men went to bring around his Cadillac (one of the regular ones, Mickey being embroiled in a dispute with the California Highway Patrol about the excessive weight of his armored car). A valet went to get Cohen pal Frankie Niccoli's Chrysler, and at 3:50 a.m., Mickey and his party stepped outside. Almost immediately a shotgun and a high-powered .30-06 rifle opened up from an empty lot across the street, and members of Mickey's party started to drop.

One of them was newspaper columnist Florabel Muir, who had been lingering inside over the morning paper as Mickey's party exited. Muir (who frankly admitted to hanging around Mickey in hopes that some shooting would start) now charged outside, into the gunfire. One of Cohen's top thugs, Neddie Herbert, had been hit and was lying wounded on the ground. Special Agent Cooper was staggering about, clutching his stomach with one hand and waving his pistol with the other. Then Muir saw Mickey, "right arm hung limp, and blood spreading on his coat near the shoulder" running toward Cooper. With his one good arm Cohen grabbed the sagging six-foot-tall lawman and stuffed him into Niccoli's Chrysler. Cohen piled in as well, and the Chrysler zoomed off—to the Hollywood Receiving Hospital. Thanks to Mickey's quick reaction, Cooper lived. The more seriously wounded Herbert wasn't so fortunate; he died four days later. Mickey himself escaped with only a shoulder wound. Florabel Muir got her exclusive, along with a sprinkling of buckshot in her bottom.

Later that night, policemen found automatic Savage and Remington shotguns in the empty lot across the street from Sherry's. A ballistics test determined that the buckshot slugs used were standard-issue police riot-control shells. Muir also noted with interest that the deputy sheriffs who seemed so diligent in ensuring that Cohen's crew was firearms-free had vanished a few minutes before the shooting.

The papers, of course, were thrilled. "The Battle of the Sunset Strip!" the press dubbed it. But who was behind the hit? Mayor Bowron blamed Manhattan crime boss Frank Costello. Others pointed to Jack Dragna, a local Italian crime boss who'd reluctantly accepted direction from Bugsy Siegel but who was known to dislike Mickey. Sergeant Stoker, the former vice officer turned county grand-jury witness, claimed the triggerman was LAPD. Cohen himself was confused by the attack. But Mickey did know one thing: He could deal with an underworld rival like Dragna. But in order to thrive as a crime lord in Los Angeles, Mickey needed a friendly—or at least tolerant—chief of police in office.

For the moment, that was impossible. In the wake of Chief Horrall's ouster, Mayor Bowron had appointed, on an emergency basis, a no-nonsense former Marine general named William Worton to run the department. One of Worton's first acts was to reconstitute the LAPD's intelligence division. Its top target: Mickey Cohen. Fortunately for Cohen, Worton was only a temporary appointment; civil service rules required the Police Commission to hire from within the department. That meant Cohen would have a chance to put a more friendly man in the position, and the diminutive gangster already knew exactly who he wanted: Thaddeus Brown, a former detective who'd headed the homicide department before winning promotion to deputy chief of patrol in 1946.

Brown was a big teddy bear of a man, enormously popular with the department's detectives and well regarded by the underworld, too. As chief of detectives, Brown insisted on knowing every detective's confidential sources. As a result, he had a wide range of acquaintances. He saw the underworld's denizens as human beings, not evil incarnate. As a result, Cohen had something of a soft spot for the man the papers called "the master detective." Brown had another, even more influential backer in Norman Chandler, the publisher of the *Los Angeles Times*. The support Norman could offer was not purely rhetorical. The Chandler family had long maintained a special—almost proprietary—interest in the LAPD. Indeed, for more than two decades the city's dominant newspaper had made it clear that a voice in police affairs was the sine qua non of the paper's political support. It was widely known that Norman Chandler controlled three of the Police Commission's five votes—and that Chandler expected them to vote for Thad Brown as chief.

In short, Brown's ascension seemed inevitable. However, it was not automatic. The Police Commission could not simply vote to promote the "master detective." Since 1923, the chief of the LAPD had been chosen under the civil service system. As a result, applicants for the top position had to take an elaborate civil service exam, composed of a written test and an oral examination. The results of the written test typically accounted for 95 percent of the total score; the oral exam plus a small adjustment for seniority contributed the other 5 percent. Candidates then received a total score and were ranked accordingly. The Police Commission was allowed to choose from among the top three candidates.

To no one's surprise, Thad Brown got the top score. What was surprising was who came in second: Deputy Chief William H. Parker, the head of the Bureau of Internal Affairs. A decorated veteran of the Second World War, wounded in Normandy during the D-day invasion, Parker had helped to de-Nazify municipal police forces in Italy and Germany as the Allies advanced. He now wanted to purge the LAPD of corruption—and Los Angeles of organized crime—in much the same way. Mickey Cohen was determined to make sure that Parker never got that chance.

"I had gambling joints all over the city," Mickey later explained, "and I needed the police just to make sure they ran efficiently." Bill Parker would not make things go smoothly.

One of the things that any crime lord needs is a line on the Police Commission, and Cohen had it. His contacts there assured him that three of the five commissioners—Agnes Albro, Henry Duque, and Bruno Newman—favored Brown. That left only Irving Snyder and Dr. J. Alexander Somerville, the sole African American police commissioner, in favor of Parker. Mickey was convinced that "the fix" was in and that Brown would be the next chief of police. The only obstacle Brown faced, Cohen's connections informed him, was that Brown's selection might be seen as a personal triumph for the little gangster. On their advice, Cohen decided to leave town for the actual decision-making period—"just to blow off any stink that could possibly come up." Along with his sometime bodyguard Johnny Stompanato (who was also known as one of Hollywood's most notorious gigolos) and his Boston terrier, Tuffy, L.A.'s underworld boss set off on a leisurely road trip to Chicago.

Cohen arrived in Chicago to shocking news. The day before the Police Commission vote, Brown-supporter Agnes Albro had unexpectedly died. The following day, the commission had voted to name Bill Parker the next chief of police. The battle for control of Los Angeles was about to begin in earnest. Though Mickey didn't know it, it was a fight Bill Parker had been preparing for his entire life.

2

The "White Spot"

*"Wherein lies the fascination of the Angel City!
Why has it become the Mecca of tourists the
world over? Is it because it is the best advertised
city in the United States? Is it that it offers
illimitable opportunities for making money and
eating fruit? Hardly that. After all the pamphlets
of the real estate agents, the boosters' clubs,
the Board of Trade and the Chamber of
Commerce have been read, something remains
unspoken—something that uncannily grips the
stranger."*

—Willard Huntington Wright, 1913

BEFORE IT WAS A CITY, Los Angeles was an idea.

Other cities were based on geographical virtues—a splendid port (San Francisco, say, or New York), an important river (St. Louis), a magnificent lake (Chicago). But nothing about the arid basin of Los Angeles (other than its mild weather) suggested the site of a great metropolis. So the men who built Los Angeles decided to advertise a different kind of virtue: moral and racial purity. Los Angeles, a settlement founded in 1781 as a Spanish pueblo, was reenvisioned as "the white spot of America," a place where native-born, white Protestants could enjoy "the magic of outdoors inviting always . . . trees in blossom throughout the year, flowers in bloom all the time" as well as "mystery, romance, charm, splendor," all safe among others of their kind. It was an image relentlessly promoted by men like Harry Chandler, owner and publisher of the *Los Angeles Times* and one of Southern California's most important real estate developers, and it worked. By 1920, Los Angeles had surpassed San Francisco to become the largest city in the west. There was just one problem with this picture of Anglo-Saxon virtue. It wasn't true. Far from being a paragon of virtue, by the early 1920s, Los Angeles had become a Shangri-la of vice.

The historic center of the city's underworld was Chinatown, "narrow, dirty, vile-smelling, [and] thoroughly picturesque," an area just east of the historic plaza that had been the center of town back in Los Angeles's pueblo days. Its opium dens introduced Angelenos to the seductions of the poppy flower; its fan tan and mah-jongg parlors catered to the area's still-sizable Chinese population; its fourteen-odd lotteries attracted gamblers of every color and nationality from across the city. Just north of Chinatown was the predominantly Mexican part of the city known as Sonoratown. There women in negligees lolled casually in the open windows of "disorderly houses," advertising their availability. According to the *Los Angeles Record*, a hundred known disorderly houses operated in the general vicinity of downtown. The citywide brothel count was 355—and growing fast. (By the mid-1920s, reformers would count 615 brothels.) That was just the high-end prostitution. Streetwalkers offered themselves on Main Street, a thriving but seedy neighborhood of taxi dance halls (so named because a dancing partner could be hired like a taxi for a short period of time), burlesque shows, and "blind pigs" (where a shot of whiskey went for ten cents a gulp). Farther south, down on Central Avenue in the thirty-block area between Fourth Street and Slauson Avenue, an even more tempting scene was taking shape, one offering narcotics, craps, color-blind sex for sale, and a strange new syncopated sound called jazz.

The city also boasted a steamy sex circuit. Upscale "ninety-six clubs"—some just blocks away from City Hall—offered "queers," "fairies," or otherwise straight men a place for a discreet "flutter" or "twentieth century" (read: oral) sex in a luxurious setting. The less well-to-do worked a circuit of downtown speakeasies, bars, public baths, and parks along Main and Hill Streets—Maxwell's, Harold's, the Crown Jewel, the Waldorf. For those who could not afford "to spend a quarter or fifty cents for a dime's worth of beer," there were the parks. The poet Hart Crane, visiting Los Angeles in 1927, would marvel at what he saw in the lush groves of bamboo and banana trees in downtown's Pershing Square. "The number of faggots cruising around here is legion," he wrote friends back East. "Here are little fairies who can quote Rimbaud before they are eighteen." The city itself was horrid, Crane wrote, but the sex was divine.

Then there was gambling. Amid the banks and stock brokerages of Spring Street, bootlegger Milton "Farmer" Page presided over a string of gambling clubs, the most imposing of which, the El Dorado, occupied the entire top floor of a downtown office building. There on a typical evening five to six hundred people would gather to play craps, poker, blackjack, roulette, and other games of skill and chance. At the corner of Spring and W. Third Streets, bookies waited to take the public's wagers on the Mexican racing tracks or on Pacific Coast League baseball games. Nearby saloons provided upstairs rooms for poker and faro, sometimes even roulette, while younger and less prosperous customers stayed in the alleys to try their luck with the dice in one of the ubiquitous games of craps. Bingo games sucked away the earnings of bored housewives; card rooms distracted their husbands. "Bunco" men (as con men were then known) preyed on the unwitting, selling naïve newcomers nonexistent stocks, gold mines, oil fields, and real estate. "Boulevard sheiks" prowled for and preyed on the growing number of working girls making their homes in Los Angeles. Among this teeming underworld's victims was a seventeen-year-old emigrant from Deadwood, South Dakota, William H. Parker III.

IT'S HARD to imagine better preparation for 1920s Los Angeles than turn-of-the-century Deadwood, a town devoted, as one wag put it, "to gold, guns, and women." Parker was born into a family that had played a large part in cleaning it up. His grandfather—the first William H. Parker— had arrived in the spring of 1877, less than a year after General Custer and the 210 men under his direct command were killed by Lakota Sioux and Cheyenne warriors at Little Big Horn, a hundred miles south of the mining camp. College educated, a former colonel in the Union Army during the Civil War who was later appointed by President Ulysses S. Grant to be the first federal collector for tax revenue and the assistant U.S. attorney in the Colorado territory, Parker cut an imposing figure. Within days of arriving in the frontier settlement, he was made captain of a hastily assembled town militia, formed to protect the booming mining camp. In 1902, he became the district attorney, a position he occupied until 1906, when he was elected to Congress. His willingness to enforce closing hours on casinos and brothels earned him a reputation as a reformer. Prosperous, fierce ("a good hater," said one acquaintance), aloof ("to many he may have appeared unapproachably chilly," noted one friend in a memorial address to the Deadwood bar), Congressman Parker was one of Deadwood's most imposing citizens—"dauntless, proud, imperious."

Congressman Parker's position should have ensured that his grandson would grow up as a member of one of Deadwood's most respected families. Instead, as he was returning home by train from his first year in Washington, the new congressman was suddenly afflicted with terrible abdominal pain. He stopped in Chicago. There a surgeon cut into the freshman representative and discovered that Parker suffered from advanced cirrhosis of the liver—a condition often associated with heavy drinking. He died two months later at the age of sixty-one, leaving behind a family of five sons and two daughters. Bill Parker would not grow up with his grandfather's wealth or prestige. Instead, he would inherit his temperament and, in time, his fondness for whiskey.

As a child, Bill grew up in a house divided. His mother, Mary Kathryn Moore, was a spirited, independent woman who was both deeply religious and good humored. By all accounts, she was intensely proud of Bill, her oldest son, who was born on June 21, 1905. Bill's father, William Henry Parker Jr., had a personality that can only be called dour. He also had a violent temper. At school, one of Parker's sisters was once asked what her father did. She answered, "Oh, my father gets up in the morning to fix breakfast and throws pots and pans around in the kitchen."

These troubles were not debilitating, at least not at first. As a young boy, Parker was diligent and bright, a dogged athlete and a gifted orator. (The Deadwood High School yearbook reported that Parker won the senior year first prize in rhetoric for his stirring recitation of William Jennings Bryan's "Cross of Gold" speech—an interesting selection for a gold-mining town.) His final report card in 1922 reveals an excellent student, with an aptitude for math and rhetoric, who enjoyed the high opinion of his teachers.

"I consider William Parker to be an unusually bright young man, endowed with mental energy and capabilities which, if properly directed, will enable him to carve out for himself a name of which all concerned may be justly proud," the principal of Deadwood High School wrote on Parker's final report card.

As an obviously intelligent young man born into a distinguished family, Bill might have been expected to follow in his father's and grandfather's footsteps and continue on to college. Instead, he stayed in Deadwood, working a series of odd jobs, delivering newspapers and selling frocks and undergarments knit by his mother to various ladies in town—and not just the ladies. By one account, Parker blushingly sold garments to the town's madams as well. The teenager's first real job, however, was at Deadwood's most prestigious hotel—the Franklin—where he got a job as a bellhop and the house detective.

In later years, Parker would occasionally allude to his work in Deadwood, suggesting that his job involved rousting guests who misbehaved and patrolling the premises for ladies of the night. In truth, he was probably more occupied with his work as a bellboy than with acts of sleuthing. The Franklin was known for its ongoing high-stakes poker game; it is unlikely that a teenage employee would have interfered much with it. Nonetheless, it's clear that the idea of being a lawman spoke to Parker's imagination. Imagination was all he had. Bill Parker seemed stuck in Deadwood.

Then, suddenly, he wasn't.

In 1922, his mother announced that she was separating from Bill's father and moving to Los Angeles and that she was taking Bill's three younger siblings with her. Bill went with her to help with the move—and to see the City of Angels for himself.

LOS ANGELES was Deadwood writ large—a boomtown on a scale never seen before or since in this country. The city was growing so quickly that residents and visitors couldn't even agree on how to pronounce its name. To some it was "Loss An-jy-lese"; to others, "Loss An-jy-lus" or even "Lows An-y-klyese"—a pronunciation the *Los Angeles Times* suspected was a deliberate eastern slur. (The paper of record insisted that the proper pronunciation was the distinctly Spanish "Loce Ahng-hail-ais," a pronunciation it printed under its masthead for several years.) Not until the 1930s did today's "Los An-ju-less" gain the clear upper hand.

Whatever its pronunciation, it was clear that people couldn't wait to get there. Model Ts crammed the old Santa Fe Trail—today's Route 66—full of Midwesterners who were California-bound. By 1922, the city's population had risen to more than 600,000. Fifteen-story skyscrapers (heights had been capped after the devastating San Francisco earthquake of 1906) lined Spring Street, the so-called Wall Street of the West. Dazzling electric signs proclaimed its next goal—2,000,000 POPULATION BY 1930! (It made it to 1,200,000.) At the corner of Wilshire and La Brea, newcomers were transfixed by something they had never seen before, neon signs, the first in the United States. Everywhere there were automobiles. On a typical workday, some 260,000 cars jammed downtown Los Angeles, making the intersection of Adams and Figueroa on the edge of downtown the busiest in the world, with more than double the traffic of its nearest rival, Forty-second Street and Fifth Avenue in New York City. Los Angeles also had one of the most extensive streetcar networks in the country. Together, the intraurban Yellow and interurban Red lines provided service over more than a thousand miles of rail and transported an average of 520,000 people into the downtown area every day. Total number of passenger trips in 1924: 110,000,000.

"All of the talk was 'boom,' 'dollars,' 'greatest in the world,' 'sure to double in price,'" marveled the author Hamlin Garland, who visited L.A. in 1923. "I have never seen so many buildings going up all at one time. . . . There are thousands in process in every direction I looked." The mingling of architectural styles was—to use a word coined in that same period—surreal. The city's neighborhoods, reported Garland, consist of "hundreds of the gay little stucco bungalows in the Spanish-Mexican, Italian-Swiss, and many other styles, a conglomeration that cannot be equaled anywhere else on earth I am quite sure." If others noticed this, they didn't seem to mind.

"The whole Middle West," Garland concluded, "wants to come here."

And no wonder. The city (to say nothing of its underworld) was a carnival. In downtown Los Angeles, the theaters and movie palaces that lined Broadway attracted thronging crowds to motley performances that mixed vaudeville performers, singers, dancers, chorus girls, acrobats, even elephants with silent films by stars like Buster Keaton, Fatty Arbuckle, Douglas Fairbanks, and Mary Pickford. Then as now, starstruck tourists could sign up for "star tours" that took them past the homes of their favorite celebrities on the beach in Santa Monica and in Beverly Hills. Streetcars packed with bands and draped with advertisements crisscrossed the city, announcing new towns every month. Elephants, lions, and circus freaks lured people out to the newest developments (or, more commonly, to a free lunch under a tent on an empty lot followed by a pitch for a "marvelous investment opportunity").

"If every conceivable trick in advertising was not resorted to, it was probably due to an oversight," wrote one early philanthropist. Along Hollywood and Wilshire Boulevards, the city's first apartment buildings were starting to rise. South of downtown was the beginning of a vast manufacturing district, home to tire fabrication and automotive assembly plants that would eventually transform bucolic Los Angeles into the country's preeminent manufacturing center. High in the Hollywood Hills, a giant sign, each letter fifty feet tall and covered with four thousand lightbulbs, promoted one of Harry Chandler's new developments, "Hollywoodland!" The "-land" later fell over, and the sign became the new city's most distinctive symbol.

Then there was the oil. Beginning in 1920, a series of spectacular discoveries just south of the city suddenly made Los Angeles into one of the world's great oil-production centers. At its acme, Southern California produced 5 percent of the world's total oil supply. Shipping out of the port of San Pedro exploded. Ordinary Angelenos became obsessive investors in local oil syndicates such as the ones organized by oilman C. C. Julian from his office suite above the palatial Loews's State Theater on Broadway. It wasn't Sacramento in 1848; it wasn't Deadwood in 1876 or the Klondike in 1897; it was bigger. For a child of Deadwood, it should have been familiar terrain. Instead, Los Angeles would prove to be a cruel instructor.

THE PARKERS settled first in Westlake (today's MacArthur Park), west of downtown, then one of the most fashionable parts of Los

Angeles. Despite having moved to a nice neighborhood, the family's position was a tenuous one. Support from Deadwood was uncertain. (Mary Parker and Bill's youngest brother, Joseph, would later move to the immigrant neighborhood of Pico Heights.) In Deadwood, the Parkers had been one of the most prominent families in town. In Los Angeles, Mary Parker was basically a single mother. Moreover, she and her family were Catholics in America's most belligerently Protestant big city, a place where the Ku Klux Klan's members at one point included the chief of the LAPD, the Los Angeles County sheriff, and the U.S. attorney for Southern California. Bill Parker did not look like one of the swarthy Mediterranean immigrants that caused Protestant Angelenos such concern. Yet at a time when anti-Catholic views circulated freely, he was in a very real sense a minority.

Parker probably didn't dwell much on these difficulties. He didn't have time. At the age of seventeen, Bill Parker was now the man in the family. Although Bill's father continued to support his family from afar, finances were tight. Bill had to find a job. And so Parker turned to Los Angeles's— and America's—fastest growing industry: the movies.

Los Angeles became the home of the movie industry almost by accident. In 1909, Col. William Selig (a minstrel show owner who filched a title from the military and the design of the Kinescope movie projector from Thomas Edison) had sent director Francis Boggs west from Chicago to shoot a western in Arizona. Arizona was hot and dull, so Boggs pressed on to the city he had visited two years earlier, Los Angeles. There he and other itinerant filmmakers found the perfect outdoor shooting environment—a mixture of cityscape and countryside, deserts and mountains, ocean and forest. Its three-thousand-mile distance from New York and the Motion Pictures Patent Company "trust," which technically (i.e., legally) held the license on the technology used by the industry, was a plus too.

By 1910, the year Los Angeles annexed Hollywood, some ten-odd motion picture companies had set up operations in the area. That same year the director D.W. Griffith completed the movie *In Old California*, the first film shot completely in Hollywood. The following year, the Nestor Film Company moved from New Jersey to the corner of Sunset and Gower Street, becoming the first Los Angeles–based motion-picture studio. Universal, Triangle, Luce, Lasky's Famous Players (later Paramount), Vitagraph (later Columbia), Metro (later part of Metro-Goldwyn-Mayer or MGM), Fox, and others soon followed. By 1915, Hollywood was synonymous with the film industry, and Los Angeles was producing between 60 and 75 percent of the country's motion pictures—a little more than a quarter of the world's total films. The First World War destroyed the foreign competition and made Hollywood the cinematic capital of the world. By 1921, its seventy-plus studios had 80 percent of the world market. In the process, Hollywood became fantastically rich. By 1919, an estimated fifteen thousand theaters in the United States alone were generating roughly $800 million a year in revenues—roughly $10 billion in today's dollars.

Parker was plankton in the Hollywood food chain. His first job was as an usher at the California Theater, an imposing Beaux Arts theater at the corner of Main and Eighth Streets. He soon switched jobs, moving two blocks north to Loews's State Theater, a glorious 2,600-seat theater, reportedly Los Angeles's most profitable movie palace, in the heart of the Broadway movie district. There (for ten to fifty cents a ticket) the public could enjoy entertainment of the most wonderful variety. It wasn't just the movies. Pit orchestras performed Gilbert and Sullivan—or Beethoven. Opera singers trilling arias shared the stage with acrobats; ballets followed circus animals; elaborate "moving tableaux" gave way to daring stunts. What tantalized audiences most, though, was something new—the femme fatale.

The first was Theodosia Goodman, a tailor's daughter from Ohio, who, in the hands of her press agents, became Theda Bara, "foreign, voluptuous, and fatal"—a woman "possessed of such combustible Circe charms," panted *Time* magazine, "that her contract forbade her to ride public conveyances or go out without a veil." Others soon followed: Pola Negri, Nita Naldi, Louise Brooks. Women weren't the only ones steaming up the screen. In 1921, Rudolph Valentino rode off with the hearts of women around the world as the Sheik, the mesmerizing Arab who kidnapped, wooed, lost, saved, and ultimately won an English lady-socialite as his bride (Agnes Ayres).

As the movies heated up, so did the imaginations of the public. No one was more vulnerable than the people most exposed—theater employees. "Love is like the measles," explained one girl usher to the *Los Angeles Times*. "You can't be around it all the time without catching the fever."

Bill Parker caught the fever.

As chief of police, Parker would become a tribune of social conservatism. As a young man, however, he was ensnared. Soon after arriving in Los Angeles while he was working as an usher, Parker met Francette Pomeroy, a beautiful, high-spirited young woman, age nineteen—almost two years older than himself. The exact circumstances of their courtship are unknown. However, it's easy to understand how Francette (who went by "Francis") might have fallen for Bill. He was an unusually handsome young man—slender, of medium height, with a high forehead, prominent nose, and large, intelligent eyes. He was smart and attentive; even then, he had a sense of presence. On August 13, 1923, the two essentially eloped and were married in a civil ceremony.

Despite (or perhaps because of) the failure of his own parents' marriage, young Bill Parker had very conventional ideas about his relationship with Francis. She did not share these ideas. On the contrary, she saw no reason why marriage should interfere with the life she previously enjoyed, which involved music, dancing, and active socializing, including a continuing association with other young men. This came as a shock to Bill. In time, Parker's family would come to view Francis as a sex addict.

Perhaps she was. More likely, Francis was an adventuresome, somewhat risqué young woman who reveled in the freedom of life in Los Angeles and who was caught off guard by Bill's traditional expectations. Whatever her activities, they were unacceptable to her husband. In February 1924, when Francis prepared to leave the house, Parker confronted her with a torrent of abuse and, according to Francis, threatened "bodily harm." Two months later, on April 15, he allegedly delivered on that threat. Francis had announced that she was going out, and Parker exploded. He followed her down the staircase, arguing furiously. When she refused to come back inside, he struck her in the face, grabbed her by the throat, and dragged her upstairs and back into the apartment.

Something horrifying was happening—to Parker and to his marriage. The handsome, ambitious young man whom Francis Pomeroy had married was vanishing, replaced by a man she would later describe in her divorce petition as "cross, cranky, peevish, irritable, aggravating, and of a generally-nagging and fault-finding attitude." He, in turn, was soon describing his wife as a "damned fool," an "idiot," a "god-damned bitch"—and worse. What Bill was like before his marriage we do not know; however, these adjectives, this intolerance of fools, would be all too familiar to the men who later worked with (and for) him. In less than two years, Los Angeles had frustrated Parker's hopes and brought out the ugliest features of his personality. Bill Parker was discovering that in Los Angeles, violence, dreams, and desire kept close company.

Bill Parker was not the only young man spurred to violence by life in "the white spot" in those days. One afternoon in the summer of 1922, just a few blocks away from where Parker was working as a movie usher, idling motorists witnessed an outburst of violence that was far more remarkable than Bill Parker's (alleged) wife-beating—a holdup of the box office of the Columbia Theater.

Any attempt to heist a box office in downtown Los Angeles, in the middle of the day, in the presence of hundreds of witnesses would have been noteworthy. But what made this band of bandits so singularly striking was their frightening, baseball bat–wielding leader. He was only nine years old. His name was Meyer Harris Cohen, but all of Los Angeles would soon come to know him simply as "Mickey."

The Combination

"The purpose of any political organization is to get the money from the gamblers . . ."
—Wilbur LeGette

MICKEY COHEN wasn't supposed to exist in Los Angeles.

"The conditions which exist here should make for the finest character building in the land," opined the *Los Angeles Times* in 1923. "The hazards of the environment are at their minimum. We should have more than the ordinary proportion of patriotism because our citizens are mainly the descendants of American pioneers. As a city we have no vast foreign districts in which strange tongues are ever heard. The community is American"—meaning, in *Times*-speak, white, native-born, and Protestant—"clear to its back-bone."

Tell that to the residents of Boyle Heights.

In a city that prided itself on homogeneity, Boyle Heights—a neighborhood across the Los Angeles River due east of downtown—was an anomaly, a mixing pot of Jews, Italians, Mexicans, Japanese, Russians, Germans, Finns, and Frenchmen. It was a neighborhood of both desperate poverty and earnest striving. The flats along the Los Angeles River were home to one of the worst slums in America—a neighborhood whose horrors, according to the photographer and social reformer Jacob Riis, exceeded the tenements of the Lower East Side. However, farther east along Brooklyn Avenue (today's Cesar Chávez Avenue) a vibrant, working-class, polyglot community had taken shape. At a time when Los Angeles was older, wealthier, and sicker than America as a whole (Southern California's supposed salubrity lured wealthy convalescents from across the country to the region), Boyle Heights was vigorous, young, and exotic. It was here that Mickey Cohen would spend his childhood—and begin his criminal career.

Boyle Heights's multiculturalism would serve that career well. Mickey grew up with close Mexican and Italian friends. (He would later boast of speaking a little "Mexican.") The experience paved the way for Mickey's later moves into the largely Italian world of organized crime. It would later lead Mickey to assemble an unusual crew, one that was half-Jewish (from New York) and half-Italian (from Cleveland). The easy mingling of Jews and Italians in Cohen's circle would frustrate Mickey's rivals and ultimately give him the clout he would need to take on one of Los Angeles's most shadowy institutions, the group of men who controlled the Los Angeles underworld who were known simply as "the Combination."

HE WAS BORN Meyer Harris Cohen on September 4, 1913, in the Brownsville section of Brooklyn, but he was always known simply as "Mickey." Just two months after his birth, Mickey's father, who (his youngest son would later recall) had been involved with "some kind of import business with Jewish fishes," died. His Russian-born wife was left to take care of the five kids. Three years later, Fanny Cohen decided to move to Los Angeles to start life anew.

Fanny, Mickey, and his sister Lillian settled into a modest apartment on Breed Street, just a block south of the newly built wooden shul that was the center of Boyle Heights's fast-growing Jewish community. Fanny opened a small grocery store around the corner on Brooklyn Avenue. The business did well enough for her to send for the rest of her family—sons Sam, Louis, Harry, and daughter Pauline. Everyone worked hard—albeit at a range of endeavors whose legality varied. By age four, Mickey was spending most of his time with his older brothers on the street, selling newspapers. Mickey's job was simple: sit on the stack of newspapers to keep them from blowing away and give passersby pleading looks. But even then, the first sprouts of criminality were taking root in little Mickey's mind: His brothers found that he was constantly giving away papers for candy and hot dogs.

Mickey soon became a full-fledged newspaper boy in his own right. At a time when newsboys typically had to scrape for a good corner, Mickey secured a prime spot at the elbow of Soto and Brooklyn Streets hawking the *Los Angeles Record* (ironically, the scourge of vice and police corruption in that era). Although his mother attempted to enroll him in kindergarten when he was four, Mickey was a reluctant student. He was always sneaking off to sell papers, particularly when a breaking story meant there were "extras" to be hawked. Indeed, Mickey so preferred making a buck to going to school that he once skipped six weeks of the first grade entirely. It took him a year and a half to graduate to second grade.

Little Mickey was a natural street urchin. He was out on the avenue so much that numbers runners were soon leaving slips with him. Local bootleggers left "packages" with him for important clients. He learned the fine points of craps and pool sharking. He even got into extortion, frightening a neighborhood barber into paying him to stay away. Naturally, Mickey soon moved into bootlegging as well.

Mickey's entrée came from his brothers Harry and Louie, who had opened a pharmacy at the corner of Pico and Bond. At first they employed Mickey afternoons as a soda jerk, but talent will out: Mickey was soon operating the still behind the store. One morning in 1920, police raided the Cohen family pharmacy and caught Mickey red-handed. That's when another defining feature of Cohen's personality came out—his dangerous temper. Instead of being taken into custody quietly, Mickey assaulted one of the arresting officers with a hot plate. He was seven.

What followed was a lesson Mickey would never forget. One of his brothers called a well-connected relative who made the charges go away. For Mickey, it was a Saul-on-the-road-to-Damascus moment. As he would later write in his memoirs, "It was all a fix. My brother had the connection." Much of his subsequent life would be devoted to the search for "the fix."

The fact that Mickey's brothers had entrusted their still to a seven-year-old might seem like conclusive proof that the brothers Cohen were not concerned with young Mickey's moral development, but in fact, such a conclusion would be unfair. Oldest brother Sam did care. Sam was a religious man. He decided to enroll Mickey in Hebrew school. Unfortunately, while waiting to meet the rabbi, Mickey "got into a beef" with another kid and slapped him in the mouth. He was promptly sent home with instructions to never appear at synagogue again.

Clearly, Mickey had a calling—a criminal one. But he was hardly a criminal mastermind, as his midday holdup of a movie theater box office demonstrated. A successful heist requires forethought and planning—a "tipster" to provide intelligence, a stolen getaway car (ideally one with "cold" plates), perhaps even a "tail" car to throw anyone who pursued you off the chase. Cohen seems not to have considered what would happen after he got his hands on the money. As a result, the police nabbed him before he could escape from the scene. This time, "the fix" wasn't "in." He was sent off to a Dickensian reform school on Fort Hill, overlooking downtown. Mickey would later describe being beaten almost every day of his seven-month stay with a shredded old bicycle tire for "any old thing." Even for a hardened street kid, it was a nightmare. When Mickey got out of this prison, he resolved never to go to school again. He had almost finished the second grade. He would not learn to read (or to add or subtract) until he was in his thirties, a shortcoming that would complicate his later life as a stick-up artist.

While Mickey started his criminal career at a precocious age, he was hardly unusual in choosing a life of crime. By late 1922, Los Angeles was experiencing an unprecedented crime wave. Statistics from the period are sketchy, but the best estimates suggest that "virtuous" Anglo-Saxon L.A. had a homicide rate that was nearly twice that of the racially mixed, immigrant metropolis New York City. In fact, with a population of only half a million people, Los Angeles was closing in fast on the total homicide tally of Great Britain, whose population was 44 million.

The cause of this surge in homicides was mysterious, but to Harry Chandler and the business establishment, its potential consequences were profoundly worrisome.

"The white spot of America," bemoaned one contributor to the *Times*, was becoming a "black spot" of crime—"so black in fact as to make it the subject of invidious comparisons whenever statistics of crime in America and Europe are cited."

Overt vice and rampant crime threatened the image that fueled Los Angeles's growth—and undergirded the fortunes of men like Harry Chandler. "Look-the-other-way" boosterism would no longer do. The image that Harry Chandler and the growth barons had so carefully cultivated was in danger. Chandler resolved to act.

BY 1922, Harry Chandler was accustomed to having his way. A member of more than thirty corporate boards; the hidden hand behind innumerable syndicates, secret trusts, and dummy corporations; a land baron who owned or controlled roughly 300,000 acres in Southern California and, across the border in Mexico, an 860,000-acre ranching and farming operation that included the largest cotton plantation in the world, Chandler was the most powerful businessman in Los Angeles. By 1922, estimates of his fortune ranged from $200 million to half a billion dollars—immense sums for the 1920s. The *Los Angeles Times* was by far the most influential and profitable paper in Southern California, with nearly double the ad linage of its nearest rival, William Randolph Hearst's *Los Angeles Examiner*. Local businessmen spoke with a mixture of awe and dread of Chandler's "thousand dollar lunches"—the occasions on which the business community was summoned to rally behind one of Chandler's civic improvement initiatives. Chandler's power was not absolute, but when he and the business community resolved to act, they generally prevailed.

Now was just such a time. Chandler quickly recruited George Cryer, a former assistant city attorney (who bore a striking resemblance to Woodrow Wilson), to run for mayor. To manage his campaign, Cryer chose a former University of Southern California football star-turned-attorney, Kent Kane

Parrot (pronounced "Perot"), a protégé of one of Chandler's closest allies in local politics, Superior Court Judge Gavin Craig.

At first, everything went well. Cryer ran an extremely well-funded campaign, and voters, at the *Los Angeles Times*'s urging, obligingly elected him mayor. Kent Parrot became his chief of staff. Mayor Cryer then set out to find a chief of police who could crack down on vice.

The mayor's first choice, a determined reformer, quit within a matter of months, frustrated at resistance within the department. Cryer's second choice, a war hero with no experience in police work, launched a vigorous crackdown on prostitution in the downtown hotels. But that was the wrong kind of crackdown. The *image* of lawlessness was bad, but certain types of lawlessness (notably prostitution and gambling) were widely seen as being good for business, as long as they were done discreetly. Outraged hoteliers soon forced his resignation. Clearly, cleaning up Los Angeles would require a delicate touch.

If Mayor Cryer was disheartened, he didn't show it. He turned next to detective Louis Oaks, who'd won acclaim for rescuing a society matron from kidnappers. But, alas, he too stumbled. First the chief was observed frequenting one of the very hotels his predecessor had attempted to close down, in the company of not one but two ladies of the night. Then he was arrested in San Bernardino in the backseat of a car with a half-dressed woman and a half-empty bottle of whiskey.

This was embarrassing, to be sure, but it was not what ended his policing career. Chief Oaks was fired only after he crossed Mayor Cryer's right-hand man, Kent Parrot. Parrot had his own man in the police department, Capt. Lee Heath. Captain Heath acted as Parrot's proxy, transferring personnel without the chief's permission and shaking down tour operators to raise funds for the Parrot-Cryer machine. Such behavior from a subordinate was problematic, to say the least. So Chief Oaks decided to dismiss Captain Heath. Parrot responded by having Oaks fired instead. He then made Heath chief.

By firing Oaks and replacing him with Heath, Kent Parrot was sending a clear message: The LAPD was now under his personal control. Harry Chandler was shocked—and furious. The LAPD was supposed to be under *his* control. For more than a decade, Chandler and his fiercely antiunion father-in-law, Gen. Harrison Gray Otis, had relied on the LAPD to do battle with radicals and union organizers.* Parrot was supposed to be a business

---

*A battle was precisely what it was. In 1910, the steelworkers union had blown up the *Times* building at First and Broadway, killing more than twenty people. Otis and Chandler responded by beefing up the LAPD and unleashing it on Communists, anarchists, union organizers, and others who threatened Los Angeles's status as an "open shop" town.

community loyalist, Harry Chandler's man on the mayor's staff. Instead, Parrot was building a rival power, one underwritten by L.A.'s booze-fueled underworld, not Harry Chandler.

Bootlegging had been a profitable pastime in Southern California since 1916, when California passed a dry law during the First World War that sought to conserve alcohol for military industrial purposes. The passage of the Volstead Act in 1920 implemented Prohibition nationwide in a far more draconian form, by outlawing beer and wine as well as spirits. It was the Volstead Act that made bootlegging a big business. Within months, high-speed motorboats were unloading Mexican and Canadian booze onto beaches from San Diego to Santa Barbara, primarily from Canadian ships that plied the route from Vancouver to Mexico. Meanwhile, convoys of trucks, many with hidden compartments, made their way up the so-called Bootleg Highway from Tecate to Tijuana to San Diego and thence to L.A. By the most conservative estimate, some 3,700,000 gallons of liquor were being illegally imported every year. Most of that was cheap hooch. However, authorities estimated that the most sophisticated bootleggers were also bringing about 150,000 cases of Scotch a year into Los Angeles. The markup on the Scotch was $35 a case, meaning that the bootleggers were grossing more than $5 million a year—about $50 million in today's dollars—on Scotch alone.

At first, much of this business was handled by precocious entrepreneurs like Tony "the Hat" Cornero, who, at the age of twenty-two, gave up his job as a taxi driver in San Francisco, moved south to Los Angeles, and started hijacking other bootleggers' liquor. In short order, *he* was the bootlegger bringing in the good Scotch, four thousand cases a run on his yacht the SS *Lilly* (whose home port was Vancouver, British Columbia). The stocky, granite-faced bootlegger with the white Stetson hats, pearl-colored gloves, and the flashing gray eyes quickly became one of Southern California's most colorful (and quotable) criminals, known for his pungent verbal broadsides against Prohibition. By one estimate, Cornero controlled about a third of Scotch imports coming into the region in these early years. However, Cornero and his gang did not have the field entirely to themselves. Another more powerful criminal cabal was plotting his demise.

In the big eastern cities, crime was largely an immigrant affair. Not in Los Angeles. Fittingly, the "white spot" of America also had a largely American-born criminal overclass. Its ringleader was Charlie "The Gray Wolf" Crawford, owner of the popular Maple Bar at Maple and Fifth Street. Crawford had learned his chops in Seattle during the years that city served as the staging ground for the turn-of-the-century Klondike gold rush in Alaska. However, in the early teens, Crawford was run out of town after he and a close associate, pimp Albert Marco, openly negotiated a lease with the city for a five-hundred-"crib" brothel on Beacon Hill. Crawford was careful not to repeat his mistakes in Los Angeles. The Maple Bar was an intimate affair. While everyone could drink downstairs, only friends of Charlie were allowed upstairs to play craps or roulette or to patronize the prostitutes. Older and wiser, Crawford prospered in Los Angeles. But it was the onset of Prohibition in 1920 that made him big.

Crawford got back in touch with Marco, who, from his base in Seattle, was able to start importing high-grade Canadian Scotch from British Columbia. The pipeline they opened to L.A. was so lucrative that Marco soon decided to move to Southern California too. There Crawford introduced him to slot machine king Robert Gans, Milton "Farmer" Page, and former LAPD vice squad officer Guy "Stringbean" McAfee. Crawford also had the all-important connection to Kent Parrot. He and his associates were prepared to pay handsomely for favors from the department, and Parrot set out to become the man who would satisfy that desire. In order to do that, he needed to establish his control over the police. Chief Oaks's firing—followed, in short order, by the appointment of Captain Heath as chief of police—left no doubt about who controlled the department.

In Seattle, Crawford had overreached. Expanding prostitution beyond the red-light district (today's Pioneer Square), partnering with Seattle police chief "Wappy" Wappenstein to use the force to collect $10 a week from the city's prostitutes—it had been too explicit, too open. In Los Angeles, the gradations of protection were more subtle. Rather than making the police direct partners, as they had in Seattle, in Los Angeles, the police were simply encouraged to crack down on Combination competitors such as Tony Cornero.

Cornero tried to buy his way out, reputedly contributing $100,000 to Mayor Cryer's second reelection campaign. But the Cryer administration just took the money and continued with the pressure. Cornero would later blame the police for some $500,000 in losses during this period. In contrast, Parrot associates such as Crawford, Page, and Marco received very different treatment from the criminal justice system. When Page was involved in his second shootout in four months at the notorious Sorrento Café in early 1925—self-defense, he claimed—he was promptly released on bail by Judge Craig, Parrot's mentor. Crackdowns on the establishments of Crawford associates likewise had a way of fizzling out: One deputy sheriff reported that on two occasions he witnessed LAPD patrol cars departing Page-owned casinos he and his colleagues were about to raid. When on yet another occasion an inexperienced young patrolman arrested pimp Marco for assault with a deadly weapon, two veteran detectives stepped in and reduced the charge to "disturbing the peace," a decision the city prosecutor defended even after it emerged that Marco, a noncitizen, was ineligible for a concealed weapons permit. So how did he get one? It turned out that Undersheriff Eugene Biscailuz, later Los Angeles County's longest-serving sheriff, had given him a license. The LAPD wasn't the only organization doing Charlie Crawford's friends favors.

In exchange for such kid-gloves treatment, Crawford and his associates gave Parrot the money he needed to run expensive political campaigns—and to resist the dictates of Harry Chandler, an assertive multimillionaire with a printing press. This alliance between city hall and the underworld was soon dubbed the Combination. The Combination supplied the money; the backlash against Chandler's reactionary political positions (he was opposed, for instance, to the cheap public power supplied by the Boulder [later Hoover] Dam) supplied many of the votes. With underworld money and populist political positions on such issues as public energy, Parrot and Mayor Cryer shrewdly built a base of supporters.

The Combination got its first true test in the mayoral election of 1925, which pitted incumbent Mayor Cryer against a conservative judge hand-picked by Harry Chandler. At issue was the question of who would control Los Angeles.

"Mr. Cryer, how much longer is Kent Parrot going to be the defacto Mayor of Los Angeles?" thundered the judge in his campaign appearances.

"Shall We Re-Elect Kent Parrot?" echoed the *Times*. The real contest, it informed its readers, was the judge "or the Boss."

Parrot replied by plastering downtown Los Angeles with posters that proclaimed that the real choice was between Chandler and Cryer. On election day, Chandler lost.

The *Times* publisher was stunned. The paper had lost control of the mayoralty before, but the Parrot-Cryer "Combination" represented something different and altogether more threatening—a standing alliance that threatened to push Harry Chandler to the margins. The paper hit back. Suddenly, the *Times* was filled with illuminating stories about how politics under Kent Parrot actually worked and editorials raving about "Boss Parrot" and "the City Hall Gang." Typical of the newspaper's new focus on vice was the *seventeen*-part series on the Cryer administration's sins published the following year.

In truth, each camp needed the other—and the LAPD. Chandler wanted the department to address the perception that Los Angeles was wracked by violent crime. He also wanted to retain control of its notorious "Red Squad," which was known for the hardball tactics it used against radicals and labor organizers. Parrot wanted the exposés to stop, without giving up his control over the police department, which he needed to protect the under-world and maintain the Combination. In short, both sides had good reasons to come to terms, and so in 1926 they did. The deal was simple: The *Times* would launch no antivice crusades; Parrot would not interfere with the operations of the Red Squad. To seal the agreement, the two sides agreed on a police chief who would satisfy both parties: James "Two Gun" Davis, an intense, blue-eyed Texan who had spent much of his career as a member of the vice squad.

With a measure of control over the police force restored, the *Times* began to downplay stories about corruption in the city. Reformers who insisted on continuing their investigations suffered misfortunes. One reform-minded council member was discovered in bed with an attractive young divorcée by LAPD vice raiders. The raiding party that was responding to the supposedly anonymous complaint included the heads of the vice and the intelligence squads—as well as a reporter from the *Los Angeles Times*. That was the system. Few dared to cross it.

BILL PARKER also found himself caught in a compromising situation with a woman, though in his case, the woman was his wife. By early 1924, Parker had become convinced that his spouse was seeing other men. On April 28, he found her at home with a young child and, suspecting the child was hers from some previous relationship, he flew into a rage. Francis insisted that the child was her sister's, which calmed her husband, for a while. In May, Bill and Francis moved in—temporarily—with Bill's mother and his youngest brother. The atmosphere was charged. Yet Francis refused to change her behavior. Parker, in return, seemed increasingly willing to respond with his fists—by Francis's account, beating her so badly on one occasion that she lost consciousness.

Parker tried to focus on his career. Working as a movie usher was no way to make a living, but by the mid-1920s good alternatives were hard to come by. The boom of the early twenties was sputtering to a stop. By 1925, some 600,000 subdivided lots stood vacant across the Los Angeles basin. Nevertheless, Parker soon found a new job as a taxi driver with the Yellow Cab Co., where he was fortunate enough to secure a stand at the newly built Biltmore Hotel on Pershing Square, the city's grandest accommodation. After a year he was promoted to supervisor, but Parker had larger ambitions than managing cabs. He wanted to be a lawyer, like his illustrious grandfather, and in 1924 he enrolled at the Southwestern School of Law.

Hindered by a full-time job and a crumbling marriage, he made little progress. In early 1925, Francis decided that she had had enough. She left

Los Angeles, returned to her hometown of Oregon City, and filed for a divorce, claiming that Parker had "made Plaintiff's life unbearable and has rendered further cohabitation with the Defendant [Parker] absolutely distasteful and made it utterly impossible for Plaintiff and Defendant to live together as husband and wife." Bill didn't bother to respond to the summons to appear in court or to contest the divorce, and on May 9, 1925, a judge in Clackamas County, Oregon, granted Francis's divorce request and awarded her possession of their one significant asset, "one Upright Sonora Phonograph," valued at $150.

Freed of his wife—a woman about whom he would never speak in subsequent years—Parker returned to the study of law with a vengeance. In 1926, he enrolled at a different institution, the Los Angeles College of Law at the University of the West. He also hit upon a new way to make a living while studying to become a lawyer: He decided to apply for a position as a policeman. Hours were flexible; the pay was adequate (about $2,000 a year, roughly what a skilled laborer earned); and benefits were good. Being a policeman was still far from a prestigious job; one public opinion survey from the era found that police officers were more respected than chauffeurs, janitors, and clerks but less respected than machinists and stenographers. But then Bill Parker would not be a policeman forever. Once he got his law degree, he planned to follow in his grandfather's footsteps and make his living as an attorney.

On April 24, 1926, Parker sat for a civil service exam. The competition was not formidable. Only about two-thirds of the men on the force had finished grade school; a mere one in ten had graduated from high school. Five months later, he received a notice stating that he had scored 85.7 on the exam, making him number 115 on the list of those eligible for a job with the police department. Never again would William Parker score so low on a civil service exam. Still, it was good enough. When his number came up, Parker was offered a position. On August 8, 1927, he joined the Los Angeles Police Department. There he made a startling discovery. In Los Angeles, the police didn't fight organized crime. They managed it.

The Bad Old Good Old Days

> "[A] smart lawyer can keep a crook out of
> jail . . . buy or bamboozle a jury, but he
> cannot prevent the cops from beating the
> hell out of a crook."
>
> —Leslie White, *Me, Detective*

FOR THE FIRST FOUR DECADES of its existence, the Los Angeles Police Department led a desultory existence. Founded in 1869 (with six paid men), the force was outmatched from the beginning. While the department proved adept at tasks such as keeping cattle out of the streets and forcing Indians into chain gangs, it showed little ability to curb the startlingly high levels of violence that prompted its creation.

"The name of this city is in Spanish the city of Angels, but with much more truth might it be called at present the city of Demons," wrote a visiting divine. "While I have been here in Los Angeles only two weeks, there have been eleven deaths, and only one of them a natural [one]."

Far from reducing the violence, the police at times contributed to it, as on the memorable occasion when the city marshal (also the city dogcatcher and tax collector) got into a shootout with one of his own officers at the corner of Temple and Main after a dispute over who should receive the reward for capturing and returning a prostitute who had escaped from one of the city's Chinese tongs.

"While there are undoubtedly good men upon the police force, the body as a whole is not a matter for our citizens to be proud of," sighed the *Los Angeles Herald* in 1900. "It is perfectly obvious to all that the policemen have not been selected for their honesty or fitness, but through political favor and for political purposes. . . . [Many officers] are over age, some under size, others unfit for duty; some do not pay their just debts, others figure prominently in divorce cases, and some receive money from sporting women for the privilege of soliciting upon the streets."

In their defense, it should be noted that police officers received no training and very little support. After being hired, officers were required to supply themselves with the gear necessary for the job: two uniforms, hats, boots, a revolver, a gun belt and cartridges, handcuffs, and a billy club. For this, they were paid $75 a month at the turn of the century—less than a milk deliveryman.

In theory, policemen of the era were charged with many tasks. Officers not only apprehended criminals, they were also responsible for preparing cases against criminals appearing in court. They picked up loose paper on the streets (blowing paper could spook horses), cleared weeds from abandoned lots, enforced foot-and-mouth disease regulations, notified businessmen of upcoming police auctions, and enforced licensing requirements. Officers also responded to fires and floods. In practice, few applied themselves to their work with much zeal. A 1904 study of the Chicago Police Department found that police officers "spent most of their time not on the streets but in saloons, restaurants, barbershops, bowling alleys, pool halls, and bootblack stands."

The activities of plainclothes detectives were more suspect still. When they operated out of saloons and dives—supposedly, in order to better monitor the underworld—it was often difficult to distinguish them from the men they were tasked with policing. Detectives routinely demanded cuts from the pickpockets, pimps, burglars, and bunco men who operated in their areas, often at the behest of local elected officials, who frequently insisted on a cut as well. Most were not particularly good at solving crimes. When something truly serious happened, for instance, the 1910 firebombing of the *Los Angeles Times*, cities turned to more capable outfits such as the William Burns Detective Agency.

In 1902, the LAPD's woes were greatly exacerbated by two ministers' "discovery" of Los Angeles's booming crib district, which centered at the time on Sanchez Street, an alley just off the historic plaza. The clergymen immediately set out to publicize the horrors of this "market for human flesh" with a series of vivid pamphlets and books (which sold very well). Inflamed churchmen descended on "hell's half-acre" to implore its prostitutes and saloonkeepers to renounce their evil ways. When that failed, they turned to the ballot, amending the city charter so as to completely outlaw all forms of prostitution, gambling, and vice within Los Angeles city limits. (Previously, such activities had been explicitly prohibited only within the central business district.) Henceforth, Los Angeles was "closed"—at least in theory.

The decision to prohibit vice put the LAPD in a difficult if not impossible situation. Faced with the threat of extinction, saloonkeepers, brewery owners, brothel operators, and gambling kingpins threw themselves into politics, donating lavishly to candidates for sheriff, district attorney, superior court judge, city council, and mayor. (Kent Parrot was simply the first to harness these funds in a systematic manner.) Their largesse was likewise available to policemen, particularly to members of the Chinatown and the Metropolitan "purity" squads willing to tip them off when the pressure to mount a raid became irresistible. As a result, officers on the front lines of the effort to police the underworld often faced a stark choice: break the law and accept bribes from the saloonkeepers, madams, and gaming house operators who were bankrolling the politicians or refuse bribes, enforce the law, and risk being fired or assigned to direct traffic on the graveyard shift down at the port of San Pedro. Not everyone chose the path of virtue.

There were moments when puritanical morals held sway. In 1912, the city council passed legislation prohibiting sexual intercourse with "any person of the opposite sex to whom he or she is not married." "A platoon of ministers" was sworn in to prowl for vice; parks and public beaches were illuminated and patrolled to prevent hanky-panky. But the reign of the morals police was short-lived. The opening of the Panama Canal in 1914 and the United States's entry into the First World War flooded Los Angeles with sailors and soldiers—populations renowned for whoring and boozing. Rationing created ample opportunities for black market profits, which in turn led to a surge in the supply of criminals. By the end of the decade, all pretense of enforcing the vice laws had basically come to an end. Los Angeles was run by the business community and the Combination. The LAPD served both as an enforcer.

It took a while for Patrolman Parker to catch on.

One night soon after his rookie probationary period had ended, Parker was leaving Central Division station, an imposing Romanesque building that also served as police headquarters up the block from the *Times*. He had just gotten into his car, ready to head off to an evening of night class at law school, when he saw an automobile weave down the First Street hill and then blow through a red light. The driver of the car was clearly drunk; Parker estimated it was moving at about sixty miles per hour. He took off in pursuit, picking up a madly whistling traffic cop along the way. Eventually, the two policemen succeeded in pulling the driver over. They found a half-empty open bottle in the car. They also discovered that the man they had stopped was John Arrington, a police reporter for the *Los Angeles Daily News*.

Today the police beat is seen as a place where novice reporters go to learn the craft—the bottom of the journalistic food chain. Not so in the 1920s. In those pretelevision days, crime was the sexiest beat in journalism, and the men (and occasionally women) who covered it were important figures. Not only were they star reporters, they also frequently functioned as political hatchet men for their publishers (a job greatly facilitated by reporters' free access to police files). Reporters supplemented their writing and (ahem) "research" with booze, poker, and occasionally extortion (publicity being something that many people were willing to pay to avoid). Veteran officers rarely crossed them. So it was hardly surprising that when Patrolman Parker hauled reporter Arrington into Central Division station and presented him to the desk sergeant for booking, he was not greeted enthusiastically. On the contrary, the sergeant on duty suggested that Parker let the newsman go. That's when a defining feature of Bill Parker's personality emerged: his stubbornness.

Infuriated at the idea that press credentials somehow inoculated the bearer from prosecution, Parker insisted that "the law was the law." Reluctantly, the desk sergeant agreed to book the newspaperman. It soon emerged that the open bottle of liquor Parker had discovered in Arrington's car was a gift from a police captain pal. Reluctantly, Parker's superiors allowed the case to go to court, where, after many testimonials to the high character and unshakable sobriety of the newsman, a judge dismissed the case. It was Parker's first lesson in how policing really worked.

Punishment, the ways in which it was or was not dispensed, provided a compelling introduction to how power was really distributed in Los Angeles. Nowhere were these realities more vivid than inside the dungeon that was the city jail. Every year fifty thousand Angelenos were arrested and passed through its halls—a significant number in a city of a million souls, and a sign that despite widespread corruption, a considerable portion of the department was still prepared to enforce Prohibition and its vice laws. Yet when a person of importance was caught in the net of vice enforcement, the legal apparatus was often forgiving. One night in 1927, the journalist and writer Louis Adamic happened to be on hand at 2:30 a.m. when "a star of world-wide fame, the sister of another famous celebrity, near stars, maids in waiting, and a bevy of attending sheiks and bull fighters" were hauled in "more or less cock-eyed drunk."

Adamic then related what happened next:

"Come along, sister, and give me a hand," the cop addresses the star. "I'm goin' to print you."

"Not by a damn sight. Let go my arm—take your paw off'n me, you mammal," she replies indignantly. . . .

The officer puts a brawny arm of enforcement around a classic waist. This is too much. He is kicked efficiently amidship. Another cop comes to the rescue of his mate. He is assaulted by the remainder of the bevy. . . . Much swearing, screeching, kicking, pulling of hair, and everything. The cops work methodically and effectively. . . . The best way of quieting a temperamental and irate movie queen, it has been found, is to sit on her.

Alas, the fun soon came to an end:

> But before this printing process is completed there is a great scurrying down the corridor and a whole brigade of bondsmen, wirepullers and fixers come charging upon the scene. The climax is quickly past. The Records are inspected to see that aliases are used, warnings issued against giving anything to the paper, and the guests prepare to depart. The star, now somewhat sobered, feels that the parting shot is expected of her—an exit is after all an exit—and drawing herself up to her full five feet six inches she withers with a single glance the offending officer who has printed her and declares so that all may hear, "You damn big bum, I'll let you know that I'm a lady."

That was how the elite were treated. In March 1929, two plainclothes officers stopped a Finnish immigrant whom they had mistaken for a suspect. Indignant, the man launched into a tirade about the police that suggested that the man held "radical" political views. The officers responded by hauling him into police headquarters and working him over with brass knuckles. Only after the man, face pulped and bloodied, abjectly proclaimed his newfound admiration for the police was he released. The district attorney brought charges against the officers in question, but they were later dismissed.

Cops sometimes acted violently because they believed the system was corrupt. "Good men would not serve on juries, nor would they take time from their private interests to act as witnesses in court trials—if they could get out of it," wrote Leslie White in his 1936 classic, *Me, Detective*. "Business men and good citizens did not want their homes robbed and their daughters raped, but they did want liquor for themselves, and prostitutes and gambling were good for business." As a result, some officers took it on themselves to dispense justice. For, as Detective White put it, "[a] smart lawyer can keep a crook out of jail . . . buy or bamboozle a jury, but he cannot prevent the cops from beating the hell out of a crook."

So some did. People arrested by the police were often detained for days—sometimes even for weeks—before being brought before a judge. Prisoners were frequently held incommunicado—no contact with family or friends, much less an attorney—until they confessed. When faced with hardened cons, the police routinely shifted prisoners into cold, dark cells without beds or chairs or into "sweat boxes." They also resorted to "the third degree." Typically, this involved round-the-clock questioning and sleep deprivation, a form of torture that almost always produced the desired confession. When it didn't—or if the police were simply pissed—the "third degree" could also involve beating prisoners with clubs, fists, or rubber hoses. Central Division station even had a special cell where such beatings occurred. "Screams have been heard and complaints from prisoners are frequent," reported one investigation of jail conditions.

Parker would later describe this period as "the bad old good old days."

Remarkably, the LAPD was actually less violent than most big-city police departments. In Chicago, prisoners were routinely beaten with phone books, manacled and hung from pipes, and teargassed. Still, Los Angeles was clearly not a city where people were equal under the law. Parker soon came to the sickening realization that Los Angeles "was in the clutch of hoodlums." *Dumb* hoodlums: IQ tests administered in the early twenties found that a significant number of police officers were "low-grade mental defectives." *Drunken*, dumb hoodlums. Sometimes, Parker would later recall, "I was the only sober man in the office."

Not reassuring words from a man who was almost certainly an alcoholic.

Parker's second arrest was more successful. Gazing out the window as he was riding home on one of the yellow Los Angeles Railway streetcars that crisscrossed the city, Parker noticed a man running toward his streetcar, carrying a woman's fur coat. Panting heavily, the man stepped onto the streetcar. He was a big guy—over six feet tall, probably weighing at least two hundred pounds—with long arms; small, deep-set eyes; and a broad chest. Something about him looked familiar. Then Parker realized that he matched the description of a man wanted by the San Francisco police who had terrorized the city for weeks by attacking people with a long knife.

Parker edged over to the man and asked, in what he hoped was a casual voice, "Say, where'd you get that coat?"

"What's it to you?" the man snarled, turning away.

Parker told the man he was a policeman and patted him down. He found—and confiscated—a long-bladed knife. Convinced that he had happened across the wanted man, Parker signaled for the motorman to stop—and informed the suspect that he was under arrest. Then he pulled the man off the streetcar and dragged him, "protesting and resisting," to a police call box, where he called for a patrol wagon. At police headquarters, the department confirmed that Parker had nabbed the man San Franciscan papers had taken to calling Jack the Ripper.

It was a major coup for a rookie officer. His superiors, doubtless, were not pleased. A rookie had no right to make such an arrest: A savvier officer would have allowed a more senior officer to take the credit. But then no one thought Bill Parker was savvy; on the contrary, he was either one of the dumbest men on the force or one of the most obstinate. Either way, he needed to be taught a lesson. So when Central Division got word one day that a shopkeeper had taken two employees hostage, the lieutenant on duty knew just who to send.

"He's got a repeating shotgun," the lieutenant said. "Take it away from him and bring him in."

"Yes, sir," Parker responded, and hurried to the shop.

When Parker arrived at the store, he saw the shopkeeper through the glass of the locked door, pacing and waving his gun. The owner saw Parker, too, and yelled at him to get back. Instead of waiting for backup, Parker went up to the store and calmly knocked on the door.

"Keep out," the owner yelled. Parker knocked again. The man with the shotgun approached the door—and started lamenting his troubles. Parker indicated that he just couldn't hear him clearly.

"Open the door so I can hear you," Parker called out to the man. As he did so, Parker rushed the gunman, grabbing the shotgun before the man could fire it. The gun was later found to contain five shells. Bill Parker had gotten lucky.

Later that year, he got lucky in another way. At some point in 1927, Parker met Helen Schultz, an eighteen-year-old telephone exchange girl, the daughter of an Austrian immigrant furniture maker in Philadelphia. In Helen, the twenty-two-year-old Parker (who by then was claiming to be twenty-five) found a kindred spirit. Helen was a devout Catholic, and she loved to hunt and fish. She was also smart, sassy, and, personality-wise, something of a pistol. (It would seem that Bill Parker had no brief for sedate women.) This time there would be no elopement. On May 1, 1928, an announcement of Parker and Helen's engagement appeared in the *Los Angeles Times*. They were married later that year.

Happy, at least in his personal life, Parker bore down on his studies. He was now plowing through night school at the Los Angeles College of Law. In 1930, he would finally receive his law degree. Then he could leave the force and follow in his grandfather's footsteps.

The Great Depression intervened. By 1930, Los Angeles had the highest personal bankruptcy rate in the country. Ruined investors were hurling themselves to their deaths from the Arroyo Seco Bridge in Pasadena with such frequency that the city was forced to erect elaborate antisuicide barriers. Nevertheless, Parker's wife, Helen, assumed that he would leave the force and go to work for a law firm as soon as he completed his degree. As the date drew nearer, however, it dawned on her that her husband might actually enjoy policing more than the practice of law.

"Statements from Bill kept cropping up about 'liking the work' [and] 'every day there is something new," Helen would later write. So one day she asked him point-blank: Would a law degree help you in a career with the police? He assured her that it would. And so the decision was made. Parker would remain a policeman.

part two/

The Struggle for Authority

5

"Jewboy"

"I wasn't the worse. Neither was I the tops."
—Mickey Cohen

BY 1927, the Parrot-Cryer Combination seemed to have Los Angeles sewn up tight. Notwithstanding the presence of a few immigrants such as pimp-turned-bootlegger Albert Marco, the criminal underworld of Los Angeles was now a decidedly WASPy affair, one that left little room for an ambitious Jewish hoodlum like Mickey Cohen. The situation was undoubtedly a frustrating one. Mickey realized early on that "putting money together" was what gave him the most pleasure in life. He also realized that bootlegging, muscle jobs, and armed robbery offered excellent opportunities for enrichment. However, without a "fix," criminal activities could have most unpleasant ramifications, as Mickey learned after his botched box office holdup. But in Los Angeles, the only outfit with a reliable "fix" was the Combination, and the Combination didn't recruit talent from the east side of the Los Angeles River. Fortunately, that very year Mickey stumbled across a way out of this dead end. His talent for fighting led him to the one group that could challenge the likes of Kent Parrot, Charlie Crawford, and Guy McAfee: the Mob.

As a condition for his release from reform school, Mickey was required to meet on a weekly basis with a "Big Brother." Mickey's was Abe Roth, a well-known fight referee. Where others saw a thuggish street scrapper, Roth saw a talented flyweight boxer. That prizefights were illegal at the time and that Mickey was on probation was no obstacle to Roth's plan. Roth soon had Mickey fighting four-round bouts in bootleg clubs and "smokers" around the city.

Mickey was not a disciplined boxer. He rarely trained in a gym, preferring instead to hire his fists out to the newsboys who controlled the most lucrative intersections in the city—the blocks downtown that could bring in $2,000, even $3,000 a year—and who consequently needed help keeping rivals off their turf. In time, Mickey and his little crew (two Jewish kids and one Latino) became those rivals, taking control of corners themselves. By 1925, he had staked out a prime corner downtown at Seventh and Spring Streets. Mickey prospered. He began to carry a roll. ("Even if I only made a couple of hundred dollars, I'd always keep it in fives and tens so it'd look big.") He developed an intense aversion to old clothes (particularly old socks). He bought a car, a patched up Model T.

Yet despite this youthful marauding, Mickey also stayed in the ring, fighting four or five nights a week around the city. He even managed to win the newsboy flyweight championship, a victory that made Mickey a minor celebrity and finally brought his boxing career to his mother's attention. When she found out what her youngest son was up to, Fanny Cohen was not pleased. Mickey's three older brothers had gone to college (at least for a while) and found good jobs. Mickey's violent hustling had to end. She ordered him to stop boxing. His friends urged the opposite: They thought he should go pro. So at age fifteen, Mickey hopped a freight train going east.

At some point in 1928, Mickey·showed up at the doorstep of brother Harry the pharmacist, who had moved to Cleveland. When Mickey told him of his plans to turn professional, Harry took one look at his five-foot, three-inch, ninety-six-pound sibling and laughed. Once he saw Mickey in the ring, however, the laughing stopped. His little brother was good. Harry began to nurse a new plan: Mickey would go pro, and he (Harry) would manage his career. A confrere told Harry that if he was serious, Mickey needed professional instruction—the best professional instruction. He needed to go to New York. And so, at the age of sixteen, Mickey Cohen was signed over to two boxing managers and sent to New York City to start training at the most famous boxing gym in the world. He was supposed to learn how to fight. Instead, he would discover a new world—the world of organized crime.

LOU STILLMAN'S GYM—Mickey's destination—was a dump. "The atmosphere," George Plimpton would later write, "was of a fetid jungle." The windows were never opened. The floors went years between cleanings. Members of the public, who could watch the action for a quarter, were encouraged to smoke; Stillman, a moody and acidulous former private eye, thought it toughened fighters up. Perhaps it did, for by 1929 the dungeonlike space on West 57th Street was the most revered gym in the world, a favorite training spot for boxers such as Jack Dempsey and, later, Joe Louis. Mickey was one of the roughly 150 fighters who rented lockers and trained there, a group whose quality ranged, in Stillman's words, from "jerk squirts to top-of-the-heaps." In his interactions with the men he was training, Stillman didn't bother to distinguish between the two.

"Big or small, champ or bum, I treat 'em all the same—bad," he once said, in what Budd Schulberg described as his "garbage disposal voice." "If you treat them like humans, they'll eat you alive."

The men surrounding Mickey were indeed a tough lot. The gym had been founded by philanthropists whose goal was not to rescue the city's toughest youth from a life of violence—there seemed to be little hope of that—but rather to encourage them to use their fists instead of knives or guns. The donors were reportedly happy with the gym's results: Stillman later calculated that only a dozen of his fighters went to the electric chair. He wasn't counting those who made their way into the rackets.

"A card of membership in Stillman's is an Open Sesame to low society in any part of the world," wrote *New Yorker* correspondent Alva Johnston in 1933. "The place is one of the centralizing institutions of the underworld; rival low-life factions meet here casually under a flag of truce, as the rival financial and social mobs fraternize at the opera."

This was sixteen-year-old Mickey Cohen's new world.

He gave it a go.

Every day Cohen did his roadwork in Central Park and then reported faithfully to Stillman's (whose motto was "Open Sundays, Mondays, & always"). He appeared on the cards on several occasions at the old Madison Square Garden. He got to know Tony Canzoneri, the featherweight champion of the world. He struck up an acquaintance with Damon Runyon, bard of the New York underworld. As a fighter, Mickey gained a reputation for scrappiness and versatility, if not talent. A natural flyweight, Mickey also routinely fought bantam and featherweight bouts. In 1933, he went up against featherweight champion Alberto "Baby" Arizmendi (like Mickey, a sometime-resident of Boyle Heights) in Tijuana, losing by a knockout in the third round. All in all, Cohen was a good, journeyman fighter. As he said later, "I wasn't the worse. Neither was I the tops."

Still, his heart wasn't in it. Boxing increasingly disgusted him. Every year in the ring brought another disfigurement—a broken nose, inch-long scars under both eyes, a two-inch scar on the left wrist. But it wasn't the pain of these injuries that upset Mickey most; rather, it was the physicality of the sport—the sweat, the blood, the blows, the tie-ups, the embraces. Mickey became compulsive about his personal hygiene. After every fight, he'd spend hours in the bathtub or shower.

Moreover, he wasn't making any money. Life as a boxer-in-training had its upsides. His managers paid his expenses, bought his clothes, and gave him pocket money. But the fact of the matter was, Mickey now never had more than $15 or $20 in his pocket. Who did? The watchful Irish and Italian men in the bleachers who periodically came in to check on their fighters' progress—men like Owney "The Killer" Madden, fresh out of Sing Sing, and Joe "the Boss" Masseria, the king of New York's Italian underworld (until his assassination in 1931). To Mickey, they were simply "the people." Even then, he knew that these were the men he wanted to associate with. He just didn't know how. So he decided to return to Cleveland and try his hand as a full-time gangster.

He was not welcomed into the fold.

Unlike New York City, where the smartest Jewish and Italian gangsters had learned to cooperate, Cleveland was still primarily Italian territory. Mickey tried to fit in by becoming a kind of honorary Italian himself, making Italian friends, picking up bits and pieces of various Italian dialects, and perfecting such forms of assault as "the Sicilian backhander." Cleveland's top Italian gangsters, brothers Frank and Tony Milano, just laughed at the "Jewboy," as they called him, who so wanted to be Sicilian. That changed when establishments across Cleveland started seeing Mickey behind the barrel of a gun. Mickey had decided that if the Cleveland outfit wouldn't take him in, he would hang out his own shingle as a "rooter," a holdup man.

Mickey's first target was a "half-ass gambling joint . . . way out the west end of Cleveland in the produce area." An informer had tipped them off to a high-stakes grocers' craps game. That night, Mickey and a few associates stormed the joint and grabbed $5,000. They struck again the following week, then two or three times a week. Mickey soon had a troupe of seven and was routinely hitting gambling joints, cafés, and whorehouses across Cleveland. It seemed a highly satisfactory life. Days were spent sleeping and playing cards. Nights were exciting and frequently rewarding, both financially and psychologically. Armed robbery, Mickey found, did wonders for his self-esteem.

"It made me equal to everybody," Mickey later recalled. "Even as small as I was, when I whipped out that big .38 it made me as big as a guy six foot ten."

Great Depression or no Great Depression, business was good. At the end of a successful heist, Mickey's little crew worked around his inability to add or subtract by stacking all the bills up separately—Lincolns here, Hamiltons there, Jacksons here (Grants were rare; Franklins, alas, were virtually unknown)—and then dividing each pile among the participants ("one for you, one for me . . .").

The Cleveland mob was remarkably calm about Mickey's behavior—until he hit a bookie parlor under its protection. Fortunately for Mickey, one member of his crew had an uncle in Buffalo who was in "the highest echelons of 'the people.'" This uncle made some phone calls to "the people" in Cleveland, and Cleveland reacted magnanimously. Instead of punishing the upstart heister, the Cleveland mob made Mickey an offer. Mickey could operate as before (as long as he stayed clear of mob-protected operations). In addition, the Cleveland outfit (as it was sometimes called) would offer him a $125-a-week retainer. In exchange, Mickey would perform certain tasks for the local mob and, on occasion, for friends elsewhere.

Cohen was delighted. He accepted at once. And, almost as quickly, he fucked up.

Among the tasks that Mickey was occasionally called on to perform was killing people. Hits followed a strict protocol. There was a pointer—someone who knew the victim and could make the target—and a triggerman. Mickey was the triggerman. One day Mickey was sent out with a pointer to take out a man who was trying to set himself up without permission from "the people" (much as Mickey himself had done). The pointer identified the victim, who was out walking with a young woman. Mickey stepped out, pulled out his revolver, and fired. The gun roared, the man went down, and the woman—clearly a lady with remarkable self-possession—started screaming,

"You shot the wrong guy! You shot the wrong guy!"

That night Mickey found out the woman was right. Pissed, he turned on his pointer.

"What's the matter with you, you rotten son of a bitch?" he shouted. He then proceeded to pistol-whip the man, breaking his jaw. Unfortunately, the man Mickey beat up was the brother of one of Cleveland's top mob leaders. Cohen, unfailingly lucky, received only a serious talking to. Unfortunately, Mickey then decided to heist a popular cafeteria that happened to be directly across the street from the 105th Street police precinct station. Cohen and an accomplice were apprehended. Although they managed to avoid conviction—the cashier obligingly agreed to confess that the robbery had been staged and was thus not really armed robbery—Cohen's criminal career in Cleveland was over. Mickey left town—for Al Capone's Chicago.

IN 1931, Al Capone was at the height of his power. Two years earlier, on Valentine's Day, members of the Capone gang dressed as police officers had lured members of the rival Bugs Moran gang to an isolated warehouse—supposedly to receive a shipment of premium whiskey at a bargain price. Moran's men thought they'd been pinched and expected nothing worse than a quick trip to the lockup. Instead, they were lined up against a wall and machine-gunned. The so-called St. Valentine's Day Massacre sealed Capone's standing as Chicago's top gangster and scandalized the nation, making Capone an international celebrity. It did not, however, make him safer. The primary target of the massacre—Bugs Moran himself—ran late to the meeting, thus missing his own execution. He was now intent on revenge. Rumors that Moran had dispatched two, four, ten gunmen followed Capone everywhere. Al Capone might be the King of Chicago, but he was a monarch who lived under the constant threat of a violent death. As a result, Capone took an interest in newly arrived gunmen, even ones as junior as Mickey Cohen.

Cohen's job in Chicago was simple: lay low at a large, Jewish-controlled gambling joint on the North Shore and scare off some neighborhood toughs who were trying to squeeze its owners. After years of associating almost entirely with Italians, Mickey "sort of had to relearn Jewish ways." He rediscovered "real good food on a Jewish style." He tried not to react violently to perceived slights ("not like [I did] with the Italians"). Then one day three "notorious tough guys"—the people Mickey was supposed to protect the casino against—came calling. Mickey opened fire before they even got through the plate-glass door. By the time the police arrived, two of the men were dead. Despite his insistence that he didn't start shooting until he saw the man pull his "rod," Cohen was arrested for murder. Fortunately for Mickey, Chicago was most definitely a city where "the fix" was "in." To his delight and astonishment, he was released the next morning after a mob representative stopped by the jail and ordered the turnkey to open up. When the jailer protested that he couldn't let a murder suspect out "just like that," Mickey's visitor called for the captain—who let Cohen out "just like that." The case never went to trial.

Soon thereafter, Mickey was summoned downtown to the Lexington Hotel to meet Al Capone himself. When Mickey walked into Capone's office, the most powerful man in Chicago (known to his friends as "Big-Hearted Al") quietly gripped the pint-sized brawler's head in his hands and kissed him on both cheeks.

"After that meeting, it was kind of like a whole new world for me," Mickey would later claim. "I wasn't just a punk kid anymore. I was someone who had done something to justify the favor of Al Capone."

In truth, Mickey probably amused Capone as much as he impressed him. Mickey had already befriended Al's little brother Mattie, an avid boxing fan. Cohen had also attracted a measure of attention because, with his broken nose and a nasty, twisting scar under his left eye, he actually looked a lot like a miniature Al Capone. He also dressed like Capone ("admiring the guy as much as I did, I may have tried to copy his ways," Mickey admitted later), heightening the "Mini-Me" effect. Court jester or respected junior gunman, it hardly mattered. Mickey had Capone's blessing and that was enough to open the doors of the Chicago underworld. He began to learn how professional criminals really worked.

"I soon found there were lots of older guys willing to teach me about how to grow up and be good at a particular piece of work I wanted to get to know about," Mickey would say later, with discreet imprecision.

Chicago was also a revelation in another way. As his friend the writer Ben Hecht would later put it, "Before coming to Chicago, Mickey knew there were numerous crooks like himself on the outskirts of society. He did not know, however, that there were ten times as many crooks in the respectable seats of government." Chicago, a city where everything seemed part of the fix, would be Mickey Cohen's model—and dream—for L.A.

6

Comrade Bill

> *"With few exceptions, no protection is afforded to the police chiefs in this country. And to this neglect, more than to any other cause, may be attributed the alliance of politics, police and crime."*
>
> —Berkeley police chief August Vollmer, 1931

WHILE MICKEY COHEN was befriending members of the Capone family, patrolman Bill Parker was struggling to advance in the Los Angeles Police Department in his own unyielding fashion. He would not pay a bribe for a cheat sheet to the civil service exam; he would not curry favor with the politicians; he would not turn a blind eye to infractions that many other officers in the department saw as routine. It was a hard way to get ahead. But Parker was also surprisingly hard to get rid of.

After his early heroics, Parker was transferred into a dead-end job at the property division. It didn't work. Parker was too nosy.

"There were some irregularities in the handling of confiscated autos," Parker later recalled (adding, with characteristic self-confidence, "I was too intelligent to conceal things from").

He was soon transferred to Hollenbeck Division, which was responsible for patrolling Mickey Cohen's old neighborhood of Boyle Heights, perhaps the "wettest" part of Los Angeles. By 1931, many police officers had lost their enthusiasm for enforcing Prohibition, which was clearly on the way out. (Its formal repeal would come two years later, in 1933.) Not Bill Parker. He immediately set out to make as many arrests as possible. Puzzled, local bootleggers were soon approaching him to ask what he wanted.

"I don't want anything," Parker angrily replied. "You're on one side of the fence, and I'm on the other." Soon thereafter, Parker was summoned to the office of the division inspector.

"Parker," he said, "what division would you like to work in?"

"What do you mean?" he replied, even though he knew full well what was happening. The liquor mob was moving him out.

"I mean," the inspector continued, "if you happened to want a transfer, where would you like to go?"

"Hollywood Division," Parker replied. Soon thereafter, he was transferred there.

Hollywood was Los Angeles's fast growing vice hot spot. But vice arrests were not exactly encouraged in his new division. Parker soon chafed at other patrolmen's "do nothing" attitude. So one night he decided to protest the policy of nonenforcement by parking directly across the street from a Hollywood house of ill repute in an effort to scare the johns away. The madam was irate, as well she might be. By one estimate, some 500 brothels were employing an estimated 2,200 prostitutes—and paying for police protection on a regular basis. Why should she, a dues-paying madam, be singled out by law enforcement? So out she stormed.

"Listen, you stupid fuck," the madam yelled at Parker. "You're ruining my business by hanging around here."

"That's the general idea," he replied.

"What's the next move?" she asked.

"The next move is to put you in jail," he said.

By the end of the week, Parker had been transferred again.

Despite such obstinacy, in the summer of 1931, Parker was made acting sergeant. His grades on the civil service exam were simply too good to ignore. Of the 505 officers who'd taken the civil service exam for sergeant, Parker received the fourth highest score. And so on July 1, he was made a sergeant and returned to Hollenbeck Division. For the first time, Parker was in a position to force other officers to adhere to a standard of conduct close to his own. Word quickly got around that when Bill Parker was at the booking desk, there would be no rough stuff.

"Take him someplace and book him if you want to start that stuff," Parker told his fellow officers; "you're not going to hit him here."

Such attitudes did not go over well with all of his fellow officers. One night in 1932, matters came to a head when a drunken member of the vice squad announced that he was going to kill Parker—and started fumbling for his gun.

"I could have killed him, but I knew I could make the doorway," Parker later recounted. So he ran. His fellow officers laughingly dismissed the entire affair as a joke and "tried to convince me the man's gun was unloaded," but Parker would have none of it.

"I got out," he said simply. He would later describe it as a night when he almost got killed.

For Mickey Cohen, boxing and armed robbery had been the path to "the people." Bill Parker found a very different—but equally unorthodox—path to prominence in the LAPD: He became a union man.

BY 1929, Los Angeles mayor George Cryer's claims to be a reformer had worn thin. One year earlier a grand jury investigation had forced the resignation of Kent Parrot's chosen district attorney and made a hero of the jury foreman, John Porter. With ties to both the Ku Klux Klan and to powerful Protestant clergymen like the Rev. Bob Shuler, Porter was an attractive figure to many Angelenos fed up with the underworld. A thriving used-auto-parts and wrecking business also gave him ample means to fund a political campaign. When Cryer announced that he would not run for a fourth term, Porter threw his hat into the race.

To block the Klansman auto wrecker, Kent Parrot turned to an auto dealer whose only other high-profile supporter was, oddly, New York Yankees slugger Babe Ruth. Reformers backed the "absolutely incorruptible" city council president William Bonelli (who would later flee to Mexico to avoid an indictment on corruption charges). After a period of uncharacteristic indecision, Harry Chandler and the *Times* hit upon the local American Legion commander, who frankly (if unhelpfully) acknowledged that he was unprepared to govern the city. With the dominant factions badly divided and the *Times*, by choosing such an oddball candidate, effectively on the sidelines, Porter won the election. Boss Parrot was no more.

With Parrot gone, the Combination began to crumble. In the summer of 1930, Charlie Crawford was gunned down in his office by a deranged young assistant district attorney. The Combination was no longer able to keep competitors out, and the price of bootleg booze plummeted. Scotch, which had once commanded $50 a case, now cost only $15, virtually wholesale prices. Gunmen robbed slot machine king Robert Gans; bookmaker Zeke Caress was kidnapped and ransomed for $50,000. Along with Gans, Guy McAfee, the vice squad officer turned vice lord, gradually consolidated his authority over the city's organized prostitution rings and downtown slot machines. But he was never able to regain the clout that Crawford had wielded.

For reformers, the weakening of the Combination should have been welcome news—and it was. But Cryer's demise and Porter's election presented Parker with a new problem. The new mayor and his most prominent supporters were viciously anti-Catholic, blaming Rome for everything from the assassinations (or attempted assassinations) of Presidents Lincoln, Garfield, McKinley, and Roosevelt to the 1910 Mexican Revolution. It is not surprising that Parker soon took an interest in strengthening rank-and-file officers' job protection. By doing so, Parker would catch the attention of the most colorful police chief in the history of the Los Angeles Police Department, Chief James "Two Gun" Davis.

THAT THE LAPD, the scourge of union organizers in America's most vociferously open-shop city, should have had a union movement is ironic. It must be said that officially it did not. Technically, Los Angeles had only the Fire and Police Protective League, officially a fraternal organization. But by the early 1930s it was well along the path to becoming a union.*

The issue that drew in Parker was job security. Simply put, officers didn't have it. There was no safe way to make a career in the LAPD. Officers like Parker who insisted on following the letter of the law risked their careers (if not their lives) during periods of corruption. Corrupt cops risked their careers during the brief but regular periods of reform that followed revelations of scandal. While policemen were theoretically under civil service protection, in practice the chief of police was still able to dismiss officers virtually at will, and officers who were dismissed lost *everything*—their pensions, benefits, everything—no matter how close to retirement they might be.

In 1934, Parker got himself elected as a sergeant representative to the Fire and Police Protective League. He quickly became a forceful advocate for patrolmen's interests, arguing effectively for a reversal of the pay cuts that had been forced on the department during the early years of the Depression. He also came to the attention of another lawyer-policeman in the department, Earle Cooke. Together, the two men began to lay the groundwork for a change to the city charter that would offer fire and police officers greater protection from political pressure.

In the summer of 1934, the Fire and Police Protective League petitioned the city council to place a charter amendment on the ballot that would "clarify procedure in disciplinary and removal actions" for firemen and police officers. This modest description was highly misleading. Parker and Cooke weren't seeking to clarify some minority ambiguity; rather, they were proposing to radically expand the protections police (and fire) officers enjoyed. Under their amendment, charges against policemen would be constrained by a one-year statute of limitations. Policemen would be entitled to counsel, and all hearings would take place before a three-person board

---

*It was also something of a racket. According to historian Gerald Woods, wealthy Angelenos purchased $1,000 memberships that brought with them preferential treatment for parking and speeding violations. (Woods, "The Progressives and the Police," 324.)

of rights whose members consisted of officers of the rank of captain or higher. Six names would be drawn out of a box; the accused policeman would then select the three officers who would sit on the panel. Moreover, the board's recommendations would be binding. The chief of police would only be able to reduce penalties, not increase them.

The city council seems to have taken this request calmly. On August 14, 1934, its members agreed to present the Fire and Police Protective League proposal to voters as Amendment No. 12-A.

The public was not highly attuned to the issue of police discipline. Surveys conducted during the mid-1930s show that the public wanted the police to be disciplined, effective, and nonpolitical. They should be "neat and military" in their appearance; they should take "a professional interest" in their work and be of at least average intelligence; and they should treat "normal" citizens with courtesy. When it came to less "normal" citizens, it was no holds barred. A majority of voters consistently endorsed *harsher* treatment for "ex-convicts, Negroes, aliens, radicals, and gangsters."

Some observers did pick up on what Parker and Cooke were trying to do. The liberal *Los Angeles Daily News* was one, correctly noting that in claiming the right to police itself the LAPD was effectively removing that right from the city's politicians. Notwithstanding the record of corruption that Los Angeles politicians had compiled, a significant number of Angelenos were hesitant to grant the department such sweeping protections. When Amendment No. 12-A went before voters on September 27, 1934, it passed by a mere 676 votes, with 84,143 in favor and 83,467 opposed. However, a narrow victory is still a victory. It was the beginning of Bill Parker's wider reputation in the department. Years later, an article in the newsletter of the LAPD's American Legion chapter would describe the (amended) Section 202 of the city charter as "our most priceless possession," and credit "Comrade Bill" as the measure's "co-author."

UNION ACTIVISM is not always the swiftest path to a police executive's affection, but Parker's legal work seems to have impressed Chief James Davis. Two more different personalities are hard to imagine. Parker was cerebral and wry. Davis was a peacock. Handsome (in a slightly puffy, heavily pomaded way), the chief loved uniforms, hats (particularly sombreros), braiding, and decorations. The Rev. Bob Shuler, a frequent critic, described him as "a man with pink complexion who looks like he had a massage every morning and his fingernails manicured." However, few voiced such criticisms directly. Manicured or not, the 240-pound Texan looked as if he could snap most of his critics in half. A close observer of the Los Angeles political scene would later describe him as "a burly, dicta-torial, somewhat sadistic, bitterly anti-labor man who saw communist in-fluence behind every telephone poll." He was also, arguably, insane. One of Davis's favorite ways to entertain dignitaries visiting the department was to have a member of his beloved pistol-shooting team shoot a cigarette out of his mouth, à la William Tell.

Davis's tactics were rough. One of his favorites was "rousting," described thusly in an admiring 1926 *Los Angeles Times* profile by police reporter (and Chandler hatchet man) Albert Nathan:

> First the word goes out of the chief's office that the "rousting" is to begin and is to be kept up for a week.
>
> Then all of the liquor squads take to the street, armed with pictures of the best known rum runners and the various members of their "mobs," and begin looking for them.
>
> As fast as any of the wanted men are located they are seized, handcuffed, loaded into a pa-trol wagon and escorted to jail. They are then locked up on charges of vagrancy or any other charge which may come to the mind of the arresting officer. In a few hours attorneys appear, writs are secured through the local courts and the prisoners are released. . . . One by one they are released and then arrested again and again. During a "rousting" a man may be arrested as many as six times, and each time has to stay in jail for one hour to two days before he gets out. After awhile the wanted men learn that every time they saunter up Spring Street they will be arrested and that they are not even safe in their homes.

Even at the time, this struck many as unlawful. "The rousting system may, as many contend, be unlawful," the *Times* conceded, but no matter: "[T]his is known and records provide it: The system works."

Nor were regular citizens exempt from his scrutiny. In 1936, Chief Davis dispatched 126 officers to sixteen highway and rail entry points on the California border to prevent "Okies" fleeing the dustbowl—he called them "the refuse of other states"—from entering California. The Los An-geles papers dubbed it (approvingly) the Bum Blockade. Inspectors from the State Relief Administration reported that officers were "exercising extra-constitutional powers of exclusion, detention, and preemptive arrest" that "seemed more like the border checkpoints of fascist Europe than those of an American state." Davis responded that 48 percent of the people turned back had criminal records.

"It is an axiom with Davis that constitutional rights are of benefit to nobody but crooks and criminals, and that no perfectly law-abiding citi-zen ever has any cause to insist on 'constitutional rights,'" reported the *Los Angeles Record* sarcastically. "Chief Davis honestly and sincerely be-lieves that the whole country would be better off if the whole question of constitutional rights was forgotten and left to the discretion of the police."

But as implausible as it may seem, Chief Davis was also something of a reformer.* One of Davis's first steps was to reinstitute rules against accepting gratuities and soliciting rewards that had lapsed under his predecessor. During his first forty-five months in office, Davis discharged 245 officers for misconduct. However, the strongest evidence for the proposition that Chief Davis was a reformer comes from his treatment of Bill Parker.

In 1934, Chief Davis turned to Parker to draft the bylaws for his beloved training facility in the hills of Elysian Park, today's Los Angeles Police Academy. Yet despite this interaction with Chief Davis, Parker's promotional path continued to be a rocky one. On June 5, 1935, Parker took the examination for lieutenant. He scored sixth on the written test, lower on the more subjective oral test, and ended up in the number ten position on the promotional eligibility list. Not until January 18, 1937, was he promoted to the position of lieutenant—and then only after two officers with lower scores had been promoted before him.

Then, suddenly, his career took off. In early 1937, Parker became Chief Davis's executive officer. In this position, he served as Chief Davis's scheduler, advisor, and gatekeeper, granting and withholding access to the chief and maintaining relationships with politicians from the mayor to city council members. He also headed the small bureau of public affairs. Work relations between the two men were formal: Parker was always "Lieutenant," never "Bill." Davis was simply "Chief." In private, however, the two men became friends. Parker (and sometimes Helen) frequently joined Davis for hunting and fishing trips with Davis's sons. Observers of departmental politics soon noted young Bill Parker's all-too-obvious ambitions. The reluctant police officer, the young man who had barely bothered with his entrance exam, now clearly aspired to one day become chief.

Soon after Parker joined the chief's staff, Davis made him an acting captain—a move that no doubt raised hackles in the department. Davis probably didn't care. He needed Parker for something big.

■ ■ ■

---

*In truth, when viewed in the context of the time, the tactics championed by Chief Davis are not as outrageous as they first appear. Most police reformers believed that improving police officers' shooting skills was an effective deterrent to the gangsterism that plagued urban America. "Routing" was a standard law enforcement tool. The Bum Blockade was less extreme than the transient forced labor camps proposed by the city's Committee on Indigent Alien Transients one year earlier. Advocates of wholesale fingerprinting were common too. August Vollmer, a Berkeley police chief and professor who became a hero to progressives in the 1920s, openly endorsed "a system of checking the movements of persons traveling from one state to another." (Vollmer, *The Police and Modern Society*, 24.)

IN 1933, voters had replaced Mayor Porter with county supervisor Frank Shaw. Shaw was not Harry Chandler's kind of candidate. For one thing, although he was ostensibly a Republican, Shaw embraced the agenda of the newly elected Franklin Delano Roosevelt. For another, Shaw had gotten his start in politics as a city council member backed by Kent Parrot, with whom he maintained close (if vague) ties. Chandler's suspicions proved to be well founded. After taking office, Frank Shaw turned to his brother Joe, recently discharged from the U.S. Navy, to help him oversee municipal affairs. Joe's title was personal secretary; however, he soon took control of every potential patronage and profit center in the city. Not surprisingly, "The Sailor" (as Joe was known) took a particular interest in the LAPD and in the Los Angeles underworld.

During the 1920s, Kent Parrot and Charlie Crawford had controlled Los Angeles. Joe was determined to revive the old police-underworld arrangements, but this time with himself on top. Where Parrot and Crawford had sought to impose a monopoly, Shaw was willing to tolerate a variety of players—as long as they all paid up and their operations didn't attract too much attention. Remnants of the Combination soon resurfaced. So did new players such as Jack Dragna, a Sicilian crime boss who focused primarily on traditional activities like extortion, prostitution, and bootlegging. (He also had a legitimate sideline as a banana importer and often referred to himself as a banana merchant.) There was plenty of money to go around. The *Hollywood Citizen-News* estimated that the L.A. underworld was generating roughly $2 million a month (20 percent of which went to selected policemen, politicians, and journalists). *Daily News* columnist Matt Weinstock put the figure even higher. His sources figured the Combination at its height was grossing about $50 million a year.

The key to it all was control of the police department. Joe Shaw was determined to make sure he had it. In principle, Chief Davis answered to the Police Commission. In practice, Shaw placed the police department's most important operations under his close supervision by insisting on making Shaw campaign manager James "Sunny Jimmy" Bolger Chief Davis's secretary. The fact that the chief's office was located in City Hall, just around the corner from the mayor's office (an arrangement instituted by Mayor Porter), further shortened Davis's leash. Bill Parker's job was to help him escape it.

IN EARLY 1937, working once more through the Fire and Police Protective League, Parker launched an effort to amend section 1999 of the city charter—this time, to extend civil service protections to the chief of police. The ballot initiative Parker drafted consisted of a single sentence: "Shall proposed charter amendment No. 14-A, amending section 1999 of the Charter clarifying the civil service status of the Chief of Police, providing that he shall not be removed except for cause and after hearing before the Board of Civil Service Commissioners, be ratified?" It seemed a modest change, but its potential consequences were immense. If it passed, the position of chief of police would no longer serve at the pleasure of the Police Commission (and the mayor who appointed its members). Instead, once sworn in, the chief of police would have a "substantial property right" in his position. The chief of police could be suspended or fired only if found guilty of a specific set of publicly aired charges after a "full, fair and impartial hearing" before the city's Board of Civil Service Commissioners. Needless to say, in a city as corrupt as Los Angeles, a full hearing was something that Mayor Shaw would never be prepared to risk. In short, Proposition 14-A would dramatically strengthen Chief Davis's position vis-à-vis the Shaws. On Tuesday, April 6, 1937, the electorate of Los Angeles approved it by a vote of 79,336 to 69,380.

It was an amendment that would change the history of Los Angeles. The Los Angeles Police Department, long subordinate to some combination of the mayor, the underworld, or the business community (or sometimes all three), now had the legal protection it needed to emerge as a power in its own right.

It also had a potent new adversary. The same year Bill Parker was attempting to erect a ring of legal protections around the chief's office that neither corrupt politicians nor the remnants of the Combination could breach, one of the most formidable figures in the history of American organized crime arrived in Los Angeles. His name was Benjamin "Bugsy" Siegel. Mickey Cohen was his muscle.

Bugsy

"Booze Barons of other climes are just bootleggers in Los Angeles. Gangsters can never build another Chicago here."

—LAPD statement, 1931

BY 1937, Bugsy Siegel was one of the most important men in organized crime. During the 1920s, Siegel and his partner, Meyer Lansky, had made names for themselves in the New York City underworld as fearless stickup men, bootleggers, and muscle-for-hire. In 1927, Siegel participated in one of the earliest efforts to coordinate bootlegging on the Atlantic seaboard. Two years later, Lansky helped organize a national crime "syndicate" at a meeting of the nation's top crime bosses in Atlantic City. In 1931, Siegel reputedly took part in the successful hit on Joe "the Boss" Masseria—the man young Mickey Cohen had seen in the bleachers at Stillman's—at a restaurant on Coney Island. The assassination made Charles "Lucky" Luciano (a longtime Lansky friend) the boss of New York and made the loose group organized by Lansky, which would soon come to be known as the Syndicate, the underworld's preeminent institution.* In short, Siegel was a figure the likes of which the L.A. underworld had never seen before. Yet Siegel did not originally move west to play the heavy. Instead, like generations of migrants before and since, he came west with dreams of health, wealth, and leisure.

Siegel first visited Los Angeles in 1933 to check in on his childhood friend George Raft. Raft, a nightclub dancer in New York, had become a Hollywood star by playing gangsters like Bugsy in the movies. (His breakthrough role came in the 1932 movie *Scarface* as the coin-flipping sidekick to the Al Capone–esque Paul Muni.) It was not the most auspicious year for a first visit to Los Angeles. That spring, a massive earthquake had leveled a wide swath of Long Beach, killing more than fifty people and badly

---

*Lansky, Luciano, and others generally spoke of "the Syndicate" rather than "the Mafia," which more properly referred to the Italian subset of the organized crime world.

shaking the confidence of the region. A quarter of the working-age population was unemployed. A vast hobo encampment (nicknamed "The Jungle") had spread along the Los Angeles River. Siegel was entranced.

He was receptive to Los Angeles for another reason as well. The same year that Siegel made his first visit to the city, Congress repealed the Twentieth Amendment, ending national Prohibition. This was something the Syndicate had long feared. What happened next, though, caught Siegel and his associates off guard. Almost overnight they became wealthy—and quasi-legitimate businessmen. Underground distribution networks could become legal liquor distributorships. The Syndicate steamers loaded with booze suddenly had a future as legal importers. Speakeasies like the 21 Club and the Stork that had once operated behind barred doors with look-out holes now hung out Welcome signs. Siegel and Lansky's car and truck rental company on Cannon Street, originally a front for bootlegging, was now a successful business in its own right. Siegel quickly became a partner in one of the biggest liquor distributorships in New York City.

Siegel's lifestyle reflected his success. In the midst of the Depression, Siegel had an apartment at Broadway and 85th and a suite at the Waldorf-Astoria, as well as a house in Scarsdale for his wife and kids. Wealth and the possibility of legitimacy had a profound psychological effect on Siegel and his associates. "Viewed from their luxurious apartments and ducal estates, jail houses became utterly repugnant," wrote newspaper columnist Florabel Muir, who'd observed Siegel's career as a hoodlum since the early 1920s.

"Caution, fathered by the urge to preserve and enjoy their vast fortunes, overtook them," she continued, adding, "There is nothing like a million dollars to bring about a conservative point of view."

Los Angeles offered the chance for a new start. If a Lower East Side tough-turned-speakeasy-"hoofer" like George Raft could transform himself into a movie star there, then perhaps a former gangster could transform himself into a gentleman of leisure. And so in 1934 Siegel moved his wife, his two daughters, and the family German shepherd to Beverly Hills and promptly set out to join the movie colony elite. He rented a luxurious house on McCarthy Drive in Beverly Hills that had once been the home of opera star Lawrence Tibbett. He enrolled his two daughters in an elite private school and an exclusive riding academy. He became a member of the Hillcrest Country Club, the social center of the film colony. He shed his New York City gangster attire (hard-shelled derby hat, fur-trimmed coats, rakish lapels) in favor of two-hundred-dollar sports coats and cashmere slacks. He took as his mistress the most flamboyant hostess in Hollywood, Dorothy di

Frasso, a New York leather goods heiress married to an Italian count. Unfortunately, Siegel then ran into a problem—an embarrassing one. He got taken—for a million dollars.

At the end of Prohibition, Siegel had about $2 million in cash. Unfortunately, he then invested much of it in the stock market. In short order, Siegel had cut his fortune in half.

"If I had kept that million," Siegel later mused to a friend, "I'd have been out of the rackets right then. But I took a big licking, and I couldn't go legitimate." Instead, he went back to what he knew best: organized crime. Los Angeles, which Siegel had once viewed as a playground, was now an opportunity.

BUGSY'S PALS back East were delighted by his decision to organize the West Coast. From Lansky and Luciano's perspective, California was a backwater—an embarrassment, really. The Combination's power had dwindled. McAfee and Gans controlled little more than prostitution and slots in the downtown core. Yet L.A.'s top Italian crime boss, Jack Dragna, had failed to step up, particularly when it came to asserting authority over fast-growing areas like the Sunset Strip. Located in unincorporated territory outside of the city of Los Angeles (and the reach of the LAPD), the Strip was the perfect vice center. But Dragna hadn't established even a proper casino. "Jack wasn't pulling the counties or the political picture together," Cohen would say later. "There was no combination; everyone was acting independently." Siegel would change that. Top New York mob boss "Lucky" Luciano contacted Dragna personally with the news that Siegel was taking change "for the good of us all."

Dragna took the news poorly. It hardly mattered. Dragna had important connections back East himself (according to Cohen, he was related to Tommy "Three-Finger Brown" Lucchese), but Siegel was a peer of the realm, an equal to anyone in the Syndicate. Mickey Cohen would later describe him as "one of the six tops . . . right up with Capone." Dragna stepped aside. Others were not so deferential.

One who declined to defer to an interloper from back East was Eddy Neales, the thirty-three-year-old owner of the Clover Club, a high-rolling Hollywood nightclub and casino just west of the Chateau Marmont above the Sunset Strip. The handsome half-Mexican, half-Caucasian Neales cut a dashing figure; the Clover Club was *the* gambling spot in a city that loved to test fortune at the tables. Neales also had a booming bookmaking business, thanks to California's decision to legalize pari-mutuel betting at racetracks in 1933.* By 1937, Neales was reputedly handling about $10 million a year in bets.

Neales didn't rely on his personal popularity to protect his operations. Milton "Farmer" Page, a major figure in the Combination, was a silent partner. Neales and partner Curly Robinson were also paying a small fortune in protection money to the Los Angeles sheriff's department, which had jurisdiction over the Sunset Strip. So it was perhaps understandable that when Siegel approached Neales and Robinson and informed them that he was looking to make a major investment in their club, they demurred. A confrontation appeared to be inevitable. Siegel recognized that he needed more muscle. So Siegel put out a call for talent. Cleveland and Chicago had just the person for the job, Mickey Cohen.

COHEN had outstayed his welcome in Chicago. At one point, he and his associates got permission from the Capone gang to open a blackjack game in the Loop. When that wasn't lucrative enough, he decided to open a craps game, despite the fact that dice games were strictly off limits in downtown Chicago. Capone accountant Jake "Greasy Thumb" Guzik personally flew in from Miami to tell Cohen to wind up his craps game. Mickey declined. Several nights later, as Mickey was standing in front of his favorite haberdashery shop, a large black car turned the corner . . . and opened fire. Mickey hesitated. He was wearing a beautiful new camelhair coat, and he hated the thought of ruining it by "flattening out" in the gutter. If the Capone gang had been serious, he figured he'd probably already be dead. Still, he didn't want to take any chances—or seem disrespectful. Into the slush he went.

Mickey was living like a man who didn't value life. Whenever he needed a buck, he'd heist a store—sometimes two or three in a day. He developed a mania for cream-colored Stetson hats, which he'd purchase for $50, wear for a few days, and then discard. When he wanted a new hat, out came the gun. When holdups alone failed to keep Mickey in new hats and flossy suits, he reopened his craps game in the Loop. He made enemies casually. In early 1937, Mickey got into a beef with a former slugger for Chicago's Yellow Cab company. One day Mickey ran into the man in a restaurant and pistol-whipped him. After getting drunk, the man tracked down Mickey and stuck a gun in his back. Cohen spun around, got his hand on the rod,

---

*Bookies offered bettors a lower "take" than racetracks such as Santa Anita (which, in addition to the house take, also collected a small tax on bets wagered), as well as better odds.

but wasn't able to wrest the firearm away from his would-be assailant. So the two men decided to go to a coffee shop to talk matters over, each with a hand firmly on the gun. They sat down at the counter. An instant later, Mickey smashed a sugar dispenser over the man's head.

"His head split open like a melon and blood flew all over the joint," Mickey noted later, with evident satisfaction. As the coffee shop erupted in screams, Cohen dashed down to the cellar to dispose of the gun. But the cops found the weapon and arrested him for attempted murder.

There was, of course, an easy way out: Mickey could tell the police that the gun wasn't his and that he'd acted in self-defense. Fingering someone for the cops, however, was something Mickey just wouldn't do. He clammed up. But for the last-minute intervention of Pop Palazzi, the Capone gang's Chicago counselor, Cohen might well have gone to prison. Instead, he was told to leave town. He went to Detroit. There he learned that Bugsy Siegel was looking for muscle in Los Angeles. Detroit wanted Mickey to go there to help out—and to keep an eye on Bugsy. So did Cleveland. And so in 1937, Mickey returned to his old hometown.

MICKEY was supposed to get in touch with Siegel as soon as he arrived in Los Angeles. Instead, he decided that he'd first make a few scores and put a little money in his pocket. If Siegel wanted to get in touch with him, well, then Siegel could come and find him. Mickey quickly hooked up with two Italian brothers, Fred and Joe Sica, who were freelance holdup men. Together, the three men went "on the heavy." They found a city that was easy pickings. Tipsters were easy to recruit. Mickey and his crew were soon heisting two or three joints a week. Brothels, shops, drugstores—any place with cash on hand was a possible target. Soon Mickey was summoning old colleagues from Cleveland, Chicago, and New York to come join him in L.A. As their confidence increased, so did the size of their targets. Were these establishments perhaps under someone else's protection? Mickey didn't know, and truth be told, he "didn't even give a shit."

"I was out with ten different broads every night," he later boasted, "and I was in every cabaret that they could possibly have in town." Bugsy Siegel was forgotten—until, that is, Mickey and his crew made a spectacularly foolish heist.

Their target was a commission bookmaking office on Franklin that handled high-roller bets and was owned by Morris Orloff, one of the biggest bookmakers in town. Mickey got in using one of his favorite ruses. At nine in the morning, he started banging on the door. The peephole opened and an ex–deputy sheriff eyed Mickey suspiciously. Mickey played it cool:

I says to the doorman, "Is Morey in?"

"Don't get here till ten o'clock or later," he says.

"I got to give him this here," I says, "and pick something up."

"Put it through the peephole," the ex-cop says.

"I can't," I says, "it's a package."

The ex-cop opened the door—and found himself staring into the barrel of Mickey's .38. Two of Mickey's associates forced their way in.

The baby-faced kid messenger tone was gone. "Lookit you cocksucker," Mickey told the lookout, "you just move and you're gone."

The man didn't move. Nor did the four other men in the room who were looking at Mickey. Mickey herded them into a corner and then announced that he was going to wait for Morey Orloff himself to arrive with the big money.

"Look kid, you got alla the money," said a big Italian man in the corner. "Whatta ya wanna stay around here. A copper could come in."

Mickey walked over to the man. He was wearing a large diamond stickpin. Mickey ripped it off.

"Listen you dago bastard," Mickey yelled at the man, "mind your own business or I'll put a phone through your head. I'm staying for Morey Orloff if I gotta stay till tomorrow."

Another man spoke up. "I'm Morey Orloff." To prove it, he showed Mickey his signet ring. That Orloff was joined at the hip with Jack Dragna, Los Angeles's top Italian crime boss, troubled Cohen not one bit. He took the signet ring too. Then, just as Mickey had hoped, an Orloff flunky arrived—with $22,000 in cash. Mickey and his crew took the money from the messenger and left.

Now Siegel was looking for Cohen. That afternoon, Mickey got a call from Champ Segal, who ran a popular barbershop next to the Brown Derby on Vine—and managed the featherweight boxing champion of the world. Segal was one of Bugsy's closest associates. He was also one of the few people in Los Angeles who knew Mickey well enough to have a phone number where he could be reached.

"Ben Siegel wants to see you." (No one called Siegel "Bugsy" to his face.)

"Ben who?" Mickey responded, vainly attempting to project innocence.

"Ben Siegel, a name you got to stand attention to," Champ replied sharply. Then, no doubt aware of how touchy Mickey was, he shifted tone. "Look, do me a favor and come on up" (to the Hollywood YMCA). Bugsy routinely spent his afternoons there, working the bag and enjoying the sauna, and he wanted to talk to Cohen. Mickey agreed.

When Mickey arrived at the Hollywood Y, he was greeted at the door by Champ and by one of Bugsy's men.

"Mr. Siegel is expectin' you," the man said curtly. He led Mickey and Champ down to the sweat room. Siegel emerged, clad in a towel and with a big smile on his face.

"Take a walk, Champ," Siegel said. Champ left. Siegel turned to Mickey.

"You were supposed to contact me when you got here," he said.

"I didn't get around to you yet," Mickey responded sullenly. "I wanted to see my family. I been busy."

"Pretty big score you got this morning," said Siegel.

Mickey said nothing.

"I want you to kick back the money," said Siegel.

"I don't know what you're talking about," Mickey replied.

Siegel smiled. "You're a good boy, but you're a little crazy. I want you to kick back that money."

"I wouldn't kick back no money for my mother," snarled Mickey. "I don't give a fuck who or what it is. When I go on a score and I put up my life and my liberty on the score, I wouldn't kick back to nobody."

"You heard what I said," Siegel said coldly.

"Go take a fuck for yourself," said Mickey. And with that, he stalked out.

Champ was waiting just outside the door. Incredulous, he ran after Cohen. "A remark like that means the death penalty," he told his charge. But Mickey was defiant.

The next day Mickey Cohen was picked up by the cops and thrown into a jail cell. Whether county or city police made the pinch is unclear. Mickey was not arraigned before a judge; there was no pretense of bringing charges. He was simply held incommunicado without bail. On day nine, Champ got him released. Again, Siegel summoned Mickey—this time to a meeting at the offices of Siegel's attorney, Jerry Giesler. Dragna associate Johnny Roselli was there as well, representing both the local Italian mob and the Chicago "Outfit" (the new name for the old Capone gang). Even to the craziest SOB in the world, it must have been clear that Mickey was now dealing directly with New York and Chicago. Not surprisingly, there was—as Mickey liked to say—"a meeting of the minds." Cohen was now fully under Siegel's arm. It was time to organize L.A., "eastern style."

MICKEY knew Eddy Neales and liked him—"a real nice sort of fellow," he'd say later, but someone "with California ways," meaning, someone who couldn't understand or accept what the Syndicate was. Neales just wanted to do his own thing. When Cohen pressed Neales's partner Curly Robinson about accepting Siegel as a partner, Robinson stalled. Siegel soon grew impatient with the act. He decided to send a message, meaning, he decided to send Mickey.

Mickey hit Neales's bookmaking operation first, targeting his commission office. Neales was in the office at the time. Cohen roughed him up, whacking him "across the mouth a few times." Instead of taking the hint, Neales went into hiding. Through his partner, Neales tried to send Mickey a conciliatory message, explaining "that he meant nothing but the best for me, but that I was too hot-tempered and had too much heat on me to join forces." Neales also warned Mickey (presciently) that his attempt "to establish things as they are in the East could never fit into the program in this part of the United States."

Mickey would have none of it. Next he hit the Clover Club itself. After raiding the cage and relieving the off tables of their cash, Mickey turned his attention to the customers, relieving one leggy young blonde of a diamond necklace. She was Betty Grable, who during the 1940s would become one of Hollywood's biggest stars.

(Years later, columnist Florabel Muir would introduce the two at a Hollywood party. Embarrassed, Cohen stammered out an apology, "if it was me." Grable just smiled. "We were insured anyway," she graciously replied.)

Neales was upset. He switched gears, threatening Siegel with police retaliation. Siegel wasn't frightened.

"That Mexican son of a bitch thinks he's comin' in with me," Siegel told Cohen. "Keep on him."

Cohen hit Neales's joints across the city five more times, wrecking each in the process. As a reward for doing Siegel's bidding, Mickey kept the proceeds from the heists for himself. When Neales turned to the sheriff's department for help, Cohen refused to back off. (Mickey's late-night visit to Deputy Sheriff Contreras's men wasn't the only factor in the sheriff department's decision to stop protecting Neales. Siegel also seems to have made a $125,000 payment to purchase some leeway from the department.) So Neales turned next to Jimmy Fox, a tough old Irishman known for his proficiency with handguns and for his excellent connections. (Fox had once shot three men in a downtown hotel room and been acquitted, implausibly, on grounds of self-defense.) As soon as Siegel heard that Neales had engaged Fox, he offered Mickey five grand to rub him out.

Soon after receiving this contract, Mickey was approached by two pharmacists, who also ran a profitable bookmaking operation out of their drugstore at the corner of Wilshire and San Vicente. They were having some problems with Fox. The pharmacists told Mickey that Fox was demanding a meeting the following evening—presumably, to put the squeeze on them—and asked if he could come too. Mickey told them he'd be glad to come and settle their problems. The pharmacist-bookmakers, dismayed by the notion that the baby-faced little fellow before them was supposed to stand between themselves and Fox, suggested that Cohen bring a few extra hands. Mickey was noncommittal.

The meeting was at the house of one of the bookmakers. Mickey arrived early, alone. When Fox arrived, he was not happy to see Mickey there, waiting for him in the kitchen. The bookmakers and one of their wives were there too. Fox got personal.

"Ya know, I'm going to tell ya something, Mickey," Fox began. "I had trouble with your brother Harry years before, and ya know, your brother ran out on me. So my feelings towards you ain't so goddamn good anyway—"

He got no further. Mickey whipped out his .38 and shot Fox on the spot. (By way of justification, Cohen later explained that Harry "was particularly close to me.") The bookmakers were stunned, then hysterical. The host's wife lost her voice for several months. Mickey calmly left—and headed downtown to the Olympic Auditorium to catch a prizefight. He didn't know if Fox was alive or dead and he didn't care. As he was leaving the auditorium, he was grabbed by Det. Jack Donahoe, one of the LAPD's toughest (and most upright) officers.

"You dirty son of a bitch," said the six-foot-one, 225-pound detective to Mickey, as he placed him under arrest. "You kill a man, and you go see a prizefight?"

For three days, Mickey languished in jail—until it became clear that Fox was going to live. Mickey claimed that Fox had drawn on him and that he had fired in self-defense. The tough Irishman declined to contradict him or comment in any way on the shooting. Cohen was released.

Imprisonment hadn't improved his mood. He blamed Eddy Neales for his three days in jail. One night while he was out with a hooker, Cohen decided that he was going to take care of Neales once and for all. Somehow he managed to acquire a key to Neales's apartment. Telling his "date" to wait in the car, Mickey slipped in and waited for the rival underworld figure to come home.

"I'm in the joint waiting to put his lights out, I hear him start opening the door. I'm ready to hit him" but then "some sixth sense told him something," Mickey later recounted. Neales "shut the door real quick and ran"—back to his business partner Curly Robinson. Eddy Neales was done with organized crime in Los Angeles. Robinson called Mickey to capitulate.

Unfortunately, Mickey's men didn't get the message fast enough. Around midnight, one of Neales's men left his Sheridan Road apartment house—alone—to get some cigarettes. Rounding the corner, he ran into Mickey's right-hand man, Hooky Rothman. This is something that no rational person ever wanted to do. A hundred and ninety pounds and built like a bull, Hooky inspired trepidation in even the toughest toughs. He was an idiot savant of assassination, brilliant at plotting a complex killing but either unable or unwilling to engage in conversation with another person. (His standard courtship line, Mickey's crew joked, was "Hello goil," followed by silence.)

"If there was a piece of work to be done, Hooky stopped eating, drinking and sleeping till it was done," Mickey commented later, approvingly.

When Neales's man saw Hooky, he was greatly relieved that the feud was over. "Hi ya, Hooky," he greeted Mickey's man. Hooky gunned him down on the spot.

"It was a bad tragedy," Mickey later reflected, "but it ended okay." Hooky was acquitted on the grounds of self-defense. Eddy Neales moved to Mexico City, just to be safe. Siegel and Cohen had run their leading bookmaking rival out of town. But the Los Angeles underworld was still not entirely under their control. The problem was the LAPD.

During his first year or so back in Los Angeles, Cohen focused on avoiding the police. Not until he met the legendary gambler Nick "the Greek" Dandolos did he realize he'd also have to deal with it.

Over dinner one night at the Brown Derby, Dandolos had a heart-to-heart with Mickey.

"You're doing it all the hard way," Nick the Greek told the uncharacteristically attentive young heister. "A smart kid doesn't have to go on the heavy to make a living." There was a better way—bookmaking.

Mickey liked "going on the heavy." As he would later tell the screenwriter Ben Hecht, "winning a street fight, knockin' over a score, havin' enough money to buy the best hats—I lived for them moments." However, Cohen had conducted so many heists during his short time in Los Angeles that he risked becoming recognizable. So at Dandolos's suggestion, he decided to go visit the Santa Anita racetrack, fifteen miles east of downtown Los Angeles, to see this business that Siegel was so interested in. He was stunned by what he saw there.

"Fifty thousand people are shovin' their money across a betting counter in open sight," he exclaimed with astonishment. Within three days, Mickey was a racetrack bookie, taking bets at his spot along the track rail. When the Pinkertons shut him down, Mickey decided to open a bookie joint of his own. Of course, to do so, Mickey would need police protection.

Fight manager Eddie Meade offered to make some introductions. Over dinner at Ruby Foo's, Meade introduced Mickey to the head of the LAPD's Hollywood vice squad, who agreed to let Mickey open a joint at Santa Monica and Western—"door open like a candy store, three-ticket windows," Mickey recalled fondly. When the day's horse racing was done, Mickey and his crew took the sheets off the walls and opened up for blackjack and poker. All the games were on the square, and the action was excellent—until, less than four months after Mickey had opened his joint, the LAPD gangster and robbery detail moved in and arrested Cohen and his top associates on suspicion of robbery. Mickey was upset. Didn't he have a deal with the police? Not exactly, his police contacts informed him. Cohen had a deal with Hollywood vice, but not with the gangster and robbery detail. And that squad had no intention of letting Mickey build up operations within city limits.

This attitude angered Mickey. Los Angeles, he fumed, was the exact opposite of eastern cities. "[I]t was a syndicate—a combination like the syndicate in Chicago or the syndicate in New York. But here, gambling and everything like they did in Jersey, Chicago, and New York was completely run by cops and stool pigeons."

Then, on the morning of January 14, 1938, an explosion ripped apart a modest house at 955 Orme Street and changed everything.

8

Dynamite

"We've got to get somebody to spill his guts."
— Jim Richardson, city editor, *Los Angeles Examiner*

IT WASN'T BUGSY SIEGEL or Mickey Cohen who toppled the Combination. Nor, despite Bill Parker's efforts, was it an honest cop. Los Angeles's ruling clique was brought down by a thirty-seven-year-old cafeteria owner named Clifford Clinton.

In a city awash in sin and suffering, Clifford Clinton was a righteous man. Stranger still, he was also a rich one, thanks to one of Southern California's hottest trends, the cafeteria. Cafeterias were to 1930s Los Angeles what coffee shops were to 1990s Seattle—ubiquitous, wildly popular, and very profitable. (In 1923, one writer punned that "Southern California" could with equal accuracy be called Sunny Cafeteria.) In 1931, Clinton took the basic idea and gave it a fantastical twist by opening Clifton's Pacific Seas, which featured a giant waterfall, jungle murals, and a Polynesian grass hut inspired by his explorations in the South Pacific, as well as a meditation garden inspired by the Garden of Gethsemane. In 1935, Clinton began work on a second establishment, the Brookdale cafeteria, which evoked Clinton's Northern California childhood with an interior that included redwood trees and a stream that fell over a waterfall before meandering through the cafeteria (past a tiny toy chapel perched upon a rocky escarpment). However, it was Clinton's response to the Great Depression that made his name.

Clinton had always been proud of his food. His cafeteria's motto was "Dine Free unless Delighted," and he meant it. The teetotaler son of Salvation Army officers, Clinton also had strong moral principles. As the Depression deepened, he went out of his way to help Angelenos in distress, offering customers a full meal (soup, salad, bread, Jell-O, and coffee) for a nickel. When it became clear that a nickel was too much for many, he opened a basement cafeteria in his South Hill Street establishment where the less fortunate could get vegetable soup over brown rice for a mere penny.

(Clinton would later estimate that he served roughly a million penny meals over the course of the decade.) Demand was so great for the so-called cave-teria that patrons lined up three hours before the restaurant opened for a meal.

Clinton's introduction to politics was accidental. In 1935, county supervisor John Anson Ford asked the thirty-five-year-old restaurant owner to inspect food operations at the County General Hospital. Clinton uncovered instances of waste and favoritism that were costing the county $120,000 a year. Retaliation was not long in coming. Soon thereafter, Clinton was visited by city health inspectors and cited for numerous violations. But Shaw's minions had messed with the wrong man. Outraged, Clinton persuaded Ford to suggest him for the 1937 county grand jury. Superior Court Judge Fletcher Bowron agreed to put forward his name, and when the 1937 grand jury convened that February, Clinton was among its members.

The county grand jury was the wildcard in Los Angeles politics. Every year, the county's fifty superior court judges appointed nineteen people to the jury, which had broad leeway to investigate wrongdoing. At least seventeen of those judges were in the pocket of the Combination; these friendly judges typically ensured that eight to twelve of the grand jury's members had close ties either to Mayor Frank Shaw's administration or to the underworld. As a result, grand juries generally managed to avoid uncovering any serious wrongdoing. A clear majority of the 1937 grand jury fit this pattern. When Clinton and three other jurors pressed for an investigation into vice conditions, the grand jury foreman refused. But Clinton was undeterred. Instead, he went directly to Mayor Shaw and asked him to bless an investigation.

Clinton's proposal put Shaw in a tough position. If the mayor refused, he risked creating the impression that he had something to hide. So over the objections of Chief Davis, Shaw endorsed Clinton's investigation. When the group unveiled its name—the Citizens Independent Vice Investigating Committee (CIVIC)—and announced that it would also be investigating municipal malfeasance, Shaw realized he had made a mistake. Clinton's public statements made it clear that he was targeting more than the city's brothels and gambling parlors; he was targeting the Combination as a whole. The mayor withdrew his support. CIVIC pressed ahead. Its volunteer investigators soon came up with a tally of vice in Los Angeles: 600 brothels, 300 gambling houses, 1,800 bookie joints, and 23,000 slot machines. The rest of the grand jury wasn't interested. It refused to accept much less publish CIVIC's report.

Clinton turned to Judge Bowron for advice. The fifty-year-old Bowron knew the underworld well. During the teens, he'd put himself through law school by working as a city reporter. Then, after serving in the Army during the First World War, he'd gotten a job as the executive secretary to California governor Friend Richardson, who appointed him to superior court. There Bowron turned his attention to the issue of corruption. Three years earlier, in 1934, Bowron had presided over a crusading county grand jury that nearly toppled District Attorney Buron Fitts. (Fitts's office had dropped a case against a millionaire real estate developer who'd allegedly raped an underage prostitute after the developer entered into a shady business deal with a member of the DA's family.) Now Bowron suggested that Clinton produce a minority grand jury report. When Clinton did so, the judge with responsibility for presiding over the grand jury ruled that it couldn't be released. Bowron issued a counterruling, and CIVIC hastily printed and distributed thousands of copies.

The report was scathing. It found that "underworld profits" were being used to finance the campaigns of "city and county officials in vital positions." In exchange, local officials were turning a blind eye to a vast network of brothels, "clip joints," gambling houses, and bookmakers. The report charged that officials from all three of the principal law enforcement agencies in the county, the district attorney's office, the sheriff's department, and the LAPD, "work in complete harmony and never interfere with the activities of important figures in the underworld."

The counterreaction was swift. Grand jury foreman John Bauer labeled Clinton an "out of control" egomaniac and charged that the cafeteriateur, rather than the underworld, was "Public Enemy #1." The *Los Angeles Times*, which was closely allied with District Attorney Fitts, echoed Bauer's allegations. When a notary appeared before the county grand jury to testify that foreman Bauer was actually a Shaw crony holding lucrative city paint contracts, Fitts, Bauer, and a squad of detectives from the DA's office arrived, uninvited, at the notary's house. The detectives then beat the hapless notary so badly that he had to be hospitalized.

Clinton came under pressure too. His real estate taxes were increased by nearly $7,000, a significant sum during the Depression. Complaints of food poisoning became commonplace. Clinton's newest cafeteria was denied a permit. But the man the newspapers had dubbed "the Cafeteria Kid" was undeterred. So Clinton's enemies upped the ante. That October, a bomb exploded in the basement of Clinton's home in Los Feliz. Fortunately Clinton, his wife, and their three children slept on the other side of the house and were unharmed. The LAPD responded by suggesting the attack was probably just a publicity ruse engineered by Clinton himself—despite the fact that a car seen speeding from the scene had license plates that tied it to the LAPD's intelligence division.

The Shaws weren't the only people playing hardball. So was former LAPD officer Harry Raymond. Raymond was an unsavory character, a twice-fired former vice squad officer with close connections to the old Combination. As the historian Gerald Woods noted dryly, "Few were better qualified to investigate vice than Raymond." Raymond had gotten involved in a picayune dispute between a friend who'd done work for Mayor Shaw's 1933 reelection campaign—and felt he was owed $2,900—and Harry Munson, a former Police Commission member who was widely considered to be the liaison between the underworld and the Shaw administration. Despite the fact that Munson's associates were clearing somewhere between $2 and $4 million a month, Munson refused to pay up. Raymond's friend decided to sue. Raymond recommended an attorney, who just happened to be Clifford Clinton's attorney as well.

Then Raymond himself got busy. His investigation soon uncovered damaging connections between the police department, the underworld, and the Shaw administration. But Raymond didn't turn this evidence over to Clinton or to prosecutors. Instead, he approached his former colleagues in the police department with a blackmail demand. In response, the decision was made to take Raymond out.

On the morning of January 14, 1938, Harry Raymond walked into the garage of his modest house at 955 Orme Street in Boyle Heights, got into his car, pressed the starter pedal, and triggered a thunderous explosion that shook the neighborhood. The car and the garage were destroyed— investigators would later determine that a heavy iron water pipe packed with dynamite had been attached to his car's undercarriage—but Raymond somehow survived, despite suffering 186 shrapnel wounds. The badly wounded Raymond summoned *Los Angeles Examiner* city editor Jim Richardson to his hospital bedside—and fingered Davis muscleman Earl Kynette.

"They told me they would get me," he whispered to the newspaperman. "They put Kynette on me. I've known for weeks he and his boys were shadowing me. They had my phone tapped. Somewhere in the neighborhood you'll find where they had their listening devices. Kynette takes his orders from City Hall and they wanted me out of the way. He's the one who rigged the bomb."

The next morning, Raymond's allegations were splashed across the front page of the *Examiner*. Raymond's attorney quickly reached out to Clifford Clinton and arranged for the wounded blackmailer to claim a more flattering connection to CIVIC. Clinton was happy to portray Raymond as a crusading investigator who had been targeted for termination because he had information that would "blow the lid off Los Angeles." A wiretapping setup was soon found, just as Raymond had alleged. Neighbors confirmed that Capt. Earl Kynette of the LAPD had indeed been surveilling Raymond in the days leading up to the explosion. Nonetheless, upon returning from a pistol shooting competition in Mexico City, Chief Davis assigned Kynette to investigate the bombing. Kynette in turn suggested that Raymond had blown himself up as part of yet another publicity stunt. This was too much for DA Fitts, who reluctantly opened an investigation into police wrongdoing. To those in the know, the situation was farcical. In a letter to U.S. senator Hiram Johnson, chamber of commerce director Frank Doherty described Fitts's investigation of the LAPD thusly: "a near psychopathic district attorney is investigating a crooked police department" that is "trying to dispense of or frighten a former crooked member of their crooked force who was spying into their crooked activities."

Chief Davis's career—and Bill Parker's—hung in the balance. Thanks to the changes in the city charter Parker and the Fire and Police Protective League had pushed through, Kynette's intelligence squad now enjoyed significant legal protections. Those advantages were on full display in the wake of the Raymond bombing. Seven members of Kynette's intelligence squad refused to testify before the grand jury about the unit's activities, citing fears of self-incrimination. Although the officers were initially suspended from duty, a review board made up of their fellow officers soon returned the men to work. But the question of Chief Davis's future—and Bill Parker's—remained.

In April 1938, the trial of Earl Kynette and his two associates got under way. The evidence against Kynette was damning. He had personally purchased the steel pipe used in the bombing. The trial also revealed that Kynette had been running a secret spy squad—one that routinely used wiretaps and dictographs to gather information on opponents of the Shaws' political machine. Among its targets were county supervisor John Anson Ford (who had run for mayor, unsuccessfully, against Frank Shaw in 1937), Judge Bowron, *Hollywood Citizen-News* publisher Harlan Palmer, and fifty other prominent Angelenos. Chief Davis clearly had some questions to answer. But when he took the stand on April 26, Davis was a disaster. Prosecutors had subpoenaed the files of the intelligence division two weeks earlier. They now confronted the chief with evidence that the LAPD intelligence squad had been monitoring county supervisors, judges, newspaper publishers, even a federal agent charged with investigating vice conditions in San Francisco who had considered launching a similar investigation into vice conditions in Los Angeles.

"Are these men criminals?" demanded one of the prosecutors.

Davis parried that everyone under observation had a criminal record—a claim that was true only if you counted parking citations. He further alleged that figures such as county supervisor John Anson Ford, Clifford Clinton, and *Hollywood Citizen-News* publisher Harlan Palmer had been in contact "with subversive elements." When pressed, Davis acknowledged that one of the intelligence squad's functions had been to investigate people "attempting to destroy confidence in the police department"—as if criticism of the police were itself a crime. Mostly, though, Davis seemed confused. His testimony at times was so incoherent that the presiding judge dismissed Davis's testimony as "a debris of words." Kynette was convicted of attempted murder, assault with intent to commit murder, and the malicious use of explosives and sentenced to ten years in prison, along with one other officer.

In an effort to salvage his position, Chief Davis disbanded the intelligence squad, reassigned more than four dozen officers, and launched sweeping vice raids throughout the city.* But it was too late.

One year earlier, Mayor Shaw had been easily reelected to a second term in office, entrenching the Chandler-Shaw-Combination triumvirate that effectively ruled Los Angeles. Clinton and the reformers now demanded that Mayor Shaw dismiss Davis as chief of police. Shaw refused. Davis was the linchpin of the arrangement by which the business establishment, the underworld, and his administration shared power. If he gave up control over the police department, the entire arrangement would come tumbling down, as the reformers well knew. Faced with this refusal, Clinton and his allies targeted the mayor himself, launching a recall effort. No big-city mayor had ever been recalled before, but by early July, Clinton had the signatures he needed to put a motion to recall Shaw on the September ballot. Now the reformers needed a candidate. That August, just one month before the election, Judge Bowron agreed to step down from the bench and run as the reform candidate. That September, voters swept Frank Shaw out of office and made Bowron mayor. Bowron immediately turned his attention to purging the LAPD—and getting rid of Chief Davis.

In theory, thanks to the charter amendments drafted by Bill Parker, Chief Davis enjoyed a bulwark of legal protections. Bowron was determined to override them. Under pressure from the new mayor, the Police Commission resigned en masse. Bowron promptly appointed a new board that was prepared to follow his instructions. Chief Davis wanted to stay and fight. However, Parker warned him that if he fought and lost, he risked losing

---

*The *Citizen-News* wryly noted that the infamous gambling joint at 732 North Highland had been raided by Lieutenant Hoy, "under whose able protection it has operated all these years."

his $330 monthly pension. Reluctantly, Davis accepted his protégé's advice. In November 1938, he resigned as chief. Parker's efforts to insulate the chief of police from political pressures had failed.

Despite his closeness to the former chief, Parker did not initially suffer from Davis's fall. The new acting chief, Insp. David Davidson, quickly reshuffled the top leadership of the force, but he affirmed Parker's position as acting captain. He also named Parker "Administrative Officer" for the department—essentially, the assistant chief of police in everything but name. Parker even moved into the previous assistant chief of police's office. Basically, Davidson was keeping Parker in the same job he'd performed before. Parker seemed to be advancing toward his dream: the chief's chair. But Mayor Bowron wasn't done yet with the LAPD.

MAYOR BOWRON was determined to eradicate the Combination. Shaw's defeat and Chief Davis's resignation had clearly dealt the underworld a major blow, but Bowron knew that its tentacles still extended deep into municipal government and into the LAPD. Soon after his election, Bowron invited Jim Richardson, city editor of the Hearst-owned *Los Angeles Examiner*, the feisty morning paper that was the *Times*'s fiercest competitor, to join him for lunch at the Jonathan Club downtown to talk strategy. The topic of their discussion was uprooting the Combination once and for all.

"We've got to find out the facts," Bowron told the newsman over lunch. "We've got to get the evidence of how it was operated, who put out the bribe money and who took it. Who are the crooks in the police department and how did the whole setup operate? We can't do much, hardly anything, until we get that information; and how are we going to get it?"

"There's only one way," Richardson responded. "We've got to get somebody to spill his guts."

A few days later, Richardson realized someone might be willing to talk: Tony Cornero. During his bootlegging days in the 1920s, Cornero had conducted a guns-blazing feud with Combination leader Milton "Farmer" Page. That feud had ended with Cornero's arrest, followed by an amazing escape to Canada. In 1929, Cornero had voluntarily returned to the United States and served two years in a federal penitentiary on McNeil Island, in the Puget Sound. He returned to Los Angeles in 1931 and hit upon a characteristically wily scheme. Rather than going up against underworld rivals and the LAPD, Cornero decided to commission gambling ships that would operate in international waters off Santa Monica Bay. Offshore gambling proved a smashing success; Cornero had reveled in one-upping his old land-based rivals. But Richardson knew Cornero still held a grudge against his old rivals in what remained of the Combination. The newspaperman thought the old bootlegger-turned-nautical casino operator might well be willing to do them one last bad turn. So he called Cornero and asked if he'd meet secretly with him—and with Mayor Bowron—to help the mayor finish off his old enemies. Cornero readily agreed. A midnight summit was arranged at Bowron's house, on a hill high above the Hollywood Bowl.

The night of the meeting, only six people were present—the mayor, his driver, the head of the Police Commission, Richardson and a colleague, and Cornero. Cornero began by explaining how the underworld operated, but what Bowron really wanted were names—names of police officers on the take.

Cornero handed Bowron a piece of paper. On it was a list of twenty-six compromised police officers. Bowron was thrilled—and puzzled.

"Thank you, Tony," the mayor told the gangster. "You have done us a big service. In fact, you've done the city of Los Angeles a big service." He paused and then continued. "But there's only one thing I can't understand. I can't understand why you're doing this. I mean, I can't see what's in it for you?"

Cornero smiled and then replied. "Well, Your Honor," he began, "you are not always going to be mayor of Los Angeles. Someday you'll be out. It may be the next election or ten years from now. I've given you the stuff to put the Syndicate out of business. Out it goes! Then comes the day when you're out too. Then the field is open again. And it will be mine. It will be open for someone else to take over. Do I make myself clear?"

"You make it clear all right," Bowron replied. The meeting was over. It was time to clean house at the LAPD.

There was just one problem. The testimony of a convicted felon like Tony Cornero was not exactly something that would hold up in court or even in an administrative hearing, given the protections that Bill Parker and the Fire and Police Protective League had so painstakingly enacted. So Mayor Bowron and his Police Commission decided to take an extraordinary step. They hired an ex-FBI man to investigate the officers in question and tap their phones. By the end of the investigation, Bowron was confident that the men were indeed corrupt. Over the course of two days, each was summoned to the mayor's office individually and asked for his resignation. When an officer hesitated—or refused—the mayor reached over to the sound recorder and played an incriminating section of the wiretap. Most of the officers agreed to resign on the spot. In two days, much of the top echelon of the department was gone. Within six months, a dozen more had followed.

The Combination had finally been smashed. In a world with Mickey

Cohen and Bugsy Siegel on the loose, it was simply too dangerous for men like Guy McAfee to operate in Los Angeles without police protection. Moreover, it seemed evident that the new mayor was determined to "close" Los Angeles. And so the organized crime figures who had held sway over the L.A. underworld since the 1920s left Los Angeles. Most relocated to a dusty little town in the Nevada desert where gambling was legal and supervision was lax—Las Vegas.

Mayor Bowron was exultant. "We've broken the most powerful ring that ever had an American city in its grip," he exulted to Richardson. "We've swept the police department clean for the first time in many years."

The sphere of police autonomy that Bill Parker had so laboriously constructed also seemed to have been swept away.

For four years, Parker and the Fire and Police Protective League had worked to restrict politicians' authority over the LAPD. On paper, chief and officers alike now enjoyed substantial legal protections. Yet when the stakes were high, those protections proved to be worthless. In a matter of months, Bowron had forced out the entire senior leadership of the police department, without a prosecutor indicting a single officer, without the Police Commission acting on a single complaint, without a single review board convening. The prospect of a powerful, independent police chief must have seemed impossibly remote.

Yet the triumph of the politicians was not complete. When Bowron's new Police Commission attempted to rescind the city charter amendments that Cooke and Parker had written—returning disciplinary authority to the chief of police (and thus to the mayor and Police Commission who appointed and oversaw him)—the city council objected. Nor did the council embrace reformers' proposals for a new city charter, one that would have greatly strengthened the mayor's rather limited powers over the executive branch of government. In short, the legal protections Parker's charters had created remained, even as Mayor Bowron drained them of their significance. They simply lay fallow, waiting for a chief who would have the skill and knowledge to breathe life into them.

IN MAY 1939, Parker got his first clear shot at becoming that chief.

In theory, promotion in the LAPD was strictly meritocratic. Under ordinary circumstances, officers sat for promotional exams roughly every two years. A written exam typically accounted for 95 percent of their scores; the remaining 5 percent was determined by an oral exam and by seniority. Officers were then ranked by their results and placed on a promotional list, from which all new appointments had to be made. But the onset of the Great Depression—and the appearance of Joe Shaw—had disrupted this process. Between 1929 and 1936, hiring in the department had essentially been frozen. In 1936, Joe Shaw had overseen a new round of civil service examinations—and, rumor had it, helpfully sold answers to the questions for all fifty positions waiting to be filled. The department's promotion lists were so suspect that Mayor Bowron's new Police Commission decided to start from scratch. It threw out the previous lists and announced a new round of competitive examinations. Among the positions up for grabs was that of chief of police.

The acting chief of police, David Davidson, disclaimed any interest in the job, saying he preferred "not to be pushed around every time a new administration took office." Capt. R. R. McDonald was known to be the mayor's favorite, yet Bowron's handpicked Police Commission nonetheless announced that it would make a purely meritocratic choice. The candidate who placed highest on the civil service exam would be the Police Commission's choice.

One hundred seventy-one officers sat for the written examination for chief, including acting captain Bill Parker. Thirty-one were called back to complete the oral portion of the test. Once again, Parker was among the top group. On June 15, 1939, Parker received his score from the Board of Civil Service Commissioners: He had received a final grade of 78.1, which placed his name eighth on the tentative eligible list. The name at the top came as a surprise to everyone: Lt. Arthur Hohmann. After several weeks of hemming and hawing, the Police Commission decided to recognize Hohmann's ranking and appointed him chief.

From the first, Bill Parker was in his sights. The services rendered to Chief Davis now stood Parker in bad stead. "Parker's loyalty and zealous attention to his office was now misinterpreted as blind loyalty to organizations and individuals and his past performance as an efficient, courageous and honest officer was discounted," wrote a friendly superior officer, B. R. Caldwell, four years after the event. Hohmann immediately created a new headquarters division—and announced that he would command it himself. R. R. McDonald was made administrative officer. Acting captain Bill Parker—now Lieutenant Parker—was out.

Demoralized by his de facto demotion and worried that he would never shake the Davis stigma, Parker seriously considered leaving the force and becoming a full-time attorney. He even lined up a few legal cases he could work on as a private attorney and drafted a letter of resignation, but at the last minute, Parker's old boss from his time at Hollywood Division, Capt. B. R. Caldwell, stepped in. Caldwell was a Parker admirer. He intervened to secure a position for Parker in the traffic accident investigation division, which he headed. This was not an inconsequential position. Managing traffic was a major problem in the world's most car-oriented big city. Traffic accidents were also a major cause of death, killing 533 people in 1941, more than ten times the number of people murdered that year. Despite feeling bruised by his treatment, Parker agreed to stay on.

Parker now had something to prove. In February 1940, he took the examination for captain and placed second on the promotion list. That May, Chief Hohmann recognized his achievement by appointing him captain. In September, Parker took the examination for Inspector of Police and again placed second. Soon thereafter, Parker won a fellowship award to Northwestern University's Traffic Institute. In the fall of 1940, he left for Chicago to study the fine points of traffic control for nine months.

The Combination got in one final dig at the new order. That fall, the generally reliable *Hollywood Citizen-News* broke the story of Bowron and Jim Richardson's secret meeting with Tony Cornero, in a highly misleading fashion: NEW VICE SETUP IN LOS ANGELES, proclaimed the banner headline. TONY CORNERO, MAYOR BOWRON AND EXAMINER CITY EDITOR IN SECRET MIDNIGHT MEETING AT MAYOR'S HOUSE. It turned out that Bowron's driver was on the Combination's payroll. Although the charge that the mayor had met with Cornero to divvy up Los Angeles was completely untrue, Bowron felt he had to respond, and so, with no little ruthlessness, he turned against the man who had decapitated the Combination, Tony Cornero.

The gambling fleet Cornero operated just offshore had long been an embarrassment. Mayor Bowron now decided that it was intolerable, so he turned up the pressure on California attorney general Earl Warren and Sheriff Eugene Biscailuz by publicly calling on them to shut down the gaming fleet. With the attention of the public upon them, Sheriff Biscailuz and Santa Monica police chief Charles Dice set out in a fleet of water taxis to arrest the offshore crime lord, who they insisted had strayed into California waters. In court, however, Cornero sprung a surprise. Santa Monica Bay, he argued, was not actually a bay at all but rather a bight, a large coastal indentation. That put his ships in international waters, out of the reach of the California courts. An appeals court agreed, and Tony "the Hat" (now "the Commodore") returned to action.

After much head-scratching, Attorney General Warren decided to try another tack: He announced that Cornero's gambling fleet was a "nuisance," which the state of California had the power to abate. A cease-and-desist warning was issued. When Cornero refused to comply, a raiding party was sent out to capture his flagship, the SS *Rex*. Cornero insisted the raiding party's members were pirates. For nine days, "the Commodore" held the raiders off with a fire hose before succumbing to hunger and surrendering the ship. The courts rejected Cornero's claims that he was a victim of piracy, and the California Supreme Court ruled that the appeals court had erred in its analysis of coastal geography. Santa Monica Bight returned to being Santa Monica Bay. Tony Cornero was out of luck for a second time.

Bugsy Siegel and Mickey Cohen, on the other hand, couldn't have been luckier. Mayor Bowron had shut down first the Combination and then Tony Cornero. Los Angeles's homegrown criminal underworld had scurried off to Las Vegas. The Los Angeles underworld was now Siegel's to command. What made the situation even sweeter was that as his influence was growing, his identity as a notorious eastern gangster remained virtually unknown. It wasn't until a wiseacre NYPD detective decided to give the Los Angeles DA's chief investigator a scare that the LAPD awoke to the fact that its nightmare of "eastern gangsters" moving into the city had already come true. The struggle for control of Los Angeles was about to move into a new phase, one that would put Bugsy Siegel and his top lieutenant, Mickey Cohen, in direct conflict with the LAPD.

Getting Away with Murder (Inc.)

"Men who have lived by the gun do not throw off the habit overnight."

—Florabel Muir

DISTRICT ATTORNEY Buron Fitts was in a tricky position. Angelenos were in a reforming mood—and Buron Fitts was the antithesis of reform. In 1936, Fitts had won reelection after essentially purchasing 12,000 votes along Central Avenue. (The *Hollywood Citizen-News* later reported that the underworld had spent $2 million—more than $30 million in today's dollars—to fund Fitts's campaign.) Knowing of his vulnerability on issues of corruption, when the Raymond bombing scandal broke, Fitts had acted with uncharacteristic vigor, ultimately convicting Joe Shaw on sixty-three counts of selling city jobs and promotions. Still, with a tough reelection campaign approaching, Fitts needed to do more. So in 1939, Fitts sent his chief investigator, Johnny Klein, to Manhattan. New York City district attorney Tom Dewey had made a name for himself by prosecuting gangsters. Klein's brief was to learn what he could about eastern gangsters who might be trying to infiltrate the City of Angels.

A former Hollywood fur salesman, Klein was not known as the savviest of investigators. When he arrived at NYPD headquarters on Centre Street to examine the department's gangster files, one of the detectives decided to have a little fun with him. He pulled forth a mug shot of Benjamin Siegel—taken in Dade County, Florida, where Siegel had been arrested for speeding.

"Now there's an outstanding citizen named Bugsy Siegel," the detective told the DA's investigator.

"Never heard of him," Klein replied.

"You never heard of him? Why, Johnny, this guy is one of the worst killers in America, and he's living right in your backyard." The detective continued, "Dewey wants this guy and would give anything to lay hands on him."

Bugsy Siegel *was* one of the worst killers in America—the FBI would later credit him with carrying out or participating in some thirty murders—but his whereabouts were hardly a secret. Every crime reporter in New York knew that Siegel was actually in New York at that very moment, staying at the Waldorf-Astoria (where he had lived for much of the 1920s, two floors below "Lucky" Luciano). And it had been a long time since Bugsy Siegel was running around indiscriminately knocking people off. Nonetheless, Klein promptly telegrammed the news of this discovery back to Los Angeles. The DA's office immediately sent a raiding party to Siegel's Beverly Hills residence—along with a reporter from the *Los Angeles Examiner*, which was delighted to have another gangster to crusade against.

The next day the *Examiner* broke the story in typical Hearst style, portraying Siegel as a Dillinger-esque outlaw on the run. To those familiar with the Syndicate's operations, the *Examiner*'s portrayal was laughable. Still, Siegel's cover was blown. The timing couldn't have been worse. Siegel had just launched an effort to sign up L.A.'s bookies for a new racing wire, the Trans-American news service. His unmasking threatened to complicate these efforts, as well as the broader effort to organize Los Angeles along eastern lines. Furious, Siegel called the Los Angeles papers. If he was really an outlaw wanted by DA Dewey, then why was he visiting New York City, unmolested, at that very moment? Siegel's consort, the Countess di Frasso, was also upset, so much so that she drove to San Simeon to make a personal appeal to William Randolph Hearst to stop the *Examiner* from further besmirching Siegel's name. These efforts floundered, for Siegel was, of course, a notorious gangster. With uncharacteristic delicacy of feeling, a despairing Siegel decided to resign from his beloved Hillcrest Country Club (though no one dared ask him to). He also decided to leave town for a bit. So he set off for Rome with the Countess di Frasso, leaving Mickey Cohen as his surrogate.

MICKEY AND BUGSY had grown close. Cohen was still raw—not to mention sullen, closemouthed, temperamental, and dangerous—but Siegel thought he had potential. As a result, he began to try, in Mickey's words, "to put some class into me . . . trying to evolve me." It wasn't easy. As a stickup-man, Mickey steered clear of flashy dressing (too memorable). White shirt, dark sunglasses, that was it. Off the job, however, Mickey continued to pay his sartorial respects to Al Capone. Siegel tried to spiff him up. He introduced Mickey to cashmere. (Mickey thought it tickled.) He also introduced Mickey to a higher class of people. For the first time in his life, Cohen "got invited to different dinner parties and . . . met people with much elegance and manners." It slowly dawned on Mickey that he'd been "living like an animal." He grew ashamed. Earnestly, he set out to improve himself. He hired a tutor to help him learn to speak grammatically.

He purchased a leather-bound set of the world's great literature, which he proudly showed off to visitors (who noted the spines were never cracked).

When a source at the Treasury Department's Bureau of Internal Revenue (precursor agency to the Internal Revenue Service) informed Siegel that the government was starting to get interested in his young sidekick, Siegel told Mickey he had to start paying taxes. It was a tough sell. ("I had a firm belief that if the government, or anybody else, wanted any part of my money they should at least be on hand to help me steal it," he said later, only half-jokingly.) The fact that Siegel prevailed on Cohen to get an accountant shows the authority that Bugsy exercised over his young protégé. Although he would later (much later) boast of thumbing his nose at Bugsy during his early days in L.A., Mickey was actually quite awed by the suave older gangster.

"I found Benny a person with brilliant intelligence," Cohen told the writer Ben Hecht in the mid-1950s. "He commanded a 1,000 percent respect and got it. Also he was tough. He come out the hard way—been through it all— muscle work, heists, killings." For someone who had dreamed of an association with "the people," working with Siegel must have seemed like a dream come true. They were not formally superior and subordinate—Mickey continued to run his own rackets and related to Bugsy more like a subcontractor on retainer than an employee—but when Siegel gave an order, Cohen jumped to. In return, Bugsy took care of Mickey, kicking him anywhere from $2,000 to $20,000 on a regular (albeit unpredictable) basis.

It was an arrangement Mickey liked. "I didn't have no wish to be a ruler," said Cohen in describing his mind-set upon first arriving in Los Angeles. "In fact that was actually contrary to my nature at the time. I just wanted to be myself—Mickey." But fate—in the form of Bugsy Siegel's itchy trigger finger—had other plans.

BUGSY AND THE COUNTESS di Frasso's trip to Rome wasn't intended just to get away from the press. Both Siegel and the multimillionaire countess had a weakness for get-rich schemes. One year earlier, they had chartered a boat to look for buried treasure off the coast of Ecuador.*

---

*Surely, this was the strangest yachting party in the history of Hollywood. The group included barber/boxing manager Champ Segal; the nephew of British foreign secretary (later prime minister) Anthony Eden; Jean Harlow's father-in-law; and a German-American captain who was also an informant for the FBI. The captain suspected the treasure expedition was actually a resupply operation for Brooklyn mob boss Louis "Lepke" Buchalter, who was on the lam. The expedition ended with Champ Segal being formally indicted on charges of mutiny. (He was later acquitted.) Neither treasure nor Louis Buchalter was found. (Muir, *Headline Happy*, 169–72.)

Now the gangster and the countess had another idea. Siegel had recently come across two chemists who claimed to have invented a new type of explosive—Atomite. Bugsy was convinced this new substance would replace dynamite and make him fabulously wealthy. With the countess's help, he hoped to sell it to the Italian military. The countess, always ready for adventure, talked to her husband, who arranged a demonstration.

For purposes of a trip to fascist Italy, di Frasso decided to recast Bugsy as "Bart"—Sir Bart, an English baronet. This was a good idea, for when the countess arrived at her husband's villa outside of Rome, she found that they had houseguests—Joseph Goebbels, Nazi Germany's propaganda minister, and Hermann Göring, Luftwaffe commander and Hitler's second in command. Although Siegel evidently had no qualms about doing business with Mussolini's military, the Nazi houseguests rubbed him the wrong way. One night he confronted the countess.

"Look, Dottie," he said, "I saw you talking to that fat bastard Göring. Why do you let him come into our building?"

The countess murmured something about social niceties, to which Siegel responded, "I'm going to kill him, and that dirty Goebbels, too. . . . It's an easy setup the way they're walking around here."

Only after the countess elaborated on the problems posed by the carabiniere—and the likely consequences for her husband—did Siegel give up on the idea. The Atomite demonstration fizzled, and "Sir Bart" and Countess di Frasso left for the French Riviera. There Siegel bumped into his old friend the actor George Raft, who was pursuing the actress Norma Shearer. Despite Atomite's inexplicable failure, Siegel seemed to be in good spirits. Raft said he was looking forward to lingering on the Riviera. Then Siegel received a cablegram from New York and his mood suddenly changed. The next day Raft noticed he was gone. The Syndicate had a problem that required Bugsy's unique talents.

The problem was Harry "Big Greenie" Greenberg. Greenberg was a former associate of Siegel and Louis "Lepke" Buchalter, the Brooklyn-based crime lord and labor racketeer. Greenberg had been arrested and deported to his native Poland, but "Big Greenie" had no intention of going back to the old country. He jumped ship in France and made it back to Montreal. From there he sent a letter to a friend in New York, implying that if his old friends in Brooklyn didn't send him a big bundle of cash, he might go talk to the authorities. Instead of sending cash, Buchalter associate Mendy Weiss sent two hitmen. "Big Greenie" checked out of his hotel just hours before the two assassins checked in. For a time, the trail went cold. Then, in the fall of 1939, "Big Greenie" was spotted in Hollywood. He had a new name (George Schachter), a new wife, and, given his lack of further communications, he'd evidently learned that blackmailing the Syndicate was a foolish thing to do. Nonetheless, at a meeting in New York, Siegel, Buchalter, New Jersey rackets boss Longy Zwillman, and Brooklyn crime overlord Albert Anastasia decided that "Big Greenie" had to go. Zwillman once again sent two gunmen to California. But the gunmen didn't like the setup and returned to New York. Bugsy being Bugsy, he decided to take care of the problem himself.

The evening before Thanksgiving, on November 22, 1939, "Big Greenie" got a call to run down to the corner drugstore to pick up a package. As he eased his old Ford convertible into a parking space outside his modest house in Hollywood, triggerman Frank Carbo walked quickly out of the shadows toward the vehicle. Bugsy Siegel was waiting in a black Mercury sedan parked down the street. Al Tannenbaum was behind him, in a stolen "crash car," ready to stop any car that pursued them. Champ Segal was parked five blocks away, ready to drive Carbo north to San Francisco where he would take a flight back to New York. From inside the Greenberg house, Ida Greenberg heard a rapid series of shots—a backfiring car, she thought, then the sound of two cars speeding down the street. When "Big Greenie" didn't reappear, she went outside to look for him. She found him in his blood-spattered car, dead from five bullets fired at point-blank range into his head.

So much for "Big Greenie"—or so it seemed. Unfortunately for Bugsy, one of his old associates back in Brooklyn was about to start talking to the DA.

Abe "Kid Twist" Reles had a reputation as one of East Brooklyn's nastiest thugs. "He had a round face, thick lips, a flat nose and small ears," noted Brooklyn assistant DA Burton Turkus. "His arms had not waited for the rest of him. They dangled to his knees, completing a generally gorilla-like figure." He also had the nasty habit of killing victims with an ice pick, which made him one of Louis Buchalter's most feared executioners.

In January 1940, two months after Greenberg's assassination, "Kid Twist" was picked up by the police on charges of robbery, assault, possession of narcotics, burglary, disorderly contact, and six charges related to various murders. For a guy like Reles, this should have been no big deal. After all, he'd been arrested forty-two times over the preceding sixteen years and had never done serious jail time. But as he languished in prison, Reles grew worried that several associates who'd also been picked up were ratting him out. So Reles informed his wife that he was willing to talk. One day, Mrs. Reles walked into the Brooklyn DA's office and announced, "My husband wants an interview with the Law."

It took twelve days and twenty-five stenographer notebooks to complete and record his confession. Reles's testimony was stunning. In two weeks' time, he clarified forty-nine unsolved murders. That wasn't even the most startling part of his story. Previously, most police officials had assumed that Reles and his associates were basically just a nasty crew of criminals who operated in and around Brownsville and East New York. Not so, Reles told the prosecutors. He revealed that Buchalter had actually assembled a group that functioned as a killing squad for a nationwide crime syndicate. For the first time, authorities realized, in Turkus's words, "that there actually existed in America an organized underworld, and that it controlled lawlessness across the United States," from Brooklyn to California. Turkus would later dub it "Murder, Inc." According to Reles, hundreds of people nationwide had been killed at its bequest. "Big Greenie" was one of them.

There was more. Reles told prosecutors that Bugsy Siegel and Buchalter lieutenant Mendy Weiss had organized the hit on "Big Greenie"—and that New York fight promoter Frank Carbo had pulled the trigger. Mickey Cohen pal Champ Segal had also been involved in the hit, Reles told authorities. He'd heard so firsthand. Reles testified that after the hit, he had overheard Siegel, Weiss, Louis Capone, and one of the original gunmen sent west to do the hit, Sholom Bernstein, discussing the rub-out. According to Reles, Bernstein had criticized the execution of the hit as something more befitting "a Wild West cowboy" than a professional assassin. In response, Siegel had allegedly replied, "I was there myself on that job. Do I look like a cowboy? I did that job myself." After Bernstein left, Reles added, Siegel had proposed whacking *him*—for fouling up ("dogging") the first hit.

Reles wasn't prosecutors' only important witness. They'd also flipped Al Tannenbaum, the other gunman Murder, Inc. had originally sent to Montreal to kill "Big Greenie." Tannenbaum was now prepared to testify that New Jersey mob boss Longy Zwillman had sent him to California with pistols for the Greenberg hit and that on the night of the murder he'd been the driver of the crash car.

A stronger case against Siegel would have been hard to imagine. With two witnesses who could link Siegel to the murder, prosecutors on both coasts went to work. Brooklyn assistant DA Burton Turkus flew to Los Angeles to brief Los Angeles district attorney Buron Fitts on the evidence. Fitts immediately assembled a raiding party. His plan was to nab Bugsy at his newly built dream mansion in Holmby Hills, one of L.A.'s most prestigious neighborhoods.

The raiding party—three cars strong, its members specially chosen for their marksmanship skills—set out for the Siegel mansion at 250 Delfern Street on the morning of August 17, 1940. They were greeted at the front door by Siegel's butler. The men informed him that they were there to see

Benjamin Siegel. The butler nodded and asked them to wait. Several minutes later, he returned and opened the door of the mansion onto a lifestyle they could scarcely conceive of. At a time when the country was mired in the seemingly unending misery of the Depression, Bugsy Siegel was living like . . . a baronet. In the bar and lounge room, eighteen-foot carved divans flanked a deeply recessed fireplace, and a choice selection of whiskeys, cognacs, and cordials was available for guests. There were six "vanity rooms" for the ladies. The dining room table was made of exotic inlaid woods and sat thirty—without extensions.

Bugsy's bed was still warm, but there was no sign of him. A member of the raiding party noticed a linen closet door ajar. Atop a pile of fresh sheets, investigators found footprints. The ceiling of the closet had a secret trapdoor that opened into the attic. There the raiding party found Bugsy Siegel in his pajamas, giggling. The gangster coolly informed his captors that he had fled because "I thought it was someone else." The police were not amused. They hauled Siegel downtown and placed him under arrest for murder. Reles and Tannenbaum were flown to Los Angeles, and on the basis of their testimony, Siegel was indicted. His request for bail was denied. Siegel would await trial at the L.A. County Jail.

MAYOR BOWRON and DA Fitts had run the remnants of the Combination out of town. Siegel's trial gave them a chance to sweep out the Syndicate as well. But almost immediately the prosecution began to experience problems—strange problems. Reporters discovered that Siegel had access to a telephone, slept in the county jail doctor's quarters, and employed another prisoner as his valet. Worst of all, he was leaving the jail virtually at will—more than eighteen times in a month and a half. The *Examiner* even spotted Siegel having lunch with the actress Wendy Barrie. In truth, he was not completely unattended. A deputy sheriff was on hand—as Siegel's driver.

Then dissension broke out between prosecutors in New York and Los Angeles. Brooklyn district attorney William O'Dwyer abruptly declined to allow Reles to return to Los Angeles to testify, saying that his prized witness, who was being guarded by a crew of eighteen policemen at an undisclosed location, had come down with a serious illness. Suspicions immediately arose that O'Dwyer, who was eyeing a run for mayor of New York, had struck a deal with the Syndicate. Prosecutors in L.A. had problems too. In 1940, Angelenos finally voted Buron Fitts out of office. His successor, former congressman John Dockweiler, was promptly embarrassed when Siegel wrote to him to request that the prosecutor-elect refund him the $30,000 he had contributed to his campaign. The DA complied. (Mickey Cohen would later claim that Siegel had actually given Dockweiler $100,000.) Siegel then used the funds to hire attorney Jerry Giesler to defend him.

Dockweiler was in a bind. Reles's testimony was essential to establishing Siegel as the mastermind of the murder plot. Without it, the new DA saw no way to secure a conviction. But O'Dwyer wouldn't give up his prized witness. As a result, on December 11, 1940, Deputy DA Vernon Ferguson, who was prosecuting the case for Dockweiler's office, went to court and requested that the murder charges against Bugsy Siegel be dismissed. That afternoon Siegel walked out of jail, a free man.

Back in New York, though, Bugsy's release proved such an embarrassment for O'Dwyer that he reversed course and agreed to let his witnesses go to Los Angeles. Dockweiler convened another jury; Al Tannenbaum flew west to testify ("under heavy guard"); and Siegel was reindicted and again arrested. The key witness, however, was Reles. Although Tannenbaum had taken part in the actual assassination itself, it was Reles who had the power to send Bugsy Siegel to the gas chamber. And it was Reles who, just before breakfast on the morning of November 12, 1941, was found dead on the roof of the building next door to the Half Moon Hotel on Coney Island, where the NYPD had him in protective custody.

What had happened to "Kid Twist"? No one knows for certain. A torn rope made from a bedsheet suggested that Reles had plunged to his death four stories below while trying to escape, though why someone facing a death sentence from the Syndicate would want to escape into Brooklyn was unclear. Perhaps Reles had simply intended to play a joke on his police protectors by demonstrating how easily he could flee. But the physical evidence suggested another explanation. Reles's body was found more than twenty feet from the wall, suggesting that Reles had been hurled out the window—defenestrated—by a policeman on the take.

Without Reles, the case against Siegel was weak. On January 19, 1942, the trial against Siegel began. While Tannenbaum was there as a witness, California law required that charges against Siegel be corroborated by independent evidence that tied the defendant to the crime—evidence the prosecution no longer had. As a result, on February 5, 1942, Judge A. A. Scott granted Siegel attorney Jerry Giesler's request to dismiss the case on grounds that no case had been made against his client. Bugsy Siegel was once again a free man.

Siegel's lengthy entanglements with the court system meant that Mickey Cohen had to take on a large organizational task. He proved to be a surprisingly talented understudy. Mickey soon took over as Siegel's liaison to the county sheriff's office. He also took responsibility for cultivating the LAPD.

"For weeks before each Thanksgiving and Christmas, I would receive calls from captains in different precincts and would be told about and given the names and addresses of some persons in their respective districts that they considered in dire straits," Mickey later related. "I would then have individual baskets made up by a good friend of mine who was in the chain market business (and who would make them up for me at wholesale prices), each basket always including a large turkey, a ham and chicken, and most other necessities for a decent Thanksgiving and Christmas." At his peak, he was sending out about three hundred baskets a year. Mickey was learning the craft of organized crime. It wasn't always turkeys and chicken.

One of Mickey's businesses was pinball and slot machines. His partner was Curly Robinson, former Clover Club owner Eddy Neales's onetime associate. Mayor Bowron had more or less succeeded in expelling slots from the city of Los Angeles, but they were still a thriving business in the county. Cohen and Robinson were determined to profit from them. Their racket was an association that every distributor in the region had to join.

But Robinson was having problems. Some of its members had gotten a bit independent minded. Expecting trouble at the next meeting, Robinson asked Cohen to come to the association's next gathering. Mickey arrived early with three of his toughest henchmen, Hooky Rothman (Cohen's right-hand man, a killing savant), "Little Jimmy" ("quiet—perfectionist—carried out instructions—tough with pistol—two time loser on heists and attempted murder"), and "Big Jimmy" ("six-foot, three-inch—ex-heavyweight pug—easygoing horse bettor—done some time in Maine for a killing"). By the time the meeting got under way, there were roughly six hundred people present.

A speaker took the stage and began to talk about the need for independence. Mickey leapt onto the platform and "busted his head open."

"Nobody come near me," he later noted. The meeting hall was silent. With Mickey and his men glowering on stage, the slot machine association fell in line. There was no more talk of autonomy. Still, on the way out, Mickey and his goons pistol-whipped "two or three other dissenters."

Slots were just a minor sideline. Cohen's real focus was on gambling.

While Siegel concentrated on signing up bookies for the Trans-American news service (an enterprise that by 1945 would be paying Benny an estimated $25,000 a month), Cohen worked on opening his own gambling joints. Initially, he steered clear of the city proper, preferring more hospitable county terrain. His first major base of operations was in Burbank, just a few blocks away from the Warner Bros. lot. Thanks to a pliable local police chief, Mickey was able to open a basic $2-a-bet bookie joint. It thrived. Back in Los Angeles, Mickey soon added a commission office that handled the kinds of big "lay-off" bets—typically anything over $5,000— that were often spread out to bookies across the country.

Commission offices thrived on a peculiarity of horse betting. Because sanctioned tracks used a pari-mutuel betting system (whereby the odds were set by the bets placed), a big bet (say $50,000) could significantly reduce the payout. Commission offices offered high rollers an alternative, where they could place big bets without lowering their payoff. Because the people placing these bets often had inside information, they also presented bookies with information that could be highly lucrative.

With this information came new friends, including a number of local politicians. One judge was so horse-crazed that he insisted that Mickey come down to his chambers and run operations from there, so that he would have access to all of Mickey's tips.

"The poor bookmakers," Mickey reflected, "were really in a quandary, as they couldn't figure out where he was getting his information and were in no position to turn down his wagers for fear of invoking the wrath of the Judge."

One afternoon as Mickey was waiting in the judge's office, he learned that the case of a small-time bookmaker was about to be heard. Mickey knew the man well; in fact, he'd robbed his establishment before. Mickey decided to peek into the courtroom and watch the proceedings. He could scarcely believe his ears when the judge handed down the sentence—thirty days in the county jail. Furious, Mickey caught the eye of the bailiff and told him that he needed to talk to the judge at once.

"The judge, thinking that I must have received word on a horse, couldn't get off the bench quick enough," Mickey later recalled. Back in his chambers, Mickey exploded, speaking "without my usual respect for him, although I did manage to keep myself somewhat under control."

"What kind of man are you, to sentence a man to jail for thirty days when you yourself are a freak for betting on the horses?"

The answer, of course, was a politician.

For a gangster, Mickey Cohen had an inadequate understanding of treachery. Not only did this make it hard to deal with politicians, it blinded him to what was happening before his very eyes with Jack Dragna.

Dragna, a short, heavyset man who favored horn-rimmed glasses, was an old-school Sicilian who liked to surround himself with Sicilians (or, barring that, at least other Italians). He had the air of someone used to dealing with money. His demeanor was more banker than muscle. Mickey didn't think much of him. Nor did he seem aware of the fact that Dragna might hold a grudge about Cohen's earlier heist. Instead, Mickey interpreted the order imposed by Siegel as the natural order of things. He saw Dragna and himself "on an even status as his two lieutenants"—with himself rising and Dragna on the way out.

"Dragna was inactive at the time, and for years had no organization at all," Mickey later recalled. "[A]nything he wanted done he came to me for." As far as Mickey was concerned, organized crime in Los Angeles was "a happy family." As for the possibility that robbing Morris Orloff and being an all-around punk might have rubbed Dragna and the Italian gangsters surrounding him the wrong way, Cohen dismissed it out of hand: "I was the guest of honor at his daughter's wedding!"

Mickey was mistaken—dangerously so. Bugsy represented New York. But Dragna had closer ties to Chicago. Although the twin capitals of the underworld generally cooperated on matters of importance, there were areas of friction. Siegel's 1942 decision to force Los Angeles bookmakers to subscribe to his wire service was one of them. At the time, most big bookies in Los Angeles were using James Ragan's Chicago-based Continental wire services—and paying a cut to Jack Dragna and Johnny Roselli, the Chicago Outfit's man in Los Angeles, for protection. Siegel didn't care. Instead, he sent Mickey Cohen to wreak havoc on the office of the Chicago wire's L.A. manager, Ragan son-in-law Russell Brophy. Even Mickey felt a little leery about this assignment. When he arrived at Brophy's main office downtown and was told Johnny Roselli was on the phone—and that he wanted to speak to Mickey—Cohen was less enthusiastic still. He knew firsthand what kind of tactics the Chicago Outfit employed. So he ducked the request. Instead, he gave the phone to his partner Joe Sica. ("I figured Italian to Italian, you know.")

"Lookit, Johnny says that whatever we've done is done, but he don't want this office busted up," Sica reported.

Which, of course, was precisely what Cohen and Sica had been sent to do.

"Tell him that I'm sorry, but this office is going up for grabs completely," Mickey replied. "Just tell him that, and hang the phone up."

Sica did. Then he and Mickey "tore that fucking office apart." Mickey beat up Brophy, hurting him so badly that Mickey decided to go on the lam. He fled to Phoenix. There he was greeted like a conquering hero by Siegel.

"You little son of a bitch," Siegel said. "You remind me of my younger days."

Mickey hid out in Phoenix for six months. Somehow (Mickey was never clear exactly how) Siegel managed to square the Brophy assault with the authorities, clearing the way for Cohen's eventual return to Los Angeles. Smoothing matters over with Jack Dragna and Johnny Roselli was a more difficult matter. After a period of dormancy, Dragna was gearing up his operations. Worse, he had opted to do so by partnering with a Los Angeles underworld figure, Jimmy Utley, whom Cohen viewed as "an out-and-out stool pigeon for the DA and attorney general's office." It aggravated Mickey, and an aggravated Mickey Cohen was a dangerous man, as Utley was about to discover.

One day soon after his return from Phoenix, Mickey sauntered out of Champ Segal's barbershop on Vine and saw Utley talking with one of the LAPD's toughest police officers, E. D. "Roughhouse" Brown, in front of Lucey's Restaurant. Mickey had long suspected that Utley was a "stool pigeon" for Brown—an informer. But if Utley was concerned about this, he didn't show it. After "Roughhouse" left, Utley waved to Mickey and Joe Sica. So Cohen and Sica walked over—and laid into Utley, pistol-whipping him "pretty badly"—in front of an estimated one hundred people.

Utley took it bravely. Despite being badly hurt, when police arrived on the scene, he insisted that he wasn't able to identify his assailants.

Jack Dragna was less understanding. He immediately got hold of Siegel and demanded a meeting with Cohen. Siegel summoned his protégé to a meeting that very night, and this time, Mickey came.

"I didn't break his ass, just with my hands," Mickey claimed, by way of self-defense. "He was talking to a fucking copper!"

Even Siegel was exasperated by this.

"What the fuck's wrong with ya?" Siegel exploded. "Don't ya know ya got to do business with these coppers? Ya wanna be a goddamn gunman all your life?"

L.A. Noir

"If you're going to gamble that kind of money, own the casa."

—20th Century Fox chairman Joseph Schenck to
Hollywood Reporter owner Billy Wilkerson

BUGSY SIEGEL wasn't the only person flexing his muscles. So was Mayor Bowron. Bowron disliked the fact that he had such limited formal control over the police department. The 1934 and 1937 charter amendments, which broadened police officers' job protections and extended them to the chief of police, were a particular sore point, which Bowron repeatedly sought to circumvent. He continued to secretly wiretap the telephone lines of senior police department officials—an activity that arguably constituted a federal felony offense—in order to ensure that the underworld did not reestablish ties with the department. Soon, the mayor was routinely demanding that Chief Hohmann fire officers caught in the wiretaps' surveillance dragnet. But Bowron, not wanting to acknowledge his illegal wiretapping, refused to explain the basis of these demands, and Hohmann refused to act without evidence. The result was a standoff—and growing tension between the city's top elected official and its top law enforcement officer.

Hohmann had been an exemplary police chief—honest and intelligent, enlightened on racial issues, and uninterested in currying favor with others. He curtailed special privileges (such as police cars and drivers for city councilmen) and ended the department's tradition of strikebreaking. Committed to professionalism, he urged his subordinates to do their duty without fear or favor because, he told them, "the days of 'Big Shot' political influence in the police department are over." He was wrong. After winning reelection in 1941, Bowron turned up the pressure on the chief. An embarrassing corruption trial involving the head of the robbery squad finally persuaded Hohmann to step aside and accept a demotion to deputy chief, clearing the way for a new, more deferential chief, C. B. Horrall.

As chief, Hohmann had appointed Horrall to a plum position, giving him responsibility for the Central, Hollenbeck, and Newton Street divisions as well as command of the elite Metropolitan Division. Now that he was chief, however, Horrall demoted Hohmann to lieutenant.. Under assault from the new chief and distraught about the sudden, tragic death of his son, Hohmann agreed to accept this second, more humiliating position— only to then turn around and sue the department to have his rank restored. Their feud further demoralized the department.

Bill Parker was demoralized too. In June 1941, he graduated from Northwestern's Traffic Institute and returned to Los Angeles. As the number two person on the inspector list, Parker had every reason to expect that he would soon receive a promotion. Instead, he found himself trapped in his position as director of the traffic bureau's accident investigation unit. Chief Horrall routinely passed him over for promotion, blandly noting that "scholastic achievements do not necessarily make the best policemen." In 1930, Parker had been trapped in the police department by the Great Depression. Now he seemed stuck again, until December 7, 1941, when history provided a way out.

The news hit official Los Angeles like a thunderclap, as the Associated Press blared

JAPS OPEN WAR ON U.S. WITH BOMBING OF HAWAII

Fleet Speeds Out to Battle Invader

Tokyo Claims Battleship Sunk and Another Set Afire with Hundreds Killed on Island; Singapore Attacked and Thailand Force Landed

The situation was actually worse than that. The U.S. Pacific fleet was not "speeding out to battle the invader." The five battleships and three destroyers that made up the backbone of the U.S. Pacific fleet were in fact sinking to the bottom of Pearl Harbor. The California coast was virtually defenseless. No one knew where the Japanese attack fleet would strike next. The situation was so dire that the War Department deliberately withheld information about the strike, lest the news trigger panic. Meanwhile, law enforcement prepared to move against what many saw as a potential "fifth column"—the city's Japanese American population.

Los Angeles was home to roughly 38,000 residents born in Japan. Another 70,000 second-generation Japanese Americans, the so-called Nisei, lived in other parts of California. The FBI had already compiled lists of politically "suspect" Japanese Americans. It turned to the LAPD to help round up the subversives.

Around noon that Sunday, police officer Harold Sullivan, who worked under Parker in the traffic division, was driving down Western Avenue on his way to work, when an acquaintance pulled up beside him at Santa Barbara Avenue (now Martin Luther King Jr. Boulevard).

"Did you hear the news?" the man asked.

"What news?" Sullivan replied.

"Why, the Japanese bombed Pearl Harbor," the man replied. Sullivan was shocked. Nothing about the attack had been broadcast over the radio. He hurried into work. At about three o'clock, he was summoned into Parker's office. Parker told him to "get three or four other guys" and report to the local FBI offices. The roundup of Los Angeles's Japanese American residents was about to begin. That night, federal agents and local officers raided Nisei homes across the region, from San Pedro to Pomona. By morning, some three hundred "subversives" were in police custody; officers and soldiers from Fort MacArthur also secured the largely Japanese fishing fleet at Terminal Island off San Pedro and put the roughly two thousand Nisei who lived on the island under guard. None were permitted to leave without police permission. Ominous reports of weapons found filled the local press. Prominent local officials appealed to the citizenry for loyalty, which Japanese American groups rushed to give. It didn't help. By Monday, Little Tokyo was shut down. Japanese-language papers were shuttered; banks were padlocked; stores, closed. By midweek, the county jail and an immigration station at Terminal Island were filled with Nisei (as well as a handful of Germans and a smattering of Italians). In February 1942, President Franklin Delano Roosevelt issued Executive Order 9066, which sent all of Los Angeles's Japanese and Japanese American residents to concentration camps in the interior. In the meantime, the War Department rushed soldiers west, fortifying the beaches, placing anti-aircraft guns throughout the city, and anchoring huge balloons with steel cables over downtown, to entangle low-flying aircraft.

For once, Bill Parker was too busy to reflect on his grievances. There was a sense that Los Angeles might be attacked at any moment. On Christmas Eve 1941, a Japanese submarine torpedoed an American ship in the Catalina Channel, just south of Los Angeles. On February 23, 1942, another sub shelled an oil storage facility in Ellwood, near Santa Barbara. Two nights later, at 2:25 a.m., the spotlights of L.A.'s civil defense forces roared to life, and anti-aircraft guns from Long Beach to Santa Monica opened fire. "The Battle of Los Angeles" had begun. It raged for two hours—until local authorities realized that jittery nerves, not Japanese bombers, had triggered the fusillade.

Parker's job at the traffic division was central to the region's preparations during this panicky period. Logistics was key to the war in the Pacific, and in Los Angeles, traffic was the key to logistics. Parker was responsible for selecting a network of roads that could function as military highways, developing plans to isolate approaches to the military targets "in the event of military action," and—should things go really wrong—for developing a master evacuation plan. He oversaw roughly two hundred other officers. Yet no matter how hard or efficiently he worked, as long as Chief Horrall was in command, there seemed to be no real prospect of advancement.

Parker's thoughts turned to the military. Perhaps the Army would recognize his skills. When he sounded out military recruitment officers, the feedback he got was encouraging. Officials at the Army's Los Angeles procurement office assured him that if he applied, he would undoubtedly receive a commission as a captain—perhaps even as a major. In February, he approached his superiors in the department about taking an unpaid leave to join the Army. At first, they resisted, but Parker was persistent, and eventually he prevailed. On April 13, 1942, he applied for a commission. Remarkably, one of his letters of recommendation was provided by former chief Arthur Hohmann, the man who had sent Parker to the traffic department. The letter represented an interesting turnaround in Hohmann's attitude toward Parker and provides rare insight into Parker's character from a close contemporary.

"Gentlemen," the letter began. "I have known Capt. William H. Parker of this department for the past thirteen years, and I am glad to commend him . . . for the following reasons:

> *1. I have such a high regard for his knowledge of right and wrong and his sense of public justice that, if I were innocent of an accusation but was thought to be guilty by an entire community of people, I would choose Capt. Parker as my counsel knowing all the while that he would rather see justice done than continue to remain popular with his contemporaries.*

> *2. If I were in command of an organization of which Capt. Parker was a member (and I have been) and I assigned Capt. Parker to perform some minor and mediocre detail of non-essential work, I would be doing so with the full knowledge that insofar as Capt. Parker was concerned that task would be the most important in the world to him for the time being, and he would do it better than anyone else I know. . . .*

Hohmann concluded by obliquely alluding to Parker's prickly personality:

This unusual admixture of fine service quality when found in one personality is very likely to be misunderstood; and, I have observed that sometimes the expression of these qualities by Capt.

Parker on occasion of public address, in staff meetings, and in private conversations, has in the past oftentimes caused his motives and objectives to be misinterpreted, misconstrued, and misquoted.

However, Hohmann continued, these faults have "improved to a marked degree, and I now feel that it would be greatly in the interest of the United States if Capt. Parker were a part of its military establishment in some governmental administrative capacity."

While waiting for a response from the Army, Parker made one last effort to advance by taking the examination for deputy chief. He placed first on the eligibility list but was not granted an interview before the Police Commission. Irate, Parker wrote to the Board of the Civil Service Commissioners to protest what he saw as a blatant violation of civil service principles. His protest was ignored. The following spring, almost one year after he had put in his application, Parker received his commission as an Army officer. The thrill he and Helen experienced as they opened the letter from the adjutant general quickly turned to disappointment. Despite assurances that he would be commissioned as a high-ranking officer, Parker was offered a commission as a mere first lieutenant. After consulting with Helen and receiving assurances that promotion would be prompt, Parker decided to accept the commission anyway. After sixteen years of service in the department, Parker was eager to be free.

His mood improved considerably when he learned that, after a month of basic training at Fort Custer, Michigan, he would be transferred to either Yale University or Harvard for three months of coursework in the Army's civil affairs training school. Parker moved east in late June, first to Michigan, and then to Cambridge, Massachusetts. Helen came west from California to be with him. Parker's time at Harvard was blissful, but in early August, classes were cut short. Lieutenant Parker was assigned to the 2675th Regiment, Allied Control Commission, North African Theater of Operations. On August 27, 1943, he shipped off to Algiers. Helen returned to Los Angeles. Parker's old patron, former chief James Davis, now the head of security at Douglas Aircraft, had arranged a job for her as an auxiliary policewoman at a Douglas aircraft assembly plant in Santa Monica.

Bill Parker wasn't the only person who saw an "out" in the war. So did Mickey Cohen.

It didn't take a middle school education to recognize that Bugsy Siegel's efforts to monopolize the wire business were damned dangerous. According to the LAPD, nearly a dozen people had died in the first few years of what it dubbed "the wire wars." At some point after the onset of the war, it appears to have dawned on Mickey that he might too. So Cohen decided to enlist.

Mickey wasn't exactly a model candidate (though there was no denying his efficiency as a killer). So he decided to grease the skids. It just so happened that his old "Big Brother," fight referee Abe Roth, was a former Army officer with considerable pull in high places. Cohen asked the silver-tongued Siegel (who, somewhat surprisingly, supported Mickey's decision to enlist) to give Roth, as Mickey put it, "all that anti-Nazi shit and stuff." Roth was amenable to Mickey's request. Even better, he had a connection who could ensure that Mickey's criminal background didn't raise any alarms. Mickey was delighted. Assured that "the fix was in," he headed to Boyle Heights to report to the neighborhood draft board.

"Lookit," he told the ladies manning the draft desk. "I want to get into the Army."

"What's your draft status?" he was asked in reply.

"I ain't been home for some time," Mickey replied evasively. (In fact, he had recently been on the lam.) "What's the big fuss about?" he continued, still confident in his fix. "I want to get in the Army. I'm ready to get in right now. What do I gotta do?"

The woman behind the desk asked for his name and then vanished into a back office. She emerged with a file—"kind of laughing and smiling."

"You can't get into the Army." The woman was holding his file. She showed it to him and then explained what it contained. The draft board had designated him a 4-F—not qualified for service in the armed forces—on grounds of mental instability.* This was embarrassing, to say the least. Rather than confess, he called his wife and informed her that he'd been made a general. Then he rushed out and purchased a $150 raincoat ("beautiful . . . tailored real good")—with epaulettes. He arrived home to find his spouse on the phone, calling everyone she knew and telling everyone, "He's in the Army! He's going away again."

It was, Mickey thought, a helluva good joke.

IN ALGERIA, Parker was assigned to the Allied Commission for Sardinia, an island off the coast of Italy that had been evacuated by the Germans in October in the face of the Anglo-American assault on Italy that had commenced earlier that year. Notwithstanding his continuing frustration about his lowly rank, Parker seemed to enjoy his experiences as a single

---

*Mickey would later insist that this classification reflected a simple misunderstanding. During an earlier court appearance, his attorney had gotten into "a beef" with a judge. The "beef" had escalated into "a big hurrah," which ended with Mickey being forced to submit to a psychological examination. Evidently, he failed. (Cohen, *In My Own Words*, 64–65.)

military man. (In Sardinia, his commanding officer would comment favorably on his "wide experience, great energy and . . ."—surprisingly—his "pleasing and happy personality.") In February 1943, Parker was transferred to England to prepare for Operation OVERLORD—the invasion of Europe. His job was to help draft a police and prison plan for France. Parker would then follow the first wave of the D-day landings as a member of the Army's civilian affairs division to help organize police operations in areas the Allies recaptured.

There was, however, one point on which Parker felt lingering unease: Helen. Relations with his wife had been strained. Despite letters that suggest a passionate reunion in Cambridge, in the months leading up to his departure from L.A., Parker's relationship with Helen had been rocky. It is not entirely clear what the problem was; Helen had rebuffed Bill's efforts to talk openly about the state of their marriage, assuring him that things were fine and that she remained committed to their marriage. Bill soon heard otherwise from friends back home. Helen, he was told, had an unusually close male friend.

FOR MICKEY COHEN, the desire to indulge—and bend the rules—meant more business. The first and most important part of it was gambling. Bookies were typically forced to pay $250 a week for the wire that provided racing results and a measure of protection. That added up. By one estimate, Bugsy Siegel's bookie take during this period amounted to roughly $500,000 a year. (He also reputedly had a multimillion-dollar salvage business that trafficked in rationed goods as well as a rumored heroin supply route.) Mickey got only a sliver of this cash. However, other Siegel-Cohen enterprises were more than enough to make Mickey a wealthy man. Cohen would later boast that the two men's loan-sharking operations "reached the proportions of a bank." They also exercised considerable sway over the city's cafés and nightclubs, lining up performers, arranging financing, and providing "dispute resolution services."

Mickey had his own operations as well, independent of Siegel. By far the most significant was the betting commission office he operated out of the back of a paint store on Beverly Boulevard. There Cohen handled big bets—$20,000, $30,000, even $40,000—from horse owners, agents, trainers, and jockeys who didn't want to diminish their payouts by betting at the racetracks. Cohen also routinely "laid off" large bets to five or six commission offices around the country. On a busy day, this amounted to anywhere from $30,000 to $150,000, of which Mickey took a 2½ to 5 percent commission. He also routinely used his insider knowledge to place bets himself.

That was the serious money side of his business. Then there was the fun stuff, like the La Brea Club, at the corner of La Brea and West Third. Mickey's personal dinner club featured fancy meals (including rationed wartime delicacies) and a high-stakes craps game. Security was tight: Some evenings, there was as much as $200,000 in cash on the table. He also opened a private club in a mansion in the posh Coldwater Canyon neighborhood, which stretches north from Beverly Hills to Mulholland Drive. There his guests—mainly denizens of the movie colony—could enjoy a good steak, listen to an attractive chanteuse ("who, when the occasion called for it, could also sing a song with a few naughty verses"), and enjoy games of chance at all hours of the night. He likewise dabbled in boxing, managing the leading contender for the title of the lightweight boxing champion of the world, William "Willie" Joyce.

Things were going so well that Cohen took a step that only the most well organized criminals could pull off: He turned his Burbank bookie joint into a casino. At first, it was a dingy place, with "an old broken-down" craps table in a room so small "that when someone wanted to go to the bathroom, the dealer had to leave the end of the table." However, it did have the advantage of a friendly police chief and a prime location—just a block or two from the Warner Bros. lot. In short order, cowboys, Indians, grass-skirted Polynesian maidens, and other extras were cramming into the former stockyard, which soon began a process of rapid expansion. Occasionally, Burbank police chief Elmer Adams (a sometime dinner guest at the Cohen household and the happy owner of a suspiciously large yacht) would bestir himself to shut down Cohen's operations, but never for long. Mickey also began to dream of opening a high-end haberdashery shop.

For Cohen, it was a golden period. But Bugsy Siegel was discontented. Despite his considerable successes, Bugsy found Los Angeles to be a frustrating place to do business. To the low- or midlevel hoodlum, the pell-mell of government jurisdictions and municipalities in the Los Angeles basin—forty-six in Los Angeles County alone—was a godsend. But for Siegel, who wanted to organize the entire area, it was a frustrating inconvenience. Even organizing the city of Los Angeles presented nearly insurmountable hurdles. According to Cohen, Siegel never succeeded in establishing a numbers game in Los Angeles not because the police force was honest but rather because he had to negotiate deals on a division-by-division basis. Siegel wanted to find a better way. So did his old partner Meyer Lansky.

Meyer and Bugsy had grown up together on the streets of New York, but after Prohibition ended, the two men had gone in different directions. Siegel had tried to set himself up as a wealthy sportsman in the movie

colony; Lansky had tried to establish himself as a businessman in the molasses business. Both failed in these endeavors—Siegel due to bad luck in
the stock market, Lansky after federal agents connected his molasses business to illicit distilleries in Ohio and New Jersey that were trying to dodge
excise taxes. As a result, both returned to the underworld. But where
Siegel delighted in strongarm stuff (leaning on bookies, union extortion,
etc.), Lansky concentrated on casinos. Still, the two men stayed in touch. In
the early 1940s, Siegel and Lansky invested together in the Colonial Inn, a
lavish casino in Hallandale, Florida. Although the Colonial Inn was a remarkable success, it still ran the risks that came with all illegal activities. As
a result, both Lansky and Siegel began to explore alternatives. Lansky
looked across the Florida Straits to Cuba. Siegel looked across the Nevada
desert to Las Vegas.

In 1931, the state of Nevada, desperate to raise revenues, had legalized
gambling. The most immediate beneficiary of this move was Reno, which
was situated on the busy Union Pacific Line between Sacramento and Salt
Lake City. However, gambling entrepreneurs also noticed the sleepy town
of Las Vegas, some 250 miles east of Los Angeles. By the late 1930s, former
Los Angeles crime bosses such as Tony Cornero and former Combination
boss Guy McAfee had opened operations there in an attempt to capitalize
on a minor boom brought about by the construction of the Hoover Dam
southeast of the city. Siegel noticed it too after he started persuading Las
Vegas bookmakers to sign up for a Syndicate-controlled racing wire. Siegel
and his Phoenix-based associate Moe Sedway could hardly miss the fact
that Las Vegas users of the wire alone were soon providing Siegel with
about $25,000 a month in revenue. No wonder he and Sedway dubbed their
Vegas service "the Golden Nugget Wire service."

Still, Las Vegas was slow to establish itself as a gambling destination. It
was hot. It was inaccessible. Compared to the classy "carpet joints" of, say,
Saratoga Springs, the casinos of downtown Las Vegas, with their sawdust
floors and hokey western themes, weren't much to look at. That began to
change in 1941, when hotelier Tommy Hull opened El Rancho Vegas. Instead of being located downtown, El Rancho Vegas was outside the city, on
the highway to Los Angeles. With its flamboyant Mission styling, manicured sixty-acre spread, steakhouse, night-club–style entertainment, and
comfortable accommodations, El Rancho Vegas wasn't just a casino, it was a
destination. (Today, this once forlorn part of Clark County is the Las Vegas
Strip.)

Siegel saw the potential to do something even larger. Las Vegas was
within driving distance of Los Angeles. As air-conditioning in automobiles
improved, it would be an increasingly easy drive. And of course, gambling

in Nevada was legal. But when Siegel made an offer on El Rancho Vegas, Hull turned him down. Instead, he decided to sell the property to an associate of Conrad Hilton. So two years later Siegel, Meyer Lansky, and other Syndicate figures purchased another, more traditional property downtown, the El Cortez. It was an excellent investment, but Siegel wanted something more. By 1945, he was looking for another investment opportunity. It was Billy Wilkerson who would provide it.

Wilkerson was the publisher of the *Hollywood Reporter*, the first movie-biz trade daily, and the man behind the Sunset Strip's choicest nightclubs. Wilkerson was also one of Hollywood's most ardent gamblers. His first nightclub, the Club Trocadero ("the Troc") was known for its backroom card game. Industry giants including Irving Thalberg, Darryl Zanuck, and Sam Goldwyn routinely played poker there with $20,000 chips. Wilkerson followed with Ciro's in 1939 and LaRue's in 1944. In the process, he shifted the locus of Los Angeles nightlife to an empty stretch of Sunset Boulevard just outside of the city limits that would soon become known as the Sunset Strip.

Wilkerson was a gambling addict. Often, he'd leave for a week or more for the nearest destination where gambling was legal—Las Vegas. During the first half of 1944, Wilkerson hit a particularly bad streak, losing almost a million dollars, a loss so large that it may have forced him to unload Ciro's. Finally, Joseph Schenck, then chairman of 20th Century Fox and a personal friend of Wilkerson's, gave him some advice.

"If you are going to gamble that kind of money," Schenck told Wilkerson, "own the *casa*."

So Wilkerson decided to build a casino—a grand one, as stylish as Ciro's, as swank as Monte Carlo, an air-conditioned luxury resort surrounded by beautiful grounds and a golf course. He would call it the Flamingo Club. Las Vegas might well have come into existence as Billy Wilkerson's town, if not for a raid one evening on the swank Sunset Towers apartment of Siegel pal Allen Smiley. Siegel and his friend the actor George Raft were visiting. The police burst in to find Siegel placing a few bets on horse races. Siegel and Smiley (but not Raft) were promptly arrested on bookmaking charges. Bugsy was indignant. All he'd been doing, he claimed, was dialing in a $1,000 bet on a race at Churchill Downs. The notion that he, personally, would be making book on some two-bit horse race was insulting. The idea that some dumb cop could just burst in and arrest him on some trumped up charge was intolerable. It was time, he resolved, to turn his full attention to Las Vegas. In the interim, Mickey Cohen could run Los Angeles.

■ ■ ■

AS THE BEVERLY HILLS police were harassing Bugsy Siegel, Bill Parker was preparing for D-day.

The invasion of Normandy began on June 6. Parker landed five days later—and was promptly wounded in a German strafing attack, for which he was awarded the Purple Heart. The news was slow to reach Los Angeles. It is a measure of Parker's standing in Los Angeles that when it did, the *Los Angeles Times* carried the following item on page two of the paper:

Lt. Parker Wins Purple Heart

Lt. William H. Parker, on miltary leave from his duties as a captain in charge of the accident prevention bureau of the Los Angeles Police Department, has been awarded the Purple Heart for injuries received in action in France, it was learned here yesterday.

He was wounded over the right eyebrow by a machine-gun bullet fired from one of two Nazi planes strafing a column of American vehicles in Normandy, according to reports.

He is serving with Army military government in France. Parker resides here at 2214 India St.

Mayor Bowron was among those who wrote Parker to wish him a speedy recovery. Chief Horrall was not.

For Parker, one brush with death seems to have been more than enough. On August 18, he wrote Helen to tell her that he'd drafted a letter "requesting that I be released from the army." Parker had what appeared to be a good case. The LAPD desperately needed experienced policemen. Throughout the war years, it had operated with only about two thousand officers, five hundred less than its authorized level. Felonies had increased by 50 percent from 1942 to 1943 alone. Juvenile delinquency was also rising quickly. But in his memo to the adjutant general, Parker chose not to emphasize Los Angeles's needs. Instead, he presented his own grievances.

"At the time I was interviewed for the commission by the Procurement Officer it was represented to me that I would receive a grade no lower than Captain as the requisition called for commissions in the grades of Captain and Major," Parker wrote, with obvious bitterness. "The Procurement Officer further stated that I would be recommended for the higher grade." He concluded with this legalistic (and hubristic) flourish:

I respectfully submit that by reason of my grade there is no position in prospect in the U.S. Army commensurate with my qualifications and thereby I request relief from active duty under the provisions of Paragraph 3, War Department Letter A.G. 210.85 (30 December 1943) PO-A-A 12 January 1944, at the expiration of my accumulated leave.

The Army was not persuaded. Parker's request was denied.

In a letter to Helen, Parker reacted by comparing himself to Christ on the road to Golgotha. He was clearly lonely and afraid of losing Helen. Parker's other correspondents continued to speak of a particularly close relationship she had with a certain male "friend." It seems clear that the relationship was a romantic one (although it is not clear whether it was merely an extended flirtation or an adulterous fling). For Parker, it must have seemed like a nightmare. It was his first marriage all over again. Distressed, Parker wrote to his bank in September asking it to cut off Helen's access to his bank account.

This was hardly an action that would go unnoticed. In early October, Helen discovered that her financial lifeline had been sundered. Far from showing chagrin at being found out, Helen went on the offensive, penning her husband a furious letter. Addressed to "First Lt. Wm. H. Parker" from "Policewoman A. Parker" (Amelia being Helen's Christian name), subject line "Being a Good Soldier," the letter boldly castigated Parker for *his* two-faced behavior:

> Last nite at about four-thirty I arrived at 2214 India Street, after a day at the plant and the usual long trek home, to find a letter written by you on the 28th of September. The salutation was "My Darling" and the closing line was "Goodnite my dear and may thy dreams be untroubled."
>
> A very strange missive to receive from you in view of the activity you have taken against me in the past couple of weeks.

At this point, her tone switched from sarcasm to anger. She castigated Parker for cutting off access to the family bank account—without notice—while he was continuing to whisper sweet nothings in his letters. She informed him that the week's vacation she'd taken off from work had been for purposes of locating a new residence after a dispute with her unreasonable landlord, not, as Parker presumably implied in some missing letter, for some tryst. She also made passing references to her loneliness—a tacit justification for her "friendship" with the mysterious "H.J."

"So now I come to the end of a story about 'a good soldier,'" she concluded, "and the end of sixteen years . . . sixteen long years when I had hoped you had built some faith in me as your wife plus being a pal thru those horrible 'political battles' and those many happy occasions when we hunted and fished together, not alone at Topaz but up north and also in the Black Hills." Her final line was pointed: "True, everything has an ending."

That Helen's initial response had been to march down to her local bank to open her own bank account she did not reveal. (The manager, a friend of Bill's, refused, prompting Helen to fume, "Were Bill's friends everywhere?")

Parker's retreat was swift, his capitulation total—or nearly so. He was desperate to shore up relations with Helen; he simply couldn't stand the prospect of another marriage disintegrating. In his subsequent letters to her, Parker was both apologetic and a bit defensive about the "the direct and harsh tactics" he had used in an effort "to learn the truth." (At one point, he would later even go so far as to suggest that "when you pause in retrospection you will realize the justice involved.") Now Helen had the upper hand, and she used it. It was she who would decide whether the marriage would endure or end.

On February 24, 1945, she wrote the decisive letter. She had spoken with "a man of religion" who had persuaded her to persevere in the marriage. Bill responded by reiterating his unwavering love for her—and warning that "the element of INDECISION must never be allowed to reenter our relationship":

> If other circumstances should arise in the future that should again throw you into a sea of doubt as to whether or not you should continue in our marriage relationship, . . . while you make up your mind as to what you desire to do you cannot expect me to stand by knowing that my entire happiness hangs in the balance and compel me to accept such a situation with the only compensation that you might possibly decide in my favor. I never want to go through that mental agony again and I do not believe that you should expect me to.

Helen accepted these conditions. Never again would she risk breaking with Bill. Henceforth, his life—and his career—would be her central concern.

ALTHOUGH PARKER HAD NOT SUCCEEDED in winning early discharge, his complaints did result in a promising new assignment—as executive officer for the G-5 section, HQ Seine Division. There he participated in the liberation of Paris (accompanying one of the first food convoys into the city). He also achieved the long-sought goal of being promoted to the rank of captain. In the spring of 1945, Parker was assigned to the U.S. Group Control Council for Germany where he renewed his acquaintance with one of the most influential figures in American policing, Col. O. W. Wilson. A star student of the pioneering police chief and criminologist August Vollmer at Berkeley in the 1920s,

Wilson had gone on to be a trailblazing police chief in Wichita, Kansas. Among his innovations was the use of marked patrol cars for routine patrol duties. (Previously, departments including the LAPD had relied on officers walking the beat.) In time, the two men would radically reshape American policing, Parker by his work in Los Angeles and Wilson through his writings and, later, by his work as superintendent of the Chicago Police Department in the 1960s.

Parker's first assignment in liberated Germany was to reorganize the Munich police force—in two months. At first, it seemed a daunting task. Organizationally, the German bureaucracy was unfamiliar. Moreover, the city was swarming with suspicious characters with opaque agendas who were trying to ingratiate themselves with the city's new occupying power. A conspiratorial milieu, tangled alliances, pervasive corruption, and extensive vice—it was all very Los Angeles.

"All my life I have been accused of being too suspicious of my fellow man," he confessed to Helen in one letter from Frankfurt. But in his efforts to reorganize the Munich and Frankfurt police departments, Parker found his skeptical approach to human nature fully borne out. "If I were permitted to relate the details of the situation that faces me," Parker boasted in another letter, "it would rival the wildest fiction."

Parker was clearly relieved to move away from the topic of his marriage to safer subjects, such as his grievances against his superiors at the LAPD. He was particularly concerned that Chief Horrall and his allies would attempt to thwart his return to the department.

"The present system of oral grading permits the superior officers to grade the candidates, as you know," he wrote in another letter to his spouse. "My position would not be too good if I had to be graded by the men who were appointed to their positions from behind me on the list. Furthermore I don't believe the Chief feels kindly toward me. . . . My present attitude is 'to hell with them.' I do not desire to be submitted to the ignominy of being passed up again."

In fact, the LAPD seems to have been eager to get Parker back. That summer, Chief Horrall contacted the Army to request that Parker be discharged from the service so that he could return to duty with the LAPD. Horrall also wrote Parker directly, claiming "the Department never did recover from the losses sustained when you left" and stating "the sooner you get back, the better and more secure everyone will feel." This was enough to prompt Parker to renew his efforts to win his release from the Army. Though reluctant to lose such an efficient officer (and worried that Parker's superiors in the Los Angeles Police Department were less enthusiastic than they let on), Colonel Wilson reluctantly agreed, and in September 1945, Parker was discharged from the Public Safety Division. The following month he came home to California.

He returned to a city transformed. The bucolic Los Angeles of blue skies, sunshine, and orange groves had disappeared (or at least withdrawn to wealthy Westside enclaves like Beverly Hills, Bel Air, and Brentwood). In its place was a new Manchester, a dark, industrial city.

Los Angeles's transformation had occurred suddenly—so suddenly that it could almost be traced to a single day: July 26, 1943. The next morning, the *Los Angeles Times* published a bewildered article on the transformation:

CITY HUNTING FOR SOURCE OF "GAS ATTACK"

Thousands Left with Sore Eyes and Throats by Irritating Fumes

With the entire downtown area engulfed by a low-hanging cloud of acrid smoke yesterday morning, city health and police authorities began investigations to determine the source of the latest "gas attack" that left thousands of Angelenos with irritated eyes, noses and throats.

Yesterday's annoyance was at least the fourth such "attack" of recent date, and by far the worst.

Visibility was cut to less than three blocks in some sections of the business district. Office workers found the noxious fumes almost unbearable. One municipal judge threatened to adjourn court this morning if the condition persists.

Warning that Los Angeles would soon become a "Deserted Village" unless the nuisance were abated, Councilman Carl Rasmussen demanded that the Health Commission make a report on what could be done about it. . . .

The culprit was smog. By late 1943, it had settled permanently over downtown Los Angeles. The noir atmosphere that the director Billy Wilder captured so brilliantly with *Double Indemnity* in 1944 was not just a symbolically fraught artifact of black-and-white film technology, it was real. Not until 1946 would denizens of downtown Los Angeles see sunshine and blue skies again. Los Angeles had become a noir city.

The Los Angeles power structure had changed as well. In the 1920s, Harry Chandler and his fellow growth barons had dreamed of transforming Los Angeles into an industrial powerhouse along the lines of Chicago. It was clear now that they had achieved their goal. By 1945, Southern California was responsible for 15 percent of the country's total industrial output. But in transforming Los Angeles into an industrial center, the business barons also brought about a change they had long feared. Aircraft companies Douglas, Northrop, and Grumman and outside companies RCA Victor, Firestone Tire, Dow Chemical, and Ford Motor Company simply didn't share the native Los Angeles business establishment's antiunion fervor. Widespread unionization, long resisted, was now a fact. The LAPD's "red squad" became a thing of the past, and with it, the business establishment's need to dominate the LAPD.

The Los Angeles business community had experienced another dramatic change as well. In 1944, Harry Chandler died. Leadership of the *Los Angeles Times* passed to his son Norman (who had become publisher in 1941). Norman was a far more genial figure than his father. However, his father's trusted associates continued to run the newspaper. Political editor Kyle Palmer was a major force in Sacramento and nationally. In Los Angeles proper, the gnomic Carlton Williams regularly attended city council meetings, routinely flashing a thumbs-up or thumbs-down to conservative members to tell them how they should vote. Under their guidance, the *Los Angeles Times* would continue to wield great power, as Fletcher Bowron would soon learn to his great sorrow.

The war had changed William Parker, too. Parker had left Los Angeles as a disgruntled midranking police officer with a stalled career. Despite his obvious talents, his prickly personality (and his association with former chief Davis) impeded his efforts to advance. He returned to Los Angeles as a decorated war hero, the highest-ranked LAPD officer to have served in the military. In a city to which veterans were relocating by the thousands every month, that put Parker in a politically powerful position. The city council took note, going so far as to pass a resolution thanking Parker for his wartime service and welcoming him back to the city. Even Chief Horrall penned a note of gratitude. Parker was determined to use that power. His first goal was to become a deputy chief.

Almost immediately, Parker ran into an obstacle—a departmental policy that required two years of service before returning officers were eligible to take promotional exams. As written, it would have prevented him from taking civil service examinations until 1947. Appeals to Chief Horrall to change the policy fell on deaf ears. So Parker went public.

One of Parker's power bases in the department was American Legion Post 381, which served LAPD veterans. At a post meeting in February 1946, Parker laid into the department for having a policy "that is out of line with the whole nation." The following day the *Los Angeles Times* played his comments on page two, in a sympathetic article titled "Policy on Police Veterans Flayed." The city attorney weighed in by issuing an opinion that the department's policy on promotions violated the state constitution, clearing the way for veterans to participate in the next round of civil service examinations. For the first time, Parker prevailed over the brass on a major policy dispute.

Parker also tended to other power bases, one of the most important of which was the Fire and Police Protective League. When Parker returned to the force, his former subordinate, the gregarious Harold Sullivan, was serving as the captain's representative to the Fire and Police Protective League. Parker wanted that position and made it clear that he expected Sullivan to step aside. Sullivan did. In early 1949, Parker became the head of the league's executive committee.

Popularity and a measure of power seemed to have boosted Parker's confidence—if not his cockiness. Soon after taking over, Parker took Sullivan and John Dick, a fire department captain, along on a lobbying trip to Sacramento. When the state legislature adjourned for the weekend without taking action on the item they had come to lobby legislators about, Parker proposed that they stay on. The men readily agreed, and the group set off for the Fairmont Hotel. There Parker demanded—and received—a suite. The men then went down to the bar, where Parker boldly struck up a conversation with "two very attractive young ladies" and a fellow who seemed to be their chaperone. The bar closed down at midnight, but Parker wasn't ready to end the evening.

"So what are you doing next?" Parker asked.

The ladies' group mentioned that they were going to an after-hours joint in another part of town. Parker asked if his group could join them. The women and their male companion readily agreed to this, so off everyone went. At the end of the evening, Parker went home with one of the women, perhaps, said Sullivan dryly, "to give her a lecture on prostitution."

This was the new Bill Parker, assertive, entitled, and worldly. And still only partially reconciled with his wife, Helen.

IN THE SPRING of 1947, Parker's newfound confidence was on display for all to see when he served as the toastmaster for the Protective League's annual civic dinner. It was the largest dinner in the league's history. Mayor Bowron was the guest of honor. By all accounts, Parker delivered a sparkling performance. That summer, Parker again garnered headlines when the French government awarded him the Croix de Guerre with Silver Star for his service during the war. At the end of the month, when the LAPD released its promotions-eligibility list, Parker topped the list of those eligible for promotion to inspector. He moved up in the legion, becoming, first, vice commander of Post 381 and then commander. Under Parker's direction, membership exploded, growing to 1,400 in 1947 (the largest annual increase of any post in the state). The next year, it topped the 2,000-person mark. In recognition, he was made membership chairman of the statewide legion.

There was just one thing that hadn't changed—the underworld. If anything, its tentacles were as tightly entwined around the city as they had been in the mid-1930s. And Parker was surprised to discover it had a new leader: Mickey Cohen.

The Sporting Life

> *"[T]o be honest with you, his getting knocked in was not a bad break for me. . . ."*
> —Mickey Cohen

MICKEY'S RISE wasn't always easy. There always seemed to be someone around who wanted to crash the party.

First, there were the uninvited guests, guys like Benny "the Meatball" Gamson from Chicago. Moody and arrogant, "the Meatball" inspired little personal affection among those who came to know him. But he had fast hands and a substantial reputation as a "mechanic," a crooked card dealer, which meant that he was much sought after by flat shops and juice joints across town. He'd frequently worked with Mickey during the days when Cohen had run wildcat casinos and card games in the Loop and on the North Shore. "The Meatball" added so much to the house advantage that Mickey had even given Gamson "a piece of the operation." In Gamson's mind, that made Mickey and him partners. So when Gamson suddenly appeared in Southern California as the war was winding down, he naturally looked Mickey up and proposed reestablishing their old relationship.

But Mickey had changed. Back in Chicago, Mickey had been little more than a punk kid with only a dim awareness of who "the people" were. Since returning to Los Angeles, he had become one of "the people" himself. In Mickey's mind, "the Meatball" simply didn't have "the get-up . . . the class, would be the only word that I could possibly find" to associate with the likes of, well, himself. So when Gamson asked Cohen to "move him in closer" with Siegel, Dragna, and Roselli, Cohen had to tell him that he couldn't do it. None of those worthies would meet with a pisher like Gamson.

Mickey tried to be nice about it, but the nicer he acted, the angrier Gamson got. Finally, Gamson told his former partner that if Siegel and Dragna wouldn't deal with him, he, Gamson, would just bring in his own crew, starting with Georgie Levinson, a noted Chicago tough. Cohen "tried to reason with him and make him understand" that that wasn't a very good idea.

"I told him, 'Lookit Ben, if we can help in [some other] way—'", but such offers only made "the Meatball" madder. To put an exclamation point on his pique, Gamson roughed up one of Mickey's old friends from Boyle Heights. Then Gamson linked up with a rival bookie named Pauley Gibbons. This would not do. It was time to hit back.

First to go was Pauley Gibbons. At 2:30 a.m. on the morning of May 2, 1946, Gibbons was accosted outside his Gale Avenue apartment by two unidentified men. According to neighbors, as soon as he saw them, Gibbons fell down on the sidewalk, screaming, "Don't kill me! Please don't kill me!" Of course they did, with seven quick shots. Gibbons's diamond and sapphire ring and a gold watch were left behind, to make it clear that this was not some robbery gone awry. To underscore the killers' opinion of Gibbons, someone paid a drunken homeless man $2 to deliver a box of horse shit (disguised as a box of flowers) to the funeral home during viewing hours. Five months later, on October 3, Gamson and Levinson met a similar fate outside Gamson's Beverly Boulevard apartment.

So much for "the Meatball."

Then there were the locals, foremost among them a family of thugs called the Shamans.

Maxie, Izzie, and Joey Shaman had enjoyed a reputation for toughness as kids growing up in Boyle Heights. They fancied they had this reputation still. Cohen henchman Hooky Rothman wasn't aware of it. When Joe Shaman started acting up one night at the La Brea Club, Hooky told little Joey, bluntly, to "behave yourself in here or get the fuck out." When Joey didn't, Hooky broke a chair over his head, worked him over a bit, and then threw him out.

When Mickey swung by that night around 4 a.m., he found out about the incident. It was a shame, he told Hooky; he'd always liked the family. Mickey later claimed that he'd thought no more about it. That seems doubtful. Word raced through Boyle Heights that six-foot, 230-pound Maxie Shaman intended to administer a beating Mickey would not soon forget. The next morning Maxie arrived at Cohen's commission office behind the paint store on Beverly Boulevard. Exactly what happened next is unclear. Mickey later claimed that Maxie and Izzie burst into his office, armed, and that he gunned down Maxie in self-defense. According to Izzie, his brother walked into Mickey's office, and Cohen blasted him, killing him in cold blood. The police preferred Izzie's story; they arrested Cohen for homicide on the spot. However, a young deputy district attorney named Frederick Napoleon Howser (who, as California attorney general, would later provide Cohen with a bodyguard) accepted Mickey's claim of self-defense, and the diminutive gangster walked.

Still, it was a setback for Mickey. The La Brea Club had become too high profile for its own good. At some point in 1945, Mickey decided to close it (though not before setting up a smaller, more intimate version of the club across the street for his closest friends). The craps game moved to a three-room suite at the Ambassador Hotel. For "seven or eight months," Cohen organized high-rolling dice games that earned him another $15,000 to $70,000 a month.

In the summer of 1947, Mickey demonstrated his growing power in an impressive and unusual (for him) manner: He decided to hold a charity dinner. The beneficiary was the Jewish paramilitary organization the Irgun.

Mickey came late to ethnic pride, but by early 1947, the outbreak of the Israeli war for independence had touched even him. He particularly admired the spunk of the Irgun, which had earned international notoriety after an attack that previous summer on Jerusalem's King David Hotel, headquarters of the British administration for Palestine, that killed ninety-three people (most of them innocent civilians). Cohen had heard that the celebrated Chicago newspaperman-turned-Hollywood screenwriter Ben Hecht was raising money for the Irgun. The Hechts had a villa in Oceanside. One day in early 1947, Mickey and associate Mike Howard decided to pay Hecht a visit. They arrived unannounced. Hecht, a man of the world, recognized his visitors at once. Howard did the talking.

"Mr. Cohen would be obliged if you told him what's what with the Jews who are fighting in Palestine," Howard announced.

According to Hecht, who later described the encounter in his memoirs, *A Child of the Century*, "Mickey looked coldly at the ocean outside my room and nodded." So Hecht told his visitors "what was what in Palestine." Cohen listened calmly as Hecht explained how David Ben-Gurion and the Haganah, the Jewish paramilitary organization that would later form the core of the Israeli Defense Forces, were betraying Irgun agents to the British. The resistance needed guns and money, Hecht explained. Howard pressed him on how he could be having fund-raising problems in a city where "the movie studios are run by the richest Jews in the whole world."

With sarcastic indignation, Hecht explained that "all the rich Jews of Hollywood were indignantly opposed to Jews fighting."

"Knockin' their own proposition, huh?" said Cohen, speaking for the first time. Then Howard quietly asked Hecht, "What city were *you* born in?"

"New York City," Hecht replied.

"What school did you go to?" persisted Howard.

"Broome Street Number Two"—on the Lower East Side, Hecht replied. That did the trick.

"I'd like to see you some more," Cohen said, gently this time. "Maybe we can fix something up." What he fixed up was a gala benefit dinner at his nightclub, Slapsie Maxie's Cafe. Hecht was the keynote speaker. When he arrived, he was stunned to find nearly a thousand people in attendance, including almost every player in the Los Angeles underworld.

"You don't have to worry," Howard whispered to Hecht. "Each and everybody here has been told exactly how much to give to the cause of the Jewish heroes. And you can rest assured there'll be no welchers." Hecht delivered an impassioned speech. Then "the bookies, toughies, and 'fancy Dans'" stood up and announced their pledges. Mickey wasn't satisfied. He turned to Howard.

"Tell 'em they're a lot o' cheap crumbs and they gotta give double." Howard obliged and then Mickey walked up on the stage and stood in the floodlights. According to Hecht, "he said nothing." He just stood and glowered.

"Man by man," continued Hecht, "the 'underworld' stood up and doubled the ante for Irgun." At the end of evening, Cohen had raised $200,000.

Cohen's clout was growing. Just a few days later, on June 20, 1947, Mickey got the break of a lifetime. It came at the expense of the man who'd made him what he was, Bugsy Siegel.

LAS VEGAS had sucked Bugsy Siegel in—and then spat him out. When Billy Wilkerson's Flamingo Casino broke ground in late 1945, he estimated that he'd need about $1.2 million to build the casino he envisioned. Lansky and Siegel had recently sold the El Cortez for a tidy profit, and in March 1946 the two men made a million-dollar investment in Wilkerson's project.

Wilkerson saw Bugsy Siegel as an investor, not a managing partner. After all, Bugsy Siegel didn't know anything about building a grand casino. He'd never even run a nightclub before. But Siegel had other ideas. By early 1947, Wilkerson had fled to Paris to escape from his former business partner.

Wilkerson was right. Siegel had never built a large establishment before, and it showed. The original budget for the new casino was $1.2 million. Siegel spent a million on plumbing alone. By the time the Flamingo opened on December 26, 1946, Siegel and his investors—who included the top leadership of the Syndicate—had plowed more than $5 million into the project. Rumors of outrageously expensive design changes started to spread. Some Syndicate chieftains became concerned that Bugsy's new girlfriend, Mob moll Virginia Hill (whom Outfit figures in Chicago had long used as a "mule" for transporting large amounts of cash) was stashing their money in Swiss bank accounts. Worse, when the Flamingo finally did open, it lost money. Siegel was forced to suspend operations to finish construction and figure out what had gone wrong. When it reopened in the spring, the Flamingo moved into the black, netting $250,000 in the three months that followed. But the hard feelings remained. There was also the matter of Siegel's attitude. Was their old friend Bugsy contrite about all the Syndicate money he'd spent? Not at all. On the contrary, he wanted even more.

At issue was the business of supplying bookies with racing information. For more than a decade, Moses Annenberg's Nationwide News Service had dominated this lucrative business.* But in 1939, Annenberg disbanded his wire operations, and leadership passed to James Ragan, who reconstituted the old monopoly as the Continental Press Service. Faced with pressure from the Outfit, Ragan went to the FBI for protection. But they weren't interested in his stories about how the old Capone mob had reemerged under new leadership. In Chicago on June 24, 1946, two shooters opened fire on Ragan while his car was stopped at the corner of State Street and Pershing Drive. Ragan was rushed to Michael Reese Hospital, where after ten blood transfusions he managed to swear out an affidavit identifying the gunman. In the weeks that followed, Ragan made a remarkable recovery—only to die suddenly on August 15. An autopsy suggested mercury poisoning. As for the gunman Ragan had identified, the affidavit identifying him was lost.

Ragan's successors got the message. They immediately sold the wire service to front men controlled by the Outfit. Bugsy Siegel did not. With Continental now in Mob hands, Chicago informed Siegel that he could go ahead and shut down the Trans-American wire. Siegel refused. He'd built a viable and highly profitable business. He wanted something in exchange for giving it up—specifically, $2 million. This demand went over poorly.

Bugsy knew the boys could get tough. When he flew into Los Angeles

---

*Annenberg purchased the General News Bureau from Chicago gambler Mont Tennes in 1927, just a few years before states such as California began to legalize horse racing and permit pari-mutuel on-track betting to bolster state revenues. The result was a huge boom in horse betting—and a vast new business for Annenberg (who also owned the *Daily Racing Form*). Just how big became evident after federal prosecutors indicted Annenberg for income tax evasion and began to dig into his businesses. Prosecutors were startled to discover that the General News Service (later renamed the Nationwide News Services, after another wire service Annenberg purchased) was AT&T's fifth largest customer. (Moore, *The Kefauver Committee*, 18.)

early on the morning of June 20, 1947, violence was on his mind. After catching a few hours of sleep at the Beverly Hills mansion that Virginia Hill was renting (from Rudolph Valentino's former manager), Bugsy headed over to associate Al Smiley's apartment, where he met with Mickey Cohen.* Siegel got right to the point.

"What kind of equipment you got?" Siegel asked him. Mickey ran down the list of weapons, hideouts, and gunmen available. Bugsy asked Mickey to send Hooky Rothman over the next day, presumably to provide extra protection. It was clear to Cohen that Bugsy "felt that there was some kind of come-off going to take place." But Bugsy hadn't seemed too worried about it. The two men had spoken out by the pool at Al Smiley's apartment. Siegel prided himself on his tan, and though Cohen noticed that he did look more tired and pallid than normal, he certainly hadn't gone into hiding.

After talking to Cohen, Siegel dropped by George Raft's Coldwater Canyon house and invited Raft to join him for dinner that night. Raft had other plans. Siegel spent the afternoon with his attorney and then went out for dinner with Al Smiley and Chick Hill, Virginia's little brother, at a new restaurant in Ocean Park. By 10:15 p.m., they were back home in Beverly Hills. Siegel and Smiley settled in on the sofa to read the early edition of the next morning's *Los Angeles Times*. At 10:45 p.m., the first of nine bullets crashed through the living room window, hitting Siegel directly in the right eye. A second bullet slammed into Bugsy's neck as Smiley dove to the floor. Seven more bullets followed as Smiley screamed "kill the lights" at Chick Hill, who had run downstairs. Then silence. When Chick turned the lights on again, Al Smiley was hiding in the fireplace and Siegel was sprawled grotesquely across the sofa, tie red with blood, head barely attached. One of his striking blue eyes was on the dining room floor. His eyelashes were found plastered on a doorjamb. The police later concluded that the gunman had rested his high-caliber rifle on a latticed pergola just twenty feet away from where Siegel and Smiley were sitting.

It was, concluded Beverly Hills police chief Clinton Anderson, "a perfectly executed hit."

"Somebody knew that Siegel would be in Beverly Hills on this one day, and that he would be at Virginia Hill's home, and when, somehow, the heavy draperies over the living-room window had been left open to give the killer a view of the room," Anderson later wrote. "The shooting was

---

*Hill herself was not there; she had left town several days earlier after a spat with Siegel and gone to Paris. (Jennings, *We Only Kill Each Other,* 189–90.)

timed exactly to occur when no police patrol car was near, and had to be done quickly since police cars were in the vicinity every 30 minutes." The only evidence the police were able to produce was a sketchy report of a black car "headed north on North Linden toward Sunset." But Chief Anderson had an idea about who might be responsible. His chief suspect was the person who would benefit most from Siegel's death—Mickey Cohen. The LAPD shared this suspicion.

MICKEY disliked Las Vegas and steered clear of Siegel's doings there. It wasn't the toll Las Vegas was taking on his mentor in crime that bothered him, it was the dust. "You have on a beautiful white-on-white shirt and a beautiful suit, and you'd come out and a goddamn sandstorm would blow up," he later groused. Still, while he tried to avoid going out to the Nevada desert, Cohen knew all about Siegel's Las Vegas troubles. He also knew that it might very well lead to violence.

"In things like this, you know, sometimes an order is given and you don't have any choice," Mickey said later. "There was no other way it could go for Benny."

Within the hour, the police were pounding at the door of Mickey's house.

"What do you want?" said Cohen when he opened the door.

But when the Beverly Hills police pinched *him* on suspicion of being involved, Mickey was indignant. Everyone knew that he and Bugsy had been "real close." "Naturally, I missed [him]," Cohen would say later. But be that as it may, Siegel's death also presented Cohen with the opportunity of a lifetime—the chance to take over the rackets in L.A.

"The people in the East called on me on all propositions," Cohen later said, " some of which I wish they had not found me home for."

The LAPD had already been watching Cohen for some time. Mickey had caught the eye of Det. John (Jack) Donahoe, a legendary figure in both the homicide and robbery squads years earlier. Donahoe figured Mickey— correctly—for a string of armed robberies in the Wilshire corridor between 1937 and 1939. He was soon picking up Mickey for questioning on a regular basis—more than once a month, by Mickey's later calculations. As the spree continued and reports of unpleasant encounters with a five-foot, five-inch gunman came in, Donahoe grew increasingly confident that Mickey was his man. Yet despite repeatedly pinching Cohen, Donahoe never seemed able to come up with charges that would stick.

In those days, Cohen was far from a charmer. The tough, tight-lipped little hoodlum whom Donahoe first encountered bore little resemblance to the talkative, press-loving gangster whom a later generation of Angelenos would come to know. Yet when you arrest someone enough, it's hard not to form a relationship. Mickey soon found that he admired the big cop. During the 1930s, robbery/homicide had been the bagman squad—the unit that handled payoffs—for the LAPD. Even after the purge of Davis-era officers, in the late thirties, a whiff of corruption still clung to the unit. Donahoe, though, was different.

"One of the finest gentleman I ever met" was Cohen's verdict: "He would never take [a] dime—never let me go—[a] strictly on the level guy."

Donahoe didn't reciprocate these sentiments. When Donahoe learned that Mickey had started dating a cute Irish dance instructor/model, LaVonne Norma Weaver, he was concerned. Donahoe seems to have had something of a soft spot for a damsel in distress, and based on what he knew about Mickey Cohen, the petite redhead was definitely in danger. Mickey had presented himself to LaVonne as a prizefighter. Donahoe took it upon himself to enlighten her as to Cohen's true identity as a stickup man.

That would have done the trick for most girls. If it didn't, Donahoe might have expected that Mickey's bizarre dating behavior would. The couple's first date was typical. First, Mickey arrived late—really late. He told LaVonne he'd pick her up at seven. He arrived at eleven. Then he swung back by his apartment so that she could meet his associates, before finally taking her to dinner at midnight.

But LaVonne was clearly a forgiving and adventuresome young woman. (In addition to dating Mickey, she was also a pilot.) Mickey's chronic tardiness and late hours didn't seem to bother her. Nor did bizarre habits such as cycling through two or three suits a day and eating ice cream and French pastries at virtually every meal. If she had any qualms about his habit of disappearing for an hour or two mid-date (while he went off to heist a joint or conduct business), she never showed it. Clearly, she did not bring burdensome conversational expectations to their relationship either. In fact, she was almost as taciturn as Mickey himself: "Actually, we never had too much conversation together," he later allowed. "She was the type of girl who didn't ask questions," said Mickey with evident satisfaction.

In the fall of 1940, the two were married, somewhat impulsively, in a wedding chapel on Western Avenue. Mickey's Boston terrier, Tuffy, was one of the witnesses. When the war ended in 1945, LaVonne wanted what every woman wanted: a new house. Moreover, she wanted it in Los Angeles's sportiest new neighborhood: Brentwood. So Mickey bought a lot near the Riviera Golf Club and started to build. But unbeknownst to Mickey, one of his general contractors was the LAPD. The Cohens' new house was wired like a recording studio. In the spring of 1947, the Cohens moved in, and the LAPD started listening.

What they heard was surprising. Cohen, so taciturn in public, was a huge talker on the telephone. Every day, he spent hours talking to bondsmen, newspapermen (and -women), bankers, and bookies—and not just in Los Angeles. Mickey's acquaintances on the East Coast reached from Miami to Boston. Topics of conversation included paying off the sheriff's office and the Los Angeles County DA's office. He also talked about doing business with California's new attorney general, Fred Howser. Large sums were discussed—a mysterious $4 million "proposition," an $8 million venture in Las Vegas. Mickey mentioned that in one three-month period alone, his operations in Burbank had netted half a million dollars. He discussed spending $30,000 during a single trip to New York. He talked about his $120,000 house. He spoke (bitterly) of spending $50,000 on LaVonne's interior decorator and on home furnishings. Evincing little understanding for the necessities of criminal conspiracy, LaVonne, in turn, was frequently overheard castigating her husband for his large phone bills.

In short, the LAPD seemed to have Cohen in its sights. But unbeknownst to the men who had tapped Mickey's manse, they also had a problem. The police had a mole.

part three/

The Enemy Within

The Double Agent

*"The heart is deceitful above all things, and
desperately wicked. Who can know it?"*

—Jeremiah

WIRETAPPER JIMMY VAUS couldn't decide whether he wanted to be a cop or a crook—so he tried to be both. In doing so, he set off on a path that led directly to Mickey Cohen.

Vaus first started working for the LAPD almost by accident. In 1946, Vaus was managing a "quiet, high-class" apartment building in Hollywood for a friend while pursuing his true passion: tinkering with electronics. Tenants at the building had started complaining about a dark-haired, well-dressed girl named Marge, whose apartment was frequented by an unusually large number of "men-friends." Marge was a B-girl downtown who made her living by tricking customers into buying her (watered-down) drinks. It seemed she was now also turning tricks on the side. So Vaus called the LAPD's Hollywood station, which promptly sent over a young vice squad officer, Charles Stoker.

Vaus explained the problem of Marge and her many "friends" to Stoker and his partner. Stoker knew the type. "Anyone visiting her now?" he asked.

Indeed there was. Vaus gave the officers her apartment number and retreated to his office. A half hour later, Stoker reappeared.

"There's someone in there with her, all right," he reported. "We could hear them talking but we couldn't hear what they were saying. We think we might hear better from outside. Do you have a ladder we could use?"

He did. Ladder supplied, Vaus returned to his office. A few minutes later, the officers were back again.

"I'm afraid we're stymied, Mr. Vaus," Stoker informed him. "There doesn't seem to be any way we can either see or hear what's going on, and in absence of evidence, we can't act."

Vaus was incredulous. "You mean, the vice squad doesn't have equipment that will enable you, in a case like this, to hear what is going on behind closed doors?" he asked.

"Nope, there's nothing like that in the Department," Stoker replied, "in a tone of voice," Vaus would later recall, "that implied I'd asked him if he'd bought the license plates for his transplanet rocket ship."

Vaus explained that it would be a simple matter to get officers the proof they needed. All he had to do was plant a concealed microphone in the room and connect it by wire to a recording device outside. Indeed, Vaus modestly continued, he'd be happy to put together such a system himself to help the officers obtain the evidence they needed against Marge.

"Come back tomorrow night, I'll have it set up and you can listen in," Vaus said.

Wiring Marge's room was a snap. When Stoker returned the following night, he was able to overhear Marge discussing prices with a customer. He promptly arrested her. Word of Sergeant Stoker's new friend soon spread to other vice squad units.* About a week after the arrest of Marge, one of the senior officers from the administrative vice unit downtown approached Vaus with a question. Could he develop a variant on a wiretap that would allow the police to listen in on conversations and also determine what telephone number had been dialed? In other words, the officer explained, "Joe Doaks walks into a drugstore, uses a particular telephone to dial a number and says, 'Joe, I'll take two dollars on horse number four in the fifth race today at Rockingham.' Could the officer working on such a case hear the conversation and know the number that had been dialed?"

The implications of the request were obvious. If the police could tap phone lines and determine whom calls were being made to, they could then pinpoint the locations of bookmakers across Los Angeles. That would give the police a big edge on the underworld.

"I think it can be done," Vaus replied. In fact, he'd already been working on just such a device, which Vaus dubbed "the impulse indicator." But it was Officer Stoker who got to it first. His target was not the bookmaking racket but rather the so-called Queen Bee of Hollywood, Hollywood madam Brenda Allen.

PROSTITUTION IN HOLLYWOOD has always been a dynastic affair. Brenda Allen had started out as a streetwalker on West Sixth Street be-

---

*Every division had its own vice squad, which led to frequent jurisdictional confusion. When he first met Jimmy Vaus, Sergeant Stoker was actually just on loan to the Hollywood Division vice squad. (He normally worked out of Central Division.) Administrative vice operated freely throughout the city and worked from headquarters downtown.

tween Union and Alvarado Streets. At some point, Allen caught the eye of Anne Forrester, the Combination's favorite madam. Allen was a quick understudy, and when Forrester went to jail, Allen took over the high-end prostitution racket. Her particular field of innovation was the call girl. Rather than risk running a "bawdy house," Allen used a telephone exchange service to manage her 114 girls. It was a lucrative business. Allen's meticulous ledgers would later reveal takes of as much as $2,400 a day, of which half, the traditional split between madam and girl, went to her.

Charles Stoker had first heard of Brenda Allen when she was a plain streetwalker named Marie Mitchell plying her business downtown. He'd been startled when he returned from the war and learned that she'd become the town's top madam. The brazenness—and cleverness—of her current arrangements aggravated him, and caused him no end of trouble. Whenever he'd arrest another prostitute, she'd complain bitterly, "Why are you arresting me while Brenda is running full-blast?"

Stoker decided he would try to take down Allen. But even finding her was a challenge. The number of the telephone exchange Brenda used was well known. Obviously, the exchange had Allen's private number. If he could get it, he could go to the phone company and get an address. But when Stoker approached the telephone exchange service and asked for Allen's number, it told him to produce a court order. So he went to the DA's office, where he was "politely but firmly given the brush off."

Stoker got the number anyway, by waiting outside the telephone exchange office and striking up an acquaintance with one of its female operators. After a week of dating, he had Allen's private number. A contact at the phone company provided a home address. But even though he now knew where Allen lived, he still couldn't prove she was orchestrating a call girl ring—until Jimmy Vaus appeared.

During his pursuit of Marge, Stoker had talked quite a bit with Vaus. He'd learned about Vaus's background as a sound engineer and his Army service. He'd heard about Jimmy's preacher daddy back in Oklahoma and about the religious radio program Vaus was hoping to launch in L.A. He'd also seen Vaus's enthusiasm for uncovering vice—and his unusual talents. So when Vaus dropped by Central Division one night and asked if he could go out with Stoker and his partner, it seemed natural to stop by Brenda Allen's spacious apartment at Ninth and Fedora Streets. There Stoker explained the problem he was having in trying to apprehend her. Stoker was delighted when Vaus responded that listening in on Allen's phone conversations was no problem at all. In fact, they could do so the very next night.

The following evening, Stoker, his two partners, and Vaus went back to Allen's apartment, this time with the appropriate wiretapping gear. One of the policemen picked the locks and then the men were in. No one had thought to bring a flashlight, so Vaus lit a match. The fact that they had illegally broken into a private residence without a court order and were now about to tap a phone line—a felony offense—seemed not to trouble the men at all. They located the telephone box, found the pair of terminals that connected to Allen's apartment, and tapped the line. Vaus had brought a lineman's handset so that they could listen in.

They didn't have to wait long for the first call. It was a woman's voice.

"Hi, Brenda, this is Marie. If anything breaks tonight call me and I'll go on it."

"Okay," Allen answered coolly. "What'll you be wearing?"

"I'll have on a full-length mink coat," the woman replied. "I'll be waiting for your call. Bye."

A few minutes later, a man called. "Got anything good tonight?"

"We've got some mighty nice books," Allen answered. "The heroine in one you'd like to read is a beaut! She has long black hair and is about five foot three and would make your reading most—enjoyable."

"Where can I get that book?" the man asked.

"On the corner of Sunset and La Brea. There is a picture on the front cover of a gal in a long mink coat. How about being there about nine o'clock?"

Stoker was thrilled. He now understood Brenda Allen's modus operandi. As calls poured in throughout the night, he also began to understand the size of her business. In fact, Allen was getting so many phone calls that the policemen in the basement were overwhelmed. Some system of recording the numbers Brenda was calling was needed. So Stocker turned to Vaus. Could he come up with something?

He could. The next night, Vaus returned with his "impulse indicator." Within three hours, Sergeant Stoker and his partners had the numbers of twenty-nine johns.

They returned the following night, to listen in . . . and collect more phone numbers. Then something odd happened. Allen dialed a number that struck Stoker as vaguely familiar. Suddenly it hit him. Allen had just dialed the confidential number of the administrative vice squad downtown. Incredulous, Stoker listened as Allen left a message for a Sergeant Jackson. A few minutes later, Sergeant Jackson called Allen back.

"Honey, I just came into the office and got your message. How's business?" Jackson asked. He then proceeded to discuss how he planned to slip away from his wife the following day to see Allen. A few minutes later, Allen called another man, to whom she complained bitterly about having to see Jackson.

When Stoker got back to the station, he discovered that "Sergeant Jackson" was Sgt. Elmer Jackson, right-hand man to administrative vice squad head Lt. Rudy Wellpott. From what Stoker had overheard, it sounded like Allen had ensnared Jackson on orders from some unnamed third party, who was probably attempting to manipulate Jackson for some sinister purpose. The next day Stoker called Jackson and told him what he'd overheard. Jackson seemed startled. He assured Stoker that he'd have nothing more to do with Brenda Allen.

Meanwhile, Jimmy Vaus was getting nervous. Wiretapping night after night was risky. Crowded into the basement with Stoker and his partners, Vaus thought they "sounded like a firemen's brigade." To minimize the danger of detection, Vaus ran a line from the apartment house down the street to Stoker's car, where they could listen in. But the night after Stoker's conversation with Jackson, the new system didn't seem to be working. There were no calls coming in. As Vaus fiddled with his equipment, he felt a hand grab his arm. He looked up—straight into the face of Brenda Allen. Allen had followed the wire to the police listening post.

Allen unleashed a stream of invective at the policemen. Then she coolly informed Stoker that he was "biting off more than he could chew." Soon thereafter, Stoker was transferred to Newton Division, where he was assigned to work narcotics. Allen's display of power disgusted him; nonetheless, Stoker resolved to have nothing more to do with vice. Instead, he concentrated on studying for the upcoming sergeants' exam, which he aced. In early 1948, he made sergeant—and, to his surprise, was transferred back to the Central Division vice squad. Once again, he was loaned out to Hollywood Division. There he learned that Brenda Allen had opened a brothel— just across the city line, off the Sunset Strip.

Stoker had no intention of letting a jurisdictional inconvenience stop him from making a good arrest. Where the city ended and the county began was famously confusing along the Strip. He decided to go ahead with the raid— and then plead ignorance if he got into trouble. But first, Stoker needed proof about what was happening in Allen's new establishment. Stoker called a friend, a sporty young executive at "a big Los Angeles firm," and asked him if he'd like to patronize Hollywood's most glamorous call house—on urgent city business. The young executive graciously agreed to help out. After calling Allen's exchange, receiving a call back, and answering her questions, he was invited over. Four beautiful girls were produced for his selection. At the end of the evening, the executive announced his intention to become a regular. He also asked Allen if he could bring some friends from the office on his next visit. The two "friends" Stoker had in mind were rookie officers at Hollywood vice.

But now that the raid was ready, Stoker's commanding officer hesitated.

He told Stoker that he needed to offer the sheriff's vice squad the chance to make the raid first. When Stoker called on Capt. Carl Pearson, county vice squad commander, Pearson paused, as if he was uncertain about how to react to the news of Stoker's imminent raid. Then he suggested that Stoker talk to Chief of Police Horrall's confidential aide on vice matters, Sgt. Guy Rudolph. A meeting was arranged at the offices of private investigator Barney Ruditsky. There Stoker was surprised to encounter an old friend, Jimmy Vaus.

Vaus had recently stopped working for Stoker, explaining that he was too busy starting his new electronics business. But it now emerged that he'd set up a wiretapping substation at Ruditsky's offices—for Sergeant Rudolph. Rudolph told Stoker that Allen was under surveillance and that it was only a matter of time until arrests were made. Stoker agreed to delay his raid. He thought no more about Vaus's presence at this meeting. Nor did Sgt. Rudolph look into Vaus's background. It was a fateful mistake. Had the police bothered to investigate Vaus's past, they would have discovered that the pudgy, eager-to-please minister's son with the cherubic face was also a petty criminal, a thief, and a hustler. In short, he was just the sort who might be willing to sell what he knew about the Brenda Allen–administrative vice squad connection to someone else who might be interested in it—someone like Mickey Cohen.

"THE HEART is deceitful above all things, and desperately wicked," said the prophet Jeremiah. "Who can know it?"

Certainly not Jimmy Vaus. Parts of his story were true: He was a preacher's son, and he did enjoy being with lawmen. Unfortunately, the self-taught electronics wizard also couldn't seem to stay clear of the law. In the years leading up to World War II, Vaus had been convicted of robbing a man in Beverly Hills—of $14. He had also been arrested for impersonating a police officer. He ran into similar difficulties during the war. Indeed, only his proficiency with a new technology called radar prevented him from being dishonorably discharged for misusing Army funds.

Two facts about Vaus's character eluded his LAPD interlocutors. The first was his avarice. The second was his growing sense of resentment. Vaus had developed marvelous eavesdropping tools for the police: a fake cane that, when pressed against a door, could detect what was said on the other side; a telescoping rod that could attach a tiny mike to a hotel room window several stories up; a remote wiretapping device that allowed police to monitor conversations from several miles away. However, he hadn't

made any money from these endeavors. At first, the excitement and gratitude shown by the police (plus, no doubt, the thrill of playing policeman)
was enough. Vaus was even flown to Washington, D.C., to teach a class on
eavesdropping at the FBI. But after a while, Vaus began to feel aggrieved
by the lack of payments. As he later put it, "The thrill of the chase was
marred by the penny-pinching of the officials."

Not that Vaus reserved his electronic talents exclusively for the LAPD.
He also worked closely with Barney Ruditsky on sensitive assignments for
clients such as Errol Flynn (who had a problem with underage girls). So
when Harry Grossman in Ruditsky's office called Vaus in late 1948 and told
him "there's a fellow I want you to meet" with a business proposition, Vaus
was naturally curious.

"Who is it?" he asked

"Mickey Cohen," Grossman replied.

"Mickey Cohen!"

Even then it was a name Vaus knew. His first thought was one of
pleasure that someone so important would want to see him.

"Where am I supposed to meet him?" asked Vaus.

"In his haberdashery around the corner from our office."

"Tell him I'll drop over."

Vaus quickly had second thoughts. What if the meeting with Mickey
was some kind of trap? Or worse still, what if Vaus's work for the police
department had infringed on one of Mickey's enterprises and Mickey
knew about it?

VAUS HAD NEVER BEEN in Michael's Haberdashery before. Stepping in, he was dazzled. "The walls were of highly polished walnut and
most of the merchandise was behind sliding doors," wrote Vaus soon after
the initial meeting. "Only a few ties, with a silk sheen, lay on the counter.
A luxurious robe on a model and a pile of finely woven shirts indicated the
garments for sale—at fabulous prices."

A clerk, "tailored to the nth degree," was watching Vaus closely, pencil-
thin eyebrow raised. Vaus felt intensely conscious of "my not-too-fat wallet."

"I'm Jimmy Vaus," he said.

A quick phone call later, and Vaus was being escorted into the rear of the
store, to Mickey Cohen's private office.

A steel-plated door separated Cohen's office from the haberdashery.
Once again, Vaus was struck by "the lavish, expensive fittings."

"There was a beautiful television set in one corner suspended from the ceiling," Vaus later recalled. "The lighting was indirect. Toward the back was a circular desk." There, beneath a huge picture of President Franklin D. Roosevelt, in a large swivel chair, sat Mickey Cohen.

Vaus was impressed: "He was short, stocky and solidly built. His tailoring was exquisite and his grooming impeccable. Not a hair was out of place. His eyes flashed, sizing one up, and then shifted to something else."

Eyeing Vaus coldly, the great man finally spoke.

"Vaus, I understand that you're the man who planted a microphone in my home for the police department. Is that right?"

It was with great relief that Vaus denied this allegation. "I don't even know where you live!" he responded.

"If there were a microphone in my home, do you think you could locate it and take it out for me?" Mickey asked, sounding slightly less severe.

"Mr. Cohen, you've got me all wrong," Vaus responded. "I'm in the business of putting them in, not of taking them out."

Mickey again fixed a cold gaze on him. Then he reached into his pocket and pulled out a "reel-sized roll" of hundred-dollar bills—the biggest wad Jimmy Vaus had ever seen. In a slow, deliberate motion, Cohen peeled off one C-note, then a second, then a third. Visions of hand-painted ties, tailored suits, and "chromium accessories for my car" floated through Vaus's mind. Before he knew it, he was on his way to the Cohen abode, accompanied by Cohen lieutenant Neddie Herbert.

When he entered the house, Vaus had to pause to catch his breath. The contrast between the lifestyles of the gangster and the policeman left him dumbstruck:

> No cop had a home this luxurious. It had obviously been decorated by a professional—only they would be this bold in their color combinations. Lemon-yellow, shades of mauve and bold tones of blue harmonized with the gleaming woodwork and indirect lighting.

Confronted with such opulence, Vaus's moral faculties, which were clearly weak to begin with, failed him entirely. "It would have been very hard to persuade a man that it was wrong to have the money sufficient to buy these creature comforts," Vaus concluded. He rushed back to his workshop and spent the night feverishly tinkering with an ultrasensitive pickup coil and a high-gain amplifier that he hoped would be capable of detecting the tiny electromagnetic current of a small bug. The following day Vaus returned to the Cohen abode on Moreno Avenue. After carefully sweeping the house, he detected a small electrical current. A carpenter was called in to cut a hole in the floor. Vaus lowered himself into the space under the house and soon found a microphone and amplifier connected to a wire. He disconnected it with a sickening feeling, for he knew that as he did so someone at the listening end was hearing their bug go dead—and that that person was a cop. Instead, he thought about what he'd buy with Mickey's money.

Neddie Herbert was delighted with Vaus's work. He asked him to stay so he could show Mickey the bug. Two hours later, when Cohen appeared, Vaus explained where and how he'd found the listening device. Mickey pulled out the roll again and peeled off a few more C-notes—a bonus for his good work. Then he offered Vaus a job.

It was a delicate moment.

Even the covetous wiretapper understood that working for both the LAPD and the city's top organized-crime boss would be a dicey proposition. But when Cohen explained what he had in mind—no lawbreaking, just consulting work—Vaus decided that working for the police and for the city's leading gangster need not be mutually exclusive. After all, was removing a bug placed illegally in Mickey Cohen's house really worse than nabbing some poor john by helping the vice squad mike his hotel room? Or breaking into a basement to plant an illegal bug? So he took the job—and took on a double life.

For eight months, Vaus pulled it off. Indeed, he thrived. With Mickey's backing, Vaus opened an electronics shop in the same Sunset Strip complex that housed Cohen's haberdashery and Cohen henchman "Happy" Meltzer's jewelry shop. Of course, it didn't last. By early 1949, Mickey had become fed up with what he saw as efforts by the vice squad to extort money from him. When police arrested "Happy" Meltzer, Cohen decided to hit back. His tool was Jimmy Vaus.

Vaus had told Cohen about the wiretaps he had done for Sergeant Stoker and about the conversations he'd overheard between Sergeant Jackson and Brenda Allen. Now he offered to help Mickey secure recordings he could use against the police. Vaus's idea was that Cohen should arrange a meeting with Lieutenant Wellpot and Sergeant Jackson at which he, Vaus, would record their extortion attempt. Mickey agreed at once. Soon after Meltzer's arrest, he contacted Jackson and Wellpott and asked to meet the two officers in his car, just off the 9000 block of Sunset. Jackson and Wellpot arrived in good spirits, presumably because they expected Mickey to agree to a payoff. They left angry when he didn't. Mickey, however, was delighted. Thanks to Vaus's efforts, Cohen now had clear evidence that the LAPD was trying to blackmail him—or so he believed. Now Mickey decided to put this evidence before the public—by bringing Vaus and his incriminating tapes to light at Meltzer's trial, which was set to commence on May 5, 1949.

Chief Horrall's boys had pushed Mickey Cohen too far, and now they would pay.

MICKEY COHEN wasn't the only person stalking Chief Horrall and the corrupt clique around him. So was Bill Parker.

In August 1947, Parker finally made inspector and was moved first to Hollywood Division and then to the San Fernando Valley bureau—far removed from the power centers in the department. But Bill Parker wasn't entirely contained. As one of the few lawyers in the department and as the architect of Section 202, Parker was a natural choice to serve as the prosecutor for the personnel bureau in trial board hearings. It was a position that gave Parker access to some of the most sensitive information in the department. He soon ran across the name of a certain sergeant—Charlie Stoker. Stoker (along with several members of Hollywood vice) had been involved in an altercation at the Gali-Gali cocktail lounge in Hollywood. A few months later, Stoker received a call from Parker, who wanted to meet with him. Stoker knew the inspector only by reputation—"a highly ambitious man," thought Stoker. Stoker, who was Catholic, also knew that Parker was known for looking out for Catholics on the force. So he agreed. But when the two men met, it wasn't the Gali-Gali cocktail lounge Parker wanted to discuss. It was the Hollywood vice squad.

Stoker allowed as to how he'd seen some questionable behavior.

Parker wasn't surprised. The entire unit was riddled with corruption, he told Stoker. He then proceeded to run down a list of specific instances of drunkenness, brutality, and extortion. Parker further informed Stoker that he intended to do everything he could to see that the current squad was dismissed. If Stoker was willing to testify to malfeasance on the squad, Parker allegedly promised he would see to it that Stoker headed the next Hollywood vice squad.

Stoker felt uneasy about betraying fellow officers, even ones who might have broken the law. Parker, Stoker concluded, "was a man compounded out of sheer ruthlessness, a man who would ride rough shod over anyone who got in the way of his becoming Chief of Police." But he had to concede "that much of what [Parker] had told me about the vice, gambling and pay-off picture in Los Angeles was true."

Nonetheless, he ducked the request, saying that he could not testify to anything about which he personally was not 100 percent certain, particularly if it concerned other officers. But Stoker would not stay silent for long.

The trial of "Happy" Meltzer began on May 5. Meltzer's defense, as presented by lead defense attorney Sam Rummel, was simple: "We will prove," declaimed Rummel, "that for a period of one and a half years before Meltzer's arrest, Lieutenant Rudy Wellpot and Sergeant Elmer V. Jackson kept up a constant extortion of Mickey Cohen." The Meltzer case, he charged, was "a frame-up" that resulted from Cohen's refusal to pay off a shakedown demand. Rummel then went on to relate a lengthy and seemingly fantastical story of late-night meetings between Cohen and Jackson in the backs of cars parked off the Sunset Strip, car chases through Beverly Hills, and B-girl payoffs down on Main Street.

As sensational as it sounded, Rummel's opening statement wasn't particularly strong. But when Rummel announced that "sound engineer J. Arthur Vaus" had recordings that would tie Sergeant Jackson to the notorious Hollywood prostitute Brenda Allen and substantiate the defense's charges that the police had tried to extort money from Cohen, the county grand jury took notice. It decided to open an investigation into the matter—after the upcoming mayoral elections.

Several weeks before the election, Parker called again and requested another meeting. Stoker agreed. After some throat-clearing about how they were both Catholics and both World War II veterans, Parker got to the point: What did Vaus know about the Brenda Allen investigation in Hollywood?

Stoker then told Parker his story—without, however, revealing that he had already spoken to the grand jury. According to Stoker, Parker listened encouragingly and then told the sergeant what he knew. There were several sources of corruption in the police administration, he said. One, controlled by Sgt. Guy Rudolph, Chief Horrall's confidential aide, had the lottery and the numbers rackets. A second source of corruption was Captain Tucker, commander of the elite "Metro" division, which, according to Stoker's account of his conversation with Parker, focused on milking Chinatown and L.A.'s prostitutes for the police department and for the city council. Finally there were Assistant Chief of Police Joe Reed, Lieutenant Wellpot, and Sergeant Jackson. Stoker claimed that Mayor Bowron was clean but also "a stupid ass, who had no idea what was going on."

Why was Parker (allegedly) telling him this?* Stoker claimed that Parker wanted him to go to the grand jury and present his own information—and Parker's—to them. With an election just weeks away, Parker continued, when the news leaked, Mayor Bowron would be forced to oust Chief Horrall and Assistant Chief Reed. Everyone knew "damned good and well" that he would be the logical man to step into Horrall's shoes.

---

*The veracity of Stoker's claims is uncertain. While elements ring true, Parker himself would later dismiss them as fabrications.

But wouldn't such a confession risk defeating Mayor Bowron?

"Hell, no," Parker (allegedly) replied. "If anything, it will insure [sic] his success." Bowron's anti-vice bona fides were impeccable. A scandal that confirmed an ongoing underworld conspiracy would simply shore him up.

So Stoker agreed to go along, telling Parker that if he could arrange for a grand jury subpoena, Stoker would tell all. He neglected to mention that he had *already* testified before the grand jury. It was a deception Parker would not forget.

ON MAY 31, 1949, Mayor Bowron was easily reelected. The following day, on June 1, the county grand jury announced that it was beginning an investigation into corruption on the police force. A week later, the *Los Angeles Daily News* began to produce a series of stories that appeared to reveal corruption at the highest level of the department. It emerged that the LAPD had been tapping Mickey's home for nearly two years. What made the story scandalous was not so much that the LAPD had bugged Cohen's home without a court order but rather that it had listened to Mickey's every conversation for two years (until the wire was removed) and yet made no move to arrest him. Instead, claimed *New York Daily News* columnist Florabel Muir, who enjoyed a nationwide following for her flamboyant descriptions of Hollywood crime, the head of the department's gangster squad had repeatedly attempted to blackmail Cohen with the transcripts.

There was also the matter of the police fraternizing with Cohen. Sergeant Jackson and Lieutenant Wellpot attempted to explain away the testimony of witnesses who placed them in Cohen's company (or establishments) and/or in Brenda Allen's proximity by arguing that they had in fact been involved in a complex undercover operation. Unfortunately for Jackson and Wellpot, Deputy Chief Richard Simon testified that the effort to build a case against Allen had been abandoned long ago. Jackson countered that he had spoken frequently to Allen because she was a valuable police informant. Then the *Daily News* produced yet another scoop. One year earlier, Jackson had been hailed in the press for killing a two-bit heister named Roy "Peewee" Lewis who had held Jackson up—with a machine gun—while he was necking in a car with his girlfriend. The *Daily News* now disclosed that the girlfriend in question was Brenda Allen.

The revelations streamed forth in torrents. Senior members of the department came forward to verify personnel chief Cecil Wisdom's claim that he had personally informed Chief Horrall of Stoker's findings concerning

Jackson, only to see them ignored. Then the *Daily News* found "Peewee" Lewis's partner, who told the paper that he and Peewee had targeted Allen and Jackson because they believed Jackson would have the $900 payoff that Allen delivered every week to the police. County grand jury testimony was supposed to be secret, but with the mayoral election behind them, the press was no longer inclined to do the mayor any favors. By mid-June, the major papers were printing what amounted to transcripts of the preceding day's testimony.

Just when a narrative highly prejudicial to the police was starting to take shape, police officers arrested Sergeant Stoker—for burglary. A beautiful policewoman, Audre Davis, came forward and tearfully claimed that love had made her an accomplice in Stoker's crime. Stoker denied it, insisting he was being targeted for embarrassing the department. (He also noted that Davis was the granddaughter of former Combination boss Charlie Crawford and that her father, former deputy chief Homer Cross, had retired to Las Vegas under suspicious circumstances.) The jury turned to Brenda Allen, who had finally been arrested, for clarification, but she only added to the confusion: She claimed to have paid off both Jackson and Stoker. Then, on July 19, someone opened fire on Mickey Cohen at Sherry's nightclub on the Sunset Strip, killing one of Cohen's henchmen and badly injuring a bodyguard provided by state attorney general Fred Howser—the same Fred Howser who had declined to prosecute Cohen for shooting Maxie Shaman four years earlier. Shell casings found across the street led to speculation that the shooter might be a policeman—payback, perhaps, for Mickey's disclosures about the vice squad.

At first, Mayor Bowron and the Police Commission defended Chief Horrall, insisting that he and his men were the victims of an underworld conspiracy. But even for a mayor who'd just won reelection, the pressure to do something was too great to resist. The cavalcade of conflicting confessions, the shootings on the Sunset Strip, the wild swirl of accusations and counteraccusations—it was all too much. Action of some sort was required. Politically, it was time for Chief Horrall and Assistant Chief Reed to go. Once again the civil service protections that the chief of police theoretically enjoyed provided no protection. On June 28, Chief Horrall retired.

Faced with a public safety crisis, Bowron did what politicians in his position do: He turned to a military man. On June 30, Mayor Bowron called General William Worton, a decorated Marine general who had literally retired earlier that day, and asked him if he'd come up from Camp Pendleton to discuss serving as the emergency chief of police for Los Angeles.

13

Internal Affairs

"Neither a slave nor a master be . . ."
—Bill Parker, quoting Abraham Lincoln,
Protective League banquet, June 30, 1949

GENERAL WORTON'S first instinct was to decline the job. The chances of making a success of it just seemed too small.

Worton knew all too well what typically befell the well-intentioned outsider who stepped into a corruption scandal. During the mid-1920s, one of his closest friends, Marine Corps general Smedley Butler (aka "The Fighting Quaker"), had agreed to serve as director of public safety in Philadelphia under similar circumstances. At first, Butler accomplished wonders, shutting down speakeasies and brothels and curbing corruption. Then he made the mistake of targeting upper-class watering holes, and was promptly forced out. Butler later described the experience as "worse than any battle I'd been in." This was saying something, considering that General Butler died in 1940 as the most-decorated officer in the history of the Marine Corps. Los Angeles seemed likely to present similar challenges to Worton. Why bother? After all, as he himself noted, "I owe this city nothing. I've never lived here. It's not my native city."

But Mayor Bowron wouldn't take no for an answer. All day, the mayor and his associates worked on Worton. Former Marine Corps commandant Alexander Vandegrift—one of the corps's towering figures, the man who had staved off an attempt to absorb the Marines into the Army just two years earlier—likewise lobbied Worton to take the job. Gradually, Worton softened. Compared to commanding the Marine Corps's Third Amphibious Corps at Okinawa, how challenging could Los Angeles be? And so, at the end of the day, rather than departing from City Hall and returning to the farm in Carlsbad that he and his wife had purchased five years earlier to enjoy in their retirement, Worton raised his hand and was sworn in as L.A.'s emergency chief of police.

"I'll be damned if I know why," he'd later say.

It didn't take long for General Worton to discover that he knew even less about policing than he'd thought.

LIKE OTHER DEPARTMENTS, the LAPD had a distinctly military appearance. Officers were uniformed and armed; ranks were hierarchical; positions had fairly explicit spans of control; and of course, violence and/or the threat of violence was routinely employed. This was no coincidence. Prior to 1937, under Chief James Davis, lines of command in the department had been notoriously unclear. The Red Squad had effectively reported to the business community; irregular officers such as Earl Kynette wielded enormous power; and police badges proliferated so widely that Davis's successors were forced to issue a new, redesigned badge. After Davis's ouster, the department's new leadership had deliberately embraced the military model of organization in an effort to curtail past abuses. Lines of command were laid out; spans of command were tightened; appearance and discipline were emphasized.

But in other ways, the department's military appearance was deceptive. Policemen were not military personnel. They were civil servants, with civil service protections that limited their work hours and sharply curtailed the chief's ability to promote and demote officers. Worton soon realized that he really had no idea how powerful he was—or even if he was in charge. So he decided to find out by doing something dramatic. At the end of his first week on the job, he announced that he was transferring fifty officers, many quite senior, "all over the place."

"Deputy chiefs were kicked around here," Worton later gleefully related. "Captains were shifted [to] where they didn't want to go."

The primary purpose of the personnel move was not so much to place officers where their talents could be better utilized—Worton had no idea who most of these officers were—but rather to find out if he *could* transfer them. He also figured "that if there was crookedness in the department . . . it would take the crooks another couple of weeks before they could get on to figuring who they could work with."

The results of this experiment were satisfactory. When one "very powerful" local politician threatened to have the new chief's job if he insisted on transferring a certain officer to the San Fernando Valley, Worton responded that if his decision wasn't upheld, he was quitting on the spot—to hell with Los Angeles. The transfer was upheld. "To make a long story short . . . I did have the power," Worton concluded. Now he had to figure out what he was going to do with it.

It was clear the LAPD faced two great challenges—eradicating gangsterism and rooting out corruption. By 1949, eradicating gangster-ism meant taking down Mickey Cohen. Rooting out corruption, how-ever, was a more treacherous matter. Chief Horrall had retired, but Assistant Chief Joe Reed—who everyone agreed was the man who really ran the department—remained in office, even as rumors of a grand jury indict-ment swirled. Moreover, both former Chief Horrall and Assistant Chief Reed still enjoyed the strong rhetorical support of Mayor Bowron, who continued to insist that the department had fallen victim to Cohen's dirty tricks. In order to navigate his way through this morass, General Worton needed guidance from someone who was both familiar with the Los Angeles–and-beyond reproach. One name came up again and again: William H. Parker.

TO SGT. CHARLES STOKER, Bill Parker was a person "of over-weening ambition—a man whose one desire was his objective—the office of Chief of Police." To many other members of the force, though, Bill Parker was a model for what a policeman should be: smart, assertive, and incorruptible. Parker's experiences and attitude held a particular appeal to the 1,400 new police officers who joined the department after the war, 90 percent of whom had served in the military. Accustomed to military disci-pline, these men were also highly attuned to bullshit. Typical of the atti-tude they brought (though perhaps a bit more cocky than most) was an ex-Navy seaman named Daryl Gates. Gates joined the police in order to earn $290 a month for a few years while working toward a law degree. He definitely did not intend to be—his words—"a dumb cop." (Gates would serve as chief of the LAPD from 1978 to 1992.)

But when Gates got to the Los Angeles Police Academy, he was impressed—not by the academy's "spit and polish" style; as a former Navy man, he'd already had plenty of that. Rather, he was struck by the abilities of his classmates. "I realized that I was one of the most undereducated [people] in the whole class, and probably, clearly, not the smartest," says Gates. One of his classmates had studied chemistry at Berkeley; another had finished two years of law school. The instructors were even more impressive—"extraordinary," says Gates. The captain responsible for overseeing the acad-emy was an ex-Marine officer and a former Olympic water polo star. Gates's lieutenant was Tom Reddin (a future chief of police). The academy's law in-structor was Buck Compton, a UCLA football and baseball star who'd joined the 101st Airborne Division in time for the Normandy invasion (and whose deeds inspired the Stephen Ambrose book *Band of Brothers*; he would later prosecute Sirhan Sirhan and serve as a California Court of Appeals judge).

The person who impressed Gates most, though, was Bill Parker.

Gates met Parker for the first time when Parker came to deliver a lecture on ethics and police history to Gates's class. "Oh, were we impressed," recalls Gates. "Oh, man. It was that kind of quality that I saw and really turned me around in terms of what this department was all about."

Parker's speech was confrontational—and riveting. He was not interested in establishing a rapport with the men or presenting himself as "a good guy." Instead, he started by cutting the men down to size.

"You're coming in, you haven't done anything to contribute to the stature or the history of this department," he told the class. "You've done nothing. We anticipate that you will do something, but you have [as yet] done nothing. You bring nothing to this department. It is what it is without you." He then proceeded to explain what the department was and what it should be.

It was, thought Gates, "an absolutely magnificent speech. It was electric." This was not a town hall–style affair. Parker entertained no questions. "He came in, gave his speech," and then left, recalls Gates.

Parker's legend was growing: D-day hero. The man who'd reorganized Axis police departments from Sardinia to Munich, purging them of fascists (a feat that seemed to bear more than a little resemblance to cleaning up the LAPD). The officer who'd stood up to Chief Horrall for veterans' rights, who'd topped both the inspector and the deputy chief promotion eligibility exams yet had to fight for promotions that were rightfully his. As for the ambition, that was obvious too. It had been since the late 1930s.

General Worton had no problem with ambition. On the contrary, he welcomed it. When he first introduced himself to his commanding staff, "I told each one of them that I wanted them to take a look at me," Worton said later. "I wanted each one of them to say, 'How are we going to get that old man's job away from him?'" The desire to earn the top job was, Worton thought, a healthy thing. "You should all want to be the chief of police of this city," he'd tell officers during his visits to the division headquarters during his first weeks on the job. "Somehow or other you should be thinking, 'How am I going to get this so-and-so out of here?'"

That Bill Parker was almost certainly thinking precisely that bothered General Worton not at all. On July 15, Angelenos woke up to the news that General Worton had moved Inspector Parker to a newly created position in his office. His duties, General Worton told the *Los Angeles Times* ("in cryptic Marine general style") would be "anything I want him to do." In fact, the meaning of Worton's move was obvious: Asst. Chief Joe Reed was being eased out. Worton's bland denials—when pressed by reporters, he simply observed that Reed had a civil service position and that the only way to vacate it was for him to resign or be removed on charges (of the sort that the county grand jury was then preparing)—only confirmed his intent. The smart money had Parker pegged as Worton's new number two. But roughly a week after Worton announced that he was bringing Parker into his office, the interim chief announced that he wanted Parker to head an entirely new bureau, Internal Affairs.

FOR DECADES, vice and its attendant, corruption, had been ineradicable parasites on the body of the LAPD. The cycle of scandal, reform, and then scandal again had driven city politics for decades. Reform-minded police chiefs had tried everything to eradicate it, putting administrative vice under the chief's tight control; disbanding administrative vice; ignoring vice; suppressing it. Internal Affairs represented something new: an entire bureau focused solely on investigating misconduct and corruption within the LAPD. Worton emphasized its importance by moving Deputy Chief Richard Simon, who headed the patrol bureau, out of City Hall and moving Parker and Internal Affairs in.

It was the perfect position for Bill Parker, for a number of reasons. First, it gave him more authority to pursue and root out corruption than he'd ever had before (vastly more authority than he had enjoyed as lead prosecutor for the department trial board). Second, it allowed him to pursue his long-cherished goal of shoring up police autonomy. By demonstrating that the department was capable of policing itself, Parker hoped to defang the small but vocal group of activists and critics who had begun to call for a board of civilians to review complaints against the department. Finally, the position gave Parker access to information—to the department's deepest secrets, both real and imagined. A new element mingled with feelings of respect—fear. Fear about what Parker was learning—and about how he might use it.

General Worton and his new team moved quickly. Under his predecessor, Chief Horrall, lines of command had grown murky. Worton clarified them, creating an organizational chart where authority and responsibility for every major function were clearly assigned. He doubled the training period for cadets at the police academy to ninety days, established a new corrections division, and ended the practice of automatically assigning all rookie officers to either the Lincoln Heights jail or traffic duty downtown, both of which tended to sour new officers on police work. The two gangster squads he inherited (each with roughly a dozen men) were combined into a single intelligence squad and instructed to work closely with the FBI and the San Francisco Police Department on antimob activities. Worton also divided the detective bureau between two inspectors, diminishing the power of that fiefdom, and placed the vice, robbery, and homicide squads under Deputy Chief Hohmann. Vice squad officers across the city were dispersed to other units. (Leaving officers in vice for years on end was, Worton thought, an invitation to corruption.) So were hundreds of other officers. The practice of accepting gifts of any sort was banned, at least in theory. The position of assistant chief was abolished too. The chief of police would no longer be able to pass responsibility for running the department to someone else.

General Worton was also keenly interested in departmental morale. Closer acquaintance with the LAPD had convinced Worton that, contrary to public perception, LAPD officers were generally dedicated and honest. But the Brenda Allen scandal had badly dented the department's self-confidence. "They didn't have the esprit of a good combat unit," Worton would later tell a reporter. So he set out to instill it, using the Corps's tried-and-true methods. The police academy became even more like Quantico. "Military bearing" became a prime objective for all LAPD officers. Worton also instituted aggressive inspections, with an emphasis on spit and polish. He often conducted them himself. Where his predecessor, Chief Horrall, had seemed content to leave departmental matters to others, General Worton was everywhere.

"He would be out prowling at night, and some guy would stop somebody to write a ticket, and this big, black car would pull up behind him, and when the officer was finished this little guy would come walking over and say, 'Hi. I'm the chief,' " recalls Bob Rock (a future acting chief). He quickly became a popular figure with his men. "He made a really diligent effort to relate to the people, to the department," says Rock.

Worton's personal style—and his efforts to instill military pride in the department—proved popular, particularly with the department's new officers, most of whom had served in the military during the war. Initially, Worton had worried about moving too quickly in this direction. However, in short order, average patrolmen were snapping to attention and saluting sharply when he appeared (even though he never formally instituted salutes).

PARKER MOVED decisively too, quickly forcing the resignation of an officer who'd been involved in a controversial shooting earlier in the year. It was an accomplishment that attracted considerable good publicity—and not the only one. One of Parker's duties for former chief James Davis had been to handle the press, and he knew how to keep his name in the headlines. On August 28, Parker presided over a huge Fire and Police dinner, lavishing praise on guest-of-honor Mayor Bowron (for seven years of regular pay raises). The following month, at a meeting of the California American Legion's three hundred top officials, Parker received a well-publicized assignment to promote "Americanism" after the convention listened to an up-and-coming Republican congressman from Whittier—Richard Nixon—warn of the dangers of a Communist insurrection. Integral to the success of this campaign, from Parker's perspective, was the removal of the cancer of organized crime, which cultivated base appetites and weakened the country when it needed to be preparing for the coming struggle with Soviet Russia. That meant dealing with the likes of Mickey Cohen.

The problems posed by Mickey were manifold. First, there was the criminal activity he was involved in. In the fall of 1949, as the county grand jury was attempting to sort out the welter of charges and countercharges between Mickey and the LAPD, another embarrassing case was headed to court, this one involving a bookmaking front company called the Guarantee Finance Corporation.

Located in unincorporated county territory, Guarantee Finance was perhaps the most audacious bookmaking operation in 1940s Los Angeles. With 74 telephones in its central gambling room, Guarantee Finance employed more than 170 runners and handled gambling in excess of $7,000,000 a year. (It was also happy to arrange high-interest loans for clients with gambling debts.) The LAPD administrative vice squad identified the operation almost immediately but found that the sheriff's vice squad was strangely uninterested in shutting it down. Frustrated, Sgt. James Fisk took matters into his own hands and raided the establishment, destroying equipment and removing betting markers. A few months later, with the operation still running, Fisk carried out a second raid. This prompted sheriff department captain Al Guasti ("Iron Man" Contreras's successor as the supervisor of the Sunset Strip) to write then-Assistant Chief of Police Joe Reed a stern letter, warning the LAPD to keep its nose out of county business. Finally, in early 1949, the state corporation commission raided the bookmaking operation and shut its operations down. The wholesale gambling operation the state raid revealed was yet another embarrassing testament to the reach of the underworld into Los Angeles.

The second thing that made Mickey seriously inconvenient was the fact that someone kept trying to kill him—in a sloppy and inept fashion. On August 2, a pipe bomb intended for Mickey exploded across the street from Cohen's Brentwood house, upsetting the neighbors and, by extension, their elected representatives. It would not do to have a resident of Brentwood die in the cross fire of a gang war. Worton decided to go after Mickey with everything he had. His first step was to sic the new intelligence squad on Cohen.

On August 3, officers searched the apartment of Cohen associate Mike Howard (Meyer Horowitz) after getting a tip that he might be dealing drugs. They didn't find any narcotics, but they did discover two unlicensed pistols. So they hauled in Howard and sent two LAPD detectives and a federal Bureau of Narcotics agent over to Cohen's house to question him about the incident.

Mickey was not happy to find police officers at his door.

"What the hell do you want?" he snarled. When he found out what they'd come to ask him about—some gun charge involving an associate— he lost it. Didn't they realize that he had guests (among them Earl Brown, *Life*'s crack crime writer, and Al Ostro of the *San Francisco Daily News*) and that it was dinnertime? He asked if the police had a warrant. They didn't.

"Well then go fuck yourself," Mickey told them. "And tell the chief to go fuck himself." Then, for good measure, he added, "Get the hell off my property, you sons of bitches."

The officers retreated. But two weeks later, in a clear indication that the police were playing by new rules, they returned and arrested him for using obscene and insulting language against a police officer. Mickey got out on bail, and a trial date was set for September 15, 1949.

The press was delighted. Mickey's journalist guests testified that Mickey had indeed questioned the legitimacy of the law officers' births. Cohen's situation looked dire, but his attorneys had a trick up their sleeves. To back his assertion that calling someone a "son of a bitch" wasn't obscene, Rummel pointed to none other than President Harry Truman, who had recently called columnist Drew Pearson the exact same thing. The courtroom laughed, the jurors retired to deliberate, and four hours later Mickey Cohen once again walked out a free man.

Within weeks, his name was back in the papers, this time in connection with one of the biggest trials in recent Hollywood history, the trial of actor Robert Mitchum. Mitchum had been busted by the sheriff's department vice squad with a joint of marijuana at a party in the Hollywood Hills, in a raid whose timing was so fortuitous as to be suspicious. Nonetheless, he was convicted and shipped off to prison for a brief stint behind bars (accompanied by a photographer from *Life* magazine). Now Paul Behrmann, a former business manager and actors' agent who had once represented Mitchum (but who had since gotten into troubles of his own with the law) came forward with a startling tale. Behrmann told DA William Simpson that Cohen was running a sex-and-extortion ring that specialized in capturing big-time businessmen and actors in compromising situations. Cohen's stable of accomplices supposedly included a party girl named "Bootsie" and the twenty-four-year-old redheaded assistant to "French lover teacher" Claude Marsan. The suggestion was made that Mitchum, too, had been set up by Cohen.

With Mickey on the loose, every day seemed to bring a new humiliation for Los Angeles area law enforcement. But the LAPD was also squeezing Cohen. Mickey had demonstrated his clout by sparking the scandal that led to Chief Horrall's ouster, but in General Worton, Cohen had arguably found a cure that was worse than the disease. It wasn't that Cohen felt fundamentally threatened by Worton; Mickey was convinced that the general "knew little or nothing of the workings of this office." However, since Chief Horrall's forced retirement, the LAPD had gone all out to make Mickey's life miserable. Constant surveillance made it difficult for Mickey to do business. A grand jury had begun to investigate Cohen's (protected) gambling operations in Glendale. There were reports that the FBI had also begun an investigation. But the worst blow of all had come from a small outfit convened at Gov. Earl Warren's behest the previous summer, the Special Crime Study Commission on Organized Crime. Although the state legislature had been careful to make the commission as toothless as possible (for example, denying its four investigators subpoena power), the commission had an asset whose tenacity could not be easily blunted—chief counsel Warren Olney III.

OLNEY CAME from one of California's most distinguished families. His grandfather was one of the founders of the Sierra Club; his father had been a justice on the California Supreme Court. Olney himself was one of Governor Warren's closest and most valued associates. He was also something of an authority on interstate gambling and the racing wire. As the head of the California attorney general's criminal division in the late 1930s (when Warren had been the state attorney general), Olney had begun to investigate bookmaking in California, with a particular focus on Moses Annenberg's Nationwide News Service. At first, Olney had struggled to figure out what was so important about the wire service. But after three days at Reno's Bank Club, it came to him. The tout sheets, the hot tips, the fluctuating pari-mutuel prices, the odds at the gate, the conditions of the track—all of that was really just a distraction. Bookies needed the wire so that they could quickly roll $2 bets from one race into $2 bets on the next race. Most gamblers weren't reading the *Daily Racing Form*, looking for an inside edge. They were betting on race after race just like gambling junkies played slots.

"Bookmaking has nothing to do with horse races," Olney concluded. "It's a strict lottery—nothing more than that." The wire delivered the information that made it possible to place bet after bet, hour after hour.

This system was generating immense amounts of money for Mickey Cohen. According to LAPD estimates, in mid-1949, Mickey had about five hundred bookmakers paying for protection (typically, $40 per week for every telephone in their operation plus $5 a week per agent). Even if the average bookie had only two telephones, this would have generated more than $160,000 a month. In exchange for such princely sums, Mickey provided attorneys and bail money for bookmakers unfortunate enough to be arrested. This service was famously speedy. In one notorious case, vice squad officers arrested a bookmaker at 3:05 p.m. only to be presented twenty-six minutes later with a bail bond and a writ of habeas corpus, signed by a judge and duly executed, ordering them to release the arrested bookie. Cohen also provided insurance against clients who engaged in "past posting"—placing bets after the race was over—in the form of a menacing visit to bettors who tried to cheat. After these visits, bettors rarely persisted in their claims.

Olney realized that there was a simple way to end it all: cut the wire. An investigation by the California Public Utilities Commission revealed that all the bookmakers in California were supplied over a single telegraphic wire leased from Western Union by the Continental Press service.* Continental then telegraphed information on odds, post times, track conditions, and results to "drops" across the nation. The Special Crime Study Commission identified eight in Southern California—front companies with unclear ownership structures and bland names such as Consolidated Publish Inc. and Southwest News. The system was fast but also vulnerable. Olney's investigators discovered that Western Union's contract with Continental

---

*Legalized pari-mutuel betting (where the odds reflect at-track wagers calculated by a pari-mutuel machine) was legal in California, but off-track bookmaking was banned, as it was in every state save Nevada. That made it impossible for Continental to collect information openly. So instead it employed undercover "signalers" or "wigglers" who transmitted odds and race results through a complicated set of signals to outside observers who typically monitored the track with high-powered binoculars and quickly relayed information to the Continental Press "drops." Drops were typically little more than a large room with fifteen to twenty telephones (each carefully registered to a false name), placed on a rack before a loudspeaker. At the beginning of the racing day, calls were placed to subscribing bookmakers and left open all day. When information came in from Chicago, an operator at the drop read it into a microphone that broadcast it out through the loudspeaker and into the battery of phones, which bookmakers on the other end heard instantly and simultaneously. The system was remarkably fast (for the pre-Internet era). Bookmakers in L.A. (who, incidentally, placed the vast majority of bets on out-of-state races) could get results from the New Orleans race tracks in as little as a minute and a half. (California Special Crime Study Commission report, March 17, 1949, 72, 79–80.)

gave state law enforcement authorities the power to request that the wire be terminated if they suspected it was being used, directly or indirectly, in violation of California law. Clearly, Continental's services were being used to violate California law, but when Olney directed the state attorney general's office to that provision, it did nothing. Finally, after months of pressure from Olney and his commission, Attorney General Howser ended his foot-dragging and presented Western Union with such a request. Western Union disconnected the wire, throwing bookmaking in California into chaos.

The halt was temporary. A mysterious new entity, the Illinois News Association, soon appeared with a request to provide a new telegraphic wire service. When the public utilities commission declined to authorize it, the "news association" sued in federal court—and lost. Undeterred, the news association appealed and sought a temporary resumption of wire service, pending the outcome of its appeal request. Attorney General Howser, ever solicitous of the underworld, declined to provide attorneys to defend the public utilities commission's action. Despite lacking counsel, the state utilities commission again prevailed.

The interruption of the wire service had a dramatic impact on gambling in Los Angeles. Without the wire, the ability to roll money quickly from one race into the next was greatly diminished. The most profitable gambling establishments, the so-called horse parlors, where bettors came into a room and placed cash bets directly, one race after the other, disappeared almost overnight. Instead, bettors were directed to call "runners," who took bets over the phone (customers were given an unlisted number and a code word) and then relayed them back to a central office, where bookies collected information via long-distance telephone calls. Volume diminished, and, as the time required to receive results increased from a few minutes to half an hour or longer, the risk of "past posting" increased. The single most lucrative source of Syndicate revenues in the Southland was being squeezed.

Mickey Cohen felt the pinch. But the impact of the wire shutoff wasn't limited to his pocketbook. The wire service was not just a source of vast profits for the Syndicate: Because every serious bookie needed it, the wire was also a tool for licensing and organizing gambling in every big city across the country. "[T]he inevitable result [of its termination]," predicted Olney, "will be the disorganization of bookmaking and the eradication of the organization upon which the Capone Syndicate could and would have based its organization of the California underworld." Cohen understood the threat. But he was preoccupied with a more pressing problem: the people who kept trying to kill him.

Mickey accepted the fact that his chosen profession entailed risks. That local crazies like Maxie Shaman would occasionally come at him was no surprise. What was a surprise was that professional hit men would repeatedly try to kill him. Bugsy Siegel had died because he'd angered virtually every other top figure in the Syndicate. Mickey hadn't. On the contrary, he'd gotten the nod to take over Bugsy's book. Manhattan mobster Frank Costello, the most influential Mob boss in the country, backed him. So did the Cleveland outfit, a far larger presence in Los Angeles than is commonly realized. A rogue hit of the sort attempted at Sherry's—one that endangered civilians and nearly killed a policeman—seemed like something no professional criminal would do.

But not only had someone made the attempt, they were continuing to do so. And if they couldn't touch Mickey directly, they were prepared to do the next best thing. They would target the members of his gang. Ironically, it was Cohen's sense of street justice (and his instinct for good PR) that made him vulnerable.

THE TROUBLE STARTED when William Randolph Hearst's *Examiner* splashed across its front page the sad story of a widow who had refused to pay a $9 radio repair bill she regarded as excessive. The radio repairman in question, Al Pearson, responded by initiating a lawsuit that led to the eventual fire sale of the widow's home, which he then purchased for $26.50. He allowed her to stay on as a tenant paying $10 a week in rent. Outraged policemen at nearby Wilshire station took up a collection.

Pearson's business practices had long attracted unfavorable attention: Police Commission chief investigator Harry Lorenson would later describe him as "the most dishonest businessman in the entire city." When Cohen heard about the incident, he saw an opportunity to burnish his image. He and seven of his boys went over to West Adams to talk with Pearson about returning the widow's house. When Pearson refused to yield to reason, Mickey's cohorts gave the recalcitrant radio repairman a severe beating, cracking his skull and fracturing his right arm—before a large crowd of cheering neighbors.

As Cohen was leaving the scene to get into his car, one of his henchmen, a three-hundred-pound former prizefighter named Jimmy Rist, rushed up.

"Hey, the guy's got a thing back there that listens to things!" he informed Mickey. "He's got everything on it that went on."

"Well, take that son of a bitch machine out of there," Cohen snapped, before jumping into his Cadillac and heading back to his office. Rist hurried back to Pearson's shop to carry out Mickey's orders. What Rist didn't know was that a neighborhood photobug had been shooting pictures of the entire episode from across the street.

Rist and his associates managed to grab the recorder. But in their haste to get away, Mickey's men made an illegal U-turn. Two rookie patrol officers spotted the car and put on their flashers. A two-block chase ensued, during which time a tire iron, a riding whip, and two pistols were thrown from the car. Cohen's men then pulled over. They were promptly arrested and taken down to the Wilshire Division station for booking. When Mickey heard about the arrest, he placed a call—to the chief of the Wilshire Division detective bureau, who hurried into the station. There he confronted the rookies, telling them they had ten minutes to get the guns, tire irons, hot plates, and stolen recorder back into Cohen's men's car. He then ordered their release.

That would have been that but for the photographer. Late that evening, Cohen got a call from a contact at the *Los Angeles Times*, informing him that a photographer had come in earlier that evening and, for $100, sold the paper negatives of his men being arrested (not realizing what he could have gotten for the negatives from Mickey). Mickey rushed down to the *Times* building and attempted to buy the negatives, but it was too late. The *Times* broke the story that tied Mickey's men to Pearson's beating, prompting Mickey to skip town. The lieutenant and sergeant involved in releasing Mickey's men were suspended and then sacked. The press had a field day. Hearst's *Examiner* likened widow Elsie Philips to Snow White; Mickey's men were dubbed the seven dwarves. Cohen and his gunmen (who included the hapless "Happy" Meltzer) were arrested. As was Mickey's habit, he quickly posted bail: $100,000 for himself, $25,000 to 50,000 for each of the dwarves. A trial was scheduled for October. Then, on September 2, 1949, Cohen henchman Frank Niccoli disappeared.

Mickey immediately suspected foul play. What he didn't yet understand was that the Dragna crew was moving to eliminate him with the assistance of his supposed friend from Cleveland, Jimmy "The Weasel" Fratianno.

In the world of organized crime, where loyalty is paramount, tribal segregation has long been the norm. But Mickey had always been different. His organization in Los Angeles had drawn on two disparate groups, Jews from New York (like the late, lamented Hooky Rothman) and Italians from Cleveland or New Jersey (like Joe and Fred Sica). Fratianno was supposed to be part of Mickey's Italian Cleveland contingent. Like Mickey, Fratianno had enjoyed a long run as a holdup man. Unlike Mickey, Jimmy had had the bad luck of being arrested while shaking down a bookmaker in 1937 and shipped off to prison. When Fratianno got out of the pen in 1945, Cohen helped him move to L.A., even springing for an expensive sanitarium sojourn to help cure Fratianno's consumption.

Far from responding gratefully to Mickey's gestures, Fratianno drifted into the sphere of Jack Dragna and his ambitious nephew Louis Tom, both of whom chafed at the notion of a Jew running the rackets. The Dragna circle soon felt comfortable enough with Fratianno to enlist him as a conspirator in an effort to regain control of the Los Angeles underworld—by rubbing out Mickey. "The Weasel" was happy to help. Their first target was Cohen henchman Frank Niccoli, who also happened to be one of Fratianno's old stickup buddies from Cleveland. At Dragna's behest, Jimmy called up Niccoli and asked him to come over for a drink. He let Niccoli finish it before having him strangled. The killers then stripped off Niccoli's clothes, stuffed the body in a mail sack, and threw it in the back of their car. A few hours later, Niccoli was interred with a sack of lime in a vineyard in Cucamonga. Niccoli's car was then abandoned at LAX.

It took Mickey several days to realize that Niccoli was missing. But Superior Court Judge Thomas Ambrose was not impressed by Cohen's claim that something awful had happened. The judge suspected that Niccoli had simply flown the coop. Reports that Niccoli had been sighted in Mexico filtered in. Police officers were dispatched to search for him in Texas. When Niccoli didn't appear in court on October 3, the first day of the trial, the $50,000 Mickey had put down as bail was forfeited.

Then, on October 10, another Cohen henchman, Davey Ogul, vanished. His car turned up two days later. Again the judge rejected Mickey's claims that foul play was involved and, when the dead man failed to present himself in court, Mickey was out another $25,000. With the police breathing down his neck, it was practically impossible to do business anyway. So on October 13 Mickey took the humiliating step of instructing his remaining henchmen to return to jail, where their safety would be guaranteed.

But where is true safety in this world? Surely not in jail. The constant attempts on his life, his miraculous escapes from death—it was enough to make a man think of Providence, for as the Psalmist said, "It is thou, Lord, only that makest me dwell in safety."

Mickey Cohen wasn't a religious man. But in the autumn of 1949, God came calling at 513 South Moreno in the form of an unlikely duo: Cohen wiretapper Jimmy Vaus and a charismatic young evangelist named Billy Graham.

14

The Evangelist

*"He has the making of one of the greatest
gospel preachers of all time."*

—the Rev. Billy Graham, commenting on Mickey Cohen

THE YEAR 1949 had been a disastrous one for Jimmy Vaus. "Happy"
Meltzer's trial and the revelations that followed had exposed him as a
double agent and placed him in considerable legal peril. And so it was that
driving home late one Saturday night in November, filled with mournful
thoughts, listening to the original singing cowboy, radio host Stuart Hamblen, Jimmy Vaus heard something that would change his life.

"A few nights ago," began Hamblen, "I went to the Big Tent at Washington and Hill, and after I heard Billy Graham preach, I accepted Christ as
my personal Savior." Hamblen was so committed to Jesus, he continued,
that he was selling his racehorses—save for his sentimental favorite, the
champion Thoroughbred El Lobo.

This was serious. Everyone who listened to Hamblen's radio program
knew he was crazy about the horses (as well as other not-strictly-religious
activities such as coon-hunting and skirt-chasin'). "He meant business if he
were selling his horses," concluded Vaus.

The next day was a Sunday. Vaus went to the beach. It was foggy and
cold. He dropped by Mickey Cohen's house in Brentwood. Mickey wasn't
home. He drove down to a bar on Washington Boulevard—and then realized, with a start, that he was headed straight for the Billy Graham revival
meeting.

By November 1949, everyone in Los Angeles knew about Billy Graham.
One month earlier, the lantern-jawed young evangelist with the fierce blue
eyes and the booming voice had arrived in town with plans to hold a series
of old-fashioned tent revival meetings. The idea was quaint. The messenger wasn't. Graham was Hollywood's idea of what a minister should be—
a six-foot, two-inch booming baritone who wore sharp, double-breasted
suits and flashy ties. Nonetheless, Graham's campaign for Christ might

well have remained a modest affair but for the mysterious intervention of William Randolph Hearst. Soon after Graham arrived in town, the editors at the morning *Los Angeles Examiner* and the evening *Herald-Express* received a terse telegram from San Simeon: "Puff Graham." The city's largest morning tabloid responded with typical élan. Graham noticed that suddenly "reporters and cameramen were crawling all over the place." Stories about Graham's "Crusade for Christ" played across the front pages of the two papers for weeks, as did breathless accounts of the goings-on within what was now dubbed "the Canvas Cathedral" ("the largest revival tent in history"). Modest crowds became impassioned mobs. And so that Sunday evening Jimmy Vaus found himself squeezing onto a back bench under the big tent, one of the roughly six thousand people who'd come to hear Graham speak.

"You know," Graham boomed through the tent, "there's a man in this audience tonight who has heard this story many times before, and who knows this is the decision he should make. . . . This is your moment of decision."

Suddenly, Vaus found himself gliding up the isle toward the platform at the front of the tent where Graham was standing. Then he was down on his knees. He left in a daze. As he was exiting the tent, a photographer's lightbulb flashed. The next day, newspaper readers awakened to the headline WIRE-TAPPER VAUS HITS SAWDUST TRAIL.

Celebrity criminal Jimmy Vaus had been born again.

It was with some nervousness that Vaus drove over to Mickey's house to explain his conversion. November had not been a good month for Mickey. After forfeiting bail on his disappearing gunmen, Mickey needed to be able to show more income from legitimate sources. So he announced plans to sell his haberdashery. Cohen carried it out with unusual style. A huge sign appeared in the haberdashery's window: MICKEY COHEN QUITS! A spotlight danced across the Los Angeles sky from the doomed store, as if its closing were a movie premiere. Curious Angelenos responded by the hundreds, helping themselves to a look into Mickey's luxurious lair (as well as a chance to purchase $25 ties at $10 prices). Vaus feared that Mickey's mood might be bad. But when he arrived at 513 Moreno, he found the gangster in good spirits. When Vaus informed Mickey that he was "going back to the Church, back into Christianity," Cohen responded, good-naturedly, "Well, what the hell else ya been?"

No, no, Vaus explained. "You're not a Christian till you give your life to Lord Jesus Christ and are born again."

Mickey was a bit unclear on the born-again thing but told Vaus "that was fine with him." Vaus summoned his courage and plowed ahead. He intended to go straight, he told Mickey, despite the financial hardships this would entail. Cohen wished him the best of luck and offered a gift of $1,500 that he happened to have in his bedroom. Vaus declined. Now that he had resolved to walk with the Lord, he didn't think it would be right to take such a sum from a notorious gangster. He left with only $500.

Vaus's conversion became the talk of the city. Billy Graham's star ascended ever higher. Graham then offered Vaus a job as a junior spokesperson, essentially, someone who would accompany Graham on his crusades and testify to the power of faith. Vaus, in turn, offered Graham something enticing: the prospect of "saving" Mickey Cohen. He arranged for Graham and radio host Stuart Hamblen to stop by the Cohen residence for a visit. Cohen's housekeeper served them hot chocolate and cookies. The men got along well. A few weeks later, Graham invited Cohen to attend a private meeting "of Hollywood personalities." At the meeting, Graham asked people who wanted him to pray for them to hold up their hands.

"Mickey lifted his hand," Graham later recounted, "and I am sincerely convinced that he wanted God."

The effort to convert Mickey Cohen had begun.

BILLY GRAHAM'S PRAYERS were apparently effective.

At 4:15 a.m. on February 6, 1950, the radar alarm designed by Jimmy Vaus went off. Mickey grabbed a shotgun and peeked out the front door. Seeing nothing, he went back to his wife's bedroom. No sooner had he gotten into LaVonne's bed than a massive explosion rocked the house. Windows throughout the neighborhood were blown out; police officers at a station three miles away felt the shock waves. When Cohen opened his eyes, his roof and most of the front of his house, including the bedroom where he normally slept, were gone. His first thought was of Tuffy (who slept beside him in an exact replica of Mickey's bed, save for the fact that his bedcovering was monogrammed "TC" rather than "MC"). Fortunately for the terrier, he had followed Mickey to LaVonne's bedroom that night. Police arrived to find Mickey in his bathrobe, shaking his head at his closet of ruined $300 suits.

Police later estimated that twenty-eight sticks of dynamite had been placed under the Cohen residence. Providence—or Lady Luck—seemed to be keeping a vigil over Mickey Cohen.

Three days later, the critical witness in the beating case of rapacious radio repairman Al Pearson came before the jury. Hazel Pearson was Al's daughter-in-law; she worked in his shop and had witnessed the attack the previous spring. But instead of offering testimony that would send Mickey and his surviving henchmen to the pen, Hazel turned on her father-in-law, whom she described as a crook and a chiseler.

"I've never really liked the man," Hazel told the all-female jury. One month later, Mickey Cohen was acquitted.

MICKEY COHEN wasn't the only person toying with a conversion experience. Interim police chief William Worton was also reaching some startling conclusions about how the LAPD should operate and how it should be run. His ideas put him on a collision course with Bill Parker.

Worton had taken over as the LAPD's emergency chief the previous July. The city charter provided for a sixty-day term, renewable once. However, when September arrived, Mayor Bowron was not ready to dispense with General Worton's services. So the city attorney was prevailed upon to issue an opinion that allowed him to continue in office. General Worton's "temporary" appointment was extended into the winter—and then again into the spring of 1950. If Mayor Bowron had had his druthers, it seems clear he would have simply appointed General Worton chief of police. But the city charter was explicit: The next chief of police had to come from within the department. It seemed an insuperable obstacle. But Worton was convinced that there was a way he could continue to direct the department without running afoul of the city charter. He would simply change what the chief of police did.

The Los Angeles Police Department's organization was unusual. Everyone described General Worton as the police chief, but in fact he was not technically in charge of the department. The Police Commission was. Worton was technically the department's "general manager." The organizational chart clearly put him under the five-member civilian board appointed by the mayor, much as corporate CEOs answer to their companies' boards. That, at least, was the theory. In practice, the Police Commission provided almost no direction to—much less oversight of—the department. There were a number of reasons for this. Unlike a corporate board whose members come primarily from business backgrounds similar to that of their CEOs, the police commissioners were civilians, not police professionals. As a result, they simply didn't have the knowledge or experience to evaluate how the chief and the department were doing.

They also didn't have the time. In addition to supervising the police department, the commission was also responsible for licensing a whole range of businesses (auto-repair shops, pawnshops, dance halls, and so forth) and approving activities (parades, public dances) that might involve the police department. This licensing task alone was enough to fully occupy the commission, which typically met one morning a week. The commission also relied almost entirely on police department personnel to conduct its investigations. Finally, even if the commission had decided to go after the department's general manager, the chief of police enjoyed something no CEO had: civil service protection. No wonder Police Commissions often made only the barest pretense of directing the department. By the end of Chief Horrall's tenure, the police chief no longer even met with the commission on a regular basis.

The more time General Worton spent in office, the more convinced he became that the entire system was flawed. The notion that the department answered to a board of civilians was nothing more than a polite fiction—and was exposed as such whenever the police department had something sensitive to handle, such as a brutality complaint. These were dealt with internally, by department personnel alone. This rubbed Worton the wrong way. So too did the fact that while the mayor was held to account, politically, for the conduct of the police department, he exercised only indirect influence over the department, through his appointees to the Police Commission.

A better model was needed, Worton concluded, and it wasn't hard to find one. Police departments in New York, Chicago, and Detroit all operated under a different management structure. In those cities, the mayor appointed a single civilian commissioner or superintendent to supervise the department. This commissioner or superintendent answered to the mayor. Day-to-day police department operations were run by a top-uniformed officer—in the NYPD, the chief of department. The Marine Corps had a similar structure. There the top-uniformed officer—the commandant—ran operations but answered to a civilian, the secretary of the Navy. Worton believed that the LAPD would benefit from a similar structure.

During the fall of 1949, he fleshed out his plan for reorganizing the department. It called for a non-civil-service commissioner who would be appointed by the mayor (subject to city council approval) to a three-year term. This commissioner would be responsible for setting goals for the department and would directly run important bureaus such as internal affairs, planning and accounting, records and identification, and communications. A uniformed police chief would serve under him and direct actual law enforcement activities. Worton believed such a reorganization could be accomplished without amending the city charter. As to who this new commissioner would be, most observers assumed that the candidate Worton had in mind was himself.

Mayor Bowron liked the idea. But Worton's plan quickly encountered opposition from powerful forces—and from at least one member of his inner circle, Bill Parker. The disciplinary system that struck Worton as ill conceived was among Parker's proudest accomplishments. With the department's top job once again in reach, Parker had no intention of standing aside while an outsider gutted the system he had created. He boldly criticized General Worton's proposed reforms. He insisted that a five-member civilian Police Commission whose members were each appointed to five-year terms would be more independent and responsive to the public than a single commissioner who answered only to the mayor would be.

"You'll get a bad city administration someday," Parker warned.

For months, the police department had stood by meekly while Mayor Bowron extended General Worton's emergency term of office in legally dubious ways and considered plans to unilaterally reorganize the department. Now the forces of the status quo ante counterattacked. General Worton had suggested that the department could be reorganized without a charter amendment. A chorus of voices arose to question this sweeping claim. Reluctantly, Mayor Bowron agreed that his acting police chief's plan would have to be submitted to the voters for their approval. As the weeks passed, it became increasingly clear that the only person who was really enthusiastic about this idea was Worton himself. Finally Mayor Bowron gave in and announced that he'd be scheduling an examination to select a new chief in the spring of 1950. Some two dozen LAPD officers promptly announced that they would sit for the examination, among them Bill Parker.

On July 10, participants' scores were announced. Parker placed first. Thad Brown and Roger Murdock placed a distant second and third. That same day, General Worton notified the Police Commission that he wished to step down from his position at the end of the month. Legally, Mayor Bowron could select any of the top three candidates, but everyone knew that the choice was really between the two heavyweights, Brown or Parker. Both men now attempted to rally their allies. In Parker's case, that meant the American Legion and the Catholic Archdiocese of Los Angeles, including its new archbishop (soon to be cardinal), James Francis McIntyre. By 1948, there were 650,000 Roman Catholics in Los Angeles, and another 55,000 were arriving from across the country every year. Msgr. Thomas O'Dwyer, the top aide to Archbishop McIntyre, sent a pointed letter to Mayor Bowron, noting Parker's many qualifications.

These were powerful backers, but Thad Brown, arguably, had even stronger allies. The LAPD had long been a strikingly Protestant organization: All but one of its previous chiefs had been Protestants. Almost all of them had also been Freemasons, as were many of the officers on the force. Brown was both. He also enjoyed the quiet support of the underworld. Thad Brown was in no way corrupt, but neither was he seen as a zealot who would attempt to eradicate the underworld altogether. The *Los Angeles Times* also supported Brown. In early August, it reported that three of the five Police Commissioners—clubwoman Agnes Albro, Henry Duque, and Bruno Newman—had settled on Brown. The Police Commission's sole African American member, J. Alexander Somerville, and Irving Snyder, the commission's Jewish member, supported Parker. Brown had the votes to become police chief—if he could keep them. For at that very moment, Agnes Albro was dying of breast cancer. Already, she was confined to bed. Brown's supporters knew they needed to move quickly. Duque and Newman proposed to convene a meeting at Albro's house to select Brown as chief. Parker vehemently objected. A meeting in a private residence would be illegal, he warned the commissioners, a clear violation of California's open meeting requirements. Brown's supporters paused. As they were debating the issue, Agnes Albro passed away.

The race was now a toss-up. "In the newspapers, it was a bigger story than baseball or the heat wave," wrote one contemporary observer. "[T]he reporters smoked out secret meetings all through City Hall. Meetings between the Mayor and his Police Commissioners; between the Mayor and the candidates; between the commissioners and the candidates."

On August 2, Mayor Bowron, General Worton, and the four members of the Police Commission sat down together. Exactly what was said was unclear, but after the meeting one of Thad Brown's supporters decided to switch his support to Parker. (Many years later, Thad Brown would claim that he had withdrawn his name from consideration because he didn't want "Bill Parker behind me, with his knife out.") To send a message of strong support for the new chief, the sole remaining Brown holdout agreed to join the pro-Parker majority in order to make the vote unanimous. And so, later that very day, the Police Commission voted unanimously to make William H. Parker Los Angeles's fortieth chief of police.

Mayor Bowron was notably lukewarm about their choice. When asked by a reporter if the appointment "met with his approval," Bowron declined to answer, suggesting instead that "all statements should come from the Police Commission."

Chief Parker waved off the mayor's lack of support. "The action of the Police Commission this afternoon was gratifying and confirms my belief that the Chief of Police must be selected without political influence," he told the press later that day.

The reality was otherwise. Parker had politicked—and prevailed. But many doubted that he would retain the position for very long.

"I know I'm supposedly coming in with a life expectancy of two weeks," he told the press after being sworn in. "We'll see."

15

"Whiskey Bill"

> *"There is a sinister criminal organization known as the Mafia operating throughout the country."*
>
> —Sen. Estes Kefauver, 1950

IT HAD BEEN a rotten vacation. Mickey had left Los Angeles a month earlier with a leisurely agenda of business and pleasure in mind. In Phoenix, he wanted to visit brother Harry and check out some drugstores he was considering purchasing. But the Phoenix police department had quickly run him out of town. The same thing had happened in Texas, where he owned an oil well. Then, when Mickey Cohen arrived at the Ambassador Hotel in Chicago on August 3, 1950, he learned that Bill Parker had been appointed chief of police. It was upsetting. "I had joints all over town, and I needed the police for coordination," Cohen would later say. Instead, the Police Commission had selected "the one cop who really gave me trouble." Just when it seemed like things could not get worse, Chicago detectives picked him up for an evening of questioning. He was released the next day and told to get out of town.

Mickey Cohen was getting too famous for his own good. Not only had he gained a dangerous new enemy in the person of Los Angeles's new police chief, he had also attracted the attention of a curious outsider, U.S. senator Estes Kefauver.

A FRESHMAN SENATOR from Tennessee, Estes Kefauver was a man of great ambition and considerable guile. In 1948, after an unremarkable decade in the House as a pro-Roosevelt, pro–Tennessee Valley Authority Democrat, Kefauver took advantage of a feud between incumbent U.S. senator Tom Stewart and Tennessee party boss Ed "The Red Snapper" Crump and slipped into the Senate. There the Yale Law School–educated senator with the vaguely Lincoln-esque looks impressed his peers with his intelligence (he had authored an academic book on monopolies)—and his womanizing ("the worst in the Senate," according to William "Fishbait" Miller, the House doorkeeper).

At some point in 1949, Kefauver hit upon the idea of investigating organized gambling. This was not a popular notion among his Senate colleagues. Democratic Senate Majority Leader Scott Lucas of Illinois relied on Cook County to offset Republican voters downstate. He was not eager to start an investigation that might expose the inner workings of Chicago politics. But Kefauver had picked his topic wisely. By 1950, organized crime had become a subject of great interest to the public. Books such as Jack Lait and Lee Mortimer's *Chicago Confidential* had city residents talking about the underworld. The American Municipal Association held a conference devoted to the subject, and both Mayor Fletcher Bowron of Los Angeles and Mayor DeLesseps Morrison of New Orleans spoke passionately and frequently about the issue. As a result, in January 1950, Kefauver was able to win passage of a measure authorizing "a full and complete study and investigation of interstate gambling and racketeering activities." Senate Judiciary Committee chairman Pat McCarran—of Nevada—responded by arranging a series of delays. But in April 1950, McCarran and Senate Majority Leader Lucas's strategy of delay collapsed when the body of a Kansas City gambling kingpin was found in a Democratic clubhouse, slumped beneath a large portrait of President Harry Truman.

The killing itself was hardly unusual: Kansas City had long been controlled by one of the country's most notorious "machines," one that did not shy away from occasional acts of violence. What made this particular slaying noteworthy was the fact that President Truman himself was a product of that same machine. (He owed both his first victory in politics—his election as a county judge in 1922—and his 1934 election to the U.S. Senate to "Boss Tom" Pendergast's Kansas City machine.) Even though "Boss Tom" had died five years earlier, the slaying in Kansas City stoked public concerns about underworld connections to government officials. Amid the ensuing controversy, the Special Senate Committee on the Investigation of Syndicated Crime in Interstate Commerce—soon known simply as the Kefauver Committee—was finally impaneled. Faced with fallout from the Kansas City slaying, President Truman also gave the Kefauver Committee a potent new tool: access to the income tax records of suspected gambling bosses. Thus armed, Kefauver revealed the investigative strategy that would catapult him to national fame. Instead of summoning witnesses to Washington, the press-savvy senator announced that his committee and its investigators would hold a series of hearings in fourteen cities across the country on "how the national crime syndicate could be smashed." In November, Senator Kefauver arrived in Los Angeles. Atop his list of witnesses was Mickey Cohen.

When Mickey received a subpoena to appear before the Kefauver Committee at the federal building downtown, all of Los Angeles expected fireworks. But when the committee convened at 9 a.m., there was no Mickey Cohen. Indignant, the commission sent investigators out to his house in Brentwood to search for the witness. They found Mickey asleep in bed. While the committee waited, Mickey got dressed with excruciating slowness. ("Being the fine dressed man I try to be, it takes time for me to get ready for an appearance.") The hearings had "been blown up so big . . . like a Hollywood premiere," and Cohen wanted to look the part of a Hollywood star. He did.

From the minute he entered a crowded courtroom in Los Angeles's federal building, "Mickey was the star of the show," reported *Time* magazine. Wearing "a natty brown suit, brown tie and deep black scowl," Cohen faced "a whole battery of newsmen, photographers, movie cameras and tape recorders."

Surveying them in much the same spirit that a feudal lord might survey his vassals, Cohen was overheard commenting, "I could spit on the sidewalk and it would make headlines."

A reporter asked the question on everyone's mind: Wasn't Mickey disrespecting the U.S. Senate by arriving late?

"Lookit, nobody notified me about the time," Mickey responded testily. "All I got was a call to come down here, and I came down, and I'm here."

For the next five hours, Mickey put on a remarkable show. One month earlier in Chicago, Harry "The Muscle" Russell, the Chicago Outfit's Florida representative, had flustered the Kefauver Committee by citing the Fifth Amendment (which protects against self-incrimination) as a justification for refusing to answer *any* questions from the committee. Mickey had no such hesitation. Speaking easily, almost casually, without notes and rarely pausing to consult attorneys Sam Rummel and Vernon Ferguson, Cohen denied every allegation thrown at him:

"I ain't never muscled no one in my life."

"I ain't never offered no policeman a bribe."

"I never pistol-whipped anyone."

"I ain't never been with no prostitute."

"I never had no part of a fix."

"I never strong-armed nobody in my life."

It was a bravura recitation of lies. But there was one issue Mickey couldn't wish away—his income.

Other Mob bosses had carefully constructed front companies or bought in to legitimate businesses in order to account for their large incomes. Frank Costello, the so-called prime minister of the underworld, insisted that he was merely a semiretired real estate investor. Jack Dragna claimed that he was a vineyard owner and banana importer. Aside from a few desultory investments (in grocery stores and a women's shoulder-pad manufacturer), Mickey had not. Even Michael's Haberdashery had never made much pretense of being a going concern. Instead, Mickey maintained that he was just a former bookmaker who now earned a modest living from gambling. But he lived like a pasha in a $120,000 house in Brentwood and purchased new Cadillacs every year for himself and his wife (to say nothing of his $15,000 armored car).

Anyone who bothered to do a quick back-of-the-envelope calculation could see that there was something suspicious about such lavish expenditures. The problem was squaring such spending with the era's high income tax rates. In 1950, a taxpayer who earned $100,000 could expect to hand nearly $60,000 of that to the federal government and another $5,000 to the state of California, leaving about $35,000 for himself. Double that hypothetical income to $200,000, and the taxpayer was left with a mere $50,000 in after-tax income. Yet by his own acknowledgment, Mickey had spent more than $200,000 on his house and about $30,000 on Cadillacs. Investigators also estimated that Cohen kept roughly eighteen men on his payroll; at his declared pay rate of "$75 to $100 a week," that added another $85,000 or so to his expenses. In order to generate, say, $125,000 in legitimate after-tax income, Mickey would had to have paid taxes on a declared yearly income of nearly a million dollars. He wasn't even close. Instead, the tax returns he had filed with the Bureau of Internal Revenue in the late 1940s reported annual incomes as low as $6,000 a year—just twice the national average income.

This should have led the Bureau of Internal Revenue to take a closer look at Mickey's finances, as it had done nearly two decades earlier in the case of Al Capone. Yet remarkably, as Warren Olney noted in the final report of the Special Crime Study Commission—a report that came out the same month that Senator Kefauver was interrogating Mickey Cohen in Los Angeles—"there has never been a racketeer, hoodlum, or gangster of first rank importance convicted of income tax fraud in California." Nor, according to comments made by Treasury Department officials at a conference on organized crime in the spring of 1949, were any such cases in the works. Local Bureau of Internal Revenue agents had actually tried to start an investigation several years earlier. But after their superiors discovered the probe, they'd been detailed to other assignments.

The Kefauver Committee had no intention of letting Mickey off so lightly. During their questioning, committee members homed in on Mickey's massive expenditures and minimal income. Grudgingly, Cohen admitted to a $40,000 home (far less than its actual value) with $48,000 worth of home furnishings. That still left a gap of $210,000 in unaccounted-for income. When pressed about the discrepancy by chief counsel Rudolph Halley, Cohen replied that over the past four years, he had borrowed about $300,000, most of which, he added, had been spent on lawyers' fees as a result of the constant "harassment from the LAPD."

Halley asked if there were any notes or collateral that could document these loans.

Mickey said there were not. People had lent him money, Cohen continued, because "they just happen to like me."

"How do you maintain that kind of credit?" Sen. Charles Tobey of New Hampshire asked.

Mickey cracked his first smile. "It's getting very weak, Senator."

The audience chuckled. By the end of the week, the investigators were gone. When a reporter asked Cohen what he thought of the experience, Mickey cracked, "All them congressional committees are a joke, a gimmick for the furtherance of a politician." Bill Parker worried him much more.

DURING PARKER'S first month on the job, four different emissaries approached him with variations on a single proposal: appointing a gambling "czar." Ostensibly, this person's job would be to curb gambling, but Parker felt his interlocutors were actually more interested in organizing it. Fearing a frame-up, Parker spoke openly about these overtures at a countywide meeting of law enforcement officers later that month. He was convinced that the various attempts to snuff out Mickey Cohen suggested that the Syndicate was preparing to move into Los Angeles in force. Los Angeles, which Parker described, in language harkening back to the 1920s, as "the last white spot among the great cities of America," risked becoming Chicago. The LAPD was determined to resist this, he told his audiences. But he warned, "I do not know how long this can be continued. There are men here ready to get their tentacles into the city and drain off large sums of money through gambling activities of various kinds."

Parker argued that if the forces of law and order were to prevail, a counteroffensive was needed. For too long, gangsters had taken advantage of the fact that when things got "hot" in one of Los Angeles County's forty-five-odd municipalities, they could just move to another. At a meeting of regional law enforcement officials, Parker proposed a new approach—a central intelligence bureau that pooled resources from all of the region's law enforcement agencies and pursued gangsters wherever they attempted to hide. Representatives from the three dozen law enforcement agencies present readily agreed to participate in such an effort. But Parker's ambitions were larger still.

"This plan goes deeper than a means of saving Los Angeles from the stigma of vice," Parker continued. "We are protecting the American philosophy of life. It is now clear that Russia is hoping we will destroy ourselves as a nation through our own avarice, greed, and corruption in government. Hence, this program has a wider application than in the Los Angeles area alone." Parker envisioned a national consortium of departments committed to information-sharing.

The assembled group was, according to one account of the meeting, "startled," both by the scope of Parker's ambitions and by his tone. In his first speeches as chief-of-police-elect, Parker had struck a hopeful—even humble—note, committing himself and his officers to the "reasonable enforcement of the law and respect for the rights and dignity of the individual—to work for the community, not rule it." But already another side of Chief Parker was appearing—the profoundly pessimistic observer of American decline, the Spengler of City Hall.

Parker was a powerful speaker in thrall to a potent theme: the corruption of American society and the perils this posed. "We have become a great nation in a material sense," Parker warned the Holy Name Society in a speech soon after becoming chief. "But this unparalleled success in the acquisition of worldly goods has been accompanied by a materialistic philosophy that threatens to destroy every vestige of human liberty.

"Egypt, Babylon, Greece, and Rome rose, then fell as strength gave way to weakness," continued Parker ominously. "It is possible that our failure to recognize the indispensability of Religion and Morality to our national welfare is leading us to the same fate that beset these brave civilizations of the past."

Whether 1950s Los Angeles was Babylon or not, Bill Parker was right about one thing, though. The underworld was moving in.

Soon after Parker was appointed chief, five of the top criminals in Los Angeles County got together in a Hollywood hotel suite to "cut up the town." The men present included Sam Rummel, Mickey Cohen's attorney and sometime business partner; Jimmy Utley, a former Cohen rival who now concentrated on bingo and abortion; Max Kleiger, bookmaker and gambler; Robert Gans, slot machine king during the heyday of the Combination in the

1930s; and Curly Robinson, his successor in the coin machine field, another Cohen partner. For hours, they discussed how to divvy up the most lucrative rackets, as well as bookmaking, gambling, bingo, and prostitution. They also discussed tactics. Since Parker wouldn't bend, the underworld decided to target Mayor Bowron. They decided to mount a recall initiative (the same measure that had brought Bowron to office in the first place in 1938). In a delightfully cynical twist, the grounds for the recall were none other than the supposed influence exercised by the underworld over Mayor Bowron, as exposed by the vicecapades of 1949.*

The LAPD heard it all. The hotel suite was bugged, courtesy the LAPD intelligence division.

The idea of an intelligence division wasn't new: Chief James E. Davis had one in the 1930s; Chief Horrall had one in the 1940s. Other units such as administrative vice and the gangster squad routinely did intelligence work too, as the bugging of Mickey Cohen's house demonstrated. But most previous intelligence work had relied heavily on wiretaps and a style of interrogation that could be summarized as "pinch-'em-and-sweat-'em." When General Worton took over the department, he wanted something different—analysis, predictions, and actionable information of the sort that military commanders received from their intelligence outfits. In short, he wanted a policing version of the Army's G-2 intelligence system.

Parker shared Worton's enthusiasm for operational intelligence. During the war, one of the new chief's most important jobs had been reorganizing and de-Nazifying the Munich police department. At the time, he had been struck by the parallels between de-Nazification and clearing the LAPD of corrupt police officers with ties to the underworld. Now that Parker was chief, he set out to realize General Worton's vision. He expanded the unit to roughly three dozen officers and appointed his most trusted associate in the department, James Hamilton, to head its operations. Both men agreed that traditional policing techniques simply did not work against the Syndicate. In the early 1940s, Bugsy Siegel had killed with impunity—and then been killed with equal impunity by a professional gunman who escaped without leaving a trace. More recently, even the most basic questions about Mickey Cohen were not fully resolved. Consider the case of Sam Rummel. Why was he, rather than Mickey, meeting to "cut up" Los Angeles? Was he Mickey's mouthpiece and junior partner, as most people assumed? Or was he playing a more subtle game? In Chicago, for instance, many astute observers of the Outfit believed that the real power rested not with so-called

---

*To bolster the impression that Bowron was in the underworld's pocket, Mickey Cohen adorned his Cadillac with a giant sign trumpeting his support for the mayor.

leaders such as Frank Nitti and Sam Giancana but rather with the men who stayed in the background, Paul Ricca, Tony Accardo, and Murray Humphreys. Might Rummel likewise be calling the shots in Los Angeles? These were the kinds of questions the intelligence division was tasked with answering.

The intelligence division didn't just watch and analyze. According to former gangster squad member Jack O'Mara, a favorite tactic was to drive new arrivals up into Coldwater Canyon or the Hollywood Hills to "have a little heart-to-heart talk with 'em, emphasize the fact that this wasn't New York, this wasn't Chicago, this wasn't Cleveland." O'Mara had his own way of driving the lesson home: He'd "put a kind of a gun to their ear and say, 'You want to sneeze?' Do you feel a sneeze coming on? A real loud sneeze?'"

Mickey's men got similar treatment, judging by a story told by former LAPD officer-turned-private-eye Fred Otash. One night, soon after the shooting at Sherry's, Otash spotted Johnny Stompanato cruising down the Sunset Strip. Otash told his partner to pull up beside him. Then he pulled their shotgun out of the gutter between the seat and the door and, when they were parallel to Stompanato, stuck the gun out the window and shouted, "Now you've had it, you motherfucker!"

"When Johnny saw the shotgun, he ducked, losing control of his new Cadillac," Otash recalled later, with obvious delight. "It went over the curb and down the hill of Sunset. He could have been killed."

Otash wasn't on the intelligence unit. He was far too unreliable and unruly for such a sensitive post. But this episode drew only a mild rebuke from downtown. Clearly, tough-guy tactics were part of the job.

"Our main purpose is to keep anyone from getting 'too big,'" Hamilton told a San Francisco newspaper years later, in discussing the exploits of his intelligence squad. "When we get word that someone has 'juice,' that he's trying to 'fix things,' and thinks he can, then we're after him.

"We're selfish about it—damned selfish. Because we know that that's the kind of a guy who's going to wreck your police department if he can. And we're going to stop him—one way or the other."

It would not be long before the unit got a dramatic test of its abilities.

AS KEFAUVER ATTEMPTED to untangle the Los Angeles underworld, the county grand jury was digging into the Guarantee Finance case. Connections to Mickey Cohen were everywhere. Sam Rummel was Guarantee Finance's attorney. Harry Sackman, Mickey's accountant, was its accountant. The company's books included one item in particular that caught the grand jury's attention: $108,000 for "juice"—payoff money. The fact that the LAPD had repeatedly (albeit extralegally) raided Guarantee Finance (which was located in unincorporated county territory), only to draw a written rebuke from the sheriff's department, made it fairly clear who was on the take. So did the astonishing testimony of Undersheriff Arthur C. Jewell before the Kefauver Committee. When pressed, Undersheriff Jewell insisted that neither he nor Sheriff Eugene Biscailuz had heard the name "Guarantee Finance" until state authorities had brought it to their attention. More astonishing still was Jewell's response to another question. The committee asked him to outline areas of illegal activities that he suspected—*suspected*—Mickey Cohen might be involved in. By the fall of 1950, every newspaper reader in Los Angeles could have answered this question at length. Not Undersheriff Jewell.

"Personally, I cannot, sir; that is honest and sincere," he told committee members.

Afterward, the county grand jury decided to look more closely at the evidence tying the sheriff's department to Guarantee Finance. The top leadership of the sheriff's department promised to cooperate. A secret meeting was convened to discuss investigation plans. The group of attendees was a small one: the foreman of the county grand jury, a representative of the district attorney's office, three county law enforcement officials, and two "servers" who would deliver affidavits to witnesses the grand jury planned to call. A list of targets—most of whom were represented by Rummel—was drawn up.

The very next day, the targets scattered. Someone had leaked the list.

The secret strategy meeting had been held on a Wednesday. The witnesses the county grand jury had intended to subpoena scattered the following day, on Thursday. On Sunday, an extraordinary rendezvous occurred. Sheriff's department captain Al Guasti, vice squad commander Carl Pearson, and vice squad sergeant Lawrence Schaffer met clandestinely with Rummel. The apparent purpose of the meeting was to coordinate a strategy whereby Rummel would cooperate with the investigation in a way that protected both himself and the sheriff's department.

Later that evening, at about 1:30 a.m., Rummel arrived back at his house in Laurel Canyon, high above what is today West Hollywood. As he walked from his floodlit garage up the steps to his Spanish colonial, a twelve-gauge shotgun roared out from behind a hedge on the property some twenty-nine feet away. The blast hit Rummel in the neck. Blood sprayed across the walk. As the getaway car screeched away—most likely up to Mulholland or over the Santa Monica Mountains into the Valley—Rummel lay on the steps, dying but not dead.

The police got there first. By the time Parker himself arrived, with Jack

Donahoe, Rummel had breathed his last breath. Surprisingly, police quickly found the murder weapon—a 1910 double-barreled Remington shotgun propped in the crook of a tree. A few minutes later, Mickey Cohen arrived, wearing a pair of slacks over his pajamas. Brushing past the police cordon, he rushed in to console Rummel's widow. Upstairs came the commotion of police setting up a command post in Rummel's den. A police lieutenant soon appeared.

"Cohen, the chief wants you upstairs."

"All right, I'll be up there," Cohen responded. But he made no move to leave the sobbing widow.

"No, he wants you up there right now," the lieutenant persisted.

Bill Parker was the last person Mickey Cohen wanted to see. By his own accounting, he was "still hot about Parker becoming chief of police." Now there he was, surrounded by obsequious aides rushing to and fro, sitting behind Rummel's desk, with Jack Donahoe standing at his side. So when Parker "starts off with this bullshit," Cohen lost it.

"Lookit, ya punk son of a bitch. As far as I'm concerned, ya should no more be chief of police than a fucking two-dollar pimp," screamed Cohen.

Suddenly, like a vet handling an angry cat, big Jack Donahoe was holding Mickey up by his neck.

"He's crazy!" Parker exclaimed. "Get him out of here. I don't want to talk to him anymore."

Mickey was hustled off. "[I]'m a son of a bitch if I didn't have his fingermarks on my throat for six days after," he said later.

THE NEXT DAY Chief Parker vowed he would find the killer. The new chief needed a win. The *Los Angeles Times* had supported his opponent; the mayor was cool to him; even the person who had done more than any other to smooth his ascent to the top—William Worton—was turning into an impediment. On the same day that Parker himself had been sworn in as chief, Bowron had named Worton to the Police Commission. Instead of the usual group of civilians who provided oversight in name only (and who in reality met once a week to hear license applications), Parker would have to answer to a board that included his former boss. This, undoubtedly, was Mayor Bowron's point.

But solving the case wouldn't be easy. The LAPD really had only one concrete piece of evidence—the murder weapon itself. It was extremely unusual to find a weapon at the scene of a professional hit. By leaving it, the killer was basically giving law enforcement the middle finger. But in this case, the killer's confidence was misplaced. In an astonishing feat of police work, the LAPD managed to trace the weapon back to Riley, Kansas, to a pawnshop frequented by a tough hood who'd recently relocated to the Los Angeles area, Tony Broncato. Broncato and his partner, Tony Trombino, were a pair of freelance gunmen who'd been questioned in connection with every major shooting in Los Angeles since Bugsy Siegel's rub-out. Unfortunately, the two Tonys had also recently turned up dead, both shot in the back of the head in a parked car just north of Sunset.

Parker suspected the Dragna crew. He and Hamilton immediately grabbed seven top suspects, including most of Dragna's muscle, and brought them into a suite of rooms they'd reserved at the Ambassador Hotel. (Reporters had staked out police headquarters, which were then located in City Hall, and Parker didn't want news of the interrogation to leak to the press.) For three days and nights, police officers interrogated the suspects, turning over alibis, looking for inconsistencies, bluffing, and threatening the suspects (who were denied sleep and access to their lawyers). As the interrogation progressed, Parker became increasingly confident that Jimmy "The Weasel" Fratianno had been the triggerman. The police even had a witness— an elderly woman who lived across the street from the crime scene. She had seen someone who fit Fratianno's physical description step out of the back-seat of the doomed men's car immediately after the shooting. Parker was elated. There was just one problem—district attorney Ernest Roll. He felt the case against Fratianno was weak.

"The Weasel" had an alibi. A waitress at a café owned by another Dragna associate, Nick Licata, said he'd been in her company the entire night of the killing. Parker thought she was lying.* But when the waitress told the grand jury Roll had reluctantly convened that two detectives had paid her a visit and attempted to persuade her to retract her statement by burning her with cigarettes, Roll declined to proceed with the case. The chief was furious, but Roll was unyielding. There would be no indictment. Parker's effort to bring Rummel's killers to justice had failed. Worse, Parker was beginning to suspect that DA Roll did not share the new police chief's interest in bringing the underworld to heel.

The LAPD proved more pliable.

Parker inherited a department with pressing problems. Los Angeles had added more than 400,000 residents during and after the Second World War, yet the police department numbered just under 4,200 officers. For a city fast approaching a population of two million people, this was a grossly

---

*He was right. After turning state's witness in 1978, Fratianno confessed to killing the two Tonys. (Demoris, *The Last Mafioso,* 54.)

inadequate number. If the department was to maintain order, it would have to do so through the most focused deployment of resources possible.

Parker moved quickly to make the department more efficient. His first act was to simplify the bureaucracy. Divisions such as business, public information, internal affairs, intelligence, and administrative vice were swept into a new bureau of administration. Under the organizational chart he inherited from General Worton, fourteen department and division heads reported directly to the chief. In the new structure, that number was reduced to eight. Parker also created a new division of planning and research, which turned its attention to everything from record-keeping procedures for chronic drunkards to training manuals to deployment patterns. The 1950 annual report epitomized the new spirit. Where previous annual reports had been dull, monochromatic, and light on statistics, Parker's first report was full of color and photographs, clear in its explanation of the department's structure, and full of relevant tables of statistics about the department's activities and about the problems it faced.

Parker's reorganization gave him more time to focus on his top priority—staying in office. There were three threats that particularly worried him. The first was a recall movement aimed at Mayor Bowron and financed by the underworld. The second was an effort at the state level to legalize gambling in California, which Parker feared would corrupt the citizenry and tempt politicians with irresistible pots of money. The third, more amorphous, threat came from political attacks on the department.

Parker realized what many of his predecessors had not—namely, that a police chief's authority ultimately depended on the level of public support he enjoyed. In ousting chiefs Davis, Hohmann, and Horrall, Mayor Bowron had repeatedly demonstrated that when the mayor wanted something, civil service protections counted for very little. Parker was also keenly aware of the fact that the average tenure of the typical LAPD chief was just two years. He was determined to avoid that fate by transforming himself into a politician to be reckoned with.

It was not an easy task. Parker did not have the backslapping personality of the typical politician. His wit was dry; his manner, reserved. He was impatient with fools. The slight Boston accent he acquired during his time in the military added a further touch of hauteur. He often spoke with an angry intensity born of resentment and conviction. But he could also be charming. People respected him—and not just in the police department. Since returning to Los Angeles after the war, Parker had risen steadily in the Fire and Police Protective League and in the American Legion. This bespoke political skills of the first order. As the head of Chief Davis's small public affairs bureau, Parker had worked closely with Davis to build support for the department, hosting lunches at the police academy, providing shooting demonstrations, and courting friends in the business community and the movie colony. He now set about using these skills to protect his new position.

From day one, Parker acted like a politician who would soon be up for re-election. The new chief maintained a frantic public schedule. He accepted almost every invitation to speak and was soon making two speeches a day, followed by another round of speeches in the evening. It was an exhausting pace, one that necessitated many hours in the car. Parker needed a driver. He asked Internal Affairs to choose a suitable candidate from among the Police Academy's recent graduates. The person selected was Daryl Gates.

Gates was the perfect physical specimen of what an LAPD officer should be: five foot, eleven inches tall and two hundred pounds of muscle. (His fellow cadets at the police academy had called him "The Bear.") He'd grown up in Highland Park, a working-class neighborhood northeast of downtown, served in the Navy during the war, returned to L.A., gotten married, and gone to the University of Southern California on the GI Bill. Like young Bill Parker, Gates wanted to be an attorney. But when his wife unexpectedly got pregnant during his senior year at USC, Gates needed a job that would support his family. He saw a job with the LAPD as a sinecure where he could finish his college degree and save some money for law school. Like Bill Parker, he was very sharp. Of the five thousand applicants who took the police entrance test, Gates placed ninth.

On Gates's first day of duty, he reported early to the office of the chief of police. When Parker arrived, Gates failed to recognize him and attempted to block him from entering the chief's office. When it came time to drive Parker back to his home in Silver Lake at the end of the day, Gates scrambled to open the back door for the chief, just as General Worton's driver had done. Parker stepped around him and got into the front seat instead. Now Gates was really nervous. He scrambled back to the driver's seat and settled in behind the wheel of the new Buick Dynaflow that was the chief's official vehicle. But he couldn't find the clutch.

Finally, in an even voice, Parker said, "You've never driven an automatic shift."

"No, sir," Gates conceded, miserably. "I don't have the slightest idea how to drive this car."

"Well, get out," Parker said. The two men switched places, and Parker drove home, with Gates in the passenger seat. He then instructed his new driver to wait there. Parker climbed up the steps and exchanged a few words with Helen. Then he came back down and taught his new driver how to operate an automatic transmission.

No word of reproach was ever uttered.

Fortunately, Daryl Gates was a fast learner, for he soon discovered that there were many evenings when Bill Parker was unable to drive himself home. Parker was a drinker—a heavy one. During the day, he was brilliant and disciplined—"a real iron ass," says Gates. Liquor never passed his lips. But nighttime was different. Out having dinner, after giving his speech, Parker sometimes loosened up and started drinking—and kept drinking. According to Gates, he drank "until his words slurred and stairs became a hazard." Disciplinarian by day, drunkard by night—it was a difficult balancing act. It was also a dangerous one.

In the fall of 1950, the day before Chief Parker was due to testify before the Kefauver Committee in Los Angeles, Captain Hamilton got a tip that the underworld was planning to take out the chief. The rub-out was supposed to happen that very night. That evening, Chief Parker was scheduled to address the Breakfast Club, a prominent business and social group, at its clubhouse in Atwater Village. Coming from downtown, the chief would typically pass through Griffith Park. The hit was supposed to occur on one of its secluded roads.

Parker reacted to the news of the planned hit calmly. Instead of canceling his appearance, he simply instructed Gates to choose a different route. He didn't even leave his wife at home. Instead, Helen sat in the backseat, holding a loaded shotgun. Gates and Parker arrived safely, but even though Hamilton had arranged for extra security at the event, Gates remained antsy. After arriving, scanning the crowd, and seeing no unfamiliar faces, Gates went outside and waited in the car. A few hours later, as things were winding down, Helen Parker came out to the car—without her husband. The minutes passed. Finally, a concerned Gates got out of the car and went to look for the chief. There was no sign of him in the hall. Worry turned to panic. Gates ran outside to alert the extra officers Hamilton had positioned outside the venue. The frantic officers searched the hall—no Parker. Finally, they found him, in a hidden barroom nursing a bourbon.

AS THE KEFAUVER HEARINGS PROGRESSED, the Treasury Department's Bureau of Internal Revenue found itself increasingly embarrassed. Warren Olney's Special Crime Study Commission had documented a striking indifference on the part of the bureau's San Francisco office to the activities of well-known crime figures. Meanwhile, the Kefauver Committee's chief investigator (himself a veteran of Olney's working group) was closing in on Mickey Cohen.

The most incriminating information came from the committee's hearings in Miami, where senators had heard testimony from a West Palm Beach bookmaker/real estate mogul named John O'Rourke. Like other big bookmakers, O'Rourke routinely "laid off" particularly big bets on other bookmakers around the country. He was also a big gambler in his own right. Mickey was a favorite partner. When quizzed about how much business he had done with Cohen, O'Rourke came up with an eye-popping $3 million figure. O'Rourke also told the astonished committee members that he'd lost roughly $80,000 to Cohen, without ever meeting Mickey in person.

When Cohen himself appeared before the committee, he was asked about this $3 million sum. Mickey insisted that the figure was misleading: $3 million was the total sum wagered, not his profit. But that still left $80,000 undeclared gambling profits. Embarrassed by such revelations, in early 1951, the Bureau of Internal Revenue commenced a vigorous investigation into Cohen's finances. A federal grand jury was soon summoning Cohen associates for closed-door hearings.

From the start, Mickey sensed trouble.

Cohen had long maintained that he was a gambler, not a gangster. Now, he told his reporter-acquaintances that he was done with even that. "Everything is going to be legitimate. . . . I'm tired. . . . I want to keep things peaceful," Mickey told the press. Brother Harry reemerged too, informing the press that he'd purchased a drugstore in Tucson and that Mickey was going to manage it. Wife LaVonne was reportedly supportive; the Arizona state pharmacy board was not. There were other signs of divestment too. The Los Angeles newspapers were buzzing with rumors that Mickey was in negotiations to sell his armored Cadillac, first to President Juan Perón of Argentina, then to Mexican President Miguel Alemán Valdés. Mickey was also sighted dining at a Sunset Strip nightclub with the Reverend Billy Graham.

It was no use. On April 6, 1951, Cohen and LaVonne were indicted on charges of allegedly evading $156,000 in income taxes between 1946 and 1948. The maximum penalty faced by the couple was twenty years in the federal penitentiary system. Still, Cohen seemed remarkably confident. On the day of the bail hearing, Mickey showed up without an attorney and, to the chagrin of Asst. U.S. Attorney Ray Kennison, convinced U.S. District Judge William Mathes to set bail at a mere $5,000. A trial date was set for early June. But there was one more spectacle scheduled before then.

Mickey was now hard-pressed for cash. The government had frozen access to the various safety deposit boxes he'd opened (under various aliases) across town. Worse, Mickey had to demonstrate to the court that the money for his defense was coming from legitimate sources. So Cohen sought out Marvin Newman, auctioneer to the stars, who in turn placed an ad in the *Los Angeles Times* trumpeting, "The Year's Most Interesting Auction . . . furnishings from the home of Mr. and Mrs. Mickey Cohen, Nationally Prominent Personality . . ." More than ten thousand people showed up for the preview. The auction itself was something of a dud. Tuffy's mahogany bed sold for just $35.

In truth, Cohen was in desperate shape. Sam Rummel, Cohen's longtime attorney who had delivered him from every previous legal scrape, was dead. Rummel's partner, Vernon Ferguson, was dying of brain cancer. Harry Sackman, Mickey's longtime accountant, had turned state's witness (though he did die suddenly of a [natural] heart attack before the trial began). In short, Cohen was going to trial utterly unprepared.

The trial began on June 4, with the prosecution asserting that it would show that Cohen had spent some $340,000 between 1946 and 1948. To the press, Mickey displayed the old bravado, confidently predicting at the end of the trial's first day that he would "beat the rap." Perhaps he really was confident. But this time, Mickey misunderstood the odds. In previous cases, such as the one recently brought against Cohen and his minions in connection with the beating of the widow-robbing radio repairman Al Pearson, Cohen had been able to present himself as something of a Robin Hood (or plead self-defense). This time, his lavish lifestyle was on trial. To secure a conviction, all the U.S. Attorney's Office had to do was persuade jurors that Cohen had "willfully" avoided paying his taxes.

The prosecution's strategy for doing this was simple: parading witnesses before the grand jury to testify about Cohen's profligate spending in the late 1940s. All told, more than a hundred people were called. Furrier A. Lispey recounted delivering a $3,000 mink and a $2,400 marten cape to LaVonne. A maître d' was brought in to recount a $600 tip. An Italian shoemaker was brought in to tell the jury about how he custom-made "two or three" pairs of shoes a week for Mr. Cohen at a cost of $65 a pair (and up). Bail bondsman Louis Glasser testified that Cohen's house and lot in Brentwood was worth a quarter of a million dollars. John O'Rourke, whose testimony in Miami before the Kefauver Committee had done so much to put Mickey in the feds' crosshairs, was also brought in to testify. He now claimed that Mickey had won between $60,000 and $70,000 from him in the past three years.

Perhaps the hardest to bear of all, though, was the prosecution's final witness—LaVonne's interior decorator. "This woman," Cohen would later rant, "who many claim robbed me of $40,000 or $50,000, got on the stand and finished me off exactly as the prosecution wanted the job done."

At the end of each witness's testimony, prosecutors added to a running chart of Cohen's spending. As the numbers climbed higher—Cohen's spending for 1947 added up to $180,000, a figure considerably higher than the $27,000 declared on his taxes—Mickey could feel the jury turning against him. His new attorneys seemed unable to stop the bleeding. Mickey tried to say that he'd lost large sums to O'Rourke in Miami as well, but O'Rourke denied it. He insisted that he never won more than a thousand dollars or so from Cohen. Attempts to assert that other expenditures had been reimbursed (and thus should not count as expenses that pointed to a large undeclared income) were likewise unsuccessful. Meanwhile, the prosecution produced evidence that Cohen had safety deposit boxes registered under fake names and stuffed with cash all over the city, Prosecutors portrayed them as further evidence of willful tax avoidance. Things were going so poorly for the defense that one day a reporter pulled Cohen aside and asked him if he knew what he was doing. The impression from the gallery, the reporter said, was that Mickey "was being thrown to the lions."

Cohen's mood darkened. His behavior became more erratic. The following day, a bailiff had to restrain Cohen when he lunged toward a Bureau of Internal Revenue agent. At other times, such as when he lingered to autograph copies of his old friend Jimmy Vaus's new book, *Why I Quit . . . Syndicated Crime* (which Mickey had written the preface to), he was the preening Hollywood celebrity.

The smoking gun, however, came in the form of a net worth statement, signed by Mickey himself, that stated he had earned $244,163.15 in taxable income over a three-year period. Cohen felt blindsided. He'd never understood or paid attention to such things. Keeping him clean was Sackman's job. Instead, by getting Mickey to sign this statement, Sackman had virtually ensured a conviction. On June 20, the court reached their verdict. Cohen was found guilty of three charges of income tax evasion and on one charge of falsifying a Bureau of Internal Revenue net worth statement. A sentencing date was set for early July. Cohen's fate was now in Judge Ben Harrison's hands.

Three weeks later, Cohen returned to court. Judge Harrison began his remarks on a remarkably mild note. "Los Angeles must take part of the responsibility for what has happened to [Cohen]," the judge began. "He was permitted to operate here as a betting commissioner with what I think was the virtual acquiescence of law enforcement officials."

The judge then expounded on the "questionable environment" in which the "personable" gambler had been raised. He also noted the many letters he had received testifying to Mickey's good side, prompting the exasperated assistant U.S. attorney to interject that the proceedings risked becoming "a society for the admiration of the good qualities of Mickey Cohen." While acknowledging that Mickey had "been a good son to his mother," the prosecutor reminded the judge that "he is here for the bad things he did."

Judge Harrison shifted course, saying that he saw no prospect of Cohen resisting the temptation of easy money.

Mickey interjected. "Right now, I could go into the drugstore business in Arizona if the authorities hadn't stopped me," he said pleadingly. But Judge Harrison brushed this aside. Instead, he sentenced Cohen to a five-year prison term, to be served at the McNeil Island federal penitentiary off the coast of Washington State in the Puget Sound. He also fined Mickey $40,000 and ordered him to pay the government the $156,000 he owed in back taxes for the years 1946–1948, plus the cost of the trial itself, another $100,000.

Cohen was stunned. It was, he would later claim, "the only crime in my whole life of which I can say I am absolutely innocent."

A request for bail was denied. Instead, Cohen was sent immediately to the county jail. A game of cat and mouse began. Cohen's attorneys filed a series of motions requesting that their client be allowed to post bail pending a decision on his appeals request. In November, a federal judge ordered Cohen released on bail. But before he could be released, prosecutors succeeded in winning an injunction and then in overturning the order. If Cohen wanted to persist in appealing his conviction, he would do so from jail. In an effort to dissuade him from doing so, law enforcement authorities set out to make Cohen's life behind bars as miserable as possible. Federal authorities insisted that Cohen be held in isolation and denied access to any visitors other than LaVonne and his attorneys. Only one exception was made to the no-visitors rule and that was for the Rev. Billy Graham, who stood by the little gangster.

"I am praying that after Mickey Cohen has paid his debt to society, he will give his heart and life to Christ," Graham told *Time* magazine that summer. "He has the making of one of the greatest gospel preachers of all time."

The feds' unsavory strategy to convince Mickey to drop his appeal request should have worked. To someone like Mickey, whose normal routine involved rising around noon, showering for an hour or so, and then changing into fresh (if not *new*) clothes and shoes, imprisonment wasn't just an ordeal; it was torture. At least, it should have been. But the feds had a problem: head jailer Charles Fitzgerald, whom Mickey would later describe as "a very good friend." Fitzgerald was a humanitarian. Under his supervision, Mickey had a way of gaining access to certain indulgences—multiple baths a day instead of just one a week, ready access to a good barber, fresh clothes, and food from outside. Cohen also found ways to exercise his innate talents: Rumor had it that he was running a variety of gambling rackets from the inside.

Eventually, the newspapers got wind of these indulgences and started reporting on Cohen's behind-bars shenanigans. In response, the federal government dispatched an investigator to Los Angeles to tighten controls. Care packages from LaVonne and the multiple baths a day were ended. Greatly stressed, Fitzgerald retired, and a new jailer was appointed. He immediately summoned Cohen to his office and "in a very excited manner that also carried an apologetic tone" informed Mickey that measures would have to be taken to knock down the rumors in the papers. Mickey replied calmly that there was no satisfying the press: If he was put into solitary confinement on the roof, he told his new jailer, some newspaper would surely report it was penthouse living. Little did Mickey know that his life was about to take a turn for the worse.

One day in early 1952, soon after Mickey's awkward interview with the new warden, Cohen was rudely awakened at five in the morning and, without even being given a chance to put on his socks or shoes, brought into the chief jailer's office. There he found the Justice Department representative and two U.S. marshals waiting for him, along with an order to transfer him immediately to the city-run Lincoln Heights Jail. Mickey Cohen was about to enter the domain of Chief William H. Parker.

Cohen was placed in solitary confinement. His cell had no windows or furniture, only a toilet and a concrete slab. No toilet paper was provided. Mickey's request to take a shower was denied. No outside food was permitted. He was not allowed to shave or to see a barber. In order to ensure that no friends on the force did him any favors, Parker and Hamilton instituted rules that barred any officer from interacting with Cohen in any way without having a lieutenant and a third officer present. When his wife, LaVonne, arrived for a visit, she was allowed four minutes—and forced to speak to Cohen through a speaking tube. Even newspapers were restricted, lest someone try to communicate with Mickey through code.

On the fourth day of his confinement, chief U.S. marshal James Boyle came to visit. He professed to be shocked (shocked!) by Cohen's conditions. "Mickey, my God, why don't you let me make arrangements to get you out of here and send you on your way to McNeil Island Penitentiary, where you will at least get some fresh air occasionally and some exercise," Boyle said, with faux sympathy.

Four days in the hands of the LAPD seemed to have done the trick. "I had to get out of the clutches of certain vultures in the LAPD," concluded Cohen. His attorney was summoned and (with a police officer present as a witness), he agreed that if Mickey couldn't take these conditions anymore, he should go ahead and request removal to McNeil Island. So Mickey did so. The next day, on March 13, Cohen was flown to Tacoma to begin serving his federal prison term.

Although their client was absent, Cohen's attorneys went forward with their appeal. It was rejected. Cohen's incarceration was now official. He would be eligible for parole in twenty-two months.

LaVonne escaped conviction, after the prosecution decided to drop their unprecedented attempt to go after a mob spouse for her husband's misdeeds. But Mickey's incarceration left her in a difficult position. His gang had largely been dismantled; his rivals were ascendant; his assets were scattered (or hidden). The guests who had flocked to Mickey's table now drifted away. One of the few people who didn't forget her was Billy Graham. Knowing that LaVonne was probably hard up for money, Graham allegedly arranged for a $5,000 gift to tide her over while Mickey was in prison. He also occasionally sent a car over to pick her up for dinner. On one occasion, soon after he'd had a chance to exchange a few words with Mickey, Graham appealed to LaVonne to turn to the Lord.

"Mickey is in a terrible frame of mind—very bitter, LaVonne," Graham said, consolingly. "Why don't you accept Christianity?"

"I am a Christian girl," said LaVonne. "A Catholic or something—I think."

Graham pressed on, confident, no doubt, that nothing less than a full-scale born again experience would suffice to save the Cohens.

"You have to give your life to the Lord," he insisted.

"The only way I would do that is if Mickey would come with me," LaVonne replied.

So far, at least, he wouldn't. But the ordeal of McNeil Island was still to come.

FOR CHIEF PARKER, the incarceration of Mickey Cohen should have been a moment to savor. But no sooner had Cohen been locked up, than Parker found himself caught in a series of scandals that threatened his job. The first came on October 7, when a police reserve officer shot and killed an unarmed eighteen-year-old college student, James Woodson Henry, whose only apparent offense was sitting in his car late at night. Henry's slaying and the poignant newspaper accounts of his parents' reaction caused a public furor. Parker responded, testily, that he could hardly dispense with the reserves when he was trying to police a city of two million people with a mere 4,189 officers, nearly 2,000 officers short of the police-to-civilian ratio suggested by most policing experts. While this was probably true, the tone of Parker's rejoinder sparked more attacks on the chief. Chastened, Parker decided to strip the reserves of their firearms. That just angered the people who had originally supported him.

L.A.'s African American community was upset with Parker too, thanks to the *California Eagle*'s reporting on an incident of police brutality that it claimed was "unsurpassed by the most vicious in the deep South." The case, which had come to public attention one month earlier, involved twenty-three-year-old George Hunter. Hunter had been waiting for the last Watts car at a Pacific Electric station when a detective allegedly accosted him. After demanding to know why he was there, the detective then insisted that he was drunk. Hunter denied it, but the detective returned with uniformed backup and arrested him. The men shoved him into a small room. There, from 3 a.m. until 7:30 a.m., he was allegedly beaten and slugged unmercifully about the head, face, and body "while being cursed, berated, and reviled with obscene language."

During the course of the beating, Hunter's real offense came out. Wrote the *Eagle* reporter, "Repeatedly, the officer blurted out, 'I'll teach you, whenever you address an officer, to say 'sir.' "[*]

White parents were fearful. The black community was indignant. One major ethnic group remained to be angered—Mexican Americans. But they didn't have to wait long. A barroom brawl between LAPD officers and a handful of young Latino men was about to explode into the greatest crisis of Chief Parker's brief tenure.

---

[*]Complaints from the African American community about disrespectful stops and brutal treatment were so commonplace that the *Los Angeles Tribune*, the city's other leading black paper, sarcastically teased General Worton when he first became chief for taking them seriously: "So naïve is this new chief . . . that he veritably pounced on a police stenographer . . . to make a note of the complaints . . . as if something was going to be done about them!!!" (*Los Angeles Tribune*, July 14, 1949.)

Dragnet

> *"When any function of government, national or local, gets out of civilian control, it becomes totalitarian."*
>
> —*Los Angeles Daily News* editorial, March 4, 1952

THE TROUBLE ARRIVED on Christmas Eve 1951, when police received a call about several young men—possibly minors—drinking a bit too heavily at the Showboat Bar, a little joint on Riverside Drive northeast of downtown. Two officers were dispatched to respond. When they arrived, they found a group of seven young men. Five of the men were Latinos—Danny and Elias Rodela, Raymond Marquez, Manuel Hernandez, and Eddie Nora. The other two—Jack and William Wilson—were Anglos. The officers asked to see some ID. The men produced it. None were underage. Nonetheless, the two police officers asked the men to finish their drinks and disperse. That's when the trouble started.

Exactly what touched off the brawl is unclear. One of the revelers, Jack Wilson, would later say that before he could comply with the officers' request, he was put in a hammerlock and dragged outside. His friends followed. One accosted one of the officers; a melee broke out. Wilson's friends would later claim that the scuffle began when they tried to prevent one of the officers from hitting a member of their party with his blackjack; the police insisted they were attacked when they asked one of the men to leave. Despite making free use of their blackjacks, the police officers got the worst of it. One officer got a black eye when one of the men got him into a headlock and punched him. The fight ended when a neighbor with a rifle broke things up. Meanwhile, someone inside the bar had called the police department for backup.

It was just after 2 a.m., Christmas morning.

From the perspective of law enforcement, assaults on police officers were unacceptable, no matter what the circumstances. So the police went back to look for the assailants. Most were picked up immediately and taken to Central Division for booking. Police kicked in the door of the last drinker involved in the brawl, Danny Rodela, at about 4 a.m. They dragged him out of bed, away from his screaming, pregnant wife, all the while hitting him with a blackjack. Unfortunately, the men who were now in custody weren't the only people who'd been out drinking. So had a great many police officers in the city of Los Angeles.

Christmas was a special holiday for the officers of the LAPD, particularly for those in Central Division. Christmas was tribute day. Dance hall operators, B-girl bar proprietors, and tavern keepers literally put bottles of whiskey out on the corner for their local patrolmen to pick up—an annual ritual of fealty that not even Chief Parker had been able to suppress. Not all of that booze went straight home. A fair amount made its way to an impromptu Christmas party at Central Division. More than a hundred officers were still there, drinking, when rumors started circulating that two officers had gotten roughed up while trying to arrest a group of Mexicans—and that one of the officers had lost an eye. By the time the prisoners were hauled in, an angry mob of officers—more than fifty strong—was ready to teach the prisoners a lesson in respect.

The prisoners were taken into an interrogation room and told to assume a spread-eagled position. Then they were kicked and beaten. The injuries the men suffered speak to the brutality of the police attack. One young man was worked over until his bladder burst. One of the victims was kicked so hard in his temples that his face was partially paralyzed. Another man's cheekbone was smashed. Frenzied officers slipped and slid across the bloody floor, struggling to land a fist or foot on the prisoners. Some even fought with each other. Onlookers yelled "cop killer," "get out of the country," and "Merry Christmas" at the men their fellow officers were pummeling. Between fifteen and fifty officers took part in the attack. Another hundred officers were in the building and had direct knowledge of the assault. When the prisoners were taken to the Lincoln Heights Jail, they were assaulted again. The prisoners were then sent to the Lincoln Heights receiving hospital. Danny Rodela arrived later, when the rumors circulating among the police were even more fantastical. He was beaten so badly that one of his kidneys was punctured. If not for three emergency blood transfusions at the old French hospital, he might well have died. After being treated, the men were returned to jail. Later, on Christmas Day, they were finally bailed out.

No one breathed a word about what had happened. The entire incident might never have come to light but for the beating of Anthony Rios.

Two months after the Christmas beatings, Rios and a friend saw two men, who appeared to be drunk, beating a third man in the parking lot of a café at First and Soto Streets in East Los Angeles. Rios attempted to intervene. The two assailants identified themselves as plainclothes officers. Rios demanded their badge numbers—and was promptly threatened with death. Then Rios and his associate were arrested for interfering with police officers. After being booked at Hollenbeck station, Rios was badly beaten. But the LAPD had messed with the wrong Chicano. Rios was an influential member of the Latino community and a Democratic County Central Committee member. He promptly sued Chief Parker and the department for $150,000. (The case was eventually dismissed.) News of his arrest and mistreatment infuriated newly elected city councilman Edward Roybal, L.A.'s first Latino councilman. Nonetheless, prosecutors in the city attorney's office insisted on prosecuting Rios. As Rios's February 27 trial date approached, other stories about police brutality and misconduct vis-à-vis Latinos began to come to light.

Parker's initial response to the Rios "incident" was ham-handed. First, he dismissed accusations of police brutality as "unwarranted." He warned that unsubstantiated complaints of police brutality were "wrecking the police department." He wouldn't even meet with the department's critics. When Councilman Roybal and a group of concerned citizens sought a meeting with Parker, he referred them to the Police Commission instead. It was in this explosive atmosphere that prosecutors announced plans to bring charges of "battery" and "disturbing the peace" against six of the seven men who had been beaten on Christmas morning by drunken police officers at Central Division station and the Lincoln Heights Jail.

The liberal *Daily News* and the *Mirror*, the Chandler-owned tabloid that competed with Hearst's *Herald-Express*, started digging. They soon located the victims of the attack and presented their account of events of the evening. The jury impaneled to prosecute the case shared these newspapers' skepticism about the official version of events. On March 12, it found only two of the six defendants guilty (on two counts of battery and one of disturbing the peace). From the bench, an irate Judge Joseph Call denounced "lawless law enforcement" and announced that "all the perfume in Arabia" would not be enough to "eliminate the stench" of police brutality. The officers involved in the beating, continued the judge, were in his estimation guilty of "assault, battery, assault with a deadly weapon, and five violations of the penal code."

"The grand jury must end this sort of thing," the judge concluded. "This should be the first order of business. And indictments should be rendered!"

Local Democrats unanimously passed a resolution condemning the "indifference of city officials . . . toward brutal police methods against citizens and minority groups." They also demanded that state attorney general Edmund (Pat) Brown initiate an inquiry into "the person and office of Chief of Police William H. Parker, the Police Commission, and other responsible officials." Stung, Chief Parker responded by announcing that he had "no objection" to a grand jury investigation. He also belatedly appointed a board of inquiry to investigate the allegations and review the report. This did little to appease his critics. On March 14, the Federal Bureau of Investigation announced that at the direction of the Justice Department it was opening an investigation into charges of police brutality against the department.

Belatedly, Parker recognized the magnitude of his problem. He abruptly changed tack. The chief now revealed that at the same time he had been publicly complaining of "unfair accusations," privately, the Bureau of Internal Affairs had been conducting a top-secret, ultrathorough investigation of its own into the beatings. In an unprecedented concession, Parker then turned a 204-page report by Internal Affairs over to the city attorney.

But Parker's story had some strange holes. When he was asked when the department's internal investigation had begun, Parker claimed that Internal Affairs had launched a vigorous investigation on December 27. He neglected to mention that many of the officers involved had in fact refused to talk to Internal Affairs.

On March 18, the county grand jury began its own investigation into the incident. Its discoveries quickly found their way into the press.

"Boys Tell Police Beating," cried the *Citizen-News*'s banner. "Jurors Told of Slugging on Christmas," announced the lead article. "Wild Party by 100 Police Described, Youth Tells of Beating at Police Yule Party," shouted the *Examiner*. Photos of bruised backs, blackened eyes, and smashed noses filled the papers. Jury foreman Raymond Thompson insisted (and DA Roll agreed) that officers who were suspects be summoned in for a lineup so the seven youths could identify their assailants. This was bitter medicine for Parker. The chief was further embarrassed when details of the initial Internal Affairs report leaked out. Its conclusion—"that none of the prisoners was physically abused in the manner alleged, if at all, while in city jail"—seemed hard to square with the photos of the men's injuries or with injuries some police officers suffered that night.

Meanwhile, more reports of police brutality were surfacing. A complement of eighteen G-men had moved into the department, requesting access to files and questioning department officials about other allegations of abuse. Parker bitterly criticized the FBI's investigation, intimating that it was an unwarranted political vendetta orchestrated by local Democrats and the Truman administration. On March 25, Councilman Roybal announced that his office had received more than fifty complaints of police brutality (ranging from "mere slappings-around" to "hospitalization of the victims with internal injuries") in the past three months alone and that he was convinced that many of these complaints had merit. Parker's appearance before the grand jury did little to quiet his critics. One source told the *Daily News* that the chief's testimony was marked by "a tendency to make windy speeches in response to simple questions."

Parker's job was in danger. The *Herald-Express* quoted "well-informed politicians" saying that taking potshots at Parker had become the favorite Los Angeles sport—"They're shooting at him." The *Mirror* insisted that it was "time to get to the bottom of these ugly rumblings of sadism and abuse of authority" (although it also carefully hedged its bets by not entirely dismissing "the possibility that Communist Party liners are fomenting antipolice prejudice"). Other papers noted that the average tenure for an LAPD chief was two years—and that Parker had been in office for nineteen months.

It wasn't just Parker's job that was in danger. So too was the department's ability to function autonomously. The first threat to the power and autonomy of the police chief had come just before Parker was made chief, during the scandalous summer of 1949, when the county grand jury took the logical step of examining how well the Police Commission oversaw the department. Its conclusion was that the Police Commission "is virtually nothing more than a licensing agency and cannot take action against officers." Newspapers such as Hearst's morning *Examiner* also took up the cry against "an autonomous, star-chamber court for the police" and a Police Commission that "has no power whatever in the internal affairs of the department." In time, these demands faded, in part because Parker himself seemed like such a straight arrow. But with what the press now called "Bloody Christmas," the old concerns returned.

Of course, Chief Parker was not without allies. He continued to command support from the city's many Legionnaires, from Los Angeles's Catholic hierarchy, and, now that he was defending it, from the force itself. Defenders pointed to the accomplishments of his traffic bureau, which had reduced vehicular homicides by half in nine years and made Los Angeles the safest big city in the world to drive in. The chamber of commerce applauded his reorganization of the department and the cost-saving innovations of the new research and planning bureau. The *Los Angeles Times* was also warming to the new chief. At a (supposedly) off-the-record meeting of civic and business leaders at the California Club (called so that Chief Parker could present his perspective on the current controversy), Parker complained that the allegations of unchecked police brutality were the result of the liberal *Daily News*'s vendetta against him.

But the most potent defense of the LAPD did not come from the city's business establishment or its dominant newspaper. It came from Hollywood, in the form of a fledgling new television show called *Dragnet*.

DEAD BODIES, distressed dames, and dangerous games. Bombshell blondes and wisecracking private eyes. High heels, handguns, and homicide. Lonely days, rainy nights, and "streets that were dark with something more than night." During the 1920s and '30s, magazines such as *Black Mask*, *Dime Detective*, and *Gun Molls* created a new genre of writing—pulp fiction (so named after the cheap pulp paper on which the magazines were printed). Schlocky and shocking, full of stock characters and lurid tales, the pulps quickly attracted big readerships. Surprisingly, they also attracted gifted writers, among them Dashiell Hammett, Raymond Chandler, and James M. Cain, who, in the 1930s, penned great books that in the 1940s became even greater movies—for example, *The Maltese Falcon*; *Double Indemnity*; *Farewell, My Lovely*; *The Postman Always Rings Twice*. In 1946, French film critic Nino Frank gave this style of filmmaking a name—"film noir."

Then there was the noir radio drama *Pat Novak for Hire*.

Pat Novak took the classic private investigator formula to the nth degree. Set on the San Francisco waterfront, it featured a world-weary boat captain with a weakness for corny quips and a knack for getting involved in other people's affairs. The show's opening lines set the blasé, world-weary tone: "Sure, I'm Pat Novak, for hire . . ." the show began, to the sound of foghorns on the waterfront. Invariably, Novak would agree to investigate a minor case—which led straight to murder. The dialogue was pure camp. Streets were "as deserted as a warm bottle of beer." Dames who "made Cleopatra look like Apple Mary" appeared in Novak's office at dusk, and spoke in voices "hot and sticky—like a furnace full of marshmallows." What made it work was the tremulous, intimate voice of Pat Novak himself—a twenty-six-year-old voice actor named Jack Webb.

Jack Webb had grown up poor, in the Bunker Hill neighborhood of Los Angeles. Early on he developed a passion for jazz and the cinema. During the war, Webb worked as a clerk for the U.S. Army Air Force in Del Rio, Texas (though later press accounts made him a B-26 crew member). Afterward, he married a young singer/actress he'd met at a jazz club before the war, Julie London—*the* Julie London. (During the war, London was a popular pinup girl. None of Webb's comrades believed that the gangly, intense twenty-two-year-old knew her—until he produced a letter.) In 1946, Webb moved to San Francisco and landed a job as a disk jockey at a local ABC-affiliated radio station, KGO. There Webb and his writing partner, Richard

Breen, created *Pat Novak for Hire*. The sensitive yet cynical PI and his extraordinarily kitschy dialogue quickly attracted a loyal following. However, Webb's big break came in 1948, when a Hollywood casting director heard one of Webb's "private-eye plays" and offered him a part in a new Eagle-Lion film, *He Walked by Night* (1948).

Eagle-Lion was a little studio with dreams of becoming the next Warner Bros. *He Walked by Night* was inspired by the recent murder of a California Highway patrolman. The film told the story of the LAPD's efforts to catch the burglar-turned-cop-killer; its highlight was an extended, real-time chase through the streets (and sewers) of Los Angeles. Webb's role was a minor one: He played the part of a technician in the crime investigation lab (in real life, Lt. Lee Jones). However, the movie shaped his career in two critical ways. The first influence was stylistic. *He Walked by Night* began with an opening disclaimer: "The record is set down here factually—as it happened. Only the names are changed—to protect the innocent." Its opening shot was an aerial pan of the city, with a dramatic voice-over: "This is Los Angeles. Our Lady the Queen of the Angels, as the Spanish named her. The fastest growing city in the nation . . ." The film also had a decidedly documentary flavor. It presented its story as one "taken from the files of the detective division." All of these elements would later appear in Jack Webb's most famous creation. The second influence was LAPD Det. Sgt. Marty Wynn, whom Webb met on the set.

Wynn had been provided by the LAPD as a technical advisor to the producers (one of whom, ironically, was Johnny Roselli, the Chicago Outfit's liaison to Hollywood, who had recently been released from the federal penitentiary after a prison sentence was mysteriously commuted). Although Wynn was supposed to instruct the director in the fine points of police procedure, once the filming got under way, he didn't have much to do. Neither did Jack Webb. As a result, both men spent a lot of time in the commissary. There the two fell to talking. When Wynn found out that Webb was a radio actor who played the part of a private eye, he took to teasing him about the silliness of radio programs like *Pat Novak*.

"It makes every cop in the country laugh when they hear this nonsense on the radio," Wynn told Webb. "Why doesn't somebody show how detectives really break a crime?"

Wynn told Webb that he ought to do it right.

"I can arrange for you to have access to cases in the police files," he told the actor. "Maybe you could do something with them."

"I doubt it, Marty," Webb responded, noting that "the fiction shows have such high ratings." But the idea stuck with Webb. In fact, he had recently started sketching out another show about a lonely PI, tentatively titled *Joe*

Friday, Room Five. What if Friday became a police officer instead? The more he thought about it, the more he liked the idea. Several weeks later, Webb called Wynn and told him that he was thinking about starting a new kind of police drama, one that portrayed police work as it really was. Wynn was pleased and, true to his word, arranged for Webb to start spending some time with Wynn and his partner, Vance Brasher.

Webb's hunger for details and verisimilitude was voracious. "How do you frisk a suspect?" "How do you kick in a door?" "How do you clean your gun?" Jack Webb was a question a minute. He was soon spending all his free time at police department headquarters in City Hall. He got permission to start taking classes at the police academy. He was learning what it meant to be a detective.

Now he needed a name. *The Cop* was quickly dismissed as disrespectful. *The Sergeant* was too military. One day during a brainstorming session, writer Herb Ellis and Webb were talking about an earlier radio program, *Calling All Cars,* when Ellis asked Webb, "What do they call it when cops go all out to catch a crook?"

"They put out a dragnet," Webb responded.

That was it. "Dragnet." Now Webb had to find a network that would broadcast his show.

His first choice, CBS, passed. No blondes, no Humphrey Bogart–style Sam Spade, no audience was the network's prediction. Webb disagreed. Authenticity was what would make his show unique. Webb went to NBC. It was desperate for programming, having recently lost prized performers Bing Crosby, Jack Benny, and Amos 'n' Andy to CBS—so desperate it was willing to give a true-to-life police documentary a go. There was just one condition: Webb had to have access to LAPD case files.

This was not necessarily an easy sell. *Pat Novak for Hire* had presented policemen in an almost uniformly bad light. (Nearly every episode featured a dumb, brutal police officer who hinders, threatens, and sometimes beats Novak as he attempts to solve the case.) So it was with some uncertainty that Wynn and Brasher took Webb to meet their captain, Jack Donahoe. They were fortunate in their choice. The good-natured Donahoe agreed to provide case notes to help Webb work up a pilot program that he could present to then-Asst. Chief Joe Reed. Webb was delighted when Reed pronounced the pilot "good and accurate." The show then went to Chief Horrall, who informed Webb "he was on the right track, reflecting the day-to-day drudgery of police work." It wasn't exactly the reaction Webb was hoping for, but it got Webb what he needed—a departmental blessing and access to its case notes. In June 1949, the first episode of radio *Dragnet* went on the air, Friday evening at 10:00 p.m.

From the start, Webb was fanatical about getting the details right. Five soundmen were employed to create a range of more than three hundred special effects. Wherever possible, the program used actual recordings from the department. Soundmen staked out the City Hall garage to capture the roar of police cruisers speeding away; they also recorded the everyday background noise of City Hall. When a script called for a long-distance phone call from Los Angeles to Fountain Green, Utah, sound engineers placed a real call, and recorded the relay clicks and point-to-point operator comments. Terminology was precise and correct. A suggestion to replace "attention all units" with the more dramatic "calling all cars" was brushed aside. Understatement rather than the exaggerated accents, over-the-top sound effects, and histrionic acting that characterized most crime radio programs was the order of the day. The most important part of the new program, though, was its central character, played by Jack Webb himself, Sgt. Joe Friday.

In those days, your typical homicide detective had a very distinctive look. "His suits are not cheap, though they don't always look well pressed," wrote newspaperwoman Agnes Underwood, "and while not loud, would hardly be called dark, conservative business numbers." Their ties, however, "shout like a movie homicide detective."

> If they are foppish about their ties, they are vainer in their searches to turn up the snazziest bands for their wrist watches. . . . The bands are dreams of matinee idols' jewelers: gold stretch, mesh, hand-tooled leather, or carved silver. If one of these lads keeps looking at his watch, he's not worried about the time, he's trying to display his newest bracelet to his associates, even if he has to roll back his shirt cuff to guarantee they'll see it.

There was "nothing sissy about the bracelet competitions," Underwood continued, "for the bands bind brawny wrists, backing up tremendous fists, made more lethal by heavy rings on the third finger of the left hand. That's one reason they don't get beaten up like movie detectives; they know how to use those fists."

Joe Friday (as played by Jack Webb) was different. He was young, tall, and almost painfully slim. (Despite being six feet tall, he weighed a mere 165 pounds, just five pounds over the LAPD's minimum weight.) He dressed casually, in sports coats and a tie, but his demeanor was anything but casual. Friday was an organization man, professional through and through, courteous in his interactions with others, but determined to resolve the case before him. Contrary to the image that later emerged, Friday was not an emotionless automaton. In fact, his most famous phrase, "Just the facts, ma'am," is one he never uttered. Nor was the original Joe Friday

the painfully square detective of the 1960 series who battled "killer reefer."
Dragnet was vérité, like reality TV. At the same time, Joe Friday was the
perfect noir hero, a jaded idealist, strangely single, who walked the mean
streets of Los Angeles but who himself was "neither tarnished nor afraid."

The radio program's success was modest. It had enough listeners to keep
it on the air (it eventually settled in on Thursdays, at 10:30 p.m.) but not
enough to make it a true hit. Nonetheless, its unorthodox depiction of or-
thodox police work attracted avid fans. Police officers were delighted; single
women were enthralled. (Many seemed to view the unattached Friday as a
desirable catch; Webb was deluged with proposals.) *Dragnet* soon picked up
a sponsor, the cigarette company Liggett & Myers, thus ensuring the program's survival. It also attracted the attention of the nation's self-styled
number one lawman, FBI director J. Edgar Hoover.

In *Dragnet*, the bureau saw a new opportunity to burnish its image. So
the FBI spoke to Liggett & Myers. Just a month after it had picked up the
radio program, the cigarette company presented Webb and NBC with an
unexpected demand: Henceforth every program would end with a tribute
to a graduate of the FBI's National Academy.

Webb, NBC, and the LAPD responded by raising hell. Neither Webb
nor NBC liked the idea of a sponsor dictating creative decisions. Moreover,
the FBI's demand missed the point of the show. *Dragnet* was all about the
day-to-day work of an *ordinary* police sergeant. The FBI's National Academy was for high-ranking officers. Honoring only them would offend ordinary patrolmen. Moreover, everyone knew that the FBI already had its
own radio program (*This Is Your F.B.I.*). Rather than provoking a fight
with the bureau, Webb and NBC decided to drop the tribute entirely.

Soon after the tribute disappeared, two agents appeared at NBC's L.A.
studio and demanded to know what had happened to the idea of honoring
an FBI Academy graduate. NBC blamed the LAPD. This was reported directly to Hoover. Worse, the memo to the director stated that the LAPD
was talking trash about the bureau, telling the network that the FBI was
"in bad repute with police departments across the country." The memo
claimed that the LAPD had even threatened to cease cooperating with the
program if the FBI was honored. Hoover was upset. He retaliated by ending FBI participation in LAPD training and refusing to admit LAPD officers to the bureau's prestigious National Academy. Although the alleged
slight to the bureau had occurred before Parker became chief, the freeze extended to Chief Parker's tenure, for reasons that are unclear. When Parker
took office, he did not receive the customary letter of congratulations from
the director.

Whether Parker knew about his department's transgressions or picked up on the terrible snub he had received from Hoover is also unclear. Passing through Washington, D.C., in the fall of 1951, Parker was granted a personal meeting with Hoover. Later, according to the FBI's L.A. special agent in charge (whose responsibilities included relaying all gossip regarding the bureau to FBI headquarters in Washington), the new chief "was very flattering in his expressions toward the Director and for the leadership he provides in law enforcement." But Parker's deference was short lived. He and the LAPD were on the verge of a series of steps that would transform the director's frigidity into outright hostility.

BY 1951, both Webb and NBC were eager to expand the radio program into a new medium—television. That meant winning the support of Bill Parker. At first, Parker was hesitant. Truth be told, he didn't much like Hollywood. The new chief blamed movies like *The Keystone Cops* for propagating an image of policemen as nincompoops. In letters to his wife, Helen, during the Second World War, he complained about having to pay to watch Hollywood films abroad. However, he did appreciate how effective moving pictures could be. During his days at the traffic division, he'd been involved in making informational films intended to educate drivers about how to use the freeways that were beginning to crisscross the basin. He understood the power of the moving picture. But the experience that really brought home to Parker just how powerful an advertisement *Dragnet* had become for the department came when he attended the International Association of Chiefs of Police conference in Miami in the fall of 1951. Everywhere he went, people addressed him as "Friday."

Still, Parker hesitated. A radio program was one thing. A television show was another. It was hard to imagine one that would live up to his own high vision for the department. But Webb was ardent in making his case—and explicit in his promises. The department would review every script. Essentially, Parker would serve as a senior producer for the show. Total commitment to the highest ideals of police professionalism would be the program's goal. Eventually Parker relented and gave Webb permission to shoot the pilot in City Hall. The episode was pulled from one of the most dramatic radio programs, "The Case of the Human Bomb." Webb was not allowed to use the LAPD's modern badge, the Series 6, though. Instead, he was restricted to the old Eagle badge—in case things went wrong.

The episode aired on Sunday, December 16, 1951. First came the famous music: *dum-da-dum-dum*. Pause. *Dum-da-dum-dum-DUM*. Then, as a picture of an LAPD sergeant's badge filled the screen, the voice-over: "Ladies and gentlemen, the story you are about to see is true. The names have been changed to protect the innocent." Several bars of music followed, then an aerial image of Los Angeles filled the screen—and the voice of Sgt. Joe Friday filled the air. "This is the city . . . Two million people. In my job, you get a chance to meet them all. I'm a cop." (How Webb managed to use the word "cop," which Parker strongly objected to, is unclear.) Parker was pleased by the dramatic story, in which Webb disarmed a bomber bent on toppling City Hall. The critics were impressed too. The *New York Times* praised the show's "terseness and understatement." Other critics hailed "the leisurely camera work, the restrained acting, and the crisp, sparing dialogue." Said the *Hollywood Reporter*, "Just about everything good that can be said about a TV film show can be said about *Dragnet*. This series is going to do more to raise the rest of the country's opinion of Los Angeles than any other show of any kind." Webb was given permission to start using the department's modern badge.

On January 3, 1952, *Dragnet* began appearing every other Thursday night on NBC. The radio drama continued as well, growing in popularity as the television show got established. To help review Webb's various and growing productions for accuracy, Parker reached down to one of the officers in his public relations bureau, Gene Roddenberry, who was paid $25 per script. Roddenberry was soon writing freelance scripts of his own for shows like *Mr. District Attorney* while also helping Chief Parker with his speeches. Then, just as *Dragnet*'s first run of fourteen episodes was coming to an end, the Bloody Christmas scandal broke. The people of Los Angeles were about to experience a serious case of cognitive dissonance. Which was the truer face of the LAPD: the carefully controlled professionalism of Sgt. Joe Friday, or the brutal realities of the Lincoln Heights Jail on a drunken Christmas Eve night?

Parker's initial response to the crisis—attack the department's critics and claim that the police department was the real victim—had been clumsy. One of the reasons for Parker's ambivalent response may well have been his own sense of personal responsibility. The commanding officer at Central Division whom investigators would later fault for the violence was Lt. Harry Fremont. Deputy Chief Harold Sullivan, who at the time headed the LAPD's patrol bureau, had resisted putting Fremont into Central Division, warning that he "was a good detective but a drunk." Sullivan even went so far as to put his reservations in writing. Parker ignored the warning. Yet in the aftermath of the beating, it was Sullivan who got transferred. Fortunately for Parker, Sullivan never breathed a word of what had happened.

Soon after his ill-received first appearance before the county grand jury, Parker changed tack. By the end of March, the newspapers were reporting that Internal Affairs was assisting the grand jury in its probe. Parker was also hinting broadly that the department might discipline officers even before the grand jury completed its investigation. Although he continued to speak out powerfully—even provocatively—in defense of the force, Parker now had a new goal: to show that no one could investigate the police department as thoroughly as the police department itself. In short, Sergeant Friday was on the job. He delivered on these promises. In the spring of 1952, the grand jury indicted eight officers on charges of "assault with force likely to do great bodily harm." Ultimately four officers were given prison sentences, a fifth officer was fined, and three officers were acquitted.

Parker went further. He ordered the transfer of fifty-four police officers with connections to Bloody Christmas, including two deputy chiefs, two inspectors, four captains, five lieutenants, and six sergeants. Another thirty-three officers were suspended, many based on evidence inadmissible in court. As it became clear that the police department was conducting a massive purge, what pressure there was to oust Parker and reform Section 202 abated. The chief still handled criticism poorly. When in their final report the grand jury faulted Parker for conditions in the jail, he couldn't resist issuing a furious retort, prompting columnist Florabel Muir and the editorial board of the *Examiner* to chide the chief for failing to acknowledge the department's foot-dragging in the matter. But the criticism now seemed a minor one. The opportunity to remove the chief from office for malfeasance, in accordance with civil service protections, was closing. Parker was determined that it would never open again.

DRAGNET wasn't the only television program that went on the air in 1952 and profoundly influenced the Los Angeles Police Department's self-image. In April 1952, just months after the first airing of *Dragnet*, another show appeared that was arguably equally influential—even though it aired on KNBH, the local NBC station, for only a few months—*The Thin Blue Line*. The title referred to a famous incident during the 1854 Crimean War when the British Army's 93rd Highland regiment—drawn up only two lines deep rather than the customary four—routed a Russian cavalry force of 2,500 men. The producer—and star—was none other than Chief William H. Parker.

The purpose of *The Thin Blue Line* was unabashedly propagandistic—to counter "current attempts to undermine public confidence in the Police Department" and "instill greater confidence in the police service." Although Parker recognized the need "to bring to the audience the type of information in which they are interested," the show he had in mind was no

Dragnet. Rather, *The Thin Blue Line* featured a panel of experts (almost always including Chief Parker himself) and a moderator, supplied by the studio. Even in 1952, this seemed a bit dull. After only five months, KNBH (which had always seen the program as public service programming, not compelling entertainment) pulled the plug on the broadcast. Nonetheless, *The Thin Blue Line* was enormously important—not as a television show, but as a metaphor. The notion that the police was all that stood between society and the void, between order and chaos, between "Americanism" and communism, was thrilling—but also treacherous. In this worldview, civilians were corrupt, weak. ("The American people are like children as far as gambling is concerned—they must be kept away from this temptation," Parker told the *Herald-Express* in October, when asked to comment on a ballot initiative that would bring Nevada-style legalized gambling to California.) Organized crime furthered this corruption and, by doing so, threatened the nation's very survival.

"Soviet Russia believes that the United States contains within itself the seeds of its own destruction, to wit: avarice, greed, and corruption," declared Parker in one often-quoted speech. "Russia believes we are rewriting the history of the decline and fall of the Roman Empire, another nation that became great and collapsed from its internal weakness."

Parker believed that a great conflict had commenced with Soviet Russia. War was already under way in Korea. To prevail in this conflict, the United States would need the virtues of Sparta, not the indulgences of the Sunset Strip. In short, Mickey Cohen and his ilk weren't just criminals. They were the unwitting agents of international communism. Police officers were thus on the front lines of protecting civilization itself.

In this vital role, Parker wanted only the very best. The 4,100-officer department was, virtually everyone agreed, terribly short staffed. Both the International Association of Chiefs of Police and the International City Managers Association believed that a ratio of three officers per thousand residents was the absolute minimum for a force capable of securing an urban area. The city of Los Angeles and its two million residents had just two police officers per thousand residents. To meet IACP standards, Los Angeles would need a minimum of two thousand new police officers. Yet the department couldn't even fill existing vacancies.

Parker thought the primary problem was low pay and the low social status of police officers. Others thought the problem had more to do with the department's standards. The notoriously subpar force of the 1920s had became an elite group by the 1950s. Parker seemed to take pride in the fact that less than 7 percent of the men who passed the civil service examination made it to the academy—and that only a fifth of those made it through the thirteen-week course. The Los Angeles Police Department had a reputation as "the West Point of police training," and Bill Parker liked it that way. His men were smart (with a minimum IQ of 110) and physically imposing (with a minimum height requirement of five feet, nine inches for men). Just as many who wanted the toughest, most challenging military assignments opted for the Marine Corps, so too were proud, aggressive officers drawn to the LAPD. Of course, they had to be. Doing the work of six thousand with just over four thousand placed unusual demands on the force. The LAPD had to be bigger, faster, more efficient, tougher.

One generation earlier, Berkeley police superintendent August Vollmer had dreamt of a professional police force whose members would not just uphold the law, but would also assess neighborhood problems like sociologists and address them like social workers. Parker had no interest in doing social work. "Law enforcement officers are neither equipped nor authorized to deal with broad social problems," he declared. "[W]e deal with effects, not causes." Eschatology interested him more than sociology. He wanted men who, like the Spartans at Thermopylae, would hold "the thin blue line until society came to its senses."

DRAGNET'S success rankled FBI director J. Edgar Hoover. So did Parker's carping about the FBI's temerity in investigating his department for potential civil rights violations. But irritation turned to anger when Parker informed "Kit" Carson, the special-agent-in-charge (SAC) of the L.A. office, that he intended to push for a resolution supporting a national clearinghouse for information on organized crime at the upcoming conference of the International Association of Chiefs of Police. Parker also informed Carson that he planned to put his name forward as a candidate for the vice presidency of the IACP, a fact Carson promptly relayed to Hoover, along with the SAC's personal assessment of Parker as "an opportunist of the first order." This was too much for Hoover. Parker's clearinghouse could become a rival to the bureau. Parker himself looked suspiciously like a rival to the director. Hoover's instructions to his underlings were clear: All SACs should contact their friends in the local law enforcement community to sabotage Parker's campaign. Parker's election attempt was soundly defeated.

Hoover was determined to monitor the threat posed by Parker. Instructions went out to the Los Angeles SAC to watch Parker closely. Washington was soon informed that Parker "was often drinking to excess and had the reputation of being obstinate and pugnacious when under the influence of alcohol." Scrawled Hoover on the bottom of one such memo, "I have no use for this fellow Parker and we should keep our guard up in all dealings with him. H."

Parker had acquired a dangerous enemy. But the Los Angeles chief of police was too preoccupied with another adversary to notice.

The Trojan Horse

"You should always have a positive side to your program and ACCENTUATE it, but likewise you should use SUBTLE FEAR."

—Cong. Norris Poulson, on how to win public office

BILL PARKER wasn't willing to tolerate Communists in city government, period. Mayor Fletcher Bowron apparently was. Ironically, the two men's disagreement on the issue of how deeply authorities should pry into individuals' political beliefs would create precisely what both men dreaded most—an opportunity for the underworld to "open" Los Angeles.

The issue was public housing. During (and immediately after) the war, Los Angeles faced an acute housing shortage. In 1949, Congress responded by passing an act authorizing the construction of more than 800,000 public housing units. Mayor Bowron sought a sizable share for Los Angeles. That summer, the city council unanimously approved a contract between the city's housing authority and the federal government that provided for the construction of 10,000 units. But public sentiment then started to change. As the housing shortage eased, the need for federally subsidized housing seemed less pressing—and more antithetical to the principle of private ownership. In 1950, Los Angeles's conservative business community, led by the *Los Angeles Times* and the chamber of commerce, persuaded the city council to overturn rent control. "Socialist housing," as they described it, was a natural next target.

A narrow majority of the city council fell in line. On December 26, 1951, by a vote of 8–7, the city council passed a resolution that directed the city housing agency to halt construction on the public housing units it had already started building. An exasperated Mayor Bowron refused, noting that work had already begun, millions of dollars had been spent, and that a contract with the federal government had already been signed. Bowron offered to renegotiate the agreement and, if necessary, reduce the number of units; however, he refused to stop work entirely. His conservative opponents responded by announcing an anti–public housing referendum for the summer of 1952.

Bowron had the law on his side. In the spring of 1952, the California Supreme Court ruled that the city council "had no right or power to rescind approval of the project or to cancel or abrogate the agreements." In late May, the state attorney general announced that in light of the Supreme Court's ruling, the anti–public housing referendum, Proposition B, would be invalid, void, and have no force or effect. Still, Bowron recognized that he had a political problem. He attempted to organize a closed-door colloquium with supporters and opponents of public housing alike to reach some consensus on the issue. But the mayor's attempts at conciliation were dashed by the release of an LAPD report (requested by the conservative chamber of commerce) that depicted public housing as a breeding ground for juvenile delinquents. Furious, Mayor Bowron accused Parker of delivering "one of the most misleading reports ever issued in my administration."

"There is nothing about a public housing project," the mayor insisted, "which inherently breeds crime."

Angelenos apparently disagreed. In June, city residents voted against public housing—379,050 "no's" versus 258,777 "yeses." Most politicians would have gotten the message. Not Mayor Bowron. Instead, in a radio address after the election, Bowron questioned whether the electorate "read and understood the question." This condescending response allowed the *Times* to accuse the mayor of "saying that the public was so dumb . . . it didn't know what it was voting about."

Bowron pressed ahead. He now proposed to build 7,000 units. Opponents responded with an explosive charge, claiming that Communists had infiltrated the Los Angeles housing authority. In particular, councilman Ed Davenport alleged that the housing authority's number two official, Frank Wilkinson, was a member of the Communist Party. The source of the information was the LAPD.

The charge emerged from a lawsuit involving a small parcel of property just north of downtown with striking views of the city, called Chávez Ravine. The city was proposing to evict a small group of private landowners in order to build public housing. Angry landowners responded by filing a lawsuit. During the trial, someone slipped an attorney for the plaintiffs an LAPD file that linked Wilkinson to the Communist Party. The accusation was a startling one. Wilkinson was the son of Dr. A. M. Wilkinson, a prominent civic activist who had worked closely with Mayor Bowron in the 1930s. The younger Wilkinson had taken loyalty oaths disavowing any connections to the Communist Party on numerous occasions. This time, however, he refused to answer questions about the subject.

Bowron had no interest in launching what he saw as a witch hunt into the background of a good friend's son. Wilkinson was a capable public official. That was enough. Morally, this may have been admirable. Politically, it proved disastrous.

By 1952, Fletcher Bowron had been mayor of Los Angeles for fourteen years. When he first became mayor, he had enjoyed support from both the left and the right. As the years passed, however, Bowron had drifted ever closer to the more conservative business community. But this had not won him their gratitude. Bowron was still his own man, as the dispute over public housing clearly showed. The business establishment wanted someone more pliable. They now resolved to put a wholly dependable ally into the mayor's office.

In December 1952, *Times* publisher Norman Chandler and Pacific Mutual Insurance president Asa Call summoned Los Angeles's business elite to a strategy session on the top floor of the *Times* building. Among the group invited were lawyers Frank Doherty and James Beebe of O'Melveny & Myers and business leaders Neil Petree, Henry Duque, and Preston Hotchkis. The top item on their agenda was choosing a new mayor. Thirty-four names were up for discussion, but when the group got to the sixteenth, everyone agreed that they had found their man. Congressman Norris Poulson was an accountant, a dyed-in-the-wool conservative who'd done yeoman's duty in Congress blocking Arizona's efforts to secure a larger allotment of water from the Colorado River. The day after Christmas, Norman Chandler called Poulson at his home in Washington and informed the congressman that a group of civic leaders wanted to draft him to run for mayor. Chandler invited Poulson to Los Angeles so that Poulson could hear their pitch. A follow-up letter described the details of their offer. In addition to promising to bankroll Poulson's campaign "generously," Chandler's letter noted that the mayor's salary was likely to be increased and that Poulson as mayor would be "entitled to strut around in a car (Cadillac) and chauffeur supplied by the city." Although Poulson privately admitted that he "knew very little about the immediate problems of Los Angeles," except for the public housing issue (which, of course, he opposed), he quickly agreed to sign on for the race. *Times* reporter Carlton Williams took charge of launching the congressman as a candidate.

Despite Parker's disagreement with Bowron on public housing and Communists in city government, Parker valued the mayor's dogged commitment to keeping Los Angeles "closed" to the underworld. Parker knew little about Poulson. So he assigned the intelligence division to investigate him. The LAPD quickly uncovered an unsettling connection to Moscow. Soon after arriving in Los Angeles for his meeting with Chandler and his associates, the intelligence division reported, Poulson had checked into a hotel and met with Joe Aidlin, a young attorney with left-wing credentials who had attracted the attention of the House Un-American Activities Committee (HUAC). Although Aidlin and Poulson had very different political leanings, in 1950 Poulson had sponsored private legislation to prevent the deportation of one of Aidlin's clients to Russia. He had also stepped in to spare an Aidlin client an appearance before HUAC. The following Christmas, Aidlin had given Poulson a small "liquor refrigerator"—price $157.35—from the Hecht's department store. Poulson also seems to have realized that accepting this gift made him vulnerable. Soon after agreeing to run for mayor, he sent Aidlin a check for the refrigerator. When he came to Los Angeles to meet with Chandler, he arranged to see Aidlin in order to explain why he was paying for this gift. What Poulson didn't know was that the LAPD's intelligence division had bugged Poulson's hotel room and was listening in.

No sooner had Poulson returned to D.C., than news of the "Red" refrigerator broke. Specifically, Poulson stood accused of protecting a suspected Communist from having to testify before HUAC in exchange for "a valuable electric refrigerator." Armed with his canceled checks that showed he had paid for the refrigerator (and bolstered by supportive coverage from the *Times* and the Hearst papers), Poulson rode the scandal out. However, his troubles with the LAPD had only begun. Several weeks later, Poulson was approached by an athletic young man (a plainclothes detective) who asked the candidate what he would do about the police department if elected.

"I just casually reached over and touched a microphone which I detected pushing out from his shirt," Poulson recounted in his unpublished memoirs. Then he walked away.

The realization that the LAPD was investigating him angered Poulson. But as the campaign progressed, Poulson's anger toward Parker was modulated by the growing realization that Chief Parker had a point: The "hoodlum element" that Mayor Bowron and Chief Parker constantly warned about was real.

This realization came slowly. First, Poulson picked up on the fact that there was a deep antipathy toward Chief William Parker in many parts of the community. "I met many, many Democrats and I noticed that they were very anti-Parker," recollected Poulson. This seemed to be particularly true of the Eastside Jewish community. Poulson's most important backer there was the newspaper publisher Sam Gach, a former Shaw associate who was also reputed to be a close personal friend of Mickey Cohen. In meetings with Poulson, Gach and associates frequently brought up the subject of Chief Parker.

"They would say that they did not want to see the city 'opened up,' but Parker and his 'Gestapo' should be controlled," recalled Poulson. At first Poulson wholeheartedly agreed. After all, he didn't like the LAPD's tough tactics either. But as the weeks passed, Poulson became increasingly uncomfortable with the drift of these discussions and the people who engaged in them. Some seemed very like "the hoodlum element" that Parker and Bowron so often inveighed against. It seemed clear what these people really wanted was a commitment to replace Parker and appoint a more "friendly" Police Commission. In a hard-fought campaign, Poulson wasn't ready to reject their support, particularly "when I wasn't positive what they represented." However, he did decide—"within myself"—that if elected he would run a clean city.

As the campaign proceeded, Poulson grew increasingly concerned about the unsavory characters flocking to his campaign. The fact that he found himself mingling with the likes of District Attorney Ernest Roll and his wife in such mixed company did nothing to allay his concerns. It was highly worrisome to find the county DA associating with such dubious characters. Poulson also discovered that there was an anti-Parker clique within the police department, just as Mickey Cohen had alleged. On one occasion, Gach took Poulson to the offices of a former LAPD captain who had hung out a shingle in Beverly Hills as an attorney. His specialty was defending officers (and others) against Parker's "Gestapo" (presumably the department's Bureau of Internal Affairs). There Gach collected a check for $1,200 for pro-Poulson newspaper advertisements and campaign work. The attorney in question (whom Poulson was surprised to see surrounded by four or five uniformed officers) informed the candidate that all he wanted was "a fair deal." Naturally, Poulson agreed to provide that. Then he took the check and fled.

Los Angeles has a nonpartisan election system that requires mayoral candidates to win an outright majority in order to become mayor. As a result, mayoral elections are generally a two-step affair: the primary typically narrows the race to two candidates and then a runoff determines the winner. In April 1953, Poulson defeated Mayor Bowron in the primaries, winning 211,000 votes to Bowron's 178,000. Bowron tried to put a game face on this loss, insisting that he had saved "his best ammunition for the finals." With Screen Actors Guild president Ronald Reagan at his side, Bowron lashed out against the "the Mammon of First Street" (i.e., Norman Chandler) and "the small group of people who control a vast commercial, financial, agricultural and industrial empire.

"Norman Chandler should run for mayor himself," Bowron asserted, before pausing to note that neither Chandler nor many of his coconspirators even lived in Los Angeles. (Chandler lived in Sierra Madre. Beebe and Hotchkis lived in San Marino.)

But even Ronald Reagan couldn't save Fletcher Bowron. Mammon retaliated, to devastating effect. Its point of attack was Mayor Bowron's alleged softness on communism. Its weapon was Chief William Parker.

On May 18—exactly one week before the general election—the House Subcommittee on Government Operations announced that it would be coming to Los Angeles to hold two days of hearings into how Communists had infiltrated the city's housing authority. Democratic members of the committee protested this brazen attempt to influence the election—to no avail. Republican congressman Clare Hoffman insisted he knew nothing about local elections and pressed ahead. The hearings were broadcast on local TV. Three former employees who had refused to answer questions about their potential membership in the Communist Party on an earlier occasion were summoned to repeat the performance for the cameras. The star witness, though, was Parker. After carefully noting that he was appearing at this sensitive time only because the committee had subpoenaed him, Parker proceeded to relate how in early 1952 he had given Mayor Bowron dossiers on ten housing agency figures with radical connections, including a dossier on Frank Wilkinson. At the committee's instruction, Parker then read the confidential dossier in its entirety. Bowron, he told the committee, had simply thrown the dossier out.

Parker's testimony was extremely damaging to the mayor. But Congressman Poulson wasn't exactly reveling in what looked increasingly like an approaching victory, for as the odds of an upset grew, the underworld became even more overt in its overtures. A former city councilman whom Poulson knew well, Roy Hampton, approached the candidate to offer him "an enormous campaign fund" if he would "pledge to appoint a friendly Police Commission and get rid of Parker." Again, Poulson begged off, promising only to "investigate this situation thoroughly."

Just days before the election, Poulson went to breakfast with someone he would later identify only as "a former deputy district attorney and now the vice president of a Los Angeles and nationally known institution." When he arrived, the candidate was startled to find the shady ex-LAPD-captain-turned-attorney and a well-known "Las Vegas gambling man" waiting for him. As he sat down to breakfast, Poulson was "really scared." The men got right to it: They offered Poulson $35,000 if he would agree to name three men to the five-member Police Commission. Poulson tried to stall. The men then insisted that "I go out and talk in the gambler's car."

Even though he suspected that he was being maneuvered into a "bugged" car, Poulson was too frightened to refuse.

"I talked in circles," Poulson wrote in his memoirs. A few days later, on April 7, Poulson defeated Bowron, 53 to 47 percent, and became Los Angeles's next mayor. Yet as Poulson left the Gaylord Hotel downtown to go to his campaign headquarters to celebrate his victory, he was "filled with mixed emotions." Thoughts of Cadillacs, chauffeurs, and a nice raise seemed far away. Poulson now had to worry about how he could avoid "opening up the town" in light of the fact that "some of the people who had supported me thought I would." Some of these people were very rough. Poulson had to decide whether he would face them with Chief Parker and his intelligence division or without them.

The Magna Carta of the Criminal

"The voice of the criminal, the Communist, and the self-appointed defender of civil liberties cries out for more and more restrictions upon police authority."

—Chief William Parker

POLICE TACTICS WERE TOUGH.

In early 1952, Chicago Outfit bosses Tony ("Joe Batters" aka "Big Tuna") Accardo and Sam Giancana decided to pay a visit to Johnny Roselli in Los Angeles en route to a vacation in Las Vegas. Accardo was well aware of the LAPD intelligence division's practice of reviewing passenger manifests so that it could intercept suspected gangsters. As a result, he took the precaution of booking his ticket as "Mr. S. Mann." Giancana booked a separate ticket as "Michael Mancuso" and avoided any interaction with Accardo on the flight. But when the two underworld figures (and Accardo's doctor) arrived, the LAPD's airport squad quickly identified the Chicago Mob bosses. Accardo and his associates left the airport with a police tail.

Accardo's party proceeded to Perino's restaurant on Wilshire Boulevard in Beverly Hills, Los Angeles's poshest dining establishment. There the men passed a pleasant meal under the watchful eye of a contingent of plainclothes policemen. As the men were finishing their meal, Lt. W. C. Hull stepped up to the table and ordered the men to produce identification. They did. The police then frisked the men, removing $12,000 in cash, at which point they were driven back to the airport and put on the next flight to Las Vegas.

The men who had stalked Accardo and Giancana came from Capt. James Hamilton's intelligence division. Its two watch lieutenants, seven sergeants, and twenty-six patrolmen (and women) conducted operations of remarkable scope. One team of officers worked full time on background checks, reviewing credit reports, bank account information, utility bills, and the like in order to monitor underworld attempts to infiltrate legitimate businesses. Another team specialized in electronic surveillance. (Olney's commission said only that "a considerable amount of information is obtained in this manner.") A three-man airport unit, manned by officers chosen for their ability to memorize hundreds of mug shots of gangsters from across the country, monitored Los Angeles International Airport twenty hours a day. It was this unit that spotted Accardo and Giancana.

Visiting gangsters were sent packing, with no regard for legal niceties. Hoodlums who were L.A. residents, such as Cohen henchmen Frank and Joe Sica, were tracked constantly by two-man teams of officers. These officers were not subtle. Indeed, the department openly stated "this scrutiny may at times border on harassment and [be aimed at] driving the subject hoodlum from our jurisdiction." The police wanted people to know they were being watched; they wanted the bad guys to feel uncomfortable. They also wanted associates of criminals to feel uncomfortable. Intelligence division officers routinely visited businessmen and casual acquaintances of known hoodlums and asked them to prove that *they* weren't involved in underworld activities by ending the relationships. The goal was to make it difficult and unpleasant for the subject of surveillance to meet with others, transact business, or have friends.

The intelligence division was also the unit that was watching mayor-elect Norris Poulson.

At first, Poulson sympathized with those who railed against Parker's "secret police." But after getting a firsthand look at the underworld, he was more understanding of police tactics. His own experiences had left him with no doubt that the underworld was actively attempting to regain control of Los Angeles. Nonetheless, Parker's black-hat operations were disturbing. No target was off limits. Indeed, soon after Parker took office, conservative councilman Ed Davenport was enraged to find two policemen hiding in a closet listening in on a meeting Davenport was having with some businessmen constituents. Local politicians saw the unit as Parker's Praetorian guard. So did Parker himself. In a letter to a priest who had written to request details about the unit, Parker openly explained that one of the division's missions was to protect the chief from political attack. In addition to "exceptional traits of characters," Parker wrote that officers who hoped to be assigned to intelligence had to be "trustworthy to the Office of the Chief of Police." The reason Parker provided for this extraordinary requirement was an interesting one: "While such loyalty to the Office might be interpreted by some to be of a personal nature"—as indeed it clearly was—"we believe such loyalty to be to the integrity of the department." Loyalty to Parker had become tantamount to police integrity.

Then there were the intelligence division files. The division maintained an alphabetical master card file "on all persons who have been brought to our attention." The protocol was precise: 5×8 card with name, physical description, photo, address, phone number, description and license of car, friends, activities, and associations. These cards were then cross-indexed with the general criminal files. Fed by the intelligence division's investigations and by a clipping service that monitored twenty newspapers across the country, the files grew quickly. How quickly was a closely held secret. No judge could subpoena these files. No Police Commission could review them, for, in another extraordinary decision, Chief Parker had ruled that these were not actually official police files. Rather, they were the personal property of the chief of police.

The potential for the abuse of power was obvious—indeed, Poulson himself had experienced it during his mayoral campaign. Yet far from expressing contrition, Chief Parker seemed to take pleasure in dropping hints about just how much he knew. "In my conversations with him," Poulson would later recall, "he would inadvertently tell what he knew about this person or that. . . . I later found out that Chief Parker had a file on MANY PEOPLE and not all communist suspects." Indeed, Parker continued to keep Poulson under surveillance, even after he became mayor. In most cities, this alone would have been a firing offense. But Parker was protected by several formidable defenses. The first was the legal defenses he had drafted in the thirties. As the liberal *Daily News* noted, Parker's 1930s reforms meant that the Police Commission "can't hire unless there is a vacancy and it can't create a vacancy unless there is grave cause and then only after a hearing." The second was his department's growing reputation as—in policing expert O. W. Wilson's constantly cited phrase—"the county's best big city police department." Just weeks before the Poulson-Bowron runoff election, the Governor's Commission on Organized Crime had issued a report praising the LAPD for its success in keeping eastern gangsters out. (It warned that they were resettling in Palm Springs instead.) Tangling with a chief whose work was garnering such accolades carried big political risks.

There was a third reason to keep Parker in office as well: fear. Los Angeles was rife with rumors that gamblers and racketeers had already "cut the town up." Poulson knew from personal experience that these rumors had some basis in fact. Firing Chief Parker would have been tantamount to inviting the underworld interests who had so frightened the mayor during his campaign to open shop in Los Angeles. Poulson viewed Parker as an admirable law enforcement officer but a "cold-blooded, self-centered individual." Ultimately, though, Poulson feared the Mob more than his chief of police. Chief Parker, announced Poulson a few weeks before his swearing in, would stay.

"Chief Parker is to remain on the job on the basis of what he does from now on," Poulson pointedly told the *Los Angeles Times*. "It will be up to the

Chief to produce and to prove to the new Police Commission—and to me—that he is the proper man to remain at the head of the Police Department."

Although he had concluded that firing Parker was simply too dangerous (politically and personally), Poulson was determined to restrain him. The mayor's strategy for doing this was to appoint a Police Commission that "would not kowtow to Chief Parker but at the same time would support a clean city and law enforcement." Since Bowron's appointees had resigned, Poulson had a chance to appoint all five police commissioners. To head the commission, Poulson turned to his top assistant, attorney Jack Irwin. Other members included John Ferraro, a former USC All-American football star who was the son-in-law of state Sen. George Luckey, one of Poulson's major Democratic backers. He also added Michael Kohn, a prominent Jewish lawyer, and Herbert Greenwood, an African American attorney who had worked in the U.S. Attorney's Office. One member of the old commission, Emmett McGaughey, a former G-man-turned-advertising executive (who was also in Poulson's church), agreed to stay on.

The message Poulson intended to send was clear: A new, more assertive Police Commission was taking over. But Poulson's stern tone and high-powered appointments didn't obscure an even more important fact: Chief Parker had just become the first police chief since 1913 to survive a change in administration. By not selecting his own candidate to be Los Angeles's top cop, Poulson was in effect conceding that his police chief was too valuable to lose. The LAPD had just taken a huge step toward the kind of autonomy Bill Parker had long dreamed of.

Parker's enemies warned the new mayor that he was making a mistake. Two weeks after Poulson was sworn in, former Police Commission member Hugh Irey published a two-part open letter to the new mayor in the *Los Angeles Mirror*. Its purpose, in the author's words, was to present "irrefutable facts to show that it is physically impossible for the Police Commission—under the present system—to be more than a figurehead for the Chief of Police." Irey described Parker as "probably the most powerful official in the city." He insisted that his goal was not to attack Parker, whom he described as a man of integrity, but rather to offer a critique of a flawed system. But Irey did paint a disturbing portrait of the police department under the new chief. He called attention to the chief's $85,000 "secret service fund." He described how the commission was powerless to conduct its own investigation into brutality cases, lacking even the authority to review the material used by the chief to formulate the report he presented to the board on any given incident. In conclusion, Irey called for full-time, paid commissioners, with investigators drawn from the detectives' bureau (which unlike the three other plainclothes units—Internal Affairs, intelligence, and administrative vice—did not work directly under Parker's personal supervision).

"Until these recommendations . . . are put into effect the Los Angeles Police Commission will continue to be a mere figurehead and rubber stamp for the Chief of Police—one of the most powerful and autocratic officials in the city," warned Irey.

Parker just scoffed.

"I've told the Police Commissioners repeatedly that anytime three of them are against me to let me know and I'll retire," he replied.

This was disingenuous. No Police Commission would ever act against the mayor on such an important issue, and Mayor Poulson had made it clear that he could not do without Parker. Irey's warnings were ignored. No changes were made to the organization of the commission. The department would continue to be run as Parker's personal fiefdom. Local observers marveled at Parker's triumph.

"Hardly anyone likes Parker, a contentious, abrasive individual who will never give Dale Carnegie lessons on 'How to Win Friends and Influence People,'" wrote the *Los Angeles Daily News*. Yet Parker had achieved something that his predecessors had not. He had become irreplaceable.

POULSON HOPED that his Police Commission would be able to restrain Chief Parker. But the limitations of the commission's structure and the dependencies on the department it fostered soon reasserted themselves. The commission met just one afternoon a week, typically for no more than an hour and a half. Most of its meetings were devoted to humdrum licensing tasks, okaying requests for parades, licensing pawnshops, vetting requests by churches to hold rummage sales, approving applications for dance halls. Its only staff were police department personnel. On those occasions when it did take up larger, policing issues, it relied on the police for guidance. Not surprisingly, the course of action it elected to pursue was almost always the one the department itself would have chosen.

If those weren't constraints enough, Chief Parker set out to actively win over the Police Commission's most important member, former Poulson campaign manager Jack Irwin. By the end of his first year in office, Irwin was routinely siding with Chief Parker over his old friend the mayor. Poulson would later blame Parker for wrecking his friendship with Irwin. Slowly, Chief Parker was gaining the upper hand.

■ ■ ■

POULSON STRUGGLED in his dealings with the chief. Parker prided himself on his analytic approach to problems, but Poulson found him to be a volatile and unpredictable partner. At times, Parker seemed to accept that the city's elected officials had an important role in governing the department, as in setting salaries. At other times, even the most basic attempts by Mayor Poulson to guide the department would set Parker off. In the spring of 1954, for instance, Mayor Poulson (an accountant by training) and City Administrative Officer Samuel Leask decided to take a close look at Parker's budget request for the coming year. In doing so, Leask discovered that 750 officers were working at clerical and office tasks that seemed to require no special policing skills. Another 56 officers were guarding 200 low-risk chronic drunks at the Bouquet Valley police farm, a facility commonly known as the dude ranch. Transferring those officers to the field would dramatically increase the number of cops on the street without altering the standards Parker insisted had provided the city with the world's greatest police force. Surely, some of the other officers could be diverted to more arduous work as well, Poulson and Leask reasoned.

But when Leask presented the idea to Parker, the chief reacted angrily. It wasn't so much the substance of the idea that annoyed Parker. Over the course of the preceding two years, Parker himself had released 109 officers for fieldwork by hiring civilian substitutes. Rather, Parker objected to the idea that Sam Leask—a man who knew nothing about policing—could swoop in and find inefficiencies that Parker had missed. At a public meeting on the police department's budget chaired by the mayor, Parker made no attempt to conceal his pique. The chief repeatedly interrupted Leask's attempts to present his analysis, going so far as to inform the astonished mayor that the management and budget of the police department were "his [meaning Parker's] own business." Parker's behavior was so boorish that Mayor Poulson, who was chairing the meeting, finally stepped in and asked Parker to let Leask speak.

Parker exploded, shouting, as he jabbed his finger at the city's chief elected official, that he would not be "intimidated" by the mayor. He even threatened to resign.

Mayor Poulson was astonished.

"You talk like you're offended and that we have no right to ask you how your department functions and how the taxpayers' money is spent," Poulson told Parker. "You immediately get angry. You talk like we were sticking our nose into something that wasn't our business. It is our business and there's no use you getting red in the face."

It was classic Parker. The chief prided himself on being rational and fact-driven; he often described critics as "emotional" or "hysterical." But in fact, Parker himself was a highly emotional man whose responses to "attacks" (real or perceived) were often more than a little hysterical. Eventually, Parker calmed down. However, he continued to resist the mayor's dictates. In the years that followed, Parker allowed the percentage of civilian employees in the department to rise only incrementally, from 23.3 percent to 25 percent.

This policy of resistance came at a high cost. Tight budgets, high standards, and attrition continued to take a terrible toll on the department. In a memo to the Police Commission in the spring of 1954, Parker noted that in July 1955 the department would have 4,453 sworn personnel—roughly the same number of officers the department had when he had become chief of police in August 1950. Yet during this same period, Los Angeles had added more than 120,000 new residents. The city was growing; its police department was not.

So far, the consequences of this situation had been minimal. Despite the comparatively small size of the LAPD, Los Angeles's crime rate remained slightly lower than in other big cities. However, crime was growing fast—faster even than the city's population. Yet while Parker desperately wanted more officers, he rejected the idea that the police had any connection to the crime rate.

"You can blame the situation on your police if you wish," he told the city council during an appearance in late 1953. "You can lay it in their laps, if you want to. Blame them even for social problems over which they have little control. . . . But let's be practical and realistic. The police do not create crime problems. . . . Nothing is solved by hysteria."

"I wish that crime were a simple plague to be solved by isolating a troublesome microbe, but it is not," Parker declared in a 1953 speech on crime and belief. "I wish it could be eliminated materialistically, by continually supplying Americans with chrome fixtures, softer beds, and shorter work hours, but I know that it cannot be thus eradicated. Certainly I do wish that the police had it within their power to solve the problem alone, but I know that they cannot." Only by restoring the citizenry's belief in the sanctity of the law could chaos be avoided, he concluded.

Parker's speeches called his audiences to a sterner morality. But the chief's worldview was fatalistic, and his analysis of society's problems discouraged practical responses. It was one thing to argue that the police weren't responsible for the increase in crime. But Parker seemed to be suggesting that neither police efforts nor any "materialistic" initiatives could address the rise in crime. Politically, this was a convenient proposition for everyone. It allowed Parker to avoid questions about why what was supposedly the nation's best police force was presiding over such dramatic increases in crime, and it allowed politicians to avoid raising taxes to expand a department run by a man many of them distrusted. It was easier to flatter the chief for creating the country's greatest police force, one that could do more with less.

But of course, Parker still faced the challenge of policing a growing city with a stagnant police force. The key to doing more with less was intelligence. Intelligence kept the underworld from buying politicians, corrupting police officers, and controlling the police department. Intelligence was the key to taking the fight to the underworld, and in the mid-1950s, the underworld seemed to be the locus of serious crime in Los Angeles. But the department's ability to collect intelligence was about to suffer a series of blows from an unexpected and formidable adversary—the courts.

FOR DECADES, police departments had enjoyed wide latitude in how they went about apprehending criminal suspects. In 1914, the U.S. Supreme Court had ruled that evidence improperly or illegally obtained could not be used at trial—a principle known today as the exclusionary rule. But the exclusionary rule applied only to federal law enforcement agencies. For local law enforcement, the proof was in the pudding. If the evidence was incriminating, courts typically asked few questions about how it was obtained. Only the most flagrant examples of police misconduct could bestir most judges to exclude evidence. The result was corner-cutting. Civil liberties advocate Hugh Manes would later note that between 1931 and 1962, the LAPD served only 631 search warrants, about 20 a year, a shockingly low number. Police routinely responded to truly serious crimes by throwing dragnets around entire neighborhoods and "tossing" hotels, motels, and even private homes in search of potential suspects. Yet in its 1949 decision *Wolf v. Colorado*, the court reiterated its opinion that the exclusionary rule did *not* apply to local law enforcement agencies.

Of course, not every method was legal. Federal statutes prohibited wiretapping, as did California state law. The prohibition was absolute: No provision was provided for law enforcement agencies to seek court permission to tap a phone line. Parker understandably viewed this as a major problem. But the department did have a work-around; it simply broke into people's homes and businesses and installed dictographs. The police department reasoned that since these were stand-alone recording devices that did not involve "tapping" a phone line, they were legal, end of story. The courts agreed—until November 1953, when the U.S. Supreme Court took up the case of *Irvine v. California*.

The case involved a suspected bookmaker (Irvine) who'd been targeted by the Long Beach Police Department. Officers had brought in a locksmith to make copies of the man's house keys, entered his house, and then installed a dictograph in his bedroom closet—all without a search warrant. The evidence obtained from the "bug" was the basis of the man's subsequent conviction. During his first trial in state court, the bookmaker had argued that by breaking into his house without a warrant, police had violated his Fourth Amendment rights to be safe from unreasonable search and seizure. The state court disagreed, as did the state appeals court. So Irvine petitioned the U.S. Supreme Court to take the case, successfully.

On February 8, 1954, the Supreme Court handed down its ruling. It noted that repeatedly entering the petitioner's home without a warrant "was a trespass and probably a burglary." The majority opinion described dictographs as "frightening instruments of surveillance and invasion of privacy, whether [used] by the policeman, the blackmailer, or the busybody.

"That officers of the law would break and enter a home, secrete such a device, even in a bedroom, and listen to the conversation of the occupants for over a month would be almost incredible if it were not admitted," the majority continued. "Few police measures have come to our attention that more flagrantly, deliberately, and persistently violated the fundamental principle declared by the Fourth Amendment as a restriction on the Federal Government." But the court nonetheless concluded that this restriction was one that applied only to the federal government.

"[I]n a prosecution in a State Court for a State crime, the Fourth Amendment does not forbid the admission of evidence obtained by an unreasonable search and seizure," wrote Justice Robert Jackson in the 5–4 majority decision. As a result, the court declined to overturn the conviction. However, in what Earl Warren biographer Jim Newton describes as the "extraordinary" final paragraph of the opinion, Justice Jackson and Chief Justice Warren took the highly unusual step of noting that federal law allowed for the prosecution of police officers who, acting under color of authority, willfully deprived a person of a federal right such as the right to be secure in one's home. The two justices then directed the court clerk to forward a copy of the record in this case, together with a copy of this opinion, to the U.S. attorney general for possible prosecution.

Parker was dumbfounded—and outraged. The highest court in the land had essentially described one of the most valuable tools in law enforcement—the dictograph—as something evil. In Parker's opinion, this description was incorrect and, in light of dictographs' long history as useful law enforcement tools, bizarre.

"Since the advent of appropriate electronic devices, the police of this state have utilized such devices to gather information and evidence concerning criminal activities," Parker responded three months later, in a speech at the Biltmore Hotel marking National Crime Prevention Week. He insisted that they did so in ways that were tightly controlled. Section 6539(h) of the California Penal Code allowed dictographs only when expressly authorized by the head of a police force or by the district attorney. The evidence thus obtained, Parker insisted, had been invaluable in the department's fight against organized crime:

> A reputed overlord of crime in this area is now serving a term in a federal prison as a result of a prosecution in which information obtained through the use of dictographic equipment contributed materially. Two reputed members of the Mafia, who escaped federal prosecution for narcotic violations when a key witness against them was found murdered, were recently convicted of crimes in the courts of this state based upon evidence obtained through a dictograph installation. The reputed head of the local Mafia is now awaiting deportation, largely as the result of a local conviction obtained through the use of a dictographic installation. One such installation alone aided our department in solving forty-three serious crimes.

If anything, Parker continued, California's total ban on wiretapping was too restrictive. Attempts by Parker and other chiefs to create a mechanism that would allow them to ask a court for permission to intercept telegraphs and tap telephones based on probable cause had stalled in the legislature, creating what Parker described in one speech as providing "a Yalu river sanctuary within the vast telegraphic and telephonic communications network of the United States within which to plan and transact their illegal activities with impunity." Parker's allusion—a reference to the river redoubt from which the Chinese Army had attacked U.S. forces during the Korean War—could hardly have been more pointed.

The position of Justice Jackson and Chief Justice Earl Warren must have been particularly galling. As California's attorney general, Warren had not hesitated to brush aside legalistic objections in his pursuit of justice (most notably, when he personally directed a police raid on Tony Cornero's gambling ship, the SS *Rex*, despite a court ruling that it was operating outside of California's territorial waters). Yet now, as chief justice of the U.S. Supreme Court, Warren seemed intent on imposing unprecedented new restrictions on law enforcement. The timing, in Parker's opinion, was terrible. Between 1950 and 1953, the LAPD had actually become smaller as Los Angeles grew. The city's crime rate was growing at an ever faster rate—a trend Parker described to the city council as "a very frightening thing." Yet instead of giving the police greater power, the judiciary was imposing new restrictions. Parker believed that by criticizing the use of dictographs (which have "solved countless serious crimes"), the court was raising the prospect that police officers might be prosecuted for what had long been standard operating procedure. In one speech, he asked his audience to consider the officer who responded to a call and saw a house-wife, prone on the floor, a probable suicide attempt at death's very door. Any officer worth his salt would kick in the door and race the woman to the hospital to pump her stomach. Was this to be treated now as trespass-ing, kidnapping, and rape?

"Certainly society cannot expect the police to risk criminal prosecution when their only sin is the valid enforcement of the law as they have been led to understand the law," Parker concluded.

This was a sensitive—and not entirely hypothetical—subject for Parker. For by his third year as chief, he himself had emerged as a major target of lawsuits. The first had come after the Bloody Christmas beating. More seri-ous was a 1951 lawsuit filed by civil rights attorney A. L. Wirin, lead attor-ney for the Southern California Civil Liberties Union. Since both the state and federal court systems were as yet unprepared to exclude evidence gath-ered illegally by local police departments, Wirin sought to shut down the LAPD's surveillance activities in another fashion—by enjoining the police department from using public money to illegally install dictographs. Parker once again detected the hand of Moscow. At a hearing, he blurted out his suspicions that the Minsk-born Wirin (whose initials stood for "Abraham Lincoln") was a Communist.

Wirin's attempts to rein in the LAPD's surveillance operations attracted broad sympathy—not least from the city's elected officials. That spring, two councilmen, Harold Harby and Ernest Debs, discovered that their work telephones had been wiretapped. Both pointed at the police. Parker vehe-mently denied the allegation, blaming the underworld instead. Given the history of wiretapping in City Hall, many doubted this denial. Just two days after the councilmen had accused the department of illegally listening in, the *Los Angeles Times* reported that the new police administration build-ing nearing completion around the corner from City Hall was chockablock with bugs and listening devices. This provided little reassurance to the city's already fearful political establishment.

Chief Parker was determined to defend—and expand—his surveillance tools. To do so, he turned to the television show *Dragnet*. By 1954, *Dragnet* had become the second most popular television show in the country (after *I Love Lucy*). The radio version (which now aired Sunday nights) also contin-ued to attract a large audience. NBC was eager to create a feature film–length version of the show. The LAPD was prepared to offer Jack Webb a particularly juicy case file to serve as the basis of the script—one that involved a spectacular gang murder—but it came with a catch. The case was solved only after the police turned to extreme tactics, including near-constant police harassment and constant surveillance. Webb accepted the deal. As a result, audiences were treated to a movie with an unusual hero—the LAPD intelligence division. With its assistance (and a skillfully placed bug), Webb cracked the case of a gangland hit—only to run into trouble in the courtroom. There, after underworld witnesses refused to testify, Friday expresses his frustration at being unable to use a wiretap too.

A female juror objects. "How do we know that all you policemen wouldn't be running around listening to all our conversations?" she asks.

"We would if you talked murder," Friday snaps back.

Even Parker supporters, such as the in-house publication of the archdiocese of Los Angeles, *The Tidings*, were somewhat disconcerted by the film's depiction of harsh police tactics. But Parker insisted that such misgivings were misinformed.

"Far from being a threat to our freedom," Parker wrote in the pages of the *California Law Review* the following spring, "the use of modern technological devices by the police may well be their most powerful tool in combating our internal enemies, and a vital necessity in the protection of our nation's security, harmony, and internal well-being."

In addition to trying to win public support for less restrictive wiretapping laws, Parker also sought broader legal protections for his officers. In the fall of 1954, Parker kicked off a campaign to persuade allies in the state legislature to pass a law shielding law enforcement officers from the threat of criminal prosecution or civil lawsuits for actions taken in the routine course of their work. But just weeks after Parker floated this proposal, state attorney general Pat Brown made an announcement that preempted Parker's efforts. Brown suggested that local district attorneys henceforth consider prosecuting police officers who broke into citizens' homes to install dictographs without a court order. Then, on April 27, 1955, the California Supreme Court suddenly and unexpectedly issued a ruling that threatened to destroy what Parker had so carefully built.

The case of *Cahan v. California* bore a striking resemblance to *Irvine*. This time it was the LAPD that had broken into the property of a suspected bookmaker, thirty-one-year-old Charlie Cahan. He was a big-time bookie, with a clearinghouse near the Coliseum, an elaborate call-back system to avoid police detection, and a network of backup "spots" across the city where debtors could place bets in person. The LAPD estimated that he was handling about $6 million a year, and his lifestyle showed it. According to an LAPD intelligence dossier, Cahan had "concubines, liquor by the case, a lavish penthouse, Cadillacs." Cahan had emerged from nowhere and become an important player virtually overnight. Many assumed he was paying for police protection. He wasn't. On the contrary, Chief Parker had instructed the intelligence division in no uncertain terms that he wanted "this son of a bitch in jail."

So the intelligence division sent a man disguised as a termite inspector into the building housing Cahan's accountants to install a dictograph. The recordings secured a conviction, and Cahan was fined $2,000, sentenced to nine days in prison, and given a five-year-probation. Cahan appealed the decision. An appeals court rejected it, but when Cahan took his case to the California Supreme Court, it was accepted. A narrow 4–3 majority threw out Cahan's conviction.

"We have been compelled to [void the conviction and impose new evidentiary guidelines] because other remedies have completely failed to secure compliance with constitutional provisions on the part of police officers," wrote Justice Roger Traynor in the majority opinion. He continued, "The courts under the old rule have been constantly required to participate in, and in effect condone, the lawless activities of law enforcement."

Traynor served notice that such practices were now coming to an end. The court struck down a California law that allowed courts to accept evidence, regardless of the manner in which it was obtained. Henceforth evidence improperly acquired would be thrown out—period. This was a fairly extreme remedy. Few other states imposed the exclusionary rule in such a blanket fashion. But the court insisted that the stakes justified such a draconian remedy.

"Today one of the foremost concerns is the police state," declared Justice Traynor bluntly. "Recent history has demonstrated all too clearly how short the step is from lawless although efficient enforcement of the law to the stamping out of human rights."

Parker's reaction was apoplectic. He described the ruling as "a terrible blow to efficient law enforcement" and warned that the decision "will probably set law enforcement back fifty years."

"The positive implication drawn from the *Cahan* case is that activities of the police are a greater social menace than are the activities of the criminal," he told the press. "This, even as a suggestion, is terrifying." State assistant attorney general Clarence Linn agreed, calling the ruling "the Magna Carta of the criminal." In a meeting with the *Mirror*, the chief revealed that in the month following the *Cahan* decision, arrests had plummeted across the board: bookmaking arrests, down 42 percent; narcotics, down 38 percent; weapons, down 20 percent. A headline in the *Mirror-News* captured the chief's sentiments perfectly: "Criminals Laugh at L.A. Police, Says Chief. Underworld Rejoices in Ruling."

Cahan offended Parker on many levels. As an attorney, he believed the ruling was ill considered and flew in the face of the doctrine of *stare decisis*, which held that courts should generally stand by earlier decisions. As a lawman, he found it insulting. But the new restrictions imposed by the courts on the police also worried Parker for a more immediate reason. For on October 9, 1955, after three years, eight months, and sixteen days in the joint, Mickey Cohen walked out of prison a free man.

The Enemy Within

"He is intent on being a respectable member of society as a senatorial nominee on getting elected. The odds are three to one that Mickey Cohen, if not stopped by a bullet, will wind up a Rotarian.'"

—Ben Hecht

WHEN MICKEY COHEN stepped off the ferry from McNeil Island at the little town of Steilacoom, near Tacoma, the press was waiting. Mickey didn't seem surprised. Even after three years in prison, he accepted press attention as his due. In fact, Cohen seemed more relaxed—and more chatty—than ever before. When asked what his next plans were, Mickey indicated that he was leaning toward opening a bar and grill, "maybe in Beverly Hills or the Miracle Mile"—this despite the fact that Cohen still owed Uncle Sam $156,123. In fact, he told the assembled press, he and a few partners had already hired an architect to draw up plans. The news was instantly telegraphed to L.A., where official reaction was not long in coming.

"There is not a chance that anyone with Cohen's record would be given a liquor license," declared Phil Davis, the Southern California liquor administrator for the state board of equalization. "I can't say he would be very welcome in Beverly Hills," agreed Beverly Hills police chief Clinton Anderson. The Los Angeles City Council voted en masse against a liquor license for Cohen, despite the fact that the city council had no say in such matters. As for Chief Parker, he suspected that Mickey's restaurant was nothing but a sham. When a reporter asked the chief if Parker had any plans to put Cohen under surveillance, he replied tersely, "The German army didn't come over and tell their plans to the Allies."

When talking to the press, Cohen projected a jaunty self-confidence. But to those who knew him well, Mickey seemed changed. Despite his long history of violence, both in the ring and on the street, he appeared to have been badly shaken by his experiences in prison.

"When I was on the Island, I saw things I couldn't believe myself. And

I thought I'd seen everything," Mickey said later. One night in particular had driven home the brutality and indifference of prison authorities:

> The middle of the night, a fella a couple of cells down starts screamin'. I call the guard and we go together to see what's the matter with the guy. The light in his cell don't turn on and the guard has to use a flashlight. The screamer is lying in a pool of blood two inches deep. When the guard investigates he discovers that this guy was trying to give himself some fun by sticking an electric light bulb up his behind. In the middle of his enjoyment the glove had busted. . . .

More startling, even, than this was what happened next: After being treated at the infirmary, the man "got a black mark for destroying government property."

Cohen was determined never to return to prison again. His aversion to further incarceration was so great that Mickey was prepared to take a desperate step: He would go straight. He decided to start by doing something that for an unlettered gangster was remarkable: He would write a book. Of course, as someone who was basically illiterate, Mickey couldn't really do this on his own. Fortunately for Cohen, Hollywood's most famous screenwriter was about to come calling.

SEVERAL MONTHS AFTER Mickey's return to Los Angeles, the screenwriter Ben Hecht was talking with the director Otto Preminger. Hecht was Hollywood's most successful screenwriter, the person responsible for such films as *Scarface* (the first gangster movie), *The Front Page* (based on his days as a newspaperman in Chicago), *Gone with the Wind* (an uncredited rewrite), *His Girl Friday*, *Spellbound*, and *Notorious*. Preminger was an Austrian Jewish émigré with a deep interest in abnormal psychology and crime. (His father had been the equivalent of the U.S. attorney general during the final years of the Austro-Hungarian Empire.) His breakout hit was the 1944 noir thriller *Laura*, which told the story of a detective investigating the slaying of a beautiful young woman who had been murdered despite—or because of—her ability to make men love her. As the investigation progressed, the detective himself fell under her spell. *Laura's* success made Preminger one of the top directors in Hollywood. In 1955, he had begun work on another noir drama, *The Man with the Golden Arm*. Based on the novel by Nelson Algren, the film told the story of a heroin addict (Frank Sinatra) with dreams of big band greatness. The aspiring drummer gets clean in prison, but after his release, he encounters two old temptations, heroin and Kim Novak. (He succumbs to one.) Hecht was helping Preminger with the screenplay. Although Preminger was not unfamiliar with the American underworld—he was, among other things, the lover of the world-famous striptease artist Gypsy Rose Lee—it still wasn't his native idiom. One day, Hecht realized that he knew someone who could provide Preminger with just the right sort of color—Mickey Cohen.

It took a while to find Cohen. The haberdashery was long since closed. The Moreno manse in Brentwood had been sold. The papers had reported LaVonne's new address in West Los Angeles—a nice apartment just off Santa Monica Boulevard near the Fox back lot (today's Century City)—but Cohen wasn't living there. Eventually, Hecht tracked him down at the Westwood Motor Inn, Mickey's temporary work address. Cohen suggested that Hecht stop by his apartment for a visit.

On the appointed day, Hecht arrived at a small, nondescript apartment building. The only outward sign of Cohen's residency within was a gleaming new Cadillac ("as luxurious and roomy as a hearse," thought Hecht). When Hecht arrived, Mickey was in the shower. It was his third of the day.* Hecht knew this could take a while, so he looked around. The apartment was tiny—"so small it was almost impossible to walk swiftly in it without bumping into the walls"—but tastefully (indeed, professionally) decorated (albeit in a "bourgeois" fashion). It was also crammed with luxury items.

"There are thirty pressed and spotless suits crowded in the closet, all in tan shades," jotted Hecht in his notebooks. "Twenty-five Chinese, Japanese, and Persian robes of silk hang there and thirty-five pairs of glistening shoes stand on the floor, neatly."

Finally, Mickey himself appeared—"nude, dressed only in green socks held up by maroon garters." He seemed lost in thought, scarcely bothering to acknowledge Hecht. Instead, he put on a new Panama hat and wandered about the small room, powdering himself with talcum, washing his hands, and looking for the perfect suit. Every twenty minutes or so, Mickey would dash over to the phone, place a call, and proceed to have a lengthy cryptic conversation "devoid of proper names." (Cohen was convinced—no doubt correctly—that his phones were tapped.) Two hours later, the two men left for dinner at Fred Sica's place.

Hecht was fascinated by Cohen's odd behavior. But Mickey soon did something that was even more surprising. He started talking. When Hecht had first met Cohen in 1947 at Hecht's home in Oceanside, Cohen had been "a calm, staring man in a dapper pastel suit." He had conveyed an

---

*Mickey's demands on the building's hot water heater were a major source of contention with the management. At his old house in Brentwood, Cohen had installed a special water heater designed for a motel. Because even that proved inadequate, Mickey had his plumber install a *hotel*-sized hot water heater instead.

unmistakable air of menace (only slightly offset by his ice-cream-and-French-pastry-fueled pudginess). In those days, Mickey sometimes went for days without saying a word.

Not anymore. The postprison Cohen was a conversationalist, at least when the mood came over him. When Hecht brought Preminger over to meet the notorious gangster, Cohen freely recounted stories of his underworld days, explaining the intricacies of the bookie business. In the process, Mickey greatly confused the director, who mistook one of Mickey's bookmaking phrases, "laying a horse" (which simply means wagering that a certain horse will lose), for a sexual act. (After the meeting, Preminger reportedly turned to Hecht and declared, "My God! Why would you take me to meet a man who lays horses?!") Mickey had even begun work on a book about his life. When he showed it to Hecht, the Oscar-winning screenwriter was astonished. Cohen's work in progress was actually pretty good. Never before had Hecht seen the criminal mind bared so openly and artlessly. But Cohen wasn't just interested in reliving his glory days. His goal, he told Hecht, was nothing less than redemption.

"I'm a different man than the wild hot Jew kid who started stickin' up joints in Cleveland, who lived from heist to heist in Chicago and Los Angeles," he told Hecht.

"What changed you?" Hecht asked.

"First, common sense," Cohen replied. "Then I wanted the respect of people—not just people in the underworld." However, the deepest change was more visceral: "I lost the crazy heat in my head," he told Hecht, "even though I seen enough dirty crooked double-crosses to keep me mad for a hundred years."

Mickey assured Hecht that he was now determined to go straight. Indeed, he had already picked a new profession. He had become a florist.

Mickey insisted that he had returned to Los Angeles "stone broke." But soon after his homecoming, Cohen somehow became the proprietor of a chain of greenhouses, with headquarters at 1402 Exposition Avenue near Normandie. Exposition Avenue was a long way from Mickey's old haunts on Sunset, but Cohen did his best to display the old razzle-dazzle, renaming the chain Michael's Greenhouses and telling the papers that he was "chucking the rackets for tropical foliage." Among his first visitors were the officers of the LAPD intelligence squad. To its officers, Mickey confided the "real" reason he had gone into the business. Exotic flowers, he told the officers, was "a tremendous racket . . . out of this world."

LaVonne thought Mickey had finally gone crazy. One month after Michael's Greenhouses came into existence, she filed for divorce. Cohen was understanding. "LaVonne had married a dashing, colorful rough-tough hoodlum and when I came home she found me quite a bit different," he piously informed the press. Cohen's parole officers seemed to believe in Cohen's reformation. There was just one problem: No one had much use for a gangster who had been scared straight.

"When I was a gangster like those characters in the movies, I tell you everybody admired me, including even the press," Mickey told Hecht one night. "Now look at the situation. . . . [S]ince I came home"—Cohen's preferred euphemism for getting out of jail—"the general public including the newspapers have been actin' sour at me, as if they were sore at my having reformed and bein' now a law abiding citizen.

"So help me, it's unusual. I ask myself, 'Can it be that the public prefers the type of person I was to the type of citizen I am now?' "

Mickey already knew the answer to that question. Of course they did.

One night after midnight, as Hecht sat at Cohen's table at one of the nightclubs he frequented nearly every evening, Hecht realized what Cohen had become. "It is a *gilgul* I'm sitting with"—a soul suspended between the stages of reincarnation. "Life won't let him in. A desperate Mickey is at the cafe table—not Mickey, the gun-flourishing heister, but a lonely knocker at the door."

Chief Parker would have none of it. Cohen was a hoodlum through and through. If Mickey thought tropical plants were a "tremendous racket," they probably were. Parker wanted every angle covered. Make sure Cohen's not strong-arming people into buying exotic tropical plants, Parker told the intelligence division. The chief's suspicions proved well founded: Several restaurateurs and bar owners confidentially informed the squad that Mickey had demanded that they pay $1,000 a month to rent a plastic fern—or else. Parker made it clear that he wanted Hamilton's men to watch every move Mickey made.

The LAPD wasn't the only law enforcement outfit tracking Cohen. So were agents from the Treasury Department. Mickey had resolutely refused to pay the federal government any of the back taxes he owed. He justified his inaction by claiming to be broke. When questioned about his new Cadillac and his lavish wardrobe, Cohen replied blandly that he enjoyed only what his friends gave (or loaned) him. Given Cohen's history of extortion, this seemed more than a little suspicious. So FBI headquarters instructed the Los Angeles office to put Cohen under surveillance. In short order, Cohen had a discreet complement of G-men with him on his nocturnal nightclub outings. What they witnessed confirmed the bureau's suspicions. Cohen, they reported, was routinely dropping $200 or $300 a night and generally spending money at a rate that only the most lucrative greenhouse in the world could provide.

The LAPD intelligence division was likewise uncovering evidence that Cohen was less reformed than he was letting on to his friend Ben Hecht. One source informed the division that Mickey was attempting to strong-arm a local linen business. The LAPD also heard rumors that Cohen, along with his old pal the great lightweight boxer Art "Golden Boy" Aragon, was fixing fights. LaVonne even called off the divorce and got back together with Mickey. Everything pointed to a full-fledged return to the life of crime.

IN THE FALL OF 1956, the LAPD gained another ally in its fight against organized crime: the thirty-year-old chief counsel of the Senate sub-committee on investigations, Robert Kennedy.

By 1956, the Kennedys were one of America's best-known families. Bobby's maternal grandfather, John F. ("Honey Fitz") Fitzgerald, had been mayor of Boston, as well as a congressman. Father Joseph was one of the country's most powerful businessmen, a prominent Wall Street investment banker, ex-ambassador to the Court of St. James, a former movie magnate (and Gloria Swanson's lover), and a high-end bootlegger. The oldest son, Joe Jr., whom Joe Sr. had been grooming for the presidency, had been killed during the Second World War; in 1946, the Navy had recognized his sacrifice by naming a destroyer after him. His brother Jack had stepped in and commenced on a remarkable rise to prominence. His Harvard College thesis, *While England Slept*, was published and became a best-selling book. During the war, he served on a PT boat. When it was cut in half by a Japanese destroyer, Lieutenant Kennedy kept his head and saved most of his men, a feat of bravery that won him a Navy and Marine Corps Medal (and a front-page story in the the *New York Times*). In 1946, he was elected to the House of Representatives from his grandfather's old district (after Joe Sr. bought out the incumbent). In 1952, Jack was elected to the U.S. Senate. Earlier that year, in 1956, Jack wrote another best-selling book, *Profiles in Courage*.

In comparison, Bobby had struggled. An indifferent student, he bounced from school to school before landing at Milton Academy. He got into Harvard, but his grades there weren't good enough to continue on to the business or law school, so he went to the University of Virginia law school instead. Upon graduating (in the middle of his class), he went to work on his brother's successful Senate campaign, where he distinguished himself with his dogged hard work. Kennedy then worked briefly for perhaps the most notorious committee in the history of the U.S. Senate—Joseph McCarthy's Senate Permanent Subcommittee on Investigations—before joining Arkansas senator John McClellan's Senate Subcommittee on Investigations as its chief counsel and staff director. There Kennedy and his boss, Senator McClellan, hit upon another subject—governmental corruption. This was an issue that provoked distinct unease in urban Democrats, many of whom were indebted to municipal machines. But Bobby brushed away such reservations. His first target would be New York City. There he discovered the world of the Irish NYPD—and the underworld.

KENNEDY'S FIRST STEP as staff director of the investigations subcommittee was to approach the Federal Bureau of Investigation for assistance. He was startled to learn that the FBI knew virtually nothing about corruption or organized crime at the city level. It simply wasn't within the bureau's jurisdiction, he was told. So he turned instead to the federal Bureau of Narcotics, the precursor to today's Drug Enforcement Administration. Two agents, Angelo Zurelo and Joseph Amato, took Bobby under their wing. They explained to Kennedy that much of the crime in New York (including, contrary to popular myth, the narcotics trade) was organized and controlled by the Sicilian mafia. They also introduced Kennedy to their partners in the New York Police Department's intelligence division, an outfit whose personnel consisted of largely Irish detectives straight out of a Damon Runyon story.

It was love at first sight.

Kennedy had long been fascinated by the experiences of his less fortunate Irish brethren. At Harvard, older brother Jack had joined an elite "final" club and generally gravitated toward what his sister Eunice would later describe as "Long Island sophisticates." Bobby sought out war veterans on the GI Bill. In the NYPD, Bobby found the ultimate tough-guy Irish institution. Kennedy couldn't get enough of it. Unbeknownst to his family or friends back in D.C., Kennedy was soon accompanying narcotics raiding parties on their nighttime forays. Often, the Bureau of Narcotics and the police would team up. Unrestrained by the Fourth Amendment, the local cops would kick in the door; narcotics agents would then storm in to make the arrests. Defendants' rights were essentially nil. Street justice was a common sight. One night, when Kennedy was out on a ridealong, the police burst into an apartment and found a man sexually abusing a two-year-old. While Kennedy watched, the police threw the man out a window as punishment.

Kennedy also fell in with the New York press, who plied him with stories of corruption in the trade union movement. They explained the unholy alliances that often resulted, whereby unions made use of the mob's "muscle," and the mobs tapped union treasuries for their own illicit businesses. Press and police alike were impressed by young Bobby's spunk. He was a fighter, figuratively and literally. One night at a bar, after an evening of rousting with the police, a fellow drinker—a big, tough-looking fellow—recognized Kennedy (who appeared regularly in the papers) and treated him to a stream of colorful insults about his family and his father. Kennedy (five foot, ten inches and 160 pounds) calmly invited the much bigger man to step outside. When the man stood up, Kennedy spun around and smashed him square in the face, breaking the man's nose. Everyone was impressed by Bobby's willingness to fight dirty, but his reporter friends wondered if he was really tough enough to take on organized crime.

The Syndicate, they stressed, was truly dangerous. Just look at what had happened to the crusading labor columnist 'Victor Riesel in the spring of 1956. One night, just after midnight, Reisel had stepped out onto a silent 51st Street and noticed a young man strolling toward him. It was the last thing Riesel ever saw. The man hurled a vial of sulfuric acid in Riesel's face, permanently blinding him. Rumor had it that the man behind the attack was Johnny Dio, a Lucchese family capo and a notorious labor union racketeer.

When told about Dio's activities, Kennedy vowed to go after him, but his reporter pals pushed him to go further. Shouldn't his committee be taking a broader look at the question of labor racketeering? Kennedy hesitated. The Senate Labor Committee might not appreciate having a young upstart intrude on their turf. Labor unions were also an important Democratic Party constituency. A high-profile investigation would undoubtedly ruffle feathers in the party. It was Washington, D.C.–based newsman Clark Mollenhoff who ultimately found the right button to push. Mollenhoff told Kennedy that racketeers were moving into the Teamsters Union in the Midwest and, in effect, dared Kennedy to check it out. When Bobby hesitated, Mollenhoff went straight for the hot button. What, are you scared? he taunted Kennedy. Are you afraid?

Soon thereafter, in August 1956, Kennedy announced that the Senate investigations subcommittee would expand its attention to the broader field of labor racketeering.* His first target was the nation's biggest and most powerful union—the Teamsters. Kennedy had heard rumors that mobsters

---

*There was another reason for Bobby Kennedy's interest in crime and municipal corruption as well, a political reason. That same August, big brother Jack made an unexpected—and ultimately unsuccessful—attempt to become Democratic presidential nominee Adlai Stevenson's running mate. The person he lost out to was none other than Sen. Estes Kefauver, who had come to national attention via his campaign against organized crime. Bobby hoped the Kennedy family would benefit in a similar fashion from his new investigation. (Thomas, *Robert Kennedy*, 73.)

had infiltrated various locals as part of an effort to gain control of the Teamsters' $250 million pension fund. But there was a problem. His reporter friends notwithstanding, Kennedy had very little information to go on. The NYPD intelligence division had some information, but it was limited to New York. The Bureau of Narcotics had a wealth of information, but it was focused on narcotics. There was one police department, though, that had made a name for itself with its relentless war on organized crime—the Los Angeles Police Department. On November 14, 1956, Kennedy and former G-man-turned-congressional-investigator Carmine Bellino flew out to Los Angeles to meet Chief Parker and intelligence division head James Hamilton. To prevent the press from getting wind of their visit, the two men traveled in secret. Kennedy used an alias, Mr. Rodgers. It would prove to be an eventful meeting.

PARKER took Kennedy's visit seriously. He directed Hamilton and Lt. Joseph Stephens, who headed the department's labor squad, to take the afternoon to meet with the Senate investigators. The men hit it off immediately. Kennedy and Bellino were impressed—and alarmed—by the material the LAPD had amassed. One example of the kinds of "strong arm" tactics employed by the mob in Southern California made a particularly vivid impression on Kennedy. It concerned a union organizer who'd gone to San Diego in defiance of warnings from the local mob. Soon after arriving, the man had been assaulted. According to Kennedy's later recounting of the story, he woke up the next day "covered in blood" and with "terrible pains in his stomach." With difficulty, he made it back to a hospital in Los Angeles, where doctors performed emergency surgery and, according to Kennedy, "removed from his backside a large cucumber." The man was later warned that if he ever returned to San Diego, he'd come back with a watermelon.

Urban myth or actual event? It didn't matter. Kennedy believed it had happened. It steeled his resolve to act.

At the end of the afternoon, Hamilton walked Kennedy out to the parking lot behind "the glass house" (as the new police administration building was called). It had been a productive day. The LAPD's wealth of information about corruption in the Teamsters reinforced Kennedy's belief that he was on to something big. So did subsequent meetings arranged by Hamilton and Stephens, which put Kennedy and Bellino in direct contact with a variety of employers, union leaders, employees, and confidential informants. Kennedy and Bellino heard from dissident members of the longshoremen's union, who complained of the leadership's radicalism and "red" sympathies.

They heard from union organizers (again in San Diego) who'd been beaten up by goons after attempting to organize retail clerks and about a Los Angeles plumbers and steamfitters local that was resisting mob attempts to muscle in on building contracts. More to the point, they heard about how local Teamsters were colluding with selected employers—employers with strong mob ties—to corner the garbage removal market in Los Angeles. Hamilton concluded by suggesting that Kennedy and Bellino take their fact-finding mission to Portland, Oregon, where crusading journalists had uncovered a wealth of incriminating evidence about corruption in the Teamsters local.

Hamilton and Kennedy met as strangers but ended the day as friends. Henceforth, the LAPD intelligence division would be an important (if largely unheralded) source of intelligence to Robert Kennedy. Kennedy's relationship with Chief Parker was different. The two men would never be friends in the way that Hamilton and Kennedy were; their personal styles were too different. But ideologically, the two men were largely in sync. In addition to sharing a faith (Roman Catholicism) and a creed (anti-communism), the two men shared a worldview: Both saw the underworld as the enemy within.

There was another similarity. Both men were battling their own internal enemies. Bobby was prone to depression ("Black Bobby," his older brother rather insensitively called him) and also to fits of anger that occasionally propelled him to violence. As a young man, Parker had shared this impulse to violence too. But the more dangerous demon for Los Angeles's proud chief of police was the demon of drink. Nowhere was that demon more in evidence than at an annual event called the Mobil Economy Run.

The Mobil Economy Run (sponsored by the Mobil Oil corporation and the U.S. Auto Club) was a coast-to-coast race designed to test the fuel efficiency of automobiles under real-life driving conditions. Automakers competed fiercely for the right to proclaim their cars the most fuel efficient in their class. But the Mobil Economy Run had another, less advertised, purpose as well. It was also a tremendous booze-fueled junket. Every year, Mobil rented a train for VIPs that ran north from Los Angeles to San Francisco, Yosemite, and Sun Valley (and thence onward east) or west to Albuquerque and then to Sun Valley and points east. Every year, Mobil invited the LAPD's chief of police and deputy chief for traffic.

On the job, Parker was a straight arrow. He took a dim view of patrol officers receiving "gifts" from merchants on their beat (though they still did). He abhorred ticket fixing and insisted on observing the strict letter of the law. Off the job (and with a little liquor in his system), he could be quite different. The Mobil Economy Run's VIP trains were all about liquoring up company guests. As soon as the train left L.A.'s Union Station, the shades came down and the bar opened. It remained open, 24/7, for the remainder of the trip.

As if determined to avoid temptation, Parker stayed away from the Mobil Economy Run during his first year as chief. In 1952, however, he succumbed. Two years later, he went along with traffic chief Harold Sullivan. The *Examiner's* automotive reporter, Slim Bernard, came too. Bernard was a character much beloved for his high jinx, so no one was surprised when, after a few drinks, Bernard somehow produced Salvation Army uniforms at the stop in Albuquerque and set out to recruit "soldiers" to solicit donations at the station. What was surprising was that Parker was happy to join the fun. Completely sloshed, he pounded away on a drum while his fellow revelers collected donations. It was a scene that made Parker's traveling companion Harold Sullivan, who didn't shy away from a few drinks on occasion himself, distinctly uncomfortable.

It got worse. By the time they reached Sun Valley, Parker (drinking all the while) was ready to lead a conga line through the hotel lobby and down the escalator. From Sullivan's perspective, Parker's behavior went well beyond boozy good fun. "He was drinking, and he had a problem," says Sullivan simply of Parker on that trip.

Parker himself presumably saw things in a different light. From that year forward, he was a Mobil Economy Run regular.

Fast-forward three years.

One day in the spring of 1957, the special bell on Sullivan's desk rang to indicate that the chief wanted to talk to him immediately. Such summons were dreaded by the deputy chiefs. Parker didn't hold regular staff meetings. By 1957, he had become quite hands off about the management of divisions that weren't under his direct control. Sullivan sometimes went weeks without discussing traffic matters with the chief. When Sullivan or another deputy chief was summoned, it typically meant that Parker was angry about something and intended to chew him out. Nonetheless, Sullivan promptly hurried down the hall to Parker's office. He was relieved to find the chief looking pensive.

"I've got a little problem," Parker told Sullivan, almost sheepishly.

"What is it?" Sullivan replied.

"Mayor Poulson wants to go on the Economy Run," Parker replied. Sullivan didn't see the difficulty. Mobil Oil would surely be delighted to have the mayor come along for the ride.

"Just call the manager and tell him that," said Sullivan. Although he was disinclined to ask favors, Parker did. Just as Sullivan predicted, the Mobil Economy Run was more than happy to extend an invitation to Mayor Poulson At the last minute, though, Poulson bowed out and sent a press aide in his stead. The aide was astonished by how much Parker drank—and (in Sullivan's words) by "what an asshole he made of himself." In short, he reported to Poulson that Los Angeles's lauded police chief was a common drunk of the worst sort. When Parker got back, the mayor confronted Parker about his public drinking, saying it was an embarrassment to the city. Parker vowed to sober up, but the binges (which typically began after work hours at the speaking engagements that filled Parker's evenings) continued—until his drinking habit brought him face to face with the possibility of a violent death.

The turning point came during a family trip to Tucson. Parker was there with his wife, Helen; his brother Joe; and his sister-in-law. The four of them were at a restaurant in Phoenix. Parker was "pulled as tight as a rubber band" that evening. The Mafia, he explained to Joe, was moving into Los Angeles. Parker was glum. He had a few B&Bs—Benedictine and brandies—too many to drive home. The next day, a subordinate called to say that one of the Los Angeles papers was reporting that a Mob figure had spotted Parker, drunk, in a Phoenix restaurant. Horrified, Parker never had another drink again.

part four

All the Way or Nothing

The Mike Wallace Interview

"I killed no men that in the first place didn't deserve killing."

—Mickey Cohen to Mike Wallace, *The Mike Wallace Interview*

CHIEF PARKER WAS RIGHT TO BE WORRIED. Mickey Cohen was looking for a way to get rid of him. But not with a bullet. He needed something subtle, like the Brenda Allen scandal in 1949. It was a difficult assignment. Los Angeles in 1957 was a very different city than it had been in 1949. Cohen was weaker, and the LAPD was immeasurably stronger. It would take an act of God to topple Chief William Parker. Fortunately, in the spring of 1957, Mickey Cohen got precisely that in the form of an invitation from the Rev. Billy Graham.

When Mickey Cohen first met Graham in 1949, Cohen was the West Coast's most famous gangster while the handsome young preacher's celebrity was still in its first blush. By 1957, the situation had changed. Graham had parlayed the success of his Los Angeles campaign into a nationwide movement. After his appearances in Los Angeles, Hearst papers across the country picked up the story of the lantern-jawed, jet blond man of God. *Time* magazine likewise hailed "the trumpet-lunged North Carolinian" with the "deep, cavernous voice" and made coverage of Graham's crusades a recurring feature of the magazine. Graham barnstormed across the country, drawing huge crowds wherever he went. No venture seemed too ambitious. He went into the movies, setting up his own production company (Billy Graham Films, later World Wide Pictures) and building a small film lot just across the street from the Walt Disney studios in Burbank; the project got so big that Graham soon teamed up with MGM for help distributing the film. He also launched a radio program on ABC, *The Hour of Decision*. But it was in 1952 that Graham took the step that would make him a household name.

One of Graham's closest friends was the Fort Worth oilman Sid Richardson. Richardson was a man with a cause: Gen. Dwight D. Eisenhower.

Richardson wanted him to run for president—and he wanted Graham to convince the general to do it. Graham took up the task assigned to him by "Mr. Sid" with alacrity, firing off a letter to the Supreme Headquarters of the Allied Powers in Brussels that was so impassioned that Eisenhower wrote Richardson to ask who this Graham fellow was.

Richardson responded by saying he'd send Graham over so Eisenhower could find out himself. The two men hit it off. When Eisenhower decided to run, he asked Graham to contribute Scripture verses to his speeches. Graham did so, but he also pressed Eisenhower about his own faith. The general confessed that he'd fallen away from the church. Graham gave him a Bible and recommended a congregation in Washington. After he was elected president, Dwight and Mamie joined it. Graham's moment as a spiritual counselor to presidents had arrived.

Graham enjoyed the perquisites that came with his proximity to temporal power, golfing at Burning Tree with Ike or his vice president, Richard Nixon; visiting American troops abroad; and establishing the National Prayer Breakfast as a de rigueur event for Washington politicians. Figuring out what to do next, though, was somewhat more challenging. First, he did a series of campus campaigns at colleges and universities across the country. Then he looked overseas. In 1954 and 1955, he toured the United Kingdom and Europe. In 1956, he visited Asia. By the time 1957 arrived, he needed something new. Graham and his advisors decided to go for something big: They would launch their biggest campaign yet in the biggest city in the world—New York City.

New York City would be the ultimate challenge. It was the citadel of secularism, with more agnostics than any other American city. It was the center of the world's media. It was a stronghold of Catholicism, with a larger Irish population than Dublin, a larger Italian population than Rome, a larger Puerto Rican population than San Juan. It was also the Jewish metropolis, home to one out of every ten of the world's Jews. Only 7.5 percent of the population belonged to mainline Protestant denominations, and most of these nominal Protestants were far removed from Graham's conservative, back-to-the-basics creed. From an evangelical standpoint, bringing New York City to Jesus was the ultimate challenge.

Protestant leaders in the city were generally supportive. A decision was made to launch the campaign in Madison Square Garden, starting on May 15. Graham and his advisors wanted to begin with something big—by saving someone who would turn every eye in New York (if not the country) toward the Manhattan crusade. Who better than the country's most notorious Jewish gangster, Mickey Cohen?

Graham and Cohen had renewed their acquaintance after Cohen's release. Cohen's apparently sincere desire for repentance was catnip to the evangelist and his circle. Graham confidant W. C. Jones began to press Mickey even more ardently to choose Christ. He and other Graham backers also offered thousands of dollars in "brotherly love gifts." Cohen was open to the idea. Being born again had certainly worked out well for his former wiretapper, Jimmy Vaus, who was now a celebrated speaker and a published author. Vaus's memoirs had even been made into a movie, *Wiretapper* (1956). A Madison Square Garden conversion would certainly gratify Mickey's undiminished desire for attention from the press. There was also, purportedly, money at stake: $15,000 to attend the Madison Square Garden crusade and another $25,000 if he converted to Christianity. That seemed like a more than fair price for Mickey's soul.

In the spring of 1957, Cohen flew to Buffalo to meet with Graham and explore the possibility of attending the upcoming Madison Square Garden campaign. The *New York Herald Tribune* broke the story: "Mickey Cohen and Bill Graham Pray and Read Bible Together," cried the headline. It quoted Mickey praising Graham for having "guided me in many things" and for being "my friend." The story also suggested that further communion between the two would be forthcoming.

"He's invited me [to the May crusade]," Cohen told the paper, "and I think I will be here for it." Cohen added that he was "very high on the Christian way of life."

The saga of L.A.'s most notorious gangster-turned-florist accepting Jesus as his personal savior promised to be the most sensational story of the summer. It demanded the attention of a journalist who would do it justice— someone who didn't hesitate to sit down with unsavory characters and ask the point-blank, personal questions that Americans wanted answers to. In short, Mickey Cohen seemed the perfect guest for Manhattan's newest media star, ABC newsman Mike Wallace.

IN THE SUMMER of 1956, Mike Wallace was the anchor of the seven and eleven o'clock news reports for New York City's Channel 5, WABD. Ted Yates, a sinewy ex-Marine from Cheyenne, Wyoming, was his producer. Wallace had been on the job for a year. Yet already he and Yates were bridling at the restrictions imposed upon them. Decades earlier George Bernard Shaw had noted that "the ablest and most highly cultivated people continually discuss religion, politics, and sex" while the masses "make it a rule that politics and religion are not to be mentioned, and take it for granted that no decent person would attempt to discuss sex." Shaw's description of Victorian England was doubly true for 1950s television, and it frustrated Wallace and Yates. The two men began to sketch out a different approach. Why not interview the people viewers most wanted to meet? Why not ask the questions viewers really wanted answers to?

That fall, Yates and Wallace managed to convince Channel 5 to replace the eleven o'clock news broadcast with an interview show. The format featured Wallace and an interesting guest—a personality from the world of politics, sports, entertainment, or religion. Yates dubbed the show *Night Beat.* It was an immediate succès de scandale. New Yorkers watched, mesmerized, as Wallace confronted bristling union leaders with pointed questions about their personal lives, quizzed actresses about their sex lives, and asked novelists about their views of God. Wallace courted conflict. His questions were relentless, his work ethic indefatigable. (*Night Beat* featured two guests for a half hour each, four nights a week.) The networks noticed. In early 1957, ABC offered Wallace a half-hour national slot that would air Sunday nights. The show would be called *The Mike Wallace Interview.* ABC president Leonard Goldenson assured Wallace that he would have the same freedom he had previously enjoyed at *Night Beat.* ("Mike, you will not be doing your job properly unless you make this building shake every couple of weeks," Goldenson reportedly told him.) Wallace jumped at the opportunity. In late April, Wallace and Yates released a list of Wallace's first guests. It included the imperial wizard of the Ku Klux Klan, the burlesque star Gypsy Rose Lee, the actor and director Orson Welles, the singer Harry Belafonte, and Mickey Cohen.

Wallace's interviews looked spontaneous, but in fact, Wallace and his production team deliberately shaped each interview into a dramatic encounter. The responsibility for researching guests and preparing a "script" of likely questions and probable answers fell to Wallace's researcher, Al Ramrus. Ramrus typically started by calling retired journalist Bill Lang, who maintained his own personal "morgue" of newspaper articles on a remarkable variety of subjects. Ramrus then checked out the three major newsweeklies—*Time, Newsweek,* and *Life*—at Hunter College and, in the case of performers, the film and theatrical division of the New York Public Library. Finally, he did a preinterview with the guest. Afterward, he drew up the "script" for Wallace. Of course, it wasn't a real script in the sense that a program like *Dragnet* was scripted. Wallace often kept the toughest questions to himself so that guests, lulled into complacency by the preinterview, would be caught off guard. Guests sometimes changed their answers. In general, though, most programs played out as Ramrus indicated they would.

Cohen presented special challenges from the start. Lang's New York–centric newspaper morgue didn't have much on Mickey, and Ramrus didn't have access to a West Coast newspaper morgue. While the national newsweeklies had plenty on Mickey during his "vicecapades" period and immediately afterward, they were sketchier on his recent activities. Nor did Ramrus have much success in talking with Cohen's associates in crime. When he reached Bugsy Siegel's ex-mistress Virginia Hill in Switzerland, Hill told him she didn't know the man.

Then there was the problem of dealing with Mickey himself.

When Ramrus contacted Mickey in Los Angeles, Cohen wasn't exactly up to speed on what a media sensation Mike Wallace had become. However, at the coaxing of the Graham camp, he eventually agreed to sit down with Wallace during his trip to New York for the campaign. Cohen let Ramrus know that in doing so he was taking a big risk. New York was full of enemies. Cohen would travel under an alias—Mr. Dunn. Ramrus himself would need to meet him at the airport—in a limo—and then take him to his hotel; the luxurious Essex House would be fine. The entire operation would have to be hush-hush. With some trepidation, Ramrus agreed to these arrangements.

On the night of May 2, 1957, Cohen's reason for caution became abundantly clear. That evening, a burly ex-boxer named Vincent "Chin" Gigante walked into the foyer of the Majestic Apartments at 115 Central Park West and followed its most famous resident, Manhattan crime boss Frank Costello (widely known in criminal and law enforcement circles as "the prime minister of the underworld") toward the elevator. As Costello was preparing to enter it, Gigante whipped out a .38 caliber pistol, yelled, "This is for you, Frank!" and shot Costello in the temple at what appeared to be point-blank range. As Costello fell to the ground, Gigante ran past the horrified doorman and leapt into a black Cadillac idling outside, which then sped away. Astonishingly, Costello lived. Startled by Gigante's cry, he had jerked away at the last moment, and the bullet had merely grazed his scalp. But the underworld was badly shaken. So, no doubt, was Ramrus. He would now be risking his life by stepping into the free-fire zone around Mickey Cohen.

WHEN COHEN FLEW into Idlewild Airport, Ramrus and the limousine Mickey had requested were there to meet him. Ramrus was nervous. He was relying on an old photo to spot the notorious gangster. To complicate things further, Ramrus had been informed that Cohen would be traveling "incognito." What that meant Ramrus could hardly guess. Moreover, Ramrus had been warned that if and when he did identify Cohen, he was under no circumstances to greet the former gangster as

"Mr. Cohen" or—heaven forbid—"Mickey." Ramrus was eager not to make that mistake. On the drive from Manhattan out to Idlewild, Ramrus repeated Mickey's cover name over and over: "Mr. Dunn, Mr. Dunn." Worriedly, Ramrus awaited the arrival of the Los Angeles flight. Anxiously, he scanned the arriving passengers for the disguised gangster. Finally, a short little man dressed "in a garment district kind of way"—pudgy, broken nose, balding, "a tough little face"—walked off the jetway. It was Mickey Cohen. He was accompanied also by a far tougher looking traveling companion, whom Cohen identified only as "Itchy." Nervously, Ramrus approached the traveling duo.

"Um, Mr. Dunn?" he said. "Hi. Mr. Dunn?"

Cohen gave him a look that made it clear he took Ramrus for some kind of dunderhead.

"I'm Mickey Cohen, kid," he replied, in a distinctly audible tone. With that the three of them were off to the Essex House on Central Park South. Ramrus had booked a one-room suite there for Mickey's use. But when Cohen arrived, he took one look at the (smallish) bathroom and declared, "This ain't gonna do." Panicky lest his odd guest depart, Ramrus rushed down to the lobby and secured a larger suite for Cohen, which met with his grumbling approval.

One task remained—conducting the preinterview. "Listen," Ramrus said, pleadingly, as Cohen and his henchman ushered him out of their room. "I need to talk to you before the interview."

"Come up later tonight, and we'll talk," Mickey replied amiably.

Ramrus returned several hours later—to a wild party. The suite was jammed with friends of Cohen, male and female, some of whom Ramrus recognized as fixtures of the New York and New Jersey underworlds. Mickey himself seemed to have secured the attention of "a young blonde girl," though, truth be told, he seemed more interested in the pineapple cheesecake from Lindy's, the famous showbiz deli on Broadway. Ramrus could see his point. The blonde looked tasty, but the cheesecake was scrumptious. Cohen waved Ramrus over. They could do the preinterview then and there, Cohen told him. Ramrus had never attempted to interview a guest in a room full of broads, wiseguys, smoke, and cheesecake, but it was clear that there was no point arguing with Cohen. So he did his best—and ate as much of the cheesecake as he could. The next day he turned over the material he had gathered to Mike Wallace. The Cohen interview was in Wallace's hands.

The next evening, on Sunday, May 19, Cohen presented himself at the ABC studios. The half-hour interview was broadcast live, with no delay. That left Wallace with no margin for error.

The interview started slowly. Wallace pressed Cohen about his "friendliness" with Billy Graham. Mickey was reticent—and somewhat incoherent. ("I just hope and feel the feeling is likewise between Billy and I.") Things picked up when Wallace turned to Cohen's criminal background. When Cohen piously claimed that he'd never been involved in drugs or prostitution, Wallace pressed him about the criminal activities he clearly had been involved with:

Wallace: Yet, you've made book, you have bootlegged. Most important of all, you've broken one of the commandments—you've killed, Mickey. How can you be proud of not dealing in prostitution and narcotics when you've killed at least one man, or how many more?

How many more, Mickey?

Cohen: I have killed no men that in the first place didn't deserve killing.

Wallace: By whose standards?

Cohen: By the standards of our way of life.

Wallace was pleased with how the interview was going. But when he urged Cohen to name the politicians whom Cohen had paid off, Mickey once again balked.

"That is not my way of life, Mike," Cohen replied firmly.

Then Wallace asked him about the LAPD. It was as if Wallace had touched Cohen with a hot iron. Suddenly, Mickey erupted. Police harassment was making it impossible for him to run his floral business, and Mickey made it clear whom he blamed.

"I have a police chief in Los Angeles who happens to be a sadistic degenerate," he said provocatively, before wandering to other topics. Wallace picked up on the statement and returned to the subject of the "apparently respectable" Chief Parker a few minutes later.

"Now, Mick," began Wallace, "without naming names, how far up in the brass do you have to bribe the cops to carry on a big-time bookmaking operation?"

"I'm going to give him much to bring a libel suit against me," replied the fuming florist. He then named Chief Parker. "He's nothing but a thief that has been—a reformed thief.

"This man here is as dishonest politically as the worst thief that accepts money for payoffs," Cohen continued. "He is a known alcoholic. He's been disgusting. He's a known degenerate. In other words, he's a sadistic degenerate of the worst type. . . . He has a man underneath him that is on an equal basis with him."

Wallace interrupted to ask the name of this underling. After being asked several times, Mickey finally answered the question. "His name," snarled Cohen, "is Captain James Hamilton, and he's probably a lower degenerate than Parker." Cohen described the intelligence division as the head of "what I call the stupidity squad."

Caught up in the excitement of the moment, Wallace pressed Mickey to expand upon his charges against "the apparently respectable Chief William Parker": "Well, Mickey, you're a reformed thief just as he's a reformed thief. Isn't it the pot calling the kettle black?"

Cohen scowled at this description before the conversation moved on to other subjects.

AFTER THE INTERVIEW was concluded, everyone agreed it had been an astonishing performance. Cohen had been raw, exciting, and revelatory. He had admitted on the air to killing people, to grossing anywhere from $200,000 to $650,000 a day through illegal bookmaking and gambling operations, to securing protection from someone "higher than the mayor of chief of police." Ramrus and the other people on set were excited about having pulled off such a dramatic interview. The feeling of euphoria didn't last long.

Mickey Cohen wasn't the only Angeleno in New York City that May 19. It just so happened that LAPD intelligence head James Hamilton was also visiting Gotham. (Parker would later deny sending him east to shadow Cohen, insisting instead that his intelligence head was in New York on vacation.) Hamilton tuned in to the evening broadcast. What he saw appalled him. The American Broadcasting Company was allowing—no, encouraging—Mickey Cohen, a known criminal, to slander Chief Parker and himself on national television. Moreover, despite concluding the interview with a statement that Cohen's views on the LAPD were exclusively his own, Mike Wallace had made comments that seemed to endorse Mickey Cohen's assessment of the police. An angry Hamilton immediately called Chief Parker in Los Angeles to tell him what was happening. He also called ABC to deliver a warning: Pull the program from your Los Angeles station or prepare to be sued.

The Mike Wallace Interview was scheduled to air on the West Coast in less than three hours. ABC had only a short interval of time during which to make a decision. Executives immediately contacted Wallace producer Ted Yates, who in turn told Wallace about the problem they'd run into. Together, Yates and Wallace hurried over to Cohen's suite at the Essex House to confer with him about Hamilton's threats. Mickey had just stepped out of the shower. He greeted his visitors calmly, clad in nothing but a towel.

Wallace and Yates explained their problem as Cohen listened calmly. At the end of their presentation, Cohen made his pronouncement.

"Mike, Ted, forget it," he said decisively. "Parker knows that I know so much about him, he wouldn't dare sue." So instead, the producers called Parker in Los Angeles and invited him to come on the show next week to defend himself. Parker indignantly refused, saying he had no intention of debating "an irresponsible character like Cohen." He further warned ABC that if it proceeded with airing the show on the West Coast, it would open itself up to charges of criminal slander. The network disregarded this warning. Instead, a few hours later, Wallace's interview with Cohen aired on the West Coast. At a news conference the next day, Chief Parker announced that he and Captain Hamilton were considering a lawsuit against ABC.

Cohen was unfazed. Soon after the interview with Wallace, Cohen went on the WINS radio station. There he repeated his charges and dared Parker to file suit. Executives at ABC were more worried. Unlike Mickey Cohen, ABC possessed legitimate income and assets, and Cohen's vituperative comments looked rather shaky in the light of day. The next day ABC offered its "sincere apologies for any personal distress resulting from this telecast." It also decided to withhold the show from the handful of stations that had not yet aired it. Parker was not mollified. He, Hamilton, and ex-mayor Fletcher Bowron responded that they would continue to explore their legal options.

A week later, ABC vice president Oliver Treyz went on the air. With a chastened Wallace standing by his side, Treyz allowed as to how something "profoundly regrettable occurred while Mr. Wallace was questioning Mickey Cohen." ABC, he continued, "retracts and withdraws in full all statements made on last Sunday's program concerning the Los Angeles city government, and specifically, Chief William H. Parker."

ABC's apology did little to assuage the anger of Parker's supporters. From Washington, D.C., Senate investigations subcommittee staff director Robert Kennedy delivered a stinging rebuke to ABC.

"Gentlemen," the letter began.

A week ago Sunday, I watched the Mike Wallace show and his guest, Mickey Cohen. I was deeply disturbed.

In the investigation that this Committee has been conducting, we have to work closely with police departments throughout the country. I want to say that no department has been more cooperative or has impressed us more with its efficiency, thoroughness and honesty than Mr. Parker's in Los Angeles.

Although I do not have a transcript here in Washington, it was my impression that Mike Wallace urged Mickey Cohen to name Captain Hamilton as a degenerate. In my estimation, I would consider Captain Hamilton as the best police officer we have worked with since our investigation began. . . .

To allow such serious and unsubstantiated charges to be made on nationwide television is grossly unfair and unjust.

> *Very truly yours,*
> *Robert Kennedy*
> *Chief Counsel*

Cohen was enraged by ABC's backtracking. From Los Angeles, he issued a statement of his own: "Any retraction made by those spineless persons in regard to the television show I appeared on with Mike Wallace on A.B.C. network does not go for me." Implicit in this response was a challenge— sue if you dare.

Parker dared. On July 8, he sued ABC, Mike Wallace, and *The Mike Wallace Interview*'s sponsors for $2 million. (Captain Hamilton and former mayor Fletcher Bowron also filed million-dollar libel lawsuits.) He did not file suit against Cohen, on the grounds that Mickey claimed to have no assets and was already deeply indebted to the federal government. ABC's attorneys sought out Mickey, hoping to discover some substance that would support his allegations. But now that ABC was calling on Cohen to show his hand, Mickey abruptly folded. Later, he would mutter only that he'd had incriminating information about Parker pinching a prostitute's ass on a yacht during a policing convention in Miami. Even if this were true, it hardly established that Parker was a bagman for the Shaws in the 1930s. ABC's attorneys realized that it was time to seek a settlement.

COHEN, meanwhile, was dealing with another problem: the wrath of his coreligionists. Ever since the idea had surfaced in the press that Cohen would convert to Christianity, Jews from across the country had been calling Michael's Greenhouses to urge Mickey against betraying his people. On the evening of Wednesday, May 22, Cohen attended the Graham campaign. But he did not come forward to be harvested for Christ, meeting privately instead with W. C. Jones and Jimmy Vaus after the rally.

The meeting reportedly was stormy. Jones berated Mickey for continuing to associate with his gangster friends. Cohen responded by angrily declaring, "If I have to give up my friends to be a Christian, I'm pulling out. I renounce it right now." Then he stormed out. With that, Mickey's Manhattan adventure came to an end.

Just days after his anticlimactic appearance at Madison Square Garden, Cohen was served with a subpoena by the FBI and flown to Chicago, where he was forced to testify at the trial of Outfit leader Paul Ricca, whom federal authorities were attempting to deport to Italy. Cohen had nothing to say. While he was more than ready to talk about himself, the old taciturnity reasserted itself when the topic turned to other gangsters. Everywhere he went, Cohen was shadowed by officers of the LAPD intelligence division. But Cohen professed to have nothing but scorn for Chief Parker's efforts to shadow and intimidate him. When, at some point the evening before his flight back to Los Angeles, Mickey slipped his LAPD security detail, he personally telegrammed Chief Parker to inform him of his flight number and arrival time in L.A. It was Cohen's personal little "fuck you."

MICKEY arrived back in Los Angeles in late May. In an attempt to stem the tide of bad news, he immediately announced that Ben Hecht had begun work on his life story, now titled *The Soul of a Gunman*. It was clear that Mickey intended to do everything he could to continue his PR blitz (despite a report from Walter Winchell that Cohen's compatriots in the underworld were getting fed up with Mickey "The Louse" Cohen's clamoring for public attention). But back in L.A., Cohen found that an unpleasant new reality awaited him. Where previously Mickey had been shadowed, he was now actively harassed. His first weekend back, two alert patrolmen saw Cohen stop his car at the corner of Santa Monica Boulevard and Western and walk over to a newsstand to buy a paper. A line of cars behind him started honking as the light changed. So the two officers went over and gave him a ticket. Cohen protested that he'd simply stopped behind a stalled car and stepped out to get a paper while the lady in the car in front of him tried to restart her engine. He refused to sign the citation. So the two officers hauled him in and booked him, on charges of causing a traffic jam. Cohen vowed to fight the charges.

"They can't get away with stuff like this," he fumed to the reporters who had rushed over when they heard that Cohen had been arrested (in riding breeches and full equestrian attire). "This is some more of Bill Parker's stuff."

Los Angeles–area law enforcement was just getting started. Prosecutors decided to throw the book at Cohen on the traffic jam charges. That summer he was convicted—and fined $11. He vowed to appeal the decision. The following month, Beverly Hills police arrested Cohen as he was tucking into a ham-and-eggs breakfast (at 2:30 p.m.) at one of his favorite restaurants. The charge was failing to register as an ex-felon. (The Beverly Hills municipal code limited convicted felons to five visits to Beverly Hills every thirty days.) Police hauled Cohen, "screaming epithets," into Chief Anderson's office for questioning. A scuffle ensued, and Anderson ordered that Cohen be charged with disorderly conduct as well. A. L. Wirin and the ACLU stepped forward to defend him, arguing that the registration requirement was unconstitutional. A Beverly Hills municipal court judge agreed and threw out the charges against Cohen. A jury later acquitted Cohen on the remaining charge.

Mickey's courtroom successes didn't extend to his business ventures. Exotic plants apparently were not, in fact, "a tremendous racket"—at least, not to someone who had never managed (or bothered) to figure out which plant was which. That summer, Cohen announced that he was leaving the greenhouse business.

"I didn't know a plant from a boxing glove," he confessed to the press, "but I would have made a go of it if those cops had left me alone. We couldn't go into the greenhouse without their hot breath wilting the plants."

Henceforth, Mickey would focus his business endeavors in an area where he was an acknowledged expert—ice cream. Together with his sister and brother-in-law (and investors from Las Vegas), Cohen was preparing to open the Carousel ice cream parlor in Brentwood. He also announced that he would be focusing on his book with Hecht and on a movie spin-off, *The Mickey Cohen Story*. Whispers of a huge movie deal soon filled the press. Cohen attorney George Bieber claimed that Cohen had been offered $200,000 in cash and 80 percent of profits but that Cohen was holding out for 20 percent of gross box office receipts. Beiber also predicted that Hecht's book would bring in $500,000 to $700,000.

Back in New York City, Mike Wallace wasn't entertaining visions of the silver screen. Instead, he was trying to save his job. ABC's promises to back Wallace through controversies were now forgotten. Instead, John Daly, the head of the network news division, stepped forward to deal with the man he saw as a loose cannon. A minder was assigned to vet the script before every show and to monitor Wallace's performances on the set—"a balding, humpty-dumpty kind of guy," as Ramrus recalled him. He was also humorless. Typical of the petty obstacles the show now faced was the minder's reaction to a proposed question for the architect Frank Lloyd Wright:

Wallace: Mr. Wright, I understand you designed a dream home for Arthur Miller and Marilyn Monroe. As an architect, what do you think of Marilyn Monroe's architecture?

"Objection," came the response from the minder. "Indecent question."

"What's indecent?" replied Wallace and Yates, innocently. The answer, of course, was the thought that had arisen in the mind of the minder.

For the most part, Wallace just brushed aside objections of this sort and did what he wanted to do. Still, the new regime was demoralizing. Although ABC eventually settled Parker's suit for $45,000, ABC's insurer, Lloyd's of London, took a dim view of the controversy. It insisted that henceforth a lawyer monitor every show, complete with cue cards. When Wallace approached a controversial subject, the attorney (who sat just outside the range of the camera) would hold up a "BE CAREFUL" cue card. The most dangerous conversational forays resulted in "STOP" or "RETREAT" cards. This was no way to run a TV show whose entire point was to be daring and provocative, and it took its toll. That December, ABC had another brush with a libel lawsuit after Wallace guest Drew Pearson charged that Senator John F. Kennedy's Pulitzer Prize–winning *Profiles in Courage* had been ghostwritten. In the spring of 1958, Philip Morris announced that it would not be renewing its sponsorship of *The Mike Wallace Interview*. Wallace's days as a national TV personality seemed numbered. The following fall, Wallace left ABC and returned to local television on Channel 13, a station even smaller than his old employer, Channel 5. Not until 1963, when Wallace managed to convince CBS News president Dick Salant to take a chance on him, did Wallace get another job at a network, this time as the host of a radio interview program and the anchor of the new *CBS Morning News*. In 1968, Wallace finally got another shot at a show that offered to make him a national media star. That program was *60 Minutes*.

MEANWHILE, back in Washington, D.C., Robert Kennedy was puzzling over a question. In keeping with Hamilton's suggestions, the investigations subcommittee had taken a close look at the behavior of Teamsters Union officials in the Pacific Northwest. They had uncovered disturbing evidence of stolen funds, including evidence that implicated Teamsters president David Beck. They had also discovered that Kennedy's friends in the New York press had been right: Certain unions—the Operating Engineers, the Hotel and Restaurant Employees, and, again, the Teamsters—did have long histories of involvement with organized crime.

There was also evidence that tied emerging Teamster leader Jimmy Hoffa to organized crime figures in Detroit, Cleveland, St. Louis, Minneapolis, and Chicago. As he considered these connections, Kennedy found himself mulling over a larger question: Was the Mafia a national, coordinated criminal enterprise, or did the phrase simply refer to the hierarchy of Italian organized crime in any given area? On November 13, 1957, Kennedy put that very question to his old acquaintance Joseph Amato, a Mob specialist with the Bureau of Narcotics.

"That is a big question to answer," Amato replied. "But we believe that there does exist today in the United Sates a society, loosely organized, for the specific purpose of smuggling narcotics and committing other crimes. . . . It has its core in Italy and it is nationwide. In fact, international."

The very next day, Kennedy and the world received definitive proof that Amato was right when New York state police decided to investigate an unusually large gathering of luxury cars and limousines at the home of Joseph "Joe the Barber" Barbara outside the little town of Apalachin (pronounced "Apple-*ay*kin") in western New York. When the state police officers arrived, Barbara's guests leapt into their cars and fled—running straight into a state police roadblock. Other gangsters ran into the woods, including (most likely) James Lanza from San Francisco, Sam Giancana of Chicago, Tommy Lucchese of New York City, and Joseph Zerilli of Detroit. Fifty-eight men were arrested. Only nineteen of the men (all of whom were Italian) were from upstate New York. The rest of the guests appeared to have come from cities all across the country and even from as far away as Cuba. John Scalisi had come from Cleveland. Santos Traficante had come from Havana. James Lanza had come from San Francisco. Frank DeSimone (the Dragnas' longtime attorney, now the family boss in his own right) had come from Los Angeles. Twenty-three of the men came from New York City and northern New Jersey, including Joseph Profaci, Joseph Bonanno, and Vito Genovese. All told, the group's members had been arrested 257 times, with more than a hundred convictions for serious offenses such as homicide, armed robbery, trafficking in narcotics, and extortion. In their pockets the police found $300,000 in cash.

It was clear that New York state police had stumbled across what appeared to be a board meeting of the Mafia. Newspapers across the country trumpeted the arrests. As astonishing as the fact that a massive international crime organization existed (and was meeting at some wiseguy's house in upstate New York) was the list of legitimate businesses these men controlled. They included "dress companies, labor organizations, trucking companies, soft drink firms, dairy products, coat manufacturers, undertaking parlors, oil companies, ladies' coat factories, real estate projects, curtain, slip cover and interior decorating, ships, restaurants, night clubs, grills, meat markets. Also vending machine sales, taxi companies, tobacco distributors, awning and siding firms, automotive conveying and hauling firms, importers of food and liquor, grocery stores and food chains, labor relations consulting firms, cement firms, waste paper removal, strap manufacture, liquor and beer distributors, textiles, shipping, ambulances, baseball clubs, news stands, motels, hotels, and juke boxes," to name just a few. In short, the underworld had burrowed deeply into the fabric of American business.

Back in Washington, Robert Kennedy had a simple question: Who were these men? Seven years earlier, the Kefauver Committee had introduced Americans to gangsters Joe Adonis and Frank Costello (whose nervous hands were famously televised during the Kefauver Committee's hearings in New York). But names such as Vito Genovese were unfamiliar. Kennedy's first reaction, naturally enough, was to turn to the Federal Bureau of Investigation. When the bureau failed to produce dossiers on these figures, Kennedy personally paid the director a visit, barging in (without an appointment) and demanding that the bureau provide the McClellan Committee with everything it had on this collection of hoods. Hoover was forced to reveal the humiliating truth. The bureau (in Kennedy's words) "didn't know anything, really, about these people who were the major gangsters in the United States." Disgusted, Kennedy and his aides turned instead to the FBI's minnow-sized rival, the Bureau of Narcotics, which was able to offer investigators a wealth of information on the activities of the men arrested in Apalachin. There was also one police department whose knowledge stood out—the LAPD.

One year earlier, the LAPD intelligence division had bugged a room of Conrad Hilton's Town House hotel, where up-and-coming Teamsters leader Jimmy Hoffa was meeting with three residents of Chicago. At the time, Hoffa was in the middle of a heated campaign for the presidency of the Teamsters Union. According to an LAPD memo on the meeting (which later turned up in the files of the Chicago Crime Commission), the men in question included Marshall Caifano, who oversaw Chicago Outfit activities in Los Angeles, and Outfit boss Murray Humphreys. The memo stated in no uncertain terms that "a member of the Executive Board is being taken before these men singly, and they are advising members of the Executive Board in no uncertain terms that Hoffa is to be the next President of the Teamsters Union." Sure enough, that fall Hoffa was elected president of the Teamsters.

The news from Apalachin—and the LAPD intelligence division's ability to tie Hoffa and the Teamsters to the Chicago Outfit—caused Kennedy to reconsider the depths of the corruption he had uncovered. The McClellan

Committee had begun its work in 1956 by focusing on dishonesty and corruption in the clothing procurement program of the military services.
That, in turn, had led to the discovery that gangsters such as Albert Anastasia and Johnny Dio had become deeply involved in both the textiles
unions and the textiles business. Apalachin had revealed an even broader
horizon of organized crime, one in which the underworld preyed upon entire industries and whole communities.

"The results of the underworld infiltration into labor-management affairs form a shocking pattern across the country," Kennedy wrote one year
later in his best-selling book *The Enemy Within*. "[T]he gangsters of today
work in a highly organized fashion and are far more powerful now than at
any time in the history of the country. They control political figures and
threaten whole communities. They have stretched their tentacles of corruption and fear into industries both large and small. They grow stronger
every day."

Parker himself couldn't have put it better. As Kennedy realized what a
profound danger organized crime posed to the American way of life, he
grew even more appreciative of the work the LAPD was doing. He also
began to seriously consider Chief Parker's idea of creating a national clearinghouse for intelligence information. Naturally, in the course of their work
together Parker and Hamilton told Robert Kennedy all about the activities
of Mickey Cohen. Not surprisingly, Robert Kennedy decided that he
wanted to meet this Mickey Cohen in person—and nail him.

William H. Parker as a rookie policeman, 1927. (Courtesy: *Herald-Examiner* Collection, Los Angeles Public Library)

Mickey Cohen as a young boxer. (Courtesy: Acme)

Chief James "Two Gun" Davis. (Courtesy: *Herald-Examiner* Collection, Los Angeles Public Library)

William Parker; his wife, Helen (holding the pistol); and Chief Davis. (Courtesy: William H. Parker Police Foundation)

Benjamin "Bugsy" Siegel (center), with his attorneys, Max Solomon and Isaac Pacht, 1944. (Courtesy: UCLA Charles E. Young Research Library Department of Special Collections, *Los Angeles Daily News* Photographic Archives, Copyright Regents of the University of California, UCLA Library)

Mayor Fletcher Bowron (seated) and Chief William Parker, 1952. (Courtesy: *Herald-Examiner* Collection, Los Angeles Public Library)

The Cohen gang. From left to right, Mike Howard, Mickey Cohen, Sol Davis, and James Rist. (Courtesy: *Herald-Examiner* Collection, Los Angeles Public Library)

Brenda Allen, Hollywood's leading madam, 1948. (Courtesy: *Herald-Examiner* Collection, Los Angeles Public Library)

Mickey Cohen, washing his hands in court. (Courtesy: *Herald-Examiner* Collection, Los Angeles Public Library)

Cohen examines his wardrobe post-bombing, 1949.
(Courtesy: S. A. Hixon, *Los Angeles Times*)

Chief William Parker and *Dragnet*
creator Jack Webb, holding a reel of
the *Dragnet* episode that attacks the
exclusionary rule. (Courtesy: Bettman/
CORBIS)

The Rev. Billy Graham, 1950. (Courtesy: *Herald-
Examiner* Collection, Los Angeles Public Library)

Mike Wallace and Mickey Cohen, 1957.
(Courtesy: Bettman/CORBIS)

Mickey Cohen, preparing to enter
Madison Square Garden for Billy
Graham's first Manhattan campaign, 1957.
(Courtesy: Bettman/CORBIS)

Lana Turner, daughter Cheryl Crane, and Johnny Stompanato with an unidentified
reporter, 1958. (Courtesy: UCLA Charles E. Young Research Library Department of
Special Collections, *Los Angeles Times* Photographic Archives, Copyright Regents of the
University of California, UCLA Library)

Mickey Cohen, holding love interest Liz Renay's new poetry album (and Mickey Jr.). (Courtesy: *LA Examiner* Negatives Collection, University of Southern California)

Candy Barr. (Author Collection)

Sandy Hagen kisses Cohen good-bye. (Courtesy: *Los Angeles Times*)

President John F. Kennedy greets Chief Parker. (Courtesy: Los Angeles Police Historical Society)

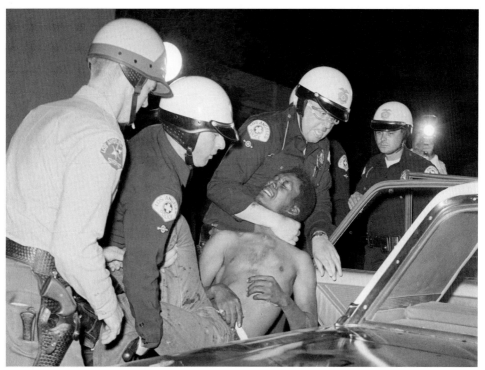

Policemen making an arrest on the second night of Watts riots in 1965. (Courtesy: Bettman/CORBIS)

Dr. Martin Luther King, addressing Watts residents at a community meeting. (Courtesy: Bettman/CORBIS)

Chief William Parker, testifying after the Watts riots. (Courtesy: *Herald-Examiner* Collection, Los Angeles Public Library)

Mickey Cohen, temporarily released from prison to attend his mother's funeral, 1969. (Courtesy: *Los Angeles Times*)

Chief William Parker, lying in state. (Courtesy: Los Angeles Police Historical Society)

21

The Electrician

*"[W]hat's the meaning in the underworld or
the racket world when somebody's 'lights are
to be put out?'"*

—Robert Kennedy to Mickey Cohen, 1959

BY LATE 1958, Mickey Cohen was back in the rackets. His target was Los Angeles's lucrative vending machine market. His modus operandi was pure muscle—threatening vending machine owners with bodily harm if they didn't pay him for protection. As word spread that Cohen was back in business, old friends resurfaced, asking favors of the sort that Cohen had once dispensed so freely. Among them was Columbia Pictures boss Harry Cohn.

Cohn had the temperament of a first-class gangster. "Bullying and contemptuous" (other common descriptions include "profane," "vulgar," "cruel," "rapacious," and "philandering"), an ardent admirer of Benito Mussolini (whose office he re-created for himself on the Columbia lot and whose picture he proudly displayed even *after* the Second World War), Cohn delighted in the fear his presence could create.

But in 1958, Cohn had a five-foot, seven-inch, 125-pound, 37-23-37 problem that all his swaggering and bullying couldn't resolve. Her stage name was Kim Novak. Novak was Columbia Pictures's—and Hollywood's—biggest star. Cohn had nurtured her career for years, grooming the young model as a successor to Rita Hayworth, purchasing the inevitable set of nude photos from a "modeling" session in the actress's youth, and carefully protecting her image. His efforts had borne fruit. In 1957, Novak had smoldered as Frank Sinatra's old flame in *The Man with the Golden Arm*. The chemistry between the two had been so hot that they'd paired up again in *Pal Joey*.

Novak's sex appeal was not confined to the silver screen. Marilyn Monroe, 20th Century Fox's screen siren, was almost a parody of the blonde bombshell. (It's no surprise that breakthrough movies such as *Gentlemen Prefer Blondes* and *How to Marry a Millionaire* cast her in comic roles.) Novak made a different impression. The alabaster-skinned beauty with the deep-set hazel eyes, platinum silver hair, and Slavic features projected a sleepy, "come hither" sensuality. And come hither they did. Frank Sinatra and Aly Khan were among the many men linked romantically to Novak during this period. There was an undeniable glamour (and great publicity) to having Columbia's leading lady chased by some of the most eligible men in the world. But at some point in early 1958, Novak seems to have begun a relationship that Harry Cohn had never anticipated. That relationship was with Sammy Davis Jr.

Sammy Davis Jr. was black. He was also a Broadway star, having recently completed a triumphant turn in the musical *Mr. Wonderful*. Davis was one of the more interesting figures of the era. He came from a venerable African American vaudeville family on his father's side. (His mother was Puerto Rican.) In addition to his prodigious musical and dancing gifts, he was a gifted raconteur and a talented photographer. He was also Jewish, having converted after a terrible auto accident in 1954 that cost him an eye. This didn't boost his standing much in Cohn's eyes. The Columbia Studio mogul hated the fact that his alabaster sex goddess was involved in a romantic relationship with a one-eyed African American entertainer—so much so that he went to Manhattan mob boss Frank Costello with a request. Cohn wanted the Mob to end Davis's relationship with Novak, using whatever means proved necessary. So Costello called Cohen (at a private number on a secure phone).

"Lookit, ya know that Harry Cohn?" Costello asked Cohen, according to Cohen's later account of their conversation.

Mickey said that he didn't know Cohn personally but that he knew of him.

"Well, lookit," Costello continued. "There's a matter come up—the guy's all right, and he's done some favors for us back here, and I want ya to listen to him out, to make a meet with him, make a meet with him for whatever he wants and go along with him in every way ya can."

Soon thereafter, Cohn called Cohen to discuss what was bothering him—the Davis-Novak relationship. After several fairly circumspect conversations, Mickey finally asked Cohn point-blank what he wanted. Cohn replied that he wanted Sammy Davis Jr. "knocked in" (i.e., "rubbed out"). In Cohen's later recounting of this story, he indignantly refused, telling Cohn, "Lookit, you're way out of line. Not only am I going to give ya a negative answer on this, but I'm going to give ya a negative answer that you better see this doesn't happen."

There's another more plausible version of the story. According to Davis biographer Gary Fishgall, Mickey Cohen visited Sammy in Las Vegas to deliver a warning and offer advice. The warning was that someone was about to put a contract out on his head. The advice was to dump Kim Novak and go find himself a nice black girl to marry. Panicked, Davis promptly called Sam Giancana in Chicago to plead for help. Giancana replied that there was only so much the Outfit could do on the West Coast. A fearful Davis broke off the relationship with Novak and abruptly married showgirl Loray White. Harry Cohn died one month later (of natural causes).

Whatever version is true, Sammy Davis Jr. apparently felt nothing but gratitude toward Mickey. When Cohen was hauled into court on April 4, 1958 (Good Friday), for assaulting a waiter who had annoyed him at a party for Davis at Frank Sinatra and Peter Lawford's Villa Capri restaurant, the entertainer came forward as a witness for the defense. (He testified that the waiter had spilled coffee on Cohen and made a rude remark.) So did another guest with a long and curious relationship with Mickey Cohen, the actor Robert Mitchum. Public violence, high-profile arrests, celebrity alibis— to a recently relapsed gangster hungry for publicity, things could hardly get better. But later that night, they did. At 9:40 p.m., Cohen associate Johnny Stompanato was stabbed to death in the home of then-girlfriend Lana Turner.

Turner, thirty-eight, was one of Hollywood's best-known (and most frequently married) actresses. According to Turner's FBI files, she was also one of the most sexually voracious. As a result, it's no surprise that she soon shacked up with Stompanato, thirty-two, a celebrity in his own right among adventuresome Hollywood actresses. "The most handsome man that I've ever known that was all man," Cohen called him. But it wasn't Stompanato's good lucks that made him Hollywood's most notorious gigolo. Rather, it was his legendary "endowment." To Mickey, though, Stompanato was kind of like a kid brother. As soon as he heard the news of Stompanato's death, he raced over to Turner's house in Beverly Hills. Attorney Jerry Giesler intercepted Cohen outside.

"If Lana sees you, she's going to fall apart altogether," Giesler told Cohen. Instead, he sent him over to the morgue to identify Stompanato's body.

In fact, Turner was terrified of Cohen. Wild rumors quickly spread. "LANA FEARS COHEN GANG VENGEANCE," cried one tabloid. The identity of the supposed killer quickly emerged—Lana's fourteen-year-old daughter, Cheryl Crane. Supposedly, she had stabbed Stompanato with a kitchen knife when she walked in on him beating her mother.

Cohen didn't believe it. Stompanato wasn't the toughest of Cohen's henchmen, but he was a former Marine. Mickey couldn't believe that a mere girl could have killed him with a knife. He suspected that Lana herself was probably the killer. Cohen wanted to see justice done.

In this, he was virtually alone. Neither prosecutors nor the public seemed upset that Johnny Stompanato was dead. The general attitude was,

Good riddance. Press accounts portrayed Stompanato as a swarthy abuser who had preyed upon the fair Turner. This offended Mickey, who believed that Stompanato and Turner genuinely loved each other. Cohen resolved to set the record straight.

The day after Stompanato's death, his apartment at the Del Capri Motel in Westwood was mysteriously sacked. A week later, love letters from Turner to Stompanato appeared in the *Herald-Express*, just as the trial of Cheryl Crane was beginning. The letters left little doubt of Turner's affection for Stompanato, whom she addressed as "daddy love" in notes signed "Tu Zincarella" (your gypsy). But this time, the resurgent gangster was out of touch with the public. The publication of private letters was seen as unseemly, and the press read them for evidence that the affair was winding down.

Cohen was puzzled by this hostile reception. But he didn't dwell on it. Perhaps he didn't care all that much about Johnny either. Or maybe he was distracted by his latest discovery, a thrice-married, hazel-eyed Marilyn Monroe look-alike named Liz Renay.

Renay was a sometime stripper (44DD-26-36) as well as an aspiring painter and occasional poet who had left New York after boyfriend Tony Coppola's longtime boss, Albert Anastasia, was rubbed out in 1957. Friends such as "Champ" Segal in New York told Renay to look up Mickey. When she did, Renay was pleasantly surprised: "His hands were soft, his nails fastidiously clean and polished. His touch was more like a caress. He wasn't at all what I expected him to be." The two hit it off and soon became a couple (though Renay would later claim that in private Mickey always "stopped short"—out of respect for Renay's boyfriend in New York). In March 1958, *Life* magazine featured a photo spread of the two of them eating ice cream sundaes at the Carousel. This was too much for LaVonne. Escorting starlets to nightclubs was one thing—that was practically part of a Hollywood gangster's job description. Flirting around town and eating ice cream with a rather notorious young woman was quite another. That June, LaVonne and Mickey returned to divorce court. This time the split was final. As alimony, Cohen agreed to pay LaVonne a dollar a year.

Meanwhile, Cohen and Hecht were making progress with his life story. On July 7, Walter Winchell reported that *The Soul of a Gunman* was finished and that Mickey Cohen had already begun selling shares in a future feature film based on his memoirs. According to Winchell, a Los Angeles psychiatrist had already invested $30,000 in the project. It soon emerged that a number of other people had made significant investments as well. Now that his client had the prospect of legitimate income at hand, Cohen attorney

George Bieber approached the Internal Revenue Service with a proposal to settle Cohen's tax problems for $200,000. Under Bieber's proposal, the government would get the first $50,000 in revenues from Cohen's life story; Cohen would get the second $50,000; and the IRS would collect the rest of the royalties until Mickey's debt was paid. Treasury agent Guy Mc-Cown expressed an interest in the deal.

Then Mickey made a misstep. On September 20, 1959, writer Dean Jennings published the first installment in what proved to be a withering four-part series about Cohen in the *Saturday Evening Post*. Entitled "The Private Life of a Hood," the article detailed Cohen's luxurious lifestyle—a lifestyle the author estimated required about $120,000 a year—at precisely the moment Cohen was denying that he had any earned income. Jennings's article also infuriated the writer Ben Hecht, who felt that by talking to Jennings, Cohen had cannibalized their proposed book. Angrily, Hecht informed Cohen that the collaboration was off. Mickey was upset (though he still harbored hopes for a lucrative movie deal).

On the whole, though, Chief Parker's problems were more acute. Cohen was reconstituting his power and hiding large sources of income from the IRS, even as he prepared to negotiate a deal that would remove the threat of federal monitoring and prosecution. Recent court decisions made it harder than ever to catch Cohen in the act. In October 1958, the state supreme court came out with yet another ruling, *People v. McShann*, that required the police to produce confidential informers in narcotics cases for cross-examination by the defense. The LAPD, warned Parker in reply, was being disarmed just as "the criminal cartels of the world" were preparing another "invasion."

"It won't be long," Parker warned, "until the Costello mob moves in here and turns this city into another Chicago."

But Cohen was not home free yet. While his attorney was seeking a deal, the Treasury Department was opening a new investigation into Cohen's finances. Investigators quickly homed in on Liz Renay. In early 1958, prosecutors in New York interrogated her about her ties to Anastasia—and her relationship with Mickey. Cohen was nonchalant about the prospect of prosecutors questioning the statuesque actress about their relationship.

"Anything she says is good enough for me," he told the *Los Angeles Times*. He even invited Chief Parker and Captain Hamilton to join them for dinner when Renay got back. "But I don't think they'd pick up the tab," he quipped. "That's a thousand-to-one shot."

The questioning of Renay continued. The U.S. attorney's office in Los Angeles convened a grand jury to investigate Mickey's lavish lifestyle. That fall, the federal grand jury summoned Renay to appear before them. She arrived at the federal courthouse resplendent in an outfit the *Los Angeles Times* described as "a tight-fitting royal blue jersey dress."

"Her red hair was set in a swirling pile," continued the anonymous scribe. "Her eyes which she said are green with brown polka dots, were dramatized by long glossy lashes and blue-shadowed eyelids." When confronted with questions about her underworld associates, Renay took the Fifth. The LAPD and the IRS seemed to have run into yet another roadblock in their effort to take down Mickey Cohen and his Syndicate associations. Fortunately for Chief Parker, though, he had another, even more powerful ally he could call upon—Robert Kennedy.

In March 1959, Robert Kennedy subpoenaed Cohen to testify before the McClellan Committee in Washington, D.C. Cohen's lawyer was Sam Dash, who would later win fame as the chief counsel of the Senate Watergate Committee. Dash took his client to meet Kennedy for the first time the day before the hearings. Cohen arrived aggrieved. He felt that he "already had a beef" with Kennedy, thanks to the stingy $8-a-day per diem authorized by Kennedy's staff. (Mickey was spending $100 a night to stay at the Washington Hilton.) Nonetheless, when Kennedy asked Cohen if he was going to answer questions at the Senate hearing tomorrow, Mickey said that he would try.

"Lookit, I'm going to answer any question that won't tend to incriminate me," he replied.

The next day, Cohen appeared as a witness—along with New Orleans crime boss Carlos Marcello ("a beautiful person, a real gentleman," according to Mickey). Kennedy began by establishing Cohen's moral character—namely, that he was an effete clotheshorse who had spent "$275 on his silk lounging pajamas, $25,000 for a specialty built bulletproof car and at one time had 300 different suits, 1,500 pairs of socks and 60 pairs of $60 shoes." Kennedy then noted that despite such lavish expenditures Cohen had declared only $1,200 in income in 1956 and $1,500 in income in 1957.

Cohen was upset about being questioned "like an out-and-out punk" by this "snotty little guy." So when Kennedy started to ask him more pointed questions about his finances, Cohen took the Fifth, declining to answer on the grounds that by doing so he might incriminate himself. Cohen's only laugh came when Kennedy asked if it was true that Cohen had gone zero for three in his professional boxing career (with three knockouts). (It wasn't. His professional boxing record seems to have been six wins, eleven losses, and one draw.)

Frustrated by Cohen's stonewalling, Kennedy called Cohen back into the hearings the next day. "I have been given to understand that you are a gentleman," he told Cohen pointedly before the cameras.

"Well, I consider myself a gentleman yeah," Cohen replied.

"Well, you sure haven't been a gentleman before this committee," Kennedy chided. "I see you're not going to answer any questions, but at least you could have answered that you *respectfully* declined to answer the questions because they may tend to incriminate you."

"That you *respectfully*?" Cohen replied, incredulous. "I'll be glad to do that—if I remember."

Then Kennedy switched gears. "Now off the record—you say you're a gentleman and all that. Let me ask you a question, and it has nothing to do with what we're here for concerning coin-operated machines, but what's the meaning in the underworld or the racket world when somebody's 'lights are to be put out'?"

It was a trick question. Cohen himself stood accused of having threatened one cigarette vending machine operator by informing him that he'd gotten a $50,000 contract to "put his lights out.'" His answer was quick in coming.

"Lookit," Mickey replied innocently, "I don't know what you're talking about. I'm not an electrician."

The audience laughed. Flushing bright red, Kennedy jumped up and headed for Mickey. But Senator McClellan grabbed Kennedy by the shoulder, to Cohen's great disappointment.

"I would have torn him apart [and] kicked his fuckin' head," Cohen said later. Instead, he and Fred Sica, highly pleased with themselves, flew up to New Jersey to visit Sica's eighty-year-old mother, who greeted Cohen by saying, "Mickey, my boy. Jimmy was supposed to get the lamp fixed, but I told him to wait for you. You fix it. You're an electrician."

To celebrate the thumb in the eye to Kennedy, the next day Cohen called the Cadillac dealership in Beverly Hills and ordered a new El Dorado Biarritz black convertible. Its list price was approximately $10,000—more than six times Cohen's declared income that year.

22

Chocolate City

"We are all members of some minority group."
—Chief William Parker

THE POLITE WORD was "Negro"—long "e," long "o." Bill Parker couldn't pronounce it correctly. Try as he might, Parker kept shortening his vowels, producing (in his odd, pseudo-Bostonian accent) something more like "nigra." The effect was jarring. When black people first heard Parker speak about race, they sometimes thought he was using the slur "nigger." When Vivian Strange, one of the few black women in the department in the early 1950s (and a fellow Roman Catholic), pointed out the chief's pronunciation problem, Parker was embarrassed. He did his best to correct himself, even going so far as to tape himself and play back his words: nigra, nigra, neegro. Parker's lack of familiarity with the word pointed to a larger challenge: Like many white Angelenos, Parker simply didn't know much about black people.

Nothing in Parker's life had prepared him to relate to African Americans. When Parker's paternal grandfather had first arrived in the Black Hills, Deadwood had been a polyglot mining camp, filled with adventurers from Wales to Nanjing, including a number of African Americans. But by the time Parker was born in 1905, that had changed. Deadwood's Chinatown, once the largest between San Francisco and the Mississippi River, had vanished; even the Chinese cemetery had been emptied of its bodies. The raucous, polyglot mining camp had given way to George Hearst's more organized Homestead Mining Company. Deadwood had become white.

The Los Angeles Parker moved to in 1922 had a similar complexion, albeit on a larger scale. Of its 520,000 residents, only about 15,000 were black. Most African American residents lived east of Main Street. The oldest black neighborhoods were near downtown, south of the rail yards along Central Avenue. By the 1920s, another sizable African American community had formed in nearby Watts. Most were drawn to the area by construction jobs building two major lines of Henry Huntington's Pacific Electric streetcar system—the north-south line from downtown L.A. to Long Beach and an east-west line from Venice to Santa Ana. When the lines were completed, they simply stayed, creating a mixed black-Latino area known as Mudtown.

As the 1920s progressed, the influx of African Americans to the Watts area accelerated. In 1926, Watts was incorporated into Los Angeles, in part to prevent the emergence of an independent, majority-black city. Three years later, the Supreme Court upheld the legality of racially restrictive housing covenants designed to keep West Slauson Avenue white. African Americans were slowly being confined to the south-central area. The upside of this concentration was political power. Unlike African Americans in the Jim Crow South, black Angelenos were never denied the right to vote. As a result, as soon as the early 1920s, black voters were seen as an important voting bloc. A handful of black political bosses soon emerged. Unfortunately, this was not a wholly positive development. These figures weren't just ward bosses; they were also crime lords. Instead of improving Central Avenue, many used their clout to create zones of protected vice. Said one police officer in the 1930s, "I know the payoff men, I know the go-betweens; but what can I do when it's sanctioned by the city's politicians?"

The situation satisfied no one. Law-abiding residents felt ignored by the police. In turn, the police came to associate Central Avenue—and African Americans in general—with crime and vice. When politics demanded a crackdown, Central Avenue was an easy target. The result was a strained relationship between African American residents and the police.

As a policeman, Parker didn't have much firsthand experience in dealing with black people. Only about 2 percent of the force was African American, a percentage that roughly reflected that of the population as a whole. Although he'd worked in the Central Division as a young policeman, his recollections of his early days as a patrolman seem largely devoid of black people. (In contrast, his stint as a sergeant in Hollenbeck in the early 1930s clearly did affect his perception of Latinos.) Had Los Angeles remained a city with only a small African American population, this might not have mattered much. But it did not. For at the same moment that Bill Parker was shipping out to join the U.S. Army, Los Angeles was becoming a major destination for African Americans.

The primary draw was jobs. The need to arm America's forces in the Pacific had transformed Los Angeles into a major industrial center. But L.A. also seemed to offer blacks an escape from the Jim Crow South, at least at first glance. African Americans responded to this new opportunity by migrating west by the thousands. In 1941, the year before Bill Parker left Los Angeles to join the U.S. Army, Los Angeles's African American population numbered approximately 70,000 residents. By the time he returned, Los Angeles had become a city with the largest African American population west of St. Louis, with an African American population of more than 125,000.

The city did not take this change particularly well. The torrent of countrified newcomers shocked black and white Angelenos alike and created serious problems for local authorities. The first and most acute problem was housing. There wasn't any, particularly at a time when even middle-class African Americans couldn't legally purchase a home in most of the Los Angeles basin. So the newcomers crowded into the only residential district that was available, Little Tokyo—the previous residents of which had been relocated to interior concentration camps up and down the coast. Soon, the area had a new name—Bronzeville. Little Tokyo had suddenly become Los Angeles's most fearful slum. It also became a center of crime. The understaffed, wartime LAPD responded poorly, with the slap of the blackjack and the crack of the truncheon. Officers policed African American neighborhoods with a heavy hand. Respect was mandatory—for officers, not residents. White officers demanded to be addressed as "Sir"—or else. (Tales of black men who were beaten and booked for drunkenness after some perceived slight were a common feature of black papers like the *California Eagle* and the *Los Angeles Sentinel*.) Black officers were, by some accounts, even rougher. According to white veterans of the 77th Street Division, black residents often requested "white justice" out of fear of what black officers might mete out.*

African Americans weren't the only minority group that often found itself at the receiving end of a policeman's baton. In 1942, L.A. county sheriff's deputies and the LAPD responded to the brutal murder of a twenty-two-year-old Latino farmworker at the Sleepy Lagoon reservoir by rounding up more than six hundred Latino youths. Many were severely beaten during their interrogations. After a flagrantly unfair trial (during which the counsel for the defense were denied the right to communicate freely with their clients), twelve of the youths were convicted of murder and another five of assault. The convictions were later overturned on appeal, and prosecutors declined to retry the case.

---

*The LAPD apparently encouraged the use of tough tactics in black neighborhoods as well. As Deputy Chief Thad Brown later told historian Gerald Woods, "You could send Negro officers to do tough jobs in the black belt, and there would be no beef." (Woods, "The Progressives and the Police," 460.)

Los Angeles even experienced something very much like a pogrom. In the summer of 1943, a handful of Chicano youths got into a fight with a group of servicemen on shore leave who'd been messing with their girlfriends. Three days later, servicemen responded with a five-day rampage through downtown and East L.A., during which time hundreds of Chicano youths, particularly those wearing "zoot suits" (whose long coats and balloon pants were widely associated with gang activity) were brutally beaten by military servicemen while the LAPD stood by. The pogrom ended only when the military placed downtown Los Angeles off-limits to all military personnel. Not since the days of the "third degree" had Los Angeles experienced such naked brutality. By 1945, it was clear that culling recent hires who should never have joined the department in the first place and improving race relations would be major challenges. Parker recognized the first challenge but not the second. By the time he faced the latter, it was too late.

WHILE COHEN thumbed his nose at Bobby Kennedy, Chief Parker found himself facing his own judicial inquiry. In the spring of 1959, a Los Angeles municipal judge, David Williams, threw out gambling charges against twenty-five African Americans, on the grounds that "the vice squad enforced gambling ordinances in a discriminatory fashion." When a resident wrote the judge to ask why he'd taken it upon himself to nullify the law, Judge Williams essentially accused the LAPD of racist law enforcement.

"I feel that when police officials instruct their subordinate officers to arrest only Negroes on a given charge, it will not be long before their newly-gained power will prompt them to enforce other statutes only against certain other groups," wrote Williams. The recipient of this letter promptly forwarded this provocative response to Chief Parker, who immediately dashed off an angry note to the judge. ("I have no knowledge of any such instruction issued in this Department, either orally or in writing.") Parker demanded that Williams defend himself.

Williams wrote back to say that he found it curious that Chief Parker thought he had the right to interject himself into someone else's private correspondence. Williams then offered a defense for his decision. He noted that over the course of the three preceding years, the only cases prosecutors had brought to him involved raids on Negro gambling games. The only white people he'd seen prosecuted on gambling charges were those swept up in raids on Negro areas. The LAPD's citywide statistics told a similar story. During the years 1957 and 1958, police had arrested 12,000 blacks on gambling charges but only 1,200 whites. Were African Americans really responsible for 90 percent of the gambling in the city of Los Angeles? Williams thought not. He suggested that the city council's police and fire committee look into why so few gambling arrests were made in "white" parts of town, such as the San Fernando Valley, Hollywood, and West Los Angeles.

The spat soon went public. Parker rejoined that blacks made up 73 percent of nationwide gambling arrests (not including bookmaking). The LAPD's arrest rate was slightly higher (around 82 percent) not because the department was more racist, he insisted, but rather because the department was dealing with unusually hardened criminals. At a meeting with the city council soon after Williams first made his remarks, Parker explained that "there are certain courts in certain states in the Deep South where people of a certain race who are accused of crimes of violence definitely can get probation if they go to California."

The black press objected strongly to this explanation. On March 19, the *California Eagle* criticized Parker for "losing his head" over the controversy with Williams. While praising his abilities as an administrator, the paper's editorial board concluded that the chief's shortcomings outweighed his virtues and called on Parker to retire. Of course, nothing came of this request. The city council conducted a cursory investigation of Judge Williams's allegations and then referred them to the Police Commission, which promptly dismissed them as "a personal attack." And so yet another investigation was stillborn.

Street-level disrespect wasn't the only thing contributing to police-minority tensions. So too did Chief Parker's principled commitment to follow where the data led him.

One of Parker's first priorities as chief of police had been to make the LAPD more efficient and more data driven. Parker's goal was crime prevention. Like most departments, the LAPD relied on crime mapping (i.e., pins on maps) to track trends and deployed its forces accordingly.

"Every department worth its salt deploys field forces on the basis of crime experience," explained Parker in a 1957 collection of speeches titled *Parker on Policing.* "Deployment is often heaviest in so-called minority sections of the city," he continued. "The reason is statistical—it is a fact that certain racial groups, at present time, commit a disproportionate share of the total crime."

Even in 1958 this was a sensitive assertion, and Parker was careful to attempt to defuse it. "[A] competent police administrator is fully aware of the multiple conditions which create this problem," he continued. "There is no inherent physical or mental weakness in any racial stock which tends it toward crime." (Indeed, Parker was fond of pointing out that racial classifications were nothing more then pseudoscience.) "But," he went on, "and this is a 'but' which must be borne constantly in mind—the police field deployment is not social agency activity. In deploying to suppress crime, we are not interested in why a certain group tends toward crime, we are interested in maintaining order."

The LAPD deployed its forces most heavily where crime was highest—in black neighborhoods. Newton Division, a crowded district of 4.8 square miles (with a population, in 1950, of 101,000 residents, most of them African Americans), was assigned 34 policemen per square mile. Hollenbeck Division, which patrolled Mexican American East L.A., had 14 patrolmen per square mile. In contrast, there were only 443 policemen assigned to the 259 square miles of the Hollywood, Wilshire, and Foothill Divisions, less than two policemen per square mile. The result of this deployment pattern was that black and Chicano residents of Los Angeles were far more likely to interact with the LAPD than were white residents of the city.

Anyone who'd spent a day on the streets of Newton Division realized that the LAPD maintained order in a certain way—with a heavy hand. In those days, most good beat officers were big, imposing men. Flagrant disrespect routinely resulted in a stiff dose of "street justice"—a bogus arrest, a painful jab with a baton, or worse. A greater police presence meant this happened more in African American parts of the city. It wasn't necessarily a racial thing. Take a tough neighborhood, add thousands of newcomers who don't know the ropes, apply police officers who believe that their personal safety depends on being tough, and you've got a recipe for trouble, regardless of the color of the people involved. But there were other reasons that the LAPD was particularly insistent on "respect."

Police departments in cities with political machines such as New York and Chicago were big organizations padded with patronage jobs. Ward bosses often reserved civil service jobs for neighborhood supporters. Such forces frequently had problems with incompetency and corruption. But they also had advantages. Officers and neighborhood residents tended to know each other. Ward bosses and precinct or division captains generally worked hand in hand. And because the number of officers relative to the population being policed was often quite large, officers knew that if they got into a scrape, there were almost always other officers close at hand. The LAPD's officers didn't have that assurance. Backup was rarely around the block. Sometimes, it was miles away. As a result, when the LAPD acted, it went in hard and fast. It was a style of policing driven in part by fear. But all that many residents saw was cocky aggression.

This left a bitter taste in black neighborhoods. While the police demanded deference and respect, many of its officers seemed unable—or unwilling—to distinguish between actual hoodlums and ordinary citizens. It was one thing to get tough with a known criminal. It was quite another to repeatedly stop and insultingly question a law-abiding citizen. But for whatever reason, that is precisely what the LAPD too often did.

In the African American press, story after story chronicled the indignities. "EVERY NEGRO A SUSPECT," screamed the *California Eagle* in a March 20, 1947, article on the police hunt for a pair of men who'd shot two police officers over the course of the preceding weekend. A shooting was, of course, a serious matter, but the police response was indiscriminate. "No Negro, no matter how little he fitted the description of the two fugitives, was immune from police search and question," continued the paper bitterly. Every few months, the paper would carry a horrifying story about a black man—or a black woman—who had suffered insult, if not assault, at the hands of the police.

"With the death this week of Dan Jense, a café owner who was brutally beaten by police in the course of a raid on his establishment, the spotlight shifts to police brutality and brings into focus the repeated complaints which have come out of minority communities for the past several years," wrote the *Eagle* in June 1949. But of course, the mainstream press didn't shift its attention to police brutality. Neither did the city's politicians. "Mayor Bowron has steadfastly defended the police in every reported incident of brutality," the *Eagle* lamented.

"The cold-blooded killing of August Salcido and the fatal beating of Herman Burns, climaxed the uninhibited 'legal lynching' campaign of terror that the police department has been carrying on against Negroes and Mexicans for some time," opined the paper on another occasion:

> Delegation after delegation has appeared before the Mayor demanding that he put a stop to the unnecessary rousting, beating and intimidating of citizens in the minority community. Bowron has promised time and again, he would check these abuses, but they have continued and grown.

The steps the mayor had taken, the paper continued, such as appointing an African American to monitor allegations of brutality, were little more than "window-dressing." With scandal again threatening the department's leadership, the paper foresaw "token raids" to divert attention from the main action.

"Any so-called 'clean-up' on the East Side [meaning east of Main Street] would be in reality a cover-up for a campaign of intimidation and police terrorism," the paper heatedly concluded.

To nonblacks, such accounts were easy to dismiss. The outspoken publisher of the *Eagle*, Charlotta Bass, was, if not a Communist, then at the very least a fellow traveler. Moreover, police department investigations rarely substantiated these dramatic tales of wrongdoing. Indeed, some proved so frivolous that the police department began to urge prosecutors to charge people who brought unwarranted complaints against the department with making false statements about the police. Even black Angelenos were sometimes skeptical of the *Eagle*, preferring instead the more conservative *Sentinel*. But the *Sentinel*, too, was replete with stories of black men and women going about their business and running afoul of the police. To African Americans, the sheer accumulation of anecdotes was compelling. White residents rarely heard or read about these stories.

AS THE HEAD of internal affairs, Bill Parker might have been expected to take a stance on such issues, but there's no evidence he did. Instead, Parker focused almost exclusively on corruption and the underworld. Yet there is reason to believe that Parker was initially seen as something of a progressive on race relations. The two commissioners who initially supported Parker for chief were Irving Snyder, who was Jewish, and Dr. J. Alexander Somerville, who was African American. Presumably, these men saw Parker as a fair-minded individual. The second reason for believing Parker would be fair-minded arose from his treatment of African American policewoman Vivian Strange.

When he was sworn in as chief, Parker made a striking promise to the rank and file: When it came to promotions, he would always pick the person at the top of the civil service eligibility list. The first test of this policy came almost immediately, when Strange became eligible to make sergeant, a rank that no African American woman had ever before attained. Strange was not popular in the department, where she had a reputation as someone who "hated" white people so much that she wouldn't ride in the same car with them. Fifty years after her promotion to sergeant, one senior LAPD commander described her as "a bitch."

Strange may (or may not) have been an unpleasant person; however, she clearly understood something that the department's white officers did not—namely, that a black woman in a car with a white man in south Los Angeles was likely to be seen as a prostitute. Insisting on driving herself to meetings in African American neighborhoods wasn't standoffish; it was an attempt to avoid humiliation. Whatever her personality, Parker did not hesitate when her name came up on the sergeant eligibility list. That November, he made Strange the LAPD's first female African American sergeant.

But those who hoped for further steps toward equality were disappointed. Parker did not change the department's unstated policy of not placing black officers in positions of command over white officers. He also dismissed the idea that the LAPD had a race-relations problem. In a March 11, 1953, letter to a resident who had written Mayor Bowron to complain about police abuse, Parker presented a rebuttal noting that over the course of the year 1952, the LAPD had received 1,068 complaints. During that same period, his letter continued, the department had made "a minimum of 1,741,860 contacts." In other words, .0006 of the officer contacts had resulted in complaints. Of those, "259 (or 24.3 percent) were substantiated and resulted in disciplinary action. . . . A total of 116 official reprimands were issued, 126 officers received a total of 1,453 days suspension. . . . Sixteen officers were terminated from the Department." To Parker, the conclusion was clear: Police misconduct was exceedingly rare, and on those occasions where misconduct did occur, it was severely punished. The possibility that the department's statistics might mislead—that complaints were discouraged, that communities of color might have become inured to behavior that would have generated waves of complaints in whiter, more affluent parts of town—was something Parker does not appear to have considered.

This represented a failure of imagination. Yet to his credit, when the facts were clear, Parker followed them to their logical conclusion. In mid-1953, Los Angeles lurched into an antigang hysteria after a group of young thugs robbed and killed a pedestrian downtown. "Rat Packs Attack," screamed the newspapers; columnists demanded that the police department hit back, often in strikingly intemperate ways. (One newspaper editorial called on the department to prevent crime by using "clubs and mailed fists"—this less than two years after the "Bloody Christmas" beatings.) Much of the public anger had a decidedly anti-Hispanic tone. Parker would have none of it. In response to an inquiry from the grand jury, Parker calmly refused to treat a lone incident as a deadly trend.

"The local juvenile gang problem is not new to this community, but has its roots deep in the social and economic make-up of this area," Parker wrote back to jury foreman Don Thompson. "The recent incidents which have unfortunately been so spectacularly reported have created a wave of hysteria, not a crime wave. Most ethnic groups at one time or another have had confused generations which physically displayed their resentment toward society. The best methods of integrating these groups into our society are well known. Those methods will solve the present problem, if citizens will continue to apply them."

To Parker, race relations were first and foremost a technical problem.

The appropriate response was to deploy skilled public relations officers, officers like one African American officer who had caught Parker's attention—Officer Tom Bradley, the same Tom Bradley who would later become Los Angeles's first African American mayor.

IN 1955, Tom Bradley was one of the LAPD's most promising African American officers. His rise had been remarkable. Bradley's parents were sharecroppers, Texas-born, who arrived in Los Angeles in 1924 with their seven-year-old son. Tom's father, Lee Bradley, soon found a job as a porter for the Santa Fe railroad. His mother, Crenner, devoted herself to the education of their son, maneuvering Bradley into the Polytechnic high school, a predominantly white institution known for its excellent athletics and strong academics. Tall, handsome, and fast, Tom Bradley excelled at both. Upon graduating, he won a track scholarship to UCLA. But after meeting Ethel Arnold (a beauty whom the *L.A. Tribune* would later describe as "the community's prettiest girl"), Bradley decided he wanted to get married. That meant he needed a job. So, during his junior year, Bradley decided to apply to become a police officer. His score on the civil service test was high, and in 1940, he joined the LAPD.

Bradley got the kind of assignments that black officers typically do—in his instance, a position in the Newton Division vice squad. His work there on a bookmaking case in 1950 caught Parker's eye. So too did his efforts to promote the department in the local press. By the autumn of 1953, Bradley was writing a regular "Police-Eye View" column for the *California Eagle*. His articles were perfectly crafted to win Parker's approval. An October 22, 1953, piece on the Police Commission described it, reverentially, as "one of the most powerful agencies of our government." This was a favorite fiction of the chief; every informed observer of Los Angeles politics knew that the Police Commission was little more than a rubber stamp. Still, it was a useful stance when the department came under political attack. Bradley also took on the department's critics in print. A January 28, 1954, column addressed the volatile issue of residents being stopped and questioned by the police. Bradley defended the practice, noting that police officers often had information that motivated the stop. Such efforts endeared him to Chief Parker. In early 1955, Parker approved Bradley's request to move to a new community relations unit. Bradley threw himself into the work with commendable zeal. In short order, he had become a member of more than 120 social, fraternal, and business groups.

Although Parker was impressed by Bradley's work, his apologetics for Chief Parker and the department met with skepticism in much of the black community. "Instead of decent human relations based on mutual respect and a negation of false and arbitrary barriers, Parker gives us the 20th century antibiotic, public relations," complained the editorial board of another African American newspaper, the *Los Angeles Tribune*, in early 1955.

African Americans were particularly upset by the police department's failure to integrate the force more aggressively. In late 1955, fire department chief John Alderson was removed from office for his point-blank refusal to integrate the fire department. Tellingly, Parker seemed to view the attempt to integrate the fire department as a quasi-subversive campaign: Intelligence division officers were sent to observe city council sessions on the issue. But when the police were confronted with similar demands, Parker maintained that LAPD was—and long had been—integrated.

Civil rights leaders thought differently.

Critics of the department noted that 60 percent of the department's 122 "active Negro personnel" were deployed to Newton and 77th Street Divisions, the two "black" divisions. Black officers were effectively excluded from other parts of the city and from many of the department's most desirable assignments.

"The Police of Los Angeles fall just a stone's throw short of being as Jim Crow as if the department were situated in the heart of Georgia, rather than California," declared the *Tribune*, somewhat melodramatically, in a February 1955 editorial.*

Despite such sniping, Parker seemed to value the job Bradley was doing. In the fall of 1958, Chief Parker personally called Bradley's home to inform him that he'd made lieutenant, only the third African American lieutenant in the history of the force.

But Bill Parker was not the trusting sort. After a series of negative articles about the department appeared in the *L.A. Sentinel*, Parker decided to take a closer look at the performance of his top community liaison officer, and so he instructed the intelligence division to put Bradley under observation. Daryl Gates was with the chief when the intelligence report came back.

"Parker told me the report said that Bradley, instead of talking the department up, was providing negative information to dissident groups, say-

---

*Parker was also buffeted from another direction—by demands that the police department do more to crack down on crime. In late 1957, the city council formally complained to the chief about "soaring" vice conditions in South-Central Los Angeles (as the area around Watts was coming to be described). Mayor Poulson weighed in as well, complaining that prostitution, bookmaking, and narcotics "flourished without apparent restraint" between 40th and 56th Streets on Central Avenue and Aaron Boulevard. Chief Parker replied, testily, that he'd be happy to clean up the area if city officials found funding to increase the size of the vice squad by 363 percent.

ing unfavorable things about Parker and the LAPD," wrote Gates in his memoirs. "That changed Parker's view of him just like that. Bradley, he fumed, was an absolute traitor to the department."

What was the nature of Bradley's transgression? While the exact offense is unknown, a 1961 intelligence division report on Bradley's appearance at a meeting sponsored by the ACLU at a private residence at 16916 San Fernando Road provides a flavor of his comments:

Mr. Bradley spoke first:—

He stated that he had worked for the City 21 years, had served on the Police Community Public Relations Unit, and had a first-hand view of Police Department/Citizen relations.

He reviewed conditions—starting back about 1947 after World War II and the Zoot Suiters, etcetera—and stated a very touchy situation was growing between the police officers and the citizens. In his opinion a lack of understanding brought about police hostilities. He stated new police candidates were given the physical and written tests and then interviewed by a psychiatrist from the University of California in Los Angeles. At the Academy recruits were treated about the same during their thirteen weeks of training. However, when the recruits left the Academy they were immediately segregated and the white officers began to get an air of superiority. Colored officers and white officers were not placed in the field as partners until about a year ago. Although, Department policy was to integrate, there was a difference between pronouncement and action, and over the years several mistakes were made and tolerated.

There seemed to be no way for line officers to communicate with top personnel concerning their grievances. The Negro officer was naturally disgusted and the white officer continued to feel more superior and better and thus bound to discriminate against the Negro in his work. . . . All in all, Mr. Bradley did not come right out and condemn the Department in the open manner that [ACLU board member] Mr. [Hugh] Manes and Mr. [Lloyd] Wright [past president of the ACLU] did, but his silence and very presence on the platform gave me and most of those present the impression that his view, and that of his two cohorts was the same.

These were remarkably mild and measured remarks, yet they, too, were processed as treacherous attacks. Clearly, Parker's threshold for "absolute treachery" was low. As punishment, Parker immediately transferred Bradley to Wilshire Division, where he was made watch lieutenant for the graveyard shift.

But Parker's efforts to punish Bradley came too late. Like Parker, Bradley had earned a law degree while on the force. As a member of the community relations detail, he had also had the chance to build a wealth of contacts—contacts he now utilized to launch himself into local politics. In 1959, Bradley joined the effort to elect a black representative to the city council. Although his chosen candidate, Eddie Atkinson, ultimately fell short (in part because of an *L.A. Times* story highlighting Atkinson's ownership of a tavern and suggesting underworld ties), Bradley impressed everyone he met. Atkinson's loss underscored one of Bradley's great strengths: A black tavern keeper was vulnerable to innuendo. A black cop like Tom Bradley wouldn't be.

PARKER saw things differently. Tom Bradley was now an enemy within—and not the only one. By the summer of 1959, one of Parker's ostensible bosses, police commissioner Herbert Greenwood, had become dissatisfied with Parker too. Where his predecessor on the board had been courtly and deferential, Greenwood was assertive and sometimes sharp. Judge Williams's earlier accusations about the department's selective enforcement of gambling ordinances led Greenwood to demand some answers. He requested that the department provide him with the information on the number, rank, and assignment of black officers. ("It is a question I'm frequently asked and I should know the answers," he explained to the *Los Angeles Times*.) According to Greenwood, Parker responded by going "into a rage, shouting that the only reason I wanted it was to attack him." Frustrated, Greenwood turned to a political ally, film star-turned-councilwoman Rosalind Wyman. But when Wyman pressed for more racial statistics from the department, Parker counterattacked, alleging that Greenwood and Wyman's request for information was nothing more than a personal smear campaign. Mayor Poulson and the four other members of the Police Commission rallied to Parker's defense. Wyman backed down, and on June 18, 1959, Greenwood resigned, releasing a statement that cited the "unhealthy attitudes" of the people in authority. Although his letter of resignation didn't cite Parker by name, his statements to the press left no doubt that the person he had in mind was the chief of police.

"We don't tell him," Greenwood said by way of explanation. "He tells us."

And so the Police Commission's sole African American member—the only member of the commission who routinely challenged the chief—stepped down. Mayor Poulson's effort to check his chief was at an end. Parker's power over the LAPD was now complete.

23

Disneyland

> *"[H]ave gangsters taken over the place that
> can destroy me?"*
>
> —Nikita Khrushchev

BILL PARKER had long conceived of the mission of the Los Angeles Police Department in lofty terms. Its task, Parker believed, was nothing less than preserving civilization itself. Organized crime was at the top of Parker's agenda not simply because he feared that it might regain control of Los Angeles but also because he believed that it weakened American society at a critical junction in the struggle against Soviet Russia. The Communist Party was Parker's ultimate adversary. The allegations of brutality, the complaints of discrimination, the calls for a civilian review board—to Parker, they were all part of Moscow's proxy war on the LAPD. Usually, the hand of the party was hidden, but in September 1959, he got a chance to clash directly with his ultimate adversary, the general secretary of the Communist Party, Nikita Khrushchev.

Earlier that year, President Eisenhower had invited Khrushchev to visit the United States, and the Soviet leader had agreed to an eleven-day trip that would crisscross the United States. Along the way, the Soviet premier was scheduled to spend one day and one night in Los Angeles. The prospect of a Khrushchev visit to Los Angeles sparked mass panic, as if a communist takeover might be affected by the mere presence of the general secretary. A hysterical protest rally was held in the Rose Bowl. As the official entrusted with Khrushchev's security, Parker was concerned. Two weeks before the visit, Parker called on the public to "support Eisenhower" in this "most difficult decision." He advised Angelenos to receive Khrushchev in a "state of aloof detachment" and to carry on with normal daily activities. Privately, though, the LAPD was preparing for the most high-security foreign visitor in the city's history. Officers would be stationed at critical locations along Khrushchev's every route. The Soviet leader would be surrounded by an envelope of LAPD officers at all times. No unauthorized contact with American civilians would be permitted. But at the very last minute, something came up. As Khrushchev flew across the country on September 19, accompanied by U.S. ambassador to the United Nations Henry Cabot Lodge, the Soviet premier made a request: He would like to tour Disneyland.

The general secretary's desire for a visit was understandable. Disneyland, which had opened in Anaheim in 1955, was one of the wonders of its age, a 160-acre, $17 million Xanadu replete with such dazzling attractions as Sleeping Beauty's castle, the Jungleland river safari ride (complete with a mechanized hippo that reared up under the boat), the Mount Matterhorn toboggan slide (with Swiss summiteers climbing the mountain), and a rocket ship that simulated a trip to the moon. With Disneyland, Walt Disney, the man whose drawings revolutionized animation, had transformed the Coney Island–style amusement park into something new, the theme park, that offered up fantasy, exoticism, and, most enticing of all, the future. Anaheim's city manager had extended an invitation to the Soviet premier when his trip to the United States had first been announced, and Khrushchev had been interested. However, when Khrushchev's advance security team went to Los Angeles to meet with Chief Parker and other local officials three weeks before his trip to the United States, the visit to Disneyland had been dropped. The fact that Khrushchev would be visiting on a Saturday posed major crowd-control problems, and his limited stay in Los Angeles meant that he would have had almost no time to enjoy the rides or see the sights. Unfortunately, this change of plans had apparently not been mentioned to Khrushchev himself. It now fell to his American hosts to deal with this request.

Khrushchev was greeted at the airport by Mayor Poulson, who delivered a terse welcome to the Soviet premier in a vacant corner of the airport. Soon thereafter, Khrushchev's request to tour Disneyland reached Chief Parker. The LAPD was stretched thin. Some five hundred officers—more than 10 percent of the force—had already been dedicated to Khrushchev's visit. Parker himself was personally commanding their operations. As the motorcade (accompanied by fifty motorcycle officers and two police helicopters) sped to Khrushchev's first event, a luncheon at 20th Century Fox, Chief Parker's car was hit by an errant tomato. The incident underscored the dangers Khrushchev faced in an unsecured environment. Parker decided to reject the premier's request. The LAPD simply could not secure the thirty-mile route to Orange County, Parker reasoned, much less a theme park located outside its jurisdiction which was likely to have forty thousand visitors with no advance notice. Disneyland, said the chief, was off limits.

This decision was not immediately relayed to the Soviet premier. Instead, upon arriving at the studio, Khrushchev was taken to the set of the movie *Can-Can* (starring Shirley MacLaine, who attempted to engage the Soviet premier in an impromptu dance). That was followed by a luncheon at the Café de Paris commissary, with 20th Century Fox president Spyros Skouras as master of ceremonies. (Frank Sinatra sat next to Mrs. Khrushchev; Bob Hope and David Niven were across the table.) By all accounts, Khrushchev was in fine spirits—as a man looking forward to an afternoon at Disneyland ought to be. Then Mrs. Khrushchev passed her husband a note, informing Khrushchev of Parker's decision. The premier's mood changed abruptly. Enraged, Khrushchev immediately lashed out in a meandering, arm-waving forty-five-minute address.

"We have come to this town where lives the cream of American art," Khrushchev began darkly.

> "But just now I was told that I could not go to Disneyland." I asked, "Why not? What is it? Do you have rocket-launching pads there? I do not know." And just listen—just listen—to what I was told—to what reason I was told. We, which means the American authorities, cannot guarantee your security if you go there.
>
> What is it? Is there an epidemic of cholera there or something? Or have gangsters taken over the place that can destroy me? Then what must I do? Commit suicide? This is the situation I am in—your guest. For me the situation is inconceivable. I cannot find words to explain this to my people!

Instead of going to Disneyland, Khrushchev's motorcade drove around UCLA and then visited a San Fernando Valley subdivision. That evening during a dinner at the Ambassador Hotel, Khrushchev vented his frustrations about Mayor Poulson's perceived rudeness. "If you persist in this," he warned, "there can be no talk of disarmament." He left for San Francisco the next day, still in a snit.

Chief Parker was offended too—by the implication that the LAPD wasn't up to protecting the Soviet premier. At a press conference the day after Khrushchev's departure, Parker described the performance of his department as "one of the greatest examples of proficiency ever demonstrated." Parker's reaction to Khrushchev's jibe about Los Angeles's gangsters is unknown.

PARKER didn't have to wait long for retribution from Moscow. In late 1959, Parker received news that the U.S. Commission on Civil Rights was planning to visit Los Angeles in order to ascertain local civil rights conditions.

The commission's interest in Los Angeles was understandable. In little over a decade, Los Angeles had become one of the most diverse cities in the country. Close to 700,000 Mexican Americans lived in L.A.—more than in any other city in the world except for Mexico City. Its Jewish population, numbering roughly 400,000 people, was exceeded only by that of New York City. Most surprising of all was the size of its black population. In 1930, only 39,000 African Americans lived in Los Angeles. By 1960, the black population numbered 424,000. Los Angeles had the fifth largest African American community in the nation (behind New York, Chicago, Philadelphia, and Detroit)—far larger than any city in the South. And roughly 1,700 new black residents were arriving every day. But instead of opportunity, many found crowded, expensive housing, low-wage jobs, and simmering racial resentment. The result, according to the Los Angeles County Commission on Human Relations, was a dangerous increase in tensions. In the second half of 1959 alone, there had been more than sixty racial "incidents," from cross burnings to telephone harassment, almost all of them instigated by whites. Naturally, the Civil Rights Commission was interested in learning more about how the city was responding. But when it contacted Parker about testifying, the chief of the LAPD declined.

For years, Parker had endured attacks on his force for brutality and discrimination. Factually, charge after charge had been disproven—at least in Parker's mind. Yet if anything, the volume and vehemence of the attacks were increasing. To Parker, the explanation was clear: Moscow was stepping up its attacks. Appearing in a public forum that was sure to be a sounding board for criticism of the police would only further its goals. Parker replied that he would provide the commission with factual evidence but he would not appear to testify before it.

Commission members were taken aback by this summary rejection. In mid-December, two staff members flew in from Washington to meet with the chief to assure him they were eager to obtain balanced testimony. Reluctantly, Parker agreed to appear before the commission. The hearings would begin January 25, 1960, and last for two days. Parker was scheduled to be the last speaker on the second morning of hearings.

The commission's staff was true to its word. While the first day of hearings did include witnesses who were critical of the police, the tone of the day was surprisingly mild. A black engineer who'd recently purchased a home in a white section of the San Fernando Valley dispensed helpful advice: sound out people in the neighborhood before trying to buy a house, look for financing at places other than traditional banks (which often

refused to give black people mortgages for houses in "white" neighborhoods), and so forth—making it sound as if pervasive residential segregation could be addressed by a few commonsense workarounds. When it
came to the conduct of the LAPD, local NAACP official Loren Miller suggested that many black residents distrusted the police department because
they'd had bad experiences with Jim Crow justice back home. In other
words, white police officers didn't have a bias against black people; black
people had a bias against police officers. This fit perfectly with Parker's
oft-stated belief that the police were the "real" embattled minority in contemporary American society.

By the time Chief Parker and his bevy of charts-toting aides arrived to
present their testimony, the commissioners were primed for Parker's point
of view. He began with a very technical presentation on the problem of
crime and policing in Los Angeles. Between the years 1950 and 1959,
crime had climbed by 132 percent. Parker attributed the increase to the fact
that the city was underpoliced (with only 1.8 officers per 1,000 residents)
and overstocked with vagabonds and criminals, "many of them deliberately shipped here by officials of other localities who want to get rid of
them." This was really no explanation at all. The crime increase was new,
yet L.A. had been underpoliced for decades, and police chiefs had complained of criminals being shipped in since the days of James Davis. But no
commissioner called Parker on this point.

Parker then segued into a discussion of Los Angeles's crime problem as
it related to the city's minority community. Police records showed that in
1958 Negroes committed crime at eleven times the rate of Caucasians.
Latinos committed crime at five times the rate of Caucasians. This was not,
the chief emphasized, a matter of some innate tendency toward crime
among blacks and Latinos. Rather, he described it as "a conflict of cultures"
and a result of the explosive growth of the African American community.

"I think there is one other statistic I will bore you with," Parker continued. "I believe this growth in population, relative growth should be of
deep interest to you in attempting to translate what you have been told in
terms of problems. The Negro population of Los Angeles has increased
58.8 percent since 1952, while the Caucasian population increased only
10.9 percent, which indicates the general type of growth in this community." In the face of "the explosive growth of this community and the inherent frictions among men, the most predatory of all animals," Parker
continued, "I would like to say, to me, it is utterly remarkable that we have
gone through this growth experience without violence, and to us it is nothing short of a miracle."

Parker then shifted to the topic of segregation. His assessment of its prevalence in Los Angeles was startling.

"There is no segregation or integration problem in this community, in my opinion, and I have been here since 1922," he asserted. "There may be an assimilation problem, I think that is inherent. But from the standpoint of integration, while there have been dislocations, this doesn't present any serious problems." Nor did the LAPD have an integration problem, the chief insisted.

"[W]e have Negro police officers; we have had them as long as I have been on the department," Parker told the commissioners. "They have been elected presidents of our classes—I doubt you have been told that—in democratic elections. There has been no integration problem. We have as much respect for them as anyone else in the department because they are individuals, they perform as individuals, and their conduct is graded on the basis of individual contact."

Parker insisted that there was no section of the city where Negroes couldn't work. He explained that he had declined to issue an order requiring black and white officers to work together because that would be "reverse discrimination." Parker said he favored integrated assignments on a voluntary basis instead.

Parker was becoming more relaxed—and more expansive. In response to a question about a witness who had recounted a story of police brutality, Parker replied with a meandering answer that concluded with one of his favorite themes: the police as "the greatest dislocated minority in America today."

"I have been very much interested in your charts where you break down crime in Los Angeles on a ratio of Caucasian, Latin, and Negro," interjected commission chairman John Hannah. "Do you have any observations as to the relationship in these groups based on the kind of housing that they have available to them or the amount of education that these young people have?"

Parker replied that "it is quite obvious" that blacks and Latinos were in the lower economic brackets but said that he hadn't "attempted to assume the role of sociologist and reach any determination" about the connections between crime and housing. (No one noted that Parker had shown no such hesitancy during the debate over public housing earlier that decade.)

"There are a few questions I would like to ask you, Mr. Parker," interrupted another commissioner. "One of them has to do with what I believe you said was a conclusion that you had reached that much of this was the result of a conflict of cultures."

"Yes, sir," Parker replied.

"Then I take it that that is a conclusion you would reach with respect to the Negro population as distinguished from the Caucasian population, suggesting that the Negro has a different culture."

"Not necessarily," Parker replied,

No, no. I think a great deal of this has been based on our experience with the Latin population more than with the Negro or the balance of Caucasian. . . . Just so we keep the record straight, I'm not singling the Negro out. The Latin population that came in here in great strength—were there before us—has presented a great problem because I worked over on the East Side when men had to work in pairs. But that has evolved into assimilation. And it's because some of these people [Mexican Americans] have been here since before we were, but some of them aren't far removed from the wild tribes of inner Mexico.

Sitting in the audience, councilman Ed Roybal could hardly believe his ears. Had Chief Parker actually described his constituents as former members of "the wild tribes of inner Mexico"? The following day, Roybal introduced a motion in the city council requesting a transcript of the previous day's hearing. By then, Chief Parker's alleged "wild tribes of inner Mexico" was the talk of the town. The city council demanded a written explanation.

Never slow to respond to an attack, Chief Parker insisted that he had been set up and misquoted. "Nobody is concerned with the rights of policemen," he fumed to the press. "I've been harassed by these elements ever since I've been chief." The chief insisted that a tape of the meeting would vindicate him.

It didn't. Forced to listen to what he said, Parker described the statement as "a slip of the tongue." He once again refused to apologize (characteristically insisting that Roybal owed *him* an apology for misinterpreting his words). He didn't have to. The *Los Angeles Times* editorial board rushed to Parker's defense, accusing not the chief of police but rather his critics of "the most offensive kind of demagoguery." Councilman Roybal reluctantly accepted the chief's explanation, and the controversy soon blew over.

That April, Parker and his wife, Helen, left Los Angeles for a fifty-five-day trip to Europe (paid for with a $45,000 settlement from ABC for Mike Wallace's interview with Mickey Cohen). The couple's trip took them to many of the places Parker had served in during the war, including Italy. Parker's visit to Italy made his carabiniere hosts nervous. Parker was, after all, one of the Mafia's most committed adversaries. What if an intrepid Mafioso decided to knock him off?

During Parker's visit to Rome, local authorities got wind of a report that gangsters who congregated at a certain café were indeed contemplating just such a hit. They presented this information to Parker and suggested that he cut his visit short. Parker scoffed at this suggestion. He would not be frightened by Mob threats. Instead, the following morning, he went to have breakfast at the café in question.

24

Showgirls

"Girls very often like me and seem attracted to me, and I find them also attractive, at times. It's talkin' to them that's the hard part."

—Mickey Cohen

THE RULES were strict and clear. Stripteases were legal in the city of Los Angeles as long as they were not "lewd and lascivious." In practice, this meant that certain rules had to be followed. The guidance provided by the city attorney's office was quite, well, explicit. Performers were required to wear G-strings and pasties. A performer was not permitted to "pass her hands over her body in such a manner that the hands touch the body at any point." The "bump and grind" was permissible—but only in "an upright position." Under no circumstances was bumping and grinding to occur "adjacent to a curtain or [an] any other object."

The biggest no-no of all, though, was touching. That was both legally off-limits and personally unwise. Strippers, then and now, tended to have personal problems and expensive needs. There was a good reason that the most successful professional gangsters, men like Meyer Lansky and Paul Ricca, were known for being faithful to their spouses. Mickey Cohen had been too, for the most part. Sure, he liked to squire starlets around town. Yes, he enjoyed "blue films" and liked a good burlesque show as much as the next man—perhaps more so. Prostitutes? They were hard to avoid in his milieu. According to Jimmy Fratianno, Cohen dropped a C-note for a professional "flutter" from time to time. However, skirt-chasing never interfered with the serious business of being a gangster. But when Bing Crosby's son introduced Cohen to Juanita Dale Slusher, better known by her stage name, Candy Barr, Mickey had a change of heart.

Candy Barr was striptease royalty, thanks in large part to her 1951 appearance in the stag film *Smart Aleck*. (Barr, then a sixteen-year-old runaway who survived by turning tricks, played the role of the teenager lured into a traveling salesman's motel room—with a friend—after a nude dip in the pool.) The one-reel, fifteen-minute film circulated widely, making Barr arguably the world's first porn star. From there, the teenaged Barr (measurements 37-22-33) dyed her hair blond and moved easily into the world of burlesque and, occasionally, the theater. Her angelic, innocent face and her heavenly but far from innocent body made her a popular performer. She was soon alternating between regular gigs in Las Vegas and Dallas (where she struck up a friendship with nightclub owner Jack Ruby). But in 1957, Dallas police arrested Barr on charges of possessing four-fifths of an ounce of marijuana. The green-eyed twenty-two-year-old performer was tried, convicted, and sentenced to fifteen years in the state prison. To Bing Crosby's son, a Candy Barr fan, it seemed a terrible injustice. He soon thought of just the person who might be able to help—Mickey Cohen.

AS A YOUNG MAN, Cohen had been shy—even prudish—when it came to the female gender. That changed in Cleveland, where he shacked up with a redheaded Irish girl named Georgia ("beautiful face and fine disposition"). Although they were never married, they lived together as man and wife until Georgia moved to Michigan and really did get married. Mickey then moved to Los Angeles.

In Los Angeles, prostitution was a big business. During his heyday, Bugsy Siegel had routinely taken a significant cut of the action (amounting to about $100,000 a year), as did the Los Angeles Sheriff Department's vice squad. As Siegel's lieutenant, responsibility for collecting from the whorehouses fell to Mickey. Cohen insisted that he refused to do it. He claimed that he wanted nothing to do with prostitution as a business.*

Ordinary women were a challenge too. Mickey was not a handsome man. In 1950, Senator Kefauver would describe him as "a simian figure, with pendulous lower lip . . . and spreading paunch." The muckraking journalist Ovid Demaris agreed: "Pint-sized and pudgy, with simian eyes, a flattened nose, and a twisting scar under his left eye." The FBI was more clinical: Cohen, one agent reported, "had a one-inch scar under each eye and one on the inner corner of his left eyebrow. His nose had been broken, and he had a two-inch scar on his left hand." Nor was he a natural conversationalist.

"Girls very often like me and seem attracted to me, and I find them also attractive, at times. It's talkin' to them that's the hard part," he said, plaintively, to Ben Hecht (one of the century's greatest conversationalists) one

---

*As is often the case with Cohen, the truth is difficult to ascertain. Early FBI reports portray Mickey as an active participant in the prostitution racket—if not as an outright pimp. See, for instance, FBI file #92-HQ-3156, Subject: "Meyer Harris Cohen," memo dated October 8, 1960.

day. "You break your back to be a gentleman when you take a girl out. They like the respect you got for them. So the next day she says, 'You know last night you didn't talk to me at all.'

" 'I didn't have nothing to say to you,' I try to explain, 'I can't make conversation out of nothing!' "

Given these drawbacks, it's easy to understand how Cohen would eventually gravitate toward professionals. His first extended fling—with the artist Liz Renay—had been something of a publicity stunt. Barr was more serious. Perhaps the fact that she'd shot her second husband one year earlier (he survived) piqued Mickey's interest. Perhaps he simply liked her act. Whatever the motivation, at Crosby's suggestion, Mickey took on Candy Barr, personally guaranteeing a $15,000 bail bond and vowing to appeal her conviction all the way to the U.S. Supreme Court.

By the spring of 1959, they were dating. Cohen lined up a gig for Barr at the Club Largo on Sunset, where she was soon earning $2,000 a week. Mickey was a nightly visitor. On April 20, readers of the columnist Art Ryan learned that Cohen had squired Candy Barr to the Saints and Sinners testimonial dinner for Milton Berle. The romance blossomed. By early May, Cohen was hinting to the press that he was considering tying the knot with Miss Barr after his divorce with LaVonne went through.

While Cohen enjoyed Candy Barr, federal authorities were stepping up their efforts to gather incriminating information on Cohen. A parade of witnesses was now passing before the federal grand jury that had been called to investigate Mickey's lavish lifestyle. Prosecutors cast a wide net, subpoenaing virtually everyone who might have seen Mickey spend money, from telephone company employees to fight promoter Harry "Babe McCoy" Rudolph to LAPD-cop-turned-private-investigator Fred Otash. Prosecutors also tightened the noose around Mickey Cohen's previous girlfriend, Liz Renay.

Renay had long been a subject of interest and was repeatedly questioned by the jury. At first, she attempted to make light of these summonses. After being called back to testify in January, she told the press that the jury was "a bunch of old meanies" and complained that the appearance had cost her a movie role. Gradually, though, the gravity of her situation began to dawn on her. Prosecutors had figured out that Cohen had turned to Renay for "loans" when he needed to pay for something with a check instead of cash. In an attempt to support Cohen's claims that he was broke, Renay initially claimed that he never paid her back. This claim was easily refuted by Western Union records that showed Cohen routinely wiring money to her account in New York. As a result, on March 12, Renay was indicted on five counts of perjury by the federal grand jury investigating Cohen's income.

She was released on $1,500 bail. Two weeks later, on March 31, while Cohen was thumbing his nose at Robert Kennedy and buying a new Cadillac, Renay pleaded innocent to the charges. Evidently, she soon had second thoughts about her situation. In July, she changed her testimony, informing the judge that she'd failed to tell the truth about the $5,500 in "loans" she'd made to Cohen, and on July 18, 1959, a federal judge gave her a three-year suspended sentence—and a clear warning to associate with the likes of Cohen no more. (She later violated the terms of the deal and ended up serving a two-year prison sentence on Terminal Island off San Pedro.)

Mickey's romance with Candy Barr was similarly ill fated. Early in the summer of 1959, she broke up with Mickey. She promptly married her hairdresser in Las Vegas. Without Cohen's high-priced lawyers throwing up delays, the law quickly closed in on Candy Barr. Soon after her nuptials, she was deported to Texas to begin her prison term.

Inwardly, Mickey grieved. Outwardly, he soldiered on. He soon found a new flame—a twenty-two-year-old stripper at the Largo named Beverly Hills. Reached by an intrepid *Los Angeles Times* reporter at noon on October 1 (Mickey was still in his pajamas and visibly sleepy), Cohen confirmed that he and Miss Hills would soon be wed. Their honeymoon was to take place in Miami, where the future Mrs. Cohen would be appearing at the Clover Club. That engagement fizzled too. By late fall, Cohen had a new love, a nineteen-year-old former carhop named Sandy Hagen, whom Cohen had "discovered" at a drive-through.

On December 2, 1959, Cohen and Hagen were having dinner at Rondelli's, an Italian restaurant in Sherman Oaks that was one of Mickey's favorite hangouts. (Cohen was widely assumed to be the stealth owner.) With them were Cohen's new canine companion, bulldog Mickey Jr., and the usual scrum of henchmen (including Candy Barr and Beverly Hills's manager). At about 11:30 p.m, Jack "The Enforcer" Whalen walked in. Whalen was probably the biggest bookmaker in the Valley at the time. As his nickname suggested, the six-foot, 250-pound Whalen was also one of the toughest. He and Mickey had something of a beef. Whalen had recently beaten up Fred Sica, one of Cohen's top men. That night "The Enforcer" was out trolling bars for delinquent borrowers, one of whom he spotted in a telephone booth in the café. Whalen walked over, grabbed the man, and proceeded to knock him around.

This was not a respectful way to conduct yourself in a rival gangster's restaurant, but Whalen didn't seem worried by Mickey's presence. In fact, he strolled over to Cohen's table afterward. What happened next is unclear. Words were exchanged; a punch may (or may not) have been thrown at one of Cohen's associates. One thing was clear though. Two shots were fired. One slammed into the ceiling. The other hit Whalen right between the eyes. Cohen got up to go wash his hands. Then he called his doctor. Then he called the fire department. Next he called the newspapers. Finally, someone called the police. By the time two patrolmen in a radio car arrived at 12:10 a.m., Whalen was dead. The policemen were disturbed to see that someone had tidied up the area around Cohen's table, a mere six feet from where the body lay. They promptly locked the doors and began to question everyone in the restaurant. Deputy Chief Thad Brown himself questioned Cohen.

Cohen's account of what had happened was vague.

"A man walked in and punched a little man at the next table," Cohen told Brown. "I never saw either before. Shots rang out. I thought someone was shooting at me, and I ducked." That was all Cohen had to say. The following day, he elaborated further—in an exclusive column for the *Herald-Express*—on the night at Rondelli's, claiming, with wild implausibility, that he'd never seen "the boys who approached the table next to him" and that he hadn't seen what happened after the shooting because he was taking off Mickey Jr.'s bib. ("You gotta wear one when you eat linguine.")

The police weren't buying it. For one thing, Cohen's Cadillac was gone. Mickey said Sandy Hagen had taken it home, but Hagen didn't have a driver's license. There was also the fact that Mickey had called quite a few people before contacting the police. Chief Parker himself soon arrived to take personal control of the investigation, but Cohen wouldn't talk to him. Outside, reporters pressed the chief about whether Cohen was a suspect.

"Obviously, he is," Parker replied. "This killing occurred at Cohen's headquarters. He was less than six feet away. We knew that the victim was going there to square a gambling beef. Then Mickey's car just happened to vanish, off the lot." Nonetheless, with no evidence tying Cohen to the shooting, he wasn't immediately booked. Instead, some thirty policemen were dispatched to round up all known Cohen henchmen for questioning.

The police then got a lucky break. Three pistols were recovered from the trash behind the restaurant. One was registered to the late Johnny Stompanato. A clearer connection to Cohen would have been hard to imagine. Police booked Cohen and four associates on charges of murder. But try as he might, Parker could find no physical evidence (such as fingerprints on the murder weapon) that tied Cohen to the shooting. None of the guns in the trash can were the murder weapon. After two nights in custody, Mickey was released on bail.

Six days later, on December 8, a Cohen lackey named Sam LoCigno presented himself (along with two attorneys) at Deputy Chief Thad Brown's office with a startling confession: LoCigno claimed that he was the person who'd shot Whalen. LoCigno insisted that the shooting had been an act of self-defense. Whalen had approached the table, said "Hello, Mr. Cohen," and then slugged one of the men at the table, George Piscitelle, before turning on LoCigno, saying, "You're next." Only then, LoCigno claimed, had he opened fire. LoCigno said that Mickey Cohen had urged him to turn himself in. (Cohen himself later told the press, modestly, that he had "induced" LoCigno to turn himself in "to save the taxpayers' money.")

Brown called in Chief Parker, who joined the interrogation. Brown and Parker quickly poked holes in LoCigno's story. When Parker asked LoCigno where the gun he'd shot Whalen with was, he replied, "I don't know." He was equally fuzzy in his response to other important questions. Parker and Brown weren't surprised. The intelligence division had long ago pegged LoCigno as nothing more than a "flunky and errand boy" for Cohen. Both felt certain that the man responsible for the shooting was Mickey himself. But try as they might, police were unable to find witnesses to make that case. Although Rondelli's had been crowded with customers at the time of the killing, no one seemed to have seen anything—with the exception of a one-eyed horse bettor who'd had eighteen highballs before the shooting started. He fingered Candy Barr's manager as the gunman. Instead, police focused on a more promising witness, a prostitute who claimed that Cohen ordered the killing, allegedly shouting, "Now, Sam, now!" just moments before the gun was fired. Unfortunately for the prosecution, however, on the witness stand, the prostitute acknowledged that she'd only heard this secondhand, from an off-duty maître d'. That was hardly enough to override LoCigno's confession.

Prosecutors tried to put a positive spin on the situation, trumpeting LoCigno's conviction as the first successful prosecution of a gangland murder in two decades. In fact, Mickey Cohen had escaped again.

THE WHALEN SHOOTING quickly moved off the front pages, replaced by politics. That July Democrats were meeting in Los Angeles to nominate the Democratic presidential candidate. Between July 11 and 15, some 45,000 visitors would descend on the city for the convention. Police Commission member John Ferraro had been chosen to be chairman of the convention's public safety committee. Ferraro, in turn, would rely heavily on Parker and the roughly three hundred officers he planned to detail to the event.

Defending the Democratic Party was, in some ways, an unlikely assignment for Chief Parker, who had become a high-profile antagonist of the party's California branch. In 1956, Parker had expressed strong support for the reelection of President Dwight Eisenhower. Parker also had close ties to the Nixon campaign through Norris Poulson's old campaign manager, Jack Irwin, who had joined the Police Commission after Poulson's election. There he quickly became a strong Parker fan. Irwin was also a friend of Vice President Richard Nixon, the Republican nominee for president that year. Irwin's connection to the vice president (and his ties to Chief Parker) worried J. Edgar Hoover. The FBI director feared that if Nixon was elected, he might attempt to ease out Hoover and replace him with Parker.

Parker was actually a double threat. Politically, he was closer to the GOP. Personally he was closer to the Kennedy camp, thanks to his relationship with Bobby. The services he would offer Sen. Jack Kennedy during the convention would further solidify Parker's Kennedy connections.

The convention began under a suffocating blanket of smog that left delegates with watery eyes and burning throats. Jacqueline Kennedy, four months pregnant, stayed away from Los Angeles entirely. Jack stayed with a few bachelor friends in a penthouse apartment in Hollywood owned by the comedian Jack Haley. Bobby stayed with brother-in-law Peter Lawford in Santa Monica. Joe Sr. monitored activities from the Beverly Hills mansion of his old friend Marion Davies, William Randolph Hearst's longtime mistress.

From the start, Parker put the LAPD at the Kennedys' disposal. At the opening reception on Sunday, Jack Kennedy, Bobby and Ethel, and Ted and Joan appeared, escorted by fifteen white-helmeted police officers and a thirty-person plainclothes detail. (In contrast, Senate Majority Leader Lyndon Baines Johnson, his wife Lady Bird, and their two daughters were left to greet the crowd on their own, assisted only by volunteer "Johnson girls" handing out long-stemmed roses as a band played the Johnson campaign song, "Everything's Coming Up Roses.") In general, though, security was light. There was no Secret Service protection. The Kennedy campaign asked that just one officer be assigned full-time to Jack. That proved insufficient. Well-wishers hemmed him in everywhere, stopping him to introduce themselves, to shake hands, to say hello. These encounters were sometimes quite frightening: on two occasions, enthusiastic supporters nearly tore off Kennedy's coat. Eventually, the campaign asked for backup. Parker upped the detail to four. Instead of mingling with the delegates, Kennedy's unit started to move him through freight elevators and basement kitchens.

The LAPD also proved to be useful during the convention. On Wednesday, July 13, 1960, some six hundred supporters of Adlai Stevenson, the Democratic Party's nominee in 1952 and 1956, swarmed the Figueroa Street entrance of the Sports Arena, where the convention was being held.

Although Stevenson insisted that he was not interested in being the party's candidate, his supporters were determined to nominate him. So they settled on the desperate stratagem of blockading the convention and then charging the floor, with the hope that they would be able to take control of the convention proceedings. The police quickly intervened, rushing forces to the entrance in order to break the blockade.

When Kennedy cinched the nomination, Parker was pleased. Yet despite Parker's genuine admiration for the Kennedy brothers, there were things about the family that made him uneasy. Several months after the convention, Parker went to visit his younger brother Joe and his sister-in-law Jane. One evening after dinner, the topic turned to the Kennedys. Bill made a fleeting comment, that "he would never believe" the things the Kennedys were involved in. Joe would later speculate that Bill spurned a job with the administration in Washington because he did not care to associate with the likes of the actor Peter Lawford and his good friend, Frank Sinatra.

Sinatra, whom Parker regarded as being "totally tied to the Mafia," was clearly a sore point. Relations between the LAPD and the entertainer had been strained since at least February 1957, when three LAPD officers had burst into Sinatra's Palm Springs house—at 4 a.m.—to serve the entertainer with a subpoena to appear before a congressional subcommittee investigating *Confidential* magazine, a scandal sheet that specialized in extorting money from celebrities with skeletons in their closets.

Exactly what kind of intelligence Parker had on the Kennedys is unknown. Once—just once—Joe picked up on a passing, uncomplimentary allusion to Kennedy-Hollywood skulduggery and expressed his doubts.

"Gee, you know, I just don't understand how that could be true, Joseph told his brother."

"Joe, you don't hear anything about what's really going on," Parker replied.

BY ALL ACCOUNTS, the department did a superb job during the convention. Hailed by the *Los Angeles Times* editorial board for its good work, Parker was later feted at the Biltmore Bowl by nearly nine hundred leading citizens. His standing had never been higher. On November 8, 1960, Sen. John F. Kennedy was elected to be the thirty-fifth president of the United States. Less than two weeks later, while out golfing with a *New York Times* reporter, the president-elect casually let drop that he was considering appointing his thirty-five-year-old brother to be the next attorney general of the United States.

The response was immediate—and negative. Bobby had never been a practicing lawyer. Most recently, he had been Jack's presidential campaign manager—hardly the nonpartisan background many hoped for in the nation's top lawman. An editorial in the *New York Times* warned against nepotism in high office. "Wise men" such as Supreme Court Justice William Douglas also criticized the prospective appointment. Privately, even JFK was doubtful. But Joe Sr. insisted that Jack needed his brother at the Justice Department precisely because he was the ultimate loyalist. Joe Sr. also wanted Bobby at Justice to protect the president from the one person in government best positioned to do JFK harm—J. Edgar Hoover. On December 16, the president announced the appointment, with his brother at his side, in front of Blair house.

The reaction in the underworld was explosive. Chicago Outfit boss Sam Giancana (who shared sometime paramour Judith Campbell Exner with Jack) immediately called Kennedy confidant Frank Sinatra and demanded to know what was going on. According to Outfit historian Gus Russo, Giancana "ended the call by slamming down the phone and then throwing it across the room."

"Eating out of the palm of his hand," the Outfit boss reportedly screamed. "That's what Frank told me. 'Jack's eatin' out of his hand.' Bullshit, that's what it is." In Los Angeles, Cohen was equally surprised. Like virtually everyone in organized crime, Mickey had assumed that "the people" had reached an understanding with Joe Sr. "Nobody in my line of work had an idea that he [JFK] was going to name Bobby Kennedy attorney general. That was the last thing anyone thought."

Parker was delighted. "It has been the pleasure of my office to work closely with Bobby Kennedy during his period as counsel for the McClellan Committee," Parker noted in a statement released by his office to the press. "This opportunity to observe his philosophies in the law enforcement field has been most gratifying." Parker confidently predicted "increased levels of support for law enforcement at all levels." He was right. Within two weeks, Kennedy had declared war on organized crime. Press reports suggested that Chief Parker might well be tapped to head the effort.

Publicly, J. Edgar Hoover welcomed Kennedy's appointment. (In fact, when JFK first floated the idea in November, Hoover had been the only major figure in Washington to express support for it.) But no one in the Kennedy family was fooled by this attempt to align himself with the new president. The antipathy between the two men was well known.

To the sixty-six-year-old J. Edgar Hoover, everything about Robert Kennedy was annoying: his sloppy dressing (Kennedy's ties were rarely straight and his shirtsleeves were rarely rolled down); his lack of regard for the dignity of his office (Kennedy often brought his ill-behaved dog, Brumus, to work, despite the fact it violated Justice Department rules, and sometimes liked to throw the football to aides in his cavernous office). Hoover was aghast to find Kennedy playing darts one day, seemingly without any concern about whether the darts hit the target or the wall. (Hoover later fumed to an associate that Kennedy was "desecrating public property.") Worst of all, though, was the obvious lack of regard for Hoover himself. Kennedy even had the audacity to "buzz" Hoover and ask him to come down to the AG's office at once instead of courteously requesting an appointment with Hoover, as previous AGs had. In contrast, Kennedy was almost ostentatious in expressing respect for the man J. Edgar Hoover increasingly regarded as a rival, LAPD chief William Parker.

OVER THE COURSE of the 1950s, Hoover's dislike of Parker had turned to hatred. Parker's cardinal sin—the offense for which he was never forgiven—had occurred seven years earlier, at a policing convention in Detroit. J. Edgar Hoover had been the honoree of a gala dinner. Although the FBI director was not there in person, his achievements had been lauded by the assembled police executives—with the notable exception of Bill Parker. After the awards ceremony, Parker wandered "from bar to bar" grumbling that Hoover wasn't the only competent police executive in the country. According to other attendees at the event, he'd also complained about the bureau's civil rights investigations into his department. Hoover was incensed. He instructed the L.A. SAC "to have no contact with Chief Parker in the future." He also suggested that friends of the bureau complain to Mayor Poulson about Parker's conduct at the Detroit convention. They did, and when Parker got back, he was summoned to the mayor's office to receive a personal rebuke from Poulson. Parker was bewildered that such minor grousing had reached the mayor. Puzzled, the chief called the L.A. SAC to clarify his comments. He asked if the bureau had put someone up to complaining to Poulson. Of course not, the SAC replied, telling Parker that it was "absurd to even entertain the thought." Meanwhile, bureau agents were instructed to monitor Parker closely.

"As the Bureau knows, Parker has a flair for sounding off," noted one memo. "He is like a rattlesnake in many respects; he is full of venom but seldom does he fail to give a warning when he is going to strike. When he is working on a new idea, he throws it out here and there to test reaction, and if he finds that his ideas are generally accepted he crystallizes them into a speech before some law enforcement groups."

The rattlesnake was now in a position to succeed Hoover as the next director of the FBI.

Parker did not lobby for the job directly. Instead, he revived his idea of a national clearinghouse that could provide big-city police departments with information on organized crime. He also resumed his criticisms of the FBI's director.

"The F.B.I. shows great interest when stolen property moves across a state line but little interest when criminals move from state to state," Parker pointedly told the *Herald-Express* in December. Although the FBI was the natural choice to take on the job of leading an organized crime clearinghouse, "they have shown no indication that they will or that they want to," Parker continued. As a result, a new agency was needed.

"I have a high opinion of the F.B.I. and Hoover," Parker continued. "They are fine firemen. But the house is burning down."

The L.A. office hastily fired off a memo to headquarters, describing the chief as "a blabbermouth." It also suggested that Parker was attempting to stir up dissension between Hoover and the new attorney general. In truth, Parker hardly needed to work at that. The Kennedys weren't exactly circumspect about whom they might prefer as FBI director. On the contrary, they openly joked about it. Just a few weeks after her husband was sworn in, Ethel Kennedy took the liberty of slipping a card into the FBI's suggestion box at main Justice. Her suggestion was for Chief Parker to replace Hoover as the head of the FBI. She helpfully signed the note "Ethel."

Ethel was a prankster. The card may have been a joke. But the joke was a pointed one because the sentiments it expressed (the desire to be done with Hoover) were obviously true. To his closest aides, Kennedy frequently criticized the director and mocked his intimate associate, Clyde Tolson. Once his brother Jack was reelected, he told friends, Hoover was out. No wonder Hoover feared that Kennedy and Parker were conspiring to dethrone him. But Hoover held a trump card—information. Eleven days after John F. Kennedy was sworn into office, Hoover forwarded a memo to RFK alerting him to a woman who was claiming to have had a sexual liaison with Jack. It was the first in a very long line of memos.

TO MICKEY COHEN, the selection of Robert Kennedy to be the attorney general was the latest development in a nightmarish autumn. On September 16, the LAPD intelligence division's painstaking efforts to document Cohen's extravagant lifestyle (along with a massive investigation by the Treasury Department and several months of intensive surveillance by

the FBI) paid dividends when prosecutors at the U.S. Attorney's Office indicted Cohen on thirteen counts of tax evasion and fraud. The sums named
were startling. Prosecutors alleged that between 1945 and 1950 and between 1956 and 1958, Cohen had evaded $400,000 in income tax. Federal
authorities also filed liens against Cohen in Los Angeles, El Paso, St. Louis,
and Cambridge, Massachusetts, in an effort to recover some of the
$135,000 he still owed in back taxes following his first tax evasion convic-
tion.

To Cohen, the case was nothing more than a personal vendetta.

"There's no question about Bobby Kennedy and Chief William Parker
having everything to do with my being indicted," he would later fume.
"[H]is squads were following me around here at the Mocambo, Ciro's,
Chasen's. They had little cameras, they would snap pictures, they would
take data."

That data was now put to damning use. The strategy pursued by the U.S.
Attorney's Office was basically the same as that used in Cohen's first trial:
prove that Cohen's expenses vastly exceeded his income. With information
provided by the intelligence division and others, Treasury Department investigators were able to reconstruct in vivid detail Cohen's free-spending
ways. A string of witnesses further bolstered their case. The landlord of
Cohen's apartment at 705 S. Barrington in Brentwood testified that after
moving in, Cohen had spent between $5,000 and $8,000 redecorating his
apartment, a sum he described as "a nominal figure" for the retired gangster.
He also noted that Mickey had paid $9,000 up front for rent and other ex-
penses. The owner of the Sportsman Lodge remembered paying Michael's
Greenhouses $9,500 for landscaping work but was rather vague on what, if
anything, had been done. A psychiatrist recalled a $10,000 gift to Cohen—
in exchange for the right to study the gangster's aberrant behavior.

Then there were the people who had invested in the Mickey Cohen life
story.

The first investor appeared as early as 1951, when Beverly Hills decorator Henry Guttman gave Cohen $10,000 for all story and screen rights to
the Cohen life story. That didn't stop Mickey from seeking other investors.
Several years later, a nightclub owner paid $15,000 for a 10 percent cut in
Cohen's book. When he tried to back out, he'd gotten a frightening phone
call from someone in New York telling him that if he didn't "straighten
things out" with Mickey, he'd "be taken care of." Other investors had followed. Comedians Jerry Lewis and Red Skelton testified to being approached
by Cohen about producing and starring in his movie. (Cohen had originally wanted Robert Mitchum to play himself.) Lewis demurred, saying
that "any productions bearing his name should involve levity." (He did

make a small investment in the project though; Mickey had been the person who first brought him to the West Coast to do a show at Slapsie Maxie's.) Skelton had also turned down Cohen's offer, pointing out that a "tall red-headed fellow" would hardly make a credible Mickey Cohen.

Then there were the "loans." By his own account, Cohen had borrowed more than $140,000 since his release from prison. Acquaintance after acquaintance appeared before the jury to relate loans in the range of $1,000 to $25,000, none of which had ever been repaid. Almost everyone said they'd happily lend Cohen more.

The most damaging testimony, though, came from Cohen's stripper paramours.

In early June 1961, Candy Barr was flown in from prison in Texas to testify. Barr told the jury that during the two months they had dated, Cohen had given $15,000 to her defense attorneys and lavished expensive presents on her, including jewelry, luggage, and a poodle. He had also picked up a $1,001.95 bill at a local clothing shop. At one point, he had even helped her flee to Mexico, arranging for her hair to be dyed black, providing phony documents, and giving her $1,700 in cash. (Barr got bored and eventually returned home.) Others put the figure even higher. Federal narcotics agent T. Jones put Cohen's spending on Barr at roughly $60,000.

The next witness after this damaging testimony was Sandy Hagen, Mickey's current fiancée. Per Judge George Boldt's orders, the twenty-two-year-old ex-model/waitress/car hop arrived wearing the mink stole Mickey had given her. Hagen insisted that she'd bought the $600 mink with her own personal funds, despite the fact that she had no apparent income. The prosecution insisted that it was a gift from Cohen, paid for with unreported income. When prosecutors proceeded to quiz Hagen about other gifts Cohen had given her, she refused to answer. She was ultimately sentenced to a week in jail for contempt of court. Hagen still refused to testify. So the prosecution moved on to another target.

On June 14, two Treasury Department agents slipped into Los Angeles and tracked down stripper Beverly Hills, just before her performance. There they served her with a subpoena to appear before the federal grand jury investigating Mickey Cohen. After meeting Miss Hills, they decided to stay for the show. Afterward, the stripper asked them sweetly, "Now that you've seen everything I've got, do I still have to appear?"

The answer was yes. And so it went. For forty days, the jury listened to the parade of witnesses—194 in total—testify about Cohen's lavish spending and unsecured personal "loans" of a sort that no sane person would voluntarily extend to a penniless ex-gangster with a small stake in an ice-cream parlor. On June 16, 1961, the United States summed up its case against

Cohen. Prosecutors claimed that in 1956 Cohen had failed to report $2,500 in income from the greenhouse. For 1957, the government had documented taxable income that exceeded $46,000 (Cohen had reported $1,272). In 1958, Cohen had failed to report at least $13,000 in income. All told, for the years 1956–58, Cohen owed the government $34,799.70 in unpaid back taxes.

Cohen's defense was simple: He insisted that these were simply loans against future income from a book and movie deal.

"I feel it's now up to God's will," Cohen told the press, after the defense rested its case. "I know in my heart I'm innocent."

The jury disagreed. After two days of deliberation, on Friday, June 30, 1961, Cohen was convicted on eight counts of income tax evasion. The next day spectators packed the 150-seat courtroom to witness Cohen's sentencing.

Judge Boldt had been a genial presence during the trial. But this particular Saturday morning he was all business. He started by asking Cohen if he had any remarks for the court.

"I can only say to your Honor very respectfully . . . [that] I made every effort to live my life in the past six years correctly, and I thought I did so," Cohen replied.

Judge Bolt thought otherwise.

"In my opinion, it is clear beyond doubt that defendant Cohen has little, if any, sense of truth, honesty, or responsibility either in his personal and financial affairs or in his obligations as a citizen of the United States," the judge said sternly.

"Notwithstanding kind and humane efforts to help Mr. Cohen's rehabilitation . . . there is no credible evidence that during the last six years he has ever engaged in any useful or commendable work or activity," Judge Boldt continued. He noted that within a short time from his first release from prison, Cohen "was in full flight on a profligate style of living, financed by many fraudulent or extorted so-called loans in a very large amount.

"If there be substantial decadence in society, as sometimes charged, Mickey Cohen is an excellent specimen," the judge continued. "The obstruction and impending weight of the collective Mickey Cohens in our national community could tip the balance to our doom in the struggle for the free way of life."

The judge then handed down his verdict—a $30,000 fine and fifteen years in prison. Cohen himself, watching calmly, seemed not to understand what had happened.

"What is the sentence anyway?" he asked reporters minutes after the verdict had been announced. When informed, he replied simply, "Well, I ain't going to say what I think until I ride with the punch a little." Mickey's reaction to the judge's lecture was succinct: "He is entitled to his opinions," Cohen said, simply.

Girlfriend Sandra Hagen put on a rather more dramatic show. Sobbing, her hands thrown up "in an attitude of prayer," she told the scribbling newsmen, "It's too long, but I'll wait for him!" The following month the government denied Cohen and Hagen's request to be married while Cohen was in federal custody as "contrary to established policies." With good behavior, Mickey would be eligible for parole in five years.

From Washington, D.C., the new attorney general called assistant U.S. attorneys Thomas Sheridan and, in Washington, Charles McNeil to congratulate them for their work on the case. He also issued a statement praising the jury.

"This was a major case and a very significant verdict," proclaimed Robert Kennedy.

Cohen's attorneys (who now included Jack Dahlstrum in addition to Sam Dash, as well as longtime Parker foe A. L. Wirin) petitioned for a new trial and asked that Mickey be freed on bond during his appeal. Judge Boldt declined both requests. Cohen's last hope for escape came in the form of a message relayed to Dahlstrum from Tom Sheridan, a special assistant to Attorney General Robert Kennedy.

"Lookit, now, don't get hot," Dahlstrum told Mickey, when he came to him with the offer. "I know you're not going to like this, but it's my duty as your attorney to relay this to you.

"The government's got three names—George Bieber, the attorney in Chicago, Tony Accardo, and Paul 'the Waiter' Ricca. If you want to cooperate with any of these three names, you can gain your freedom."

Mickey responded by instructing Dahlstrum to tell Sheridan and Kennedy that they could go fuck themselves.

At daybreak on the morning of Friday, July 28, deputy U.S. marshals removed Cohen from the L.A. County Jail and flew him to his new home: Alcatraz. It was an unusual destination for an income tax evader. Cohen had little doubt the choice was Bobby Kennedy's doing.

ALCATRAZ was like no prison Cohen had ever been in before. "It was a crumbling dungeon," Cohen would later write. The prison blocks were always bathed in the cold ocean clamminess. There was no hot water to shave with, no newspapers, no radio, no television, no magazines. "You never seen a bar of candy there, only on Christmas," lamented the man who had once wooed Candy Barr. The yard was a mere fifty feet long.

Inmates got only forty-five minutes a day outside. Life inside was dank and dangerous. Mickey did have a few good friends in the joint, such as one-time Siegel associate Frank Carbo, Harlem crime boss "Bumpy" Johnson, and Alvin Karpis, the head of the notorious Ma Barker–Alvin Karpis bank-robbing gang in the 1930s. But even the prestige of the Syndicate afforded little protection against his stir-crazy, ultraviolent fellow prisoners.

"The atmosphere was such that you lived in fear," Cohen would later recall. "Like if you're walking around a corner, you're liable to get a shiv in your back."

After three months on "the Rock," Cohen was abruptly summoned to the warden's office.

"Well, I guess you got the good news," the warden began, reluctantly.

"What good news?" Cohen replied.

Cohen had been released on bail—freed on a writ signed by U.S. Supreme Court Justice William Douglas, who had decided that he could return to Los Angeles to await a decision by the U.S. Court of Appeals for the Ninth Circuit on his income tax conviction appeal. It was the first time an inmate from Alcatraz had ever been released on bail.

Mickey was exultant. After stepping off the boat in San Francisco, he promptly made his way to the luxurious Fairmont Hotel on Nob Hill for a night of pampering. How Cohen paid for the evening—or managed to purchase a luxury class ticket to Los Angeles the next day—is unclear. But despite these splurges, this time Cohen appeared to have learned a lesson. When Cohen (looking natty in a black monogrammed Alpaca sweater, open white-on-black sport shirt, and black-and-white checkered pants) presented himself at his bondsman's to sign the note required for his $100,000 bail, he announced to the amused press corps that he had turned down an offer to borrow a Caddy for the duration of the appeals process and would be driving a Volkswagen instead.

Reporters noted that he "killed the engine twice, had trouble adjusting the seat and then tried to take off with the brake on" on the way out.

Then, two weeks later, something shocking happened. Cohen and four others were indicted for murder in connection with the December 2, 1959, death of Jack Whalen. LoCigno had started to talk behind bars. In the process, he'd given authorities an important new lead, which prosecutors argued led straight to Mickey Cohen.

25

The Muslim Cult

" 'Civil disobedience' . . . simply means the
violation of local laws that someone has
decided are not based on morality of
justice. "

—William Parker

POLICE LIEUTENANT Tom Bradley didn't immediately realize that his transfer from public relations to Wilshire Division was a form of punishment. Instead, he seems to have viewed the move as an opportunity. Wilshire Division had long been largely off-limits to black officers. The appointment of a black lieutenant—even to the midnight shift—seemed like a huge step forward. Chief Parker's comments before the U.S. Commission on Civil Rights were also encouraging. Bradley decided that the time was right to attempt a major goal—desegregating the radio cars.

As watch commander, Bradley had considerable authority. Soon after moving to Wilshire Division, he gave the order that henceforth all radio cars in that division would be integrated. But Bradley knew he would need the chief to back him up. At least some white officers were sure to complain and resist. So he sent a request up the chain of command asking Chief Parker to support the new policy. Bradley's proposal was tough: If officers didn't go along with the new policy, they would be out of a job, "just like any other type of insubordination."

Parker refused. Without backup from the brass, Bradley's integration was doomed. Just as he had feared, some white officers under his command complained loudly of reverse discrimination and sabotaged assignments by calling in sick on the days they were paired with black officers. Without support from his superiors, Bradley was unable to respond effectively to such disobedience. Bradley's efforts to integrate Wilshire slowly withered. As for Bradley himself, with a law degree in hand and pension eligibility fast approaching, he began to consider a new career—in politics.

■ ■ ■

IN JUNE 1959, at roughly the same time Lieutenant Bradley was beginning to seriously consider a political career, Officer Francisco Leon responded to a report of an auto theft. He soon spotted the stolen car and set off in pursuit. The car chase ended with a hail of bullets and the sixteen-year-old African American car thief dead. The shooting of an unarmed teenager led to demands for an investigation. County coroner Theodore Curphey announced that he would convene a coroner's jury to determine whether the shooting had been justified or an act of criminal homicide. He then made a provocative announcement: The coroner's jury, he declared, would be composed entirely of Negroes.

The NAACP immediately objected. For years the group had protested the selection of all-white coroner juries, but this was reverse segregation, the group argued. So Dr. Curphey amended his plan. The coroner's jury would have six black jurors—a majority—and four Caucasians. On June 29, 1960, the coroner's jury handed down the recommendation that Officer Leon be prosecuted for homicide.

Chief Parker exploded. The coroner himself had originally stated "that he saw no basis for prosecution in this case," Parker stated. The intentional selection of a majority Negro jury was, Parker charged, a reckless experiment in whether "a Negro jury could be unprejudiced." As far as Parker was concerned, by recommending that Officer Leon be prosecuted for murder, the jury had essentially answered the question—in the negative.

Soon after the verdict, Parker addressed the issue of why groups like the NAACP and the ACLU were always on the attack against the police department. It was not because of actual police brutality, Parker told his audience. No, complaints of police brutality represented something else entirely; they were an example of that most nefarious of totalitarian propaganda techniques, "The Big Lie," an untruth so colossal that most people were unable to grasp that it was wholly fabricated. Pioneered by the Nazis, adopted by the Communists, this was the technique now being deployed against the LAPD. Those who used it—notably the NAACP and ACLU—did so knowingly, as part of a plan to undermine American democracy. As Parker told the Bond Club, "The type of democracy they [the NAACP and ACLU] are trying to sell is represented by *People's World*," the weekly newspaper of the Communist Party of the United States.

Whether because of the department's actions or the "Big Lie," by early 1961 one thing was certain: Chief Parker had become a deeply unpopular figure in the black community—even as the black community was becoming an increasingly important part of the city. A mayoral election was fast approaching, and the conduct of the police department under incumbent mayor Norris Poulson promised to be a significant issue. That presented Poulson's primary opponent, Rep. Sam Yorty, with both an opportunity and a danger.

Yorty was one of the oddest figures in California politics. Elected to Congress in 1936 as a radical liberal, he had run for mayor of Los Angeles during the 1938 mayoral recall as the favored candidate of Red Hollywood. He'd been soundly thrashed. Two years later, he ran for a seat on the city council and lost again. Instead, he settled for a seat in the California assembly. There he reinvented himself as a hard-core anti-Communist. It didn't help. In 1940, he failed in his attempt to win election to the U.S. Senate. In 1945, he lost another mayoral election. He returned to Congress in 1950 and, four years later, promptly lost another Senate election. During the 1960 election, Yorty, ostensibly a Democrat, endorsed Richard Nixon. Kennedy's victory promised two years of misery in Washington. So he decided to run for mayor again instead. In January 1961, he formally entered the race.

This time, Yorty's timing was good. After two terms as mayor, Poulson seemed burnt out. A few months earlier, he'd announced that he wouldn't seek a third term. The resulting cries of anguish from the downtown business establishment persuaded him to run one more time. Yorty now took aim at that establishment, which was led, as always, by the *Los Angeles Times*. He positioned himself as the champion of the "little guy" and as someone who would pay attention to the needs of the fast-growing San Fernando Valley. When Poulson supporters mocked him for enthusiastically discussing new methods of trash collection, Yorty embraced the moniker "Trashcan Sam." The candidate's populist message played well. So did his direct, colloquial style, which was highly effective in the still newish medium of television. One of Yorty's supporters was George Putnam, the news anchor at KTTV (and the inspiration for the character Ted Baxter on *The Mary Tyler Moore Show*), which was actually owned by the *Los Angeles Times*. In the old days, the Chandlers would never have tolerated a mixed message. Now, for whatever reason, they did. While the *Times* took the mayor's side, Putnam was allowed to tout Yorty.

Poulson, meanwhile, struggled with rumors. A long-standing throat ailment was alleged to be cancer. Yorty's team also maintained that Poulson had acquired a $250,000 ranch in Oregon during his time in office. (In reality, it was a much smaller property owned by his wife.) Then, in the final weeks of the campaign, Poulson came down with laryngitis. Photographs

of the incumbent mayor in the hospital filled the papers in the days leading up to the primary election, which the mayor lost. Under Los Angeles's system of nonpartisan elections, a runoff election was scheduled for
June 1.

The anti-Yorty forces, led by *Times*man Carlton Williams, played tough,
delving into some dubious ties between Yorty, the Teamsters, and Las
Vegas gambling interests. The day after Yorty placed first in the primary
vote, Poulson contended that Yorty's campaign was "backed by the underworld." Yorty responded by filing a $2.2 million libel suit. He countered
that Poulson was controlled by an "overworld" consisting of Carlton
Williams and the downtown business establishment. Yorty also stepped up
his attacks on the police.

In his public appearances, he was always careful to distinguish between
Chief Parker, whom he promised to keep on, and the Police Commission,
which he criticized mercilessly. But as election day approached, Yorty
sharpened his rhetoric against the chief, describing the current police commissioners as "Parker's appointees," promising to clean house, and insinuat-
ing that Parker would probably resign as well. In private, and to select black
audiences, Yorty may have gone even further. Many Parker foes certainly
believed they had received a firm promise that as mayor Yorty would force
Parker out. Yorty also promised to fully integrate the department. Not surprisingly, candidate Yorty soon noticed that he was being trailed by plainclothes officers from the LAPD intelligence division.

In fact, Yorty did have some worrisome connections. One of his earliest and strongest supporters was Jimmy Bolger, the man the Shaws had
put into former chief James Davis's office as a secretary (and minder).
After Davis's forced resignation, Bolger had found refuge on the Board of
Public Works, which for many years was the bastion of the old Frank
Shaw camp. Bolger was a notorious figure, one widely considered to have
been a direct link to the underworld in the 1930s. It was natural that
Parker would be concerned about his reappearance. Yorty was less understanding. Like Poulson before him, he was soon fuming about the
LAPD's "Gestapo-like tactics" and complaining that the incumbent mayor
was attempting to scare law-and-order voters with the specter of Parker's
dismissal.

Ultimately, however, it was race that decided the election.

One day before the general election, on May 30, Memorial Day, a black
youth attempted to sneak onto a merry-go-round at Griffith Park. An attendant tried to make the seventeen-year-old pay. At this point, accounts of
what happened diverge. The attendant and his employer claimed they were

assaulted; others claimed that the seventeen-year-old fare-jumper was roughed up. A fight broke out; police officers rushed to the scene; and soon a mini-riot was under way, pitting roughly two hundred black rioters against a considerably smaller number of policemen. Dozens of black rioters and four LAPD officers were injured in the brawl.

The next day, newspapers splashed news of the incident across their front pages. The *Los Angeles Times* insisted that the incident was not a race riot—and that Los Angeles was not Alabama. But the city's African American voters drew a different conclusion. Voters in South Los Angeles shifted decisively toward Yorty, who won by sixteen thousand votes. That shift, wrote the *Los Angeles Times* one week later, was "perhaps the single biggest factor in Mayor Poulson's defeat."

It now fell to Mayor Yorty to decide what he would do with his police chief. At his first postelection press conference, Yorty's tone was harsh.

"I have confidence in [Parker] as an administrator, but as a public relations expert I think he could stand a lot of schooling and a lot of direction," Yorty told the press. In the days that followed, Yorty was even more outspoken in his criticisms of the department. It was "perfectly obvious," he told reporters, that "the department was used to check the history, from childhood to current date, of everybody even remotely connected with my campaign and even my [law] clients." Asked if the mayor-elect thought Parker was aware of such activities, Yorty replied, "[H]e had to be." Yorty further described such activities as illegal and vowed to investigate the department further after he was sworn in on July 1. There was thus considerable anticipation about the outcome of the two men's first private meeting. Reporters observed a grim-faced Chief Parker heading into his conference with the mayor. They also noted what reporters described as "a bulging briefcase." The two men emerged all smiles. An understanding had been reached. Yorty would replace most of the men on the Police Commission, but Parker would stay on as chief, with the mayor's full support.

Rumor had it that Chief Parker had shown Mayor Yorty his file.

"BLACK AND BLUE" brawls at Griffith Park were just one of Parker's worries. By the time Mayor Yorty took office, Southern California police agencies had identified a new and altogether more worrisome adversary. Police called it The Muslim Cult. Its members preferred the Nation of Islam.

In the fall of 1959, the LAPD circulated a briefing and training memo from the Culver City Police Department that set forth the basic facts about the organization (as law enforcement understood it):

Briefing and Training Memo from the Culver City Police Department, Classified and Restricted, 11/1/1959

Introduction

Nation of Islam

Or

The "Muslim Cult"

In 1931, a pseudo-religious group was organized in the United States and called the "Muslims." This group adopted, in part, many of the rituals of the true Islamic movements. The Muslim cult, however, is not a legitimate member of the Moslem religion and its existence is denounced by the leaders of the true Moslem Church in the United States. . . .

Relatively little has been known of the "Muslims" until recently, partially because it has been a secret organization and partially because it was felt that any attendant publicity would create some fanatical attractiveness to its recruitment program. However, within the last three months, this cult has been exposed in scores of national magazines and newspapers and by many national and local TV commentators as a purveyor of racial tensions and unrest.

It has been determined that the "Muslim" cult is nation-wide—well-organized and well-financed, militant, and growing. The known membership in New York is over 3,000, in Indianapolis over 500, and in Los Angeles, membership figures range from 600 to 3,000.

There are reportedly 3,000 Muslims in the Los Angeles area associated with either Muhhamed's Eastside temple at 1106 ½ E. Vernon Street, Los Angeles, or Muhammad's Temple of Islam No. 27, located at 1480 W. Jefferson Blvd, Los Angeles. Both temples are headed by Henry X, minister. None of the members use their last names but use the letter 'X.' The reason being that their last names are not really theirs but names handed to them by the masters of slaves. They supposedly will continue to use no last name until the Caucasian race is eliminated.

THE REPORT acknowledged that "to date, there have been relatively few 'incidents' attributed to the 'Muslims' on the local scene"; however, it predicted that it was only a matter of time until a clash occurred.

"Any organization that advocates racial hatred must provide violence and action to satisfy the appetites of its members and to stimulate its program," wrote the Culver City police. When it did, police predicted that officers would find a formidable adversary in the group's paramilitary arm, the so-called Fruit of Islam.

"These men are selected for their physical prowess and are adept at aggressive tactics and Judo," continued the memo:

> They are almost psychotic in their hatred of Caucasians and are comparable to the Mau Mau or Kamikaze in their dedication and fanaticism. It has been reported that many temples have gun clubs in which this militant group are trained in weapons. . . . It has been stated locally, that the members of this cult will kill any police officer when the opportunity presents itself, regardless of the circumstances or outcome.

Little did the Culver City police anticipate that the LAPD would fire the first shot.

AT ABOUT eleven on Friday night, April 27, 1962, Officers Frank Tomlinson and Stanley Kensic spotted two Negro males standing behind the open trunk of a 1954 Buick outside of the Muslim Temple at 5606 South Broadway, Mosque 27. The two men seemed to be examining something in a black garment bag. Despite the fact that he was getting married the next day, Kensic decided to stop and ask the two men some questions. Tomlinson, who was completing his one-year rookie probation period that very night, flicked on the cruiser's lights, and the officers double-parked near the two men. Kensic asked if the men were Black Muslims.

"Yes, sir," came the prompt reply.

The officers had heard about the dangerous new cult before. Seven months earlier, two Black Muslims had gotten into a brawl at a market on Western Avenue near Venice Boulevard, when the manager attempted to stop them from distributing their newspaper, *Mr. Muhammad Speaks*, outside. Since then, police had received regular warnings about the Muslims at roll call. As a precaution, Kensic and Tomlinson decided to frisk the men for weapons. They found none. They then checked the Buick's tags against their hot list of stolen cars. Again, nothing. The officers asked the two men where the clothes came from. Monroe X Jones was beginning to explain that he worked for a drycleaner, when the officers decided to separate the two men. Kensic would later testify that he said, "Come with me." Fred X Jingles, the other party present, heard something different: "Let's separate these niggers."

Jingles pushed away Kensic's hands. Although he wasn't fighting back, the attitude worried Kensic, who promptly grabbed Jingles's arm and spun him around, slamming the man onto the trunk of the Buick. A bystander ran into the temple to call for help. Instead of going limp, Jingles fought back. Jones now slipped away from Officer Tomlinson and pulled Kensic off his friend. A fight broke out. As Tomlinson ran to help his partner, he was grabbed by another Muslim. The scene was briefly interrupted when a black off-duty special deputy driving down Broadway stopped and fired a warning shot. Officer Tomlinson now had a chance to regain control of the situation. But instead of composing himself, drawing his gun, ordering the crowd to freeze, and then radioing for help, Tomlinson pulled out his sap and attempted to hit the nearest Muslim. At that very moment, the black special deputy motorist fired into the crowd, wounding Jingles. In the confusion, Jones grabbed Kensic's gun—and shot Tomlinson. An African American policeman who happened to be driving by jumped out and fired a shot into the air to disperse the crowd. Then he radioed for help. Meanwhile, Black Muslims were racing back to the temple from across the neighborhood.

Police cruisers poured into the neighborhood. Instead of sealing off the area and ascertaining just what had happened, officers charged the building, swinging nightsticks wildly. Two Muslims who fought with the police were shot. So were two who sought to flee or surrender. One died; another was permanently disabled. Four more men were badly injured. Other Muslims fought back, ineffectually. Inside the men's room, police beat a dozen of the men who'd been involved in the melee. The battle was over.

The following day, Chief Parker went to visit Officer Kensic at Central Receiving Hospital. Afterward, Parker called the Friday-night incident "the most brutal conflict I've seen" in his thirty-five years on the force and described Kensic's injuries as the result of a vicious attack by a "hate organization which is dedicated to the destruction of the Caucasian race."

The Nation of Islam sent in one of its most prominent leaders too—its "national minister," Malcolm X. At a press conference at the Statler Hilton Hotel (which Malcolm X began with the sobering words "Seven innocent, unarmed black men were shot in cold blood"), the controversial Black Muslim leader denounced Chief Parker as a man "intoxicated with power and his own ego."

But Malcolm X wasn't there for funeral publicity. He was determined to bring the LAPD to justice. Suspecting that police would seek to prosecute the men it had arrested in order to justify the seven shootings, he set to work lining up the services of one of the city's most respected African American attorneys, Earl Broady. A former policeman and now a proud resident of Beverly Hills, Broady initially rejected these overtures. He thought of Black Muslims as riffraff and saw Parker as a reformer, albeit an autocratic one. However, Malcolm X's persistence and his lucid explanations of what was at stake—plus the largest retainer fee Broady had ever been offered—eventually prevailed.*

Malcolm X's efforts put the NAACP in an awkward situation. Although he was loath to associate his organization with the Nation of Islam, executive director Roy Wilkins suspected there was considerable truth to Malcolm X's version of what had happened. Eventually, the NAACP decided to join the civil suit. Meanwhile, the LAPD counterattacked. Parker arranged for a group of Negro leaders, many of them ministers hostile to the Black Muslims, to endorse a campaign to eradicate the Nation of Islam. But when the group convened before the county board of supervisors on May 8, protesters shouted them down. Both the ministers and the supervisors were shaken. Not since the days of the Zoot Suit Riots, said one supervisor, had he felt such tension. The ministers decided to amend their request. Now, they proposed to work with the police to eradicate the Nation of Islam *and* police brutality. Three days later a group of twenty-five ministers met with Chief Parker. But when one of the participants, Rev. H. H. Brookins, broached a recent order to require two officers per car in Negro areas, Chief Parker declared, "I didn't come here to be lectured," and stalked out. Horrified, the head of the Police Commission persuaded Parker to return. But at the end of the meeting Parker complained that "the Negro people" seemed unable to conduct a civil exchange with him.

This was too much. Rev. J. Raymond Henderson decided to hold a protest at his Second Baptist Church, one of the largest congregations in the west. On the evening of Sunday, May 13, nearly three thousand people packed the church, among them the exotic Muslim leader from New York, Malcolm X. As a non-Christian, he was not allowed to step into the worship area. But when he rose from his front-row seat and asked to address the audience, Reverand Henderson allowed him to proceed. Malcolm X's speech was so mesmerizing, an undercover LAPD officer reported, that when Reverend Henderson tried to interrupt his diatribe about police brutality, the reverend's own congregation booed their minister into silence.

The LAPD was losing the black community.

In early June, a group called the United Clergymen for Central Los Angeles denounced Parker as "anti-Negro" and asked Mayor Yorty to personally

---

*"On May 14, an all-white coroner's jury acquitted the officer involved in the point-blank shooting of one of the men at the mosque, Ronald X Stokes. Stokes had been shot with his hands raised because the officer who killed him felt endangered. The jury's deliberations took less than thirty minutes. The Black Muslims were not treated so leniently. Despite Broady's efforts, on July 14, 1963, eleven members of the Nation of Islam were convicted on a variety of charges and given prison sentences ranging from one to ten years. ("Sentences Reimposed on 11 Black Muslims," *Los Angeles Times*, March 3, 1965.)

investigate complaints of verbal and physical brutality. Parker responded that this was nothing more than an attempt by Communist sympathizers to use the technique of the "Big Lie" against the department. Mayor Yorty rushed to his police chief's defense.

"I doubt if there is any city in the United States with more Negroes in government than Los Angeles," Yorty told the press, noting that he himself was a member of the NAACP and that both his civil service and police commissions were dominated by minorities. This was technically true. The Police Commission's five members did include a black attorney, a Latino doctor, and a Jewish lawyer. But these men hardly served as Parker's boss. On the contrary, Parker himself had chosen at least one of the minority members, African American attorney Elbert Hudson. As for the constant drumbeat of allegations about police brutality, Yorty dismissed them as "wild and exaggerated" and echoed Parker's suggestion that they were Communist inspired. That summer Parker flew to Washington, D.C., to brief Attorney General Robert Kennedy on the Black Muslim menace.

Chief Parker ignored—or mocked—those who sought to draw attention to African American grievances. When in early 1963, the Episcopal bishop of California drew attention to "the bad psychological pattern" between police and minority groups, Parker hit back, dismissing the prelate as an uninformed San Franciscan.

"The Negro community here has praised us long and loud," Parker insisted. "We have the best relationship with Negroes of any big city in America today."

Chief Parker and Mayor Yorty's brush-off inspired black Angelenos to take action. The following year, in 1963, three African Americans were elected or appointed to the city council, Billy Mills, Gilbert Lindsay, and Tom Bradley. All had made police accountability a major part of their campaign platforms. All soon discovered that they could make no headway against Chief Parker.

That August, America watched while civil rights demonstrators converged in Washington, D.C., for a march to demand jobs and freedom for all Americans. To many Americans, the Rev. Dr. Martin Luther King's "I Have a Dream" speech was a thrilling paean to the promises of freedom. To Chief Parker, it was an invitation to revolt. Immediately after the March on Washington, law enforcement and National Guard officials met to draft a plan to respond to civil disorder. An emergency plan was developed, numbering nearly a hundred pages in length. Later that fall, LAPD officials wrote a memo on police-guard coordination that included a provision that would permit the use of hand grenades against protesters.

The emergence of a civil rights movement founded on the concept of civil disobedience likewise disturbed Parker greatly—more greatly than the conditions that prompted its emergence. Parker seemed to believe that Los Angeles already was as integrated as it could be, short of embracing "reverse discrimination" (i.e., forcing white people to work with and live next to black people when they would rather not). When asked how he would have responded to civil rights demonstrations had he been the chief of police in Birmingham, Parker ducked the question. "Los Angeles is not Birmingham," he replied. To Parker, the willingness of Los Angeles–area civil rights organizations to criticize the LAPD—a department that Chief Parker firmly believed had done "a magnificent job" with race relations— afforded the final proof that the civil rights movement was essentially pro-Communist and antipolice.

In Chief Parker's world, race relations had a "through the looking glass" quality. The LAPD arrested a higher percentage of minorities than other big-city police departments because it enforced the law more equally than other departments. Race relations in Los Angeles seemed bad because race relations were so good that the city had become a target for agitators. Unnamed forces, Parker insisted, had chosen Los Angeles as "a proving ground" for their strategy of damaging the police precisely because it took racial complaints so seriously. Fortunately, the chief asserted, it wasn't working. "Negroes," he confidently asserted in the summer of 1963, "aren't ready to make big demonstrations." Nor would he permit the threat of disorder to intimidate the department into unilaterally disarming.

"This city can't be sandbagged by some threat of disorder into destroying itself," he told *Los Angeles Times* columnist Paul Coates in the summer of 1963. "We have the most advanced department in the nation in human relations."

The country's greatest police department would not allow its youngest great city to go up in flames.

26

The Gas Chamber

"Don't worry about me."
—Mickey Cohen

IN JANUARY 1962, the U.S. Court of Appeals for the Ninth Circuit upheld Cohen's tax conviction. Mickey returned to Alcatraz. But two weeks
later, U.S. Supreme Court Justice William Douglas stepped in again, allowing Mickey to leave on bail once more while the U.S. Supreme Court considered his final appeal. Soon thereafter, a reporter for the *Valley News*
found him living quietly in a rented house in Van Nuys. He complained
about the lack of closet space and the small hot water heater. He explained
that he and Hagen were engaged and hoped to be married as soon as he
won his income tax appeal. He was even working on a new version of his
life story, tentatively titled *The Poison Has Left Me*. Meanwhile, on March 5,
1962, Mickey Cohen's trial for the murder of Jack Whalen got under way.
If convicted, Cohen faced the possibility of the gas chamber.

Cohen's indictment arose from statements LoCigno had made in prison.
Mickey's junior henchman had confessed to a priest that he had not, in
fact, shot Whalen but had agreed to be the fall guy after Mickey Cohen
promised him a large cash payoff and a short prison term. He'd gotten neither. The priest in turn tipped off prosecutors in L.A. to the fact that LoCigno
might be willing to talk. An agent then came up to pay LoCigno a visit. "I
didn't do the shooting," he told the agent in their first meeting. "I can't tell
you who did but I can get someone to lead you to the gun." A friend of
LoCigno's took investigators to a popular make-out spot on Mulholland
Drive. There police found a rusty revolver that matched the type of gun
fired in the Whalen killing. They quickly traced the gun's ownership to another member of Mickey's party, Roger Leonard.

Although he was willing to talk with authorities, LoCigno wasn't willing to finger Leonard or anyone else as the actual gunman. Instead, at the
second trial, LoCigno largely repeated the account he had given the jury in

his first trial. The prosecution tried to offset this problem with a new witness—a USC student/model who had been dating Candy Barr's manager at the time. The fearless coed testified that Barr's manager had warned her that "there's going to be trouble at Rondelli's" and later said, "it was stupid to put all the guns in the trashcan." However, she didn't identify Mickey as the gunman either, and much of her testimony came perilously close to hearsay. The gun police had recovered following LoCigno's suggestions was too rusty to be positively identified as the murder weapon. In short, prosecutors had very little in the way of new evidence that could tie Mickey to the shooting.

Cohen's attorneys did not hesitate to make this point. "If you convict Mickey Cohen in this case," declared his attorney during his closing statement on April 4, "you'll be convicting him only because he's Mickey Cohen, not because he's guilty." The following day, after a four-hour closing argument accusing Cohen and his attorneys of weaving "a web of deceit" around what prosecutors claimed was a premeditated conspiracy to kill Jack Whalen, the prosecution rested its case. On Thursday, the jury—eleven women and one man—retired to deliberate. By the end of the day Friday, they still had not reached a verdict. The presiding judge ordered them sequestered over the weekend.

On day four of the jury's deliberations, newspaper columnist Paul Coates tracked down Cohen and found him "half-dozing in a Beverly Hills barber's chair." A manicurist was buffing his nails. A shoeshine boy was hard at work polishing his brand-new Florsheims. As Coates pondered the question of how a man who at any moment could be condemned to death could be so relaxed, the radio crackled to life.

"Here's another bulletin," the newscaster announced excitedly. "The Mickey Cohen murder trial jury, failing for the fourth day to reach a verdict, has been locked up again for the night."

"Mickey's barber gasped," wrote Coates.

"The pressure—the suspense. It must be terrible," the barber suggested. Mickey just grunted.

"This is a crazy town," he finally answered. "They accuse me of bumping a guy off. So what do they do? They turn me loose and lock up my jury!"

The next day, the jury in Cohen's case informed the judge that it was hopelessly deadlocked. Nine members of the jury were ready to acquit. Three insisted on holding out for a conviction. Reluctantly, Judge Lewis Drucker declared a mistrial.

"Although much testimony of the defendants was discredited and there was some admitted perjury, I consider the totality of the evidence against them shows no conspiracy exists," declared the judge. With that, the murder charges were dismissed. Mickey Cohen had once again beaten the rap.

Cohen had dodged the gas chamber. But he couldn't avoid a return trip to Alcatraz. Later that spring, the Supreme Court rejected his appeals request in his tax-evasion case. In early May, he bid Sandy Hagen and an estimated two hundred fans and autograph seekers farewell as he surrendered to authorities at the federal building in downtown Los Angeles. His mandatory release date was early 1972. Kissing Hagen good-bye, Mickey declared to the assembled crowd, "I followed the concept of life man should—except for that gambling operation."

THE FOLLOWING FEBRUARY, Mickey Cohen was moved from Alcatraz to the federal penitentiary in Atlanta. There he took over Vito Genovese's old job in the electric shop, along with Genovese's hot plate and shower. Mickey typically got off work a bit early, so he could make it to the showers first, for an extra-long rinse. But that particular day, when Cohen headed to the showers, wrapped in a towel, he found himself face to face with an unexpected visitor, Attorney General Robert Kennedy.

Kennedy had come to offer the hoodlum one last opportunity to turn state's witness for the government. "How the hell are you going to live fifteen years in this goddamn chicken coop?" he asked Cohen.

"Don't worry about me," Cohen replied. Then he proceeded to the shower.

Compared to Alcatraz, Atlanta was "paradise." Cohen could listen to the radio and read the newspaper—even watch television from time to time. He slowly adjusted to prison hours—waking up at five thirty or six, going to sleep early, when lights went out. To stay in shape, "I did a lot of shadow boxing and knee bends." He thought about appeals strategies and wrote letters to his attorneys. He engaged in "shop talk" with "certain guys from Philadelphia, Chicago, and New York." He also made nice with other inmates.

"[Y]ou say hello to everybody, particularly if you're somebody with a name. See, if you don't, they'll say, 'Who the hell does that son of a bitch think he is? He thinks he's a big shot?'" From such small slights, shocking violence could sometimes erupt.

Cohen was playing it smart. But sometimes, even the smartest card player gets dealt a bad hand. That's what happened to Mickey on August 14, 1963, when a deranged inmate, Estes McDonald, escaped from medical supervision. After scaling a chain-link fence and crossing the prison yard, he found Mickey Cohen inside watching TV—and viciously brained him with a three-foot-long lead pipe. By the time prison authorities restrained McDonald, Cohen was a bloody heap, his skull visibly indented. It took him six hours to regain consciousness. It was another two days before prison doctors were confident that Cohen would survive. Prison authorities tried to put a happy face on the situation for Sandy Hagen and Cohen family members, but the damage done was severe. Mickey's legs were partially paralyzed. His arms were essentially useless. His voice was slurred. Cohen had to beg the prison bull for a special allotment of six rolls of toilet paper a day, simply to dry the tears that now rolled down his cheeks spontaneously, uncontrollably.

In October, Cohen was transferred to a special medical facility in Springfield, Missouri, for brain surgery. It was only partially successful. Cohen was still unable to walk following the operation and could use only one arm. Cohen was sent to Los Angeles for therapy—under armed guard. As a result of intensive physical therapy there, considerable progress was made. By the end of his time in Los Angeles, Cohen was able to move with the assistance of a walker. Progress was rewarded with a transfer back to Springfield. There, for most of the next eleven months, he was kept in solitary confinement, ostensibly for his protection. Cohen responded by filing a $10 million lawsuit against the government for negligence in allowing the convict who had attacked him to escape.

In March 1964, Cohen's old friend Ben Hecht wrote the gangster a sympathetic letter. "Dear Mickey," it began.

> *You are not in the only jail there is. There is another jail called "old age" in which I am beginning to serve time. Like you, I am not allowed to complain or protest—Rose won't stand for it.*
>
> *I hope they let you look at television so that you can keep up on the shenanigans that the "holier than thous" continue to commit and perform. I was going to write a letter to Attorney General Kennedy about you—I inquired of a friend of his how he might react to such a letter. I was told he would react loudly and angrily rant against it. . . .*
>
> *If there is such a thing as "Good luck" in the place where you are, I hope you find it.*
>
> *Sincerely, Ben Hecht*

Hecht died one month later. Cohen seemed trapped in a living death. Disconsolate, he wrote the faithful Sandy Hagen, telling her that she should wait for him no more.

"I may never come out of here alive, and the best I'm going to come out is terribly crippled," he wrote. "I won't be in no position to be any good to you or anyone else."

Ever obedient, Hagen complied with Mickey's instructions. She married and disappeared from the newspapers, never to be found again. Cohen was now truly alone.

BILL PARKER was also struggling against a failing body. In May 1964, Parker left Los Angeles for the Mayo Clinic. The papers reported he would be gone for a week of "skin and arthritic treatment." In fact, it appears that he was undergoing serious gastrointestinal surgery. Associates were shocked at his appearance upon his return. Parker was gaunt and appeared to have aged several years. However, surgery didn't seem to have diminished his zest for rhetorical combat. When later that summer rioting broke out in four eastern cities after clashes between police officers and African Americans, Parker was adamant that Los Angeles would see no similar large-scale disturbances. At appearances throughout the city, the chief returned to his theory of outside agitators, noting that most of the protesters who turned out for civil rights demonstrations in Los Angeles weren't even black.

Yet signs of racial strife were everywhere. That April, black youths had clashed with police on multiple occasions, first at a track meet at Jefferson High School, then, two weeks later, at the scene of a traffic accident. (Parker blamed "social unrest and resentment against all forms of governmental authority" for the disturbances.) In May, California assistant attorney general Howard Jewell warned, in a report to the state AG, that the bitter conflict between Parker and civil rights leaders risked sparking rioting unless the tensions were addressed. Judge Loren Miller, a member of the Jewell Commission, was even more pessimistic.

"Violence in Los Angeles is inevitable," wrote Miller. "Nothing can or will be done about it until after the fact. Then there will be the appointment of a commission which will damn the civil rights leaders and the Chief alike."

Parker vehemently disagreed.

"I doubt that Los Angeles will become part of the battleground of the racial conflict that is raging in the United States today," Parker told the Sigma Delta Chi journalism fraternity that fall. "This city is ten years ahead of other major metropolitan areas in assimilating the Negro minority." Real unrest would only become a danger, Parker told the Sherman Oaks Rotary Club in the spring of 1964, if "the current soft attitude on the part of the republic to crime and Civil Rights demonstrations" continued.

Even with three African Americans on the city council, no one could check Chief Parker's course. Councilman Bradley became so frustrated with the situation that in the spring of 1965, he even introduced legislation that would have made the chief of police *more* powerful. Bradley's rationale was that it was time to end the charade that the Police Commission directed the department and hold accountable the man who really did. But like most of Bradley's other attempts to restrain Parker, it failed. Bill Parker would chart his own destiny.

27

Watts

"This community has done a magnificent job [with race relations]. We're afraid to tell the truth, because it would prove this is the Garden of Eden."

—Chief William Parker, June 25, 1963

ON WEDNESDAY EVENING, August 11, 1965, a California Highway Patrol motorcycle officer, Lee Minikus, was waved down by a passing African American motorist. The motorist told Minikus that he'd just seen a white Buick headed up Avalon Boulevard, driving recklessly—"like he might be drunk or something." Minikus, who was white, set off in pursuit and soon caught up with the speeding car. He pulled it over at 116th and Avalon. Its driver was twenty-one-year-old Marquette Frye. His stepbrother Ronald, twenty-two, was also in the car. Office Minikus asked Marquette for his license. He didn't have one. Smelling alcohol, Officer Minikus asked Marquette to get out of the car to perform the standard field sobriety test. Frye failed the test. Minikus went back to his motorcycle and radioed for his partner, who was patrolling the nearby Harbor Freeway. He also called for a patrol car to take Marquette in to be booked and a tow truck for the car. It was a minute or two after seven o'clock in the evening.

Minikus told Marquette that he was under arrest. Still good-natured, Marquette asked Minikus if his brother or some other family member could take the car home. They were only a block away. Officer Minikus said that he could not. Department procedure called for towing away and impounding the car. At that very moment, an ex-girlfriend of Marquette's walked by. Seeing that Marquette was about to be arrested, she hurried over to the apartment where he lived to fetch Marquette and Ronald's mother. When she arrived at the scene to find a second motorcycle patrolman (Minikus's partner), a transportation car, and the tow truck, Mrs. Frye got upset—at Marquette. She started to scold him for drinking. Up until this point in the arrest, Marquette had been subdued but cooperative. Now, his mood changed. He pushed away his mother and allegedly started shouting, "You motherfucking white cops, you're not taking me anywhere!" yelling that they would have to kill him before he would go to jail.

It was a sweltering day. Since Monday, temperatures had been in the mid-nineties—fifteen degrees hotter than it had been all summer. A yellow-gray blanket of smog lay heavy across the city. In 1965, air conditioners were still a rarity in this part of Watts, a working-class neighborhood of newly built two-story apartment buildings and bungalows. As a result, residents tried to spend as much time outside as they could. The neighborhood was full of people that evening—people who were naturally curious to know what all the ruckus was about. By the time Marquette got angry, a crowd of roughly a hundred bystanders had gathered. Some of them started to murmur, angrily. Minikus's partner slipped off and radioed a code 1199—officer needs help. He returned with a baton used for riot control. The officer in the patrol car grabbed his shotgun.

The crowd, now numbering perhaps 150 people, was starting to turn hostile. "Hit those blue-eyed bastards!" a voice yelled. While one highway patrol officer waved his shotgun at the crowd, the two motorcycle patrol officers attempted to grab Marquette. A scuffle broke out as California Highway Patrol reinforcements arrived at the scene. Marquette was struck by a baton and collapsed on the ground. Mrs. Frye jumped onto the back of one of the arresting officers, screaming, "You white Southern bastard!" Little brother Ronald got into the mix too. By 7:23 p.m., all the Fryes were under arrest. The crowd was now screaming.

"Leave the old lady alone!" someone cried.

"Those white motherfuckers got no cause to do that," yelled someone else.

"We've got no rights at all—it's just like Selma," shouted someone else.

The number of onlookers swelled to between 250 and 300 persons. The crowd was getting more and more agitated. Who didn't know about the shootout three years earlier with the Nation of Islam? Who didn't know that just one year earlier white Californians had voted to maintain housing segregation, to keep black Angelenos confined to the ghetto? Picking up on the mood, one of the highway patrol officers slipped off to radio for more backup. Soon three more highway patrol officers appeared. Minikus and his partner were now struggling with Marquette and his stepbrother—and with Mrs. Frye. Another officer swung his nightstick at Marquette, hitting him on the forehead and opening a nasty cut. As this was going on, the first LAPD units arrived at the scene.

The arresting officers caught the crowd's mood. They knew things could get violent. The patrol cars and the tow truck pulled away fast. But as the motorcycle patrolmen revved their engines, one of the officers felt a wad of spit hit the back of his neck. He and his partner stopped and plunged back into the crowd, grabbing the woman they thought was responsible, who started screaming that she hadn't done anything. The patrol cars returned to the scene, where the crowd, enraged by police mistreatment of a pregnant black woman (as the rumor now had it) was screaming for blood.

"Motherfuckers! Blue-eyed devils! Motherfuckers!"

Another man started urging the crowd to respond; the highway patrol arrested him as well. Then they left to take the Fryes to be booked at a local sheriff's substation. By 7:40 p.m., the police were again pulling away. A youth hurled a bottle at one of the retreating patrol cars, hitting its rear fender with a crash. This time the police did not return, but instead of dispersing, the assembled crowd headed out into the neighborhood, intent on venting their anger. White motorists passing through the area soon found themselves pelted with stones and, in some cases, beaten. One of the people driving through the area was Chief Parker's protégé, Daryl Gates.

Gates had enjoyed a rapid ascent in Parker's police department. In 1963, Parker confidant James Hamilton, the longtime head of the Los Angeles Police Department's intelligence division, had left the department to go to the National Football League. (The NFL was having problems with gambling and organized crime, and Robert Kennedy had recommended his old friend as the perfect person to clean it up.) No position in the department was more sensitive; Parker tapped Gates to fill it. After two years of exemplary service in that position and another outstanding performance on the civil service exam, in June 1965 Gates became (at the age of thirty-eight) one of the youngest inspectors in the history of the LAPD. A *Herald-Examiner* story on the appointment noted that Gates was "rumored to be Parker's choice as a successor." He was assigned to command Patrol Area 3—Highland Park, Hollywood, Hollenbeck, and Central Division. But in early August, the inspector who was normally in charge of Patrol Area 2—South-Central and southwest L.A.—went on vacation. As a result, those areas were added to Gates's command.

On the evening of August 11, Gates was heading over to check on security at the Harvey Aluminum Company plant at 190th and Normandie, where workers were out on strike. Over the radio he heard a dispatcher alerting all units to "a major 415"—a large-scale civil disturbance. Gates was about a mile from the intersection of Avalon and 116th Street. He decided to drive over and see what was going on.

What he saw was mayhem. "A kind of crazed carnival atmosphere had broken out," Gates recalled later in his memoirs. "Laughing, shouting, hurling anything they could find, people were running helter-skelter through the streets. Cars—ours and those of unsuspecting motorists—were pelted with rocks and bottles." But, as Gates noted, "no single mob had formed." Moreover, most of the violence was confined to an eight-block area that centered on the scene of the Frye arrest. There was still a chance to control the chaos.

The police had regrouped at a gas station just off the Imperial Highway, where an ad hoc command post had been set up. As the ranking officer, Gates took charge of the field office. Using the roughly twenty patrol cars on hand, Gates attempted to cordon off the area. It was seventy police officers against a mob of five hundred, eight hundred, a thousand—no one really knew for sure. That wasn't counting reporters, whose presence seemed to spur the youths to additional acts of violence. Nonetheless, by the early hours of the morning it appeared that the police had managed to contain the violence. By 3 or 4 a.m. in the morning, the rock-throwing had died down and the streets had largely cleared. Deputy Chief Murdock, with whom Gates had been in communication all evening, gave the order for the exhausted police officers to retire.

LOS ANGELES was not having a race riot.

If officers on the street were attuned to the possibility of spontaneous racial violence, Chief Parker was not. Even as the violence spread, Parker told a *Los Angeles Times* reporter that the city was not experiencing a race riot—where blacks attacked whites—"since all the rioters were Negroes." Rather, what Los Angeles was witnessing was an outburst of childish emotionalism—"people who gave vent to their emotions on a hot night when the temperature didn't get below 72 degrees."

In fact, Parker's police department had been caught off guard—despite ample warnings. Earlier that summer, for instance, Chief Parker received a letter from B. J. Smith, director of the Research Analysis Corporation in McLean, Virginia. Smith noted that Rochester, Philadelphia, New York, and Newark had all experienced race riots during the summer of 1964. How was the country's greatest police department preparing for the possibility of urban violence? Smith's questions were timely: "What are the signs or indications of impending civil disturbance? What measures can be taken to avert this trouble? What techniques are most effective for controlling and discrediting demonstrations and riots?"

Chief Parker's response, in a letter written on May 12, was telling. "The Los Angeles Police Department has never experienced an insurgency situation," he replied. Moreover, it never expected to. "There have been no occurrences of civil disturbances nor serious conditions which might initiate such a situation in this city." He concluded the letter by referring Smith to cities that had.

It was a curious response. Parker's apocalyptic imagination was well developed. Just a few weeks after receiving Smith's letter, for instance, Parker sat down for a radio interview with ultra-right-wing radio host Dean Manion. The tone of their conversation was dark. Parker told his listeners that America was in the midst of a slow-motion socialist revolution: "The difficulty encountered in this socialistic trend is that it is a revolution and it is not entirely a bloodless one, I assure you." Yet somehow the prophet of social anarchy seemed unwilling to accept the possibility that anarchy might erupt in his own city, even after it already had.

THURSDAY MORNING dawned uneasy. The violence had stopped, but no one knew what would happen that night. Eager to defuse the tensions, the Los Angeles County Human Relations Committee scheduled a 2 p.m. community meeting at Athens Park, eleven blocks from the scene of the rioting. Community leaders from across Watts and, indeed, the city appeared—before a huge throng of print, television, and radio reporters— to urge the residents of Watts not to resort to violence. The meeting started well. Even the combative Mrs. Frye urged residents "to help me and the others calm this situation down so that we will not have a riot tonight." But as the event continued, a different mood swept through the crowd. Appeals to calm gave way to expressions of grievance. In a moment of confusion, an African American high school student dashed up to the microphones and informed the crowd that black youths would attack the white areas adjacent to Watts that evening. His remarks were widely carried by the media.

Chief Parker did not attend the meeting. Nor would he agree to meet with those whom he dismissively called the "so-called" Negro leaders, who he believed were attempting to "relieve the Negro people of any responsibility in this situation." Instead, the chief spoke to the press. His comments were not helpful. When asked about the causes of the unrest, Parker replied that the trouble started "when one person threw a rock, and like monkeys in a zoo, others started throwing rocks." Calls by assemblyman Mervyn Dymally to announce the immediate establishment of a civilian police review board were dismissed as "a vicious canard." Parker believed it was now time to meet force with force. After being briefed on what had transpired at the Athens Park meeting, Parker called the adjutant general of the California National Guard to inform him that Los Angeles might well need the Guard. But calling out the Guard was something that only the governor could do and Governor Brown was in Greece on a trip. As a result, the authority to call out the Guard rested with Lt. Gov. Glenn Anderson, who was in Santa Barbara. That evening, Parker called Anderson to brief him on the situation. The lieutenant governor decided to drive back to his house in Los Angeles that evening so he could assess the situation for himself.

At roughly the same time, a delegation of African American activists was meeting with deputy chief Roger Murdock. The activists wanted no visible police presence in Watts that evening. They believed the sight of police would only spur further violence. Instead, they asked the department to deploy only black officers—in civilian clothes and unmarked cars.

Deputy Chief Murdock rejected this proposal out of hand. All day long, he, Daryl Gates, and Inspectors John Powers and Pete Hagan had been working to craft a plan to control South-Central Los Angeles. Their strategy was to deploy units from across the city—as well as roughly 150 deputy sheriffs from the 77th Street station. The hope was that the heavy presence of officers on the street would deter the rioters. Gates would deploy with a contingent of officers to the north of the Imperial Freeway; Inspector John Powers would come in from the south.

THE EVENING began uneventfully—so much so that Gates and the other inspectors decided to treat themselves to a celebratory dinner. But when Gates arrived at the center of field operations, it was clear that things were going badly, even worse than the night before.

The LAPD's training in riot control had taught officers how to handle large groups of people—a mass protest heading down the street. The police mass in formation, split the rioters into two, and disperse them down two different streets. That, at least, was what the training manuals said. But this was different. There was no mass of marchers or rioters to confront. Instead, it was guerrilla warfare. Shots were being fired, Molotov cocktails thrown. Assailants disappeared down alleys and over fences seconds after they appeared. All around, windows and storefronts were being smashed and stores looted. Buildings were starting to go up in flames. Gates realized with horror that the LAPD's field deployment was "a complete abject failure." Confronted with tactics they had never imagined, much less trained against, the LAPD was adrift.

Orders from headquarters that came over the squawking radios only added to the problem. While the burden of directing the department's overall response had fallen primarily on Deputy Chief Murdock, Chief Parker was also taking a role in directing the department's response. Unfortunately, it was not a particularly helpful one. On the first night of the riots, Gates recalls Chief Parker "barking out orders on the radio."

"Get everyone out of their cars! Everybody out of their cars."

Eventually, Gates turned the radio off.

Around midnight, the comedian and civil rights activist Dick Gregory suddenly appeared at Gates's command post. He wanted to address the rioters. Initially Gates refused to provide a bullhorn or an accompaniment of officers, but he was overruled. So Gregory went out—and was promptly shot in the leg. His quick-witted reply: "All right, goddamn it. You shot me. Now go home."

They didn't. By 4 a.m., some one hundred people had been injured and stores up and down Avalon had been looted and burned. Yet once again, the police were optimistic. Gates "sensed that the worst was over" and reported that the situation was "under control." Other senior officers echoed this sentiment. When a member of Lieutenant Governor Anderson's staff called the department's emergency control center early Friday morning to get an update, the sergeant on duty told him that "the situation was well in hand." Reassured, Anderson left Los Angeles at 7:25 a.m. Friday morning for Berkeley, where he was scheduled to attend a meeting as a member of the finance committee of the university's board of regents.

Half an hour later, the looting resumed. Rioters no longer felt they had to wait for the cover of night to act. By 9 a.m. looters were emptying the commercial sections of Watts along 103rd Street and north on Central Avenue. Chief Parker spoke with Mayor Yorty soon thereafter. Both men agreed that it was time to call in the Guard. Yet oddly, Mayor Yorty then left Los Angeles for a previously scheduled speaking arrangement in San Francisco.

At 9:45 a.m., Parker convened an emergency staff meeting to discuss the situation. A liaison for the National Guard was present. In the course of the meeting, Chief Parker indicated that he expected the department would need one thousand Guardsmen to restore order. Yet not until 10:50 a.m. did Parker call Governor Brown's executive secretary to formally request the Guard. But Governor Brown was still in Greece. The person who did have the authority to call out the Guard was Lieutenant Governor Anderson, and Anderson was unreachable, in transit to Berkeley.

Speed was of the essence. By midmorning, police estimates put the size of the mob rampaging through the commercial section of Watts at three thousand. Ambulance drivers and firefighters were refusing to enter the area without armed escorts, escorts the undermanned LAPD could not provide. At that very moment, the 850-man strong Third Brigade of the National Guard was marshaling twelve miles away in Long Beach, in preparation for a weekend of training exercises at Camp Roberts near Santa Barbara.

The brigade was fully armed and could have deployed to Watts in an hour's time. If the Third Brigade proceeded on to Santa Barbara instead, they would be two and a half hours away from the city.

At 11 a.m., Governor Brown's executive secretary finally reached Lieutenant Governor Anderson in Berkeley and relayed Chief Parker's request for the Guard. Still Anderson hesitated. He did not trust Bill Parker. Instead of acting on the chief's request or contacting National Guard officers in Los Angeles for an independent assessment of the situation, Anderson decided that he would return to Los Angeles to see the situation for himself. A National Guard plane was dispatched to Oakland to pick him up. From there he flew to Sacramento for a further round of consultations with state Guard officials. At 1:35 p.m., he left for Los Angeles. By the time he arrived at 3:30, rioters were turning their attention to burning the buildings they had emptied out. Sniper fire kept away the fire trucks. By now, the police had ceded the neighborhood to the mob. Photographs show officers watching while looters stroll out of stores carrying new appliances.

But Parker's police weren't worried about public relations. The looting had drifted north, to Broadway. By late afternoon, it was clear that the rioting threatened the downtown area if not the city as a whole.

That's when Chief Parker left for the weekend.

The LAPD had a policy. Every weekend on a rotating basis, one of the deputy chiefs took over as the duty chief, with primary responsibility for running the department. That weekend, duty chief responsibility fell to deputy chief Harold Sullivan, who commanded the traffic division. With uncontained rioting threatening the central city, this might have seemed like a bad weekend to shift responsibility for running the department to one of the deputy chiefs. But Bill Parker was by then a sick man. The job had aged him—ravaged him really. And on the afternoon of Friday, August 13, as a large swath of his city was going up in flames, Chief Parker felt bad. When Sullivan went to Parker and asked the chief what he wanted to do about the weekend, he replied, "You take care of things." Then Bill Parker went home.

The LAPD was now Harold Sullivan's to command.

Sullivan was a traffic guy. He thought in terms of freeways, and he understood how they bifurcated the city in terms of race and class. Two were particularly important. The first was the Harbor Freeway. Built during the 1950s to connect downtown Los Angeles to the port at San Pedro, the Harbor Freeway sliced through the westernmost edge of the African American neighborhoods of Watts. To the west of the Harbor Freeway was the more affluent (and whiter) neighborhood of Crenshaw, as well as (farther north) the cynosure of Los Angeles's gilded youth, the exclusive University of Southern California. To the east was the ghetto. As a result, living west of the 110 soon became a highly desirable goal—and a sign of success—for African American Angelenos.

The other important freeway was the Santa Monica Freeway (then an unnamed spur of interstate 110), which ran west from downtown Los Angeles to Santa Monica. As a socioeconomic barrrier, "the 10" was even more significant. To the north lay Los Angeles's most affluent neighborhoods and municipalities—Hancock Park, Beverly Hills, Brentwood. These were the homes of the white elite. South of the 10 was the city of the working class. Sullivan recognized that the freeway was not just a class or racial barrier. It was also a massive concrete wall. The Harbor Freeway was indefensible, punctuated as it was by dozens of over- and underpasses. The Santa Monica Freeway was different. Sullivan quickly calculated that between downtown and Beverly Hills, only a small number of underpasses connected south Los Angeles to the affluent neighborhoods to the north. He dispatched a contingent of reserve traffic officers to those critical underpasses, with firm instructions to seal them off and let no one through. California Highway Patrol officers soon arrived, to reinforce the blockades. The rich northern part of the city was now safe. As for Watts and Central Avenue, until the National Guard arrived, there was nothing authorities felt they could do. They were left to burn.

Soon after arriving in Los Angeles, Lieutenant Governor Anderson spoke to Hale Champion, the state finance director back in Sacramento. Champion was aghast at what was unfolding. Moreover, he had gotten through to Governor Brown in Athens. Brown felt the Guard should be called out at once and that the possibility of a citywide curfew should be seriously considered. He also told Champion that he was flying back to California immediately. Spurred by this piece of news, Anderson finally decided to call out the Guard. At four o'clock, he announced the decision to the press. An hour later, he finally signed the proclamation. By six, 1,300 guardsmen had assembled in the local armories. By seven, they were en route to two local staging areas. Yet not until 10 p.m. would the first Guardsmen actually be deployed.

Remarkably, no one had died during the first two days of rioting in Watts. That changed Friday night. Sometime between six and seven, the first resident of Watts died, an African American caught in the crossfire between police and looters. He would not be the last.

Friday night brought something no American city had ever seen before: a full-scale urban war, one in which firemen and ambulances were fair game.

Snipers repeatedly opened fire on the hundred-odd engine companies that were fighting fires in the area. That night, a fireman was crushed and killed by a falling wall. As the shooting intensified, the dying began. At six thirty, twenty-one-year-old Leon Watson was gunned down, standing outside a barbershop. Two hours later, a deputy sheriff was fatally shot with his own gun while struggling with three suspects. The killing came quickly now. One hour later an unarmed Watts resident was killed by police outside a liquor store. Three unarmed companions were wounded. The next civilian died three minutes later. The next, two minutes after that. And so it went. The streets of Watts were washed with blood.

Desperate to restore order, police officers and sheriff's department deputies joined with more than a thousand Guardsmen, on foot, to sweep the streets. By 3 a.m., some 3,300 Guardsmen had been deployed. Yet still the violence raged. Throughout the night, hundreds of reports of snipers firing on the police were called into the 77th Street station. Not until the following evening, when Lieutenant Governor Anderson imposed an eight o'clock curfew on a forty-six-square-mile area of South Los Angeles and more than 13,000 National Guardsmen had deployed, was order restored. That Sunday, Chief Parker reappeared on the airwaves. His presence was not helpful. An attempt to assert that authorities had re-gained control—"Now we're on top and they're on the bottom"—was misinterpreted by many as an endorsement of white supremacy. Not until Tuesday morning was the curfew lifted. More than a thousand people had been wounded and treated in area hospitals. Thirty-four people had died during the rioting. Nearly four thousand people had been ar-rested. Six hundred buildings had been damaged by looting and fire, pri-marily grocery stores, liquor stores, furniture shops, clothing stores, and pawnshops (which seem to have been targeted primarily as repositories for guns). Some 261 buildings were totally destroyed. But as the fires died down, a new conflict flared up. At issue was the question of who was to blame.

TO GROUPS like the NAACP, the ACLU, SNCC, and others on the left, responsibility clearly rested with Chief Parker, Sam Yorty, and the Los Angeles power structure. Community organizer Saul Alinksy recom-mended that both Parker and Cardinal McIntyre—"that unchristian, prehis-toric muttonhead"—be removed. As the embers of Watts still burned, Dr. Martin Luther King arrived in Los Angeles, where he criticized the Parker/Yorty administration and described the riots as "a sort of blind and

misguided revolt against the nation and authority."* King's critical yet conciliatory comments were not welcomed. Governor Brown described King's
visit as "untimely." African American Angelenos were hardly more welcoming. At a meeting in Westminster, he was heckled by the predominantly
black crowd. One member of the crowd stood up and said that the community needed "people like Parker and Yorty down here—not Dr. King.
They're the ones responsible for what's going on."

King agreed and promised to do everything he could to get the mayor
and the police chief to attend a meeting, adding, "I know you will be courteous to them." The crowd laughed. Neither Yorty nor Parker had set foot
in Watts since the riots.

Still, King tried to follow through on his promise. Mayor Yorty was not
receptive. In a closed-door meeting, Yorty excoriated the civil rights leader
for daring to mention "lawlessness, killing, looting, and burning in the
same context as our police department." He also rejected the idea of a civilian police review board. King left Los Angeles shaken by white obstinacy
and by the rise of a new black militancy.

To Mayor Sam Yorty and Chief Parker, the cause of the riots was clear—
and had nothing to do with King's psychological mumbo jumbo. The quick
spread of Molotov cocktails, the inflammatory printed handbills that appeared in Watts on Thursday, the reports of men addressing the crowds
with bullhorns, the movements of youths in cars through areas of great
destruction—Parker felt like everything pointed to the involvement of the
Communist Party, the Black Muslims, or both. Parker did not believe that
radicals had started the violence; he did believe that they had moved into a
chaotic situation and made it immeasurably worse. His department, with
its vaunted intelligence apparatus, had not failed. Instead, they had engaged with a deadly foe. Even as the violence on the street wound down,
the LAPD prepared to hit back.

At 2 a.m. on the morning of August 18, just days after the violence had
finally subsided, the LAPD launched an all-out attack on what it saw as
the epicenter of the violence—the Muslim Temple at 5606 South Broadway, headquarters for the Los Angeles chapter of the Nation of Islam. The
ostensible cause of the raid was an early-morning anonymous phone call
to Newton Division, claiming that the Black Muslims were stockpiling

---

*In a November 13, 1965, *Saturday Review* article, King offered the following explanation of
why rioting had broken out in Los Angeles: "Los Angeles could have expected riots because
it is the luminous symbol of luxurious living for whites. Watts is closer to it and yet further
from it than any other Negro community in the country. The looting in Watts was a form of
social protest very common through the ages as a dramatic and destructive gesture of the
poor toward symbols of their needs."

weapons. As the police were breaking down the door, they came under fire—or so they later claimed. Officers later explained that "pellets" had started "pounding" their cars. So the police opened fire. In all, somewhere between five hundred and a thousand rounds of ammunition slammed into the two-story stucco structure. Eventually, the occupants of the Temple signaled that they were ready to surrender. Fifty-nine Nation of Islam members were arrested. No guns were found. Three weeks later, a judge blamed the incident on the LAPD's "imagination" and dismissed charges against the nineteen men charged with felony offenses. When African American councilman Billy Mills demanded that Parker come before the council to explain the raid, Parker refused, saying, "I suggest he read the City Charter and find out what his powers and limitations are."

The following day, the *Los Angeles Times* noted with evident satisfaction that the "taboo" on white men entering the Temple "had been broken." The paper further reported that while no guns had been found, the temple was full of seditious literature, including hundreds of leaflets that provocatively read, "Stop Police Brutality." Police actions only bolstered the Black Muslims' standing. Soon thereafter, Marquette Frye, the young man whose stop had sparked the Watts riots, joined the Nation of Islam.

THE STREETS of Watts weren't the only place where the LAPD went on the offensive. During the riots, the ailing chief had at times withdrawn from command decisions. However, he had kept up a busy schedule of television appearances, during which he forcefully criticized the rioters and defended the department. Now that the riots were over, Parker was ferocious in defending his men's performance and his own legacy. Instead of sulking or hiding, he launched a media blitz.

Watts was not a failure of the department, the chief insisted. What had happened was a bad Highway Patrol stop on a hot day that gave the Communist Party and its allies the opening they had long hoped for. It did not matter that the men with the bullhorns were later identified as members of local community groups or that the cars moving with suspicious ease through the combat zone almost certainly contained gang members, not Communist Party organizers. The LAPD had not failed. Nor had Chief William Parker. He had not missed black Los Angeles's anger and alienation. On the contrary, Chief Parker maintained that Watts had proved him right.

As evidence of a large conspiracy failed to turn up, Chief Parker turned to another explanation—one that emphasized black migration, the civil rights movement, and mass psychology. He was not shy about making his

case. "A great deal of the courage of these rioters was based on the continu-
ous attacks of civil rights organizations on the police," declared Parker on
CBS Reports later that month.

"They're attempting to reach these groups . . . by catering to their emotions," declared Parker (an emotional man who had no patience for that
quality in others). " 'You're dislocated, you're abandoned; you're abused
due to color,' " Parker continued, mimicking and mocking the attitudes of
civil rights supporters. The civil rights movement had unleashed the
virus of civil disobedience—the belief that people "don't have to obey the
law because the law is unjust." At the same time, a huge surge of black
migration had "flooded a community that wasn't prepared to meet
them." (Parker didn't hide his own feelings about the matter: "We didn't
want these people to come in," he told the panel.)* Both factors laid the
foundations for the uprising. One thing was for certain: The LAPD was
not to blame.

"I think we are almost sadistic in the way we're trying to punish ourselves over this thing without realizing what we have destroyed is a sense
of responsibility for our own actions," continued Chief Parker. "We have
developed a shallow materialist society where everyone is a victim of their
environment and are therefore not to be blamed for anything. . . . If you
want to continue to live in that society, good luck to you."

On August 29, Parker appeared on *Meet the Press*, the most respected of
the Sunday news shows. There he faced off against host Lawrence Spivak
and journalists from NBC News, *Time*, and the *Washington Post*. The questioning was polite—Parker was introduced as the most respected law enforcement officer in the United States, after J. Edgar Hoover—but pointed.
Parker was asked about the causes of the riots, the lack of black officers on
the force, and the persistent allegations of police abuse against minorities.
His responses were unyielding. The rioting was sparked by a botched arrest by the California Highway Patrol. The LAPD had only a handful of
Negro lieutenants because it was hard to find qualified Negroes willing to
work in such an underpaid, underappreciated profession. Isolated verbal
abuse of minorities was perhaps a problem, but so was the fact that eight
hundred of his officers had been physically assaulted in the performance of
their duties during the course of the previous year.

The response to these appearances was overwhelmingly positive. Parker
claimed that in the weeks following the riots and his media appearances, he

---

*During the same interview, Parker also made it clear that "less than one percent" of L.A.
County's 600,000 African American residents were involved in the violence.

received 125,000 telegrams and letters—"ninety-nine percent of them favorable." The city council, the American Legion, the Downtown Businessmen's Association—virtually every major interest group in the city rushed to proclaim its admiration for Los Angeles's indispensable chief of police.

CALIFORNIA Governor Pat Brown begged to differ. By 1965, Brown was an old foe of Parker's, having clashed repeatedly with him over wiretaps, capital punishment, and other criminal justice issues. Brown suspected that frustration over discrimination and high unemployment was behind the riots, not Communist agitators or some spreading malaise of lawlessness. On August 19, he appointed an independent commission, the Governor's Commission on the Los Angeles Riots, headed by former director of Central Intelligence John McCone, to examine the cause and course of the riots. Brown charged the commission with delivering a thorough report as quickly as possible. The commission heard directly from more than seventy-nine witnesses; its staff interviewed hundreds of people, including ninety arrested during the riots. Twenty-six consultants queried another ten thousand people.

The testimony of many of the African Americans who appeared before the commission and Chief Parker, Police Commission president John Ferraro, and Mayor Yorty was strikingly at odds. Witnesses such as councilman Tom Bradley and state assemblyman Mervyn Dymally expressed some sympathy for the plight of law enforcement officers attempting to patrol a dangerous ghetto. Yet they also insisted that the LAPD was both too slow to enforce the law in black neighborhoods and, when it did act, too often did so disrespectfully—sometimes even brutally. Negroes, testified Assemblyman Dymally, "generally expected the worst from police and got it."

Parker, Ferraro, and Yorty rejected this critique. In his testimony before the McCone Commission on September 17, Parker put forward his analysis of what had happened—to a strikingly sympathetic audience. According to Chief Parker, Watts reflected the general decline of law and order throughout the United States. Parker's rambling testimony, with its strange third-person references to himself (e.g., Negro leaders "seem to think that if Parker can be destroyed officially, then they will have no more trouble in imposing their will upon the police of America . . . because nobody else will dare stand up" to them) would later be described by the historian Robert Fogelson as "bordering on the paranoid." But McCone and most white Angelenos found it perfectly reasonable.

Civil rights leaders attacked Parker for provocative comments, particularly his "we're on top and they're on bottom" statement. Critics interpreted this as an endorsement of the status quo. It was possible that Parker's remarks in that particular instance were simply descriptive. But there is no mistaking the drift of Chief Parker's comments. Despite his earlier experiences as a Catholic in an aggressively Protestant city, Parker had never been sympathetic to the civil rights movement. Its embrace of civil disobedience horrified him. He did not see the history of hundreds of years of legal oppression. He did not see the horrifying indignities that African Americans in his own department such as Vivian Strange or Tom Bradley (who once dressed up as a workman in order to go look at a house in a majority-white neighborhood he was considering buying so as not to draw unwanted attention) routinely faced. This was a tragic failure of empathy for the chief of a great African American city.

Yet for many years, Parker's comments on race had a certain balance: He criticized civil disobedience but also disdained the "pseudoscience" of racism. He foresaw a time when "assimilation" would remove racial conflicts. But as the 1960s progressed, any sense of balance fell away. Bill Parker had denied that blacks in Los Angeles experienced racism in any significant way. Now he actively played on white fears of black and brown violence to rally support for the police department.

"It is estimated that by 1970," he told viewers of ABC's *Newsmaker* program on August 14, "forty-five percent of the metropolitan area will be Negro; that excludes the San Fernando Valley. . . . If you want any protection for your home and family, you're going to have to get in and support a strong police department. If you don't, come 1970, God help you!"

Given such comments, it is hardly surprising that Chief Parker's relationship with his critics did not improve. Back in Los Angeles at a city council meeting in September, Councilman Bradley attempted to pin down Parker on the "shadowy organization" that Parker constantly (albeit elliptically) referred to in his talks about the Watts riots.

"Can you identify the organization?" Bradley asked the chief.

"I have my suspicions," replied Parker. Then he turned the question around on Bradley. "Perhaps you can. You're closer to those people."

PARKER'S combative appearances belied his fragile health. That October, he returned to the Mayo Clinic, this time for heart surgery. In his absence, the department took a few small steps toward a less combative posture, assigning African American lieutenants to five critical divisions (Public Information, Newton, 77th Street, University, and Wilshire) to serve as community relations officers. But when rumors began to circulate that Parker might be about to retire, Yorty urged him to return to the job.

On December 2, 1965, the day before Parker was scheduled to return to Los Angeles, the Governor's Commission on the Los Angeles Riots, which was known simply as the McCone Commission, issued its report. Written largely by commission vice chairman Warren Christopher, it attempted to tack between the two camps. The rioting was dismissed as the handiwork of a disgruntled few, not a mass uprising driven by legitimate concerns. As to whether the LAPD's style of policing was to blame for the outbreak of violence, the McCone Commission report was coy. It reported "evidences [of] a deep and longstanding schism between a substantial portion of the Negro community and the Police Department," and mentioned the frequent complaints of "police brutality" (a phrase the report placed in prophylactic quotation marks, lest the commission be accused of confirming that such things occurred). The report also noted that "generally speaking, the Negro community does not harbor the same angry feeling toward the Sheriff or his staff as it does toward the Los Angeles police." Indeed, the McCone Commission correctly observed that "Chief of Police Parker appears to be the focal point of the criticism within the Negro community."

"He is a man distrusted by most Negroes," the report continued. "Many Negroes feel that he carries a deep hatred of the Negro community."

But the commission raised these issues only to dismiss them. "Chief Parker's statements to us and collateral evidence such as his record of fairness to Negro officers are inconsistent with his having such an attitude," the commission declared. "Despite the depth of feeling against Chief Parker . . . he is recognized, even by many of his most vocal critics, as a capable Chief who directs an efficient police force that serves well this entire community." This, of course, was precisely the proposition that many African Americans rejected. Christopher concluded the section on the policing with the Parkeresque declaration: "Our society is held together by respect for law." The police, it continued, were "the thin thread" that bound our society together. "If police authority is destroyed . . . chaos might easily result." The commission also echoed Parker's rhetoric about the civil rights movement: "Throughout the nation unpunished violence and disobedience to law were widely reported and almost daily there were exhortations here and elsewhere to take the most extreme and illegal remedies to right a wide variety of wrongs, real and supposed."

The report's criticism of the Police Commission was more pointed. It noted, with wonder, that "no one, not a single witness, has criticized the

Board for the conduct of the police, although the Board is the final authority in such matters. We interpret this as evidence that the Board of Police Commissioners is not visibly exercising authority over the Department vested in it by the City Charter." Yet the commission's recommendations—that the Police Commission meet more frequently, request more staff, and get more involved, were strikingly naïve. The Police Commission's powerlessness was not simply a matter of its occasional meetings and limited resources. It also reflected a deliberate, decade-long strategy by Chief Parker to assert the prerogatives of the professional policeman over those of the casually involved citizen. A mere exhortation was hardly an effective remedy against as skilled a politician as Bill Parker.

To many on the left, the McCone Commission's report was a bitter disappointment. A January 1966 assessment by the California advisory committee to the U.S. Commission on Civil Rights criticized the report for ignoring warnings, such as the one sounded by assistant attorney general Howard Jewell, that the bitter conflict between Parker and civil rights leaders might well lead to riots. But to Parker, even mild criticism smacked of a personal attack.

Back on the job after a six-week period of rest and recuperation, he responded with characteristic bluntness.

"I think they're afraid I'm going to run for governor," Parker told the *Los Angeles Times*. "[T]his is just a political attack on me in an attempt to use the Police Department as a scapegoat and to repeat the completely false charge that the Police Department caused the rioting."

In fact, it was Mayor Yorty who was planning to run for governor against Pat Brown—as a law-and-order conservative. Not surprisingly, Yorty backed Parker's response to Watts 100 percent. Politically, Parker had become a potent symbol of law and order. Personally, Yorty worried about Parker's health. On December 16, Yorty wrote to the Police Commission to propose appointing a civilian police administrator to assist Parker in his job. Nothing came of the idea.

Forced to choose between Chief Parker and his critics, L.A.'s elected politicians went with the police. In March 1966, the city council voted to *commend* Chief Parker for his management of the department and the "pattern of realistic human relations" he had established with the city's African American community. Only three members of the council, Tom Bradley, Gilbert Lindsay, and Billy Mills, voted against this curiously worded expression of support.

Parker's popularity dissuaded the city's elected officials from criticizing him directly. "It's most plausible that Chief Parker is the most powerful man in Los Angeles," mused *Los Angeles Times* publisher Otis Chandler to a *Washington Post* reporter that summer. "He is the white community's savior, their symbol of security."

Privately, however, many recognized that Parker was the major obstacle to improved race relations in the city. On March 4, 1966, an FBI agent who'd attended a special panel on Watts at the National Association of District Attorneys in Tucson reported on his conversation with L.A. district attorney Evelle Younger and Judge Earl Broady, a member of the McCone Commission and an African American. Both Younger and Broady described Parker's "ingrained action [*sic*] against Negroes" as "the major stumbling block to any problem of effective community relations." Younger also identified the LAPD's failure to recognize or promote black officers as a major problem. Both men said that they believed Parker would have resigned by now if not for demands from civil rights groups such as the Congress of Racial Equality that he step down. (Parker didn't want to lose face.) Younger also confided that Chief Parker was a very sick man. Less than a week later, Parker was hospitalized for "a temporary cardiac incapacity." Not until June 1 was Parker able to resume command of the department.

On July 5, 1966, Chief Parker sent a memorandum to the city council that represented a serious attempt to come to terms with the city's public safety needs. In it, Parker returned to one of his favorite themes: the need to increase the size of the LAPD. The memo noted that in October 1965, L.A.'s ratio of police officers per thousand residents had fallen to a mere 1.87—little more than half of New York's 3.31 officers per thousand. Yet while L.A.'s population had risen 17 percent since 1958 (and serious crime had risen 47 percent), the size of the police department had actually fallen. One table comparing the number of police per 1,000 residents in Chicago, New York, and Los Angeles made a powerful case for Parker's argument that Los Angeles had made a disastrous decision to underinvest in its police force:

	1950	1955	1960	1964	% change
NY	2.37	2.65	3.02	3.31	+39.7%
Chicago	2.00	2.03	2.82	2.89	+44.5%
L.A.	2.22	1.99	1.88	1.84	−17.1%

The memo concluded by noting that "if the recommended [police] manpower rate for 1958 were projected to a police-officer-per-thousand ratio in 1965, Los Angeles would need 11,010 police officers"—double the size of the current force. As for the chances of this happening, even Parker considered the idea "academic." Thanks to his insistence on high standards (of a certain sort), the LAPD couldn't even fill the much smaller number of positions that were currently available. But Parker's fundamental analysis was almost certainly correct. Los Angeles was underpoliced—criminally so. It still is.

On the evening of July 16, 1966, Bill Parker went to a banquet at the Statler Hilton Hotel to receive an award from the Second Marine Division, which was celebrating its seventeenth annual reunion. He received a plaque citing him as one of the nation's foremost police chiefs. After a few brief remarks, he walked back to his table, where Helen was sitting, while a thousand Marine Corps veterans gave him a standing ovation. He sat down, then, suddenly, he leaned back and started gasping for air. Slowly he crumpled to the floor. His heart had finally failed him. After almost thirty-nine years on the force, Chief William H. Parker was dead. He was sixty-one years old.

The public responded to Parker's death with an outpouring of grief. Mayor Yorty declared himself to be "shocked and heart-broken."

"Los Angeles and America will sadly miss our courageous and beloved Police Chief Parker," Yorty declared. "He was a monument of strength against the criminal elements."

Governor Pat Brown (a frequent Parker antagonist) praised the chief for his "courageous commitment to the rule of law." Even adversaries such as A. L. Wirin had admiring words. Although they had "disagreed sharply on most subjects," the civil liberties attorney declared, "I have admired him throughout the years as an efficient and dedicated police officer."

Said councilman Tom Bradley, "I regret the death of a man who did much to change the image and practices of the police department, although he often spoke from emotion without considering the effect of his words."

Only Thomas Kilgore, the western representative for Dr. Martin Luther King's Southern Christian Leadership Conference, seemed willing to dissent: "His death will be a loss in the sense he put together a strong, disciplined police force. But I think his death will be a relief to the minority community, who believe he woefully misunderstood the social revolution taking place."

At the funeral home, Parker's casket was given a twenty-four-hour police honor guard. The day before the funeral, Parker's body was brought to the City Hall rotunda to lie in state. More than three thousand mourners came to pay their respects and view Parker's body. The funeral itself was scheduled for 10 a.m. the following day at St. Vibiana's cathedral. Police and church officials alike were caught off guard by the massive turnout. Thousands of Angelenos—including Gov. Pat Brown, Republican gubernatorial nominee Ronald Reagan, and Mayor Sam Yorty—and police chiefs from sixty cities filled the cathedral for the requiem high mass, with Cardinal James Francis McIntyre as the officiant. Another 1,500 people lined Main Street to listen to the mass on loudspeakers and, afterward, to observe the hearse carrying Parker's body, escorted by 150 LAPD motorcycle officers. The funeral procession to Parker's grave site at the San Fernando Mission Cemetery was seven miles long. There, a military honor guard buried Chief Parker with full honors while the American Legion Police Post 381 band played "Hail to the Chief" as the casket was moved to the grave site. Taps was played, a rifle volley fired, and then Chief Parker was lowered into the earth.

28

R.I.P.

"I don't want to be rude, but I got to beg off this thing."

—Mickey Cohen

WILLIAM PARKER was dead, but the system he had created lived on.

On July 18, Parker's old rival, chief of detectives Thad Brown, was sworn in as chief of police. This time, FBI director J. Edgar Hoover was quick to convey his congratulations. The new chief responded in the proper fashion. ("It is encouraging to know that I may rely upon your confidence and support in the great task that lies ahead," gushed Brown in reply.) But Thad Brown was only an interim chief. From the beginning, he made it clear that he would not take part in the civil service examination that would select the next permanent chief of police.

During his life, Parker had made no secret of who he thought the next chief should be. "Meet Gates," he'd tell other (more senior) officers in the department. "This officer is going to be chief someday." But a few months before his death, Parker had confided to his young protégé his doubts that this would come to pass.

"I've always thought you would be the next chief, but if I have to leave now, you're too young," he told Gates. "You don't even have your twenty years in."

"What difference does that make?" Gates asked.

"You can't afford to take this job unless you have twenty years, and you have your retirement benefits. Because if something happens, if you're forced to resign, you wouldn't want to stay at a lower rank. So you'd leave and you wouldn't have anything," Parker replied. Parker died when Gates had been on the force for nineteen years. Nonetheless, after Parker's death when the civil service exam for a new chief was held, Gates took the test, as an inspector. But the top score—and the position of chief—went instead to Gates's old instructor at the Police Academy, Tom Reddin. One of Reddin's first actions was to request the intelligence file on himself.

"The notions in it," he later recalled, "were almost laughable, and most of them were wrong." But this did not lead Reddin to disband the intelligence unit. Instead, he expanded its operations further. Even the department's oldest friends fell within its purview, including the former attorney general of the United States, Robert Kennedy.

IN EARLY 1968, Robert Kennedy began a last-minute campaign for the Democratic presidential nomination. On June 5, Kennedy scored a huge win over front-runner Eugene McCarthy in the California Democratic primary. The celebration party was held at the Ambassador Hotel on Wilshire Boulevard.

In 1960, the LAPD had provided security to John F. Kennedy during the Democratic convention. (Secret Service protection was not then offered to candidates before they became the nominee.) The LAPD would normally have provided security at the Ambassador. However, Kennedy's staff wanted no police officers to be visible. Just two months earlier, Dr. Martin Luther King had been assassinated in Memphis. The presence of uniformed officers at the Ambassador was seen as simply too provocative. Instead they relied solely on former FBI agent William Barry and two professional athletes he employed.

"Kennedy's people were adamant, if not abusive, in their demands that the police not even come close to the senator while he was in Los Angeles," recalled Daryl Gates.

But under normal circumstances, that wouldn't have been the end of the story. For many years, the LAPD had secretly protected (and monitored) the activities of visiting VIPs by ensuring that local livery companies used undercover policemen as drivers. Most VIPs never knew, but Kennedy's people did. They arranged for their own driver. As a result, there was no chance that a plainclothes LAPD officer would be at Kennedy's side when, shortly after midnight, the candidate slipped out of the fifth-floor ballroom of the Ambassador Hotel, where he'd just delivered a rousing victory speech and, exiting through its kitchen, encountered Sirhan Sirhan, a Palestinian angry about Kennedy's support of Israel during the Six-Day War. As Kennedy was shaking hands with a busboy, Sirhan stepped out from beside a refrigerator and opened fire with a .22 caliber pistol. Two bullets entered the senator's upper torso. One, fired from a distance of one inch away, entered the back of his head.

Four LAPD patrol cars were circling the Ambassador. The police arrived within minutes, after Kennedy's entourage, which included Kennedy's bodyguard and the writer George Plimpton, had wrestled Sirhan to the ground.

Kennedy was rushed to the Central Receiving Hospital, and then taken across the street to Good Samaritan Hospital for surgery. It was no use. Twenty-six hours later, at 1:44 a.m., June 6, 1968, Robert Kennedy was pronounced dead.

SEVERAL WEEKS LATER, the warden at the federal penitentiary in Springfield called Mickey Cohen into his office.

"There's a call from Washington, and he's going to call back, like, say, one o'clock, so get showered and prepared," he said, brusquely.

When Cohen returned, he found his old pal the columnist Drew Pearson on the line. Needless to say, it was highly unusual for the warden of a federal prison to put a newspaper columnist through to an inmate.

"We're going for [Vice President Hubert] Humphrey for president," Pearson informed him, "and I'll assure you that if he becomes our president, you're going to be given a medical parole."

This sounded good. Naturally, though, Mickey wanted to know why Pearson was willing to do such a tremendous favor.

"I'm gonna use you again in the campaign against Nixon," Pearson informed him. When Nixon first ran for the U.S. Senate in 1950, his campaign manager and attorney, Murray Chotiner, had asked Mickey Cohen to raise $75,000 for the campaign, a considerable sum in those days. Cohen responded by throwing a fund-raiser at the Knickerbocker Hotel. Said Cohen later: "It was all gamblers from Vegas, all gambling money, there wasn't a legitimate person in the room." Cohen had told Pearson about it. Now the columnist wanted to go public with the information.

Cohen was amenable. He'd long since soured on Nixon, whom he considered to be a "rough hustler, like a goddamn small-town ward politician" who dressed like "maybe . . . a three-card Monte dealer" and was an anti-Semite to boot. "Go ahead if that's the way to go," Cohen replied.

A series of accusatory columns by Pearson duly appeared. Mickey was ecstatic. Pearson assured him that a medical parole was simply a matter of time.

"I got a definite promise from LBJ that one way or another, if Humphrey wins or loses, you're going to get a parole or a medical parole at least," Pearson assured him. News of the payoff spread throughout Washington. Rival columnist Jack Anderson ran a story saying that President Lyndon Johnson was considering a Cohen pardon as a reward for "dirt" Cohen had provided to Drew Pearson on Richard Nixon.

Cohen wrote brother Harry to let him know that "the fix was in." It wasn't. Humphrey lost, and LBJ left office without granting Mickey a medical parole. Mickey didn't even bother to ask his old acquaintance Richard Nixon. There was nothing for Cohen to do but serve out the remainder of his sentence.

ON JANUARY 6, 1972, Mickey was released from the Springfield federal penitentiary. Despite extensive physical therapy for nearly a decade, Mickey still needed help with the most basic tasks, such as getting dressed and standing up. Age, ice cream, and, of course, his nearly fatal braining with the lead pipe had made Mickey an old man. But life beckoned still. The night before his release, Cohen bade good-bye to such dear friends as Johnny Dio. "Before you leave a prison after eleven years of being incarcerated," he said later, "the most exciting day is the day before."

Once again, a crowd of reporters gathered for Cohen's release. The frumpy little man who emerged wearing a white T-shirt, windbreaker, and rolled-up chinos bore little resemblance to the suave prisoner who had entered prison a decade earlier. "To hell with this rotten joint," Cohen muttered, as he was helped to brother Harry, who'd come to pick him up—in a brand-new white Cadillac. Their first stop was Hamby's restaurant in downtown Springfield, where Mickey gorged himself—two orders of ham and eggs, three glasses of fresh-squeezed orange juice, and a Danish pastry. Then he got a shave, a haircut, a massage, and a manicure. As always, he left a tip that was "extraordinary . . . particularly for a small town." Then he went to a hotel and showered "for a couple of hours, I guess."

From Springfield, Mickey and Harry, along with a young man named Jim Smith, who suddenly appeared in the capacity of caretaker, drove to Hot Springs, to visit bootlegger Owney "The Killer" Madden's widow and soak in the waters. (Owney had passed away during Mickey's time in the joint.) Cohen hoped that the hot springs would help him "correct my walking at least forty to fifty percent, anyway." Instead, several weeks of hydrotherapy weakened him badly. The food, however, was marvelous. The manager of the Arlington Hotel "still remembered me from my heydays" and made sure Mickey got plenty of Italian cuisine.

"They brought out big silver things full of food, and the chef himself was out there dishing it out—every kind of pasta, every kind of chicken, veal, everything you could imagine," Cohen recalled.

Then it was on to New Orleans, to see Carlos Marcello. ("We talked about the old times, among other things.") Only then did Mickey Cohen return to Los Angeles.

What he found there stunned him. The Sunset Strip he had once known was gone. Its elegant nightclubs were shuttered. Teenage punks and rock 'n' roll had taken over what had once been Hollywood's grandest boulevard. Elegance was no more. Broads now walked around "with skirts up to their neck." Harry and Cohen caretaker Jim Smith tried to explain the fashion for miniskirts and, well, the sixties, but it was hard to understand. Even crime was bewildering and different.

"Today, it's a whole new setup, because you got punks running around. Kids go in, and people give them their money, and they still kill them afterwards," Mickey lamented. In fact, Mickey Cohen was about to discover just how strange the new criminal underworld was.

In February 1974, Patty Hearst, the granddaughter of William Randolph Hearst, was kidnapped from her apartment in Berkeley by one of the decade's most bizarre criminal terrorist groups, the Symbionese Liberation Army. Founded by an escaped African American convict who had adopted the nom de guerre "Cinque" (after the leader of the 1839 slave ship rebellion on the *Amistad*), the SLA espoused a strange blend of Maoist terrorism and Black Power ideology. In the early 1970s, the group assassinated a popular African American Berkeley school superintendent. Several members were convicted and incarcerated for the killing. Hearst was originally seized in order to facilitate a hostage exchange. But two months after her kidnapping, the story took a bizarre twist: Hearst took part in a bank robbery—as an SLA member. The video footage of Patty Hearst—who had adopted the name Tania—was a news sensation. The Bay Area was now too hot for the SLA. So Cinque decided to go south to his hometown of Los Angeles. That's when Patty's father Randolph called Mickey Cohen.

Mickey Cohen had always revered William Randolph Hearst.

"He was a benefactor for me throughout my career and when I needed him," Mickey would later explain, perhaps in reference to the Hearst papers' favorable coverage of Mickey during the Al Pearson beating trial. "There was nothing the Hearst people could call on me for that I would refuse or not attempt to do."

So when Randolph Hearst called Mickey (at the recommendation of the *San Francisco Chronicle*'s crime reporter) and asked if he'd be willing to use his contacts in the underworld to locate Patty, Cohen was happy to oblige. Calling on certain acquaintances in the African American "sporting world," Cohen soon made contact with some figures who might—or might not—have been SLA members or associates. A half dozen meetings ensued, all of them preceded by elaborate, multicar evasive maneuvers intended to throw off any cops who were trailing Cohen. Mickey was frankly jittery at the early meetings. Although he respected SLA members for their skill as lamsters, Cohen didn't get the underground anti–Vietnam War movement. The SLA guys, in turn, viewed Cohen as a "square" because he didn't drink and had never tried drugs. After a while, though, things got chummy. So chummy that Cohen felt a deal was within reach. Through his reporter-contact at the *Chronicle*, Cohen summoned Patty's parents down from San Francisco to L.A.

They met over dinner at Gatsby's. Patty's mother was nervous, probably because the maître d' came over early to inform them that they were being monitored by men from the LAPD intelligence division. She told Mickey that she was worried that her daughter might now be so committed to the SLA that she would not return to her parents' custody willingly. That didn't seem to concern Mickey. But what Catherine Hearst said next did.

"We may be making a mistake bringing Patty back," Mrs. Hearst continued quietly. "We may be bringing her back to do thirty, forty years in prison."

That was it for Mickey.

"Lookit," he told them, "if the situation is such that you folks don't know whether she's going to go to prison or not, I don't want no part of it." It was against Cohen's code of ethics to send a lamster to prison. Cohen was done with the Hearsts.

"I don't want to be rude," he told them, "but I got to beg off this thing."

Mickey's muscle days were over. But as the threat of violence that had long been associated with him dissipated, he now became what, arguably, he'd long wanted to be—a celebrity. When he went to the fights, real celebrities like Frank Sinatra, Sammy Davis Jr., and Redd Foxx would come over to say hello. (Mickey appreciated the fact that Sinatra always greeted him with a kiss on the cheek and the more formal "Michael.") Although Cohen's tips were sadly reduced ("I maybe used to tip a barber twenty dollars, I maybe tip five dollars now"), he still wore tailor-made clothes and luxurious robes. He still dined at restaurants such as Chasen's, Perino's, and Mateo's, even though it now took him four or five hours to get dressed to his standards. At theaters such as the Shubert, Cohen was a fixture on opening night. His sources of income remained mysterious. (His attorneys had won a settlement from the government for failing to protect Cohen in prison; however, the government had reclaimed most of the money as payment owed it for overdue taxes.) Friends like Frank Sinatra once more kicked in "gifts" to tide him over. Rumor had it that Cohen had resumed bookmaking.

In September 1975, Mickey checked into UCLA Medical Center, complaining of pain from an ulcer. It turned out he had stomach cancer. His doctors informed him that he had only months to live. Mickey used the

time to relate his life story to the writer John Peer Nugent. The highly idio-
syncratic result was *In My Own Words*. The following summer, Mickey
Cohen died at home in his sleep, leaving $3,000 in cash, which the IRS
promptly took. With back taxes, penalties, and interest, he still owed the
U.S. government $496,535.23.

Epilogue

"This city is plagued by hostility, rage and resentment. It could happen again."

—former FBI director William Webster, October 1992

IN 1969, LAPD officer-turned-councilman Tom Bradley decided to challenge incumbent mayor Sam Yorty for the city's top elected office. Bradley presented himself as a statesman who would address the city's biggest issues—rapid transit, business growth, racial harmony. His base of support came primarily from the city's African American community, which made up nearly 20 percent of the population, and from the liberal, heavily Jewish Westside, but it also included some surprising members of the city's downtown business community, most notably the *Los Angeles Times*. To this formidable challenge, Yorty responded with a simple and devastating rejoinder: If Bradley was elected, Yorty charged, the police force would resign en masse, leaving (white) Angelenos defenseless before the (black and brown) criminal hordes.

Just before the vote, chief of police Tom Reddin resigned to take a job as a news commentator (at a salary of $100,000 a year). Rumors immediately arose that Reddin had left rather than face the possibility of serving under Mayor Bradley. Despite Reddin's denials that politics played a role in his decision, Bradley lost the general election.

Reddin's decision to step down gave Gates another shot at the chief's position. This time, however, the recently divorced inspector scored poorly on the oral portion of the civil service exam and placed third on the list. At the top was Deputy Chief Ed Davis, whom the historian Gerald Woods would later describe as "a Protestant version of Bill Parker." Like Parker, Davis was an innovator. His concept of "team policing" (which Davis referred to as "the basic car plan") called for assigning officers to small geographic areas where they could work with residents to identify and solve crime problems. It prefigured what is today called community policing. Davis also eliminated the practice of awarding black officers low scores on the oral component of civil service exams, which had long limited the promotion of African Americans. But if Davis's reforms were in some ways progressive, his personal style was not. Like Parker, he was also an outspoken cultural conservative. No one was safe from his derision. White liberals were derided as "swimming-pool Communists." Homosexuals were "fruits." In general, Davis encouraged his officers to treat "the counterculture" as an enemy.

Few dared to complain. In 1973, Bradley once again challenged Yorty, along with California state assembly speaker Jesse Unruh and former police chief Tom Reddin. This time, Bradley was the front-runner. He carefully crafted a "law and order" platform that promised unyielding support for the police. This time, he won, beating Yorty soundly in another runoff to become Los Angeles's first African American mayor.

It took Bradley two more years to take control of the Police Commission. Only then, in 1975, did the commission order the department's Public Disorder Intelligence Division and Organized Crime Intelligence Division (the successors to Parker and Reddin's intelligence division) to destroy the intelligence files the department had amassed over the course of the preceding four-odd decades. Some two million dossiers were shredded.* But both intelligence divisions were retained. Together, they continued to employ nearly two hundred officers.

IN JANUARY 1978, after eight years as chief of police, Ed Davis resigned in order to pursue a career in politics. He was not interested in running for mayor. ("That position has no power. I have more power than the mayor.") Only one position in California state government seemed like a clear step up—being governor. By making a run for statewide office, Davis gave Daryl Gates the opportunity he had been dreaming of since his very first days in the department, when Chief Parker first began to school him as his successor.

Mayor Bradley didn't want him. The mayor was fed up with what his associates referred to as "the LAPD mentality"—an attitude that even Daryl Gates would later describe as "independence bordering on arrogance." Standing in his way was the system Bill Parker had created.

---

*Former intelligence division chief Daryl Gates would later insist this was much ado about nothing: "Many of those 'files' were 3 × 5 index cards used to reference files which contained only newspapers clippings." Even if this is true, that still meant that the LAPD had collected, by Gates's own estimation, "highly sensitive information" roughly 100,000 "subversives." This was intelligence gathering on a very large scale. (Gates, *Chief,* 226.)

Los Angeles's civil service code still required the Police Commission to select a new chief from one of the top three scorers on the combined written/oral promotional exam, although it had been amended to provide for the possibility of an outside candidate. Rumor had it that Santa Monica police chief George Tielsch (who'd previously headed the Seattle Police Department) was Bradley's top choice. But at the end of the examination process, Daryl Gates was number one on the eligibility list.

The Police Commission hesitated. Selecting someone other than the top-ranked candidate would be a big political risk. As it considered its choice, police commissioner Jim Fisk asked for a private meeting with Gates.

Fisk had been one of the LAPD's most talented new officers. Like Bradley, he had joined the department in 1940. He quickly established himself as one of the department's bravest policemen and routinely topped the civil service examinations. However, Fisk also had a reputation as a liberal. He was passed over by Parker for a position as deputy chief in the mid-1950s. Tapped to lead the department's community relations effort after Watts, he was passed over for the position of chief after Parker died, despite having the highest civil service score. When Reddin retired, the Police Commission again ignored Fisk's top score to select Ed Davis as police chief. Fisk left to teach at UCLA until he was summoned back by Mayor Bradley. As a member of the Police Commission, he was supposedly one of the department's five bosses. As a result, Fisk might well have expected that when he asked Gates to be more "flexible"—to show some willingness to take direction from the Police Commission—the assistant chief would have responded positively.

"Okay. What issue do you want me to compromise on?" Gates replied.

The Police Commission was under pressure to contain the department's rising costs (which were increasing, in no small measure, as a result of a pay increase Gates himself had championed as assistant chief). Fisk explained that he and his fellow commissioners felt that one way to mitigate the problem would be to prune the number of upper-level positions in the department. Gates listened noncommittally. He knew that one of his rivals for the top position, deputy chief Bob Vernon, had presented the commission with a detailed plan for trimming top management. Yet when Gates appeared before the full Police Commission and was asked if he'd be willing to eliminate upper-management positions, his reply was a simple "No."

"Why not?" Fisk asked.

"You know," Gates replied, "you people are really amazing. On the one hand, you talk very strongly about affirmative action, about moving blacks and Hispanics and women up in the organization. At the same time you want to cut out all of these top jobs. How are you going to have vacancies to move people into when you've slashed all these positions from the top?"

It was a remarkably insouciant response—and vintage Gates. Instead of offering a concession that would allow the Police Commission to choose him and save face, Gates was in effect daring them to pick someone else. They didn't have the nerve to. On March 24, 1978, Daryl Gates was named the next chief of police. He was sworn in four days later. The system that Bill Parker had created could not be broken. Chief Gates soon settled in as a chief in the Parker mold. Then came the evening of Saturday, March 2, 1991. As in Watts, it started with the California Highway Patrol.

TIM AND MELANIE SINGER were a husband-and-wife Highway Patrol team. On the night of March 2, they were patrolling the Foothill Freeway north of Los Angeles. They were headed toward Simi Valley when, in their rearview mirror, they spotted a white Hyundai gaining on them, fast. They pulled over and watched it blow past at upward of a hundred miles per hour. They gave chase, but the car ignored the patrol car's sirens. Instead, it accelerated. Units from the LAPD joined the chase. The Hyundai exited the freeway on Paxton Street, maintaining speeds of up to eighty-five miles per hour on residential streets, and tore through a red light at Van Nuys and Foothills, nearly causing a collision, before a pickup truck that was partially blocking the road brought the car to a stop just beyond the intersection of Osborne and Foothills, near the darkened entrance to Hansen Dam Park.

There were three passengers in the car, all black men. Two passengers got out and, following police instructions, lay down prone on the ground. The driver of the car hesitated and then slowly climbed out. Across the street, the sirens and police helicopter awakened a plumbing supply store manager, who'd recently purchased a video camera. He dressed and stumbled out to his balcony with the camcorder. Then he turned it on and captured nine minutes and twenty seconds of footage that showed a large black man charging the police. An officer swung his baton at the man, knocking him down. The officer kept swinging as the man writhed across the ground. A large group of officers stood by, arms folded. The man was then taken into custody. The videographer was disturbed by what seemed to be a brutal and blatant example of "street justice." The next day, he offered his tape first to the LAPD and then to CNN. Neither was interested. On Monday, the videographer took it to a local television station, KTLA. That evening, KTLA put the tape up on the ten o'clock news. By Tuesday morning, CNN (which had an affiliate agreement with KTLA) had started to put an edited version on the air, one that had cut out the driver's initial charge at the police. NBC had a tape by later in the day. The beating of Rodney King was now playing endlessly across the country.

The LAPD hierarchy was shocked by what they saw, although many commanders saw something very different from what the public did. LAPD Sgt. Charles Duke, a martial arts consultant, was distressed by how ineffectively the arresting officer used his baton. Other officers were disturbed by the failure of the supervising sergeant to make use of the large numbers of officers who had arrived at the scene and stood by watching. But the brass had no interest in examining the possibility that poor training had played a role in the beating. Instead, Chief Gates described the beating as an "aberration" and promised a full investigation. Mayor Bradley vowed that "appropriate action" would be taken against the officers involved. County DA Ira Reiner immediately convened a grand jury and within two weeks of the incident, four of the officers involved were indicted.

Mayor Bradley decided the time was right to assert his authority over the police department—authority that, legally, he did not have. On April 1, he announced the formation of "an independent commission" on the Los Angeles Police Department. Its chairman was attorney Warren Christopher, former vice chairman of the McCone Commission, deputy attorney general under President Lyndon Johnson, deputy secretary of state under President Jimmy Carter, and a partner at O'Melveny & Myers, the city's most powerful law firm. The day after announcing the appointment, Bradley asked Gates for his resignation. Gates refused.

The Police Commission, whose members were Bradley loyalists, met secretly (in violation of state law) and then informed the chief that they were voting to put him on unpaid leave to investigate "serious allegations of mismanagement." This angered the chief. It was Mayor Bradley, not he, who had recently been dogged by a series of allegations about improper entanglements with businessmen seeking favors from the city. Gates said he'd see them in court. The city council, led by John Ferraro, pressured the Police Commission to reinstate Gates. Finally, after a judge issued a restraining order against the commission's attempted action, Ferraro managed to persuade Bradley and Gates to agree to a truce. Privately, though, Gates had come to believe that Bradley "had brought to Los Angeles a rat's nest of impropriety not seen since the days of the Shaw regime of the 1930s." Meanwhile, the prosecutors' case against the officers involved in the beating moved forward.

Three months later, on July 9, the Christopher Commission issued its report—and called for Chief Gates's resignation. Its conclusions were damning. The report described a department with a small number of "problem officers," who employed deadly force yet who never seemed to receive serious punishment. The commission criticized the department's retreat from community policing and spoke directly to the culture Daryl Gates had inherited and intensified:

> L.A.P.D. officers are trained to command and to confront, not to communicate. Regardless of their training, officers who are expected to produce high citation and arrest statistics and low response times do not also have time to explain their actions, to apologize when they make a mistake, or even to ask about problems in a neighborhood.

The historian Lou Cannon would later characterize the Christopher Commission report as "an impressive and penetrating indictment of the Los Angeles Police Department and its 'siege mentality.'" But Cannon noted that it was also seriously flawed.

One of the commission's most troubling findings was that the LAPD harbored a number of officers with racist sentiments. The evidence for this proposition came primarily from the text messages officers had sent to each other from their patrol cars' MDT units. Over the course of six months, the commission had reviewed six million text messages. Most had been about routine police matters, but a small yet "disturbing" subset suggested a culture of excessive force and racism. Examples cited included references to "kicking" witnesses, "queen cars," and—worst of all—"monkey-slapping time." It looked bad—Christopher would describe these texts as "abhorrent"—but only to someone who knew nothing at all about police lingo. "Kicking" a suspect meant releasing him. "Monkey-slapping time" was slang for goofing off. A "queen car" was not an automobile driven by homosexuals but rather a unit from a station assigned to a special duty. When the police department reviewed the texts in question (and eliminated phrases such as "Praise the lord and pass the ammunition" from the list of objectionable statements), it found 277 references to incidents that appeared to involve misconduct and 12 racial slurs—out of 6 million text messages. It is hard to imagine any big-city police department (or, for that matter, any institution at all) doing better. Not surprisingly, Gates responded by calling the group's report "a travesty."

Inaccurate though it was in many of its details, the Christopher Commission nonetheless identified what was in many ways the deepest source of tension between Bradley and Gates—namely, the police chief's extraordinary lack of accountability to the city's elected officials. That more than anything was Parker's legacy. Warren Christopher proposed to end it. Under a ballot proposition endorsed by his commission, the Police Commission would select three candidates, rank their preferences, and then send the list to the mayor to make the final choice, subject to the city council's approval. The Police Commission would be able to fire the chief at any point, with the mayor's concurrence. (The city council would also be able to overturn the Police Commission and mayor's decision with a two-thirds vote.)

Gates immediately recognized that the true goal of the commission was "controlling the police." Protégé of Bill Parker that he was, he vowed to fight it. Otherwise, "the chief would be silenced by the politicians and subject to the mayor's every whim. . . . The L.A.P.D. would become politicized for the first time since the corrupt 1930s."

That it might simply become accountable to the people's chosen representatives apparently never occurred to him. But Gates did understand that pressure to oust him was mounting. Fed up with being under assault, he was more than ready to leave—but he wanted to leave on his own terms. In late July, Gates announced that he would step down as chief the following year, in the spring of 1992. Until then, however, Gates resolved that he would do everything he could to preserve the chief's prerogatives for his successor. Capping the police chief's tenure and changing lines of authority in the department would require a change to the city charter. That would require a citywide referendum, one that would most likely be scheduled for the next round of municipal elections in June 1992. Chief Gates vowed to fight it.

Meanwhile, the lawyers for the officers indicted in the Rodney King beating were preparing motions that would transfer the trial to a location outside of L.A. County. But prosecutors weren't particularly worried. No trial had been moved outside of Los Angeles since 1978. On November 26, 1991, however, Judge Stanley Weisberg agreed to do just that. He transferred the case to Simi Valley, a bedroom community of 100,000 people northwest of Los Angeles in Ventura County. Simi Valley was conservative, 80 percent white (and just 1.5 percent black), and popular with LAPD retirees. A more favorable venue for the police officers was hard to imagine.

JURY SELECTION BEGAN in February 1992. At the end of the month, prosecutors faced an all-white jury. On March 2, 1992, one day short of the first anniversary of the Rodney King incident, the trial got under way. In the mind of the public, the Rodney King beating was a straightforward case of police brutality. But in the courtroom, matters weren't so clear-cut. Rodney King had led the police on a high-speed car chase. As the arresting officers feared, he was an intoxicated ex-con. Tests for PCP proved inconclusive, but officers' fears were understandable in light of what had occurred before the famous videotape started running. King had thrown off four officers who attempted to "swarm" him and had then shaken off two attempts to subdue him with a Taser, before charging the police. All of these factors lent credence to the claims made by officers on the scene that they believed they were dealing with someone high on PCP, whom they were endeavoring to subdue without shooting him. On the afternoon of April 29, 1992, the jury acquitted the four police officers on all but one of the charges.

The jury in Simi Valley had been out for deliberation for almost a week. As the days passed, anxiety in South-Central Los Angeles had steadily grown. Watts had come as a horrible surprise, a massive riot whose precipitating incident had been a random California Highway Patrol stop. But by 1992, most residents of Los Angeles understood the possibility of urban violence. When the jury told the presiding judge it had reached a verdict, the court immediately informed the LAPD—and delayed the courtroom opening of the verdict for two hours, a decision that gave the LAPD time to prepare. But with a handful of exceptions, no preparations were made.

For a department that had long been obsessed with its failure to contain the Watts riots, the apparent lack of concern about what might ensue in the event of an acquittal was curious. But even if no operational preparations for trouble had commenced, it would have been reasonable to expect that the LAPD now had the tactics, training, and materiel to respond to a Watts-style insurrection. After all, Chief Gates himself had seen the inadequacies of the department's earlier preparations. He had also seen the danger of withdrawing from a riot area in the hope that an outbreak of violence would burn itself out. LAPD policy was clear: The department would respond with overwhelming force (which included two armored personnel carriers) to any outbreak of civil unrest, arresting and prosecuting everyone involved and cordoning off the area so that the violence would not spread.

At least, that was the theory. But as angry crowds gathered at the intersection of 55th and Normandie, the LAPD once again seemed utterly unprepared. Worse, it seemed complacent. Requests to deploy the elite Metro unit in riot gear had been rebuffed on the theory that "riots don't happen during the daytime." No tear gas had been distributed; requests to deploy rubber bullets had been rejected; and no instructions had been provided to officers at the 77th Street station, which was located in the heart of South-Central. By 5:30 p.m., rioting had begun. Its epicenter was the intersection of Florence and Normandie. As in Watts, a crowd had assembled near the scene where police were making an arrest—and the crowd was quickly turning ugly. The LAPD now faced its post-Watts moment of truth. But instead of clearing the mob and seizing control of the intersection, as post-Watts operating procedure called for, LAPD personnel on the scene pulled back. By 5:45, the rioters had the streets to themselves.

The mood at police headquarters (known since 1969 as Parker Center) was oddly unconcerned. In recent months, the once-defiant Gates had become disengaged. Everyone expected that he would resign soon but no one knew when. As for Mayor Bradley, who had not spoken to his police chief in thirteen months, he seemed more concerned about the possibility that the LAPD might spark violence by overreacting than about the violence that was already unfolding. Neither man seemed able to grasp the reality of what was happening. When a reporter stopped Chief Gates at half past six that evening and asked how the LAPD was responding to the growing unrest, he paused and then placidly replied that the department was responding "calmly, maturely, and professionally." Then he left for a fund-raiser in Mandeville Canyon in distant Brentwood. Its purpose was to raise money to oppose Amendment F, the amendment to the city charter proposed by the Christopher Commission that would give the mayor authority to select the police chief and limit future police chiefs to two five-year terms.

BACK IN SOUTH-CENTRAL, the Watts riots seemed to be replaying themselves. Once again, the rioters broke into the liquor stores first, then the pawnshops, where they found an ample supply of guns. Once again, confusion reigned at 77th Street station. No effort was made to regain control of the street. No perimeter was established to contain the violence. The major routes into South-Central were not sealed off. Meanwhile, the area's gangs took control of the streets, much as they had back in 1965. White motorists who ventured into the riot zone were dragged out of their cars and beaten. The most horrifying episode involved a white big-rig truck driver, Reginald Denny, who was pulled out of his cab by a handful of black youths, kicked, beaten with a claw hammer, and then nearly killed by a youth, Damian Williams, who struck Denny on the head with a block of concrete. As Chief Gates drove toward Brentwood—and Mayor Bradley drove toward the launch of his "Operation Cool Response"—Angelenos watched in horror as news helicopters hovering overhead televised Williams doing a touchdown-style dance and flashing the symbol of the Eight Tray Gangster Crips.* Not until 8:15 p.m. did Gates return to Parker Center.

In 1965, Parker had pushed early and hard for the National Guard while

---

*Denny lived only because four other neighborhood residents—African Americans all—saw what was happening on television and rushed out to the intersection in question. Finding Denny, one member of the party, a truck driver, drove him to a nearby hospital, where a team of five surgeons [two of them African Americans] managed to save his life. (Cannon, *Official Negligence*, 308–309.)

Lt. Gov. Glenn Anderson hesitated. In 1992, it was Gov. Pete Wilson who pushed hardest for the Guard. At 9 p.m. that night, Wilson finally prevailed upon Mayor Bradley and Chief Gates to allow him to summon the National Guard. Not until later that night when he went out into the field did Gates grasp the magnitude of the disaster that was unfolding—and the extent of the LAPD's failure. The staging area at 77th Street station was complete chaos. The most basic tenets of riot control, such as cordoning off the area where violence was occurring, had not been observed. Gates had trusted his commanders, and they had failed him. The chief, who treated his senior commanders much more kindly than Chief Parker had, erupted in rage. Then, like a ghost, he disappeared into the night with his driver and a security aide.

In the early hours of the morning, two officers guarding a church at the corner of Arlington and Vernon were startled to see the chief pull up. Gates asked if they needed anything. One of the officers requested a Diet Coke from a nearby convenience store. "No problem," said the chief. A few minutes later, Gates's driver returned—without the soda. Gates wanted them to light their safety flares so that no one would run into their car by accident.

"There's a riot going on, and the chief is micromanaging how our car was parked," one of the officers later marveled. He laughed at this advice. The other officer was more upset. She'd really wanted a Diet Coke.

Gates did not return to the command post until 6 a.m. that morning. Only then, on Thursday morning, did the LAPD request assistance from the sheriff's department, which was prepared to lend the department up to five hundred officers. That night, the National Guard at last began to deploy. Not until Monday morning, May 4, was the violence finally stopped. By then, fifty-four people had died, more than two thousand had been injured and treated in hospital emergency rooms, and more than eight hundred buildings had burned—four times the number destroyed during the Watts riots. Because of the LAPD's failure to cordon off the area where the violence started, the looting and violence spread much farther than it had in 1965. Venice and Hollywood saw outbreaks of violence. Homeowners in posh Hancock Park and elsewhere hired mercenaries to protect their neighborhoods. Ultimately, property damages exceeded $900 million.

As the historian Lou Cannon has noted, there was a terrible irony to what had transpired:

> Ironically, the L.A.P.D. was unprepared for the riots largely because Gates had not demonstrated the independence he feared would be stripped from future chiefs. Instead of standing up to Mayor Bradley and the black leaders who feared that aggressive police deployment might

cause a provocation, Gates had attempted to appease politicians by ordering the department to keep a low profile during jury deliberations.

By failing to respond forcefully to the riots, the LAPD had shown, in effect, that it had already lost its independence.

On June 2, just a month after the riots had ended, the voters of Los Angeles made it official. Prior to the riots, Warren Christopher had drafted Charter Amendment F, which limited the police chief's tenure to two five-year terms, stripped civil service protections from the chief's position, and allowed the Police Commission to remove a chief for reasons other than misconduct. Charter Amendment F also targeted the protections Parker had won for the rank and file, adding a civilian to the department's internal disciplinary panels and generally weakening procedural protections for police officers. Yet despite the unfavorable publicity that had followed the release of the Rodney King video, Amendment F's electoral prospects had been uncertain. That changed after the riots. The vote now offered voters a chance to weigh in on the performance of Chief Gates. On June 2, 1992, by a two-to-one margin, voters approved Christopher's charter amendment. Daryl Gates retired three weeks later. The system Bill Parker had created was finally dead.

Acknowledgments

THIS BOOK BEGAN five years ago, when I went to Los Angeles to report a story on LAPD chief William Bratton for *Governing* magazine. I had lived in Los Angeles previously and had been fascinated by its history. As a result, I was more interested in the history of the department than I might otherwise have been. I soon found myself pondering a puzzle: How did the police department of James "Two Gun" Davis and "Bloody Christmas"—the *L.A. Confidential* LAPD, as it were—suddenly become the *Dragnet* LAPD? How did a department that had answered for decades to corrupt politicians come to answer to no one? The more deeply I read, the more convinced I became that the answer was bound up in the life of Chief William H. Parker.

I knew Parker only as a name, an esteemed but controversial police chief whom criminologists associated with what they call "the professional model" of policing. To his many admirers, he was a saint and a prophet. To his many detractors, he was an "arrogant racist" who nearly destroyed the west's greatest city. I approached him as a person. For that initial introduction, I must first thank Sgt. Steve Williams and Regina Menez of the William H. Parker Police Foundation, and Parker Foundation president Kenneth Esteves for generously opening the archive records to me. Retired LAPD officer Dennis DeNoi was an early and enthusiastic guide to their contents. After a week of reading in the archives, I was convinced that the story of Chief Parker's LAPD was central to the history of Los Angeles and determined to write about it. My agent, Jill Kneerim, offered encouragement and wise counsel from the start. She pushed this book in all the right ways.

The Los Angeles Police Department was exceptionally supportive from the beginning. The Police Commission, the city attorney's office, and Chief Bratton gave me access to internal departmental records from the period, making me only the second outside researcher so favored. I gratefully acknowledge their help and support. Todd Gaydowski, records management officer for the City of Los Angeles, facilitated my every request. Mary Grady, Richard Tefank, and Tamryn Catania were unfailingly helpful.

I owe a particular debt of gratitude to the first researcher given access to the LAPD's departmental files, Arizona State University professor Edward Escobar. Professor Escobar pointed me to one of the city's most valuable historical resources, the LAPD scrapbooks housed at the City Records Center atop the Piper Technical Center downtown. Professor Escobar also invited me into his own home for a week to review copies of LAPD files from the 1950s and 1960s that were deaccessioned by the department in 1999. His personal collection now constitutes the most complete repository of official records from this era. I greatly appreciate his hospitality and admire his trailblazing work in the history of Chicano Los Angeles.

At Piper Tech, I passed many fascinating months in the company of city archivists Jay Jones and Mike Holland, who patiently explained to me the intricacies of Police Commission and city council minutes and their associated files, while keeping me fueled with delectable home-roasted coffee. Todd Gaydowski was my guide to the LAPD's chief of police files. Former Los Angeles archivist–turned–L.A. City Historical Society–dynamo Hynda Rudd also offered encouragement and advice. To Todd, Jay, Mike, and Hynda, my sincere thanks.

Other archives also offered valuable assistance during the course of my research. The staff of the Newberry Library in Chicago provided enthusiastic assistance working with the Ben Hecht Collection. It was my week in Chicago that convinced me that Mickey Cohen, as both a product and a leader of the underworld, was the central antagonist in Parker's story and an essential part of the history of Los Angeles. Back in Los Angeles, UCLA's Special Collections was a home away from home. The Joseph Shaw, Harold Story, and Norris Poulson Collections all added greatly to my understanding of midcentury Los Angeles; interacting with UCLA staff was a daily pleasure. My sincere thanks to Angela Riggio, Genie Guerard, Robert Montoya, Aislinn Catherine Sotelo, and everyone there who helped me. Six weeks at the Huntington Library exploring the papers of former mayor Fletcher Bowron made me envy academics. My thanks to Laura Stalker for making that possible. In Washington, D.C., John Martin and the staff of the Library of Congress helped me do an amazing amount of West Coast research from the East Coast.

Los Angeles Police Historical Society executive director Glynn Martin offered generous support and gentle corrections throughout. Former LAPD captain Will Gartland helped me connect with numerous veterans of Parker's LAPD. Thank you to Arthur Sjoquist and everyone else who spoke to me. My special thanks to Joseph Parker, former chief Daryl Gates, former acting chief Bob Rock, former deputy chief Harold Sullivan, and Parker-era Police Commission members Frank Hathaway and Elbert Hudson. In Houston, Joseph and Jane Parker shared their time and reminiscences generously. Their recollections made Chief Parker come alive.

Among the pleasures afforded me by this book was the chance to return to Santa Monica. Numerous friends, old and new, welcomed my family back to our old neighborhood. Ashley Salisbury repeatedly offered her sharp editorial eye as well as her delightful company; Marc and Jessica Evans offered friendship, encouragement, and dazzling generosity in all things. Yong-nam Jun brightened many a lunch at Philippe; Eric Moses provided insights and company; Andrew Sabl and Miriam Laugesen, a home to live in. Ana Lopez and Marva Bennett took care of our family like their own. From New York, Michael Cohen offered excellent suggestions and much-appreciated support. Robin Toone spared me from several legal errors.

I owe a special debt of gratitude to my editor at *Governing*, Alan Ehrenhalt, and his wife, Suzanne. Thank you for your support, your excellent edits, and for giving me a job when I returned to D.C. My editor at Harmony Books, John Glusman, pushed me to find the story (and waited patiently while I did). This book is better off for it.

Finally, thank you to my family. To my parents, John and Sally, without a lifetime of support, I would never have attempted to write this book. Without your many trips to Santa Monica, I would never have succeeded. Oliver and Tom, what wonders you are.

The last paragraph goes to my wife, Melinda, who moved back to L.A. and made innumerable sacrifices over the course of five years so that I could write this book. I am profoundly grateful for your support, friendship, and love. It is to you that this book is dedicated.

Chapter One: The Mickey Mouse Mafia

Page 3. "[A] dead-rotten law enforcement": Stoker, *Thicker'n Thieves*, 131.

Page 3. Mickey Cohen was not a man: "Year Passes but Murder Not Solved: Search for Woman's Slayer Recalls Other Mysteries," *Los Angeles Times*, February 14, 1949; Stoker, *Thicker'n Thieves*, 199. Quotes from Cohen come primarily from his published memoirs (as told to John Peer Nugent), *In My Own Words*; Muir, *Headline Happy*; and Vaus's *Why I Quit . . . Syndicated Crime*, as cited below.

Page 4. "I looked": Hecht, "Mickey Notes," 4, Hecht Papers, Newberry Library.

Page 4. The fact of the matter was: Demaris, *The Last Mafioso*, 30–31.

Page 4. "Power's a funny thing": Cohen, *In My Own Words*, 81.

Page 5. Administrative vice's response was: California Special Crime Study Commission on Organized Crime report, Sacramento, January 31, 1950, 32. See "Cohen Introduces Sound Recorder," *Los Angeles Times*, May 6, 1949, 10, for an account of the incidents of the evening. "Cohen to Testify in Partner's Case: Deputy Sheriff Denies Policeman's Story That Meltzer Displayed Gun at Arrest," *Los Angeles Times*, May 10, 1949, A8, would seem to verify Mickey's claim that the gun was planted. However, historian Gerald Woods, "The Progressives and the Police," claims that strong circumstantial evidence linked the gun to Meltzer (404).

Page 5. Mickey was furious: Stoker, *Thicker'n Thieves*, 179. "Brenda's Revenge," *Time* magazine, July 11, 1949.

Page 8. As Mickey started to: Mickey's claim to have driven all the way back to Wilshire without looking up seems implausible given the two miles of curves he would have had to traverse on San Vicente Boulevard.

Page 8. Cohen didn't report: Cohen, *In My Own Words*, 122–23; Jennings, "Private Life of a Hood, Part III," October 4, 1958.

Page 8. The evening of: Cohen, *In My Own Words*, 125–29. Muir, *Headline Happy*, 202–10.

Page 8. By 3:30: Some accounts of the shooting mention only the shotgun (or two shotguns). See Muir, *Headline Happy*, 205, 207–209; Cohen, *In My Own Words*, 126.

Page 9. Later that night: Muir, *Headline Happy*, 202–209; "Full Story of Mob Shooting of Cohen," *Los Angeles Daily News*, July 20, 1949.

Page 9. The papers, of course: Howser was actively attempting to organize and extort money from Northern California bookmakers, slot machine operators, and other gamblers. Fox, *Blood and Power,* 291.

Page 10. Brown was a big teddy: Author interview with Daryl Gates, December 10, 2004; McDougal, *Privileged Son,* p. 194.

Page 11. "I had gambling joints: Cohen, *In My Own Words,* 146–47.

Page 11. Cohen arrived in Chicago: Woods, "The Progressives and the Police," 418.

Chapter Two: The "White Spot"

Page 12. "Wherein lies the fascination . . .": Wright, "Los Angeles–The Chemically Pure," *The Smart Set Anthology,* 101.

Page 12. Other cities were based: Findley, "The Economic Boom of the 'Twenties in Los Angeles," 252; "The Soul of the City," *Los Angeles Times,* June 24, 1923, II4; Fogelson, *The Fragmented Metropolis,* 80; Davis, "The View from Spring Street: White-Collar Men in the City of Angeles," Sitton and Deverell, eds., *Metropolis in the Making,* 180. The "white spot" metaphor began innocently, as a description of business conditions in Los Angeles in the early 1920s, but soon took on troubling racial connotations.

Page 12. The historic center of: Percival, "In Our Cathay," *Los Angeles Times,* December 4, 1898, 6. See also AnneMarie Kooistra, "Angels for Sale," 25 and 29 for maps of L.A.'s historic tenderloin district, as well as 91, 174–75; Henstell, *Sunshine and Wealth,* 89; Woods, "The Progressives and Police," 57; Sitton "Did the Ruling Class Rule at City Hall in 1920s Los Angeles?" in *Metropolis in the Making,* 309.

Page 13. The city also boasted: Hurewitz, *Bohemian Los Angeles and the Making of Modern Politics,* 104; Mann, *Behind the Screen,* 89.

Page 14. Congressman Parker's position: "Col W. H. Parker Called By Death: South Dakota Congressman Passed Away Yesterday—Speaker Cannon Expresses Deep Regret," clipping from Deadwood newspaper, William H. Parker Foundation archives.

Page 15. As a child, Bill: The oldest Parker sibling, Catherine Irene, was born on August 29, 1903. Bill was born two years later, on June 21, 1905, followed by Alfred on May 29, 1908; Mary Ann in 1911; and Joseph on April 10, 1918. Author interview with Joseph Parker, Houston, Texas, December 12–13, 2004.

Page 15. As an obviously intelligent: Sjoquist, "The Story of Bill," *The Link,* 1994; Domanick, *To Protect and to Serve,* 91.

Page 15. In later years, Parker: See "Police Instincts of Bill Parker Flourished Early," *Los Angeles Mirror-News,* June 18, 1957, for a typical (and improbable) account of this period in Parker's life.

Page 16. Los Angeles was Deadwood: In 1934, the United States Geographical Board recognized the most popular variant, today's "Los An-ju-less." Henstell, *Sunshine and Wealth,* 26. However, controversies about the proper pronunciation lingered into the 1950s. "With a Soft G," *Time* magazine, September 22, 1952.

Page 16. Whatever its pronunciation: John Anson Ford, who moved to L.A. in 1920 from Chicago, recounts the wagon trail–like quality of the migration in this description of the journey: "We had not expected to find so many other motorists, equipped very much as we were, all heading for California. On long level stretches of the dirt roadway each day we could see cars ahead and behind us, perhaps half a mile apart. Each car was followed by a long plume of dust. These automobiles, laden with camping equipment, household goods, and the unkempt appearance of both children and adults, made them easily distinguishable from local farmers or city dwellers. An amazingly large segment of the nation was on the move—and that move was to California." Ford, *Honest Politics My Theme*, 52–53; Woods, "The Progressives and the Police," 75; Starr, *Material Dreams*, 80.

Page 17. "The whole Middle West": Garland, *Diaries*, 40.

Page 17. "If every conceivable trick: http://www.npr.org/programs/morning/features/patc/hollywoodsign/index.html.

Page 17. Then there was the: Fogelson, *The Fragmented Metropolis*, 127. See also Tygiel, "Metropolis in the Making," 1–9.

Page 17. The Parkers settled first: "Champion 'Ag-inner' of Universe Is Shuler, Belligerent Local Pastor Holds All Records for Attacks Upon Everybody, Everything," *Los Angeles Times*, June 1, 1930, A2; Starr, *Material Dreams*, 136–39.

Page 18. By 1910, the year: http://www.life.com/Life/lifebooks/hollywood/intro.html; Starr, *Material Dreams*, 98; Ross, "How Hollywood Became Hollywood," in Sitton and Deverell, eds., *Metropolis in the Making*, 262.

Page 19. Parker was plankton in: "Plans Submitted for Fine Theater: Picture Palace to Follow Elaborate Spanish Architecture," *Los Angeles Times*, July 11, 1920, V1.

Page 19. The first was Theodosia: "Milestones," *Time* magazine, April 18, 1955.

Page 19. As the movies heated: Dixon, "Problems of a Working Girl: Queer Aspects of Human Nature Exhibited to Quiet and Watchful Theater Workers, Says Love is Catching 'Like the Measles," *Los Angeles Times*, July 15, 1919, II2.

Page 19. As chief of police: Parker's claim to have been born in 1902 rather than 1905 dates to this era, raising the possibility that he lied about his age so that he could claim to be slightly older than Francis. Divorce petition, Francette Pomeroy, Oregon City, OR.

Page 20. Despite (or perhaps because of): Author interview with Joseph Parker, Houston, Texas, December 12–13, 2004. It should be noted that my account of Bill's first marriage comes almost entirely from his wife's divorce petition. Such accounts are invariably one-sided; exaggerating spousal cruelty was a common tactic for achieving a speedy divorce. It should also be remembered that Bill's response to his wife's behavior would have struck many men as wholly justified at the time.

Page 21. Any attempt to heist: Reid, *Mickey Cohen: Mobster*, 39. See also unpublished notes for Mickey Cohen biography dated February 6, 1959, Ben Hecht Papers, Newberry Library, Box 7.

Chapter Three: The Combination

Page 22. "The purpose of any political": Woods, "The Progressives and the Police," 315, 341.

Page 23. He was born Meyer: There is some confusion about Mickey's birth date. Cohen himself generally claimed that he was born in 1913; however, his funeral marker says he was born in 1914. Still other evidence points to a 1911 birth date. See Lewis, *Hollywood's Celebrity Gangster*, 1; Cohen, *In My Own Words*, 3. Other accounts of Mickey's life say that his father was a grocer.

Page 23. Fanny, Mickey, and sister: Boyle Heights's Jewish population jumped from 10,000 in 1917 to 43,000 in 1923, making it home to about a third of Los Angeles's

Jewish population. Romo, *History of a Barrio*, 65. The current brick Breed Street Shul was finished several years later, in 1923.

Page 23. Mickey soon became a: Clarke and Saldana, "True Life Story of Mickey Cohen," *Los Angeles Daily News*, July 1949. This is the beginning of a nine-part series on Mickey that is a valuable, though not always reliable, guide to his life. See also "Cohen Began as a Spoiled Brat," the second installment in the series.

Page 24. Mickey's entrée came from: Mickey's exact age at the time of this incident is somewhat unclear. In *Mickey Cohen: Mobster*, Ed Reid says that this occurred when he was seven (37–39). In his autobiography, *In My Own Words*, Cohen says that this incident occurred when he was nine (5).

Page 24. What followed was a: Cohen, *In My Own Words*, Chapter One.

Page 24. Clearly, Mickey had a: The FBI would later estimate his IQ to be 98. Cohen FBI files.

Page 24. While Mickey started his: The following year Los Angeles would surpass it—a lead L.A. would maintain until the 1990s. Klein, *The History of Forgetting*, 75. However, Woods, "The Progressives and the Police," 73, disputes the belief, widespread at the time, that Los Angeles was suffering a crime wave.

Page 25. "The white spot of . . .": "The Soul of the City," *Los Angeles Times*, June 24, 1923, II4.

Page 25. By 1922, Harry Chandler: In 1909, progressive reformers had dismantled the old ward system that had allowed Democrats, Catholics, and Jews to be elected to political office in favor of a system that provided for only citywide at-large elections. The result was a city government dominated by *Times* readers—white, middle-class Protestant Republicans. Woods, "The Progressives and the Police," 9.

The *Times* newsroom claimed that Chandler was the eleventh wealthiest man in the world. Gottlieb and Wolt, *Thinking Big*, 125; "The White Spot Glistens Brightly," *Los Angeles Times*, July 17, 1921, II; Taylor, "It Costs $1000 to Have Lunch with Harry Chandler," *Saturday Evening Post*, December 16, 1939.

Page 25. Now was just such: Sitton, "Did the Ruling Class Rule at City Hall in 1920s Los Angeles?" in Sitton and Deverell, eds., *Metropolis in the Making*, 305.

Page 26. At first, everything went: Fogelson, *Fragmented Metropolis*, 219. Los Angeles mayors initially served only two-year terms, hence the high tally.

Page 26. This was embarrassing: Sitton, "The 'Boss' Without a Machine: Kent K. Parrot and Los Angeles Politics in the 1920s."

Page 26. By firing Oaks and: Sitton, "The 'Boss' Without a Machine: Kent K. Parrot and Los Angeles Politics in the 1920s."

Page 27. Bootlegging had been a profitable: Henstell, *Sunshine and Wealth*, 60.

Page 27. At first, much of: Anderson, *Beverly Hills Is My Beat*, 130. See also Nathan, "How Whiskey Smugglers Buy and Land Cargoes, Well-Organized Groups Engaged in Desperate Game of Rum-Running," *Los Angeles Times*, August 8, 1926, B5; Rappleye, *All-American Mafioso*, 40; and Henstell, *Sunshine and Wealth*, 60. It is not surprising that Nathan neglects to mention Combination figures such as Guy McAfee, who had ties to the Chandler-favored Cryer administration.

Page 27. In the big eastern: Law enforcement was too. Historian Robert Fogelson has argued that people engaged in both professions for similar reasons, notably out of a desire for upward social mobility. According to Fogelson, this is one of the reasons why graft and corruption were so prevalent in urban police departments: Many of the men who staffed them were as interested in getting ahead as the men who were paying them off. See Fogelson, *Big City Police* 29, 35.

For more on Crawford, see "Crawford Career Hectic, Politician Gained Wide Notoriety as 'Pay-Off Man' in Morris Lavine Extortion Case," *Los Angeles Times*, May 21, 1931, 2. See also Woods, "The Progressives and the Police," 305–6.

Page 28. Crawford got back in: The exact relationship between Crawford and Marco is unclear. While Crawford seems to have kept a hand in prostitution, he was apparently more of a political fixer; Marco, in contrast, was more hands on. Most accounts of the era accord Crawford the position of primacy; however, some describe Marco as the leader of the Combination. Others point to Guy McAfee, "Detective McAfee is Exonerated," *Los Angeles Times*, September 23, 1916, I9.

Page 28. Cornero tried to buy: I say "seemed overt" because in this instance, Farmer's claim of self-defense was actually quite plausible. Nonetheless, in general it was clear that Farmer enjoyed considerable advantages, including (somewhat later) having his personal attorney on the Police Commission. Woods, "The Progressives and the Police," 233, 237.

Page 29. "Mr. Cryer, how much . . .": "Bledsoe Hurls Defy at Cryer, Challenges Parrot's Status as De-Facto Mayor," *Los Angeles Times*, April 23, 1925.

Page 29. "Shall We Re-Elect . . ." "Shall We Re-Elect Kent Parrot?" *Los Angeles Times*, April 23, 1925, A1.

Page 29. The *Times* publisher was: For a discussion of Parrot's sway over the LAPD, see "Oaks Names Kent Parrot, Charges Lawyer Interfered in Police Department, 'Dictatorial and Threatening,'" *Los Angeles Times*, July 29, 1923, I14; "Dark Trails to City Hall are Uncovered: How Negro Politicians Make and Unmake Police Vice Squad Told in Heath Case," *Los Angeles Times*, August 17, 1923, II1; and "Kent Parrot Accused by Richards as 'Sinister,' Retiring Harbor Commissioner Names Him as Would-Be Boss," *Los Angeles Times*, August 1, 1923, II1; Sitton, "The 'Boss' Without a Machine," 372–73.

Page 29. In truth, each camp: Sitton, "Did the Ruling Class Rule at City Hall in 1920s Los Angeles?" 312. See also Domanick, *To Protect and Serve*, 40–49, for an extended and colorful discussion of James Davis.

Page 30. With a measure of: The arrest of councilman Carl Jacobson was a variant on a common police racket known as the badger game, an extortion racket made possible by the fact that extramarital sex was actually illegal in Los Angeles. The setup was simple: Working with an unmarried female accomplice, the police arranged an assignation, usually at a downtown hotel, and then burst in to make an arrest—unless, that is, they received a payoff. In this instance, however, Councilman Jacobson boldly refused to go with the usual script. Insisting that he had been framed, he demanded a trial and was acquitted. He later sued Crawford, vice lord Albert Marco, Callie Grimes (the would-be temptress), and five police officers. However, they, too, were acquitted, leaving the question of exactly what happened in Ms. Grimes's bedroom hopelessly unsettled. "Crawford Career Hectic," *Los Angeles Times*, May 21, 1931, 2. See also Woods, "The Progressives and the Police," 252–55.

Page 30. Parker tried to focus: Starr, *Material Dreams*, 70.

Page 31. Freed of his wife: Fogelson, *Big City Police*, 82, 103. Author interview with Joseph Parker, Houston, Texas, December 12–13, 2004.

Page 31. On April 24, 1926: Fogelson, *Big City Police*, 102; letter from the Board of Civil Service Commissioners, September 28, 1926, William H. Parker Police Foundation Archives. Note that Police Commission minutes misrecord his name as "William H. Park."

Chapter Four: The Bad Old Good Old Days

Page 32. "[A] smart lawyer can . . .": White, *Me, Detective*, 188; Sjoquist, *History of the Los Angeles Police Department*, 37.

Page 32. "The name of this city . . .": Fogelson, *Fragmented Metropolis*, 26, quoting the diary of the Rev. James L. Woods, November 24, 1854 (at the Huntington Library).

Page 32. "While there are undoubtedly . . .": "Committee of Safety Makes Its Report," *Los Angeles Herald*, November 8, 1900; Fogelson, *Big City Police*, 9.

Page 32. In their defense: Woods, "The Progressives and the Police," 24.

Page 33. The activities of plainclothes: Fogelson, *Big City Police*, 51.

Page 33. In 1902, the LAPD's: Kooistra, "Angeles for Sale," 25. Reverend Kendall's *Queen of the Red-Lights*, which is based on Pearl Morton, is an excellent introduction to the genre.

Page 33. The decision to prohibit: Woods, "The Progressives and the Police," 49.

Page 34. There were moments when: Kooistra, "Angeles for Sale," 71.

Page 34. One night soon after: For one of Parker's several accounts of this episode, see Dean Jennings, "Portrait of a Police Chief," 84. In the 1930s, Arrington was the reputed bagman for the Combination's gambling interests.

Page 34. Today the police beat: New York City was something of an exception. There the profusion of publications put reporters in a more supplicatory position. Muir, *Headline Happy*, 41.

Page 35. Infuriated at the idea: Jacoby, "Highlights in the Life of the Chief of Police," *Eight Ball*, March 1966, William H. Parker Police Foundation archives.

Page 35. " 'Come along, sister, and . . .' ": Quoted in Starr, *Material Dreams*, 170–71. That same year, the old police station/stockade was torn down and the new Lincoln Heights Jail was built in its place. Ted Thackrey, "Memories—Lincoln Heights Jail Closing," *Los Angeles Herald-Examiner*, June 27, 1965.

Page 36. Cops sometimes acted violently: White, *Me, Detective*, 188; Woods, "The Progressives and the Police," 225.

The existence of "the third degree" was a hotly debated topic at the time. Police chiefs denied its existence. Critics insisted that it was routinely used. To some extent, both sides were talking past each other. Police chiefs defined the "third degree" as torture, critics as coercive pressure. The analogy to current-day interrogation tactics for suspected terrorists is very close. See also Wickersham Commission, 146–47; and Hopkins, *Lawless Law Enforcement*.

Page 37. Remarkably, the LAPD was: Carte and Carte, *Police Reform in the United States*, 60. See also Hopkins, *Lawless Law Enforcement*.

Page 37. Parker told the man: "Why Hoodlums Hate Bill Parker," *Readers Digest*, March 1960, 239, condensed from *National Civic Review* (September 1959).

Page 38. "Open the door so . . .": Stump, "LA's Chief Parker."

Page 38. Later that year: Wedding announcement, *Los Angeles Times*, May 1, 1928, 24.

Page 38. The Great Depression intervened: Starr, *The Dream Endures*, 165.

Page 39. "Statements from Bill kept . . .": Letter from Helen, William H. Parker Police Foundation archive.

Chapter Five: "Jewboy"

Page 43. "I wasn't the worse . . .": Cohen manuscript, Hecht Papers, Newberry Library. Mickey would later claim to have fought seventy-nine pro fights, including five against past, present, or future world champions. Cohen biographer Brad Lewis counts a more modest (but still impressive) record of sixty wins (twenty-five by knockout) and sixteen losses. Lewis, *Hollywood's Celebrity Gangster*, 14.

Page 43. As a condition for his: Unpublished Cohen manuscript, Hecht Papers, Newberry Library.

Page 43. Mickey was not: Cohen, *In My Own Words*, 6–8.

Page 44. Yet despite this youthful: Reid, *Mickey Cohen*, 39–40.

Page 44. Lou Stillman's gym: Schulberg, *The Harder They Fall*, 90.

Page 45. The men surrounding Mickey: "Lou Stillman, Legendary Boxing Figure, Is Dead," *New York Times* obituary, August 20, 1969. The *Times*'s obituary credits the "open sesame to low society" remark to Damon Runyon, suggesting that perhaps Runyon used it first.

Page 45. "A card of membership . . .": Johnston, "The Cauliflower King-I," *The New Yorker*, April 8, 1933, 24.

Page 45. Moreover, he wasn't making: Establishing with any precision when Mickey returned to Cleveland is difficult. Ben Hecht writes that Mickey returned in 1932/3, which would make any meeting with Al Capone himself unlikely, given Capone's 1931 conviction for income tax evasion. However, a document in the Newberry Library's Hecht Papers that was apparently prepared by Mickey himself says he returned to Cleveland at age seventeen, which would have been the year 1930.

Page 46. Unlike New York City: Moe Dalitz had established important relations with the various Italian gangs that held sway over different parts of Cleveland, but he had not yet made Cleveland his primary base of operations.

Page 46. Great Depression or no: Cohen, *In My Own Words*, 15–16.

Page 48. Cohen's job in Chicago: Ben Hecht presents a somewhat different account of this incident, saying that Mickey was given a "louse book" to operate, one that catered to ten- and twenty-cent horse bettors, on the North Side. Quoting Cohen, Hecht writes, "The first thing I know a Chicago tough guy calls on me where I'm running my little louse book and says he has been engaged for twenty dollars to put the muscle on me. I don't ask who engaged him but I said, 'I'm going to give you a chance to prove you're a tough guy.' And I pulled my gun. In that time I would of felt undressed if I wasn't carryin' a gun. The tough guy ran behind a door and I blasted him through the door which is the last I saw of him."

Page 48. "After that meeting, . . .": Reid also claims that Mickey didn't arrive in Chicago until well after Al Capone's 1931 arrest. However, the volume and detail of Cohen's recollections from this period make it doubtful that his Chicago recollections were entirely fabricated.

Chapter Six: Comrade Bill

Page 50. "With few exceptions": Wickersham Commission, Nos. 1–14, 43.

Page 51. Hollywood was Los Angeles's fast: Kooistra, "Angeles for Sale," 88, quoting *Bob Shuler's Magazine.*

Page 51. "Listen, you stupid fuck,": Jennings, "Portrait of a Police Chief," 87.

Page 51. Despite such obstinacy: In 1930, the written examination accounted for 95 percent of officers' scores, with marksmanship and seniority accounting for the remaining 5 percent. Memorandum to the general manager civil service, "Subject: Facts on Chief Parker's Exam Records," June 1, 1966, William H. Parker Police Foundation archives. This memo provides a comprehensive overview of Parker's history in the department.

Page 51. "Take him someplace and . . .": Domanick, *To Protect and to Serve*, 85.

Page 51. "I got out,": Stump, "L.A.'s Chief Parker."

Page 52. By 1929, Los Angeles: One of the more startling features of this era is the widespread acceptance of the Klan, which permeated 1920s Los Angeles. Throughout this period, the Police Commission, which was responsible for regulating a wide variety of public events, routinely approved a regular Saturday night Ku Klux Klan dance on Santa Monica Boulevard. Palmer, "Porter or Bonelli for City's Next Mayor," *Los Angeles Times*, May 26, 1929, B1.

Page 52. To block the Klansman: Sitton, *John Randolph Haynes*, 218. Parrot retired to Santa Barbara and effectively withdrew from politics. In the mid-1930s, the Los Angeles papers would attempt to resurrect the specter of Parrot; Woods, "The Progressives and the Police," 311.

Page 53. That the LAPD: In 1919, the Boston police department became the first police force to attempt to affiliate with the American Federation of Labor. When officers went on strike, a week of chaotic looting and rioting ensued. Massachusetts governor Calvin Coolidge called in the National Guard to secure the city. Coolidge then dismissed the eleven hundred officers who had walked off their jobs, a show of resolution that paved the way to his successful run for the White House. Afterward, Boston hired a new police department and granted its officers almost all of the benefits the strikers had originally demanded.

Page 53. The issue that drew: In 1931, the Fire and Police Protective League tried again and was able to persuade the electorate to amend the charter to specify that officers could only be dismissed for "good cause." It also gave officers accused of misdeeds a chance to appear before a board of inquiry consisting of three captains, randomly chosen. Again, the practical results were disappointing. Captains were not exactly eager to challenge the chief or his superiors. Town Hall, "A Study of the Los Angeles City Charter," 116–17, 108–109.

Page 53. In 1934, Parker got: Leadership of the union was divided evenly between the police department, which named two police representatives, a sergeant representative, a lieutenant representative, and a captain or higher representative to the organization's board, and the fire department, which named two firemen, an engineer, a captain, and a chief representative to the board. These elections were not exactly democratic exercises. According to former Deputy Chief Harold Sullivan, the lieutenants exercised great control over police activities on the board, which makes Parker's election all the more mysterious. Author interview with Harold Sullivan, July 7, 2007, Los Angeles, CA.

Page 53. In the summer of 1934: See City Council Minutes, August 14, 1934, pp. 234–35.

Page 54. The city council seems: City Council Meetings, vol. 248, August 14, 1934, pp. 235–36; City Council Minutes, August 15, 1934, p. 269, for the final text of Amendment No. 12-A. The city council also debated an amendment to abolish the Police Commission that day. It narrowly lost.

Page 54. The public was not: Carte and Carte, *Police Reform in the United States*, 105.

Page 54. Some observers did pick: City Council Minutes, vol. 249 (October 5, 1934), 18. The *Los Angeles Times* misreports the vote count as 83,521 ayes to 83,244 nayes. "Complete Vote Received for Thursday's Election," *Los Angeles Times*, September 30, 1934, 5.

For further discussions of Section 202, see also Escobar, "Bloody Christmas," 176–77.

Page 54. Union activism is not: Domanick, *To Protect and to Serve*, 22–23. The quote comes from the Harold Story Papers, Special Collections, UCLA, Los Angeles, CA.

Page 55. Even at the time: Nathan, " 'Rousting' System Earns Curses of the Rum-Runners, Chief Davis's Raids Keep Whiskey Ring in Harried State," *Los Angeles Times*, August 22, 1926, B6.

Page 55. Nor were regular citizens: LAPD officers were deputized by the counties in question and thus authorized to make arrests. Woods, "The Progressives and the Police," 342; Bass and Donovan, "The Los Angeles Police Department" in *The Development of Los Angeles City Government: An Institutional History, 1850–2000*, 154.

Page 55. "It is an axiom with . . .": Domanick, *To Protect and to Serve*, 53; Henstell, *Sunshine and Wealth*, 50. Both may well be quoting Gerald Woods, who in turn is almost certainly quoting an unidentified article in the *L.A. Record*.

Page 56. But as implausible as: Woods, "The Progressives and the Police," 322, 259.

Page 56. In 1934, Chief Davis: See "Facts on Chief Parker's Exam Records," Assistant General Manager Civil Service, June 1, 1966, William H. Parker Police Foundation archives, Los Angeles, CA.

Page 56. Then, suddenly, his career: See Deputy Chief B. R. Caldwell's letter to HQ, Los Angeles Procurement District, February 23, 1943, for a detailed (if occasionally opaque) discussion of Parker's career from 1933 through 1943. William H. Parker Police Foundation, Los Angeles, CA. See also Domanick, *To Protect and to Serve*, 28.

Page 57. In 1933, voters had: Woods, "The Progressives and the Police," 316–17; Sitton, *Los Angeles Transformed*, 12–13.

Page 57. During the 1920s, Kent: Kooistra, "Angeles for Sale," provides an excellent account of McAfee's activities throughout the 1930s. See also the October 9, 1953, FBI memo on Jack Dragna (Dragna FBI file 94–250); Weinstock, *My L.A.*, 56; and Woods, "The Progressives and the Police," 335.

Page 57. The key to it all: Donner, *The Age of Surveillance*, 59–64.

Chapter Seven: Bugsy

Page 59. "Booze barons"; "Are Gangsters Building Another Chicago Here?" *Los Angeles Times*, March 29, 1931, A1.

Page 59. By 1937, Bugsy Siegel: Jennings, *We Only Kill Each Other*, 29–31. Readers interested in a more sober assessment of Siegel should consult Robert Lacey's *Little Man: Meyer Lansky and the Gangster Life*.

Page 59. Siegel first visited Los Angeles: In addition to appearing as a dancer in vaudeville shows and on Broadway, Raft was also a regular presence at Jimmy Durante's Club Durante and at Texas Guinan's El Fey. This did not mean that Raft himself was in any way fey. In addition to being a sometime prizefighter, he was a close associate of Manhattan beer king Owney Madden. Such tough guy–showbiz connections were quite common in the 1920s. Bootlegger Waxey Gordon was an enthusiastic backer of such Broadway musicals as *Strike Me Pink*, even going so far as to order his gunmen to turn out in tuxedos for opening night. (Wisely, he also had them check their guns at the coat check.) Muir, *Headline Happy*, 159.

Page 60. He was receptive: Muir, *Headline Happy*, 160–64, discusses Siegel's post-Prohibition quasilegitmacy (and stock market troubles). See also Lacey, *Little Man*, 68, 79–80.

Page 60. Siegel's lifestyle reflected his: Jennings, *We Only Kill Each Other*, 27, 30.

Page 60. "Caution, fathered by the . . .": Muir, *Headline Happy*, 161.

Page 60. Los Angeles offered the: Muir, *Headline Happy*, 157–62. Siegel himself sometimes put the date of his arrival in Los Angeles one year later, in 1935. "Siegel Denies Buchalter Aid: Film Colony Figure Testifies on Removal Fight," *Los Angeles Times*, May 27, 1941, A1.

Page 61. "If I had kept . . .": Jennings, *We Only Kill Each Other*, 36–38; Muir, *Headline Happy*, 162–65.

Page 61. Bugsy's pals back East: See Hecht, "Mickey Notes," 1, Hecht Papers, Newberry Library; Cohen, *In My Own Words*, 41.

Page 61. One who declined to: A 2 percent take would have generated a healthy $200,000 a year in bookie action—not bad for the Great Depression. Hecht, "Mickey Notes," 4–5, Hecht Papers, Newberry Library.

Page 62. Cohen had outstayed his: In his autobiography, Cohen claims that he didn't take a dive (30). In his earlier conversations with Ben Hecht, however, he admitted that he did. Cohen manuscript, 19, Hecht Papers, Newberry Library.

Page 62. Mickey was living like: Taxi companies routinely employed violence to secure the best stands. Payoffs to police were also common. In Los Angeles, independent cabbies' frustration with the dominant Yellow Cab company (which was widely believed to have struck a deal with the police) boiled over into full-scale riots on more than one occasion in the 1930s. Cohen manuscript, 21–23, Hecht Papers, Newberry Library.

Page 64. "I says": Hecht manuscript, 82–84 Hecht Papers, Newberry Library; Cohen, *In My Own Words*, 36–37.

Page 65. The next day Mickey: This account draws heavily on Ben Hecht's account and is strikingly different from the blustering story Mickey tells in his autobiography. Hecht Papers, Newberry Library.

Page 66. (Years later, columnist Florabel . . .): Cohen, *In My Own Words*, 45.

Page 66. Cohen hit Neales's joints: Notes in the Ben Hecht Papers suggest that Siegel paid the sheriff's department $125,000 on at least one occasion. Hecht, "Mickey Notes," 4, Hecht Papers, Newberry Library. In the early 1950s, the California Commission on Organized Crime discovered links between Sheriff Biscailuz and Irving Glasser, a notorious bondsman closely associated with Siegel and Cohen. Woods, "The Progressives and the Police," 402.

Page 66. Soon after: Cohen manuscript, n.p., Hecht Papers, Newberry Library.

Page 67. "Ya know, I'm going . . .": Cohen, *In My Own Words*, 41.

Page 68. "It was a bad . . .": Unpublished manuscript, Hecht Papers, Newberry Library.

Page 68. During his first: Hecht manuscript, 9–10, Hecht Papers, Newberry Library.

Page 69. This attitude angered Mickey: Cohen, *In My Own Words*, 41.

Chapter Eight: Dynamite

Page 70. "We've got to get": Richardson, *For the Life of Me,* 224.

Page 70. In a city awash: McWilliams, *Southern California,* 170.

Page 70. Clinton had always been: "Penny Money At Cafe: Clinton 'Caveteria' Caters to Customers of Lean Purse," *Los Angeles Times,* October 14, 1932, A8. See also Starr, *The Dream Endures,* 165–66.

Page 71. Clinton's introduction to politics: Ford, *Honest Politics My Theme,* 86–87, 90.

Page 71. The county grand jury: Woods, "The Progressives and the Police," 339, 351.

Page 71. Clinton turned to Judge: The case was one of statutory rape; the victim was actually a prostitute supplied by a madam who specialized in underage girls. In the lead-up to Fitts's decision not to prosecute, one of the developer's employees arranged to purchase property from the DA's parents for a strikingly generous price. Fitts's investigators then prevented the girl in question from testifying by holding her in isolation in a downtown hotel. Richardson, *For the Life of Me,* 176.

Page 72. The report was scathing: Woods, "The Progressives and the Police," 356–57; Starr, *The Dream Endures,* 168–69; Parrish, *For the People,* 127.

Page 72. The counterreaction was: McDougal, *Privileged Son,* 44; Starr, *The Dream Endures,* 169. For more evidence of Fitts's thuggery, see Richardson's account of when a Fitts investigator jabbed a gun in his belly, *For the Life of Me,* 177.

Page 72. Clinton came under pressure: Starr, *The Dream Endures,* 169; Woods, "The Progressives and the Police," 355.

Page 73. The Shaws weren't: Woods, "The Progressives and the Police," 261, 357. See Richardson, *For the Life of Me,* 220, for a more positive assessment of Raymond.

Page 73. Then Raymond himself got: Sitton, *Los Angeles Transformed,* 16–17. Gerald Woods speculated that Raymond was targeted for a hit out of fear that he might testify to the Combination's connections with the Shaw machine in the upcoming trial of Shaw campaign assistant (and former Police Commission member) Harry Munson (357–58). Tom Sitton finds evidence that Raymond also approached the Combination with a shakedown request.

Page 73. On the morning of: Underwood, *Newspaperwoman,* 175.

Page 73. "They told me they . . .": Richardson, *For the Life of Me,* 221–22.

Page 73. The next morning, Raymond's: See Weinstock, *My L.A.,* 56–57, for an account of the connections between Raymond, Clinton, and the Combination; Sitton, *Los Angeles Transformed,* 17–18.

Page 74. Chief Davis's career: Domanick, *To Protect and to Serve,* 77–78.

Page 74. In April 1938, the: Underwood, *Newspaperwoman,* 176–78.

Page 74. Davis parried that everyone: "Davis Defends Police Spying at Bombing Trial, Bitter Clashes Mark Chief's Day on Stand," *Los Angeles Times,* April 27, 1941, 1. See also Domanick, *To Protect and to Serve,* 76; Woods, "The Progressives and the Police," 361; and "The Case of Earl Kynette," *Los Angeles Herald-Examiner,* July 8, 1966.

Page 75. One year earlier, Mayor: See Sitton, *Los Angeles Transformed,* 18–23, for the definitive account of the race.

Page 75. In theory, thanks to: Sitton, *Los Angeles Transformed,* 32.

Page 76. Despite his closeness to: "Chief Shifts 28 Officers in New Shake-Up of Police," *Los Angeles Times,* March 9, 1939, 2.

Page 76. A few days later: Gambling ships first appeared off the coast as early as 1923, but it was Tony Cornero who had the audacity to reconceive of them as floating casinos. He would die of a heart attack eighteen years later at a craps table in Las Vegas, just months before he, Milton "Farmer" Page, and other Combination figures finished building the world's largest casino, The Stardust. At Cornero's request, a band played "The Wabash Cannonball" at his funeral. Richardson, *For the Life of Me*, 227.

Page 77. There was just one: "Chief Shifts 28 Officers in New Shake-Up of Police," *Los Angeles Times*, March 9, 1939, 2.

Page 78. Mayor Bowron was exultant.: Richardson, *For the Life of Me*, 219–28; Woods, "The Progressives and the Police," 367.

Page 78. Yet the triumph of: Los Angeles's city charter sharply curtailed the power of the mayor. City departments operated under the control of general managers who enjoyed civil-service protection and who answered to independent boards of commissioners. Mayors enjoyed only the right to nominate commissioners (who then had to be approved by the city council), though mayors frequently sought to expand their authority by demanding written resignations in advance. Woods, "The Progressives and the Police," 370.

Page 78. In theory, promotion in: Author interview with Harold Sullivan, July 26, 2007.

Page 79. The acting chief of: Woods, "The Progressives and the Police," 371.

Page 79. One hundred seventy-one: See William H. Parker Police Foundation archives for this and other Civil Service board notices.

Page 79. From the first, Bill: Letter of recommendation from Inspector E. B. Caldwell, Parker Foundation archives; "Police Due for Shake-up Tomorrow, Chief Announces: New Divisions Will Be Organized and Shifts Made of Many Uniformed Officers in Sweeping Program," *Los Angeles Times*, November 30, 1939. See also Sjoquist, *History of the Los Angeles Police Department*, 84.

Page 79. Demoralized by his de facto: Letter from Caldwell to HQ Los Angeles Officer Procurement District, February 23, 1939, William H. Parker Police Foundation archives.

Chapter Nine: Getting Away with Murder (Inc.)

Page 82. "Men who have lived": Muir, *Headline Happy*, 161.

Page 82. District Attorney Buron Fitts: Central Avenue played an important and unique role in Los Angeles politics. During the 1920s, its large and fast-growing African American population emerged as one of the only reliable voting blocks in the city. A handful of political bosses controlled many of these votes and were sometimes able to demand considerable freedom for illicit activities, a situation that greatly frustrated African American progressives like Charlotta Bass Hayes, publisher of the *California Eagle*. Parrish, *For the People*, 127; Woods, "The Progressives and the Police," 347.

Page 82. "You never heard of . . .": Jennings, *We Only Kill Each Other*, 60.

Page 82. Bugsy Siegel *was* one: Jennings, *We Only Kill Each Other*, 27.

Page 83. The next day the: Muir, *Headline Happy*, 167–69; Richardson, *For the Life of Me*, 4–5.

Page 83. Mickey and Bugsy: Cohen, *In My Own Words*, 58.

Page 84. "I found Benny a . . .": Later (much later) Cohen would circulate stories of how he'd stood up to "the Bug" at their first meeting (while generally omitting the story of what happened to him as a result). Cohen, *In My Own Words*, 38. Cohen's comments to Ben Hecht in the mid-1950s make it clear that even at his craziest, Mickey knew how powerful Siegel was. Hecht Papers, Newberry Library.

Page 84. It was an arrangement: Cohen, *In My Own Words,* 36.

Page 85. Only after the countess: Jennings, *We Only Kill Each Other,* 74–78, provides a somewhat fanciful account of this episode.

Page 86. The evening before Thanksgiving: "Widow of Victim Heard at Murder Trial of Siegel: Heard Shots Killing Mate," *Los Angeles Times,* January 27, 1942, A1; "Siegel and Carbo Identified as Murder Aides, Tannenbaum Tells Killing," *Los Angeles Times,* January 28, 1942, A1.

Page 86. Abe "Kid Twist" Reles: Turkus and Feder, *Murder, Inc.,* 52.

Page 86. In January 1940, two: Nash, *World Encyclopedia of Organized Crime,* 331.

Page 86. It took twelve days: Turkus and Feder, *Murder, Inc.,* 67.

Page 87. Reles wasn't prosecutors' only: "Murder Plot Story Filed: Testimony Transcript in Siegel Case Gives Gang," *Los Angeles Times,* August 31, 1940, A1.

Page 87. The raiding party—three: Jennings, *We Only Kill Each Other,* 47–48.

Page 88. Bugsy's bed was still: "Siegel's Attic Capture Told, Witnesses at Death Trial Describe Hunt in Suspect's Mansion," *Los Angeles Times,* January 31, 1942, A1. See also Jennings, *We Only Kill Each Other,* 100–101; Muir, *Happy Holidays,* 176–77.

Page 89. Dockweiler was in a: Dean Jennings argues that O'Dwyer was on the take (*We Only Kill Each Other,* 121). Jerry Giesler argued that prosecutors in L.A. were on the take (*The Jerry Giesler Story,* 237–38).

Page 89. Back in New York: "Plunge Fatal to Gangster, State Witness Against Buchalter and Others Attempts to Escape," *Los Angeles Times,* November 13, 1941, 2.

Page 89. What had happened to: "Abe Reles Killed Trying to Escape, Sheet Rope Fails After He Lowers Himself from 6th to 5th Floor, Motive Puzzles Police," *New York Times,* November 13, 1941, 29. Jennings, *We Only Kill Each Other,* 128–29, makes the case for defenestration.

Page 89. Without Reles, the prosecution's: Giesler, *The Jerry Giesler Story,* 239–40.

Page 90. But Robinson: For an assessment of his gang and an account of the meeting, see Hecht notes, Ben Hecht Papers, Newberry Library, Chicago.

Page 91. "The poor bookmakers": Ben Hecht Papers, Newberry Library, Chicago.

Page 92. "Dragna was inactive at: Cohen would later claim that he had been attuned to the danger of a resentful Dragna all along (*In My Own Words,* 63). This is the wisdom of hindsight.

Page 92. Sica did. Then he: Cohen, *In My Own Words,* 62.

Page 93. Utley took it bravely: "Report Hints Cohen Had Part in Slayings," *Los Angeles Times,* June 16, 1959; "Mad Gunman Captured, Mickey Cohen Tells Inside Story of L.A.," *Los Angeles Times,* November 18, 1950, 1.

Page 93. Jack Dragna was less: Cohen, *In My Own Words,* 63–64.

Chapter Ten: L.A. Noir

Page 94. "If you're going to . . .": Wilkerson III, *The Man Who Invented Las Vegas,* 12.

Page 94. Bugsy Siegel wasn't: For more on Hohmann, see Sjoquist, *History of the Los Angeles Police Department,* 84; and Woods, "The Progressives and the Police," 380.

Page 94. Hohmann had been: Woods, "The Progressives and the Police," 381.

Page 94. As chief, Hohmann had: "Special Police Groups Press Fight on Crime, Cities Combat Increased Felonies with Crack Units; in Los Angeles It's 'Metro,'" *Los Angeles Times*, February, 23, 1964.

Page 95. Bill Parker was demoralized: Woods, "The Progressives and the Police," 420.

Page 95. JAPS OPEN WAR ON: AP headline immediately following Pearl Harbor.

Page 95. The situation was actually: The guns at Fort MacArthur, which was supposed to protect the U.S. naval station at San Pedro/Long Beach, would have been useless against a carrier-based aerial attack. Verge, *Paradise Transformed*, 33–34, 22.

Page 96. "Why, the Japanese bombed . . .": Verge, *Paradise Transformed*, 22; author interview with Harold Sullivan, July 26, 2007. Concerns about Japanese fishing vessels reflected well-founded worries about Japanese espionage. Since at least 1939, the Japanese military had used Mexican-based fishing vessels to monitor the Pacific fleet based at Long Beach. That same year, Japanese agents had recruited a Nisei former sailor as an intelligence agent and managed to steal important code books. Verge, *Paradise Transformed*, 10.

The efficiency of the operation was no coincidence. One official involved in the raid told the *Times*, "Although we had our plans set, the Japanese attack caught us a bit early." "Japanese Aliens' Roundup Starts: F.B.I. Hunting Down 300 Subversives and Plans to Hold 3000 Today," *Los Angeles Times*, December 8, 1941, 1; "Round Up of Japanese Aliens in Southland Now Totals 500: Officers, Working with F.B.I., Continue Hunt; Asiatic, Who Had Pledged Loyalty, Found with Guns," *Los Angeles Times*, December 9, 1941, 4; "Little Tokyo Banks and Concerns Shut, Even Saloons Padlocked; Extra Police on Duty to Prevent Riots," *Los Angeles Times*, December 9, 1941, 4.

Page 96. For once, Bill Parker: Verge, *Paradise Transformed*, 23–24.

Page 97. Parker's thoughts turned to: Captain Robert L. Dennis to HQ, Los Angeles Officer Procurement District, February 23, 1943, William H. Parker Police Foundation archives.

Page 98. However, Hohmann continued, these: Arthur Hohmman to HQ Los Angeles Officer Procurement District, February 19, 1943, William H. Parker Police Foundation archives. The conclusion of Hohmann's letter also suggests that Hohmann may have personally blocked Parker's earlier attempts to enlist in the military, which if true would be another interesting twist in what was clearly a complex relationship.

Page 98. His mood improved considerably: Col. Jesse Miller, Director, Military Government Division, to First Lt. William Parker, May 11, 1943, William H. Parker Police Foundation archives. For Parker's impressions of New England, see his June 30, 1943, letter to Helen, William H. Parker Police Foundation archives.

Page 99. It was, Mickey thought: Cohen, *In My Own Words*, 65.

Page 99. In Algeria, Parker was: Brig. Gen. J. K. Dunlop, Regional Allied Commissioner, letter of reference, January 15, 1944, William H. Parker Police Foundation archives.

Page 100. There was, however, one: Letter to Helen Parker, March 12, 1945, William H. Parker Police Foundation archives.

Page 100. For Mickey Cohen, the: The $500,000 estimates came from Carey McWilliams, Jennings, *We Only Kill Each Other*, and puts his take at $120,000 a year.

Page 100. Mickey had his own: Cohen would later estimate that his was one of approximately two hundred major bookmaking commission offices nationwide at the time. Cohen manuscript, Ben Hecht Papers, Newberry Library.

Page 101. Things were going so: The de jure owner of the stock farm was actually a former LAPD officer, Jack Dineen. California Special Crime Study Commission report, January 31, 1950, 32.

Page 102. Meyer and Bugsy had: Lacey, *Little Big Man*, 79–81.

Page 102. In 1931, the state: Russo, *The Outfit*, 292.

Page 103. Wilkerson was the publisher: Weller, *Dancing at Ciro's*, 88–89.

Page 103. So Wilkerson decided to: Wilkerson III, *The Man Who Invented Las Vegas*, 49. For a judicious account of Bugsy Siegel's much smaller role in the creation of Las Vegas, see Johnson, "Siegel, Bugsy." See also Muir, *Headline Happy*, 193–94.

Page 104. The invasion of Normandy: Related in letter to Helen, September 9, 1944, William H. Parker Police Foundation archives.

Page 104. Lt. Parker Wins Purple: "Lt. Parker Wins Purple Heat," *Los Angeles Times*, August 6, 1944, 2.

Page 104. For Parker, one brush: Verge, *Paradise Transformed*, 113–14.

Page 105. I respectfully submit that: "Memorandum for the Adjutant General, Subject: Relief from Active Duty," undated, William H. Parker Police Foundation archives.

Page 106. "So now I come: Bill Parker to Helen, October 8, 1944, William H. Parker Police Foundation archives.

Page 106. That Helen's initial response: In her address book, William H. Parker Police Foundation archives.

Page 106. Parker's retreat was swift: Parker letter to Helen, December 10, 1944, William H. Parker Police Foundation archives.

Page 106. On February 24, 1945: The tiffs, of course, continued. Within a matter of weeks, Bill was writing somewhat carping letters complaining of the quality of Helen's letters. Almost none of Helen's letters have survived, making it difficult to evaluate this claim.

Page 107. Parker's first assignment in: Parker letter to Helen, May 26, 1945, William H. Parker Police Foundation archives.

Page 107. "All my life I . . .": Parker letter to Helen, undated but from Frankfurt, William H. Parker Police Foundation archives.

Page 107. In fact, the LAPD: C. B. Horrall to Capt. W. H. Parker, June 26, 1945, William H. Parker Police Foundation archives. Parker's July 19, 1945, letter to Helen contains details of Parker's deliberations with Colonel Wilson, William H. Parker Police Foundation archives.

Page 109. The Los Angeles business: McDougal, *Privileged Son*, 2, 176.

Page 110. Parker also tended to: "W. H. Parker Heads Fire Police League," *Los Angeles Examiner*, January 7, 1949.

Page 110. The group mentioned that: Author interview with Harold Sullivan, July 26, 2007.

Page 110. In the spring of 1947: "Parker's the One in '51, Los Angeles Police Post 381, American Legion, Unanimously Presents William H. 'Bill' Parker for the Office of COMMANDER of THE AMERICAN LEGION, DEPARTMENT of CALIFORNIA, for the Year 1951–52," August 1950 (Number Three), William H. Parker Police

Foundation archives. See also "Police Post Gets Membership Drive Trophy," *L.A. Fire and Police Protective League News*, 1947, William H. Parker Police Foundation archives.

Chapter Eleven: The Sporting Life

Page 112. "[T]o be honest with . . .": Cohen, *In My Own Words*, 81.

Page 112. First, there were: Cohen, *In My Own Words*, 51–52.

Page 113. So much for "the: See Lewis, *Hollywood's Celebrity Gangster*, 57, for an account of the killing. The January 1950 study of the state of California's Special Crime Study Commission report said that the LAPD suspected "Hooky" Rothman and Joseph "Scotty" Ellenberg of being the gunmen, although they never found evidence to arrest and prosecute them (13). Mob figure Jimmy Fratianno identified Rothman as the triggerman (Demaris, *The Last Mafioso*, 25). The excrement anecdote comes from Anderson, *Beverly Hills Is My Beat*, 137.

Page 113. When Mickey swung by: The shooting occurred on May 15, 1945. See Cohen, *In My Own Words*, 71–73. Lewis, *Hollywood's Celebrity Gangster*, offers very different accounts (53–54).

Page 114. Still, it was a: The date of these dice games is uncertain. Later news accounts suggest they may have occurred in the late forties. See "Cohen Admits Big Gambling Take in Hotel Dice Games," *Chicago Tribune*, 3. Intriguingly, this article also notes that from 1947 onward, the Ambassador was owned by J. Myer Schine, whose son, David Schine, emerged in the 1950s as an intimate of Senator McCarthy's chief investigator, Roy Cohn. Cohn, a bitter opponent of Robert Kennedy, would later become a prominent organized crime defense lawyer.

Page 115. "I'd like to see . . .": Hecht, *A Child of the Century*, 610–11.

Page 115. Tell 'em they're a . . .": Hecht, *A Child of the Century*, 612.

Page 115. Wilkerson was right.: Muir, *Headline Happy*, 190–91; Russo, *The Outfit*, 295.

Page 116. At issue was the: May, "The History of the Race Wire Service."

Page 116. Bugsy knew the boys: Anderson, *Beverly Hills Is My Beat*, 144–45; Cohen, *In My Own Words*, 79; Jennings, *We Only Kill Each Other*, 198–210.

Page 117. After talking to Cohen: Jennings, *We Only Kill Each Other*, 208–9.

Page 118. "The people in the . . .": Cohen, *In My Own Words*, 81.

Page 118. "The LAPD had already: "Capt. Jack Donahoe of Police Retires, Handled Many Famous Cases," *Los Angeles Herald-Examiner*, March 8, 1962, B1.

Page 119. "One of the finest . . .": Cohen manuscript, Ben Hecht Papers, Newberry Library, 8.

Page 119. In the fall of: Cohen manuscript, Ben Hecht Papers, Newberry Library, 8–9; Lewis, *Hollywood's Celebrity Gangster*, 38.

Page 120. What they heard was: For more on Howser's checkered career, see Warren Olney, "Law Enforcement and Judicial Administration in the Earl Warren Era," Earl Warren Oral History Project, University of California, 1981; "Hidden Microphones Hear Cohen Secrets, Police Device Records Intimate Talks in Home," *Los Angeles Times*, August 16, 1949, 1.

Chapter Twelve: The Double Agent

Page 123. "The heart is deceitful": Jeremiah 17:9, King James Bible.

Page 123. Vaus first started: Vaus, *Why I Quit . . . Syndicated Crime*, 18–21.

Page 124. "Come back tomorrow night . . .": Vaus, *Why I Quit . . . Syndicated Crime*, 18–20. See also Stoker, *Thicker'N Thieves*, 82–86.

Page 124. Prostitution in Hollywood has: Rasmussen, "History of Hollywood Madams Is Long, Lurid," *Los Angeles Times*, November 30, 1997, B3.

Page 125. Charles Stoker had first: Vaus, *Why I Quit . . . Syndicated Crime*, 23; Stoker, *Thicker 'n Thieves*, 81.

Page 126. When Stoker got back: Stoker, *Thicker'N Thieves*, 85–87.

Page 127. Allen unleashed a stream: Stoker, *Thicker'N Thieves*, 91.

Page 127. Stoker had no: Stoker, *Thicker N'Thieves*, 94–95.

Page 128. Two facts: Vaus, *Why I Quit . . . Syndicated Crime*, 30–34, 36–46, 52.

Page 129. Vaus had never been: Vaus, *Why I Quit . . . Syndicated Crime*, 37.

Page 130. "No cop had a": Vaus, *Why I Quit . . . Syndicated Crime*, 39.

Page 131. Vaus had told Cohen: Stoker, *Thicker'N Thieves*, 94.

Page 132. In August 1947, Parker: Stoker provides the sole account of this meeting (142–43). Given the questions that would later emerge about his motivations and veracity, it should be treated with caution.

Page 132. Stoker felt uneasy about: Stoker, *Thicker'N Thieves*, 222–23.

Page 133. Soon after Stoker's: Stoker, *Thicker N'Thieves*, 181–85, 187–90.

Page 133. So Stoker agreed to: Stoker's account of this meeting (186–88) and indeed this period is intensely controversial. Parker himself would later completely disavow Stoker's account of events, even claiming by late 1949 that Sgt. Elmer Jackson's involvement with Brenda Allen was in fact a frame-up. Yet certain parts of Stoker's account ring true. First, the evidence against Sergeant Jackson (though not the chief himself) seems strong. Second, the picture of Parker Stoker presents has notable similarities to that presented by Fred Otash, another maverick LAPD officer, in his book, *Investigation Hollywood!*. Other figures who knew Parker well likewise believe that he was prepared to use the kinds of extreme tactics described by Stoker to become chief.

Page 134. On May 31, 1949: Woods, "The Progressives and the Police," 407.

Page 134. There was also the: "CONVICT DESCRIBES KILLING BY L.A. COP: Slaying of 'Peewee' Lewis Described at San Quentin," *Los Angeles Daily News*, June 7, 1949.

Page 134. The revelations streamed forth: Woods, "The Progressives and the Police," 407.

Page 134. Just when a narrative: Audre Davis's later arrest certainly doesn't bolster her credibility. Nonetheless, historian Gerald Woods insists that prosecutors had developed "a strong circumstantial case against [Stoker]." The county grand jury thought otherwise; it declined to convict Stoker. See also, "Policewoman Implicates Sgt. Stoker in Burglary Love for Vice Squad Man Admitted by Audrey [sic] Davis," *Los Angeles Times*, July 3, 1949.

Page 135. At first, Mayor Bowron: "Police Commission Commends Horrall: Full Confidence in Chief and Staff Expressed in Written Statement," *Los Angeles Times*, March 24, 1947. One month later, on July 27, Chief Horrall, Asst. Chief

Joe Reed, and Capt. Cecil Wisdom were indicted for perjury. Sergeant Jackson and Lieutenant Wellpott were also indicted on perjury and for accepting bribes. However, none of the men were ultimately convicted. In retrospect, the case against Chief Horrall, who was known for his strikingly hands-off management style, seems weakest. He was almost surely innocent. As for Sergeant Jackson and his associates, the most accurate verdict would be "not proven." Woods, "The Progressive and the Police," 408.

Page 135. Faced with a public: See Benis Frank, interviewer, "Oral History Transcript: General William Worton," 307.

Chapter Thirteen: Internal Affairs

Page 136. "I'll be damned if . . .": See Benis Frank, interviewer, "Oral History Transcript: General William Worton," 310.

Page 137. Like other departments, the: Chief Davis eventually handed over a list of 7,800 people who'd received badges. It included such luminaries as Shirley Temple (a Davis favorite), King Vidor, Louis B. Mayer, and Bela Lugosi. Larry Harnisch, "Mayor Investigates Honorary L.A.P.D. Badges," October 28, 1938, *Daily Mirror blog*, accessed October 28, 2008.

Page 137. The primary purpose of: See Benis Frank, interviewer, "Oral History Transcript: General William Worton," 309.

Page 138. To Sgt. Charles Stoker: Stoker, *Thicker'N Thieves*, 222; "New Police Chief on Job, to tell Program in Week," *Los Angeles Times*, July 1, 1949, 1; Daryl Gates, *Chief*, 15.

Page 139. It was, thought Gates: Author interview with Daryl Gates, December 10, 2004.

Page 139. That Bill Parker was: "Chief Names Staff Inspector in Top Level Police Changes: Parker Given Number Two Post," *Los Angeles Times*, July 15, 1949, 1.

Page 140. For decades, vice and: "Police Shift Offices Due to City Hall Jam," *Los Angeles Times*, August 19, 1949, 2.

Page 140. General Worton and his: Woods, "The Progressives and the Police," 409–10; "Ex-Marine Tightened Up Los Angeles Police," *Chicago Sun-Times*, March 12, 1952.

Page 141. General Worton was also: "Novice Chief Brings New Confidence . . . ," *San Francisco Call-Bulletin*, May 10, 1995.

Page 141. "He would be": Author interview with Bob Rock, December 10, 2004, Los Angeles, CA.

Page 141. Parker moved decisively too: "Police Officer Keyes Resigns Under Attack," *Los Angeles Times*, July 26, 1942.

Page 143. "Well then go fuck . . .": " 'Innocent' in Cussing, Says Mickey Cohen," *Los Angeles Mirror*, August 31, 1949.

Page 143. Within weeks, his name: Server, *Baby, I Don't Care*, 166, 203–204. See also "Americana," *Time*, January 31, 1949. Mitchum's conviction on drug possession charges was overturned in 1951, which suggests that the accusations against Mickey may well have been true.

Page 144. With Mickey on the: Warren was backed up by five high-powered commissioners: former U.S. ambassador to Russia Adm. William H. Standley; former Union Pacific president William M. Jeffers; mining magnate Harvey Mudd; Gen. Kenyon Joyce, onetime deputy president of the Allied Control Commission for Italy; and Gerald H. Hagar, Oakland, past president of the Star Bar. "Warren

Picks First of Crime Commissions: Jeffers and Mudd Among Those Named Under New State Law," *Los Angeles Times*, October 22, 1947.

Page 144. "Bookmaking has nothing to . . .": Fox, *Blood and Power*, 288.

Page 145. This system was: California Special Crime Study Commission report, January 31, 1950.

Page 145. Olney realized that there: Special Crime Study Commission report, March 17, 1949, 72, 79–80.

Page 146. The interruption of the: Special Crime Study Commission report, March 7, 1949, 16–25.

Page 146. Mickey accepted the fact: In fact, by the late 1940s, Anthony Milano, underboss of the Mayfield Street gang during Mickey's Cleveland days and brother to Cleveland mob boss Frank Milano, lived virtually around the corner from Mickey, in an imposing private residence off Sunset Boulevard. Ostensibly, Milano was now the president of an eastern bank (a six-year-sentence stint in the federal penitentiary in Leavenworth evidently posing no obstacles to a career in finance). In practice, the LAPD noted that he was in contact with Mickey on an almost daily basis. Special Crime Study Commission report, January 31, 1950, 29–30.

Ovid Demaris's book *The Last Mafioso*, which presents Jimmy Fratianno's perspective on the period, suggests that Mickey was genuinely surprised by efforts to rub him out. Not everyone agrees. Rob Wagner's *Red Ink, White Lies* argues that Cohen rejected Syndicate demands to share his underworld profits, thus triggering an entirely predictable gang war (229).

Page 147. The trouble started: Cohen, *In My Own Words*, 95–100. There are multiple accounts of exactly what happened with the photographs. See also Jennings, "The Private Life of a Hood," conclusion, October 11, 1958, 114.

Page 148. Rist and his associates: "Bowron Asks Grand Jury Action in Police Scandal, Two Officers Suspended; Cohen Posts $100,000 Bail," *Los Angeles Times*, March 23, 1949, 1.

Page 148. In the world of: Mickey's experiences in Cleveland contributed greatly to his multicultural precociousness. In the early thirties, the Cleveland underworld had been divided between two essentially cooperative groups, the Italian Mayfield Road gang, run by "Big Al" Polizzi, and the Jewish Cleveland Syndicate, whose leaders included Louis Rothkopf, Moe Dalitz, and Morris Kleinman. These two groups worked together closely in what was known as the Combination. Interestingly, during his days in Cleveland, Mickey had worked primarily with the Italian gangsters, particularly Mayfield Road gang underboss Tony Milano. Demaris, *The Last Mafioso*, 8–9.

Page 148. Far from responding gratefully: Demaris, *The Last Mafioso*, 24.

Chapter Fourteen: The Evangelist

Page 150. "He has the making . . .": "Jigs and Judgments," *Time*, July 23, 1951.

Page 150. "A few nights": Vaus, *Why I Quit . . . Syndicated Crime*, 71–72.

Page 150. By November 1949, everyone: "Heaven, Hell & Judgment Day," *Time*, March 20, 1950.

Page 151. Suddenly, Vaus found himself: *Los Angeles Times*, November 8, 1949; Vaus, *Why I Quit . . . Syndicated Crime*, 71–76.

Page 151. It was with some: *Life*, January 16, 1950; "Portrait of a Punk," *Cosmopolitan*.

It is difficult to know how much financial pain Mickey was really feeling. In an article written several months after Vaus's visit with Cohen, one of the most astute observers of the Southern California scene, lawyer/journalist Carey McWilliams, estimated that Mickey was receiving payoffs in the amount of $427,000 a year. Given the fact that the state public utility commission had effectively choked off the wire service that was once the most profitable part of Mickey's portfolio, that number seems high. Columnist Florabel Muir, who was close to Mickey and had excellent sources in the underworld, believed that Cohen was under real financial pressure. Of course, Mickey had other activities— extortion, slot machines, perhaps narcotics—which undoubtedly helped offset at least some of the pain.

Page 152. "Mickey lifted his hand": See Cohen, *In My Own Words*, 106–107, for an account of the meeting. Sensitive to charges that he had considered betraying his faith, Cohen plays down the conversion angle. Compare Cohen's account with Graham's, "The New Evangelist," *Time* cover story, October 25, 1954.

Page 152. At 4:15 a.m. on February: Lewis, *Hollywood's Celebrity Gangster*, 137; Demaris, *The Last Mafioso*, 40.

Page 152. Police later estimated that: Leppard, "Mr. Lucky Thrives on Borrowed Time," *Los Angeles Herald-Express*, December 3, 1959.

Page 154. During the fall of: Woods, "The Progressives and the Police," 411–12.

Page 155. These were powerful backers: Author interview with Daryl Gates, December 10, 2004.

Page 156. The race was now: Webb, *The Badge*, 250–52.

Page 156. On August 2: "Parker Appointed New Police Chief Head, Patrol Division Head Promoted in Climax to Hot Battle Over Worton's Successor," *Los Angeles Times*, August 3, 1950, 1. See also Woods, "The Progressives and the Police," 418. In describing Parker as the LAPD's fortieth police chief, I discount Dr. Alexander Hope, who headed the volunteer Los Angeles Rangers (Sjoquist, *History of the Los Angeles Police Department*, 36). I also count previous chiefs who served more than one term, such as James E. Davis, only once.

Page 156. Mayor Bowron was notably: *Los Angeles Times*, August 3, 1950. Later that day, Bowron issued a more positive statement on the Parker appointment.

Page 156. "I know I'm supposedly . . .": "Los Angeles Police Chief: William Henry Parker 3d," *New York Times*, August 114, 1965, 8.

Chapter Fifteen: "Whiskey Bill"

Page 157. "There is a sinister . . .": Kefauver Committee report, quoted in Turking and Feder, *Murder, Inc.*, 426.

Page 157. It had been a: Mickey would later deny being held overnight. "That was always newspaper bullshit," he claimed. "They'd say to me, 'How long ya going to be in town?' I'd say, 'I'm leaving at such and such a time on Wednesday.' So they'd give the story to the newspapers that, 'We ordered him to leave town by Wednesday'" (*In My Own Words*, 147). This is probably boasting.

Page 157. A freshman senator from: Russo, *The Outfit*, 259.

Page 158. At some point in: Moore, *The Kefauver Committee and the Politics of Crime, 1950–52*, 49. See also Russo, *The Outfit*, 251–52.

Page 158. The killing itself was: "Truman Speeds War on Crime; Mickey Cohen Pay-off Charged, Racketeers' Tax Returns to Be Eyed," *Los Angeles Times*, June 2, 1951, 1.

Page 159. "Lookit, nobody notified me . . .": Cohen, *In My Own Words*, 148; Russo, *The Outfit*, 255.

Page 159. "I ain't never muscled . . .": "I Ain't Never . . . ," *Time*, November 27, 1950.

Page 160. Other Mob bosses had: Dragna's legitimate businesses included a 538-acre vineyard near Puente and a Panama-flagged frigate that shuttled bananas between Long Beach and Panama. Special Crime Study Commission report, January 31, 1950, 25–26. For Mickey's legitimate holdings, see "Portrait of a Punk," *Cosmopolitan*. The Kefauver Commission was particularly well informed about Mickey because its chief investigator, Harold Robinson, had come from Warren Olney's special crime study commission. Warren Olney, "Law Enforcement and Judicial Administration," 297.

Page 160. Anyone who bothered to: Calculations come from the Final Report of the Special Crime Study Commission, November 15, 1950, 37.

Page 160. This should have led: Final Report of the Special Crime Study Commission, November 15, 1950, 39.

Page 161. Mickey cracked his first: "MAD GUNMAN CAPTURED, Mickey Cohen Tells Inside Story of L.A., Bland Gangster Spars with Counsel in Quiz; Sheriff Also Testifies," *Los Angeles Times*, November 18, 1950, 1.

Page 161. The audience chuckled: Cohen, *In My Own Words*, 148.

Page 161. During Parker's first month: Webb, *The Badge*, 253.

Page 161. Parker argued that if: The idea for an interagency intelligence agency was not new. In the fall of 1947, District Attorney William Simpson, Sheriff Eugene Biscailuz, and Police Chief C. B. Horrall had announced the creation of a similar entity. "Police Network in 20 Cities to Keep Constant Tab on Mobs," *Los Angeles Daily News*, November 11, 1947. However, Parker revived the idea and gave it a concerted push that previously had been lacking.

Page 162. "This plan goes deeper . . .": Webb, *The Badge*, 253.

Page 162. The assembled group was: "Parker Declares City Is White Spot of Nation," *Los Angeles Times*, August 9, 1950.

Page 162. "[W]e have become a . . .": Parker, "Religion and Morality," in *Parker on Police*, 18.

Page 163. The idea of an: "Worton Shifts 33 in Police Shake-Up: Top Flight Officer Named Intelligence Aide to Chief in Reorganization Move," *Los Angeles Times*, August 4, 1949. Earlier in his career, Worton himself had been a special intelligence officer in the Navy's Office of Naval Intelligence. "Worton 'Man of the Year' in the *Los Angeles Mirror* Mailbag Vote," December 30, 1949.

Page 163. Parker shared Worton's enthusiasm: Chief Parker, for one, seems to have suspected this. Kefauver, *Crime in America*, 241.

Page 164. The intelligence division didn't: Lieberman, "Crusaders in the Underworld: The LAPD Takes On Organized Crime," *Los Angeles Times*, October 26, 2008.

Page 164. "When Johnny saw the . . .": Otash, *Investigation Hollywood*, 184.

Page 164. "We're selfish about it . . .": "Novice Chief Brings New Confidence . . . ," *San Francisco Call-Bulletin*, May 10, 1955.

Page 164. As Kefauver attempted to: Because Guarantee Finance operated as a "fifty-fifty book," with management and participating bookies sharing expenses, the cost of juice was almost certainly twice that figure—$216,000. Kefauver, *Crime in America*, 240.

Page 165. Later that evening, at: *Scene of the Crime*, 126–27.

Page 166. Mickey was hustled off: Cohen, *In My Own Words*, 150–51.

Page 166. But solving the case: The LAPD was right. However, the two Tonys were killed not because the police were closing in on them for the Rummell shooting—they had no involvement in that—but rather because the two men had recently heisted a big bookmaking operation in Las Vegas. Demaris, *The Last Mafioso*, 51–54.

Page 167. "The Weasel" had an: Stump, "L.A.'s Chief Parker—America's Most Hated Cop," *Cavalier Magazine*, July 1958. See also Demaris, *The Last Mafioso*, 56–60, for Fratianno's account of the interrogation.

Page 168. Parker moved quickly to: Woods, "The Progressives and the Police," 425–26.

Page 169. "Well, get out," Parker: Gates, *Chief*, Chapters One and Two. Gates's characterizations of Parker are often ungenerous, as when Gates describes Parker as "a stern, cantankerous man with a reputation as a bully" (25). Throughout the earlier pages of his memoir, Gates presents himself as an independent-minded rebel, eager to break free of Parker's tutelage. Yet in the version of Gates's memoirs annotated by Helen Parker (available for perusal at the William H. Parker Police Foundation) a very different and in some ways more plausible picture of the young Gates emerges as an officer whom Parker had to push out into the field. There is probably at least some truth to this alternative account.

Page 170. Fortunately, Daryl Gates was: Helen Parker would later deny claims that Parker was a heavy drinker, insisting that her husband simply enjoyed a cocktail or two at the end of the day. This claim can be set aside. Gates's testimony on this point is compelling and corroborated by others, such as Deputy Chief Harold Sullivan.

Page 170. As the Kefauver hearings: Gates, *Chief*, 37. Other federal law enforcement agencies had likewise missed opportunities to go after the little gangster. The Bureau of Narcotics had identified Cohen's close associate, Joe Sica, as the principal supplier of heroin in Southern California and the San Joaquin Valley, but had failed to place him as a member of Cohen's inner circle. More curious still was the conduct of the FBI. While the bureau developed a large file on Cohen activities, it showed no inclination to develop a case it could take to prosecutors. This was entirely in keeping with the FBI's long-standing lack of interest in prosecuting organized crime, which director J. Edgar Hoover insisted was primarily local and thus a matter for local law enforcement to address.

Page 171. When Cohen himself appeared: "Cohen Deals Going Before Jury Today, Federal Inquirers Expected to Hear of Borrowings," *Los Angeles Times*, February 9, 1951, A1.

Page 171. Cohen had long maintained: Lewis, *Hollywood's Celebrity Gangster*, 169. He ultimately sold it to the Texas Stock Car Racing Association instead. "Mickey Cohen Cashes In on His Glaring Notoriety," *New York Times*, April 3, 1951, 28.

Page 171. It was no use: Lewis, *Hollywood's Celebrity Gangster*, 169.

Page 172. The trial began on: Cohen manuscript, Ben Hecht Papers, Newberry Library, n.p.

Page 172. The prosecution's strategy: "Cohen Profits Told as Tax Case Opens, Federal Prosecutor Attacks Gangster's Story of Loans," *Los Angeles Times*, June 5, 1951, 2; Cohen manuscript, Ben Hecht Papers, Newberry Library, n.p.

Page 172. Perhaps the hardest to: Cohen manuscript, Ben Hecht Papers, Newberry Library, n.p.

Page 173. At the end of: Lewis, *Hollywood's Celebrity Gangster*, 172–75; Cohen manuscript, Ben Hecht Papers, Newberry Library, n.p.

Page 173. The smoking gun: Jennings, "The Private Life of a Hood," conclusion, October 11, 1958, 116.

Page 174. Mickey interjected. "Right now, . . .": Cohen would later claim that Sackman had set him up. The supposed rationale for the double-cross had to do with the problems Sackman himself was experiencing with the revenue bureau in connection with the Guarantee Finance Company. By offering the bureau Cohen, Mickey believed that Sackman was trying to save himself. This theory may be true. During the sentencing, Judge Harris would go so far as to state that Cohen "had talked himself into this case" by giving the revenue bureau a false statement when he could simply have remained silent. "Mickey Cohen Gets 5 Years, $10,000 Fine," *Los Angeles Times*, July 10, 1951, 1; Hill, "5-Year Term Given to Mickey Cohen; Judge Finds Gambler 'Not So Bad,'" *New York Times*, July 10, 1951, 1.

Page 174. A request: The description that follows comes from Cohen manuscript, Hecht Papers, Newberry Library.

Page 174. "I am praying that . . .": "Jigs & Judgments," *Time*, July 23, 1951.

Page 175. One day in early: "Mickey Shifted to New Jail to End 'Privileges,' Crowding at County Bastille the Official Cause," *Hollywood Citizen-News*, February 8, 1952.

Page 175. Cohen was placed in: "Cohen 'Safe' in U.S. Cell, Moved to Federal Pen, Brutality By Police Told," *Los Angeles Herald-Express*, February 14, 1952.

Page 175. "Mickey, my God, why: Cohen manuscript, Ben Hecht Papers, Newberry Library.

Page 176. Although their client was: Lewis, *Hollywood's Celebrity Gangster*, 124.

Page 176. "Mickey is in": Hecht, "Mickey Notes," 9, Hecht Papers, Newberry Library.

Chapter Sixteen: Dragnet

Page 178. The trouble arrived on: See Edward Escobar's definitive article, "Bloody Christmas and the Irony of Police Professionalism: The Los Angeles Police Department, Mexican Americans, and Police Reform in the 1950s," 171. This incident also inspired the opening scenes of the James Ellroy book (later movie) *L.A. Confidential*.

Page 178. From the perspective of: Said the arresting officer later, "Sure I hit him. He was kicking at me with his feet. I only used necessary force to subdue him." "Parker Clams Up on Jury Quiz," *Los Angeles Daily News*, March 27, 1952; Escobar, "Bloody Christmas and the Irony of Police Professionalism," 187.

Page 179. Christmas was a special: Author interview with Harold Sullivan, July 26, 2007. The department would later insist, implausibly, that officers at Central station were consuming only ice cream, pie and cake, and coffee that evening. "'Cops So Drunk They Fought Each Other to Beat Us,'" *Los Angeles Herald-Express*, March 19, 1952.

Page 179. The prisoners were taken: "6 on Trial Tell More Police Brutalities," *Los Angeles Daily News*, March 6, 1952. See also "Wild Party by 100 Police Described, Youth Tells of Beatings at Police Yule Party," *Los Angeles Examiner*, March 19, 1952; "'Cops So Drunk They Fought Each Other to Beat Us,'" *Los Angeles*

Herald-Express, March 19, 1952; "Bare Yule Police Brutality Transcript," *Los Angeles Daily News*, May 13, 1952.

Page 179. Two months after the: Escobar, "Bloody Christmas," 185. "East side" was a phrase originally used to describe the area east of Main Street.

Page 180. Parker's initial response to: "Chief Shrugs at Claim of Cop Brutality, Police Brutality Gets Brush-off by Chief Parker," *Los Angeles Mirror*, February 27, 1952; "Chief Parker Hits Brutality Stories," *Los Angeles Times*, February 28, 1952. In Parker's defense, it should be noted that the particular cause of the chief's complaint—an allegation by a Latino doctor that a police officer had fired on him—did indeed prove to be unsubstantiated.

Page 180. The liberal *Daily News*: *Los Angeles Times*, March 6, 1952.

Page 180. Local Democrats unanimously passed: "PARKER FORCED TO ACT ON BRUTALITY, Cop Brutality Quiz Demanded by L.A. Judge," *Los Angeles Mirror*, March 13, 1952; "F.B.I. Probing L.A. Police Brutality," *Los Angeles Times*, March 14, 1952.

Page 181. Belatedly, Parker recognized the: See "Florabel Muir Reporting," *Los Angeles Mirror*, March 14, 1953, for a column on the chief's change of heart.

Page 181. But Parker's story had: "Florabel Muir Reporting," *Los Angeles Mirror*, March 20, 1952.

Page 181. "Boys Tell Police Beating,": March 19, 1952; "An Inadequate Answer," *Los Angeles Examiner* editorial, May 2, 1952, describes the initial Internal Affairs' report, which found no evidence of abuse.

Page 181. Meanwhile, more reports of: "Move for Action on L.A. Police Brutality Charges," *Los Angeles Daily News*, February 26, 1952; "Parker Clams Up on Jury Quiz," *Los Angeles Daily News*, March 27, 1952.

Page 182. Parker's job was in: "Police Brutality Probe Is Overdue," *Los Angeles Mirror*, March 14, 1952; Webb, *The Badge*, 174–75.

Page 182. The first threat to: "Grand Jury to Attack Police Trials System," *Los Angeles Examiner*, September 7, 1949; "Law for Policemen Took," *Los Angeles Examiner*, editorial, November 14, 1949.

Page 182. Of course, Chief Parker: See the March 28, 1953, untitled *Daily News* editorial for a rebuttal of these charges.

Page 183. *Pat Novak* took the: Hayde, *My Name's* Friday, 13. See also Wikipedia, http://en.wikipedia.org/wiki/pat_nuyak&equals$fur-hire.

Page 183. Jack Webb had grown: Unless otherwise noted, the biographical information that follows comes from Michael Hayde, *My Name's Friday*. The chronology of events that led to this job offer is not entirely clear. Owen McClaine, the casting agent for *He Walked by Night*, claims to have heard Webb's "private eye plays"—presumably, *Pat Novak*—and then offered him the job. But Jack Webb did not start playing the lead role in *Pat Novak* until 1949, when the program went national on ABC—one year after he appeared in *He Walked by Night*.

Page 184. "I doubt it, Marty,": Hayde, *My Name's Friday*, 18–19.

Page 186. Joe Friday (as played: See Raymond Chandler's essay "The Simple Art of Murder" for more on the noir hero.

Page 187. The radio program's success: "Real Thriller," *Time*, May 15, 1950.

Page 187. Soon after the tribute: A July 17, 1958, memo from the FBI's L.A. SAC to Hoover described Parker as a "Traffic Officer" prior to his appointment to the position of chief of police "with whom office had practically no contact."

Page 187. Whether Parker knew about: Hayde, *My Name's Friday*, 31–33. See August 2, 1963, FBI memo, Parker FBI file, for the origins of the FBI feud. See December 4, 1951, memo from SAC, Los Angeles, to Director, FBI, for Parker's praise of Hoover.

Page 188. The episode aired on: Hayde, *My Name's Friday*, 46.

Page 189. Parker's initial response to: On July 18, 1959, the FBI's San Francisco SAC sent a confidential memo to J. Edgar Hoover, reporting on a recent off-the-record confab Parker had held with Bay Area law enforcement officials about community relations that provides rare insight into the chief's thoughts about the Bloody Christmas affair. According to the SAC, Parker stated that "certain of his men were undoubtedly in the wrong." Parker further noted that "a number of his young officers were also wrong in 'clamming up' when his own inspectors attempted to investigate the beatings, and that had these officers not done this, the entire matter might in all probability have been settled within the department." Also author interview with Harold Sullivan, July 26, 2007.

Page 189. Soon after his ill-received: "Parker Hints at Crackdown, Own Cleanup May Forestall Jury Action," *Hollywood Citizen-News*, March 27, 1952; "Grand Jury Indicts Eight Officers in Beating Case," *Los Angeles Times*, April 23, 1952; "Bloody Christmas—One Year Later," *Los Angeles Mirror* editorial, December 6, 1952.

Page 190. Parker went further: Webb, *The Badge*, 174–75; "36 L.A. Policemen Face Discipline for Brutality," *Los Angeles Times*, June 17, 1952; "Grand Jury Turns Heat on Parker, Report Hits Police Dept. Conditions," *Los Angeles Daily News*, April 2, 1952; "An Inadequate Answer," *Los Angeles Examiner* editorial, May 2, 1952.
A July 29, 1952, memo from the L.A. SAC to Hoover asserted that Parker had not been popular in the department before the FBI's civil rights investigation commenced but that Parker's strong defense of the department had "earned him support since." Nonetheless, the SAC claimed that Parker's position "is still somewhat precarious" as "it is generally known that the Mayor is hostile to him, as are a number of the Los Angeles Police Commissioners." The following month Mayor Bowron would categorically deny any intention of removing Parker. "Bowron Denies Parker Ouster," *Los Angeles Herald-Examiner*, May 27, 1952.

Page 190. *Dragnet* wasn't the only: A July 18, 1952, "confidential memo" from the FBI's San Francisco SAC to Director Hoover reports that the L.A. business community had also printed a brochure titled "The Thin Blue Line" to distribute to members of the public. Whether the phrase was first used for the pamphlet or for the TV show is unclear.

Page 190. The purpose of: April 1, 1952, letter from Parker to the Police Commission, William H. Parker Police Foundation archives.

Page 191. "Soviet Russia believes that . . .": Parker, *Parker on Police*, 30. See also Charles Reith, *The Blind Eye of History*, 209–23, for a viewpoint that profoundly influenced Parker.

Page 191. In this vital role: Woods, "The Progressives and the Police," 430.

Page 191. Parker thought the primary: Woods, "The Progressives and the Police," 429.

Page 192. One generation earlier, Berkeley: Parker, *Parker on Police*, 12.

Page 192. Hoover was determined to: See memorandum to Mr. DeLoach, December 12, 1960, for summary of bureau's relationship with Parker, Parker FBI files.

Chapter Seventeen: The Trojan Horse

Page 194. "You should always have . . .": Poulson, *The Genealogy and Life Story*, 91.

Page 195. "There is nothing about . . .": "Chief Parker Expected to Quit in Bowron Row," *Los Angeles Examiner*, May 27, 1952; Sitton, *Los Angeles Transformed*, 171; Parson, *Making a Better World*, 112, 115.

Page 195. The charge emerged from: The residents of Chávez Ravine would later be evicted for another reason—to make way for Dodger Stadium.

Page 196. Bowron had no interest: Sitton, *Los Angeles Transformed*, 171.

Page 196. In December 1952: The Cadillac soon broke down, and Poulson replaced it with a fuel-efficient Rambler, much to the horror of West Coast oil and gas companies. Parson, *Making a Better World*, 127; Poulson, *The Genealogy and Life Story*, 132–34.

Page 197. "I just casually reached . . .": Poulson, *The Genealogy and Life Story*, 144.

Page 197. "They would say that . . .": Poulson, *The Genealogy and Life Story*, 144.

Page 199. the House Subcommittee on: "Verbal Battles by Lawyers Rock Public Housing Quiz," *Los Angeles Times*, May 21, 1953. Parson, *Making a Better World*, 203–208, provides a complete transcript of the LAPD's Wilkinson file.

Page 200. "I talked in circles,": Poulson, *The Genealogy and Life Story*, 144–45.

Chapter Eighteen: The Magna Carta of the Criminal

Page 201. "The voice of the . . .": Webb, *The Badge*, 244.

Page 201. Accardo's party proceeded to: Russo, *The Outfit*, 302. The *Los Angeles Mirror* presents a slightly different version of the incident, which features a verbal confrontation at the airport. "Chicago Hoodlum Chased by Cops, Goes to 'Vegas,'" *Mirror*, January 16, 1953. See also Davidson, "The Mafia Can't Crack Los Angeles," *Saturday Evening Post*, July 31, 1965. Fittingly, Perino's was also a famous gangster-movie restaurant, a place that featured in such films as *Scarface*, *Bugsy*, and *Mulholland Drive*. It was torn down in the spring of 2005 (http://franklinavenue.blogspot.com/2005/04/perinos-no-more.html, accessed July 16, 2008).

Page 202. Then there were the: Parker to Rev. John Birth, director, Catholic Youth Organization, April 28, 1953, William H. Parker Police Foundation archives. See Weeks, "Story of Chief Parker, Enemy of the Criminal," for a disingenuous attempt to explain away the "personal" intelligence files. *Los Angeles Mirror*, June 17, 1957, 1.

Page 203. The potential for the: Poulson, *The Genealogy and Life Story*, 140. The *Daily News* was speaking out against a proposal that surfaced that summer to give the police chief even more power over the department. "Give Police Board, not the Chief, More Power," *Los Angeles Daily News*, July 2, 1953; *Los Angeles Times*, May 12, 1953.

Page 203. There was a third: Coates, "Midnight Memo to the Mayor," *Los Angeles Mirror*, July 20, 1953; Poulson, *The Genealogy and Life Story*, 140, 147.

Page 203. "Chief Parker is to . . .": "Poulson Pledges War on Gangsters: Mayor-Elect Maps Plans with Parker; Shake-Up of Police Commission Indicated," *Los Angeles Times*, June 17, 1953.

Page 204. Although he had concluded: Poulson, *The Genealogy and Life Story*, 147; "4 Named to Police Board by Poulson," *Hollywood Citizen-News*, July 2, 1953.

Page 204. The message Poulson intended: Woods, "The Progressives and the Police," 151–52.

Page 205. "Until these recommendations . . .": Irey, "An Open Letter to the Mayor: Ex-Official Tells LA Police Stymie," *Los Angeles Mirror*, July 13, 1953; Irey, "Police Dept. 'Split' Bared," *Los Angeles Mirror*, July 14, 1953.

Page 205. "Hardly anyone likes Parker, . . .": Parker's relationship with the press had taken a turn for the worse earlier in the year, when he shut down a poker game involving reporters and the police that had been going on since time immemorial. At the chief's insistence, a sign was put up that read "No more card playing. By order of the Chief of Police." Parker would later claim that he was moved to act after discovering that one unfortunate reporter had run up a $2,000 debt. The press itself seems to have viewed the crackdown case as pure vindictiveness. In a scathing story about the controversy, the *Daily News* complained of the chief's "incredible inability to get along with newsmen or take criticism." "Speaking of Snoopers," *Los Angeles Daily News*, January 19, 1953.

Page 205. Poulson hoped that his: Commission members received a stipend of $20 per meeting but were otherwise unpaid. Mayor Poulson's predecessor, Fletcher Bowron, had also wrestled with this problem, when confronted with the prospect of having the ornery, independent-minded Parker as chief. His solution had been to place William Worton on the Police Commission board. Harry Frawley, "Police Board Will Use More Power—Mayor," *Valley Times*, August 8, 1950. It didn't work. Parker's allies on the city council ferociously resisted a few early efforts by Worton to discipline the new chief. In the summer of 1951, General Worton resigned from the Police Commission and was gone. "Newman and Worton Quit Police Board," *Los Angeles Times*, July 18, 1951, 1.

Page 205. If those weren't constraints: In his memoirs, Poulson would later accuse Parker of deliberately undermining the mayor's relationship with Poulson. This is probably true; however, Parker undoubtedly also benefited from an incident that occurred that very summer. Soon after Irwin joined the Police Commission, he was approached by Herbert Hallner, chief investigator for the state board, with a proposition: If Irwin would "cooperate" with a group of "citizens" attempting to win permission to open, he would be "well taken care of." It was common knowledge that the group of citizens in question was a front for Jimmy Utley, Mickey Cohen's sometime underworld rival. Irwin quickly informed Parker and Poulson of the approach, and with Irwin's continuing assistance, the department arranged a successful sting operation aimed at the corrupt investigator. The incident undoubtedly heightened Irwin's regard for the chief. See "Cal. Employe [*sic*] Accused as Bunco Go-Between," *Los Angeles Daily News*, September 2, 1953.

Page 206. Poulson struggled in his: "Responses to Questions of the Los Angeles City Council Concerning a Juvenile Gang Attack on a Citizen in Downtown Los Angeles Which Resulted in His Death, Given by Los Angels [*sic*] Chief of Police W. H. Parker on December 8, 1953," Police Department files, Escobar collection, Tucson, AZ.

Page 206. But when Leask presented: Memorandum from Parker to the Board of Police Commissioners, "Subject: Progress Report—August 9, 1950, to January 1, 1953," January 7, 1953, Escobar collection, Tucson, AZ.

Page 206. "You talk like you're . . .": "Charge 750 Police in Office Jobs, Quiz Chief," *Los Angeles Herald-Express*, May 5, 1954; Williams, "Mayor and Parker in Sharp Clashes: Poulson, Police Chief and Leask Argue Heatedly at Public Hearing on City Budget," *Los Angeles Times*, May 6, 1954, 1.

Page 206. It was classic Parker.: Gerald Woods put it aptly in his 1,310-page dissertation, "The Progressives and the Police": "A most contentious man, he could not abide the same quality in others. . . . He brooked no criticism of himself, his politics or his subordinates. . . . Parker's description of society provided a concise analysis of the chief himself. Americans, he said, were 'emotional people, responsive to stimuli administered to us through communicative media; we are immature and subjective about problems, and there is an unwillingness for us to accept our mistakes.' His enemies could not have said it better" (432).

Page 207. So far, the consequences: Memorandum from Parker to the Board of Police Commissioners, "Subject: Progress Report—August 9, 1950, to January 1, 1953," January 7, 1953, Escobar collection.

Page 207. I wish it could: Parker, *Parker on Police*, 16.

Page 208. For decades, police departments: For instance, in the spring of 1955, Judge Aubrey Irwin dismissed a case against Hollywood playboy LeRoy B. ("Skippy") Malouf after concluding that Malouf had been framed by the police. " 'Planted' Fur Story Acquits Malouf in Theft," *Los Angeles Times,* April 7, 1955, p. 4.

See the depiction of police work as approved by the department in *He Walked by Night*.

Page 208. Of course, not every: Parker would later argue that technically wiretapping per se was not illegal under federal statutes but rather the divulging of information from a wiretap was. Parker, "Laws on Wiretapping," letter to the *Los Angeles Times*, January 23, 1955.

Page 209. "[I]n a prosecution": *Irvine v. California,* 347 U.S. 128 (1954); Newton, *Justice for All*, 338. No case was ever brought against the officers involved.

Page 210. The position of: "Chance on the High Sea," *Time*, August 14, 1939; Warren, *The Memoirs of Earl Warren*, 255; Parker, "Responses to Questions of the Los Angeles City Council Concerning a Juvenile Gang Attack on a Citizen in Downtown Los Angeles," December 8, 1953, Escobar collection.

Page 211. "Certainly society cannot expect . . .": City News Service, "Parker Hits at Highest Court Ruling in Irvine 'Bookie' Case," *L.A. Journal*, February 19, 1954.

Page 211. This was a sensitive: Wirin's lawsuit was finally rejected on May 31, 1955. "Judge Rules He Cannot Stop Police Microphones, Lacks Jurisdiction on Use of Public Funds for Installation, McCoy Says," *Los Angeles Times*, July 1, 1955.

Page 211. Wirin's attempts to rein: *Los Angeles Herald-Express*, April 19, 1954; *Los Angeles Times*, April 5, 1954.

Page 212. "We would if you . . .": Lieberman, " 'Dragnet' Tales Drawn from LAPD Files Burnished the Department's Image," *Los Angeles Times*, October 30, 2008.

Page 212. "Far from being a . . .": Mooring, "Chief Gives Opinion of 'Bad Cop' Films," *The Tidings*, October 22, 1954; "Telephone Tap Defended by Chief Parker," *Los Angeles Mirror–Daily News*, March 7, 1955. In 1968, Congress passed legislation (known as Title III) governing federal law enforcement's use of electronic surveillance that adopted precisely that procedure. California, however, declined to follow suit. Until quite recently, California state law criminalized all wiretaps that did not have the consent of both parties, with an exception only for certain narcotics-related law-enforcement matters. See Privacy Rights Clearinghouse, http://www.privacyrights.org/fs/fs9-wrtp.htm#wt2, accessed July 26, 2008.

Page 212. In addition to trying: "Police Warned on Secret Wire Taps, Officers Subject to Liability for Illegal Entry, Brown Says," *Los Angeles Times*, September 4, 1954.

Page 212. The case of *Cahan*: Lieberman, "Cop Befriends Crook," *Los Angeles Times*, October 29, 2008.

Page 213. Traynor served notice that: Liptak, "U.S. Is Alone in Rejecting All Evidence if Police Err," *New York Times*, July 19, 2008.

Page 213. "Today one of the . . .": "Hidden Mike Barred, Beverly Bookie Case Upset by High Court," *Hollywood Citizen-News*, April 28, 1955.

Page 213. "The positive implication drawn: Earlier that year the Chandlers' *Mirror* had bought out Manchester Boddy's *Daily News*, creating the *Mirror-News*. For Parker's statistics, see "Criminals Laugh at LA Police, Says Chief. Underworld Rejoices in Ruling," *Los Angeles Mirror–Daily News*, May 31, 1955.

Chapter Nineteen: The Enemy Within

Page 215. "He is intent on . . .": Hecht Papers, Newberry Library, Chicago.

Page 215. "There is not a: "Mickey Can't have L.A. Bar, Officers Rule," *Hollywood Citizen-News*, October 10, 1955.

Page 215. "When I was on . . .": Cohen, Hecht manuscript, 63, Hecht Papers, Newberry Library.

Page 216. Several months after: The timing of the meeting between Hecht, Preminger, and Cohen is problematic. Brad Lewis's *Hollywood's Celebrity Gangster* places the meeting in the late 1940s or 1950s, well before the 1955 film was made (71). It is nonetheless possible that Preminger was reading Nelson Algren's book, published in 1949.

Page 217. On the appointed: Hecht manuscript, 1–3, 18–19, Hecht Papers, Newberry Library.

Page 218. Not anymore. The postprison: Hecht manuscript, 13–14, Hecht Papers, Newberry Library. See also Cohen to Hecht, March 22, 1964, Hecht Papers, Newberry Library. Cohen, *In My Own Words*, 64, offers a slightly different recollection.

According to Hecht, Mickey originally brought him a 150-page typed manuscript that he said he had dictated. "Mickey Cohen Takes Manuscript to Author," *Los Angeles Times*, August 4, 1957, 34. The Newberry Library contains fragments of this apparent manuscript.

Page 218. LaVonne thought Mickey: Lewis, *Hollywood's Celebrity Gangster*, 193, 196.

Page 219. One night after midnight: The word *gilgul* means "cycle" in Hebrew and refers to a concept of reincarnation from the Kabbalistic tradition. Hecht manuscript, 16–17, 70–71, Hecht Papers, Newberry Library.

Page 219. Chief Parker would have: Lieberman, "Cop Befriends Crook," *Los Angeles Times*, October 29, 2008.

Page 220. By 1956, the Kennedys: The extent of Joseph Kennedy's involvement in bootlegging is often exaggerated. Contrary to public myth, the Kennedy family fortune was not based on illegal liquor. Joseph Kennedy's father, P. J., had owned a series of saloons and liquor distributorships well before Prohibition, but it was Kennedy's financial prowess (and his decision to bail out before the crash of 1929), as well as a series of savvy investments in Hollywood that increased the family's resources so dramatically in the late 1920s and 1930s. That said, even though it was hardly necessary financially, Kennedy seems to have occasionally dabbled in bootlegging. See Fox, *Blood and Power*, 19–20; Thomas, *Robert Kennedy: His Life*, 41.

Page 221. Kennedy had long been: Thomas, *Robert Kennedy: His Life*, 62–3, 71.

Page 222. Soon thereafter, in August: Thomas, *Robert Kennedy: His Life*, 72; Kennedy, *The Enemy Within, 18–21*.

Page 223. Parker took Kennedy's visit: Thomas, *Robert Kennedy: His Life*, 74.

Page 223. At the end of: Kennedy, *The Enemy Within*, 8.

Page 225. One day in the: Author interview with Harold Sullivan, July 26, 2007.

Page 226. The turning point came: Author interview with Joe Parker, December 12–13, 2004.

Chapter Twenty: The Mike Wallace Interview

Page 229. "I killed no men . . .": Mickey Cohen to Mike Wallace, May 19, 1957; Wallace and Gates, *Close Encounters*, 49.

Page 229. When Mickey Cohen: In 1950, Graham switched from describing his revivals as "Campaigns" to calling them "Crusades." Graham, *Just As I Am*, 163.

Page 230. Richardson responded by saying: Graham, *Just As I Am*, 150, 162, 174–75, 190–92.

Page 230. Graham and Cohen had: See Jennings, "The Private Life of a Hood," conclusion, October 11, 1958, for an admission from "Picked for Cohen Role in Film, Skelton Says," *Los Angeles Times*, May 25, 1961, 2. W. C. Jones admitted to only about $18,000 in gifts.

Page 231. "He's invited me . . .": "Mickey Cohen Sees Billy Graham, Talks on Religion, Former Mobster Goes to N.Y. for Conference," *Los Angeles Times*, April 2, 1957, B1.

Page 231. In the summer of: Adams, "Mike Wallace Puts Out Dragnet to Line Up 'Talent' for His New Show," *New York Times*, April 21, 1957, 105; Wallace and Gates, *Close Encounters*, 21–24, 32–33.

Page 232. That fall: Wallace and Gates, *Close Encounters*, 45.

Page 232. Wallace's interviews: Author interview with Al Ramrus, March 18, 2008; Wallace and Gates, *Close Encounters*, 31–32.

Page 233. When Ramrus contacted Mickey: Cohen, *In My Own Words*, 171. The claim that Billy Graham pushed Cohen to talk to Mike Wallace should be viewed with a certain degree of skepticism since Mickey himself is the sole source for this claim. Jennings, "Private Life of a Hood, Part III," October 4, 1958, reports that Cohen also received $1,800 for expenses.

Page 233. When Cohen flew: Author inteview with Al Ramrus, March 18, 2008, provides most of the account that follows. See also Wallace and Gates, *Close Encounters*, 48–53. Wallace recalled another companion named Arlene—presumably the nightclub dancer Arlene Stevens—and places Mickey in the Hampshire House. Wallace, *Between You and Me*, 160–67.

Page 235. "I have a police chief": Wallace and Gates, *Close Encounters*, 50; Wallace, *Between You and Me*, 161–63.

Page 236. "Well, Mickey, you're a . . .": "Important Story," *Time*, June 3, 1957; "Parker Seeks Grand Jury Action Over Cohen Blast," *Los Angeles Times*, May 21, 1957, B1.

Page 236. Mickey Cohen wasn't: See Harnisch, "Cohen Talks," for an interesting discussion of the controversy about whether to air the episode on the West Coast and an explanation of kinescope technology. Harnish, *Daily Mirror* blog (http://latimesblogs.latimes.com/thedailymirror/2007/05/cohen-talks.html).

Page 236. The *Mike Wallace Interview*: Wallace and Gates, *Close Encounters,* 50–51; Wallace, *Between You and Me,* 163–64.

Page 238. Cohen was enraged by: "A.B.C.-TV Retracts Remarks by Cohen," *New York Times,* May 27, 1957, 44.

Page 238. Cohen, meanwhile, was dealing: "Cohen Attends Graham Rally in New York," *Los Angeles Times,* May 22, 1957, 10. See also Jennings, "The Private Life of a Hood," conclusion, October 11, 1958. Brad Lewis, *Hollywood's Celebrity Gangster,* says Cohen was paid $15,000 to attend the rally (206). There are no further records of direct encounters between the two men, although evidently Graham's father-in-law, Dr. Nelson Bell, himself a distinguished preacher, stayed in touch.

Page 239. "They can't get away . . .": "Cohen Booked for Not Signing Traffic Ticket," *Los Angeles Times,* May 26, 1957, 1; "Mickey Cohen's Traffic Trial Off to Salty Start, Policemen Who Made Arrest Testify That Defendant Delayed Autos at Intersection," *Los Angeles Times,* July 11, 1957, 5.

Page 240. Los Angeles–area: "Cohen Found Guilty, Gets $11 Traffic Fine," *Los Angeles Times,* November 12, 1957, 5; "Cohen Jailed for Failure to Register," *Los Angeles Mirror,* September 26, 1957, accessed October 12, 2008, via Larry Harnisch's *Daily Mirror* blog (http://latimesblogs.latimes.com/thedailymirror/mickey_cohen/index.html); "Jury Acquits Mickey Cohen on Disturbing Peace Charge, Ex-Convict Ruling May Affect Case," *Los Angeles Times,* December 17, 1957, 2.

Page 240. "I didn't know a . . .": Lewis, *Hollywood's Celebrity Gangster,* 208. The profitability of the greenhouse business is somewhat unclear. For a positive assessment of its cash flow, see Salazar, "Violence Marks Cohen's History," *Los Angeles Times,* July 2, 1961.

Page 240. Henceforth, Mickey would focus: "Chicago Attorney Glad to Stake Mickey Cohen, Admits $22,500 Loan; Says Ex-Gambler Stands to Make Fortune on Life Story," *Los Angeles Times,* June 9, 1958, 19.

Page 240. Back in New York: Ramrus interview, March 18, 2008; Wallace and Gates, *Close Encounters,* 52–53.

Page 241. For the most part: Wallace and Gates, *Close Encounters,* 52.

Page 242. "That is a big . . .": Fox, *Blood and Power,* 325–26.

Page 242. The very next day: Fox, *Blood and Power,* 326. For a different account of the gangsters' response to the police raid, see Hilty, *Robert Kennedy, Brother Protector,* 124.

Page 242. It was clear that: Ben Hecht Papers, Newberry Library.

Page 243. Back in Washington, Robert: Thomas, *Robert Kennedy: His Life,* 82.

Page 243. One year earlier the: Russo, *The Outfit,* 317.

Page 244. "The results of the . . .": Kennedy, *The Enemy Within,* 229.

Chapter Twenty-one: The Electrician

Page 245. "[W]hat's the meaning in . . .": Cohen, *In My Own Words,* 193–95.

Page 245. By late 1958, Mickey: Otash, *Investigation Hollywood!,* 179–86.

Page 245. Cohen had the temperament: Gabler, *An Empire of Their Own,* 152.

Page 245. But in 1958, Cohn: "A Star Is Made," *Time,* July 29, 1957.

Page 246. There's another more plausible: There are many versions of this episode in Davis's life. See Fishgall, *Gonna Do Great Things,* 114, for the most convincing.

Page 247. Whatever version: Jennings, "Private Life of a Hood," part two, September 27, 1958, 117.

Page 247. In this, he was: Cohen, *In My Own Words*, 187.

Page 248. The day after Stompanato's: See, for instance, "Lana's Romance with Stompanato Cools: Star Asks to Be Left Alone," *Chicago Daily Tribune*, April 10, 1958, 8.

Page 248. Renay was a sometime: Renay, *My Face for the World to See*, 129–32.

Page 248. Meanwhile, Cohen and Hecht: "$200,000 Tax Writeoff Offer to Cohen Told," *Los Angeles Times*, June 8, 1961, 29.

Page 249. On the whole, though: "Lawmen Blast High Court Order to Identify Informants in Arrests: Ruling Termed Crippling in Drive on Dope," *Los Angeles Mirror-News*, October 2, 1958; "Poulson Cuts Police Budget by $6 Million, Commissioner Promptly Warns Mayor that City Faces Criminal Invastion," *Los Angeles Times*, May 1, 1959.

Page 249. "It won't be long,": Woods, "The Progressives and Police," 446.

Page 249. "Anything she says is . . .": "Mickey Cohen Proud of Actress in Murder Quiz, Admits Liz Renay, Questioned in Anastasia Case, Loaned Him $10,000 He's Repaying," *Los Angeles Times*, February 27, 1958, C12.

Page 250. "Her red hair was . . .": "Girl Friend of Mickey Cohen Quizzed Again, Won't Tell Treasury Agent About Gifts from Bodyguard of Slain Anastasia," *Los Angeles Times*, September 10, 1958, B1.

Page 250. The next day, Cohen: Lewis, *Hollywood's Celebrity Gangster*, 244. See also http://www.boxrec.com/list_bouts.php?human_id=166332&cat=boxer, accessed 10/25/2008.

Page 251. To celebrate the thumb: Cohen, *In My Own Words*, 193–97.

Chapter Twenty-two: Chocolate City

Page 252. "We are all members . . .": Webb, *The Badge*, 244.

Page 252. The polite word was: To his credit, Parker recognized that this was a problem soon after he became chief and set to work on curbing this unfortunate tendency. "Ex-Sergeant Strange Praises Chief Parker, Remembers Sincerity," *Los Angeles Times*, November 20, 1996, C12.

Page 253. As the 1920s progressed: Bass and Donovan, "The Los Angeles Police Department," 155.

Page 253. As a policeman, Parker: During Chief Davis's tenure as chief, Parker might also have dealt with Lt. Homer Garrott, an African American lieutenant whom Davis made an acting captain. Lomax, "Bradley Makes 'Loot' Just in Time for the Vote on the Police Pay Raise," *Los Angeles Tribune*, October 31, 1958.

Page 253. The primary draw: Parson, *Making a Better World*, xi.

Page 255. Los Angeles even: Escobar, *Race, Police, and the Making of a Political Identity*, 186–203. PBS's American Experience documentary *The Zoot Suit Riots* also provides an excellent account of the era (http://www.pbs.org/wgbh/amex/zoot/index.html; accessed 2/21/2008).

Page 255. "I feel that when . . .": David Williams to Herb Schurter, April 1, 1959; Parker to Williams, April 13, 1959; Williams to Parker, April 21, 1959, LAPD records, CRC.

Page 255. Williams wrote back to: Woods, "The Progressives and the Police," 471.

See also Williams's July 9, 1959, letter to Councilman John Holland, Council File No. 89512, CRC.

Page 256. The spat soon went: "Parker Hits Influx of Parolees to L.A.: Tells City Council of Huge Rise in Crime," *Los Angeles Herald-Express*, March 13, 1959.

Page 256. The black press: Memorandum to the City Council from the Police Commission, "Subject: Council File No. 89512," August 6, 1959, CRC. See also FBI September 4, 1959, report, captioned "Top Hoodlum Program," Parker FBI file.

Page 256. One of Parker's first: This approach dates back to at least the early 1920s, when August Vollmer had pioneered the use of crime maps as a guide to deploy his elite "crime crushers" unit during his year as chief of police in Los Angeles. Today's LAPD uses the computer-mapping tool COMPSTAT in a strikingly similar fashion.

Page 257. The LAPD deployed: Civil Rights Congress, "Is the Police Department Above the Law?" pamphlet, Southern California Library, Los Angeles.

Page 257. Anyone who'd spent: See Wambaugh, *The Blue Knight*, for an excellent (if fictitious) description of the mind of a beat cop in the 1960s.

Page 258. "Any so-called . . .": "Police Investigation Points Up Brutality In Minority Community," *California Eagle*, June 30, 1949.

Page 259. Strange may (or may not): It is worth noting that Strange, like Parker, was a devout Roman Catholic, a fact that undoubtedly elevated her in Parker's estimation. Nor did Sergeant Strange's promotion put her in a position to command white officers. She worked in community relations, in effect as a liaison to the black community. "Ex-Sergeant Strange Praises Chief Parker, Remembers Sincerity," *Los Angeles Times*, November 20, 1996, C12.

Page 260. This represented a failure: "Responses to Questions of the Los Angeles City Council Concerning a Juvenile Gang Attack on a Citizen in Downtown Los Angeles Which Resulted in His Death, Given by Los Angeles Chief of Police W H Parker on December 8, 1953," Los Angeles Police Department files, CRC.

Page 260. "The local juvenile gang . . .": January 29, 1954, Parker letter to Don Thompson, 1953 county grand jury foreman, in response to a letter from him asking about rat packs, Escobar collection.

Page 261. In 1955, Tom Bradley: See Lomax, "Bradley Makes 'Loot' Just in Time for the Vote on the Police Pay Raise," *Los Angeles Tribune*, October 31, 1958, for a glowing account of Bradley's early career.

Page 261. Bradley got the kind: In an August 18, 1955, letter to Seattle police chief H. J. Lawrence, Parker described Bradley's work in the following terms: "In our Public Information Division, we have a Community Relations unit which is staffed by a Negro sergeant and a Mexican officer. The outstanding job that these men have done in dealing with the minority elements of the community has created respect and confidence in this Department. Some of their most valuable contributions have been working with the minority press to prevent the publication of unsubstantiated reports which tended to arouse animosities in the community. They have also developed a close personal liaison with influential leaders in the minority communities. A copy of their job outline is also enclosed." Los Angeles Police department files, Escobar collection.

Page 262. "Parker told me the . . .": Gates, *Chief*, 66.

Page 262. Parker was also buffeted: Woods, "The Progressives and the Police," 441. According to Bradley's authorized biography, Bradley was out fishing when Parker called, and wife Ethel answered the phone. Characteristically, the sphinxlike

Bradley had not informed her that he had taken the exam for lieutenant. (He had also neglected to tell her he was joining the police department or, later, taking the bar exam.) Ethel decided to turn the tables on Bradley this time. She ordered a lieutenant's uniform and let Bradley discover it when he opened his closet. Bradley was so excited that he forgot about the fish in the car. Ethel found them there the next morning. (Payne and Ratzan, *Tom Bradley, the Impossible Dream*, 53.)

This homey anecdote may be untrue. Press accounts from the time state that it was acting chief Richard Simon who promoted Bradley to lieutenant while Parker was away on a fishing trip. (See Lomax, "Bradley Makes 'Loot' Just in Time for the Vote on the Police Pay Raise," *Los Angeles Tribune*, October 31, 1958.) It is possible that Bradley, who was always attuned to the need to reassure white voters of his crime-fighting credentials, changed the story for his biographer in an attempt to claim support from Parker where none had existed. Bradley's strikingly respectful treatment of Parker in his biography lends further credence to this interpretation.

Page 263. Mr. Bradley spoke first: Lomax, "Bradley Makes 'Loot,' Just in Time for the Vote on the Police Pay Raise," *Los Angeles Tribune*, October 31, 1958, reports Bradley's move to Wilshire as a new position befitting Bradley's promotion.

Page 264. "We don't tell him,": "Police Board Member Flays Parker, Quits," *Los Angeles Times*, June 16, 1959; Woods, "The Progressives and Police," 465–66.

Chapter Twenty-three: Disneyland

Page 265. "[Have] gangsters taken over . . .": "The Elemental Force," *Time*, September 28, 1959.

Page 265. Earlier that year, President: "Parker Plans Security for Khrushchev Visit," *Los Angeles Times*, September 7, 1959; "Keep Cool with Mr. K, Chief Parker Tells L.A.," *Los Angeles Mirror-News*, September 7, 1959, 1.

Page 266. Khrushchev was greeted at: In fact, LAPD officers had escorted dignitaries to Disneyland before, including former President Harry Truman. See "Parker Rejects Mr. K. Gripe, Russ Police OKd Ban on Disneyland Tour," *Los Angeles Herald-Express*, September 21, 1959, A6.

Page 267. "We have come to . . .": "The Elemental Force," *Time*, September 28, 1959.

Page 267. Instead of going to: Sherman, "Mr. K Hurls Hot Retort at Poulson," *Los Angeles Times*, September 20, 1959, 1.

Page 267. Chief Parker was offended: "Parker Rejects Mr. K. Gripe, Russ Police OKd Ban on Disneyland Tour," *Los Angeles Herald-Express*, September 21, 1959, A6.

Page 268. The commission's interest in: Sherman, "L.A. Negroes Only Part of Over-All Minority Problem: Concentration of Race Here Is Fifth Largest in United States," *Los Angeles Times*, January 24, 1961, 2.

Page 268. The commission's staff was: "Brutal Tactics Told at Hearing," *Los Angeles Mirror*, January 26, 1960.

Page 269. By the time Chief: Of course, this hardly explained the crime surge, as Los Angeles had been severely underpoliced even before 1950 (and, according to the police complaints dating back to the 1930s, besieged with criminal vagabonds).

Page 270. Parker insisted that there: "Parker Angrily Denies Racial Discrimination: Presents Charts of City Districts, Tells of Undesirables Shipped into Los Angeles," *Los Angeles Times*, January 27, 1960, B2. See also Becker, "Police Brutality on Coast Denied: Los Angeles Chief Answers Charges of Anti-Negro Tactics by His Force," *New York Times*, January 27, 1960, 18. Parker's testimony provoked the following sarcastic letter from Beavers:

Dear Mr. Parker:
Reference is made to your statement to the Civil Rights Commission, as published in the newspapers.
   Your expressions to the effect that opportunities for promotion within the Police Department are based upon qualifications without regard to race, color or creed, encourages the hope that certain discriminatory practices in existence as of July 10, 1959, have been eliminated. It is common knowledge that there are several Negro officers whose educational backgrounds, characters and years of service fully qualify them for assignment to various divisions in the Police Department in which no Negroes were serving seven months ago.
   We note your denial of racial bias did not include an explanation as to why no Negro officers are assigned to the following seven divisions: central Detective Bureau—Homicide—Robbery—Forgery—Auto Theft—Burglary—Narcotics—Administrative Vice and Internal Affairs.
   Your supplying this additional explanation or giving information as to steps being taken to more fully utilize the talents and skills of this group of officers in these various divisions of your organization will be deeply appreciated.

   Very truly yours,
   George Beavers

Page 270. Parker was becoming more: Fumed Parker, "They [the police] were being blamed for all the ills of humanity; they were constantly being bombarded, and I have been nothing but harassed by these elements since I was chief of police. I have been sued repeatedly. I have a suit pending now in the Federal court under the Federal Civil Rights Act."

Page 271. Sitting in the audience: In response to a question from Commissioner Johnson about integration in the department, Parker insisted, in effect, that the department already was integrated—but in a very sly fashion. "Officers may be assigned together and sometimes they are, but not as a matter of discrimination, no . . ." the Chief replied. Consciously mingling partners would be nothing more than "reverse discrimination." Parker attempted a similar move when asked to name the highest-ranking black officers in the department. Parker pointed to Lt. Roscoe Washington and said the only thing holding him back was his performance on the *written* exam—this despite the fact that black officers routinely received low *oral* evaluations. By insisting the problem was a written exam—no bias there!—Parker was, with lawyerly skill, deflecting attention away from the problem of orals scores.

Page 271. Never slow to respond: "Racial Bias Accusations False, Says Chief Parker. Explains Police Problem," *Los Angeles Mirror-News*, January 27, 1960, A.

Page 271. It didn't. Forced to: "Council Hears Parker's Recording on 'Wild Tribes,' Chief Denies Slur, Refuses to Apologize," *Los Angeles Times*, February 3, 1960. See also "Demagoguery Loses a Round," *Los Angeles Times*, February 5, 1960.

Chapter Twenty-four: Showgirls

Page 273. "Girls very often like . . .": Hecht manuscript, 39 Hecht Papers, Newberry Library.

Page 273. The rules were strict: "Lid Off L.A.!" Coates, *Los Angeles Mirror-News*, February 15, 1952.

Page 273. Candy Barr was striptease: Shteir, *Striptease*, 297.

Page 274. Ordinary women were a: Lewis, *Hollywood's Celebrity Gangster*, xii–xiii.

Page 275. By the spring of: Ryan, "Dot-dot-dot—It's Just Like Downtown," *Los Angeles Times*, April 20, 1959, B5.

Page 275. Renay had long been: "Liz Renay Indicted on Perjury Charges: Mickey Cohen's Actress Friend Accused of Lying About Raising $5,500 in Loans," *Los Angeles Times*, March 13, 1959, 4.

Page 276. Inwardly, Mickey grieved: Hulse, "Mickey Cohen to Wed Striptease Dancer, 22," *Los Angeles Times*, October 2, 1959, 4.

Page 276. On December 2, 1959: "Cohen Suspect in Slaying, Restaurant's Guests Flee After Shooting," *Los Angeles Mirror-News*, December 3, 1959; Cohen, "Cohen's Own Story of Café Shooting," *Los Angeles Herald*, December 3, 1959. For more background on Whalen, see also Lieberman, "Cop Befriends a Crook," *Los Angeles Times*, October 29, 2008.

Page 277. "A man walked in . . .": Korman, "Hoodlum Shot to Death, Victim Ripe for Killing, Police Report," *Chicago Daily Tribune*, December 4, 1950, 14.

Page 277. "Obviously, he is,": "Shooting Takes Place Six Feet from Mickey," *Los Angeles Mirror-News*, December 3, 1958.

Page 277. The police then got: "Mickey Cohen Jailed in Murder of Bookie," *Los Angeles Times*, December 4, 1959, 1.

Page 277. Six days later: "Slayer of Bookmaker Surrenders to Police," *Los Angeles Times*, December 9, 1959, 1.

Page 278. Brown called in Chief: "Witnesses Deny They Saw Whalen Shooting," *Los Angeles Times*, March 11, 1960, B32. See also Lieberman, "Noir Justice Catches Up with Mickey Cohen," *Los Angeles Times*, November 1, 2008; "Admits Slaying Bookie, Claims It Was 'Self Defense,' " *Los Angeles Examiner*, December 9, 1959.

Page 278. Prosecutors tried to put: Lieberman, "Noir Justice Catches Up with Mickey Cohen," *Los Angeles Times*, November 1, 2008.

Page 278. The Whalen shooting quickly: Blake, "First Such Convention in City Brings With It Host of New Problems," *Los Angeles Times*, May 30, 1960.

Page 279. The convention began under: "Kennedy's 'Pad' in L.A.—Dirty Shirts and Disorder," *San Francisco Call-Bulletin*, July 15, 1960.

Page 279. From the start, Parker: "Noise, Cheers, Applause, Songs—and 3 Candidates," *Kansas City Times*, April 11, 1960; "Big Squeeze Boosts Police for Kennedy," *Los Angeles Mirror*, July 11, 1960.

Page 279. The LAPD also proved: Fleming, "Stevenson Supporters Try to Invade Arena, Extra Police Rushed to Entrance as Chanting Crowd of 600 Mills About," *Los Angeles Times*, July 14, 1960.

Page 280. By all accounts, the: See, for instance, "The Bright Badge of the L.A.P.D.," *Los Angeles Times* editorial, August 9, 1960, B4.

Page 281. "Eating out of the . . .": Russo, *The Outfit*, 407.

Page 281. Parker was delighted.: "Parker Hails Kennedy as Crime Foe," *Los Angeles Times*, December 17, 1960, 12; "Chief Parker May Head US Crime Probers," *Los Angeles Herald-Express*, December 22, 1960.

Page 281. To the sixty-six: Thomas, *Robert Kennedy: His Life*, 114.

Page 283. "I have a high: "Chief Parker May Head US Crime Probers," *Los Angeles Herald-Express*, December 22, 1960; White, "Parker Takes Swipe at FBI," *Los Angeles Mirror*, December 22, 1960.

Page 283. Ethel was a prankster: Thomas, *Robert Kennedy: His Life*, 117.

Page 283. To Mickey Cohen, the: More specifically, prosecutors charged Cohen with evading roughly $30,000 in taxes between 1956 and 1958 and also with avoiding another $347,000 in taxes (plus interest and penalties) between 1945 and 1950, in addition to several other infringements of the law. See Korman, "Convict Cohen a Second Time Tax Offender: Guilty of Beating U.S. out of $400,000," *Chicago Tribune*, July 1, 1961, 3. Cohen's previous tax conviction had been for avoiding $130,000 in taxes between 1946 and 1948. The decision to charge Cohen with concealing even more income in the immediate postwar years reflected new discoveries about Cohen's gambling income from that era.

Page 284. "There's no question about . . .": Cohen, *In My Own Words*, 195–96.

Page 284. The first investor appeared: "Cohen's Story Contract Presented at His Trial," *Los Angeles Times*, May 19, 1961, 30; "$9,000 Advance for Cohen, Screenplay Told," *Los Angeles Times*, May 20, 1961, 11; Korman, "2 FILM COMICS ADD SPICE TO COHEN'S TRIAL: Jerry Lewis, Skelton on Witness Stand," *Chicago Daily Tribune*, May 25, 1961, A7; "Ben Hecht Sees Cohen as Top Book Material," *Los Angeles Times*, May 18, 1961, B2.

Page 285. The next witness after: "Candy Barr Tells About Being Cohen's 'Sweetie:' Jailed Stripper Testifies How Ex-Hoodlum Helped Her Flee U.S. to Mexico Hideway," *Los Angeles Times*, June 3, 1961, 12.

Page 285. The answer was yes: Caen, "Another World: Search for the Prize Topper," *Los Angeles Times*, June 15, 1960, B5; "U.S. Rests Cohen Income Tax Case," *Los Angeles Times*, June 17, 1961, 9.

Page 286. "I feel it's now . . .": "Cohen Defense Claims He Was Losing Money," *Los Angeles Times*, June 24, 1961, 11.

Page 287. Mickey responded by instructing: Cohen, *In My Own Words*, 205.

Page 288. Reporters noted that he: "Mickey Cohen Jaunty Again—in Volkswagen," *Los Angeles Times*, October 20, 1961, 26.

Page 288. Then, two weeks later: "Mickey Cohen, 4 Others Indicted in Murder Plot, All Accused in Dec. 2, 1959 Slaying of Jack Whalen in Sherman Oaks Cafe," *Los Angeles Times*, November 1, 1961, 2.

Chapter Twenty-five: The Muslim Cult

Page 289. "'Civil disobedience' . . . simply means . . .": Manion, "Anarchy Imminent," May 30, 1965.

Page 289. Police lieutenant Tom Bradley: Indeed, Bradley's promotion and appointment to Wilshire Division was widely seen as a promotion in the black community. Lomax, "Bradley Makes 'Loot,' Just in Time for the Vote on the Police Pay Raise," *Los Angeles Tribune*, October 31, 1958.

Page 291. Poulson, meanwhile, struggled with: Los Angeles has nonpartisan primaries. Any candidate who wins more than 50 percent of the vote in the primary automatically wins election to the office in question. If no candidate wins an outright majority, then the two top vote-getters meet for a rematch in the general election. The top vote-getter in that election then claims the contested office.

Page 292. In his public appearances: See "All Elections Promises Kept, Yorty Asserts. But Black Leaders Flat Contradict His Claim That He Never Promised to Fire Chief Parker," *Los Angeles Herald-Examiner*, July 9, 1962.

Page 292. In fact, Yorty did: Ainsworth, *Maverick Mayor*, 129, 132–33.

Page 293. The next day, newspapers: *Los Angeles Times*, June 9, 1961. See "Two Cited Under Lynch Law After Park Riot," *Los Angeles Times*, June 2, 1961, for an account of the case. See also "This Is not Alabama," *Los Angeles Times* editorial, June 1, 1960.

Page 293. "I have confidence in . . .": Gottlieb and Wolt, *Thinking Big*, 364–65; "Yorty, Parker Clash: Chief Denies Charge of Ballot 'Gestapo,' " *Los Angeles Examiner*, June 9, 1961.

Page 293. Rumor had it that: The rumor seems to have started with councilman Carl Rundberg, who after the mayor and police chief's meeting, expressed a desire to know "what Parker had on Yorty." Parker denied the allegation, but Rundberg rejoined that he personally had heard Parker play back recordings of negative remarks made by Yorty about the police. See *Hollywood Citizen-News*, February 18, 1963.

Daryl Gates would later categorically deny that Parker collected dirt on Yorty and other politicians. Perhaps this is true (although Yorty's allegations seem similar to those leveled by Norris Poulson in 1952). What is striking, though, is that most observers at the time believed he did and feared the chief accordingly. Author interview with Daryl Gates, December 10, 2004.

Page 295. The officers had heard: "Six Muslim Suspects Held in Row at Market," *Los Angeles Times*, September 3, 1961; Branch, *Pillar of Fire*, 4–15.

Page 297. Malcolm X's efforts put: Branch, *Pillar of Fire*, 11. See *Los Angeles Sentinel*, May 17, 1962, for a slightly different account.

Page 297. In early June, a: Woods, "The Progressives and the Police," 476.

Page 298. "The Negro community here . . .": "Parker Assails Bishop's View of Negro Policy," *Los Angeles Times*, January 18, 1963, A1.

Page 299. "This city can't be . . .": Woods, "The Progressives and the Police," 475–76.

Chapter Twenty-six: The Gas Chamber

Page 300. "Don't worry": Cohen, *In My Own Words*, 214.

Page 300. Cohen's indictment arose from: Reid, *Mickey Cohen*, 69; "Officers Out to Get Cohen, LoCigno Says," *Los Angeles Times*, March 22, 1962, A2.

Page 300. Although he was willing: "Under Table, Didn't See Slayer, Cohen Says," *Los Angeles Times*, March 29, 1962, 30.

Page 301. Cohen's attorneys did not: "Cohen's Defense Closes Murder Trial Argument," *Los Angeles Times*, April 5, 1962, 34.

Page 301. "This is a crazy town . . .": Coates, "A Cool Customer in a Hot Spot," *Los Angeles Times*, April 15, 1962, B7.

Page 301. "Although much testimony of . . .": "Mickey Cohen Murder Charges Dismissed," *Los Angeles Times*, March 19, 1962, 2. LoCigno's earlier conviction had been vacated by an appeals court. However, he did not go free. Later that fall, he was convicted of manslaughter and sentenced to one to ten years' imprisonment. "Lo Cigno Rules Guilty of Manslaughter," *Los Angeles Times*, November 15, 1962, B8.

Page 302. Cohen had dodged the: Lewis, *Hollywood's Celebrity Gangster,* 278–79, 280–81.

Page 302. "Don't worry about me,": Cohen, *In My Own Words,* 214.

Page 303. In October, Cohen was: "Mickey Cohen Sues U.S.," *New York Times,* February 18, 1964, 22; Lewis, *Hollywood's Celebrity Gangster,* 284–86.

Page 304. "Violence in Los Angeles . . .": "An Analysis of the McCone Commission Report," California Advisory Committee to the United States Commission on Civil Rights, January 1966, LAPD official records box 84638, CRC.

Page 304. "I doubt that Los . . .": "Police Chief William H. Parker Speaks," a compilation of Parker statements prepared by the Community Relations Conference of Southern California, 2400 South Western Avenue, Los Angeles, California, available in Parker's FBI file, 62-96042-109.

Chapter Twenty-seven: Watts

Page 306. "This community has done . . .": Woods, "The Progressives and the Police," 475–76.

Page 306. Minikus told Marquette that: My account of the beginning of the riots comes from Robert Conot's *Rivers of Blood, Years of Darkness* (6–29) and from the Governor's Commission on the Los Angeles Riots report (the so-called McCone Commission), issued December 5, 1965, reprinted in Robert Fogelson, ed., *Mass Violence in America* (10–23). Frye would later challenge this account, claiming that the Highway Patrol officer had been preparing to release him until other officers arrived with a nastier attitude. See Horne, *The Fire Next Time,* 54.

Page 307. It was a sweltering: Conot, *Rivers of Blood, Years of Darkness,* 6.

Page 308. Gates had enjoyed a: *Los Angeles Herald-Examiner,* June 2, 1965, CRC scrapbook.

Page 308. What he saw was: Gates, *Chief,* 90.

Page 309. The police had regrouped: In fact, thanks to the strike at Harvey Aluminum, L.A. County sheriff Peter Pritchess had also placed a sizable number of deputy sheriffs on alert near the area—roughly two hundred. Nothing prevented Deputy Chief Murdock from calling them in as assistance. Yet no calls were made that night to the sheriff's department. Conot, *Rivers of Blood, Years of Darkness,* 50, 65.

This characterization of the early morning comes from the McCone Commission report, cited above. Gates, *Chief,* 90–91, portrays events of the first morning in a less positive light.

Page 310. Chief Parker did not: " 'Pseudoleaders Who Can't Lead,' Blamed by Parker," *Los Angeles Herald-Examiner,* August 15, 1965; "Los Angeles Police Chief William H. Parker 3d," *New York Times,* August 14, 1965.

Page 312. Around midnight, the comedian: Gregory, *Call On My Soul,* 111.

Page 312. They didn't. By 4: Gates, *Chief,* 99.

Page 312. At 9:45 a.m., Parker: Parker would later claim that Colonel Quick, the National Guard liaison present at the 9:45 LAPD staff meeting, had received the request and promised the chief to submit it immediately. Colonel Quick, in contrast, would recall a more general conversation, one that did not include a direct and specific request for the Guard.

Page 313. At 11 a.m., Governor Brown's: Anderson did order the Guard to marshal forces at local armories at 5 p.m. Friday afternoon, in the event a call-up was necessary. Anderson would tell the McCone Commission that he had been advised that a five o'clock call out was the earliest time feasible for a guard deployment. Unaware of the location of the Third Brigade, the lieutenant governor thus felt that he had the afternoon to investigate and deliberate.

Page 313. To Parker, it was: Gottlieb and Wolt, *Thinking Big*, 378.

Page 314. The other important freeway: Author interview with Harold Sullivan, July 26, 2007.

Page 315. Friday night brought something: Horne, *Fire This Time*, 72.

Page 315. Desperate to restore order: According to the McCone Commission, the maximum deployment of the LAPD during the riots was 934 officers; the maximum for the sheriff's department was 719 officers. For an account of Parker's television appearance, see Conot, *Rivers of Blood, Years of Darkness*, 348–49.

Page 315. To groups like: Horwitt, *Let Them Call Me Rebel*, xv.

Page 316. Still, King tried to: Horne, *Fire This Time*, 183.

Page 316. To Mayor Sam Yorty: Parker's concerns about communist agitation would at one time have been quite understandable. According to Horne, during the 1940s, Los Angeles "had one of the highest concentrations of Communists in the nation," with roughly 4,000 card-carrying members. However, by 1965, the power the party once held over Hollywood's unions and the city's trade unions— and in L.A.'s African American community—had been broken. In comparison, the Nation of Islam (which Parker insisted on viewing as some adjunct of the party) emphasized an almost Booker T. Washington–like ideology of black self-sufficiency. Horne, *Fire This Time*, 5, 11. See also Hertel and Blake, "Parker Hints Muslims Took Part in Rioting," *Los Angeles Times*, August 17, 1965.

Page 316. At 2 a.m. on the: LAPD informant Louis Tackwood would later claim that he had instigated the call at the department's behest. Horne, *Fire This Time*, 126; Erwin Baker, "Mills Tells Parker to Explain Raid: Chief Denies Councilman Has Right to Quiz Him on Muslims," *Los Angeles Times*, November 9, 1965, 3. Parker later agreed to testify. "L.A. Councilmen to Hear Parker," *Valley-Times*, September 11, 1965.

Page 317. The following day, the: Horne, *Fire This Time*, 127–28.

Page 318. On August 29: "Chief William Parker Speaks," Parker FBI file.

Page 319. California governor Pat Brown: Fogelson, "White on Black," 114.

Page 319. The testimony of many: Fogelson, "White on Black," 124, quoting testimony of Mervyn Dymally, "statement prepared for the Governor's Commission on the Los Angeles Riots," October 11, 1965, 2.

Page 319. Parker, Ferraro, and Yorty: Fogelson, "White on Black," 126, quoting testimony of Mervyn Dymally, "statement prepared for the Governor's Commission on the Los Angeles Riots," October 11, 1965, 2.

Page 319. Civil rights leaders attacked: See Rustin, "The Watts 'Manifesto' and the McCone Report," 147, for the typical reading of this statement.

Page 320. "I have my suspicions": "Riot Hearings Boil, Parker, Bradley in Row Over 'Mystery Man,'" *Los Angeles Herald-Examiner*, September 14, 1965. See also *Dallas Morning News*, September 14, 1965.

Page 320. Parker's combative appearances belied: Memorandum from Acting Chief Richard Simon to Police Commission, "Subject: Request for Five Additional Positions of Lt of Police to Be Community Relations Officers," October 12, 1965, CRC.

Page 321. But the commission raised: See the section of the McCone Commission report entitled "Law Enforcement—the Thin Thread"; Rustin, "The Watts 'Manifesto' and the McCone Report," 153.

Page 322. "I think they're afraid: *Los Angeles Times*, January 24, 1966.

Page 322. Parker's popularity dissuaded the: von Hoffman, "L.A. Chief Overlooked a Bad Heart to Serve," *Washington Post*, July 18, 1966, A1.

Page 323. Privately, however, many recognized: FBI memorandum to Mr. Felt from H. L. Edars, "Subject: NDAA Midyear Meeting, Tucson, AZ," March 4, 1966, Parker FBI file; "Parker Out of Hospital, Will Rest," *Hollywood Citizen-News*, March 15, 1965.

Page 323. The memo concluded by: It should also be noted that Parker believed that, after rising 130 percent in nine years, crime had "plateaued." Newsom, "Men Efficient, Vigilant, Brave, Chief Relates," *Hollywood Citizen-News*, June 20, 1965.

Page 324. On the evening of: West, "Chief Parker Collapses, Dies at Award Banquet, Stricken During Standing Ovation by Marine Veterans," *Los Angeles Times*, July 16, 1966.

Page 324. "His death will be: Houston, "Police Chief Parker's Death Mourned in City and State, Meeting May Be Today to Name his Successor," *Los Angeles Times*, July 19, 1966; "Friends, Critics Praise Parker," *Los Angeles Herald-Examiner*, June 18, 1966.

Page 324. At the funeral home: "6000 Pay Last Tribute to Parker, Chief Eulogized in Congress," *Los Angeles Herald-Examiner*, July 21, 1966, A16.

Chapter Twenty-eight: R.I.P.

Page 326. "I don't want to . . .": Lewis, *Hollywood's Gangster Celebrity*, 318.

Page 327. "The notions in it,": Domanick, *To Protect and to Serve*, 155–56; Woods, "The Progressives and the Police," 502.

Page 327. Four LAPD patrol cars: Gates, *Chief*, 147–53. Information about the LAPD's secret policy of providing police escorts to visiting dignitaries comes from an author interview with former police commissioner Frank Hathaway, February 17, 2008.

Page 328. "I'm gonna use you . . .": Cohen, *In My Own Words*, 233.

Page 328. "I got a definite . . .": Cohen, *In My Own Words*, 234–36.

Page 329. Once again, a crowd: Lewis, *Hollywood's Celebrity Gangster*, 307.

Page 329. Then it was on: Cohen, *In My Own Words*, 238–43.

Page 331. In September 1975, Mickey: Lewis, *Hollywood's Celebrity Gangster*, 325.

Epilogue

Page 333. "This city is plagued . . .": Mydans, " 'It Could Happen Again,' Report on Los Angeles Riots Blames Police and City," *New York Times*, October 25, 1992.

Page 333. In 1969, LAPD: Woods, "The Progressives and the Police," 504.

Page 333. Just before: "Politics and the LAPD," *Los Angeles Times*, April 11, 1969, C6.

Page 333. Reddin's decision to step: Woods, "The Progressives and the Police," 505; Cannon, *Official Negligence*, 88.

Page 334. It took Bradley: Dominick, *To Protect and to Serve*, 160, 294.

Page 334. In January 1978, after: Cannon, *Official Negligence*, 90. After his resignation in 1978, Davis did run for office, winning election as a Republican to the state senate in 1980.

Page 334. Mayor Bradley didn't want: Gates, *Chief*, 174.

Page 335. "You know," Gates replied: Gates, *Chief*, 176.

Page 336. There were three passengers: Lou Cannon's *Official Negligence* provides a convincing—and strikingly revisionist—account of the Rodney King beatings. For anyone interested in the history of Los Angeles, the LAPD, or policing in general, Cannon's book is a must-read.

Page 337. The LAPD hierarchy was: Gates, *Chief*, 316, 318.

Page 337. The Police Commission, whose: Gates, *Chief*, 340.

Page 337. Three months later, on: Cannon, *Official Negligence*, 142–44.

Page 338. One of the commission's most: Gates, *Chief*, 348–49; Cannon, *Official Negligence*, 139.

Page 339. Gates immediately recognized that: Gates, *Chief*, 351.

Page 340. At least, that was: Cannon, *Official Negligence*, 264.

Page 341. The mood at police: Cannon, *Official Negligence*, 300.

Page 342. Gates did not return: Cannon, *Official Negligence*, 305, 341.

Page 343. On June 2: Cannon, *Official Negligence*, 356; "Final Election Returns," *Los Angeles Times*, June 4, 1992, A20. See also Sahagun, "Riots Transform Campaign on Police Reform," *Los Angeles Times*, May 31, 1992, B1; and Berger, "Elections '92 LAPD Disciplinary System to Undergo Major Restructuring Police," *Los Angeles Times*, June 4, 1992, B3.

Select Bibliography

A Note on Sources:

Many of the periodicals cited in the Notes and below came from the LAPD scrapbooks at the City Records Center (CRC) in Los Angeles. Often these clippings lack page numbers or even headlines. I have tried to provide the most complete citation possible, citing the paper's name at the time of each article publication. (The scrapbooks may be reviewed in person at the City Records Center at the Piper Technical Center downtown.)

Files identified as LAPD departmental records are stored at the CRC but are not available to the general public.

Adams, Val. "Mike Wallace Puts Out Dragnet to Line Up 'Talent' for His New Show," *New York Times*, April 21, 1957.

Ainsworth, Ed. *Maverick Mayor: A Biography of Sam Yorty, Mayor of Los Angeles*. Garden City, N.Y.: Doubleday, 1966.

Alexander, David. *Star Trek Creator: The Authorized Biography of Gene Roddenberry*. New York: ROC, 1994.

Anderson, Clinton. *Beverly Hills Is My Beat*. Englewood Cliffs, N.J.: Prentice-Hall, 1960.

Baker, Erwin. "Mills Tells Parker to Explain Raid: Chief Denies Councilman Has Right to Quiz Him on Muslims," *Los Angeles Times,* November 9, 1965.

Bass, Sandra, and John T. Donovan. "The Los Angeles Police Department" in *The Development of Los Angeles City Government: An Institutional History, 1850–2000*. Los Angeles: Los Angeles City Historical Society, 2007.

Becker, Bill. "Police Brutality on Coast Denied: Los Angeles Chief Answers Charges of Anti-Negro Tactics by His Force," *New York Times*, January 27, 1960.

Berger, Leslie. "Elections '92 LAPD Disciplinary System to Undergo Major Restructuring Police," *Los Angeles Times,* June 4, 1992.

Blake, Gene. "First Such Convention in City Brings with It Host of New Problems," *Los Angeles Times*, May 30, 1960.

Branch, Taylor. *Pillar of Fire: America in the King Years 1963–65*. New York: Simon and Schuster, 1998.

———. *At Canaan's Edge: America in the King Years 1965–1968*. New York: Simon & Schuster, 2006.

Caen, Herb. "Another World: Search for the Prize Topper," *Los Angeles Times*, June 15, 1960.

Caldwell, B. R. Letter to HQ, Los Angeles Procurement District, February 23, 1943. William H. Parker Police Foundation archives.

California Advisory Committee to the United States Commission on Civil Rights. "An Analysis of the McCone Commission Report." January 1966. LAPD official records box 84638, City Records Center.

California Eagle. "Police Investigation Points Up Brutality In Minority Community." June 30, 1949.

California Special Crime Study Commission on Organized Crime reports. March 7, 1949; January 31, 1950; November 15, 1950; and May 11, 1953. Sacramento, California.

Cannon, Lou. *Official Negligence: How Rodney King and the Riots Changed Los Angeles and the LAPD*. New York: Times Books, 1997.

Carte, Gene, and Elaine Carte. *Police Reform in the United States: The Era of August Vollmer*. Berkeley: University of California Press, 1975.

Chandler, Raymond. "The Simple Art of Murder." *The Atlantic Monthly*. December 1944.

———. *The Big Sleep and Farewell, My Lovely*. New York: The Modern Library, 1995.

Chicago Daily Tribune. "Lana's Romance with Stompanato Cools: Star Asks to Be Left Alone." April 10, 1958.

Chicago Sun-Times. "Ex-Marine Tightened Up Los Angeles Police." March 12, 1952.

Chicago Tribune. "Cohen Admits Big Gambling Take in Hotel Dice Games," June 22, 1961.

City Council Minutes. August 14, 1934, 234–35.

———. Vol. 249, October 5, 1934, 18. Los Angeles City Archives, Piper Technical Center.

———. Vol. 247, June 14, 1934, 248. See also the attached city council files, Los Angeles City Archives, Piper Technical Center, File No. 3140 (1934).

———. Vol. 248, August 14, 1934, 235–36. See City Council Minutes, August 15, 1934.

———. Memorandum to the City Council from the Police Commission, "Subject: Council File No. 89512," August 6, 1959, CRC.

City News Service. "Parker Hits at Highest Court Ruling in Irvine 'Bookie' Case," *Los Angeles Journal*, February 19, 1954.

Civil Rights Congress, "Is the Police Department Above the Law?" pamphlet, Southern California Library, Los Angeles.

Clarke, John, and Joseph Saldana, "True Life Story of Mickey Cohen." July 1949.

Coates, Paul. "Midnight Memo to the Mayor," *Los Angeles Mirror*. July 20, 1953.

———. "Lid Off L.A.!" *Los Angeles Mirror-News*, February 15, 1952.

———. "A Cool Customer in a Hot Spot." *Los Angeles Times*, April 15, 1962.

Cohen, Michael. "Cohen's Own Story of Café Shooting." *Los Angeles Herald*, December 3, 1959. CRC scrapbook.

Cohen, Mickey. Unpublished manuscript, n.p., Hecht Papers, Newberry Library, Chicago.

Cohen, Mickey, as told to John Peer Nugent. *In My Own Words*. Englewood Cliffs, N.J.: Prentice-Hall, Inc., 1975.

Cohen letter to Hecht, March 22, 1964. Newberry Library, Chicago.

Conot, Robert. *Rivers of Blood, Years of Darkness: The Unforgettable Classic Account of the Watts Riot*. New York: Bantam, 1967.

Cosmopolitan. "Portrait of a Punk."

Davidson, Bill. "The Mafia Can't Crack Los Angeles." *Saturday Evening Post*, July 31, 1965.

Davis, Clark. "The View from Spring Street: White-Collar Men in the City of Angeles" in *Metropolis in the Making*.

Demaris, Ovid. *The Last Mafioso: The Treacherous World of Jimmy Fratianno*. New York: Times Books, 1981.

Dixon, Jane. "Problems of a Working Girl: Queer Aspects of Human Nature Exhibited to Quiet and Watchful Theater Workers, Says Love Is Catching 'Like the Measles.'" *Los Angeles Times*, July 15, 1919.

Domanick, Joe. *To Protect and to Serve: The LAPD's Century of War in the City of Dreams*. New York: Pocket Books, 1994.

Donner, Frank. *The Age of Surveillance: The Aims and Methods of America's Political Intelligence System*. New York: Random House, 1980.

Escobar, Edward. *Race, Police, and the Making of a Political Identity: Mexican-Americans and the Los Angeles Police Department 1900–1945*. Los Angeles: University of California Press, 1999.

——— "Bloody Christmas and the Irony of Police Professionalism: The Los Angeles Police Department, Mexican Americans, and Police Reform in the 1950s," *Pacific Historical Review* 72, 2.

Ethington, Philip. "The Global Spaces of Los Angeles, 1920s–1930s" in Gyan Prakash and Kevin Kruse, eds., *The Spaces of the Modern City*. Princeton, NJ: Princeton University Press, 2008.

Federal Bureau of Investigation, Freedom of Information Act files: Meyer Harris Cohen, File #7-HQ-5908, 58-HQ-6129, 92-HQ-3156; James Dragna; William H. Parker (see in particular August 2, 1963, memo, Parker FBI file, for the origins of the FBI feud); Johnny Roselli; Bugsy Siegel; and Lana Turner.

Findley, James Clifford. "The Economic Boom of the 'Twenties in Los Angeles," unpublished dissertation, Claremont (California) Graduate School, 1958.

Fishgall, Gary. *Gonna Do Great Things: The Life of Sammy Davis, Jr.* New York: Simon & Schuster, 2003.

Fleming, Lou. "Stevenson Supporters Try to Invade Arena, Extra Police Rushed to Entrance as Chanting Crowd of 600 Mills About." *Los Angeles Times*, July 14, 1960.

Fogelson, Robert. *Big City Police*. Cambridge, Mass.: Harvard University Press, 1977.

———. *The Fragmented Metropolis: Los Angeles, 1850–1930*. Los Angeles: University of California Press, 1993.

———, ed. *Mass Violence in America: The Los Angeles Riots*. New York: Arno Press, 1969.

————. "White on Black: A Critique of the McCone Commission Report on the Los Angeles Riots" in Robert Fogelson, ed. *The Los Angeles Riots*. New York: Arno Press, 1969.

Ford, John Anson. *Honest Politics My Theme*. New York: Vantage Press, 1978.

Fox, Stephen. *Blood and Power: Organized Crime in Twentieth-Century America*. New York: Penguin, 1989.

Frank, Benis, interviewer. "Oral History Transcript: General William Worton." Washington, D.C.: Historical Division, Headquarters, U.S. Marine Corps.

Frawley, Harry. "Police Board Will Use More Power—Mayor." *Valley Times*, August 8, 1950.

Friedrich, Otto. *City of Nets: A Portrait of Hollywood in the 1940's*. New York: Harper & Row, 1986.

Gabler, Neil. *An Empire of Their Own: How the Jews Invented Hollywood*. New York: Doubleday, 1989.

Garland, Hamlin. *Diaries*. San Marino, Calif.: Huntington Library, 1968, p. 40.

Gates, Daryl. *Chief: My Life in the L.A.P.D.* New York: Bantam Books, 1992.

Giesler, Jerry. *Hollywood Lawyer: The Jerry Giesler Story*. New York: Simon & Schuster, 1960.

Gottlieb, Robert, and Irene Wolt. *Thinking Big: The Story of the Los Angeles Times and Its Publishers and Their Impact on Southern California*. New York: Putnam, 1977.

Governor's Commission on the Los Angeles Riots, issued December 5, 1965. Reprinted in Robert Fogelson, ed. *Mass Violence in America: The Los Angeles Riots*.

Graham, Billy. *Just As I Am*. New York: Harper SanFrancisco, 1997.

Gregory, Dick. *Callus on My Soul: A Memoir*. New York: Kensington Books, 2002.

Harnisch, Larry. "Cohen Talks." *Daily Mirror Blog*, http://latimesblogs.latimes.com/thedailymirror/2007/05/cohen_talks.html.

Hayde, Michael. *My Name's Friday: The Unauthorized but True Story of* Dragnet *and the Films of Jack Webb*. Nashville: Cumberland House, 2001.

Hecht, Ben. Unpublished draft of Mickey Cohen biography dated February 6, 1959. Box 7. Ben Hecht Papers, Newberry Library, Chicago, IL.

————. *A Child of the Century*. New York: Simon & Schuster, 1954.

Henstell, Bruce. *Sunshine and Wealth: Los Angeles in the Twenties and Thirties*. San Francisco: Chronicle Books, 1984.

Hertel, Howard, and Gene Blake. "Parker Hints Muslims Took Part in Rioting." August 17, 1965.

Hill. Gladwin. "5-Year Term Given to Mickey Cohen; Judge Finds Gambler 'Not So Bad." *New York Times*, July 10, 1951.

Hilty, James W. *Robert Kennedy, Brother Protector*. Philadelphia: Temple University Press, 1997.

Hollywood Citizen-News. "Mickey Shifted to New Jail to End 'Privileges,' Crowding at County Bastille the Official Cause," February 8, 1952, CRC scrapbooks.

————. "Parker Hints at Crackdown, Own Cleanup May Forestall Jury Action," March 27, 1952.

————. "4 Named to Police Board by Poulson," July 2, 1953.

———. "Hidden Mike Barred, Beverly Bookie Case Upset by High Court," April 28, 1955.

———. "Mickey Can't Have L.A. Bar, Officers Rule," October 10, 1955.

———. Untitled article, February 18, 1963.

———. "Parker Out of Hospital, Will Rest," March 15, 1965.

Hopkins, Ernest Jerome. *Our Lawless Police: A Study of Unlawful Law Enforcement.* New York: Viking, 1931.

Horne, Gerald. *Fire This Time: The Watts Uprising and the 1960s.* Charlottesville, VA: University of Virginia Press, 1995.

Horwitt, Sanford. *Let Them Call Me Rebel.* New York: Knopf, 1989.

Hulse, Jerry. "Mickey Cohen to Wed Striptease Dancer, 22." *Los Angeles Times,* October 2, 1959.

Hurewitz, Daniel. *Bohemian Los Angeles and the Making of Modern Politics.* Los Angeles: University of California Press, 2007.

Houston, Paul. "Police Chief Parker's Death Mourned in City and State, Meeting May Be Today to Name His Successor." *Los Angeles Times,* June 19, 1966.

Irey, Hugh, "An Open Letter to the Mayor: Ex-Official Tells LA Police Stymie." *Los Angeles Mirror,* July 13, 1953.

———. "Police Dept. 'Split' Bared." *Los Angeles Mirror,* July 14, 1953.

Jacoby, Norman. "Highlights in the Life of the Chief of Police." *Eight Ball,* March 1966. William H. Parker Police Foundation archives.

Jennings, Dean. *We Only Kill Each Other: The Life and Bad Times of Bugsy Siegel.* New York: Penguin, 1992.

———. "MICKEY COHEN: The Private Life of a Hood." *Saturday Evening Post,* parts 1–4, September 20, 1958; September 27, 1958; October 4, 1958; and October, 1958.

———. "Portrait of a Police Chief." *Saturday Evening Post,* May 7, 1960.

Johnson, David R. "Siegel, Bugsy." http://anb.org/articles/20/20-01749.html; American National Biography Online Feb. 2000, access date: July 17, 2006.

Johnston, Alva. "The Cauliflower King-I." *The New Yorker,* April 8, 1933.

Kansas City Times. "Noise, Cheers, Applause, Songs—and 3 Candidates." April 11, 1960, CRC scrapbooks.

Kefauver, Estes. *Crime in America.* Garden City, N.Y.: Doubleday & Company, 1951.

Kendall, Sydney. *The Queen of the Red-Lights,* pamphlet published by W. J. Phillips, 1906. Special Collections, UCLA. Los Angeles, CA.

Kennedy, Robert. *The Enemy Within.* New York: Popular Library, 1960.

King Jr., Martin Luther. "Beyond the Los Angeles Riots." *Saturday Review,* November 13, 1965, 33–35, 105.

Klein, Norman. *The History of Forgetting: Los Angeles and the Erasure of Memory.* New York: Verso, 1997.

Kooistra, AnnMarie. "Angels for Sale: The History of Prostitution in Los Angeles, 1880–1940." University of Southern California Dissertation, August 2003.

Korman, Seymour. "Hoodlum Shot to Death, Victim Ripe for Killing, Police Report." *Chicago Daily Tribune,* December 4, 1950.

———. "2 FILM COMICS ADD SPICE TO COHEN'S TRIAL: Jerry Lewis, Skelton on Witness Stand." *Los Angeles Times,* May 25, 1961.

———. "Convict Cohen a Second Time Tax Offender: Guilty of Beating U.S. Out of $400,000," *Chicago Tribune,* July 1, 1961.

Kyle, Palmer. "Porter or Bonelli for City's Next Mayor." *Los Angeles Times,* May 26, 1929.

Lacey, Robert. *Little Man: Meyer Lansky and the Gangster Life.* Boston: Little, Brown, and Company, 1991.

Leppard, Stan. "Mr. Lucky Thrives on Borrowed Time." *Los Angeles Herald & Express,* December 3, 1959.

Lieberman, Paul. "Cop Befriends a Crook" *Los Angeles Times,* October 29, 2008, http://www.latimes.com/news/local/la-me-gangster29-2008oct29,0,4555503,full.story.

———. "Crusaders in the Underworld: The LAPD Takes On Organized Crime." *Los Angeles Times,* October 26, 2008.

———. "Noir Justice Catches Up with Mickey Cohen," November 1, 2008. "Up with Mickey Cohen." *Los Angeles Times,* November 1, 2008.

———. " 'Dragnet' Tales Drawn from LAPD Files Burnished the Department's Image." *Los Angeles Times,* October 30, 2008, http://www.latimes.com/news/local/la-me-gangsterwebb30-2008oct30,0,6588206.story.

Lewis, Brad. *Hollywood's Celebrity Gangster: The Incredible Life and Times of Mickey Cohen.* New York: Enigma Books, 2007.

Life magazine. "Trouble in Los Angeles," January 16, 1950.

Liptak, Adam. "U.S. Is Alone in Rejecting All Evidence If Police Err." *New York Times,* July 19, 2008.

Lomax, Almena. "Bradley Makes 'Loot,' Just in Time for the Vote on the Police Pay Raise." *Los Angeles Tribune,* October 31, 1958.

Los Angeles Daily News. "CONVICT DESCRIBES KILLING BY L.A. COP: Slaying of 'Peewee' Lewis Described at San Quentin." June 7, 1949.

———. "Police Network in 20 Cities to Keep Constant Tab on Mobs." November 11, 1947.

Los Angeles Examiner. "W. H. Parker Heads Fire Police League." January 7, 1949.

———. "Grand Jury to Attack Police Trials System." September 7, 1949.

———. "Law for Policemen Took," editorial, November 14, 1949.

———. "Wild Party by 100 Police Described, Youth Tells of Beatings at Police Yule Party," March 19, 1952.

———. "An Inadequate Answer," editorial, May 2, 1952.

———. "Chief Parker Expected to Quit in Bowron Row," May 27, 1952.

———. "Admits Slaying Bookie, Claims It Was 'Self Defense,' " December 9, 1959.

———. "Yorty, Parker Clash: Chief Denies Charge of Ballot 'Gestapo,' " June 9, 1961.

Los Angeles Herald. "Committee of Safety Makes Its Report," November 8, 1900.

Los Angeles Herald-Examiner. "Bowron Denies Parker Ouster," May 27, 1952.

———. "All Election Promises Kept, Yorty Asserts. But Black Leaders Flat Contradict His Claim That He Never Promised to Fire Chief Parker," July 9, 1962.

————. " 'Pseudoleaders Who Can't Lead,' Blamed by Parker," August 15, 1965.

————. "Riot Hearings Boil, Parker, Bradley in Row Over 'Mystery Man,' " September 14, 1965.

————. "The Case of Earl Kynette," July 8, 1966.

————. "Friends, Critics Praise Parker," July 18, 1966.

————. "6000 Pay Last Tribute to Parker, Chief Eulogized in Congress," July 21, 1966.

Los Angeles Herald-Express. "Cohen 'Safe' in U.S. Cell, Moved to Federal Pen, Brutality by Police Told," February 14, 1952.

————. " 'Cops So Drunk They Fought Each Other to Beat Us,' " March 19, 1952.

————. "Charge 750 Police in Office Jobs, Quiz Chief," May 5, 1954.

————. "Parker Hits Influx of Parolees to L.A.: Tells City Council of Huge Rise in Crime," March 13, 1959.

————. "Parker Rejects Mr. K. Gripe, Russ Police OKd Ban on Disneyland Tour," September 21, 1959.

————. "Chief Parker May Head US Crime Probers," December 22, 1960.

Los Angeles Mirror. "Mayor Investigates Honorary L.A.P.D. Badges," October 28, 1938, via Larry Harnisch's *Daily Mirror* blog (http://latimesblogs.latimes.com/thedailymirror/2008/10/mayor-investiga.html).

————. " 'Innocent' in Cussing, Says Mickey Cohen," August 31, 1949.

————. "Worton 'Man of the Year' in *Mirror* Mailbag Vote," December 30, 1949.

————. "Full Story of Mob Shooting of Cohen." July 20, 1949.

————. "Move for Action on L.A. Police Brutality Charges." February 26, 1952.

————. "6 on Trial Tell More Police Brutalities." March 6, 1952.

————. "Parker Clams Up on Jury Quiz." March 27, 1952.

————. "Grand Jury Turns Heat on Parker, Report Hits Police Dept. Conditions." April 29, 1952.

————. "Bare Yule Police Brutality Transcript." May 13, 1952.

————. "Speaking of Snoopers." January 19, 1953.

————. "Chief Shrugs at Claim of Cop Brutality, Police Brutality Gets Brush-off by Chief Parker," February 27, 1952.

————. "PARKER FORCED TO ACT ON BRUTALITY: Cop Brutality Quiz Demanded by L.A. Judge." March 13, 1952.

————. "Florabel Muir Reporting," March 20, 1952.

————. "Bloody Christmas—One Year Later," editorial, December 6, 1952.

————. "Chicago Hoodlum Chased by Cops, Goes to 'Vegas,' " January 16, 1953.

————. "Give Police Board, Not the Chief, More Power." July 2, 1953.

————. "Cal. Employe [*sic*] Accused as Bunco Go-Between." September 2, 1953.

————. "Cohen Jailed for Failure to Register," September 26, 1957, accessed via the *Los Angeles Times*'s invaluable *Daily Mirror* blog (http://latimesblogs.latimes.com/thedailymirror/mickey_cohen/index.html), October 12, 2008.

————. "Brutal Tactics Told at Hearing," January 26, 1960.

————. "Big Squeeze Boosts Police for Kennedy," July 11, 1960.

————. "Criminals Laugh at LA Police, Says Chief. Underworld Rejoices in Ruling," May 31, 1955.

Los Angeles Mirror–Daily News. "Telephone Tap Defended by Chief Parker," March 7, 1955.

———. "Police Instincts of Bill Parker Flourished Early," June 18, 1957.

Los Angeles Mirror-News. "PARKER FORCED TO ACT ON BRUTALITY, Cop Brutality Quiz Demanded by L.A. Judge," March 13, 1952.

———. "Police Brutality Probe Is Overdue," March 14, 1952.

———. "Lawmen Blast High Court Order to Identify Informants in Arrests: Ruling Termed Crippling in Drive on Dope," October 2, 1958.

———. "Shooting Takes Place Six Feet From Mickey," December 3, 1958.

———. "Keep Cool with Mr. K, Chief Parker tells L.A.," September 7, 1959.

———. "Cohen Suspect in Slaying, Restaurant's Guests Flee After Shooting," December 3, 1959.

———. "Racial Bias Accusations False, Says Chief Parker. Explains Police Problem," January 27, 1960.

Los Angeles Police Departments records, City Records Center (CRC), Los Angeles.

Los Angeles Sentinel, May 17, 1962.

Los Angeles Times. "Detective McAfee is Exonerated," September 23, 1916.

———. "Plans Submitted for Fine Theater: Picture Palace to Follow Elaborate Spanish Architecture," July 11, 1920.

———. "The White Spot Glistens Brightly," July 17, 1921.

———. "The Soul of the City," June 24, 1923.

———. "Oaks Names Kent Parrot, Charges Lawyer Interfered in Police Department, 'Dictatorial and Threatening,'" July 29, 1923.

———. "Kent Parrot Accused by Richards as 'Sinister,' Retiring Harbor Commissioner Names Him as Would-Be Boss," August 1, 1923.

———. "Dark Trails to City Hall are Uncovered: Now Negro Politicians Make and Unmake Police Vice Squad Told in Heath Case," August 17, 1923.

———. "Shall We Re-Elect Kent Parrot?" April 23, 1925.

———. "Bledsoe Hurls Defy at Cryer, Challenges Parrot's Status as De-Facto Mayor," April 23, 1925.

———. "Champion 'Ag-inner' of Universe Is Shuler, Belligerent Local Pastor Holds All Records for Attacks Upon Everybody, Everything," June 1, 1930.

———. "Crawford Career Hectic, Politician Gained Wide Notoriety as 'Pay-Off Man' in Morris Lavine Extortion Case," May 21, 1931.

———. "ARE GANGSTERS BUILDING ANOTHER CHICAGO HERE?: Police Officially Deny It; Admit Privately Facts," March 29, 1931.

———. "Penny Money At Cafe: Clinton 'Caveteria' Caters to Customers of Lean Purse," October 14, 1932.

———. "Complete Vote Received for Thursday's Election," September 30, 1934.

———. "Chief Shifts 28 Officers in New Shake-Up of Police," March 9, 1939.

———. "Davis Defends Police Spying at Bombing Trial, Bitter Clashes Mark Chief's Day on Stand," April 27, 1939.

———. "Police Due for Shake-up Tomorrow, Chief Announces: New Divisions Will Be Organized and Shifts Made of Many Uniformed Officers in Sweeping Program," November 30, 1939.

———. "Policewoman Implicates Sgt. Stoker in Burglary, Love for Vice Squad Man Admitted by Audrey [sic] Davis," July 3, 1949.

———. "Murder Plot Story Filed: Testimony Transcript in Siegel Case Gives Gang," August 31, 1940.

———. "Siegel Denies Buchalter Aid: Film Colony Figure Testifies on Removal Fight," May 27, 1941.

———. "Plunge Fatal to Gangster, State Witness Against Buchalter and Others Attempts to Escape," November 13, 1941.

———. "Japanese Aliens' Roundup Starts: F.B.I. Hunting Down 300 Subversives and Plans to Hold 3000 Today," December 8, 1941.

———. "Little Tokyo Banks and Concerns Shut, Even Saloons Padlocked; Extra Police on Duty to Prevent Riots," December 9, 1941.

———. "Round Up of Japanese Aliens in Southland Now Totals 500: Officers, Working with F.B.I., Continue Hunt; Asiatic, Who Had Pledged Loyalty, Found with Guns," December 9, 1941.

———. "Widow of Victim Heard at Murder Trial of Siegel: Heard Shots Killing Mate," January 27, 1942.

———. "Siegel and Carbo Identified as Murder Aides, Tannenbaum Tells Killing," January 28, 1942.

———. "Siegel's Attic Capture Told, Witnesses at Death Trial Describe Hunt in Suspect's Mansion," January 31, 1942.

———. "Police Officer Keyes Resigns Under Attack," July 26, 1942.

———. "Warren Picks First of Crime Commissions: Jeffers and Mudd Among Those Named Under New State Law," October 22, 1947.

———. "Year Passes but Murder Not Solved: Search for Woman's Slayer Recalls Other Mysteries," February 14, 1949.

———. "Bowron Asks Grand Jury Action in Police Scandal, Two Officers Suspended; Cohen Posts $100,000 Bail," March 23, 1949.

———. "Cohen Introduces Sound Recorder," May 6, 1949.

———. "Cohen to Testify in Partner's Case: Deputy Sheriff Denies Policeman's Story That Meltzer Displayed Gun at Arrest," May 10, 1949.

———. "New Police Chief on Job, to Tell Program in Week," July 1, 1949.

———. "Chief Names Staff Inspector in Top Level Police Changes: Parker Given Number Two Post," July 15, 1949.

———. "Worton Shifts 33 in Police Shake-Up: Top Flight Officer Named Intelligence Aide to Chief in Reorganization Move," August 4, 1949.

———. "Hidden Microphones Hear Cohen Secrets, Police Device Records Intimate Talks in Home," August 16, 1949.

———. "Police Shift Offices Due to City Hall Jam," August 19, 1949.

———. "Parker Appointed New Police Chief Head, Patrol Division Head Promoted in Climax to Hot Battle Over Worton's Successor," August 3, 1950.

———. "Parker Declares City Is White Spot of Nation," August 9, 1950.

———. "Mad Gunman Captured, Mickey Cohen Tells Inside Story of L.A.," November 18, 1950.

———. "Cohen Deals Going Before Jury Today, Federal Inquirers Expected to Hear of Borrowings," February 9, 1951.

————. "Truman Speeds War on Crime; Mickey Cohen Pay-off Charged, Racketeers' Tax Returns to Be Eyed," June 2, 1951.

————. "Cohen Profits Told as Tax Case Opens, Federal Prosecutor Attacks Gangster's Story of Loans," June 5, 1951.

————. "Mickey Cohen Gets 5 Years, $10,000 Fine," July 10, 1951.

————. "Newman and Worton Quit Police Board," July 18, 1951.

————. "Chief Parker Hits Brutality Stories," February 28, 1952.

————. "F.B.I. Probing L.A. Police Brutality," March 14, 1952.

————. "Under Table, Didn't See Slayer, Cohen Says," March 29, 1952, 30.

————. "Grand Jury Indicts Eight Officers in Beating Case," April 23, 1952.

————. "36 L.A. Policemen Face Discipline for Brutality," June 17, 1952.

————. "Verbal Battles by Lawyers Rock Public Housing Quiz," May 21, 1953.

————. "Poulson Pledges War on Gangsters: Mayor-Elect Maps Plans with Parker; Shake-Up of Police Commission Indicated," June 17, 1953.

————. "Police Warned on Secret Wire Taps, Officers Subject to Liability for Illegal Entry, Brown Says," September 4, 1954.

————. " 'Planted' Fur Story Acquits Malouf in Theft," April 7, 1955.

————. "Judge Rules He Cannot Stop Police Microphones, Lacks Jurisdiction on Use of Public Funds for Installation, McCoy Says," July 1, 1955.

————. "Mickey Cohen Sees Billy Graham, Talks on Religion, Former Mobster Goes to N.Y. for Conference," March 2, 1957.

————. "Parker Seeks Grand Jury Action Over Cohen Blast," May 21, 1957.

————. "Cohen Attends Graham Rally in New York," May 22, 1957.

————. "Cohen Booked for Not Signing Traffic Ticket," May 26, 1957.

————. "Mickey Cohen's Traffic Trial Off to Salty Start, Policemen Who Made Arrest Testify that Defendant Delayed Autos at Intersection," July 11, 1957.

————. "Mickey Cohen Takes Manuscript to Author," August 4, 1957.

————. "Cohen Found Guilty, Gets $11 Traffic Fine," November 12, 1957.

————. "Jury Acquits Mickey Cohen on Disturbing Peace Charge, Ex-Convict Ruling May Affect Case," December 17, 1957.

————. "Mickey Cohen Proud of Actress in Murder Quiz, Admits Liz Renay, Questioned in Anastasia Case, Loaned Him $10,000 He's Repaying," February 27, 1958.

————. "Chicago Attorney Glad to Stake Mickey Cohen, Admits $22,500 Loan; Says Ex-Gambler Stands to Make Fortune on Life Story," June 9, 1958.

————. "Girl Friend of Mickey Cohen Quizzed Again, Won't Tell Treasury Agent About Gifts from Bodyguard of Slain Anastasia," September 10, 1958.

————. "Liz Renay Indicted on Perjury Charges: Mickey Cohen's Actress Friend Accused of Lying About Raising $5,500 in Loans," March 13, 1959.

————. "Under Table, Didn't See Slayer, Cohen Says," March 29, 1959.

————. "Poulson Cuts Police Budget by $6 Million, Commissioner Promptly Warns Mayor That City Faces Criminal Invasion," May 1, 1959.

————. "Report Hints Cohen Had Part in Slayings," June 16, 1959.

————. "Police Board Member Flays Parker, Quits," June 19, 1959.

————. "Parker Plans Security for Khrushchev Visit," September 7, 1959.

————. "Mickey Cohen Jailed in Murder of Bookie," December 4, 1959.

————. "Slayer of Bookmaker Surrenders to Police," December 9, 1959.

————. "Parker Angrily Denies Racial Discrimination: Presents Charts of City Districts, Tells of Undesirables Shipped into Los Angeles," January 27, 1960.

————. "Council Hears Parker's Recording on 'Wild Tribes,' Chief Denies Slur, Refuses to Apologize," February 3, 1960.

————. "Demagoguery Loses a Round," February 5, 1960.

————. "Witnesses Deny They Saw Whalen Shooting," March 11, 1960.

————. "This Is Not Alabama," editorial, June 1, 1960.

————. "The Bright Badge of the L.A.P.D.," editorial, August 9, 1960.

————. "MAD GUNMAN CAPTURED, Mickey Cohen Tells Inside Story of L.A., Bland Gangster Spars with Counsel in Quiz; Sheriff Also Testifies," November 18, 1960.

————. "Parker Hails Kennedy as Crime Foe," December 17, 1960.

————. "Ben Hecht Sees Cohen as Top Book Material," May 18, 1961.

————. "Cohen's Story Contract Presented at His Trial," May 19, 1961.

————. "$9,000 Advance for Cohen, Screenplay Told," May 20, 1961.

————. "Picked for Cohen Role in Film, Skelton says," May 25, 1961.

————. "Two Cited Under Lynch Law After Park Riot," June 2, 1961.

————. "Candy Barr Tells About Being Cohen's 'Sweetie': Jailed Stripper Testifies How Ex-Hoodlum Helped Her Flee U.S. to Mexico Hideaway," June 3, 1961.

————. "$200,000 Tax Writeoff Offer to Cohen Told," June 8, 1961.

————. "U.S. Rests Cohen Income Tax Case," June 17, 1961.

————. "Cohen Defense Claims He Was Losing Money," June 24, 1961.

————. "Six Muslim Suspects Held in Row at Market," September 3, 1961.

————. "Mickey Cohen Jaunty Again—in Volkswagen," October 20, 1961.

————. "Mickey Cohen, 4 Others Indicted in Murder Plot, All Accused in Dec. 2, 1959 Slaying of Jack Whalen in Sherman Oaks Cafe," November 1, 1961.

————. "Mickey Cohen Murder Charges Dismissed," March 19, 1962.

————. "Officers Out to Get Cohen, LoCigno Says," March 22, 1962.

————. "Under Table, Didn't See Slayer, Cohen Says," March 29, 1962.

————. "Cohen's Defense Closes Murder Trial Argument," April 5, 1962.

————. "Lo Cigno Rules Guilty of Manslaughter," November 15, 1962.

————. "Parker Assails Bishop's View of Negro Policy," January 18, 1963.

————. "Special Police Groups Press Fight on Crime, Cities Combat Increased Felonies with Crack Units; in Los Angeles It's 'Metro,'" February 23, 1964.

————. Sentences Reimposed on 11 Black Muslims," March 3, 1965.

————. "Ex-Sergeant Strange Praises Chief Parker, Remembers Sincerity," July 20, 1966.

————. "Politics and the LAPD," April 11, 1969.

Los Angeles Tribune. "Truman Speeds War on Crime; Mickey Cohen Pay-off Charged, Racketeers' Tax Returns to Be Eyed." June 2, 1950.

Manion, Dean. "Anarchy Imminent: Local Police Hobbled in Efforts to Stem Crime." May 30, 1965, Manion forum, South Bend, Indiana. William H. Parker Police Foundation, Los Angeles, CA.

Mann, William. *Behind the Screen: How Gays and Lesbians Shaped Hollywood, 1910–1969.* New York: Viking, 2001.

May, Allan. "The History of the Race Wire Service," http://crimemagazine.com/racewire3.htm, Crime: An Encyclopedia of Crime, 08-06-2000, access date: January 28, 2008.

McDougal, Dennis. *Privileged Son, Otis Chandler and the Rise and Fall of the L.A. Times Dynasty.* Cambridge, Mass.: Perseus, 2001.

McWilliams, Carey. *Southern California: An Island on the Land.* Salt Lake City: Gibbs Smith, 1999.

Moore, William Howard. *The Kefauver Committee and the Politics of Crime, 1950–1952.* Columbia, MO: University of Missouri Press, 1974.

Mooring, William. "Chief Gives Opinion of 'Bad Cop' Films." *The Tidings,* October 22, 1954.

Muir, Florabel. *Headline Happy.* New York: Henry Holt and Company, 1950.

Mydans, Seth. " 'It Could Happen Again,' Report on Los Angeles Riots Blames Police and City." *New York Times,* October 25, 1992.

Nash, Robert Jay. *World Encyclopedia of Organized Crime.* New York: Da Capo Press, 1993.

Nathan, Albert. "How Whiskey Smugglers Buy and Land Cargoes, Well-Organized Groups Engaged in Desperate Game of Rum-Running," *Los Angeles Times,* August 8, 1926.

———. " 'Rousting' System Earns Curses of the Rum-Runners, Chief Davis's Raids Keep Whiskey Ring in Harried State," *Los Angeles Times,* August 22, 1926.

Newsom, Jim. "Men Efficient, Vigilant, Brave, Chief Relates." *Hollywood Citizen News,* June 20, 1965.

Newton, Jim. *Justice for All: Earl Warren and the Nation He Made.* New York: Riverhead Books, 2006.

New York Times. "Abe Reles Killed Trying to Escape, Sheet Rope Fails After He Lowers Himself from 6th to 5th Floor, Motive Puzzles Police," November 3, 1941.

———. "Mickey Cohen Cashes In on His Glaring Notoriety," April 3, 1951.

———. "A.B.C.-TV Retracts Remarks by Cohen," May 27, 1957.

———. "Mickey Cohen Sues U.S.," February 18, 1964.

———. "Los Angeles Police Chief: William Henry Parker 3d," August 14, 1965.

———. "Lou Stillman, Legendary Boxing Figure, Is Dead," obituary, August 20, 1969.

Olney, Warren. "Law Enforcement and Judicial Administration in the Earl Warren Era." Earl Warren Oral History Project, University of California, 1981.

Otash, Fred. *Investigation Hollywood!* Chicago: Regnery, 1976.

Parker, William H. "Police Chief William H. Parker Speakers," a compilation of Parker statements prepared by the Community Relations Conference of Southern California, 2400 South Western Avenue, Los Angeles, CA, Parker FBI file, 62-96042-109.

————. January 7, 1953, memo to the Board of Police Commissioners, Subject: Progress Report, August 9, 1950 to January 1, 1953. LAPD records. Originally CRC Box 35314, now Escobar collection, Tucson, AZ.

————. "Responses to Questions of the Los Angeles City Council Concerning a Juvenile Gang Attack on a Citizen in Downtown Los Angeles," December 8, 1953. Originally CRC Box 35324, now Escobar collection, Tucson, AZ.

————. Parker letter, January 29, 1954, to Don Thompson: 1953 county grand jury foreman, in response to a letter from him asking about rat packs. Originally CRC box 35300, now Escobar collection, Tucson, AZ.

————. "Laws on Wiretapping," letter to the *Los Angeles Times*, January 23, 1955.

————. *Parker on Police.* Springfield, IL: Charles C. Thomas Publisher, 1957.

William H. Parker Police Foundation archives, Los Angeles, CA. "Col W. H. Parker Called by Death: South Dakota Congressman Passed Away Yesterday—Speaker Cannon Expresses Deep Regret," clipping from Deadwood newspaper.

————. Letter from the Board of Civil Service Commissioners, September 28, 1926.

————. "Memorandum for the Adjutant General, Subject: Relief from Active Duty," undated.

————. Letter from Arthur Hohmman to HQ Los Angeles Officer Procurement District, February 19, 1943.

————. Letter from Captain Robert L. Dennis to HQ, Los Angeles Officer Procurement District, February 23, 1943.

————. Col. Jesse Miller, Director, Military Government Division, to First Lt. William Parker, May 11, 1943.

————. Letter from C. B. Horrall to Capt. W. H. Parker, June 26, 1945.

————. "Police Post Gets Membership Drive Trophy." *L.A. Fire and Police Protective League News*, 1947.

————. "Parker's the One in '51, Los Angeles Police Post 381, American Legion, unanimously presents William H. 'Bill' Parker for the office of COMMANDER OF THE AMERICAN LEGION, DEPARTMENT OF CALIFORNIA, for the year 1951–52," August 1950, Number Three.

————. "Facts on Chief Parker's Exam Records," Assistant General Manager Civil Service, June 1, 1966.

Parrish, Michael. *For the People: Inside the Los Angeles County District's Office, 1850–2000.* Santa Monica: Angel City Press, 2001.

Parson, Donald Craig. *Making a Better World: Public Housing, the Red Scare, and the Direction of Modern Los Angeles.* Minneapolis: University of Minnesota Press, 2005.

Payne, James Gregory, and Scott Ratzan. *Tom Bradley, The Impossible Dream: a Biography.* Charlottesville: University of Virginia Press, 1986.

Percival, Olive, "In Our Cathay." *Los Angeles Times*, December 4, 1898.

Poulson, Norris. *The Genealogy and Life Story of Erna and Norris Poulson.* Department of Special Collections and Digital Collections, Department of Special Collections, UCLA, Los Angeles, CA.

Rappleye, Charles. *All-American Mafioso: The Johnny Rosselli Story.* New York: Doubleday, 1991.

Rasmussen, Cecilia, "History of Hollywood Madams Is Long, Lurid." *Los Angeles Times,* November 30, 1967.

Ratzan, Scott, and James Gregory Payne. *Tom Bradley, the Impossible Dream.* Santa Monica, Calif.: Roundtable Publishers, 1986.

Readers Digest. "Why Hoodlums Hate Bill Parker," March 1960, 239, condensed from *National Civic Review* (September 1959).

Reid, Ed. *Mickey Cohen: Mobster.* New York: Pinnacle Books, 1973.

Reith, Charles. *The Blind Eye of History: A Study of the Origins of the Present Police Era.* London: Faber and Faber, 1952.

Renay, Liz. *My Face for the World to See.* New York: Bantam Books, 1971.

Richardson, James. *For the Life of Me: Memoirs of a City Editor.* New York: Putnam, 1954.

Romo, Richardo. *History of a Barrio: East Los Angeles.* Austin: University of Texas Press, 1983.

Ross, Steven. "How Hollywood Became Hollywood," in Tom Sitton and William Deverell, eds. *Metropolis in the Making: Los Angeles in the 1920s.* Los Angeles: University of California Press, 2001.

Russo, Gus. *The Outfit: The Role of Chicago's Underworld in the Shaping of Modern America.* New York: Bloomsbury, 2001.

Rustin, Bayard. "The Watts 'Manifesto' and the McCone Report." *Commentary,* August 1966.

Ryan, Art. "Dot-dot-dot—It's Just Like Downtown." *Los Angeles Times,* April 20, 1959.

Sahagun, Louis. "Riots Transform Campaign on Police Reform." *Los Angeles Times,* May 31, 1992.

Salazar, Ruben. "Violence Marks Cohen's History." *Los Angeles Times,* July 2, 1961.

San Francisco Call-Bulletin. "Novice Chief Brings New Confidence. . . ." May 10, 1955.

———. "Kennedy's 'Pad' in L.A.—Dirty Shirts and Disorder," July 15, 1960.

Scene of the Crime: Photographs from the L.A.P.D. Archive. New York: Harry Abrams, 2004.

Schulberg, Budd. *The Harder They Fall.* New York: Random House, 1947.

Server, Lee. *Baby, I Don't Care.* New York: St. Martin's, 2001.

Sherman, Gene. "Mr. K Hurls Hot Retort at Poulson," *Los Angeles Times,* September 20, 1959.

———. "L.A. Negroes Only Part of Over-All Minority Problem: Concentration of Race Here Is Fifth Largest in United States." *Los Angeles Times,* January 24, 1961.

Shteir, Rachel. *Striptease: The Untold History of the Girlie Show.* New York: Oxford, 2004.

Sifakis, Carl. *The Mafia Encyclopedia.* New York: Checkmark Books, 2005.

Simon, Richard. Memorandum to the Police Commission, "Subject: Request for Five Additional Positions of Lt of Police to Be Community Relations Officers," October 12, 1965. LAPD records, CRC.

Sitton, Tom. *John Randolph Haynes: California Progressive.* Palo Alto: Stanford University Press, 1992.

———. *Los Angeles Transformed: Fletcher Bowron's Urban Reform Revival, 1938–1953.* Albuquerque: University of New Mexico Press, 2005.

————. "The 'Boss' Without a Machine: Kent K. Parrot and Los Angeles Politics in the 1920s," *Southern California Quarterly,* Winter 1985 (volume LXVII, number 4).

————. "Did the Ruling Class Rule at City Hall in 1920s Los Angeles?" in Tom Sitton and William Deverell, eds. *Metropolis in the Making: Los Angeles in the 1920s.* Los Angeles: University of California Press, 2001.

Sjoquist, Arthur. *History of the Los Angeles Police Department.* Los Angeles: Los Angeles Police Revolver and Athletic Club, 1984.

————. "The Story of Bill." *The Link,* 1994.

Starr, Kevin. *Material Dreams: Southern California Through the 1920s.* New York: Oxford University Press, 1990.

————. *Endangered Dreams: The Great Depression in California.* New York: Oxford University Press, 1996.

————. *The Dream Endures: California Enters the 1940s.* New York: Oxford University Press, 1997.

Stevens, Steve, and Craig Lockwood. *King of the Sunset Strip: Hangin' with Mickey Cohen and the Hollywood Mob.* Nashville: Cumberland House, 2006.

Stoker, Charles. *Thicker'N Thieves: The Factual Expose of Police Pay-Offs, Graft, Political Corruption and Prostitution in Los Angeles and Hollywood.* Santa Monica: Sidereal Company. 1951.

Stump, Al. "L.A.'s Chief Parker—America's Most Hated Cop." *Cavalier Magazine,* July 1958.

Taylor. Frank. "It Costs $1000 to Have Lunch with Harry Chandler." *Saturday Evening Post,* December, 16, 1939.

Thackrey, Ted. "Memories—Lincoln Heights Jail Closing." *Los Angeles Herald-Examiner,* June 27, 1965. CRC.

Thomas, Evans. *Robert Kennedy: His Life.* New York: Simon & Schuster, 2000.

Time magazine, "Chance on the High Seas," August 14, 1939.

————. "Americana," January 31, 1949.

————. "Brenda's Revenge," July 11, 1949.

————. "Heaven, Hell & Judgment Day," March 20, 1950.

————. "Real Thriller," May 15, 1950.

————. "Jigs and Judgments," July 23, 1951.

————. "With a Soft G," September 22, 1952.

————. "The New Evangelist," October 25, 1954, cover story.

————. "Important Story," June 3, 1957.

————. "A Star is Made," July 29, 1957.

————. "The Elemental Force," September 28, 1959.

Town Hall, *A Study of the Los Angeles City Charter: A Report of the Municipal and County Government Section of Town Hall.* Los Angeles: Town Hall (John Randolph Haynes and Dora Haynes Foundation), 1963.

Turkus, Burton, and Sid Feder. *Murder, Inc.: The Story of the Syndicate.* New York: Da Capo Press, 1951.

Underwood, Agnes. *Newspaperwoman.* New York: Harper & Brothers, 1949.

Valley Times. "L.A. Councilmen to Hear Parker," September 11, 1965.

Vaus, Jim. *Why I Quit . . . Syndicated Crime.* Los Angeles: Scripture Outlet, Inc., 1951.

Verge, Arthur. *Paradise Transformed: Los Angeles During the Second World War.* Dubuque, IA: Kendall Hunt, 1993.

Vollmer, August. *The Police and Modern Society.* Berkeley: University of California Press, 1936.

von Hoffman, Nicholas. "L.A. Chief Overlooked a Bad Heart to Serve." *Washington Post,* July 18, 1966, A1.

Wagner, Rob Leicester. *Red Ink, White Lies: The Rise and Fall of Los Angeles Newspapers 1920–1962.* Upland, Calif.: Dragonfly Press, 2000.

Wallace, Mike. *Between You and Me: A Memoir.* New York: Hyperion, 2005.

Wallace, Mike, and Gary Paul Gates. *Close Encounters: Mike Wallace's Own Story.* New York: William Morrow, 1984.

Wambaugh, Joseph. *The Blue Knight.* New York: Grand Central Publishing, 2008.

Warren, Earl. *The Memoirs of Earl Warren.* Garden City, New York: Doubleday & Company, 1977.

Webb, Jack. *The Badge.* Englewood Cliffs, N.J.: Prentice-Hall, 1958.

Weeks, Paul, "Story of Chief Parker, Enemy of the Criminal." *Los Angeles Mirror,* June 17, 1957, 1, accessible at http://latimesblogs.latimes.com/thedailymirror/2007/06/william_parker.html.

Weinstock, Matt. *My L.A.* New York: Current Books, 1947.

Weller, Sheila. *Dancing at Ciro's: A Family's Love, Loss, and Scandal on the Sunset Strip.* New York: St. Martin's Griffin, 2003.

West, Dick. "Chief Parker Collapses, Dies at Award Banquet, Stricken During Standing Ovation by Marine Veterans." *Los Angeles Times,* July 16, 1966.

White, Art. "Parker Takes Swipe at FBI." *Los Angeles Mirror,* December 22, 1960.

White, Leslie. *Me, Detective.* New York: Harcourt, Brace, 1936.

Wickersham Commission. "Nos. 1–14." Washington, D.C.: GPO, 1930.

Wilkerson III, W. R. *The Man Who Invented Las Vegas.* Bellingham, Wash.: Ciro's Books, 2000.

Williams, Carlton. "Mayor and Parker in Sharp Clashes: Poulson, Police Chief and Leask Argue Heatedly at Public Hearing on City Budget." *Los Angeles Times,* May 6, 1954.

Williams, David. July 9, 1959, letter to Councilman John Holland, Council File No. 89512. LAPD records, CRC. See also April 1, 1959, letter to Herb Schurter and April 21, 1959, letter to Parker. LAPD records, CRC.

Woods. "Ex-Marine Tightened Up Los Angeles Police." *Chicago Sun-Times,* March 12, 1952.

Woods, J. Gerald. "The Progressives and the Police: Urban Reform and the Professionalization of the Los Angeles Police," UCLA dissertation, 1973.

Wright, Willard Huntington. "Los Angeles—The Chemically Pure." *The Smart Set,* March 1913. Reprinted in Burton Roscoe and Groff Conklin, eds. *The Smart Set Anthology,* New York.

Credits

GRATEFUL ACKNOWLEDGMENT is given for permission to use material from the following sources:

Archives and photograph collection, William H. Parker Police Foundation, Los Angeles, California.

Photographs, the Los Angeles Police Historical Society, Los Angeles, California.

LAPD official departmental records, the Los Angeles Police Department; the Los Angeles Police Commission; the office of the Los Angeles City Attorney; and the City Records Center, Los Angeles, California.

The Genealogy and Life Story of Erna and Norris Poulson, by Norris Poulson, Department of Special Collections and Digital Collections, Department of Special Collections, UCLA, Los Angeles, California.

Photographs, USC Special Collections, University of Southern California, Los Angeles, California.

Photographs, *Los Angeles Times*, Los Angeles, California.

Photograph Collection, Los Angeles Public Library, Los Angeles, California.

Ben Hecht Papers, Newberry Library, Chicago, Illinois; the Hecht Estate; and the William Morris Agency.

Personal collection, Edward Escobar, Tucson, Arizona.

Index

About the Author

JOHN BUNTIN is a staff writer at *Governing* magazine, where he covers crime and urban affairs. A native of Mississippi, Buntin graduated from Princeton University's Woodrow Wilson School of Public and International Affairs and has worked as a case writer for Harvard University's John F. Kennedy School of Government. A former resident of Southern California, he now lives in Washington, D.C., with his family.

For more information, please visit www.johnbuntin.com.